Cambridge Studies in Biological and Evolutionary Anthropology 62

African Genesis: Perspectives on Hominin Evolution

The announcement of the first African hominin species, *Australopithecus africanus*, from Taung, South Africa in 1924, launched the study of fossil man in Africa. New discoveries continue to confirm the importance of this region to our understanding of human evolution.

Outlining major developments since Raymond Dart's description of the Taung skull, and, in particular, the impact of the pioneering work of Phillip V. Tobias, this book is a valuable companion for students and researchers of human origins. It presents a summary of the current state of palaeoanthropology, reviewing the ideas that are central to the field, and provides a perspective on how future developments will shape our knowledge about hominin emergence in Africa. A wide range of key themes are covered, from the earliest fossils from Chad and Kenya, to the origins of bipedalism and the debate about how and where modern humans evolved and dispersed across Africa and beyond.

SALLY C. REYNOLDS is an honorary research staff member of the Institute for Human Evolution, University of the Witwatersrand, South Africa and Liverpool John Moores University, UK. She conducts research on the world-famous Sterkfontein Cave fossils and is interested in the relationships between geomorphology, mosaic habitats and extinction in hominins and other mammals.

ANDREW GALLAGHER is a Lecturer in the School of Anatomical Sciences, University of Witwatersrand. His principal research focuses on the evolutionary significance of size variation in hominin evolution and the functional morphology of the locomotor system.

Cambridge Studies in Biological and Evolutionary Anthropology

Series editors

African Genesis

Perspectives on Hominin Evolution

Edited by

SALLY C. REYNOLDS
University of the Witwatersrand, South Africa

ANDREW GALLAGHER
University of the Witwatersrand, South Africa

CAMBRIDGE
UNIVERSITY PRESS

CAMBRIDGE UNIVERSITY PRESS
Cambridge, New York, Melbourne, Madrid, Cape Town,
Singapore, São Paulo, Delhi, Mexico City

Cambridge University Press
The Edinburgh Building, Cambridge CB2 8RU, UK

Published in the United States of America by Cambridge University Press, New York

www.cambridge.org
Information on this title: www.cambridge.org/9781107019959

© Cambridge University Press 2012

First published 2012

Printed in the United Kingdom at the University Press, Cambridge

A catalogue record for this publication is available from the British Library

Library of Congress Cataloguing in Publication data
African genesis : perspectives on hominin evolution / [edited by] Sally C. Reynolds,
Andrew Gallagher.
    pages cm. – (Cambridge studies in biological and evolutionary anthropology)
    Includes bibliographical references and index.
    ISBN 978-1-107-01995-9
    1. Fossil hominids.   2. Human evolution.   I. Reynolds, Sally C., editor of compilation.
    II. Gallagher, Andrew, 1975 – editor of compilation.
    GN282.A27   2012
    599.93′8–dc23   2011049201

ISBN 978-1-107-01995-9 Hardback

Contents

Contributors

Lee R. Berger, Institute for Human Evolution, University of the Witwatersrand, Private Bag 3, PO Wits, Joahnnesburg, 2050, South Africa

Fred L. Bookstein, Department of Anthropology, University of Vienna, Althanstr. 14, A-1090 Vienna, Austria and College of Arts and Sciences, University of Washington, 180 Nickerson Street #309 WA 98109 Seattle, USA

Günter Bräuer, Abteilung für Humanbiologie, Universität Hamburg, Allende Platz 2, 20146 Hamburg, Germany

Michel Brunet, Collège de France, Chaire de Paléontologie humaine, 75231 Paris Cedex, France and Université de Poitiers Faculté des Sciences, Institut International de Paléoprimatologie et Paléontologie humaine, IPHEP et UMR CNRS 6046, 86022 Poitiers Cedex, France

Steven E. Churchill, Department of Biological Anthropology and Anatomy, Duke University, Durham, NC 27708 USA

Ronald J. Clarke, Institute for Human Evolution, University of the Witwatersrand, Private Bag 3, PO Wits, Joahnnesburg, 2050, South Africa

M. Christopher Dean, Research Department of Cell and Developmental Biology, University College London, Gower Street, London, WC1E 6BT, UK

Michelle S. M. Drapeau, Département d'anthropologie, Université de Montréal, CP 6128 Succ. Centre-ville, Montréal, QC. H3C 3J7, Canada

Sarah Elton, Hull York Medical School, University of Hull, Cottingham Road, Hull, HU6 7RX, UK

Dean Falk, School for Advanced Research, Santa Fe, NM 87505, USA and Department of Anthropology, Florida State University, Tallahassee, FL 32306, USA

Andrew Gallagher, School of Anatomical Sciences, University of the Witwatersrand Medical School, 7 York Road, Parktown, 2193, Johannesburg,

South Africa and Department of Anthropology and Development Studies, University of Johannesburg, Auckland Park, 2006, Johannesburg, South Africa

John A. J. Gowlett, British Academy Centenary Project, University of Liverpool, Liverpool L69 3GS, UK

Colin Groves, School of Archaeology and Anthropology, Australian National University, Canberra, Australia

Philipp Gunz, Department of Anthropology, University of Vienna, Althanstr. 14, A-1090 Vienna, Austria and Department of Human Evolution, Max Planck Institute for Evolutionary Anthropology, Deutscher Platz 6, D-04103 Leipzig, Germany

Adam Hartstone-Rose, Pennsylvania State University, 205 Hawthorn, 3000 Ivy Side Park, Altoona, PA 16601 USA

Jason Hemingway, School of Anatomical Sciences, University of the Witwatersrand Medical School, 7 York Road, Parktown, 2193, Johannesburg, South Africa

Ralph L. Holloway, Department of Anthropology, Columbia University, 1200 Amsterdam Ave, New York, USA

Vance T. Hutchinson, Department of Anthropology, Tulane University, New Orleans, LA 70118 USA

William L. Jungers, Department of Anatomical Sciences, School of Medicine, Stony Brook University, Stony Brook, New York, USA

Ivor Janković, Institute for Anthropological Research, Amruševa 8, 10000, Zagreb, Croatia

Kevin L. Kuykendall, Department of Archaeology, University of Sheffield, Northgate House, West Street, Sheffield S1 4ET, UK

Sang-Hee Lee, Department of Anthropology, University of California, Riverside, Riverside, CA 92521–0418, USA

Julia Lee-Thorp, Department of Archaeological Science, University of Bradford, Bradford BD7 1DP, UK

Paul R. Manger, School of Anatomical Sciences, University of the Witwatersrand Medical School, 7 York Road, Parktown, 2193, Johannesburg, South Africa

Emma Mbua, National Museums of Kenya, PO Box 40658, Nairobi, Kenya

Henry M. McHenry, Department of Anthropology, University of California, Davis, CA, USA

Philipp Mitteroecker, Department of Theoretical Biology, University of Vienna, Austria and Department of Anthropology, University of Vienna, Althanstr. 14, A-1090, Vienna, Austria

Simon Neubauer, Department of Human Evolution, Max Planck Institute for Evolutionary Anthropology, Leipzig, Germany and Department of Anthropology, University of Vienna, Althanstr. 14, A-1090 Vienna, Austria

Osbjorn M. Pearson, Department of Anthropology, MSC 01–1040, University of New Mexico, Albuquerque, NM 87131, USA

Travis R. Pickering, Department of Anthropology, University of Wisconsin-Madison, 1180 Observatory Drive, 5240 Social Building, Madison, WI 53706, USA and Institute for Human Evolution, University of the Witwatersrand, Private Bag 3, PO Wits, Johannesburg, 2050, South Africa

Martin Pickford, Collège de France, 75231 Paris Cedex, France and Département Histoire de la Terre, Paris, France

Sally C. Reynolds, Institute for Human Evolution, University of the Witwatersrand, Private Bag 3, PO Wits, Joahnnesburg, 2050, South Africa and Liverpool John Moores University, School of Natural Sciences and Psychology, James Parsons Building, Byrom St., Liverpool L3 3AF, UK

Brian G. Richmond, Center for the Advanced Study of Hominid Paleobiology, Department of Anthropology, George Washington University, USA and Human Origins Program, National Museum of Natural History, Smithsonian Institution, Washington, DC, USA

Avraham Ronen, Zinman Institute of Archaeology, University of Haifa, Haifa 31905, Israel and Max Stern Academic College of Emek Yezreel, Emek Yezreel 19300, Israel

Darryl J. de Ruiter, Department of Anthropology, Texas A&M University, College Station, TX 77843, USA

Brigitte Senut, Muséum National d'Histoire Naturelle, Département Histoire de la Terre Paléontologie (USM 203), UMR 5143 CNRS, Paris, France

Fred H. Smith, Department of Sociology and Anthropology, Campus Box 4660, Illinois State University, Normal, IL 61790–4660, USA

Muhammad A. Spocter, School of Anatomical Sciences, University of the Witwatersrand Medical School, 7 York Road, Parktown, 2193, Johannesburg, South Africa

Matt Sponheimer, Department of Anthropology, University of Colorado at Boulder, Boulder CO 80309, USA

J. Francis Thackeray, Institute for Human Evolution, University of the Witwatersrand, Private Bag 3, PO Wits, Joahnnesburg, 2050, South Africa

Phillip V. Tobias, School of Anatomical Sciences, University of the Witwatersrand Medical School, 7 York Road, Parktown, 2193, Johannesburg, South Africa

Peter S. Ungar, Department of Anthropology, University of Arkansas, Fayetteville, AR, USA

Lyn Wadley, Institute for Human Evolution, University of the Witwatersrand, Private Bag 3, PO Wits, Joahnnesburg, 2050, South Africa

Gerhard W. Weber, Department of Anthropology, University of Vienna, Althanstr. 14, A-1090 Vienna, Austria

Milford H. Wolpoff, Paleoanthropology Laboratory, Department of Anthropology, University of Michigan, MI, 48109–1107 USA

B. Headman Zondo, Bernard Price Institute for Palaeontology, School of GeoSciences, University of the Witwatersrand, South Africa

Foreword

As the Honorary President of the African Genesis symposium committee, it was a great pleasure to welcome delegates from many countries to a meeting that served two purposes: to celebrate the discovery of the Taung child, the type specimen of *Australopithecus africanus* and, secondly, to honour Professor Phillip Tobias, the doyen of palaeoanthropology in Africa, the continent from which humanity evolved.

It was awesome to hear presentations by Michel Brunet, Brigitte Senut and Martin Pickford, regarding the type specimens of *Sahelanthropus* and *Orrorin*, from Chad and Kenya respectively, dated between 6 and 7 million years before the present. To place things in perspective there was a lecture by David Begun on African hominin origins, with reference to Miocene primates. This was followed by colloquia on the origin, adaptations and radiations of australopithecines; on hominid evolutionary ecology in the Plio-Pleistocene; on origins and diversity of *Homo* in the early Pleistocene; and on the origins, evolution and behaviour of *Homo sapiens* in the Late Pleistocene.

Speaker after speaker paid tribute to Professor Tobias whose enthusiasm has evidently encouraged many palaeoanthropologists who have worked on hominid fossils curated by the School of Anatomical Sciences at the University of the Witwatersrand. The collections at Wits have grown substantially since the description of the Taung child by Professor Raymond Dart in 1925.

The description of 'Little Foot', an extraordinary australopithecine discovered at Sterkfontein by Ron Clarke, Nkwane Molefe and Stephen Motsumi, was dramatic. Here was a palaeoanthropologist's dream. If *Sahelanthropus* and *Orrorin* were breathtaking, this new discovery in the Cradle of Humankind was even more so. A virtually complete skeleton, initially dated at 3.3 million years on the basis of fauna and palaeomagnetism, has been found *in situ* in the Silberberg Grotto and awaits formal description. Ron Clarke's presentation made South Africans proud of their heritage, and proud of the work that is being done in this part of the African continent.

In addition to formal lectures by invited speakers, there were many excellent posters presented by students who represent a new generation of palaeoanthropologists.

I would like to express my sincere gratitude to the organising committee of the African Genesis symposium for their dedicated efforts that made the event the stunning success that it was. Thanks are also extended to the many sponsors, especially to De Beers, the Department of Science and Technology, the Anglo-American Chairman's Fund, the Wenner Gren Foundation for Anthropological Research, the National Research Foundation, the Palaeontology Scientific Trust (PAST), First National Bank, the French Embassy in South Africa, the Canadian Embassy and the School of Anatomical Sciences at the University of the Witwatersrand. Special thanks are extended to Sally Reynolds for her sterling efforts with regard to the publication of this compilation of papers, and to Cambridge University Press for accepting the proceedings of the African Genesis symposium as part of their Cambridge Studies in Biological and Evolutionary Anthropology series.

Francis Thackeray
Honorary President
African Genesis: a symposium on hominid evolution in Africa

Acknowledgements

We would like to extend our thanks to the University of the Witwatersrand Medical School for hosting the conference and to all the participants who joined us for this marvellous event. Francis Thackeray, in his role as President of the Symposium, was a kind and genial host. We would like to acknowledge the hospitality of the Mayor of the City of Johannesburg, Amos Masondo and the staff of the Cradle Restaurant (Cradle of Humankind) for our delegates. We are grateful to Professor Laurence Chait for the bust of Phillip Tobias that has been installed at Sterkfontein.

Our generous sponsors made this symposium unforgettable; specifically we acknowledge De Beers, the Department of Science and Technology (DST), the Anglo-American Chairman's Fund, the Wenner Gren Foundation for Anthropological Research, the National Research Foundation (NRF), the Palaeontology Scientific Trust (PAST), First National Bank, the French Embassy in South Africa, the Canadian Embassy and Rick Menell. The fossil exhibit was a highlight of the conference and Stephanie Potze and the staff of the Ditsong National Museum of Natural History (formerly the Transvaal Museum, Pretoria) are thanked for granting permission to display the original fossils of Sterkfontein's 'Mrs. Ples' and Raymond Dart's 'Taung child' together for the first time.

To all our colleagues and friends at Wits Medical School, including Colin Menter, Muhammad 'Spoc' Spocter, Meredith Robinson, Jason Hemingway, Manoj Chiba, Kavita Chibba, Ishana Ryan, Candice Hutchinson, Adhil 'Bugs' Bhagwandin and the late Heather White: thank you for your camaraderie, patience and loyal support.

Our thanks are due to Martin Griffiths and Lynette Talbot at Cambridge University Press for their invaluable help in the production of this volume. We also owe a special mention to Bernard Wood for his support of this project.

Finally, Sally would like to extend her gratitude to her parents, Chris and Jenni Reynolds for all their support of this volume. In particular, she would like to acknowledge the patience, encouragement and editorial support of her mother, Jenni.

Sally C. Reynolds
Andrew Gallagher

1   *African Genesis: an evolving paradigm*

SALLY C. REYNOLDS

Introduction

The Late Miocene and Early Pliocene hominin fossil record confirms Africa as
the birthplace of humanity. Raymond Dart's announcement of the first species
of 'ape-man' in the journal *Nature* (Dart, 1925) forever changed our perceptions of Africa's place in the 'human story' and firmly established the field
of African palaeoanthropology. We palaeoanthropologists, past, present and
future, owe a significant debt to Dart's discovery and his recognition of its
importance. But Dart's work was just the beginning of a long and proud legacy of excavation and research in southern Africa, and new discoveries continue to confirm the importance of this region to our understanding of human
evolution.

The African Genesis symposium, held at the University of the Witwatersrand
Medical School, Johannesburg, South Africa between 8 and 14 January 2006,
celebrated the 80th anniversary of Dart's publication of the Taung child and
the 80th birthday of a remarkable man, Professor Phillip V. Tobias. Tobias
continued the tradition established by his mentor Dart, and his mentor before
him: a long line of mentors and students stretching back more than 500 years
(Ungar and Tobias, Chapter 2). Tobias, in turn, continues to collaborate with
colleagues and former students on a variety of new perspectives on the fossil
hominin material (e.g. Lockwood and Tobias, 2002; Holloway *et al.*, 2004;
Curnoe and Tobias, 2006; Moggi-Cecci *et al.*, 2006). His commitment to education and scientific rigour established a strong foundation for our scholarly
community.

Phillip Tobias's contributions encompass the systematic study of all aspects
of human evolution and he continues to inspire students and colleagues worldwide. In his role of palaeoanthropologist, he described new fossil discoveries
(Leakey *et al.*, 1964; Hughes and Tobias, 1977), headed the excavation programme at Sterkfontein for many years and studied deposits of Sterkfontein,

African Genesis: Perspectives on Hominin Evolution, eds. Sally C. Reynolds and Andrew
Gallagher. Published by Cambridge University Press. © Cambridge University Press 2012.

such as the Silberberg Grotto in which Ron Clarke would later discover a near -complete *Australopithecus* skeleton (Tobias, 1979; Clarke and Tobias, 1995). Tobias's seminal publications include two monographs on the comparative morphology and evolutionary significance of two hominin taxa, *Australopithecus boisei* and the enigmatic *Homo habilis* from Bed 1 Olduvai Gorge, Tanzania (Tobias, 1967, 1991).

The African Genesis conference and this subsequent volume outline the major developments since Dart's announcement and description of Taung and gauge the consensus between various subdisciplines concerning the broader issues of hominin emergence in our ancestral homeland. This chapter reviews and summarises the main topics linking the contributions in this volume. These are loosely grouped into four parts: (I) the search for origins, whether these be in the earliest African Miocene deposits, in new excavations or in the new interpretation of previously studied hominin assemblages (Chapters 3–7); (II) hominin cranial, postcranial and dental morphology (Chapters 8–16); (III) the processes of modern human origins and dispersals (Chapters 17–21) and (IV) faunal context of hominin discoveries and the inferences about the evolution of human behaviour through time (Chapters 22–27).

At the end of the volume overview, I discuss the other significant discoveries of the last two decades that have helped to change our perspectives of our science and our origins.

Part I (Chapters 3–7)

In search of origins: evolutionary theory, new species and paths into the past

Colin Groves (Chapter 3) reviews the search for a species concept that is grounded in biology, but still applicable to the fossil record. He examines this important concept in three parts: first, how species can be identified; second, how speciation occurs and third, how these concepts can be meaningfully applied to the diversity of species of hominins identified in the fossil record. Groves also offers a new scheme of classification for the hominins and posits the modes of speciation and dispersal that may have led to the fossil evidence observed.

Michel Brunet (Chapter 4) discusses the environment of a new hominin genus, *Sahelanthropus tchadensis*, from the Chadian deposits of Toros-Menalla that date to approximately 7.0 million years old (Ma). Evidence that this hominin lived in an environment similar to the modern-day Okavango Delta (Botswana) provides an important reminder of how much the interpretation of early hominin environments has changed since Yves Coppen's 'East Side Story' (Coppens, 1983). The prevailing view of human evolution from Dart (1925) until the discovery of *Sahelanthropus* was that early (Miocene) hominins evolved in savannah environments, specifically in southern and eastern Africa. Recent discoveries, both within Africa and elsewhere, show that several other regions contain important aspects of the human story and that our Miocene ancestors were clearly not exclusively associated with savannah environments (e.g. Brunet *et al.*, 2002).

Brigitte Senut (Chapter 5) provides an insightful and thorough review of Miocene hominoids, with a consideration of their modes of locomotion. While most Miocene hominoids can be considered primarily adapted to arboreal locomotion, significant morphological differences exist in the shoulder, elbow and wrist joints of known Miocene apes, which indicate considerable diversity in locomotor mode, relative to modes seen in extant primates. Senut also explores the possibility that hominin adaptations to bipedality may have arisen in closed, forested environments.

Martin Pickford (Chapter 6) echoes the idea that recent fossil discoveries have radically altered our understanding of Miocene hominins. The discovery of the 6.0 million-year-old bipedal hominin *Orrorin tugenensis* in the Lukeino Formation, Kenya, in 2000, has shed doubt on what the last common ancestor (LCA) between humans and apes may have looked like. *Orrorin* appears very different from the hypothetical LCA, which was predicted to possess large canines and be a knuckle-walker (Pickford *et al.,* 2002). Ape-like specimens recovered in the same levels as *Orrorin* (Pickford and Senut, 2005) suggest that the LCA must have existed some time before the appearance of *Orrorin* at 6 Ma (Senut and Pickford, 2004). These finds indicate that *Orrorin,* along with the older *Sahelanthropus* from Chad and the somewhat younger *Ardipithecus* from the Lower Aramis Member of the Sangatole Ethiopia were all bipedal and inhabiting closed, forested environments.

Ronald J. Clarke (Chapter 7) presents an historical review of 40 years of excavation at the world famous site of Sterkfontein, where the first adult specimen of *Australopithecus africanus* was discovered by Robert Broom in 1936 (Broom, 1936). Clarke reviews the most important fossil discoveries made at Sterkfontein during the long-running research project started by Phillip V. Tobias and A. R. Hughes in 1966. The Sterkfontein excavation project has had several remarkable results, not just in terms of impressive hominin discoveries such as the StW 53 cranium (Hughes and Tobias, 1977), which has been recently redated to 1.8–1.4 Ma based on seriation methods (Herries *et al.*, 2009) but also insight into fossil plants (Bamford, 1999), in-depth taphonomic studies (Pickering, 1999; Kibii, 2004; Pickering *et al.*, 2000) and a deeper understanding of the complexity of cave breccias and site formation processes

(Kuman, 1994; Clarke, 1994; Kuman and Clarke, 2000; Reynolds *et al.*, 2007). Clarke's discovery of a near-complete hominin skeleton (StW 573), dating to between 3.3 Ma and 2.2 Ma (Partridge *et al.*, 1999; Walker *et al.*, 2006) has shed much light on aspects of the *Australopithecus* postcranial morphology (e.g. Clarke and Tobias, 1995; Clarke, 1998, 1999).

Part II (Chapters 8–16)

Hominin morphology through time: brains, bodies and teeth

Dean Falk (Chapter 8) reviews the development of endocast studies, comparing the scientific and public response to the first endocast to be discovered and described by Dart (1925; see also Holloway, Chapter 9) to the most recent endocast to cause controversy and comment within the palaeoanthropological community, that of *Homo floresiensis*, LB1, which was found on the Indonesian island of Flores in 2004 and is dated to between 38 ka and 18 ka (Morwood *et al.*, 2004). Work by Falk and colleagues on the endocast of the *H. floresiensis* specimens indicate that 'global, rather than mosaic, cortical reorganisation' occurred and that the cerebral cortex of this species has derived features that span the entire surface (Falk *et al.*, 2005; 2007). She concludes that both brain size and neurological reorganisation characterise human evolution (Gould, 2001; Falk, Chapter 8).

Ralph L. Holloway (Chapter 9) provides his perspective on Dart's original interpretation of the position of the lunate sulcus in *Australopithecus africanus* (Dart, 1925). Holloway reviews the issue of brain reorganisation and the development of the three areas of brain research (i.e. palaeoneurology, comparative neuroanatomy and molecular genomics). As Holloway and other authors point out, the process of *Australopithecus* brain reorganisation was probably more complex that that first envisioned by Dart (1925), with a mosaic pattern of brain enlargement and simultaneous reorganisation of the brain being a likely scenario (Falk, Chapter 8; Holloway, Chapter 9). More recently, work undertaken by Holloway and colleagues on the Sterkfontein *Australopithecus* cranium StW 505 suggests 'cortical reorganisation preceded brain enlargement in hominin evolution' (Holloway *et al.*, 2004: 290).

In Chapter 10, Paul R. Manger and his colleagues explore the relationship between hominin body size and brain size, compared with other primates. The analysis by Manger and colleagues of body and brain size estimates of a range of humans and extant primates, as well as fossil hominins, indicates that the relationship between brain and body size is the same for fossil hominins and modern humans (Manger *et al.*, Chapter 10). They propose two key transitions that have shaped our present brain–body mass relationship. The first occurred at the origin of the primates, where scaling laws governing non-primate mammalian orders diverged from the Order Primates. The second putative event occurred at the origin of the hominin lineage, where scaling laws appear altered in favour of further positive allometry. When they are combined, these two shifts towards positive allometry together explain the present *H. sapiens'* large brain relative to all other mammals. The authors suggest that the large human brain is a highly successful 'spandrel' (*sensu* Gould and Lewontin, 1979), for which the causes are as yet unclear, but which may well be environmental in origin.

Henry M. McHenry's contribution (Chapter 11) is a case study of recent comparative physiological investigations into hominin energetics. Recent experimental data reveal that energy expenditure during bipedal progression in chimpanzees (*Pan*) does not substantially exceed that incurred during terrestrial quadrupedalism. These results confirm earlier ideas that energetics imposed no obstacle to the transition from a terrestrial quadrupedal gait to bipedalism and that even the earliest bipeds may have enjoyed an energetic advantage (Taylor and Rowntree, 1973). The extant African hominins (*Gorilla, Pan, Homo*) display poorly adapted terrestrial gaits compared with quadrupedal mammals of a similar size, including the large cercopithecine monkeys such as *Papio* (McHenry, Chapter 11).

Michelle S. M. Drapeau (Chapter 12) presents a novel perspective on the 'transitional' morphology of the upper limb in *Australopithecus afarensis*. Drapeau and her colleagues have undertaken a revised synthesis of comparative hominin upper limb morphology during the past decade (Drapeau, 2004; Drapeau *et al.*, 2005). While the upper limb of the earliest hominins remains undoubtedly primitive, tantalising evidence has emerged for a remarkable suite of morphological features that strongly suggest that *Australopithecus* engaged their upper limbs in novel manual activities that have no corollaries among the extant hominins. This new evidence may provide some support for the cladistic inference that the common ancestor of the panin–hominin dichotomy may have regularly engaged in enhanced manual activities as part of an expanding and more sophisticated terrestrial ecological repertoire (e.g. Panger *et al.*, 2002).

The contribution by Brian G. Richmond and William L. Jungers (Chapter 13) examines the proximal femoral morphology of Plio-Pleistocene early hominins with specific reference to the femoral specimens assigned to the 6-Ma *O. tugenensis* from Kenya and the Indonesian small hominin species, *H. floresiensis* (Senut *et al.*, 2001; Brown *et al.*, 2004). As discussed in an earlier section, the precise biomechanical attributes of the *Orrorin* femoral neck are problematic, but morphometric analysis by Richmond and Jungers (2008; Chapter 13) confirm that the affinities of the *Orrorin* specimen are in agreement with the Upper Miocene age and its being a bipedal, basal hominin with similarities to Plio-Pleistocene *Australopithecus* and *Paranthropus* rather than with Lower Pleistocene *Homo* (McHenry and Corruccini, 1976, 1978). As for the much-debated 'Hobbit' species, the study by the authors of the proximal femoral anatomy of the *H. floresiensis* specimen (LB1/9) indicate that it is not a small modern human, but possesses a primitive morphology suggesting that it is a distinct hominin species that existed on the island of Flores in the Late Pleistocene (Morwood *et al.*, 2004).

M. Christopher Dean (Chapter 14) explores the types of data that can be gleaned from even very badly weathered dental specimens that preserve little macroscopic detail. The specimen discussed is a hemimandible fragment (KNM-ER 1817) recovered from the Okote Member of Koobi Fora, Kenya, dating to between 1.65 and 1.55 Ma (Wood, 1991). This specimen could be assigned only to Hominidae gen. et sp. indet., but the size of the mandible suggested that it probably represents *Paranthropus boisei* (Leakey, 1974; Wood, 1991). Using microscopy techniques, Dean provides information about rates of dentine formation and root extension times and offers insights into differences between dental traits in modern humans and extinct hominins. His results indicate that molar roots in *P. boisei* may have had faster rates of root extension than those of modern human molars at the same developmental stage and illustrate the powerful insights that can be gained using microscopic techniques.

Kevin L. Kuykendall (Chapter 15) examines the evolutionary development, in particular the morphology of the cusps and the enamel–dentine junction (EDJ), of the *Paranthropus* molar specimen from the Pliocene site of Gondolin. This site lies within the Cradle of Humankind, (South Africa) and has been dated faunally to between 2.0 and 1.5 Ma (Menter *et al.*, 1999). Initial published reports described the isolated lower molar (GDA-2) as '*Paranthropus* sp. indet.' (Menter *et al.*, 1999). The specimen is an 'unexpected variant'; exceeding the size variation for all known southern African *Paranthropus* specimens and falling more closely within the range of eastern African specimens. Although a larger sample of the 'hyper-robust' variant form would allow further investigation into the environmental context and life history of what was, presumably, a large body-sized *Paranthropus* subpopulation, Kuykendall points out that such investigations must await the further recovery of more 'hyper-robust' specimens for study.

Gerhard W. Weber and his colleagues (Chapter 16) review how technology is being used to digitise and analyse specimens as part of a new subdiscipline of anthropology called 'virtual anthropology' (VA; Weber *et al.*, 2001). As an illustration of this new approach, reconstructions of fossil specimens are presented, including that of a Makapansgat cranium (MLD37/38) and Sterkfontein crania Sts 71 and StW 505. New analyses can correct for various taphonomic problems associated with fossil specimens, such as deformation or incomplete preservation. It is also possible to compare digitally enhanced reconstructions to several other reconstructions simultaneously. Virtual anthropology promises many benefits to students of palaeoanthropology, since several teams of researchers can work on different digital versions of the same fossil specimen simultaneously. Comparisons between fossils can be made without the constraints of travel or funding, thus aiding the access of researchers to fossils around the world and also facilitating new and integrative analyses, which have hitherto been difficult, if not almost impossible, to undertake.

Part III (Chapters 17–21)

Modern human origins: patterns and processes

Steven E. Churchill and his colleagues (Chapter 17) present new body-size estimations of fossil *Homo* species of the African Middle Pleistocene, from such sites as Berg Aukas (Namibia) and Kabwe (Zambia). When orbit and femur data are compared with modern sub-Saharan African *H. sapiens*, the data suggest that the majority of Middle Pleistocene *Homo* individuals are larger than both early and modern *H. sapiens* counterparts. A possible reason for the increased body size may have been the requirement for increased body mass and muscularity to ensure success in hunting large-bodied prey species (Churchill and Rhodes, 2006).

Milford H. Wolpoff and Sang-Hee Lee (Chapter 18) consider the role that the continent of Africa played in providing significant genetic contributions to the modern human gene pool. Given the limited genetic data available, the authors instead employ measures of phenetic, rather than phylogenetic, similarities. The authors consider the hypothesis that the taxon represented by the Middle Pleistocene Bodo cranium (Middle Awash region, Ethiopia) is ancestral to lineages of later hominins, represented by the morphology of the Herto cranium from Herto Bouri (Ethiopia), dating to between 160 ka and 154 ka (Clark *et al.*, 2003) as well as samples of European Neandertals. Their results do not support the hypothesis that Herto and European Neandertals are the very different endpoints of two divergent lineages. Instead, the authors contend that some amount of gene flow, perhaps facilitated by as little as 24 to 74 matings between archaic and anatomically modern humans, would preserve overall levels of genetic similarity (Hawks and Cochran, 2006). The authors conclude that the genetic origins of modern humans must comprise combinations of African *H. sapiens* and Neandertal genes.

Fred H. Smith and his colleagues (Chapter 19) consider how within-African population movements have affected the morphological patterns observed within anatomically modern humans. Based on the geologically earliest fossils of anatomically modern humans from eastern Africa (specifically the sites of Omo Kibish and Herto, Ethiopia, which date to between 196 ka and 104 ka, and 160 ka and 154 ka, respectively), Smith and colleagues propose an assimilation model whereby these original populations spread out from eastern Africa and into southern and northern Africa and gradually assimilated the pre-existing archaic humans in these regions. Later and better dated sites in this region, such as Border Cave, show no such mosaic of features, suggesting that by approximately 74 ka (Grün *et al.*, 2003), the assimilation of modern humans into southern Africa is already complete. The authors contend that this is essentially extinction by assimilation, similar to a process of extinction by hybridisation (Levin, 2002). Given the wealth of sites in Africa, the process of human population movements and developments indicates that within-African movements were as important as those that occurred when modern humans left Africa.

The contribution by Emma Mbua and Günter Bräuer (Chapter 20) considers the exact mode of speciation prior to the emergence of the suite of facial and cranial features considered 'anatomically modern'. Several authors approach the fossil variation in *H.sapiens* differently, with some considering the mixture of archaic and modern *Homo* specimens as the African transitional group (ATG; Smith 1993, 2002). Mbua and Bräuer address this issue with a new morphological analysis of cranial features, designed to differentiate between long-term, diachronic changes and multiple speciation events. Rather than splitting the Middle Pleistocene anatomical variation into a range of separate species (as discussed in Bräuer, 2008), the authors advocate the approach that the modernisation of the *Homo* lineage began with the species represented by the Bodo cranium and continued to develop as a single species, *H. sapiens*, dispersing out from eastern Africa, as is suggested by Smith and colleagues (Chapter 19).

Osbjorn M. Pearson (Chapter 21) examines the genetic, anatomical and archaeological data available for the emergence of modern humans. The definition of what exactly constitutes modern human behaviour has long been subject to debate and McBrearty and Brooks (2000) have shown that the Later Stone Age (LSA) appearance was not a sudden revolution from the Middle Stone Age (MSA), rather a gradual accretion of increasingly modern behavioural and technological traits. Pearson considers that 'precocious' early behavioural changes such as the use of ochre and backed pieces by 300 ka at the Zambian sites of Twin Rivers and Kalambo Falls (Barham, 2002a,b) and the even earlier appearance of prepared core technology and blade production at Kapthurin,

Kenya, by 500 to 400 ka (McBrearty, 2001) represent nascent modern behaviours, which, in some cases, became locally extinct and were later re-invented (Shennan, 2001; d'Errico, 2003). Pearson contends that the capacity for 'modern' behaviour may have preceded the appearance of anatomically modern humans.

Part IV (Chapters 22–27)

In search of context: hominin environments, behaviour and lithic cultures

Darryl J. de Ruiter and colleagues (Chapter 22) examine the fauna associated with the extinct hominin *P. robustus*, from the Cradle of Humankind sites (Gauteng Province, South Africa). Using faunal data from Pleistocene sites such as Sterkfontein, Swartkrans and Kromdraai, they identify a pattern of arid-habitat avoidance for this species, which is in agreement with stable light isotope studies that indicate that this species had a mixed diet (Sponheimer *et al.*, 2006). The authors suggest that this species would have modified its landscape use in times of environmental and climatic fluctuations to make use of open grassland areas (their less favoured habitats) in order to exploit fallback resources such as insects, sedges and tubers.

Extant primates and their extinct counterparts form the basis of Sarah Elton's contribution (Chapter 23), which reviews the community of 11 monkey species in southern Africa that underwent fundamental community changes and extinctions during the Plio-Pleistocene. The South African cercopithecid fossil record over the past 3 Ma is characterised by high species diversity at the beginning of the period, followed by a reduction in diversity in the Pleistocene, which appears to have been due in part to cooling, drying shifts in climate and the spread of grassland habitats. The surviving monkey species, the baboon (*Papio hamadryas ursinus*) and vervet monkey *(Chlorocebus aethiops)* are eclectic feeders that can exist in environments extensively modified by humans. This ability to coexist with humans, since as early as the Late Pleistocene, has probably been the key to their ongoing success in Africa. In addition, the inferred role of the hominins during the Plio-Pleistocene may have been the generalist niche presently occupied by the baboons and vervets.

Travis R. Pickering's contribution (Chapter 24) considers our evolving view of hominin behaviour by reviewing Raymond Dart's 'killer ape' hypothesis (Dart, 1949), an idea much popularised in the decades after its publication (Ardrey, 1961). Central to this idea was the notion that broken bones found with the hominins were used by them as tools for inter- and intraspecies violence. Subsequent careful research by C. K. (Bob) Brain illustrated the role of carnivore damage in creating the distinctive damage patterns, thereby refuting Dart's killer ape model and establishing the subdiscipline of taphonomy (Brain, 1981). Pickering also reviews one of the present debates of hominin behaviour, the issue of when and how hominins gained access to carcasses. Did hominins obtain animal tissue by scavenging carnivore kills, or instead by hunting and /or aggressive scavenging? Dart's killer ape hypothesis may have a ring of truth to it in at least one instance: the evidence for cannibalism suggested by butchery marks on the StW 53 cranium does suggest that early hominins may have been capable of violence, although the context and intention of this behaviour is as yet unclear (Pickering *et al.*, 2000).

John A. J. Gowlett (Chapter 25) examines Acheulean stone tools from African sites dating to between 1.1 and 0.2 Ma, such as Casablanca (Morocco) and Kilombe and Baringo (Kenya), to deduce the internalised, shared concepts of desirable tool attributes in the minds of the toolmakers. Acheulean bifaces, while showing much size variation, possess a consistent pattern of production that remains constant at a variety of sites across Africa. As tools became larger, the increasing size and weight demanded that stone tool makers adjust their designs to preserve the utility of these tools (e.g. Crompton and Gowlett, 1993). These demands suggest that ancient humans were capable of controlling four or five of the most important lithic variables simultaneously (Gowlett, 2006). They indicate that the toolmakers tended to manipulate the variables relating to the tool-forms in a consistent manner, across temporal and geographic ranges, leading Gowlett to conclude that the concepts were affected by external experiences and their unique cultural traditions. Based on this evidence, he also argues that the shared attributes indicate systematic or collective social communication by the Acheulean toolmakers.

Lyn Wadley (Chapter 26) discusses the interpretations and significance of the Sibudu Cave (KwaZulu-Natal Province). Sibudu is the third South African site to document the transition between the Middle Stone Age Still Bay industry and the subsequent enigmatic, microlithic, Howiesons Poort industry (Wadley, 2007). The sequence is detailed enough to offer intriguing signs of behaviour: changes in the types of species hunted through time, as well as changes in the use of raw materials for tools. Wadley observes that notable shifts in material culture and subsistence strategies appear to coincide with marked changes in the environment at the site. She stresses the need for ongoing excavation efforts in southern Africa, since more evidence for the Still Bay and Howiesons Poort succession, such as has been recovered at Sibudu, is necessary to understand the origins of modern behaviour in the region.

Avraham Ronen (Chapter 27) explores the development of the awareness of death, combined with a review of deliberate funerary practices. The oldest known burials of both *H. neanderthalensis* and *H. sapiens* date to the Middle Palaeolithic period (specifically between 130 and 100 ka) and were found in the Mount Carmel and Galilee regions of Israel. Ronen argues that burial practices indicate that both humans and Neandertals likely possessed similarly developed syntactical language skills, an awareness of death and, possibly, a concept of an afterlife.

Review of other scientific developments

The African Genesis conference aimed to review the major developments since Dart's description of the Taung skull and to gauge consensus between various subdisciplines. Major groundbreaking work has been done in the intervening decades and we now possess greater insight into the biology, intelligence, genetics and behaviour of hominins.

In the last two decades, rich new fossil hominin sites at Drimolen and Malapa, both in the Cradle of Humankind have been discovered (Keyser *et al.*, 2000; Berger *et al.*, 2010). The new species of *Australopithecus sediba* from Malapa dating to 1.95 to 1.78 Ma has been interpreted as representing a species of late *Australopithecus* – early *Homo* (Berger *et al.*, 2010). Other well known and much debated fossils, such as Sterkfontein cranium StW 53, first assigned to *H. habilis*, have been reassigned as the type specimen of a new species: *H. gautengensis* (Curnoe, 2010). Re-examination of *Paranthropus robustus* males has provided insights into the life histories and social organisation of an extinct hominin (Lockwood *et al.*, 2007). We have shifted our emphasis from single sites and have started to widen our view and examine the landscape around hominin sites and consider what features attracted the hominins to these regions (Bailey *et al.*, 2011; Reynolds *et al.*, 2011).

Hominins from Late Miocene and Pliocene, such as *Sahelanthropus*, *Orrorin*, *Ardipithecus* and *Kenyanthropus* have been discovered in central and eastern Africa and, surprisingly, these species appear to have lived in closed, wooded or mosaic environments (Senut *et al.*, 2001; Leakey *et al.*, 2001; Brunet *et al.*, 2002; White *et al.*, 2009). This lays to rest the savannah hypothesis (Dart, 1925), at least for the earlier part of the hominin fossil record, that was long considered pivotal to our African genesis.

In southern Africa, stable light isotope analysis has enabled us to gain insight into the diets of hominin species, leading to unexpectedly high levels of variation, both in *Australopithecus africanus* from Sterkfontein (e.g. van der Merwe *et al.*, 2003) and clear evidence of seasonal and annual dietary variation in *Paranthropus robustus* (Sponheimer *et al.*, 2006). Recent microwear texture analysis results for these hominins are consistent with this result (Scott *et al.*,

2005). Later genera, such as *P. robustus*, show a pattern of habitat avoidance of open, grassland habitats (de Ruiter *et al.*, Chapter 22). Our interpretation of cave deposits now encompasses the appreciation of climate- and time-averaging, which has bearing on how morphological variation and faunal communities should be interpreted in the fossil record (O'Regan and Reynolds, 2009; Hopley and Maslin, 2010).

New species, such as the 'Hobbit' (*H. florisensis*) from Indonesia and early *Homo* dating to approximately 1.75 Ma from the site of Dmanisi, Republic of Georgia (Vekua *et al.*, 2002) clearly show that important chapters of our ancestors' history were written outside of Africa. Other important firsts, such as abstract art and personal adornment, long thought to have developed outside of Africa, appear to have originated in Blombos Cave in South Africa at about 75 ka (Henshilwood *et al.*, 2004, 2009). Genetic studies on modern humans have shed light onto our evolution in unexpected ways: a genetic mutation that may be in part responsible for speech – the *FOXP2* gene – has been found (Enard *et al.*, 2002) and more importantly, a later study indicated that the Neandertals also possessed this critical mutation (Krause *et al.*, 2007). We have sequenced the genome of Neandertals and discovered that they are 'likely to have had a role in the genetic ancestry of present-day humans outside of Africa' (Green *et al.*, 2010: 722).

Recent excavations in the rainforests of central Africa have yielded a Chimpanzee Stone Age and a history of stone tool modification that stretched back at least 4300 years in the Côte d'Ivoire (Mercader *et al.*, 2007). Stone tool using and possibly even stone tool manufacture may no longer be exclusively associated with our lineage.

All of these discoveries have given us insights into what makes us human. Previously our concept of human behaviour included bipedality, syntactical speech, toolmaking and an awareness of death. Slowly but surely, these definitions are being revised as new discoveries challenge our perceptions. Through it all, the efforts and creativity of palaeoanthropologists all over the world ensure that the next 80 years of our field will continue to surprise, shock and delight all of us who follow the paths into the past.

Conclusion

The study of human origins from southern African sites began in the 1920s and the pace of the field has quickened considerably over the last two decades or so. When Raymond Dart's description of the Taung child was first published in 1925, his ideas met with mixed reactions. Recent discoveries at the Cradle of Humankind fossil sites, as well at Blombos Cave, illustrate how the southern

African region continues to produce new evidence to aid our understanding of human evolution and the role southern Africa played in the human story. It is thanks to tireless pioneers working in Africa that the important role of this continent can be fully appreciated. Phillip V. Tobias is one of those pioneers and he in turn has nurtured and encouraged several new generations of researchers. His scholarly legacy is that the systematic study of all aspects of human evolution continues, both in South Africa, where so many human 'firsts' have been recorded, but also all around the world.

Acknowledgements

My thanks are due to Professor Tobias for being the inspiration for the conference and this volume. Andrew Gallagher and I extend our thanks to all our colleagues who attended the African Genesis conference and to the authors whose contributions have made this book such a privilege to edit. Andrew Gallagher, Brian G. Richmond, Peter S. Ungar and Osbjorn M. Pearson all made helpful comments on this chapter.

References

Ardrey R. (1961). *African Genesis: a Personal Investigation into the Animal Origins and Nature of Man*. New York: Atheneum.

Bailey, G. N., Reynolds, S. C. and King, G. C. P. (2011). Landscapes of human evolution: models and methods of tectonic geomorphology and the reconstruction of hominin landscapes. *Journal of Human Evolution*, **60**(3): 257–80.

Bamford, M. (1999). Pliocene fossil woods from an early hominid cave deposit, Sterkfontein, South Africa. *South African Journal of Science*, **95**: 231–7.

Barham, L. S. (2002a). Systematic pigment use in the Middle Pleistocene of South-Central Africa. *Current Anthropology*, **43**: 181–90.

  (2002b). Backed tools in Middle Pleistocene Central Africa and their evolutionary significance. *Journal of Human Evolution*, **43**: 585–603.

Berger, L. R., de Ruiter, D. J., Churchill, S. E. *et al.* (2010). *Australopithecus sediba*: a new species of *Homo*-like australopith from South Africa. *Science*, **328**: 195–204.

Brain, C. K. (1981). *The Hunters or the Hunted? An Introduction to African Cave Taphonomy*. Chicago: University of Chicago Press.

Bräuer, G. (2008). The origin of modern anatomy: by speciation or intraspecific evolution? *Evolutionary Anthropology*, **17**: 22–37.

Broom, R. (1936). A new fossil anthropoid skull from South Africa. *Nature*, **138**: 486–8.

Brown, P., Sutikna, T., Morwood, M. J. *et al.* (2004). A new small-bodied hominin from the Late Pleistocene of Flores, Indonesia. *Nature*, **431**: 1055–61.

Brunet, M., Guy, F., Pilbeam, D. *et al.* (2002). A new hominid from the Upper Miocene of Chad, Central Africa. *Nature*, **418**: 145–51.

Churchill, S. E. and Rhodes, J. A. (2006). How strong were the Neandertals? Leverage and muscularity at the shoulder and elbow in Mousterian foragers. *Periodicum Biologorum*, **108**: 457–70.

Clark, J., Beyene, Y., WoldeGabriel, G. *et al.* (2003). Stratigraphic, chronological and behavioural context of Pleistocene *Homo sapiens* from Middle Awash, Ethiopia. *Nature*, **423**: 747–52.

Clarke, R. J. and Tobias, P. V. (1995). Sterkfontein Member 2 foot-bones of the oldest South African hominid. *Science*, **269**: 521–4.

Clarke, R. J. (1994). On some new interpretations of Sterkfontein stratigraphy. *South African Journal of Science*, **90**: 211–14.

(1998). First ever discovery of a well-preserved skull and associated skeleton of *Australopithecus*. *South African Journal of Science*, **94**: 460–3.

(1999). Discovery of complete arm and hand of the 3.3 million-year-old *Australopithecus* skeleton from Sterkfontein. *South African Journal of Science*, **95**: 477–80.

Coppens, Y. (1983). Les plus anciens fossiles d'Hominidés. In *Recent Advances in the Evolution of Primates*. Pontificiae Academiae Scientiarum Scripta Varia, pp. 1–9.

Crompton, R. H. and Gowlett, J. A. J. (1993). Allometry and multidimensional form in Acheulean bifaces from Kilombe, Kenya. *Journal of Human Evolution*, **25**: 175–99.

Curnoe, D. (2010). A review of early *Homo* in southern Africa focusing on cranial, mandibular and dental remains, with the description of a new species (*Homo gautengensis* sp. nov.). *Homo – Journal of Comparative Human Biology*, **6**(31): 151–77.

Curnoe, D. and Tobias, P. V. (2006). Description, new reconstruction, comparative anatomy and classification of the Sterkfontein StW 53 cranium, with discussions about the taxonomy of other southern African early *Homo* remains. *Journal of Human Evolution*, **50**: 36–77.

Dart, R. A. (1925). *Australopithecus africanus*: the man-ape of South Africa. *Nature*, **115**: 195–9.

(1949). The bone-bludgeon hunting technique of *Australopithecus*. *South African Journal of Science*, **2**: 150–2.

Enard, W., Przeworski, M., Fisher, S. E. *et al.* (2002). Molecular evolution of *FOXP2*, a gene involved in speech and language. *Nature*, **418**: 869–72.

d'Errico, F. (2003). The invisible frontier: a multiple species model for the origin of behavioral modernity. *Evolutionary Anthropology*, **12**: 188–202.

Drapeau, M. S. M. (2004). Functional anatomy of the olecranon process in hominoids and Plio-Pleistocene hominins. *American Journal of Physical Anthropology*, **124**: 297–314.

Drapeau, M. S. M., Ward, C. V., Kimbel, W. H. *et al.* (2005). Associated cranial and forelimb remains attributed to *Australopithecus afarensis* from Hadar, Ethiopia. *Journal of Human Evolution*, **48**: 593–642.

Falk, D., Hildebolt, C., Smith, K. *et al.* (2005). The brain of LB1, *Homo floresiensis*. *Science*, **308**: 242–5.

(2007). Brain shape in human microcephalics and *Homo floresiensis*. *Proceedings of the National Academy of Sciences, USA*, **104**: 2513–18.

Gould, S. J. (2001). Size matters and function counts. In Falk, D. and Gibson, K. R. (eds.), *Evolutionary Anatomy of the Primate Cerebral Cortex*. Cambridge: Cambridge University Press, pp. xiii–xvii.

Gould, S. J. and Lewontin, R. C. (1979). The spandrels of San Marco and the Panglossian paradigm: a critique of the adaptationist programme. *Proceedings of the Royal Society London B*, **205**: 581–98.

Gowlett, J. A. J. (2006). The elements of design form in Acheulian bifaces: modes, modalities, rules and language. In Goren-Inbar, N. and Sharon, G. (eds.), *Axe Age: Acheulian Tool-making from Quarry to Discard*. London: Equinox, pp. 50–67.

Green, R. E., Krause, J., Briggs, A. W. *et al.* (2010). A draft sequence of the Neandertal genome. *Science*, **328**: 710–22.

Grün, R., Beaumont, P., Tobias, P. and Eggins, S. (2003). On the age of Border Cave 5 human mandible. *Journal of Human Evolution*, **45**: 155–67.

Hawks, J. and Cochran, G. (2006). Dynamics of adaptive introgression from archaic to modern humans. *PaleoAnthropology*, **2006**: 101–15.

Henshilwood, C., D'Errico, F., Vanhaeren, M. *et al.* (2004). Middle Stone Age shell beads from South Africa. *Science*, **304**: 404.

Henshilwood, C. S., d'Errico, F. and Watts, I. (2009). Engraved ochres from the Middle Stone Age levels at Blombos Cave, South Africa. *Journal of Human Evolution*, **57**: 27–47.

Herries, A. I. R., Curnoe, D. and Adams, J. W. (2009). A multi-disciplinary seriation of early *Homo* and *Paranthropus* bearing palaeocaves in southern Africa. *Quaternary International*, **202**(1–2), 14–28.

Holloway, R. L, Clarke, R. J. and Tobias, P. V. (2004). Posterior lunate sulcus in *Australopithecus africanus*: was Dart right? *Comptes Rendus Palevol.*, **3**: 287–93.

Hopley, P. J. and Maslin, M. A. (2010). Climate-averaging of terrestrial faunas: an example from the Plio-Pleistocene of South Africa. *Paleobiology*, **36**(1): 32–50.

Hughes, A. R. and Tobias, P. V. (1977). A fossil skull probably of the genus *Homo* from Sterkfontein, Transvaal. *Nature*, **265**: 310–12.

Keyser, A. W., Menter, C. G., Moggi-Cecchi, J. *et al.* (2000). Drimolen: a new hominid-bearing site in Gauteng, South Africa. *South African Journal of Science*, **96**: 193–7.

Kibii, J. M. (2004). Comparative taxonomic, taphonomic and palaeoenvironmental analysis of 4–2.3 million year old australopithecine cave infills at Sterkfontein. PhD thesis, University of the Witwatersrand.

Krause, J., Lalueza-Fox, C., Orlando, L. *et al.* (2007). The derived *FOXP2* variant of modern humans was shared with Neandertals. *Current Biology*, **17**: 1–5.

Kuman, K. (1994). The archaeology of Sterkfontein: past and present. *Journal of Human Evolution*, **27**: 471–95.

Kuman, K. and Clarke, R. J. (2000). Stratigraphy, artefact industries and hominid associations for Sterkfontein, Member 5. *Journal of Human Evolution*, **38**: 827–47.

Leakey, R. E. F. (1974). Further evidence of Lower Pleistocene hominids from East Rudolf, North Kenya. *Nature*, **248**, 653–6.

Leakey, L. S. B., Tobias, P. V. and Napier, J. R. (1964). A new species of the genus *Homo* from Olduvai Gorge. *Nature*, **202**: 7–9.

Leakey, M. G., Spoor, F., Brown, F. H. *et al.* (2001). New hominin genus from eastern Africa shows diverse middle Pliocene lineages. *Nature*, **410**: 433–40.

Levin, D. (2002). Hybridization and extinction. *American Scientist*, **90**: 254–61.

Lockwood, C. A. and Tobias, P. V. (2002). Morphology and affinities of new hominin cranial remains from Member 4 of the Sterkfontein Formation, Gauteng Province, South Africa. *Journal of Human Evolution*, **42**: 389–450.

Lockwood, C. A., Menter, C. G., Moggi-Cecci, J. *et al.* (2007). Extended male growth in a fossil hominin species. *Science*, **318**: 1443–6.

McHenry, H. M. and Corruccini, R. S. (1976). Fossil hominid femora and the evolution of walking. *Nature*, **259**: 657–8.

(1978).The femur in early human evolution. *American Journal of Physical Anthropology*, **49**: 473–88.

McBrearty, S. (2001). The Middle Pleistocene of East Africa. In Barham, L. and Robson-Brown, K. (eds.), *Human Roots – Africa and Asia in the Middle Pleistocene*. Bristol, England: Western Academic & Specialist Press Limited, pp. 81–98.

McBrearty, S. and Brooks, A. S. (2000). The revolution that wasn't: a new interpretation of the origin of modern human behavior. *Journal of Human Evolution*, **39**: 453–563.

Menter, C., Kuykendall, K. L., Keyser, A. W. *et al.* (1999). First record of hominid teeth from the Plio-Pleistocene site of Gondolin, South Africa. *Journal of Human Evolution*, **37**: 299–307.

Mercader, J., Barton, H., Gillespie, J. *et al.* (2007). 4,300-year-old chimpanzee sites and the origins of percussive stone technology. *Proceedings of the National Academy of Sciences* **104**(9): 3043–8.

Moggi-Cecchi, J., Grine, F. E. and Tobias, P. V. (2006). Early hominid dental remains from Members 4 and 5 of the Sterkfontein Formation (1966–1996 excavations): catalogue, individual associations, morphological descriptions and initial metric analyses. *Journal of Human Evolution*, **50**: 239–328.

Morwood, M. J., Soejono, R. P., Roberts, R. G. *et al.* (2004). Archaeology and age of a new hominin from Flores in eastern Indonesia. *Nature*, **431**: 1087–91.

O'Regan, H. J. and Reynolds, S. C. (2009). An ecological reassessment of the southern African carnivore guild: a case study from Member 4, Sterkfontein, South Africa. *Journal of Human Evolution*, **57**: 212–22.

Panger, M. A., Brooks, A. S., Richmond, B. G. *et al.* (2002). Older than the Oldowan? Rethinking the emergence of hominin tool use. *Evolutionary Anthropology*, **11**: 235–45.

Partridge, T. C., Shaw, J., Heslop, D. and Clarke, R. J. (1999). The new hominid skeleton from Sterkfontein, South Africa: age and preliminary assessment. *Journal of Quaternary Science*, **14**(4): 293–8.

Pickford, M. and Senut, B. (2005). Hominoid teeth with chimpanzee- and gorilla-like features from the Miocene of Kenya: implications for the chronology of the ape–human divergence and biogeography of Miocene hominoids. *Anthropological Science*, **113**: 95–102.

Pickford, M., Senut, B., Gommery, D. *et al.* (2002). Bipedalism in *Orrorin tugenensis* revealed by its femora. *Comptes Rendus Palevol*, **1**: 191–203.

Pickering, T. R. (1999). Taphonomic interpretations of the Sterkfontein early hominid site (Gauteng, South Africa) reconsidered in light of recent evidence. PhD thesis, University of Wisconsin, Madison. University Microfilms, Ann Arbor, Michigan.

Pickering, T. R., White, T. D. and Toth, N. (2000). Cutmarks on a Plio-Pleistocene hominid from Sterkfontein, South Africa. *American Journal of Physical Anthropology* **111**: 579–84.

Scott, R. S., Ungar P. S., Bergstrom, T. S. *et al.* (2005). Dental microwear texture analysis shows within-species diet variability in fossil hominins. *Nature*, **436**: 693–5.

Senut, B., Pickford, M., Gommery, D. *et al.* (2001). First hominid from the Miocene (Lukeino Formation, Kenya). *Comptes Rendus de l'Académie des Sciences*, **332**: 137–44.

Senut, B. and Pickford, M. (2004). La dichotomie grands singes – homme revisitée. *Comptes Rendus Palevol*, **3**: 265–76.

Shennan, S. (2001). Demography and cultural innovation: a model and its implications for the emergence of modern human culture. *Cambridge Archaeological Journal*, **11**: 5–16.

Smith, F. (1993). Models and realities in modern human origins: the African fossil evidence. In Aitken, M., Stringer, C. & Mellars, P. (eds.), *The Origins of Modern Humans and the Impact of Chronometric Dating*. Princeton: Princeton University Press, pp. 234–48.

   (2002). Migrations, radiations, and continuity: patterns in the evolution of Middle and Late Pleistocene humans. In Hartwig, W. (ed). *The Primate Fossil Record*. Cambridge: Cambridge University Press, pp. 437–56.

Sponheimer, M., Passey, B. H., de Ruiter, D. J. *et al.* (2006). Isotopic evidence for dietary variability in the early hominin *Paranthropus robustus*. *Science*, **314**, 980–2.

Reynolds, S. C., Clarke, R. J. and Kuman, K. (2007). The view from the Lincoln Cave: mid- to late Pleistocene fossil deposits from Sterkfontein hominid site, South Africa. *Journal of Human Evolution*, **53**(3): 260–71.

Reynolds, S. C., Bailey, G. and King, G. C. P. (2011). Landscapes and their relation to hominin habitats: case studies from *Australopithecus* sites in eastern and southern Africa. *Journal of Human Evolution*, **60**(3): 281–98.

Richmond, B. G. and Jungers, W. L. (2008). *Orrorin tugenensis* femoral morphology and the evolution of hominin bipedalism. *Science*, **319**: 662–1665.

Taylor, R. C. and Rowntree, V. J. (1973). Running on two or four legs: which consumes more energy? *Science*, **179**: 186–7.

Tobias, P. V. (1967). *Olduvai Gorge Volume 2: the Cranium and Maxilliary Dentition of* Australopithecus (Zinjanthropus) boisei. Cambridge: Cambridge University Press.

(1979). The Silberberg Grotto, Sterkfontein, Transvaal, and its importance in palaeo-anthropological research. *South African Journal of Science*, **75**: 161–4.

(1991). *Olduvai Gorge Volume 4: the Skulls, Teeth and Endocasts of* Homo habilis. Cambridge: Cambridge University Press.

van der Merwe, N. J., Thackeray, J. F., Lee-Thorp, J. A. and Luyt, J. (2003). The carbon isotope ecology and diet of *Australopithecus africanus* at Sterkfontein, South Africa. *Journal of Human Evolution*, **44**, 581–97.

Vekua, A., Lordkipanidze, D., Rightmire, G. P. *et al.* (2002). A new skull of early *Homo* from Dmanisi, Georgia. *Science*, **297**(5578): 85–9.

Wadley, L. (2007). Announcing a Still Bay Industry at Sibudu Cave, *Journal of Human Evolution*, **52**: 681–9.

Walker, J., Cliff, R. A. and Latham, A. G. (2006). U-Pb isotopic age of the StW 573 hominid from Sterkfontein, *South Africa. Science*, **314**: 1592–4.

Weber, G. W., Schäfer, K., Prossinger, H. *et al.* (2001). Virtual anthropology: the digital evolution in anthropological sciences. *Journal of Physiological Anthropology and Applied Human Sciences*, **20**: 69–80.

White, T. D., Ambrose, S. H., Suwa, G. *et al.* (2009). Macrovertebrate paleontology and the Pliocene habitat of *Ardipithecus ramidus. Science*, **326**: 87–93.

Wood, B. A. (1991). *Koobi Fora Research Project. Volume 4. Hominid Cranial Remains*. Oxford: Clarendon Press.

2 *Academic genealogy*

PETER S. UNGAR AND

PHILLIP V. TOBIAS

Time, the Refreshing River:[1] an academic genealogy extending more than half a millennium.

We are like dwarfs on the shoulders of giants, so that we can see more than they, and things at a greater distance…not by virtue of any sharpness of sight on our part, or any physical distinction…but because we are carried high and raised up by their giant size.

(John of Salisbury, 1159 quoting Bernard of Chartres)[2]

Introduction

Palaeoanthropologists often justify the study of human evolution as important to our understanding of where we as a species have been, where we are today, and where we will go in the future. Following the same logic, palaeoanthropologists should be better able to understand their own intellectual traditions with an appreciation of their academic genealogies. The history of palaeoanthropology and the personalities of its practitioners have had a profound impact on our field and the way we have phrased hypotheses, gathered data and interpreted our results (Cartmill *et al.* 1986; Landau 1991).

It may in this light come as a surprise that little formal work has been published on academic genealogies of palaeoanthropologists. Academic lineages have been well documented and detailed for a number of disciplines. The Mathematics Genealogy Project at North Dakota State University, for example, has been recognised by the *Chronicle of Higher Education*, *Science* magazine and other media outlets. This well funded, web-based project now boasts an academic tree listing more than one

---

[1] This phrase, from a poem by W. H. Auden, was used by Joseph Needham as the title of one of his books of essays (1943).
[2] Quoted in Rees (2006).

African Genesis: Perspectives on Hominin Evolution, eds. Sally C. Reynolds and Andrew Gallagher. Published by Cambridge University Press. © Cambridge University Press 2012.

hundred thousand individuals with roots dating back hundreds of years. Similar web-based genealogy databases are available for chemistry, physics, linguistics, computer science, neuroscience, philosophy, and other disciplines.

So why not palaeoanthropology? Our field is relatively young, but its intellectual roots span back through the centuries to the great medical schools of the European Renaissance. Surely we could benefit from, take comfort in, or at least gain some wry amusement out of, an understanding of our academic pedigrees. This chapter presents an academic genealogy of intellectual ancestry and descent shared to varying degrees by many palaeoanthropologists. It works backward from one of us (PVT), and reaches across four continents and more than five hundred years (Figure 2.1).

Figure 2.1. Academic lineage described in this chapter. Individuals are placed according to the dates of their highest relevant degrees.

Approaches to this genealogy

This exercise is by its nature an oversimplification. To be sure, no individual academic is influenced by only one mentor. In this sense, a genealogical plexus of blood vessels is probably a reasonable analogy, especially for the academic pedigree of an anatomical scientist! Our intellectual family tree more closely resembles a tangle of lianas connecting back and forth in seeming indecipherable chaos. Add to this the fact that ancestors came from many different academic traditions and that some individuals are better documented than others, and the task of tracing an academic genealogy becomes a formidable undertaking.

First and foremost, we must carefully define 'mentor' to make sense out of any academic genealogy. For this chapter, we identify a mentor as the individual who had the most documented influence on the student in the discipline of palaeoanthropology, or before the advent of palaeoanthropology, in the academic field for which that student became best known. This could be a teacher, a doctoral dissertation, research or clinical advisor, or a graduate or postdoctoral mentor. Academic genealogy is not an exact science. Some student and mentor relationships are obvious, whereas others are more difficult to establish and must be selected as 'best choice' among several possibilities.

Most of the individuals in this genealogy are well known from biographies, published or unpublished letters, detailed obituaries and other documents. This is fortunate, as the strength of a chain is only as good as its weakest link. Relationships between each mentor–student pair and facts about each individual were gathered from the primary literature and confirmed with demonstrably independent sources whenever possible. Rationales for ascribing relationships for less obvious links are offered as necessary.

Information on each individual is presented in a separate section. These sections provide only basic biographic facts because the emphasis here is on the linkages between mentor and student. Details provided include formal education and degrees, academic positions held and major contributions in research and teaching. Occasional anecdotes and quotations are also offered to give the reader a sense of these academicians as 'real people'. References to more detailed biographic information are presented at the end of each section.

Phillip Vallentine Tobias (1925–)

Mentor: Raymond Arthur Dart

Phillip Tobias was born in Durban, South Africa in 1925. His university education began at the University of the Witwatersrand in 1942, where he earned BSc and BSc Honours degrees (1946, 1947), the medical degrees MB, BCh

(1950) and a PhD (1953) for a thesis entitled *Chromosomes, Sex-Cells and Evolution in the Gerbil*. He was awarded a DSc degree for his works on hominid evolution in 1967. Tobias mentions Raymond Dart first among the 'veritable *Senatus Academicus*' that helped shape his academic career (Tobias, 2005). While Joseph Gillman advised Tobias on his cytogenetics doctoral thesis, Dart was clearly his mentor in palaeoanthropology – from the classroom to the laboratory and into the field.

Tobias was appointed demonstrator and instructor in histology and physiology at the University of the Witwatersrand in 1945. He served as lecturer (1951–2), senior lecturer (1953–8), professor and chair (1959–90) of anatomy, and as dean of the Faculty of Medicine (1980–2) at the University of the Witwatersrand, Johannesburg. He remains today professor emeritus and honorary professorial research fellow at that institution. Tobias is a captivating and respected teacher and lecturer, as well as a caring and diligent mentor. One of Tobias's academic protégés, Frederick Grine (1990), wrote of his 'extraordinarily thorough, painstaking and incisive comments, suggestions and criticisms', noting that his 'unfailing encouragement and wise counsel have truly been inspirational'. Tobias has had many academic descendants to date, spanning at this point at least four academic generations. These include the first author of this article, Peter Ungar, who was Frederick Grine's student. Ungar himself has now mentored several students, who today are in the process of training their own. And so it continues.

Phillip Tobias is best known for his landmark descriptions of early hominins. He has authored over 1150 works to date, spanning a dizzying variety of topics from genetics to human evolution, and anatomy, growth and development, to the history and philosophy of science. He has received numerous awards and honorary degrees, including three Nobel Prize nominations. He is a Fellow of the Royal Society (London) and a Foreign Associate of the National Academy of Sciences of the USA, Commander of the Order of Merit of France and Commander of the National Order of Merit of Italy. He has maintained an inspiring stance against apartheid from 1949 onward.

References: Sperber, 1990; Tobias, 2005; Koenig, 2005.

Raymond Arthur Dart (1893–1988)

*Mentor: Grafton Elliot Smith, but see also
James Thomas Wilson*

Raymond Dart was born in Toowong, Brisbane, Australia in 1893. His university education began in 1910 at the University of Queensland, where he received a BSc in 1913 and MSc in 1914. He enrolled in the University of Sydney in 1913, where he received his MB and ChM in 1917 and MD in 1927. Dart studied anatomy under James Thomas Wilson and served as his assistant between 1914 and 1917. He wrote more than four decades later that Wilson's influence on him was 'so great that even today, I find myself guided by the standards he implanted in my young mind' (Dart, 1959).

Following brief military service, Dart was appointed senior demonstrator under Grafton Elliot Smith at University College, London. In 1919 he continued his studies of neuroanatomy. Smith had a tremendous influence on Dart's interests in palaeoanthropology and thus may be considered Dart's primary mentor for this genealogy. Dart left London at the end of 1922 to accept a post as professor of anatomy in the Medical School at the University of the Witwatersrand, Johannesburg, South Africa. He served as professor and head of the Department of Anatomy from 1923 to 1958. Concurrently he was dean of the Faculty of Medicine from 1925 to 1943. Dart was a 'brilliant, gifted teacher who brought all the passion and conviction of a missionary preacher to his classes' (Fagan, 1989). Raymond Dart's best known accomplishment is his recognition of the human-like qualities in the famous Taung child skull discovered in 1924 and assigned by him to a new genus and species, *Australopithecus africanus*. His claim flew in the face of the prevailing paradigm, that mankind had evolved in Asia. He doggedly championed his view that it represented a species whose members have taken steps in a human direction and from the middle of the twentieth century saw its almost universal acceptance. He and his team recovered from the site of Makapansgat some 300 km north of Johannesburg further remains of *Australopithecus*, but his association with that site generated another revolutionary claim, namely that the thousands of broken bones had been artificially smashed and shaped by the australopithecines. Although his claim for a bone, tooth and horn culture has not been supported, the impact of that work catalysed the development of the field of taphonomy. Dart pioneered studies on the evolution of the human upright posture and made many contributions in southern African archaeology. It has been said of him that he was 'a maker of men' and this is perhaps his most lasting contribution. Raymond Dart played a major role in building up the infant Medical School of the University of the Witwatersrand, Johannesburg, including the establishment of the Witwatersrand Medical Library (now the Health Sciences Library), university courses for physiotherapists, occupational therapists and nurses, and the Medical BSc and honours degrees, which laid a foundation for many of the distinguished graduates of this School.

References: Dart, 1959; Wheelhouse, 1983; Tobias, 1984; Tobias, 1989; Fagan, 1989; Wheelhouse and Smithford, 2001.

Grafton Elliot Smith (1871–1937)

Mentor: James Thomas Wilson

Grafton Elliot Smith was born in Grafton, New South Wales, Australia in 1871. He entered the University of Sydney in 1888 to study medicine, and graduated as MB and ChM in 1893. He received an MD in 1895 for his dissertation on the anatomy and histology of the non-placental mammal brain. Smith served as a demonstrator of anatomy under his mentor James Thomas Wilson from 1894–6. He continued his research at Cambridge until 1900.

Elliot Smith's first professorship was the chair of anatomy at the University of Cairo from 1900 to 1909. During that time he continued to develop his research on neuroanatomy, but added Egyptian bioarchaeology, human evolution and the origin and spread of civilisation to his repertoire of interests. He accepted the chair of anatomy at the Victoria University of Manchester, where he served until 1919. He then filled the chair of anatomy at University College, London until his retirement in 1936. Smith mentored many students and staff during his career, and more than twenty went on to fill chairs of anatomy. He must have been an inspiring lecturer, as Raymond Dart recounted after hearing him speak for the first time, 'I fell under his spell that night and prayed that at some time I would be allowed to work under him' (Dart, 1959).

Elliot Smith was a remarkably prolific researcher with some 434 works to his credit, including eight books. He is perhaps best known for his work on the infamous Piltdown man and on hyperdiffusionism, but he published on an amazing assortment of topics, from mammalian comparative neuroanatomy to many aspects of human evolution, and the bioarchaeology of Dynastic Egypt. Elliot Smith received many accolades, including a Knighthood in 1934, and Cross of the French Legion of Honour in 1936.

References: Wilson, 1938; Dart, 1959; Elkin and MacIntosh, 1974; Blunt, 1988; Morison, 1997.

James Thomas Wilson (1861–1945)

Mentor: William Turner

James Thomas Wilson was born in 1861 at Moniaive, Dumfriesshire, Scotland. He began his medical training at the University of Edinburgh in 1879 and received his BM degree there in 1883. After a surgical rotation at the Royal Infirmary in Edinburgh and a year as a surgeon on a cargo ship at sea, he returned to the University of Edinburgh as demonstrator of anatomy under William Turner for two winter sessions. Of his mentor, Wilson later wrote

'I cannot omit a special reference to the Edinburgh School of Anatomy in which I received not only my early anatomical instruction, but my later training as a teacher of anatomy under my old chief Sir William Turner, to whom as in private duty bound, I must pay tribute' (Morison, 1997).

Wilson began his career as demonstrator of anatomy in the Medical School at the University of Sydney in 1887. He remained in Sydney for more than three decades, later serving as professor of anatomy and as dean of the Faculty of Medicine. He also served as director of the Prince Alfred Hospital and held numerous other appointments. Wilson returned to Britain in 1920 to fill the chair of anatomy at Cambridge University, a position he held until his retirement in 1934. Wilson was evidently not the most exciting of lecturers. His pupil, Elliot Smith, once wrote that his boring osteology lectures 'rapidly killed all interest in the subject' (Morison, 1997). Nevertheless, he was an excellent research mentor, 'advising, criticizing, and above all, encouraging, all with great vehemence' (Morison, 1997).

Wilson's best known publications involve the anatomy, physiology and embryology of native Australian mammals, but he also published on other subjects, including human anatomy. Like his mentor before him, Wilson took an active role in military affairs, ascending through the ranks to Lieutenant-Colonel in the Australian Intelligence Corps and Honorary Colonel in the Censorship Service.

References: Hill, 1949; Smith, 1950; Morison, 1997.

Sir William Turner (1832–1916)

Mentor: Sir James Paget

William Turner was born in Lancaster, England in 1832. He began his medical training as an apprentice to a local general practitioner in 1848 and his formal education two years later when he enrolled in St. Bartholomew's Hospital Medical School to work under James Paget. Turner was qualified to practise by the Royal College of Surgeons and took honours in chemistry at the London University in 1853. He became the favourite pupil of Paget, who recommended him for the post of demonstrator at the University of Edinburgh in 1853.

Turner served the University of Edinburgh from 1854 to his death in 1916, first as demonstrator, then as professor, dean of the Faculty, and finally principal and vice-chancellor. He took a great interest in his students and trained, encouraged and guided them. It should come as no surprise then that, according to Hill (1949), 'round about the turn of the century, the vast majority of professors of anatomy in the [British] Empire had been pupils of William Turner'. Turner had a distinguished career in the Volunteer Service, becoming a decorated Lieutenant Colonel. He was knighted in 1886 and created Knight Commander of the Order of Bath in 1901.

Turner was Britain's leading anatomist for much of the nineteenth century, and had a diverse portfolio of interests. He published more than 200 works on topics ranging from human craniology to mammalian placentation. William Turner advised Charles Darwin during the development of natural selection theory, and was among the first researchers to look to comparative anatomy for evidence of evolution.

References: Keith, 1916; M. A. (anon), 1917; Morison, 1997; Anon, 2002; Magee, 2003.

Sir James Paget (1814–1899)

Mentor: Peter Mere Latham

James Paget was born in Great Yarmouth, Norfolk, England in 1814. His medical education began in 1830 with apprenticeship to a general practitioner-surgeon in Great Yarmouth. In 1834, he moved to London and became a student at St. Bartholomew's Hospital. Paget spent much of his time attending the ward rounds of Peter Mere Latham, and served under Latham as clinical clerk between 1835 and 1836, when he was qualified to practise by the Royal College of Surgeons.

Paget's teaching, research and clinical appointments, and accomplishments are too many to list here. He spent most of his career at St. Bartholomew's Hospital Medical School, where he served first as the curator of the anatomy and pathology museum, then as demonstrator, lecturer, warden and, ultimately, surgeon. He also served as professor at the Royal College of Surgeons and ran a very busy private practice, seeing up to 200 patients a day at the hospital! He was appointed Surgeon Extraordinary to Queen Victoria in 1858, Surgeon-in-Ordinary to the Prince of Wales in 1863 and was conferred a baronetcy in 1871. He resigned from St. Bartholomew's Hospital that year, but continued to practise medicine and hold various appointments, including that of President of the Royal College of Surgeons and Vice-Chancellor of the University of London.

Paget is best known as one of the founding fathers of scientific medical pathology, and his name is associated with Paget's disease of the bone and nipple. His works include *Lectures on Tumours* (1851) and *Lectures on Surgical Pathology* (1853) and numerous papers on cancer, syphilis and typhoid. Despite all this, teaching remained important to Paget. He wrote to his pupil William Turner 'I can feel with and for you the immense pleasure of lecturing to full benches of attentive men. Many and great as have been the pleasures that I have derived from my profession, none has been as great as this' (Paget, 1901).

References: Paget, 1901; Roberts, 1989; Coppes-Zantinga and Coppes, 2000; Royal College of Physicians, 2006a.

Peter Mere Latham (1789–1875)

Mentor: Thomas Bateman

Peter Mere Latham was born in London, England in 1789. After taking a BA at Brasenose College in Oxford in 1810, he began medical studies at St. Bartholomew's Hospital and at the Carey Street Dispensary under the tutelage of Thomas Bateman. He earned an MA in 1813, MB in 1814 and MD from St. Bartholomew's Hospital in 1816.

Latham worked as a physician at the Middlesex Hospital between 1815 and 1824, and then at St. Bartholomew's Hospital until ill health forced him to resign in 1841 (though he maintained a small private practice until 1865). Latham had a decorated clinical career, including an appointment as Physician Extraordinary to Queen Victoria from 1837 to his death in 1875. Latham became a lecturer in medicine at St. Bartholomew's Hospital Medical School in 1836, and taught students there for many years. He was a very dedicated teacher and he wrote passionately on medical education reform. As for his teaching, his pupil James Paget wrote, 'I think there were none who did not thoroughly admire him, and imitate him in his mode of study, and very gratefully remember his teachings' (Paget, 1901). On his lecturing style, however, Paget added curiously 'he was very pompous; sometimes almost laughably so, especially if he had to speak of general rules relating either to personal conduct or to modes of study; but this only helped the memory of his hearers' (Paget, 1901).

Latham is remembered for his descriptions of clinical symptoms and physical findings in cardiology as presented in his *Essays on Some Diseases of the Heart* (1828) and *Lectures on Clinical Medicine Comprising Diseases of the Heart* (1845). He is also remembered for his pioneering work on auscultation and percussion, published in *Lectures on Subjects Connected with Clinical Medicine* in 1836.

References: Munk, 1878; Paget, 1901; Spaulding, 1971; Fleming, 1997; Royal College of Physicians, 2006b.

Thomas Bateman (1778–1821)

Mentor: Robert Willan

Thomas Bateman was born in Whitby, Yorkshire, England in 1778. His early medical training began with an apprenticeship to an apothecary in Whitby. Bateman's formal studies began in 1797 at the Windmill Street School of Anatomy and St. George's Hospital in London. He then matriculated at the University of Edinburgh in 1798, and received an MD in 1801 for a thesis on *Haemorrhoea Petechialis*. He returned to London that year and began training under Robert Willan. Bateman quickly became Willan's disciple, championing his mentor's works (and gratefully acknowledging his indebtedness to Willan) for many years.

Bateman began work as a physician at both the Fever Institution and the Carey Street Dispensary in 1804. He continued practising until ill health forced his resignation from the institution in 1818 and from the dispensary the following year. He died in 1821 at the age of 42. He evidently mentored several young physicians during his years at the dispensary, and was a serious and intense teacher. Rumsey (1827) wrote 'the simplicity of his language and conscientious fidelity of his whole mind to his office, were admirably calculated to fix the attention and attachment of a scholar. No levity unworthy of his learning or his subject ever dishonoured either'.

Bateman is known for continuing Willan's work to describe skin diseases and standardise dermatology nomenclature. His *Practical Synopsis of Cutaneous Diseases According to the Arrangement of Dr. Willan* in 1813 and *Delineations of Cutaneous Diseases, Exhibiting the Characteristic Appearances of the Principal Genera and Species, Comprised in the Classification of Willan* in 1817 are considered to have been the most influential textbooks of dermatology in the nineteenth century. Bateman is credited with identifying and describing several skin diseases, among them *Herpes iris* of Bateman and eczema. He published a collection of papers as the *Reports on the Diseases of London and the State of the Weather* that drew much attention, as well as other works based on his practice at the Fever Institution.

References: Bateman, 1812; Rumsey, 1827; Booth, 1999; Levell, 2000; J. R. (anon), 2006; Royal College of Physicians, 2006c.

Robert Willan (1757–1812)

Mentor: William Cullen

Robert Willan was born at The Hill, near Sedbergh in Yorkshire, England in 1757. He began his medical training in Edinburgh in 1777, studying medicine under William Cullen and other teachers at the university. Cullen's influence is evidenced in Willan's later work classifying skin lesions, which followed his mentor's efforts to categorise diseases using the Linnaean system (see below), just as Erasmus Darwin was to do. Willan received his MD in Edinburgh in 1780 for a thesis on inflammation of the liver.

After two years of private practice in Darlington, Willan moved to London. He was appointed physician to the newly established Carey Street Dispensary in 1783, where he treated patients and mentored some forty young physicians during his tenure. Such dispensaries catered for the poor, disheveled masses, providing Willan with a 'dermatological goldmine' (Booth, 1999) upon which to base the research for which he became best known. He resigned from the dispensary in 1783, but continued to practise medicine until he became ill in 1811. Willan died in 1812.

Willan is recognised for bringing order to the discipline of dermatology with his classifications and descriptions of skin lesions. These he codified in his very successful treatise *On Cutaneous Diseases*. He has been called the father of modern dermatology, and his name remains attached to *lupus vulgaris* (Willan's lupus) and *psoriasis vulgaris* (Willan's lepra). He also wrote on a host of other medical topics ranging from the history of leprosy to the advantages of vaccination.

References: Bateman, 1812; Beswick, 1957; Hare, 1973; Sharma, 1983; Doig *et al.*, 1993; Booth, 1999.

William Cullen (1710–1790)

Mentor: Andrew Plummer

William Cullen was born in Hamilton, Lanarkshire, Scotland in 1710. His early medical training was informal, involving apprenticeships in Glasgow and London. He began his formal medical education by attending winter classes in 1734–5 and 1735–6 at the University of Edinburgh. While he earned his MD in Glasgow in 1740, genealogists consider Andrew Plummer to have been his principal mentor, as Cullen was evidently greatly influenced by Plummer and his lectures in Edinburgh (Kerker, 1955; Gaffney and Marley, 2002).

Cullen began lecturing on medicine at the University of Glasgow in 1744, and was appointed to its first lectureship in chemistry three years later. He taught chemistry and medicine in Glasgow until 1755, when he returned to Edinburgh to share a professorship with Plummer until his mentor died the following year. Cullen continued at Edinburgh until 1789, and died the following year. William Cullen is best remembered as a teacher and mentor. He was, by all accounts, a lucid and enthusiastic lecturer, more concerned with getting his points across than with formality. In one famous quotation, he referred to Carolus Linnaeus's writings as 'the most uncouth jargon and minute pedantry' he had ever seen!

He is, nevertheless, well known for applying the Linnaean system to classify diseases by symptom. Cullen wrote many popular medical textbooks widely used throughout Europe and North America during the late eighteenth and early nineteenth centuries. His *First Lines of the Practice of Physic* and *A Treatise of the Materia Medica*, for example, set the standard for decades. In fact, it was in these works that he coined the term 'neurosis'. On the other hand, while he is best known as a founding father of chemistry in Britain, he wrote only one research paper related to this field – an examination of the cooling effects of evaporating fluids.

References: Thomson, 1832; Wightman, 1955; Kerker, 1955; Doig *et al.*, 1993; Gaffney and Marley, 2002; Doyle, 2005b.

Andrew Plummer (1697–1756)

Mentor: Herman Boerhaave

Andrew Plummer was born in Edinburgh, Scotland, in 1697. He began his university studies in the arts at the University of Edinburgh from 1712 to 1717, but then switched to medicine, matriculating at the University of Leiden in 1720 under the direction of Herman Boerhaave. Of Boerhaave's impact on Plummer, Kerker (1955: 38) wrote that Plummer 'could not have failed to succumb to his influence'. Plummer graduated MD in 1722 for a thesis *De phthisi pulmonali a catarrho orto*. He then returned to Scotland in 1724 and passed the licentiate examination of the Royal College of Physicians of Edinburgh permitting him to practise medicine.

Plummer and three other Leiden alumni began teaching medicine and chemistry at the new Edinburgh Dispensary in 1725, 'according to the method of the celebrated Herman Boerhaave' (Doyle, 2005a). The four were appointed professors, without salary, at the University of Edinburgh the following year, effectively founding the medical school. Plummer continued his private practice, taught chemistry and helped develop and run the group's pharmaceutical laboratory. He continued this work until his death in 1756. Plummer was evidently a better chemist than teacher, as one student, Oliver Goldsmith, wrote, 'Plumer [sic] professor of chymistry understands his busines [sic] well but delivers himself so ill that he is but little regarded' (Doyle, 2005a). John Fothergill later recounted 'had not a native diffidence veil'd his talents as a praelector he would have been among the foremost in the pupils' esteem' (Doyle, 2005a).

Plummer published papers on clinical medicine and chemistry, including *Remarks on chemical solutions and precipitations* and *Experiments on neutral salts, compounded of different acid liquors, and alcaline salts, fixt and volatile.* He is best known for formulating Plummer's pills – a preparation of calomel, antimony sulfide and mercuric acid used, rather ineffectively, for more than a century as a panacea for numerous ailments.

References: Kerker, 1955; Underwood, 1977; Gaffney and Marley, 2002; Doyle, 2005a.

Herman Boerhaave (1668–1738)

Mentor: Burchard de Volder

Herman Boerhaave was born in 1668 in the parsonage at Voorhout near Leiden, the Netherlands. He entered the University of Leiden in 1684, and attended the lectures and demonstrations of Burchard de Volder. Boerhaave earned a doctorate in philosophy in 1690, after which De Volder promoted him to magister. Boerhaave later edited De Volder's *Oratio de novis et antique.* The pupil's respect for his mentor is clear in the preface, where he praises De Volder's 'sharpness of mind (*acerrimam ingenii aciem*), by which he exceeded everyone else' (Knoeff, 2002). Boerhaave also earned an MD from Harderwyck in 1693.

Boerhaave practised as a physician in Leiden for some years, and then was appointed to teach medicine at the University of Leiden in 1701. He worked at Leiden until his death in 1738, much of the time holding simultaneous chairs in botany, clinical medicine and chemistry. Boerhaave has been called one of the great teachers of all time (Kerker, 1955), and was named *communis Europae praeceptor* (the common teacher of Europe) by Albrecht von Haller (Underwood, 1977). Many of Boerhaave's students, such as Carl Linnaeus and Andrew Plummer, became some of the most influential academicians in the world.

Boerhaave wrote the medical textbooks *Institutiones medicae* and *Aphorismi de cognoscendis et curandis morbis*, and his *Elementa Chemiae* was among the most influential texts of the eighteenth century. He is considered the father of physical chemistry, with contributions including the introduction of exact measurements to chemistry, demonstration that water is a product of combustion, proof that heat is weightless and performance of the first calorimetric studies.

References: Kerker, 1955; Lindeboom, 1968; Underwood, 1977; Luyendijk-Elshout, 1998; Kidd and Modlin, 1999; Knoeff, 2002.

Burchard de Volder (1643–1709)

Mentor: Franciscus Sylvius

Burchard de Volder was born in Amsterdam, the Netherlands in 1643. He began to study medicine and philosophy in Amsterdam, and took an MA at Utrecht in 1660. He continued his education in Leiden, falling under the influence of Franciscus Sylvius. He earned an MD in 1664, with a dissertation *Theses de la Nature, très opposes aux idées Péripateticiennes*. De Volder then went back to Amsterdam to establish a medical practice, but returned to Leiden in 1670 following an offer of the chair of logic. During his time in Leiden, De Volder served also as professor of mathematics. He was appointed rector by William of Orange (then also the King of England) in 1697. De Volder taught the classics, mathematics and physics in Leiden, but resigned from his professorship due to illness in 1705.

Burchard de Volder did not produce a great volume of works, but his contributions were influential. His work reflected the ideas of his mentor Sylvius, and offers insights on some of De Volder's contemporaries including Spinoza, Descartes, Newton, Huygens and Boyle. De Volder argued for the integration of mathematics and physics in his *Oratio de conjungendis philosophicis et mathematicis disciplinis* (1682) and later for the integration of these with medicine in *De rationis viribus et usu in scientiis* (1698). He published studies on the weight of air and invented an air pump. He set up the first physics laboratory in Leiden and his lectures and demonstrations on gases and the atmosphere had a clear impact, especially on his most renowned student, Herman Boerhaave.

References: Partington, 1961; Klever, 1988; Gaffney and Marley, 2002; Knoeff, 2002.

Franciscus Sylvius (1614–1672)

Mentor: Emanuel Stupanus

Franciscus Sylvius (François Dubois or De le Boë) was born in Hanau, Germany, in 1614. He began his formal education with courses in Sedan and at other universities in Germany and France, ultimately receiving his MB at the University of Leiden in 1634. Sylvius obtained his MD in Basel in 1637 for this thesis, *Disputatio medica de animale motu einsque laesionibus*, under the direction of Emanuel Stupanus. The strong Paracelsian tradition at Basel clearly exerted an influence on Sylvius, as is evident in his later works.

Sylvius practised for a short time in Hanau, and then returned to Leiden to give private lectures on anatomy. He started a lucrative practice in Amsterdam in 1641, but was drawn back to Leiden by an appointment as professor of medicine in 1658. Sylvius remained at the University of Leiden, ultimately becoming *rector magnificus* from 1669–70. Sylvius was evidently a great teacher, and 'his clear, elegant and sometimes eloquent speech, slow enough to be followed by even somewhat dull intellects, drew around his chair an immense concourse of pupils who regarded him with strong affection' (Baker, 1909). He himself wrote 'I have endeavoured with all my might to make sure that my auditors should profit as much as possible from my industry and labor and go out as excellent physicians' (Baker, 1909). Indeed, Sylvius drew students from all over Europe, teaching them anatomy, chemistry and clinical medicine.

Sylvius conducted research on anatomy, physiology and pathology. He was a leading proponent of the school of Iatrochemistry, a doctrine that held that life and disease processes are based on chemical actions, and that medicine could be understood in terms of universal rules of physics and chemistry. The basic idea was a good one, but it fell apart quickly when Sylvius tried to unite the Galenic notions of humoral medicine with seventeeth-century chemistry. Much of this work is laid out in *Praxeos medicae idea nova* published in 1671. We know the name of Franciscus Sylvius today by his research on the structure of the brain, and particularly by his recognition of the 'Sylvian fissure' (lateral sulcus) as described in *Disputationes Medicae* (1663), 'Sylvian ventricle' (cave of septum pellucidum), 'Sylvian fossa' (lateral cerebral fossa) and a number of other eponymously designated entities. However, the 'Sylvian aqueduct' (cerebral aqueduct) owes its name to Jacobus Sylvius (1478–1555).

References: Baker, 1909; Baumann, 1949; Gubster, 1966; Underwood, 1972; van Gijn, 2001.

Emanuel Stupanus (1587–1664)

Mentor: Johannes Nicolaus Stupanus

Emanuel Stupanus (Emanuele Stupano) was born in Basel, Switzerland, in 1587. His formal education began in Geneva under Esaïe Colladone and Caspar Laurentius, and he attended classes at various universities in Germany, France and Italy. Stupanus returned to the University of Basel to earn his MD with highest honours conferred by mathematics professor Petrus Ryffius (Peter Ryff), who studied under Theodor Zwinger (see below) in 1613. Emanuel served an apprenticeship under his father, Johannes Nicolaus, until 1620 when he replaced the older Stupanus as professor of theoretical medicine. We know little about Emanuel's teaching prowess, though Baumann (1949) reported that 'as promoter he seems not to have been unattractive'.

Emanuel Stupanus was a very active scholar, producing dozens of works spanning a career of more than forty years. His known works include *Vere' Aureorum Aphorismorum Hippocratis enarrationes & commentaria aphoristica Nova Methodo eiusmodiin ordinem digesta* (1615) and his translation and completion of Bartholomew Castelli's *Lexicon Medicum Graeco-Latinum* (1628). He published on a broad range of medical subjects.

References: Hofmann, 1698; Burckhardt, 1917; Baumann, 1949.

Johannes Nicolaus Stupanus (1542–1621)

Mentor: Theodor Zwinger

Johannes Nicolaus Stupanus (Juan Nicolás Stupano) was born in 1542 in Chiavenna, Italy. He took his formal education at the University of Basel, receiving his BA in 1563, MA in 1565 and MD in 1569 under the direction of Theodor Zwinger. Stupanus began teaching as professor of logic and rhetoric at the Basel Academy in 1560, and was appointed professor of theoretical medicine at the University of Basel in 1589, where he replaced Zwinger in 1589. He resigned from the University of Basel in 1620.

Stupanus senior was a prolific researcher and writer, publishing many works on physiology, pathology and diagnostic medicine. He was evidently a fervent advocate of the Paracelsian approach that presaged Sylvius's Iatrochemical School. Johannes Nicolaus Stupanus translated many works from Italian into Latin. These included texts on astronomy, the works of Machiavelli (*Prince, Discorsi*) and histories (including a history of Naples by Pandulphis). He is best known for his treatise *Medicina Theorica* (1614).

References: Hofmann, 1698; Koelbing, 1970.

Theodor Zwinger (1533–1588)

Mentor: Gabriele Falloppio

Theodor Zwinger (Theodoro Zuingero) was born in 1533 in Basel, Switzerland. He studied in Basel, Lyon and Paris, where he attended the lectures of Petrus Ramus. Zwinger then studied anatomy at the University of Padua, perhaps the most renowned Medical School of the European Renaissance. He received his medical degree in 1559 at the University of Padua under the direction of Gabriele Falloppio. Zwinger took a faculty position in the medical school at the University of Basel in 1559, and was elected chair of Greek in 1565, ethics in 1571 and theoretical medicine in 1580.

Zwinger was an accomplished physician and philosopher known for his contributions in many fields. He is best remembered for his *Theatrum vitae humanae*, first published in 1565. This work is said to be 'the most comprehensive compilation of knowledge ever achieved by a single human being in the Early Modern Period' (Zedelmaier, 2008). As for his teaching and mentoring, little is known, though Blair (2008) does refer to a letter from the medical students at the University of Basel asking him to speak more slowly because of difficulty keeping up with him.

References: Herzog, 1778; Haeser, 1881; Dufournier, 1936; Kolb, 1951; Karcher, 1956; Bietenholz, 1971; Portmann, 1988; Blair, 2008; Zedelmaier, 2008.

Gabriele Falloppio (1523–1562)

Mentor: Antonio Musa Brasavola

Gabriele Falloppio (Gabriel Fallopius, Gabriello Falloppio) was born in Modena, Italy in 1523. He began his studies in anatomy in 1544 in Modena with Niccolo Machella, and is said to have spent some time at the University of Padua with Ratteo Realdo Colombo. He evidently completed his education at the University of Ferrara in 1548, under the direction of Antonio Musa Brasavola and Giovanni Battista Canano. Academic genealogists consider Brasavola to have been his mentor. Falloppio briefly taught pharmacy at Ferrara, but became professor of anatomy at the University of Pisa in 1549 and, in 1551, chair of anatomy and surgery at the University of Padua, where he also held a professorship in botany.

Falloppio was an outstanding teacher and anatomist. Hamilton (1831) reported that his lectures both at Pisa and Padua 'attracted crowds of auditors', and that he was 'most methodical in teaching'. According to O'Malley (2008), Falloppio 'lectured and demonstrated with such success as to attract a number of later to be distinguished students'. While several works are attributed to him, only *Observations anatomica* (1561) was published during his lifetime. This important book includes a series of commentaries and criticisms on Vesalius's *De humane corporis fabricate*. Falloppio is perhaps best known for his meticulous dissections and his descriptions of the vestibulococclear system, deciduous teeth and female reproductive tract, including the tubes that now bear his name.

References: Hamilton, 1831; Walsh, 1913; Sanchez, 2009.

Antonio Musa Brasavola (1500–1555)

Mentor: Nicolo Leoniceno

Antonio Musa Brasavola (Brassavola, Brasavoli) was born in 1500 in Ferrara. He attended universities in Padua, Bologna and Paris before returning to Ferrara, where he studied medicine under Nicholas Leoniceno and Giovanni Manardi. Brasavola's biography of Leoniceno, entitled *Praeceptor meus* (*My teacher*) makes the student–mentor relationship clear. Brasavola received his medical degree in 1521, though began lecturing in logic at Ferrara in 1519. While his tenure at Ferrara was interrupted periodically by breaks for private practice, Brasavola taught logic there until 1527, natural philosophy until 1536 and medicine until his death in 1555.

Brasavola was evidently a dedicated teacher. Thorndike (1941) tells of Brasavola being informed whilst lecturing that his house was on fire, and of his instance on finishing the lecture before leaving! He was also a well respected medical doctor, and served as court physician for Ercolo II, the Duke of Este, and for a time attended Pope Paul III in Rome. Brasavola also consulted for King Francis I of France, Kaiser Charles V of Germany and King Henry VIII of England, and treated patients from all walks of life. His principal research interests were in botany and pharmacology, and he is known for performing the first recorded successful tracheostomy. Brasavola was a prolific author, with more than forty major works to his credit. Some of the best know are *Examen omnium simplicium medicamentorum, quorum in officinis usus est* (1537), a witty imaginary conversation in which he introduced several new pharmaceuticals, and his commentaries on Hippocrates and Galen, *In octo libros aphorismorum Hippocratis & Galeni commentaria & annotationes* (1541), *In libros de ratione victus in morbis acutis Hippocratis & Galeni commentaria & annotationes* (1546) and *Index refertissimus in omnes Galeni libros* (1556).

References: Panoucke, 1820; Hamilton, 1831; Bottoni, 1892; Garrison, 1913; Thorndike, 1941; Nutton, 1997.

Nicolo Leoniceno (1428–1524)

Nicolo Leoniceno (Nicolaus Leoninus, Nicolo da Lonigo) was born in Lonigo in 1428. He studied Latin and Greek under Ognibene da Lonigo in Vicenza, but moved to Padua in 1446. He completed his education in philosophy and medicine at the University of Padua in 1453. Most academic genealogies list Pelope, or Pietro, Roccabonella as Leoniceno's primary mentor, but we have been unable to find confirmation in either case. Pietro Roccabonella, for example, evidently did not become professor of medicine at Padua until 1465. It is possible that Pietro's grandfather, Niccolo Roccabonella, was Leoniceno's mentor, as Niccolo also taught medicine at Padua, but more research is needed to evaluate this possibility. Leoniceno taught philosophy and medicine at the University of Ferrara for an extraordinary 60 years, from 1464 until his death in 1524, with sabbaticals to teach at Bologna in 1483 and 1508–9. He was also an accomplished clinician.

Leoniceno saw himself as an educator first, his motto being *Plus ago docens omnes medicos* (Nutton, 1997). He is best remembered for his translations of ancient Greek texts by Galen, Hippocrates and others. Among his many works, two stand out: his criticism of Pliny, Avicenna, Serapio and others in *De Plinii et plurium aliorum in medicina erroribus liber ad doct. Virum Angelum Politianum* (1492) and the documentation of a syphilis pandemic that spread across Europe in the late 1400s in *Libellus de epidemia, quam vulgo morbum gallicum vocant* (1497).

References: Castigloni, 1941; Major, 1954; Pepe, 1986; Nutton, 1997.

Discussion

The twists and turns of research focus and interests presented in this genealogy are a product of the personalities of the individuals involved and the historical contexts in which they lived. Linnaean taxonomy led Willan to his classification of skin lesions, and Darwinian Natural Selection led Turner to comparative anatomy. While their styles varied from 'diffident' (Plummer) to 'pompous' (Latham), most of the men in this genealogy shared a remarkable drive and enthusiasm for teaching and research. Some, such as Falloppio, Sylvius, Boerhaave and Cullen, were excellent teachers, whereas others, such as Elliot Smith and Paget, are best remembered for their scientific contributions. Several, including Plummer, Wilson and Dart laboured to establish new departments modelled on their own almae matres, demonstrating yet again how the kernels of academic thought can be passed from mentor to pupil over centuries.

In the end, it is likely that none of these men would have been the academicians they turned out to be without the contributions of their mentors.

Acknowledgements

We are grateful to Kristin Krueger and Jessica Scott for finding and gathering many of the background references used to confirm the links in this genealogy. We thank Daniel Levine and Lynda Coon for their help translating Latin texts and Jacob Adler for pointing out that Sylvius's mentor's name was Stupanus (not Stupaeus). We also thank Blaine Schubert and Qian Wang for discussions that led to this project.

References

Anon (2002). *Sir William Turner, 1832–1916. Surgeon's News 1.* Edinburgh.

Baker, F. (1909). The two Sylviuses. An historical study. *Johns Hopkins Hospital Bulletin*, **20**: 329–39.

Bateman, T. A. (1812). A biographical memoir of the late Dr. Willan. *Edinburgh Medical and Surgical Journal*, **8**: 502–12.

Baumann, E. D. (1949). *Francois dele Boë, Sylvius*. Leiden: Brill.

Beswick, T. S. (1957). Robert Willan: the solution to a ninety-year-old mystery. *Journal of the History of Medicine and Allied Sciences*, **12**: 349–65.

Bietenholz, P. G. (1971). *Basle and France in the Sixteenth Century. The Basle Humanists and Printers in their Contacts with Francophone Culture.* Toronto-Buffalo and Geneva: University of Toronto Press and Libraire Droz.

Blair, A. (2008). Student manuscripts and the textbook. In Campi, E., De Angelis, S. and Groeing, A.-S. (eds.), *Scholarly Knowledge: Textbooks in Early Modern Europe.* Geneva: Libraire Droz S.A, pp. 39–74.

Blunt, M. (1988). Sir Grafton Elliot Smith (1871–1937). In Ritchie, J. (ed), *Australian Dictionary of Biography*, Volume 12. Melbourne: Melbourne University Press. pp. 645–6.

Booth, C. C. (1999). Robert Willan MD FRS (1757–1812): Dermatologist of the millennium. *Journal of the Royal Society of Medicine*, **92**: 313–18.

Bottoni, A. (1892). *Cinque Secoli d'Universita a Ferrara, MCCCXCI-MDCCCXCI.* Bologna: Stabilimento Tip, Ramorani E. Albertazzi.

Burckhardt, A. (1917). *Geschichte der Medizinischen Fakultaet zu Basel, 1460–1900.* Basel: Reinhardt.

Cartmill, M., Pilbeam, D. and Isaac, G. (1986). One hundred years of paleoanthropology. *American Scientist*, **74**: 410–20.

Castiglioni, A. (1941). *A History of Medicine.* New York: Alfred A. Knopf.

Coppes-Zantinga, A. R. and Coppes, M. J. (2000). Sir James Paget (1814–1889): a great academic Victorian. *Journal of the American College of Surgeons*, **191**: 70–4.

Dart, R. A. (1959). *Adventures with the Missing Link.* New York: Harper and Brothers.

Doig, A., Ferguson, J. P. S., Milne, I. A. and Passmore, R. (1993). *William Cullen and the Eighteenth Century Medical World.* Edinburgh: Edinburgh University Press.

Doyle, W. P. (2005a). *Andrew Plummer (1697–1756). http://www.chem.ed.ac.uk/about/ professors/plummer.html.* Edinburgh: Chemistry Webmaster, School of Chemistry, University of Edinburgh.

    (2005b). *William Cullen (1710–1790). http://www.chem.ed.ac.uk/about/professors/ cullen.html.* Edinburgh: Chemistry Webmaster, School of Chemistry, University of Edinburgh.

Dufournier, B. (1936). Th. Zwinger de bale et la scolastique de l'histoire au XVIe siecle. *Revue d'Histoire Moderne*, **11**: 323–35.

Elkin, A. P. and MacIntosh, N. W. G. (1974). *Grafton Elliot Smith: the Man and his Work.* Sydney: Sydney University Press.

Fagan, B. (1989). The passion of Raymond Dart. *Archaeology*, **42**: 18–&.

Fleming, P. R. (1997). *A Short History of Cardiology.* Amsterdam: Rodopi.

Gaffney, J. S. and Marley, N. A. (2002). Chemical genealogy of an atmospheric chemist: James N. Pitts, Jr., a case study. *Fourth Conference on Atmospheric Chemistry Symposium: Urban, Regional, and Global-Scale Impacts of Air Pollutants 82nd American Meteorological Society National Meeting, Orlando, FL 2002, Proceedings Volume, Paper* P1.3: 181–6.

Garrison, F. H. (1913). *An Introduction to the History of Medicine.* Philadelphia: W. B. Saunders.

Grine, F. E. (1990). Deciduous dental features of the Kalahari San: comparison of nonmetrical traits. In Sperber, G.H. (ed.), *From Apes to Angels: Essays in Anthropology in Honor of Phillip V. Tobias.* New York: Wiley-Liss, pp. 153–70.

Gubster, A. (1966). The positiones variae medicae of Franciscus Sylvius. *Bulletin of the History of Medicine*, **40**: 72–80.

Haeser, H. (1881) *Lehrbuch der Geschichte der Medicin: Geschichte der Medicin in der neuren zeit.* Jena: Verlag Von Gustav Fischer.

Hamilton, W. (1831). *The History of Medicine, Surgery, and Anatomy, from the Creation of the World, to the Commencement of the Nineteenth Century.* London: Henry Colburn and Richard Bentley.

Hare, P. J. (1973). A note on Robert Willan's Edinburgh days. *British Journal of Dermatology*, **88**: 615.

Herzog (1778). *Athenae Rauricae. Sive Gatalogus Professorum Academiae Basiliensis Ab A. MCCCCLX ad A. MDCCLXXVII Cum Brevi Singulorum Biographia. Adiecta Est Recensio Omnium Eiusdem Academiae Rectorum.* Basel: Car. Aug. Serini.

Hill, J. P. (1949). James Thomas Wilson. *Obituary Notices of Fellows of the Royal Society*, **6**: 18.

Hofmann, J. J. (1698). *Lexicon Universale, Historiam Sacram.* Leiden: Jacob Hackius, Cornel. Boutesteyn, Petr. Vander Aa., & Jord. Luchtmans.

J. R. (anon) (2006). *The Life of Thomas Bateman.* London: Longman, Hurst, Reese, Orme and Brown.

Karcher, J. (1956). *Theodor Zwinger und sein Zeitgenossen. Episode aus dem Ringen der Basler Arzte um die Grandlehren der Medizin im Zeitalter des barocks. Studien zur Geschichte der Wissenschaften in Basel, III.* Basel: Helbing und Lichtenhahn.

Keith, A. (1916). Sir William Turner, K.C.B., F.R.S. *Man*, **16**: 65–71.

Kerker, M. (1955). Herman Boerhaave and the development of pneumatic chemistry. *Isis*, **46**: 36–49.

Kidd, M. and Modlin, I. M. (1999). The luminati of Leiden: from Bintius to Boerhaave. *World Journal of Surgery*, **23**: 1307–14.

Klever, W. N. A. (1988). Burchard De Volder (1643–1709), a Crypto-Spinozist on a Leiden Cathedra. *Lias*, **15**: 191–240.

Knoeff, R. (2002). *Herman Boerhaave (1668–1738). Calvinist Chemist and Physican.* Amsterdam.

Koelbing, H. M. (1970). Johannes Nicolaus Stupanus, Rhaetus (1542–1621). In *Äskulap in Graubünden*. pp. 628–46.

Koenig, R. (2005). South Africa's bone man: 80 and still digging into the past. *Science*, **310**: 608–9.

Kolb, W. (1951). *Geschichte des anatomischen Unterrichtes an der Universität zu Basel, 1460–1900*. Basel: B. Schwabe.

Landau, M. (1991). *Narratives of Human Evolution*. New Haven: Yale University Press.

Levell, N. J. (2000). Thomas Bateman MD FLS 1778–1821. *British Journal of Dermatology*, **143**: 9–15.

Lindeboom, G. A. (1968). *Herman Boerhaave: the Man and his Work*. London: Methuen Press.

Luyendijk-Elshout, A. M. (1998). Herman Boerhaave. *Journal of the History of the Neurosciences*, **7**: 52–4.

M. A. (anon) (1917). Sir William Turner. *Proceedings of the Royal Society of London Series B*, **89**: 622.

Magee, R. (2003). Sir William Turner and his studies on the mammalian placenta. *ANZ Journal of Surgery*, **73**: 449–52.

Major, R. H. (1954). *A History of Medicine*. Springfield, IL: Charles C. Thomas.

Morison, P. (1997). *J. T. Wilson and the Fraternity of Duckmaloi*. Amsterdam: Rodopi Press.

Munk, W. (1878). *The Role of the Royal College of Physicians of London*, Volume 3. London: Royal College of Physicians.

Nutton, V. (1997). The rise of medical humanism: Ferrara, 1464–1555. *Renaissance Studies*, **11**: 2–19.

O'Malley, C. D. (2008). Falloppio, Gabriele. In *Complete Dictionary of Scientific Biography*, Vol. 4. Detroit: Charles Scribner's Sons. pp. 519–21.

Paget, S. (1901). *Memoirs and Letters of Sir James Paget*, 2nd edn. London: Longmans, Green and Company.

Panckoucke, C. L. F. (1820–1822). *Dictionare des Sciences Medicales Biographie Medicale*. Paris: C.L.F. Panckoucke.

Partington, J. R. (1961). *A History of Chemistry*. Volume 2. New York: St. Martins Press.

Pepe, L. (1986). Scienziati e stabilimenti scientifici a Ferrara. *Museologia Scientifica*, **3**:113–19.

Portmann, M.-L. (1988). Theodor Zwinger (1533–1588), ein Basler Humanistenarzt. *Schweizerische Rundschau fur Medizin Praxis*, **77**: 1110–13.

Rees, N. (2006). *Brewer's Famous Quotations*. London: Weidenfeld and Nicolson.

Roberts, S. (1989). *Sir James Paget: the Rise of Clinical Surgery*. London: Royal Society of Medicine.

Royal College of Physicians (2006a). *A biography of Sir James Paget*. Published online at www.aim25.ac.uk: The National Archives.

(2006b). *Latham, Peter Mere (1789–1875)*. Published online at www.aim25.ac.uk: The National Archives.

(2006c). *A Biography of Thomas Bateman.* Published online at www.aim25.ac.uk: The National Archives.

Rumsey, J. (1827). *Some Account of the Life and Character of the Late Thomas Bateman.* London: Longman, Rees, Orme, Brown and Green.

Sanchez, O. F. (2009). Curiosidades en Medicina: Gabrielle Falloppio. *Revisita Medica de Rosario*, **75**:112–13.

Sharma, O. P. (1983). Robert Willan remembered. *Journal of the American Academy of Dermatology*, **9**: 971–6.

Smith, S. A. (1950). The life and work of James Thomas Wilson. *Bulletin of the Post-Graduate Committee in Medicine, University of Sydney*, **6**: 1–12.

Spaulding, W. B. (1971). Peter Mere Latham (1789–1875): a great medical educator. *Canadian Medical Association Journal*, **104**: 1109–14.

Sperber, G. H. (1990). *From Apes to Angels: Essays in Anthropology in Honor of Phillip V. Tobias.* New York: Wiley-Liss.

Thomson, J. (1832). *Account of the Life, Lectures, and Writings of William Cullen.* Volume 1. Edinburgh: Blackwood Press.

Thorndike, L. (1941). *A History of Magic and Experimental Science, VI.* New York: MacMillan.

Tobias, P. V. (1984). *Dart, Taung, and the Missing Link: An Essay on the Life and Work of Emeritus Professor Raymond Dart, Based on a Tribute to Professor Dart on His 90th Birthday, Delivered at the University of the Witwatersrand, Johannesburg, on 22 June 1983.* Johannesburg: Witwatersrand University Press.

(1989). Dart, Raymond Arthur (1893–1988). *Nature*, **337**: 211.

(2005). *Into the Past: A Memoir.* Johannesburg: Picador Africa.

Underwood, E. A. (1972). Fransciscus Sylvius and his Iatrochemical School. *Endeavor*, **31**: 73–6.

(1977). *Boerhaave's Men at Leyden and After.* Edinburgh: Edinburgh University Press.

van Gijn, J. (2001). Franciscus Sylvius (1614–1672). *Journal of Neurology*, **248**: 915–16.

Walsh, J. J. (1913). Fallopio, Gabriello, anatomist. In Herbermann, C. G., Pace, E. A., Pallen, C. B., Shahan, T. J. and Wynne, J. J. (eds.), *The Catholic Encyclopedia: An International Work of Reference on the Constitution, Doctrine, Discipline, and History of the Catholic Church.* New York: The Encyclopedia Press, p. 722.

Wheelhouse, F. (1983). *Raymond Arthur Dart.* Sydney: Transpareon Press.

Wheelhouse, F. and Smithford, K. S. (2001). *Dart: Scientist and Man of Grit.* Sydney: Transpareon Press.

Wightman, W. P. D. (1955). William Cullen and the teaching of Chemistry. *Annals of Science* **11**: 154–65.

Wilson, J. T. (1938). Sir Grafton Elliot Smith (1871–1937). *Obituary Notices of the Fellows of the Royal Society*, **2**: 322–33.

Zedelmaier, H. (2008). Navigieren im Text-Universum. Theodor Zwingers *Theatrum Vitae Humanae. Metaphorik*, **14**: 113–35.

Part I

In search of origins: evolutionary theory, new species and paths into the past

3   *Speciation in hominin evolution*

COLIN GROVES

Abstract

In this chapter, I survey ideas of the concept of species, as they apply to the
human evolutionary record. I discuss the question of the meaning of a genus,
concluding that all species since the separation of the human line from that
of the chimpanzee (and possibly including the chimpanzee lineage as well)
should be placed in a single genus, for which the prior available name is *Homo*.
How new species arise is a yet more controversial topic, and I list the variety of
modes of speciation that have been proposed, with predictions as to what the
results of some of these modes might look like, making suggestions as to how
they might apply in palaeoanthropology.

Speciation in hominin evolution

We can expect that human beings were subject to the same evolutionary
forces and principles as other sexually reproducing animals, at any rate in
the earlier stages of the evolution of the human clade (until cultural factors
became so pervasive as to be overriding). This at once requires that we examine the question of species in the human clade, because it is at the point of
speciation and (more controversially) during the course of a species' existence, that evolutionary change takes place. First, therefore, we must ask:
what is a species?

The evolutionary species

There is widespread agreement that, in all important respects, the basic unit of
biology is the species, and that it is the evolutionary species concept (Simpson,

African Genesis: Perspectives on Hominin Evolution, eds. Sally C. Reynolds and Andrew
Gallagher. Published by Cambridge University Press. © Cambridge University Press 2012.

1961) that most closely represents what a species is and why it is important. Simpson's definition has two parts:

- a species is a lineage evolving separately from others
- and with its own unitary evolutionary role and tendencies.

The first part suggests that it sustains itself, in large part at least, from its own genetic resources; the second part specifies that it occupies a unique biological space, which includes a unique role in the natural world. Such a definition focuses attention on why the concept of species is important, but is of little help when it comes to actually recognising a species when we meet it – more to the point, how we can distinguish one species from another. This is where the controversies begin.

The biological species concept (BSC) is associated with the names of Mayr and Dobzhansky; it gradually took shape, and was fully formalised by Mayr (1963). This concept requires that a species be reproductively isolated from other species: broadly speaking, that under natural conditions it should not exchange genes with other species (the popular idea that two species are 'unable' to interbreed is a misunderstanding: it is not that they *cannot* interbreed, it is that they *do not*). This concept remained virtually unchallenged until the 1970s, despite the fact that it is applicable only in cases of sympatry or parapatry, and of course contemporaneity – concerning allopatric populations, or populations in different time periods, it is silent. The most recent major taxonomic study that utilises the BSC (Mayr and Diamond, 2001) recommends that one compare the sort of differences that characterise allopatric populations with the differences between sympatric pairs of their closest relatives, as do Coyne and Orr (2004), in adopting a looser version of the BSC. This in effect sets up different standards of comparison in different taxonomic groups. If a genus contains a pair of sympatric sibling species (species that differ only slightly, inconspicuously), the standard for species recognition will be set much 'lower' than in a genus in which sympatric species pairs are grossly different. It is the search for objective standards – for an operational means of distinguishing species – that has been responsible for the controversies that marked taxonomic discussions over the past 15 or 20 years.

Among the attempts to make the species concept more operational, at least as far as sexually reproducing animals are concerned, the recognition species concept (Paterson, 1986: 63) has been perhaps especially influential: a species according to this concept is 'that most inclusive population of biparental organisms which share a common fertilization system'. While admitting that this concept stands to be misunderstood, and the 'specific mate recognition systems' on which it depends can be understood only by extensive fieldwork, it has certainly been extremely productive in identifying cryptic species (meaning those whose morphological differences are not obvious), especially in nocturnal mammals such as bushbabies (Primates, family Galagidae).

The most nearly operational characterisation of species is provided by the phylogenetic species concept (PSC) as defined by Cracraft (1983, 1989, 1997). This definition, like Simpson's, has two parts: a species is the smallest cluster of individual organisms:

- within which there is a parental pattern of ancestry and descent
- and that is diagnosably distinct from other such clusters by a unique combination of fixed character states.

The first part of the definition specifies that we are talking about populations; the second part specifies how we may distinguish these populations. As pointed out to me during the course of the African Genesis symposium by W. L. Jungers, Eldredge and Cracraft (1980: 92) had earlier provided a definition of phylogenetic species that in some respects is less prone to potential misunderstanding: 'A species is a diagnosable cluster of individuals within which there is a parental pattern of ancestry and descent, beyond which there is not, and which exhibits a pattern of phylogenetic ancestry and descent among units of like kind.' This makes it absolutely clear that species are indeed evolving populations. Note, however, that although the PSC is the most nearly objective concept that is available, the inference that we are dealing with a population remains all-too-often just that: an inference, virtually untestable. The assumption that we are dealing with a population is one that all species concepts must make, and its inferential nature is something that we have to live with.

What is 'diagnosably distinct'? In order to diagnose anything, one must be able to characterise it without any exceptions. Thus 'diagnosably distinct' implies the following:

- 100% difference from other species
- every individual can be assigned to its species by some character or other
- given age and sex variation
- except for demonstrable hybrids between different species
- there are fixed differences
- these differences must be heritable, of course
- there are character-state gaps between species.

In other words, species are defined not by 'how much difference', but 'what difference' there is from other species: not quantity but quality. As Nelson and Platnick (1981:12) put it succinctly: 'species are simply the smallest detected samples of self-perpetuating organisms that have unique sets of characters'. For further discussion of the nature of the PSC, and its relationship to the subspecies concept, see Kimbel and Rak (1993), Groves (2001) and Cotterill (2003).

The question of the recognition of a species from a single specimen often arises in palaeontology, indeed in the living fauna as well (Groves, 2000). When a single specimen falls outside the range of variation of a comparative sample in several apparently independent character states, or is metrically outside the range of variation as represented by, for example, the 3-standard-deviation limits, then the null hypothesis (that it represents the same species) may be considered falsified.

It may occur in the fossil record that we have a hypothesised ancestor–descendent sequence without clear breaks, yet samples at one end of the sequence are diagnosably distinct from those at the other. A potential case is outlined by Kimbel *et al.* (2006). How would such a case be treated? Kimbel and Rak (1993) proffered one solution: 'we recognize temporally disjunct clusters of specimens that are separately diagnosable by apomorphies as distinct species...[whereas] temporally contiguous clusters of specimens that are not separately diagnosable, but rather evince continuous character change over time, represent a single, unbroken lineage (species) in our view' (Kimbel and Rak, 1993: 472).

What if there is demonstrable cladogenesis within a given fossil sequence; where do species begin and end? Kornet and McAllister (1993) proposed the composite species concept (CSC), in which species is:

- the set of all organisms belonging to an originator internodon
- and all organisms belonging to any of its descendant internodons
- excluding further originator internodons and their descendant internodons

– meaning that a new species begins at the branch-point above which a new character state becomes fixed (an originator internodon), and ends at the branch-point above which the next new character state becomes fixed (the next originator internodon). Accordingly, species are lineages, but they must be diagnosable lineages.

One must, of course, be certain where the branching points occur for this concept to be successfully applied. In most cases this will not be known, and the PSC, identifying the smallest diagnosable clusters, will be the safest concept to adopt (as per Kimbel and Rak, 1993: see above). The principle is that, in species recognition as in other branches of science, Type I errors (false positives) are more tolerable than Type II errors (false negatives): it is simpler to combine erroneously separated categories than to unscramble those that have been erroneously lumped.

What is a genus?

Although objectivity seems an achievable goal (the population assumption always granted) where species are concerned, in the case of the higher categories in taxonomy subjectivity rules. A genus (or indeed a family, an order, a class and so on) should be monophyletic, but there are no other guidelines. Essentially, a genus is what one thinks it ought to be. If we are speaking scientifically, then this is an unsatisfactory state of affairs.

The founder of the principle of phylogenetic systematics, Hennig (1952–1966), sought some objectivity, and proposed to link taxonomic 'higher ranks' to time depth, but realised fully that it would not quite work, because genera of invertebrates are much more broadly drawn than those in vertebrates, especially birds and mammals. His proposal was revived by Goodman *et al.* (1998); it was supported by Avise and Johns (1999), and has been put into practice a few times (see for example Groves, 2001), but has not yet achieved wide acceptance.

Goodman *et al.* (1998) accepted that, because of different standard practices in different animal groups, there have to be different standards for different groups if there is to be communication among specialists in a particular subfield: an entomologist's genus characteristically goes back to the Eocene, an ornithologist's only to the Pliocene, if that. In mammals, as proposed by Goodman *et al.* (1998), living genera should go back earlier than the Miocene–Pliocene boundary: 7 million years would, they suggest, be a reasonable time depth for a mammalian genus, which seems to do least violence to presently adopted practice. Thus, if two species-groups separated, using either the fossil record or the molecular clock, more than 7 million years ago they should be placed in different genera; if they separated noticeably less than 7 million years ago, they should be placed in the same genus. In extinct mammals, the time depth should be equivalent (i.e. a genus lasts 7 million years).

Consequences for palaeoanthropology would be that most, probably all, members of the human lineage would belong to a single genus, *Homo* (whether the living chimpanzees should be placed in the same genus is a question not considered here, although it has many proponents). Before palaeoanthropologists reject such a proposition out of hand, let us consider the present position. First, we have at least one genus, *Australopithecus*, which is admittedly paraphyletic (and the recent ascription of a second species to *Ardipithecus* renders that genus probably paraphyletic as well); to render *Australopithecus* monophyletic would require separating all species except for the type species, *A. africanus*, into genera of their own, probably a whole series of them. Second, the literature is beset by arguments as to whether certain species should be split off into their own genera: the desirability or otherwise of recognising the genus *Paranthropus* is the most persistent example. To a major extent, arguments about phylogeny are hedged about with thoughts of what damage this might do to taxonomy, because the name of the genus is the first word in the name of the species. It is surely not desirable that nomenclature, with its useful information-retrieval function, should be at the mercy of the latest phylogenetic hypothesis.

A list of phylogenetic species in the hominin fossil record under the Goodman *et al.* (1998) scheme follows. This scheme presents the species in descending order according to their approximate geological ages. In line with the recommendation of Article 51.1 of the *International Code of Zoological Nomenclature* (4th edition, 1999), each specific name is followed by its author(s) and date; these are not bibliographic citations, however. Where more than two individuals are authors of the scientific name, all but the first abbreviated to '*et al.*', the presence of parentheses () indicates that the specific name in question was first proposed with a different generic name.

Proposed scheme

Homo tugenensis (*Orrorin*: Senut *et al.*, 2001). Lukeino Fm., Kenya, ±6 Ma.

Homo kadabba (*Ardipithecus*: Haile-Selassie, 2001). Middle Awash, Ethiopia, 5.8–5.2 Ma.

Homo ramidus (*Ardipithecus*: White *et al.*, 1994). Aramis, Ethiopia, 4.4 Ma.

Homo anamensis (M. Leakey *et al.*, 1995). Kanapoi and Allia Bay, Kenya, 4.17– 3.9Ma.

Homo afarensis (Johanson, 1978). Hadar, Laetoli, Maka, etc., E.Africa, 3.6–3.0 Ma.

Homo platyops (M. Leakey *et al.*, 2001). Lomekwi, Kenya, *c.* 3.5–3.3 Ma (*Kenyanthropus*: M. Leakey *et al.*, 2001).

Homo africanus (Dart, 1925). Taung, Sterkfontein, Makapangat, S.Africa, 3–?2.5 Ma (*Australopithecus*: Dart, 1925).

Homo garhi (Asfaw *et al.*, 1999). Bouri, Ethiopia, 2.5 Ma.

Homo walkeri (Ferguson, 1989). Lomekwi, Kenya, 2.5 Ma.

Homo robustus (Broom, 1938). Kromdraai, Swartkrans, Drimolen, S.Africa, ?1.6 Ma (*Paranthropus*: Broom, 1938).

Homo boisei (L. Leakey, 1959). Olduvai, Peninj, Koobi Fora, Omo, Chemeron, Konso, E.Africa; Malema, Malawi, 2.3–1.0 Ma (*Zinjanthropus*: L. Leakey, 1959).

Homo rudolfensis (Alexeev, 1986). Koobi Fora, Kenya, 1.9 Ma; Uraha, Malawi, 3.3 Ma.

Homo floresiensis (Brown *et al.*, 2004). Liang Bua, Flores, ?95–12 ka.

Homo habilis L. Leakey, *et al.*, 1964. Olduvai, Koobi Fora, Hadar, E. Africa, 2.3–1.6 Ma.

Homo georgicus Gabounia *et al.*, 2002. Dmanisi, Georgia, 1.8 Ma.

Homo ergaster Groves & Mazák, 1975. Koobi Fora, Nariokotome, Kenya, 1.8–1.5 Ma.

Homo louisleakeyi Kretzoi, 1984. Olduvai, Tanzania, 1.48–1.33 Ma.

Homo antecessor Bermúdez de Castro *et al.*, 1997. Gran Dolina (Atapuerca), Spain; ?Ceprano, Italy; 0.8 Ma.

Homo erectus (Dubois, 1892). Sangiran, Trinil, ?Perning, Java, ?1.9–0.8 Ma (*Pithecanthropus*: Dubois, 1894).

Homo soloensis Oppenoorth, 1932. Ngandong, Sambanugmacan, Ngawi, Java, ?100–<30 Ma (*Javanthropus*: Oppenoorth, 1932).

Homo pekinensis (Black, 1927). Zhoukoudian, Nanjing, Hexian, China, 550–250 ka (*Sinanthropus*: Black, 1927).

Homo heidelbergensis Schoetensack, 1908. Mauer, Bilzingsleben, Germany; Petralona, Greece; Kabwe, Zambia; Ndutu, Tanzania; Bodo, Ethiopia, 600–?300 ka (*Palaeanthropus*: Bonarelli, 1907).

Homo neanderthalensis King, 1864. European sites; Tabun, Amud, Israel; Shanidar, Iraq; Teshik-Tash, Uzbekistan; *c.* 300–30 ka (*Archanthropus*: Arldt, 1915).

Homo sapiens Linnaeus, 1758. Omo/Kibish, Herto, Ethiopia, 195 ka – worldwide, present day.

The species listed above are those that seem, in the present state of analysis, to be diagnosable under the PSC, except that within *Homo afarensis* it is likely that the Hadar sample is diagnosably distinct from the sample from the type locality, Laetoli (see Kimbel *et al.*, 2006). The species have been listed in approximate, but not exact, time sequence; for example, *Homo floresiensis* is listed among what seem to be its closest relatives (Argue *et al.*, 2006), not among other Late Pleistocene species. Fossil specimens left unallocated in this scheme include some that remain controversial (*Sahelanthropus* from Chad), or are not yet analysed (Daka, from Ethiopia), or are too fragmentary (Gongwangling, China).

The available name of the species represented by the so-called Black Skull is not *aethiopicus*, as has unfortunately become widespread, but *walkeri*; the name of the species represented by Olduvai Hominid 9 is *louisleakeyi* (Groves, 1999); the other specific names are those in more general use.

How do new species arise?

Speciation, in the PSC, is the origin of one or more new species that are diagnosably distinct from the parent species and/or each other. Typically, it is thought of as consequent on lineage splitting (cladogenesis). Phyletic speciation (anagenesis) used to be taken for granted prior to what may be called the 'punctuated equilibrium revolution' of the 1970s, but appears to have been neglected theoretically since Petry (1982). I will not consider phyletic speciation here.

The mechanisms of speciation, in the lineage splitting sense, are a perpetual topic of discussion (White, 1978; Groves, 1989). For those who regard speciation as equivalent to the achievement of reproductive isolation, it is the question of sympatry that is crucial: a species, under the BSC, is not a 'real species' until reproductive isolation has been at least partially achieved, and indeed it is the intrinsic interest of the origin of reproductive isolation that appears to be the motivation for many authors, including Coyne and Orr (2004), to continue their adherence to the BSC. The problem of how reproductive isolation arises should not be allowed to overshadow the problem of divergence; the relationship between the two is not inherently independent, nor is it necessarily an invariant sequence (divergence followed by reproductive isolation). Once we acknowledge that the relationship between the two processes is complex, we may ask the interesting questions, such as: is reproductive isolation a by-product of divergence, or is it selected for once sympatry has been achieved, or can it even precede divergence?

In what follows, I will treat speciation modes largely geographically, but with special attention to two particular mechanisms (hybridisation and centrifugal speciation) that fit uneasily into any of the geographic modes although they are broadly speaking of the sympatric/parapatric type:

- Allopatry
  - ◦ Type 1 – population subdivision
  - ◦ Type 2 – founder effect
- Parapatry
- Stasipatry
- Sympatry
- Hybridisation
- Centrifugal modes

Allopatry Type 1 (dichopatric speciation: Cracraft, 1984)

The standard model of speciation is allopatric; indeed, it is the only model accepted by some authors (Mayr, 1963 and elsewhere). Whether the population splits evenly into two (dichopatric) or a small part of it hives off from the main population (founder effect, or peripatric) has somewhat different results.

The typical form of dichopatric speciation is simple population division by a barrier:

- a barrier arises (a river changes course, for example), splitting the population into two
- the two daughter populations slowly diverge
- divergence will be accelerated if, as is common, there was some clinal variation across the parent population
- the two daughter populations are comparable in size so there is no population bottleneck
- the result is that neither daughter species is entirely plesiomorphic with respect to the other.

Equivalent in its effect to the barrier case is the extinction of intermediate populations in a cline. This happens when climate change shrinks a species' available habitat to two or more isolates. If the surviving populations are sufficiently far apart along the cline so that their gene pools are largely distinct, the result is almost 'instant speciation'. (There is a fear that the biodiversity crisis at the present time may well be having some such effect, as formerly widespread species become restricted to dispersed quasi-insular populations.)

A special case will be that of a progressive cline (Grubb, 2000). This is when apomorphic character states are concentrated towards one end of the cline. The result of such a population splitting in two is that one daughter species will be plesiomorphic in most of its features, the other predominantly apomorphic.

Allopatry Type 2 – founder effect (peripatric speciation: Mayr, 1982)

In this mode of allopatric speciation, a small segment of the population becomes cut off from the rest: it differs from Type 1 in the extreme asymmetry of the split. A small sample drawn from a population will not possess a typical selection of the polymorphic alleles, such that alleles that are rare in the parent population may even predominate in the small isolate. One or more of these unusual alleles may drift towards fixation; or in the new environment, both extrinsic and intrinsic (i.e. the environment of the unusual combination of genes), and freed from gene flow from the main population, they may be selected for. The result is one highly autapomorphic species with a small range, plus one wholly plesiomorphic widespread species. As the latter is identical to the parent species, it seems mandatory to treat it as the same (*pace* Hennig, 1952).

Starting as it does from a small population base, the future of the peri-patric isolate is, in theory, not rosy. Nonetheless for Mayr (1963, 1982) and the punctuated equilibrium proponents (Eldredge and Gould, 1972), this is the predominant mode of speciation. Indeed, a population that starts from a small population base does not necessarily lose genetic variability as long as it expands rapidly (Lande and Barrowclough, 1987), so the problem may not be so much the small initial size of the isolate as its presumably restricted oppor-tunity to disperse into unoccupied habitat. If this problem can be overcome, it does seem plausible that founder effect speciation will have the potential to achieve its mooted importance.

Parapatry

Allopatric speciation is the divergence of populations that are not in genetic contact. In parapatry, however, the two populations (candidates for speci-ation) meet and exchange genes along a mutual boundary; gene flow is not as potentially extensive as in the case of sympatry, but there will be, in principle, some gene flow, and this can be a problem for speciation. The most plausible model is called 'clinal speciation' by White (1978), whereby a step in a cline becomes steeper over time due to intensified selection (White calls this area-effect speciation), and the strong spatial differences in gene complexes become incompatible.

The most striking form of parapatric speciation, illustrating how differ-ences in gene complexes can build up across distance until they become incompatible, is ring species. In such a case, a species spreads its range around some barrier, until the two ends of its distribution come into contact, and prove genetically incompatible. The 'classic example' of this used to be the circumpolar distribution of the herring gull (*Larus argentatus*) com-plex, but this has recently turned out to be wrong: there are now known to be quite a number of different, geographically replacing species in this com-plex (Liebers *et al.*, 2004). Instead, we have a new ornithological exemplar, the Greenish Warbler (*Phylloscopus trochiloides*), closely analysed by Irwin *et al.* (2005). This species lives in suitable habitat around the Tibetan Plateau, with both morphological and molecular character states changing gradually northwest and northeast of its apparent homeland in the southern Himalayas, until in central Siberia the two streams meet and seem to be reproductively incompatible.

In parapatric speciation, reproductive isolation must evolve by reinforce-ment, whereas in allopatric speciation, reproductive isolation may evolve as a by-product of a divergence, if there is evidence for it at all.

Stasipatry (White, 1978)

This mode of speciation concerns chromosomal mutations. It was first detected by White (1978) in grasshoppers, but its widespread applicability remains untested. It is a special model of parapatric or sympatric speciation:

> First, a chromosomal rearrangement arises. If it protects an advantageous linkage group, and if there is a degree of inbreeding – in a coarse-grained environment; or in some types of social system, such as one-male groups, as in guenons (*Cercopithecus*) – it may spread.

The heterozygotes between the rearrangement and the plesiomorphic karyotype have reduced fertility, but as soon as homozygotes begin to be generated they are essentially fertile only with each other, and are reproductively isolated from the parent form.

Sympatry

The possibility of sympatric speciation has been raised from time to time, but is still extremely controversial. Mayr (1963) dismissed it out of hand, and continued to do so (Mayr and Diamond, 2001). Even in the event that the well-argued examples find wide acceptance, it may still be questioned whether the model applies outside such organisms as Rift Lake cichlids (especially Lakes Malawi and Tanganyika). There are three potential modes that have been argued, the first mainly on theoretical grounds (but see Bush, 1969), the other two as explanatory models for the observed mega-diversity of lake fish faunas:

- ecological races exhibiting assortative mating (Maynard Smith, 1966)
- disruptive selection promoted by competition for a key resource (Dieckmann and Doebeli, 1999)
- sexual selection (Kondrashov and Kondrashov, 1999).

Hybrid speciation (recombinational speciation: Coyne and Orr, 2004)

The idea that new species may arise not by the splitting of one into two, but by the fusion of two into one, is not new but has taken on a new lease of life because of certain molecular findings in mammals.

Hybrids often show unexpected genetic features. Quite common is a high frequency in some hybrid zones of alleles (called hybrizymes by Woodruff, 1989) that are otherwise rare, or even unknown, in the parent populations.

Morphological anomalies, presumably the morphological phenotypes from the same phenomenon, are also known (Arntzen and Wallis, 1991). Their genesis has been much discussed; suggestions are that they may result from the disruption of parental epistasis, recombination within loci, increased mutation or relaxed selection.

At least one primate species is plausibly of hybrid origin (Tosi *et al.*, 2000): *Macaca arctoides*, the Stumptail macaque of mainland Southeast Asia (from southern China to the Isthmus of Kra in peninsular Thailand). The mitochondrial DNA of this species most closely resembles that of *M. fascicularis* (the Crab-eating or Longtailed macaque of Southeast Asia), whereas the Y-chromosome DNA assorts with those of *M. assamensis* and *M. thibetana*, from the northern part of Southeast Asia and central China. The discrepancy is so marked (the mitochondrial and Y-chromosome sister groups belonging to widely separated species groups) that the only plausible hypothesis seems to be that *M. arctoides* results from a hybridisation event between these two groups; this, from molecular clock calculations, would have occurred about one million years ago. Note that *M. arctoides* is a highly autapomorphic – not to say totally bizarre – species, and no one could possibly have detected its real origin from its morphology alone.

This case illustrates a likely, but not inevitable, scenario: males of one of the parent species are dominant to the other (in the simplest case, they are larger in size), so that they are able to displace males of the other species and mate with their females. The hybridisation will therefore be predominantly one-way, and the hybrid species inherits the Y-chromosome DNA of one parent species and the mtDNA of the other.

Hybrid speciation is a different phenomenon from the apparently quite common situation whereby the interbreeding of two species is followed by backcrossing; as Coyne and Orr (2004) pointed out, this will lead to the local extinction of the rarer of the two parental species, with one of the non-recombining portions of its genome (typically the mtDNA) remaining as a lasting legacy. For hybrid speciation to occur, the hybridised population should be isolated from both parent species so that backcrossing cannot occur, or is rare.

The role of centrifugal forces

The centrifugal mode is called centrifugal speciation by Groves (1989), but describes not so much the generation of a new species as the geography of its consequences. The principle is as follows: the centre of the distribution of a species or genus has denser populations than the periphery, hence the centre generates more evolutionary novelties through mutation and recombination, and selection (as opposed to drift) is a more powerful force. The result is that the more central populations and taxa will tend to be more derived, and more primitive taxa, and populations retaining more plesiomorphic states, will tend to be peripherally distributed.

How do we recognise these modes in the fossil record?

Are there ways in which the fossil record may yield information on how species may have been generated? I suggest that there are, and that if we can disentangle potential modes of speciation it may tell us something about the biogeography, in particular, of hominins at that time, and perhaps even give insights on ecology and behaviour. This is because, when we examine pairs of sister species, the different modes of speciation yield somewhat different expectations as to what we may find as a consequence of their operation:

Allopatry Type 1 – neither of the two sister species retains the ancestral morphology; both are changed, and about equally, from the putative ancestral species.

Allopatry Type 2 (founder effect) – one of the two sister species retains the ancestral morphology, the other is much changed. If we are lucky, and the record at that point is sufficiently good, we will see the founder-effect species slowly spreading from its small original range.

Parapatry – probably impossible to differentiate from Allopatry Type 1.

Stasipatry – there seems not a hope of detecting this in the fossil record!

Sympatry – we will see, again if the record is sufficiently good, a new species differentiating very rapidly in the middle of the range of its parent species.

Hybridisation – a species exhibits apparent mixed characteristics at first, but rapidly develops its own unique features.

Centrifugal mode – plesiomorphic states are unexpectedly concentrated in a peripheral population.

Possibilities

A brief survey of the time-slices that are afforded to us in the human fossil record already suggests possible modes of speciation. Further discoveries will help to test these hypotheses.

The 3.5 Ma time-slice

Homo platyops cf. H. afarensis

In this species pair, *H. platyops* differs in possessing a range of apomorphies, including small teeth, weak prognathism and facial flatness. This assumes that the relatively poorly known Laetoli, Maka and Fejej populations of *H. afarensis* have the same facial features as are better known for the later Hadar sample.

The known distribution of *H. platyops* is very restricted, and inserts within the much wider range of *H. afarensis*. This is the sort of picture one would expect from sympatric speciation: a novel species with autapomorphic character states (*H. platyops*) has arisen from a central part of the range of a widespread plesiomorphic species (*H. afarensis*) and, apparently, has spread no further.

The 2.5 Ma time-slice: 1 'Robust australopithecines'

Homo walkeri (KNM-ER 17000, the Black Skull) exhibits both apomorphic and plesiomorphic states when compared to its contemporaries *H. africanus* and *H. garhi*, which may be treated as a unit for present purposes. The apomorphic states include very large cheekteeth (a parallelism with *H. garhi*) and dished face; plesiomorphic conditions compared to both its contemporaries include strong prognathism, smooth nasal sill and strong postorbital constriction.

Apomorphic and plesiomorphic states thus appear in both units. This situation is most plausibly seen as a consequence of allopatric speciation Type 1 (dichopatric); a widespread species has split into two equal daughters, which continue to diverge in allopatry.

The 2.5 Ma time-slice: 2 'Gracile australopithecines'

The differences of *Homo garhi* from *H. africanus* are mainly plesiomorphic: frontal trigon, no facial pillars, presence of I^2-C' diastema, and convex subnasal clivus. Only the huge cheekteeth are apomorphic compared to *H. africanus*.

This suggests that Allopatry Type 2 (founder effect) may be responsible. A widespread species, the centrally distributed *H. garhi*, has budded off a peripheral isolate, *H. africanus* in South Africa. This scenario will be tested when East African sites between 3.0 and 2.5 Ma become better known.

But there is a twist to this story. The only apomorphic state in *H. garhi* is megadonty, and it is of great interest that this condition is shared with the only so far known contemporary East African species, *H. walkeri*. There are two problems that arise from this. The first problem concerns the identity of Omo-18, the type specimen of *Paraustralopithecus aethiopicus*. There is little that can be said for sure about this specimen, except that it is megadont. The name *aethiopicus* for it is preoccupied if used with either *Homo* or *Australopithecus* (though not if it is used with *Paranthropus*, see Groves, 1999), but it is worth pointing out that it could as easily belong to *H. garhi* as to the species represented by the Black Skull.

A more interesting question is this: what if the huge cheekteeth of *H. garhi*, rather than being a parallelism with *H. walkeri*, are a legacy of hybridisation?

The 1.8 Ma time-slice

Homo georgicus (taking that concept to cover all of the Dmanisi sample) differs from its exact contemporary, *H. ergaster*, apparently exclusively by plesiomorphic conditions, including the smaller endocranial volume (ECV), narrow pyriform aperture, strong postorbital constriction, U-shaped dental arcade and forward position of anterior marginal tubercle of mandible. Yet, if we take an African, presumably East African, homeland for granted (but see Kingdon, 2003), it is *H. georgicus* that is the product of dispersal, not the more apomorphic *H. ergaster*. This is exactly the pattern one expects as a result of centrifugal speciation. It is, however, not only a northeasterly relative of *H. ergaster* that exhibits plesiomorphic differences. Grine has in several places (see for example Grine *et al.*, 1996) maintained that certain South African specimens, notably SK847, resemble *H. ergaster* in many respects but retain notable plesiomorphic character states. The question irresistibly arises whether the Swartkrans and Dmanisi samples represent the same, formerly widespread, species, from which *H. ergaster* has arisen centrally by centrifugal mechanisms. A comparison between the two should be of considerable interest in this light.

Summary

Speciation is the study of divergence as well as of the achievement of reproductive isolation. Divergence may occur alone, or the two processes may occur in tandem, or together. Speciation is usually envisaged as occurring in allopatry in its initial stages, but parapatric and even sympatric speciation are being increasingly taken seriously, while speciation by hybridisation is known to have occurred in several mammals including primates.

Different modes of speciation predict different character state polarities and different geographies in sister species, and in the human fossil record one can make working hypotheses of the speciation modes that are likely to have operated.

If the genus *Homo* is expanded to incorporate all known species of the human clade, its time depth will be more commensurate with that of other mammalian genera, while phylogenetic hypotheses will no longer need to drag nomenclatural changes in their wake.

Acknowledgements

I thank the organisers of the African Genesis symposium for inviting me to such a thrilling and absorbing fest, and for their wonderful hospitality: especially Sally Reynolds, Andrew Gallagher and Colin Menter, the late Heather White, and, of course, Phillip Tobias in whose honour it was held. I would like to thank some of the other delegates for helpful comments during the symposium, in particular Alison Brooks, Ron Clarke, Ray Corbey, Bill Jungers and Milford Wolpoff. I would finally like to thank the referees of this chapter for their extremely helpful comments: Jason Hemingway, Jonathan Kingdon, Sally Reynolds, and the late Peter Grubb, a fine scientist and wonderful friend, to whose memory I dedicate this contribution.

References

Argue, D., Donlon, D, Groves, C. *et al.* (2006). *Homo floresiensis*: microcephalic, pygmoid, *Australopithecus*, or *Homo*? *Journal of Human Evolution*, **51**: 360–74.

Arntzen, J. W. and Wallis, G. P. (1991). Restricted gene flow in a moving hybrid zone of the newts *Triturus cristatus* and *T.marmoratus* in western France. *Evolution*, **45**: 805–26.

Avise, J. C. and Johns, G. C. (1999). Proposal for a standardized temporal scheme of biological classification for extant species. *Proceedings of the National Academy of Sciences USA*, **96**:7358–63.

Bush, G. L. (1969). Sympatric host race formation and speciation in frugivorous flies of the genus *Rhagoletis* (Diptera, Tephritidae). *Evolution*, **23**: 237–51.

Cotterill, F. P. D. (2003). Species concepts and the real diversity of antelopes. In Plowman, A. (ed.), *Ecology and Conservation of Small Antelope*. Fürth: Filander Verlag, pp. 59–118.

Coyne, J. A. and Orr. H. A. (2004). *Speciation*. Sunderland, MA: Sinauer Associates, Inc.

Cracraft, J. (1983). Species concepts and speciation analysis. *Current Ornithology*, 1:159–87.

(1984). The terminology of allopatric speciation. Systematic. *Zoology*, **33**: 115–16.

(1989). Speciation and its ontology: the empirical consequences of alternative species concepts for understanding patterns and processes of differentiation. In Otte, D. and Endler, J. A. (eds.), *Speciation and its Consequences*. Sunderland: Sinauer Associates, pp. 28–59.

(1997). Species concepts in systematics and conservation biology: an ornithological viewpoint. In Claridge, M. F., Dawah, A. A. and Wilson, M. R. (eds.), *Species: The Units of Biodiversity*. New York: Chapman and Hall, pp. 325–39

Dieckmann, U. and Doebeli, M. (1999). On the origin of species by sympatric speciation. *Nature*, **400**: 354–7.

Eldredge, N. and Cracraft, J. (1980). *Phylogenetic Patterns and the Evolutionary Process*. New York: Columbia University Press.

Eldredge N, and Gould, S. J. (1972). Punctuated equilibria: an alternative to phyletic gradualism. In Schopf, T. J. M. (ed.), *Models in Paleobiology*. San Francisco: Freeman Cooper & Co, pp. 83–115.

Goodman, M., Porter, C. A., Czelusniak, J. *et al.* (1998). Toward a phylogenetic classification of Primates based on DNA evidence complemented by fossil evidence. *Molecular Phylogenetics and Evolution*, **9**: 585–98.

Grine, F. E., Jungers, W. L. and Schultz, J. (1996). Phenetic affinities among early *Homo* crania from East and South Africa. *Journal of Human Evolution*, **30**: 189–225.

Groves, C. P. (1989). *A Theory of Human and Primate Evolution*. Oxford: Oxford University Press.

(1999). Nomenclature of African Plio-Pleistocene hominins. *Journal of Human Evolution*, **37**: 869–72.

(2000). The genus *Cheirogaleus*: unrecognised biodiversity in Dwarf Lemurs. *International Journal of Primatology*, **21**: 943–62.

(2001). *Primate Taxonomy*. Washington: Smithsonian Institution Press.

Grubb, P. (2000). Morphoclinal evolution in ungulates. In Vrba, E. S. and Schaller, G. B. (eds), *Antelopes, Deer, and Relatives*. New Haven and London: Yale University Press, pp. 156–70.

Hennig, W. (1952–1966 translation). *Phylogenetic Systematics*. Urbana: University of Illinois Press.

International Commission on Zoological Nomenclature (1999). *International Code of Zoological Nomenclature*, 4th edition. London: International Commision on Zoological Nomenclature.

Irwin, D. E., Bensch, S., Irwin, J. H. *et al.* (2005). Speciation by distance in a ring species. *Science*, **307**: 414–16.

Kimbel, W. H. and Rak, Y. (1993). The importance of species taxa in palaeoanthropology and an argument for the phylogenetic concept of the species category. In Kimbel, W. H. and Martin, L. B. (eds.), *Species, Species Concepts, and Primate Evolution*. New York and London: Plenum Press, pp. 461–84.

Kimbel, W. H., Lockwood, C. A., Ward, C. V. *et al.* (2006). Was *Australopithecus anamensis* ancestral to *A. afarensis*? A case of anagenesis in the hominin fossil record. *Journal Human. Evolution*, **51**: 134–52.

Kingdon, J. (2003). *Lowly Origin: Where, When, and Why Our Ancestors First Stood Up*. Princeton: Princeton University Press.

Kondrashov, A. S. and Kondrashov, S. A. (1999). Interactions among quantitative traits in the course of sympatric speciation. *Nature*, **400**: 351–4.

Kornet, D. J. and McAllister, J. W. (1993). The composite species concept. In Kornet, D. J. (ed.), *Reconstructing Species: Demarcations in Genealogical Networks*. Leiden: Rijksherbarium, pp.61–89.

Lande, R. and Barrowclough, G. F. (1987). Effective population size, genetic variation, and their use in population management. In Soule, M. E. (ed.), *Viable Populations for Conservation*. Cambridge: Cambridge University Press, pp. 87–123.

Liebers, D., de Knijff, P. and Helbig, A. J. (2004). The herring gull complex is not a ring species. *Proceedings of the Royal Society London B*, **271**: 893–901.

Maynard Smith, J. (1966). Sympatric speciation. *American Naturalist*, **100**: 637–50.

Mayr, E. (1963). *Animal Species and Evolution*. Harvard: Harvard University Press. (1982). Speciation and macroevolution. *Evolution*, **36**: 1119–32.

Mayr, E. and Diamond, J. (2001). *The Birds of Northern Melanesia: Speciation, Ecology, and Biogeography*. Oxford: Oxford University Press.

Nelson, G. and Platnick, N. I. (1981). *Systematics and Biogeography; Cladistics and Vicariance*. New York: Columbia University Press.

Paterson, H. E. H. (1986). Environment and species. *South African Journal of Science*, **82**: 62–5.

Petry, D. (1982). The pattern of phyletic speciation. *Paleobiology*, **8**: 56–66.

Simpson, G. G. (1961). *Principles of Animal Taxonomy*. New York: Columbia University Press.

Tosi, A. J., Morales, J. C. and Melnick, D. J. (2000). Comparison of Y chromosome and mtDNA phylogenies leads to unique inferences of macaque evolutionary history. *Molecular Phylogenetics and Evolution*, **17**: 133–44.

White, M. J. D. (1978). *Modes of Speciation*. San Francisco: W. H. Freeman.

Woodruff, D. D. (1989). Genetic anomalies associated with *Cerion* hybrid zones: the origin and maintenance of new electromorphic variants called hybrizymes. *Biological Journal of the Linnean Society*, **36**: 281–94.

4   *Searching for a new paradigm for hominid origins in Chad (Central Africa)*

MICHEL BRUNET

Abstract

The idea of an ascendance for our species is quite recent (about 150 years ago). But questions remain: who was this ancestor, and where and when did he arise? In the 1980s, early hominids were known only from southern and eastern Africa. Digging in Djurab desert (Northern Chad) from 1994 onwards, the Mission Paléoanthropologique Franco-Tchadienne (MPFT) team unearthed first a new australopithecine (dated to 3.5 Ma, Brunet *et al.*, 1995; Lebatard *et al.*, 2008), the first ever found west of the Rift Valley and a later new hominid *Sahelanthropus tchadensis* (Brunet *et al.*, 2002a) from the late Miocene, dated to 7 Ma (Vignaud *et al.*, 2002; Lebatard *et al.*, 2008). This earliest known hominid is a new milestone suggesting that an exclusively southern or eastern African origin of the hominid clade is likely to be incorrect. In the last decade our roots have descended deeper into the Lower Pliocene (4.4 Ma) to the Late Miocene (7 Ma) with three new species: *Ardipithecus kadabba* (5.8–5.2 Ma, Middle Awash, Ethiopia), *Orrorin tugenensis* (c. 6 Ma, Lukeino, Kenya) and the oldest one *Sahelanthropus tchadensis* (c. 7 Ma). *S. tchadensis* displays a unique combination of derived characters that clearly shows hominid affinities that are close, temporally speaking, to the last common ancestor between chimpanzees and humans, and that it cannot be related to chimpanzees or gorillas. In Chad, the Late Miocene sedimentological and palaeobiological data indicate the presence of a mosaic environment probably very similar to the present Okavango Delta (Central Kalahari, Bostwana). As with the other Late Miocene hominids, *S. tchadensis* was a bipedal animal living in a wooded habitat.

It is now clear that the earliest hominids did not inhabit savannah environments, nor were they living only in South and East Africa. In the light of this new evidence, our early hominid history must now be reconsidered within a completely new paradigm.

African Genesis: Perspectives on Hominin Evolution, eds. Sally C. Reynolds and Andrew Gallagher. Published by Cambridge University Press. © Cambridge University Press 2012.

63

Introduction

During the last 150 years, we have discovered unexpected ancestors, numerous close relatives and our deep geological roots. But who was our ancestor? Where and when did he arise?

The new deal...west of the Rift Valley

In the 1980s the distribution of hominid remains in Africa showed the earliest prehumans coming from East Africa (Ethiopia and Tanzania) (Figure 4.1). This led Coppens (1983) to propose an 'East Side Story' palaeoscenario: early

1 Taung	14 Kanapoi
2 Drimolen	15 Chemeron
3 Sterkfontein	16 W. Turkana
4 Swartkrans	17 Koobi Fora
5 Kromdraai	18 Allia Bay
6 Makapansgat	19 Omo
7 Malema	20 Konso
8 Laetoli	21 Maka
9 Olduvai	22 Aramis
10 Peninj	23 Hadar
11 Lukeino	24 Koro-Toro
12 Chesowanja	25 Toros-Menalla
13 Lothagam	

Figure 4.1. Map of Africa showing the main Mio-Pliocene hominid localities.

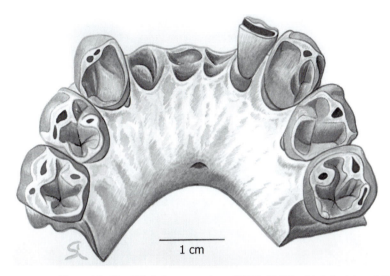

Figure 4.2. Mandible holotype specimen (KT12–95-H1) of *A. bahrelghazali* (Brunet *et al.*, 1996).

hominids appeared and evolved in the Pliocene primary savannah east of the Rift Valley, while the tropical forest, west of the Rift Valley, was thought to represent the early African ape habitat. In 1994, I obtained a research permit from the Chadian authorities to conduct a geological and palaeontological survey in the Djurab desert, northern Chad. One year later (January 1995), east of Koro-Toro, we recovered a lower Pliocene vertebrate faunal assemblage including a partial lower jaw specimen (nicknamed 'Abel'), which belongs to a new australopithecine species and the first ever to be found west of the Rift Valley (Brunet *et al.*, 1995): *A. bahrelghazali* (Brunet *et al.*, 1996; Figure 4.2).

Since 1995, other australopithecine sites have been discovered in the Koro-Toro area (Brunet *et al.*, 1997), all with similar faunal assemblages and whose mammal species (proboscidians, suids, rhinocerotids and equids) indicate a biochronological age of around 3.5 Ma. Apart from these discoveries, our geological and palaeontological survey in the Djurab desert from 1994 to 1997 yielded three new fossiliferous areas that were biochronologically and radiometrically dated to: (1) the early Pliocene (4.5–4 Ma), at Kollé; (2) the Mio-Pliocene boundary (5.5–5 Ma), at Kossoum Bougoudi; and (3) to the Late Miocene (7 Ma), at Toros-Menalla (TM) (Brunet *et al.*, 1998, 2000; Lebatard *et al.*, 2008). To date, more than 500 fossiliferous localities have been discovered in the Djurab desert, representing up to 20 000 taxonomically recognised vertebrate remains.

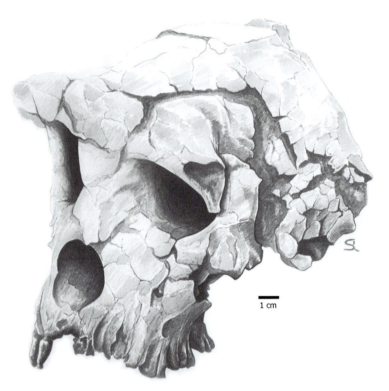

1 cm

Figure 4.3. Cranium holotype specimen (TM 266–01–060–1) of *S. tchadensis* (Brunet *et al.*, 2002a).

In 2001, the MPFT team unearthed a new hominid genus, *Sahelanthropus tchadensis* (Brunet *et al.*, 2002a), from the locality TM 266. The holotype cranium (Figure 4.3), nicknamed 'Toumaï', is associated with a faunal assemblage containing more than 70 species. The mammalian component of the fauna indicates a biochronological age congruent with the radiometric age close to 7 Ma (Vignaud *et al.*, 2002; Lebatard *et al.*, 2008). This earliest known hominid, *S. tchadensis*, uncovered at least 2600 km west of the Rift valley, is another new milestone in our evolutionary history, suggesting that the concept of an exclusively eastern or southern African origin of the hominid clade is in need of revision.

Sahelanthropus tchadensis emerged during a period of scientific discovery that was characterised by the discovery of geologically older ancestral species deriving from Late Miocene sediments: *Ardipithecus kadabba* (5.8–5.2 Ma, Ethiopia; Haile-Selassie, 2001; Haile-Selassie *et al.*, 2004), *Orrorin tugenensis* (*c.* 6 Ma, Kenya; Senut *et al.*, 2001) and *Sahelanthropus tchadensis* (7 Ma, Chad; Brunet *et al.*, 2002a).

In many respects, one might say that the discoveries since 1994 have a scientific significance equivalent to that of Dart's groundbreaking discovery: *Australopithecus africanus* (Dart, 1925) for palaeoanthropologists of our era. During the last ten years the framework of the hominid evolutionary history has been completed altered. We possess a completely new understanding of the environments inhabited by the early hominids. Subsequently, the models established in the 1980s must be reconsidered. The hominids discovered during the last decade, while extending the geographical and temporal limits of our family, show original associations of characters and morphotypes that force us to revise our definitions of the Hominidae per se. Ultimately, what we require is a completely new paradigm.

The Chadian hominids

The material referred to the Chadian australopithecine 'Abel' consists of an anterior lower jaw (Figure 4.2), the horizontal ramus complete until the lower fourth premolar (P_4), and an upper right third premolar (P^3). This hominin possesses a new mosaic of derived and primitive anatomical characters, specifically: the flat anterior face of the lower jaw; a subvertical symphysis, bulbous in its outline with a shallow genioglossal fossa; an incisiform and very asymmetrical canine with a strong bifid lingual crest. Each premolar exhibits a pattern of three pulp canal roots and the P_4s are sub-molariform in shape, and show a large talonid. This original combination of anatomical features has been interpreted as being sufficiently distinct to warrant a new species named *Australopithecus barhelghazali* (Brunet *et al.*, 1996).

To date, only three late Miocene species may claim the 'enviable status' to be among the earliest hominids. Two of them are from eastern Africa: *Ardipithecus kadabba* (5.8–5.2 Ma, Ethiopia; Haile-Selassie, 2001; Haile-Selassie *et al.*, 2004) and *Orrorin tugenensis* (*c.* 6 Ma, Kenya; Senut *et al.*, 2001); the third one, the oldest known hominid, is from central Africa: *Sahelanthropus tchadensis* (7 Ma, Chad; Brunet *et al.*, 2002a; Lebatard *et al.*, 2008). The geographic location of the type site of *S. tchadensis*, lying 2600 km west of the Rift Valley, along with its great antiquity, suggest an early and widespread hominid distribution in Africa (by 6 million years ago, at least). The material referred to the Chadian hominid 'Toumaï' consists of a near-complete cranium, although distorted (Figure 4.3). This cranium has now been reconstructed using 3D stereolithocast methods (Figures 4.4 and 4.6) and has been associated with several mandibular fragments and isolated teeth (Figure 4.5). *Sahelanthropus*

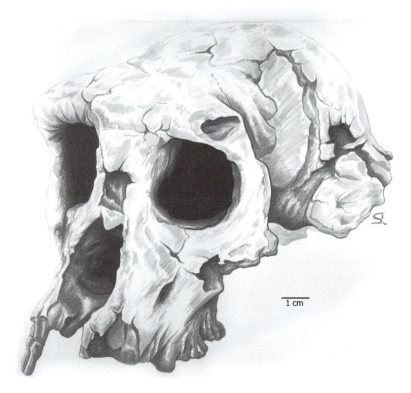

Figure 4.4. Stereolithocast of the *S. tchadensis* cranium 3D reconstruction.

tchadensis displays a unique combination of primitive and derived characters. Identifiable derived features of *S. tchadensis* are: a relatively flat face with an anteroposteriorly short premaxilla; an anteriorly positioned foramen magnum linked to a rather short basioccipital and a sub-horizontal nuchal plane; a downward lipping of the nuchal crest. The lower jaw shows a vertical symphysis with weak transverse tori. For the dentition, the most notable anatomical features are: a non-honing C/P$_3$ complex; a lack of a diastema between C and P$_3$; small-crowned canines with a long root, the upper one without any honing distal crest and the lower one with a large distal tubercle, both shoulders being very low; a P^3 with a strongly sloping buccal surface; postcanine teeth with maximum radial enamel thickness intermediate between chimpanzees and australopithecines; and bulbous, slightly crenulated postcanine occlusal morphology. It is interesting to note that all the hominid mandibular specimens from Toros-Menalla have the same root pattern in the postcanine teeth, with two roots and three separate pulp canals for each premolar.

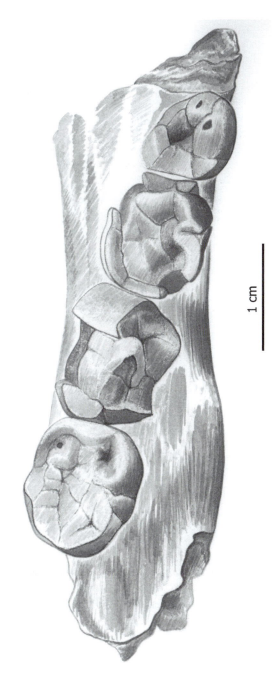

1 cm

Figure 4.5. Right lower jaw paratype specimen (TM 266–02–154–1) of *S. tchadensis*.

Figure 4.6. Artist's representation of the Toumaï bust.

For a primate anatomist and evolutionary biologist, these traits indicate that *S. tchadensis* cannot be related to chimpanzees or gorillas but rather suggest that this species is related to later bipedal hominids. *Sahelanthropus tchadensis* may be temporally close to the common ancestor of chimpanzees and humans (Brunet *et al.*, 2002a,b; 2005; Zollichofer *et al.*, 2005; Guy *et al.*, 2005). Other authors who focus only on the primitive traits of this genus reach understandably different conclusions: that *S. tchadensis* is related to apes and corresponds to a female palaeogorilla (Wolpoff *et al.*, 2002, 2006; Pickford, 2005). Our results suggest otherwise.

Coppens's East Side palaeoscenario (1983) initially emphasised the important role played by savannah environments in early hominid evolution. In the light of this new evidence, does this model still hold?

Late Miocene hominid environments: the new story

The sedimentological evidence from the Late Miocene Toros-Menalla fossil-iferous area demonstrates successive wet (mega-lake Chad events) and arid periods (desertic events) over the last 7 Ma. These successive events are iden-tified by a sedimentological series of aeolian sandstones (indicative of deser-tic episodes), perilacustrine sandstones (showing lacustrine transgressions), and green pelite and diatomite (associated with true lacustrine environments) (Vignaud *et al.*, 2002; Schuster *et al.*, 2006). *Sahelanthropus tchadensis* and the associated vertebrate fossils assemblage have been uncovered from the perilacustrine sandstones (from the anthracotheriid unit). Sedimentological data agree with the reconstruction of a mosaic environment, indicating a veg-etated perilacustrine belt between lake and desert (Vignaud *et al.*, 2002). The Okavango Delta in the central Kalahari (Botswana) appears to be a good mod-ern analogue of similar habitat diversity (mosaic of lacustrine and riparian waters, swamps, patches of forest, wooded savannah, grassland and desertic areas) (Brunet *et al.*, 2005). The palaeoenvironment of *S. tchadensis* did not correspond to our initial expectations for habitats of an early hominin, and although the exact habitat of the TM 266 hominid among this mosaic of avail-able habitat types is still uncertain, we now presume it was dwelling in a wooded habitat.

Other significant hominid discoveries associated with wooded environ-ments also cast doubt on the role played by open environment or savannah, that was presumed to have favoured the adoption of bipedal posture in the course of hominid evolution, most notably the discoveries from the Middle Awash (Ethiopia, *Ardipithecus ramidus* and *Ar. kadabba*) and also the Lukeino Formation (Kenya, *Orrorin tugenensis*). Instead, sedimentological and faunal data suggest wooded environments for *Ar. ramidus* (White *et al.,* 1994; WoldeGabriel *et al.,* 1994) and *Ar. kadabba* (WoldeGabriel *et al.,* 2001). In 2001 those authors noted (p. 177): 'It therefore seems increasingly likely that early hominids did not frequent open habitats until after 4.4 Ma. Before that, they may have been confined to woodland and forest habitats.' A wooded habi-tat (open woodland with denser stands of trees in the vicinity) has been also suggested for the Kenyan hominin *Orrorin tugenensis* (Pickford *et al.*, 2002).

According to the recent description of a nearly complete skeleton of *Ar. ram-idus* (Aramis, Ethiopia, 4.4 Ma, White *et al.*, 1994), it appears that this hominid was a climbing biped, both terrestrial and arboreal, with an opposable grasp-ing big toe (without arched feet and walking flat-footed), living in a woodland landscape (Lovejoy, 2009; Lovejoy *et al.*, 2009a,b,c,d; Suwa *et al.*, 2009a,b; White *et al.*, 2009a,b). This is of fundamental importance, since the three Late

Miocene taxa *Ar. kadabba* (Haile-Selassie, 2001; Haile-Selassie *et al.*, 2004), *Or. tugenensis* (Galik *et al.*, 2004; Pickford *et al.*, 2002; Senut *et al.*, 2001, Ohman *et al.*, 2005; White, 2006) and *S. tchadensis* (Brunet *et al.*, 2002, 2004; Zollikofer *et al.*, 2005; Guy *et al.*, 2005) are probably habitual bipeds. These findings require the reconsideration of earlier savannah models in relation to the origin of hominins.

A new paradigm for a new early hominid history

During the last 150 years, most of the models for hominid evolution have been overturned by successive discoveries. This clearly highlights the importance of fieldwork, as well as the sobering realisation that our understanding of our evolutionary history has, at most, a life expectancy that usually does not go beyond new findings. In the last decade the number of recognised hominid taxa and the length of our geological roots (from 3.6 Ma in the 1970s to 7 Ma in the 2010s) have doubled. These new hominids, while extending the geographical and temporal limits of our family, present new morphotypes with original associations of anatomical characters representing a new evolutionary grade (Brunet, 2009) before *Homo* and *Australopithecus*. Thirty years ago, available fossil hominin remains led us to consider eastern African savannah as the cradle of humankind. Now, it appears that the earliest members of our family favoured wooded environments and were not restricted to eastern or southern Africa but were rather living in a wider geographic region, including at least central and eastern Africa.

In Chad, the biochronological age of *Sahelanthropus tchadensis* indicates that the divergence between chimpanzee and human lineages occurred before 7 Ma, which is earlier than generally acknowledged by molecular phylogeneticists (Kumar and Hedges, 1998; Pilbeam 2002) and still earlier than recently published by Patterson *et al.*, 2006.

Besides, from a palaeobiogeographical point of view, published results derived from fieldwork shows that central Africa was, at least between 7 and 3 Ma, an area marked by crisscrossing sporadic faunal exchanges with northern and eastern Africa (Boisserie *et al.*, 2003, 2005; Brunet *et al.*, 1995, 1996, 1997, 1998, 2000, 2002a, b; 2004; Brunet and White, 2001; Geraads *et al.*, 2001; Lihoreau *et al.*, 2006; Likius *et al.*, 2003; Mackaye *et al.*, 2005; Peigné *et al.*, 2005; Vignaud *et al.*, 2002).

Better identifying the migratory patterns and the faunal exchanges between northern, central, eastern and southern Africa during the Mio-Pliocene is a key element indispensable for a new understanding of the origin and dispersal of the first members of the human group and therefore its evolutionary history.

We need more data from these geographic areas and notably from northeastern Africa (Libya, Egypt, Sudan and so forth). Palaeontologists and paleoanthropologists will therefore have to conduct more and more geological and palaeontological field surveys in these areas.

Acknowledgements

We thank the Chadian Authorities (Ministère de l'Education Nationale de l'Enseignement Supérieur et de la Recherche, Université de N'djamena, CNAR), the Ministère Français de l'Education Nationale (Faculté des Sciences, Université de Poitiers), Ministère de la Recherche (CNRS : Département EDD, SDV and ECLIPSE; Projet ANR 05-BLAN-0235), Ministère des Affaires Etrangères (DCSUR, Paris and SCAC, Projet FSP 2005–54 de la Coopération Franco-Tchadienne, Ambassade de France à N'djamena) to the Région Poitou-Charentes, the NSF program RHOI (co-PI's F.C. Howell and T.D. White), and to the Armée Française, MAM and Epervier for logistical support. We are grateful to many colleagues and friends for their help. We thank also all the other MPFT members who joined us for field missions, and more especially S. Riffaut, for drawings, X.Valentin and A. Bernet for technical support. We are most grateful to G. Florent and C. Noël for their administrative guidance of the MPFT team.

References

Boisserie, J.-R., Brunet, M., Likius, A. *et al.* (2003). Hippopotamids from the Djurab Pliocene faunas, Chad, Central Africa. *Journal African Earth Sciences*, **36**: 15–27.

Boisserie, J.-R., Likius, A., Vignaud, P. *et al.* (2005). A new late Miocene hippopotamid from Toros-Menalla, Chad. *Journal Vertebrate Paleontology*, **25**(3): 665–73.

Brunet, M. (2002). Reply to Wolpoff M. H., Senut B., Pickford M., Hawks J. (2002) Sahelanthropus or 'Sahelpithecus'? *Nature*, **419**: 582.

(2009). Origine et évolution des hominidés: Toumaï une confirmation éclatante de la prédiction de Darwin, *Comptes Rendus Palevol.*, **8**: 311–19.

Brunet, M. and White, T. D. (2001). Deux nouvelles espèces de Suini (Mammalia, Suidae) du continent africain (Ethiopie; Tchad). *Comptes Rendus Académie des Science*, **332**: 51–7.

Brunet, M., Beauvillain, A., Coppens, Y. *et al.* (1995). The first australopithecine 2 500 kilometres west of the Rift Valley (Chad). *Nature*, **378**: 273–4.

(1996). *Australopithecus bahrelghazali*, une nouvelle espèce d'homnidié ancien de la région de Koro Toro (Tchad). *Comptes Rendus Académie des Sciences*, **322**: 907–13.

Brunet, M., Beauvillain, A., Geraads, D. *et al.* (1997). Tchad: un nouveau site à Hominidés Pliocène. *Comptes Rendus Académie des Sciences*, **324**: 341–5.

(1998). Tchad: découverte d'une faune de mammifères du Pliocène inférieur. *Comptes Rendus Académie des Sciences*, **326**: 153–8.

Brunet, M., Beauvillain, A., Billiou, D. *et al.* (2000). Chad: discovery of a vertebrate fauna close to the Mio-Pliocene boundary. *Journal Vertebrate Paleontology*, **20**: 205–9.

Brunet, M., Guy, F., Pilbeam, D. *et al.* (2002). A new hominid from the Upper Miocene of Chad, Central Africa. *Nature*, **418**: 145–51.

Brunet, M., Guy, F., Boisserie, J.-R. *et al.* (2004). Toumaï, Miocène supérieur du Tchad, le nouveau doyen du rameau humain. *Comptes Rendus Palevol*, **3**:275–83.

Brunet, M., Guy, F., Pilbeam, D. *et al.* (2005). New material of the earliest hominid from the Upper Miocene of Chad. *Nature*, **434**: 752–5.

Coppens, Y. (1983). Les plus anciens fossiles d'Hominidés. In *Recent Advances in the evolution of Primates*. Pontificiae Academiae Scientiarum Scripta Varia, pp. 1–9.

Dart, R. (1925). *Australopithecus africanus*, the man-ape of South Africa. *Nature*, **115**: 195–9.

Galik, K., Senut, B., Pickford, M. *et al.* (2004). External and internal morphology of the BAR 1002–00 *Orrorin tugenensis* femur. *Science*, **305**:1450–3.

Geraads, D., Brunet, M., Mackaye, H. T. *et al.* (2001). Fossil Bovidae (Mammalia) from the Koro Toro Australopithecine sites, Chad. *Journal of Vertebrate Paleontology*, **21**: 335–46.

Guy, F., Lieberman, D. E., Pilbeam, D. *et al.* (2005). Morphological affinities of the *Sahelanthropus tchadensis* (Late Miocene Hominid, Chad) cranium. *Proceedings of the National Academy of Sciences USA*, **102**: 18836–41.

Haile-Selassie, Y. (2001) Late Miocene hominids from the Middle Awash, Ethiopia. *Nature*, **412**: 178–81.

Haile-Selassie, Y., Suwa, G., and White, T. (2004) Late Miocene hominids from the Middle Awash, Ethiopia, and early hominid dental evolution. *Nature*, **303**: 1503–5.

Kumar, S. and Hedges, S. B. (1998). A molecular timescale for vertebrate evolution. *Nature*, **392**: 917–19.

Lebetard, A. E., Bourles, D. L., Duringer, P. *et al.* (2008). Cosmogenic nuclide dating of *Sahelanthropus tchadensis* and *Australopithecus bahrelghazali*: Mio-Pliocene hominids from Chad. *Proceedings of the National Academy of Sciences USA*, **105**: 3226–31.

Lovejoy, C. O. (2009). Reexamining human origins in light of *Ardipithecus ramidus*. *Science*, **326**: 74e1–74e8.

Lovejoy, C. O., Latimer, B., Suwa, G., Asfaw, B. and White, T. D. (2009a). Combining prehension and propulsion: the foot of *Ardipithecus ramidus*. *Science*, **326**: 72e1–72e8.

Lovejoy, C. O., Simpson, S. W., White, T. D. *et al.* (2009b). Careful climbing in the Miocene: the forelimbs of *Ardipithecus ramidus* and humans are primitive. *Science*, **326**: 70e1–70e8.

Lovejoy, C. O., Suwa, G., Simpson, S. W. *et al.* (2009c). The great divides: *Ardipithecus ramidus* reveals the postcrania of our last common ancestors with African apes. *Science*, **326**, 100–6.

Lovejoy, C. O., Suwa, G., Spurlock, L. *et al.* (2009d). The pelvis and femur of *Ardipithecus ramidus*: the emergence of upright walking. *Science*, **326**: 71e1–71e6.

Lihoreau, F., Boisserie, J. R., Viriot, L. *et al.* (2006). Anthracothere dental anatomy reveals a late Miocene Chado-Libyan bioprovince. *Proceedings of the National Academy of Science USA*, **103**(23): 8763–7.

Likius, A., Brunet, M., Geraads, D. *et al.* (2003). Le plus vieux Camelidae (Mammalia, Artiodactyla) d'Afrique: limite Mio-Pliocène, Tchad. *Bulletin Société Géolologique de France*, **174**: 187–93.

Mackaye, H. T., Brunet, M. and Tassy, P. (2005). *Selenetherium kolleensis* nov. gen. nov. sp. un nouveau Proboscidea (Mammalia) dans le Pliocène tchadien, *Géobios Lyon*, **38**: 765–77.

Ohman, J., Lovejoy, C. O. and White, T. D. (2005). Questions about *Orrorin* femur. *Science*, **307**: 845b.

Patterson, N., Richter, D. J., Gnerre, S. *et al.* (2006) Genetic evidence for complex speciation of humans and chimpanzees. *Nature*, **441**: 1103–8.

Peigné, S., Bonis, L., Likius, A. *et al.* (2005) New de machairodontine (Carnivora, Felidae) from the Late Miocene hominid locality of Toros-Menalla, Chad. *Comptes Rendus Palevol*, **4**: 243–53.

Pickford, M. (2005) Orientation of the foramen magnum in Late Miocene to extant African apes and hominids. *Anthropologie* (Brno) XLIII/2–3: 191–8.

Pickford, M., Senut, B., Gommery D. *et al.* (2002) Bipedalism in *Orrorin tugenensis* revealed by its femora. *Comptes Rendus Palevol*, **1**: 191–203.

Pilbeam, D. (2002) Perspectives on the Miocene Hominoidea. In Hartwig, W. (ed.), *The Primate Fossil Record*. Cambridge: Cambridge University Press, pp. 303–10.

Schuster, M., Duringer, P., Ghienne, J. F. *et al.* (2006). The age of the Sahara Desert. *Science*, **311**: 821.

Senut, B., Pickford, M., Gommery, D. *et al.* (2001) First hominid from the Miocene (Lukeino formation, Kenya). *Comptes Rendus Académie des Science*, **332**:137–44.

Suwa, G., Asfaw, B., Kono, R. T. *et al.* (2009a). The *Ardipithecus ramidus* skull and its implications for hominid origins. *Science*, **326**: 68e1–68e7.

Suwa, G., Kono, R. T., Simpson, S. W. *et al.* (2009b). Paleobiological implications of the *Ardipithecus ramidus* dentition. *Science*, **326**: 94–9.

Vignaud, P., Duringer, P., Mackaye, H. T. *et al.* (2002). Geology and palaeontology of the Upper Miocene Toros-Menalla hominid locality, Chad. *Nature*, **418**: 152–5.

White, T. D. (2006) Early hominid femora: the inside story. *Comptes Rendus Palevol*, **5**: 99–108.

White, T. D., Suwa, G. and Asfaw, B. (1994). *Australopithecus ramidus*, a new species of early hominid from Aramis, Ethiopia. *Nature*, **371**: 306–12.

White T. D., Asfaw, B., Beyene, Y. *et al.* (2009a). *Ardipithecus ramidus* and the paleobiology of early hominids. *Science*, **326**: 65–86.

White T. D., Ambrose, S. H., Suwa, G. *et al.* (2009b). Macrovertebrate paleontology and the Pliocene habitat of *Ardipithecus ramidus. Science*, **326**: 87–93.

WoldeGabriel, G., White T. D., Suwa G. *et al.* (1994). Ecological and temporal placement of early Pliocene hominids at Aramis, Ethiopia. *Nature*, **371**: 330–3.

WoldeGabriel, G., Haile-Selassie, Y., Rennek, P. R. *et al.* (2001) Geology and palaeontology of the Late Miocene Middle Awash valley, Afar rift, Ethiopia. *Nature*, **412**: 175–8.

Wolpoff, M. H., Senut B., Pickford M. *et al.* (2002). *Sahelanthropus* or "*Sahelpithecus*"? *Nature*, **419**: 581–2.

Wolpoff, M. H., Hawks, J., Senut, B. *et al.* (2006). An ape or *the* ape: is the Toumaï cranium TM 266 a hominid? *PaleoAnthropology*, **2006**: 36–50.

Zollikofer, C., Ponce de León, M., Lieberman, D. E. *et al.* (2005). Virtual cranial reconstruction of *Sahelanthropus tchadensis. Nature*, **434**: 755–9.

5   *From hominoid arboreality to hominid bipedalism*

BRIGITTE SENUT

Abstract

During the 2000s, several new taxa of putative hominids have been described from the Upper Miocene of Africa: *Orrorin tugenensis* from the Tugen Hills, Kenya (6.1 to 5.7 Ma), *Ardipithecus kadabba* from the Middle Awash, Ethiopia (5.7 to 5.2 Ma) and *Sahelanthropus tchadensis* from Toros-Menalla, Chad (7 to 6 Ma). Bipedal locomotion has been claimed for all these taxa, but only *Orrorin* exhibits clear features of bipedalism. One drawback to the study of human origins is that scholars usually tend to compare the fossils only with modern apes (usually chimpanzees) and with modern humans; the modern apes often erroneously being considered as primitive and humans as derived. Miocene apes possess a higher diversity of locomotor repertoires than modern ones and it appears reductionist to focus only on modern hominoids to understand how bipedalism emerged. It is crucial to take into consideration the locomotion of Miocene apes knowing that even if these hominoids could occasionally walk bipedally, their bones did not exhibit the morphology of later bipedal hominids. Miocene large hominoids were arboreal animals adapted to climbing. The locomotor repertoire of early hominids was a mixture of bipedal locomotion and climbing, as indicated by the morphology of the limbs of *Orrorin* and *Australopithecus*. The study of locomotion must be carried out in an environmental context. When we consider the Miocene apes, it appears that they inhabited forest (dry or humid) or wooded environments; arboreal life was a survival strategy, for feeding and escaping from predators. Palaeontological and depositional data from the Lukeino Formation, Kenya, indicate that Late Miocene hominids lived in forested environments. Despite the usual belief, prevalent since Darwin, that humans and thus bipedalism emerged in a savanna environment, it appears that the emergence of hominids took place in a closed habitat and that bipedalism might have had its origins in an arboreal way of life.

African Genesis: Perspectives on Hominin Evolution, eds. Sally C. Reynolds and Andrew Gallagher. Published by Cambridge University Press. © Cambridge University Press 2012.

Introduction

Research on the origin of hominid locomotion or of bipedalism has been biased by the fact that most studies conducted on australopithecines have been done by comparing them with modern African apes and extant humans. In general, they were expected to fit one or the other mode of locomotion. However, modern animals are highly derived and the extant apes represent just the extant part of the great diversity of the non-human hominoid world. Fossil hominoids had their own ways of moving, some of which no longer exist today. Comparisons with modern animals are essential for understanding the movements, but are not sufficient to reconstruct the locomotor complexes of fossil taxa; the skeletons of fossil apes must be taken into account.

Moreover, the study of locomotion in hominoids has been pervasively biased for the last 35 years by the representation of human evolution by Rudi Zallinger published in the book by Francis Clark Howell in the late 1960s (Howell, 1968: pp. 41–5) on the evolution of mankind. Since that date, this particular hypothesis on the origins of bipedalism has been widely disseminated. The scenario presented by Zallinger is that we evolved from a terrestrial knuckle-walker that became more and more erect through time to culminate in the modern type of bipedalism. However, it appears that fossil apes were much more diverse than previously thought, and while the origins of bipedalism have been hotly debated (did it emerge from knuckle-walking? climbing? terrestrial quadrupedalism? arboreal quadrupedalism?) (Tuttle, 1977; Coppens and Senut, 1991; Richmond and Strait, 2000), the various hypotheses have been widely discussed but mostly on the basis of comparisons with living primates. However, the most satisfactory way forward is to take into account the locomotor record of the fossil hominoids that existed prior to hominids (Senut, 2003, 2006a) (Figure 5.1).

Another problem that arises from the reconstruction of past locomotion is that most of the time such studies do not include environmental data. But locomotion takes place in an environment and animals do not move in the same way on the ground as in the trees. However, Coppens (1983) with the 'East Side Story' reminds us that the holistic, naturalistic approach to the study of hominids is the only way to understand our origins, and even if the hypothesis is debated, it cannot be completely rejected (Senut, 2006a). Following Darwin's ideas on the origins of humankind, our environmental history has been dominated by the 'savanna hypothesis', which suggests that humans emerged in a savanna-like environment where they became bipedal and could use stone tools. But does this hypothesis conform to the latest data on palaeoenvironments?

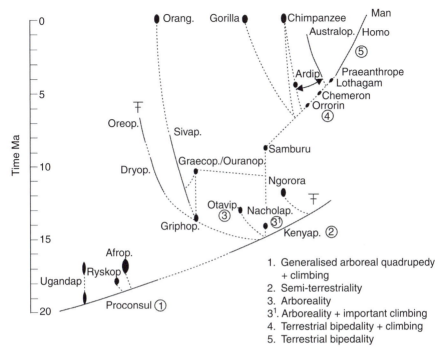

Figure 5.1. Proposition of evolution of locomotion in hominoids (from Senut, 2003).

The Miocene apes: the diversity in arboreal primates

Many palaeoprimatologists have proposed that most Miocene apes were com-
mitted arboreal dwellers. However, the mode of locomotion of these primates
has been debated: ape-like, monkey-like or both? (Rose, 1983). Up to the 1970s
to 1980s, few detailed studies of the locomotor behaviour of fossil non-human
hominoids were done, due partly to the paucity of specimens, but also to the
fact that scholars were more inclined to work on bipedalism of early hominids,
and also to the fact that priority was given to the teeth, mandibles and skulls
(when available). Moreover, some postcranial specimens were wrongly identified (confusion with carnivores or even reptiles is not rare). From the 1980s
onwards, new field expeditions in the Miocene of Africa and Eurasia led to the
discovery of specimens including partial skeletons that led to the rethinking of
our locomotor history. Humans being hominoids, it seems obvious that understanding Miocene apes would help to understand our own ancestry, but even
today some scientists still concentrate on comparisons between fossil hominids
and modern African apes. But when studying the evolution of a functional

locomotor complex such as arboreality, it is essential not to limit the comparisons to extant apes, but to take into account not only other arboreal primates such as Platyrrhine monkeys and guenons, but also fossil apes (Senut, 1991, 2003; Nakatsukasa, 2004).

Miocene apes are highly diverse, ranging in size from gibbons (*Micropithecus*) to gorillas (*Ugandapithecus*). In the rest of the chapter, we will focus only on median to large hominoids, the smaller ones being too distant from our origins.

Africa

Early Miocene

Several hominoids are known from the Early Miocene of Eastern Africa and can be classified into two genera: *Ugandapithecus* and *Proconsul*. *Ugandapithecus* is the oldest, at around 20 to 19 Ma in Eastern Uganda (from Napak and Moroto), and from Western Kenya (Meswa Bridge, Songhor, Koru for example).

Ugandapithecus

The bulk of the postcranial elements of large apes collected from the volcano-sedimentary deposits at Napak in Uganda is usually described as *Proconsul major* (Bishop, 1964; Andrews, 1978; Martin, 1981; Gommery et al., 1998, Harrison, 2002). Additional dental and postcranial material discovered by the Uganda Palaeontology Expedition in 1985 and during 1998 to 2000 suggests that this large hominoid differs from *Proconsul* at the generic level, for which the genus *Ugandapithecus* was erected (Senut et al., 2000). A detailed analysis has been published (Pickford et al., 2009). *Ugandapithecus* is known only by isolated postcranial elements but these are well enough represented (femora, humerus, scapula and calcaneum) to allow us partly to reconstruct the locomotion (Gommery et al., 1998, 2002; Senut et al. 2010). Several femoral fragments are known that exhibit a clear cranial orientation of the femoral neck. The high collo-diaphyseal angle augments abuction and lateral rotation of the thigh (Rose, 1983; Ward et al., 1993). The morphology of the intertrochanteric crest, which is salient and oblique terminating at the lesser trochanter, and the presence of two distinct posterior fossettes are remarkable. The digital fossa is deep and isolated from an intertrochanteric depression, which is short and deeper than in modern African apes. The morphology suggests that the *m. obturatorii* and *musculi gemelli* (abductors and external rotators of the thigh, activated in quadrupedal walking and climbing) might have been powerful. The greater trochanter is located well below the femoral head and the insertion for the *m. gluteus minimus* projects strongly laterally. The insertions for the *m. gluteus medius* and the *m. gluteus minimus* are close to each other, as is the case in chimpanzees. The femoral shaft is bowed anteriorly and the tibia is strongly medio-laterally compressed. The flattening of the posterior face and the curvatures of the shaft recall the morphology seen in modern hominoids, in particular chimpanzees. In size, it is close to extant female gorillas (Rafferty *et al.*, 1995). The features suggest quadrupedal walking and powerful climbing.

Proconsul

Proconsul is certainly the lower Miocene ape with the best known locomotor apparatus due to the discovery of an almost complete skeleton on Rusinga Island, Kenya, in 1951 (Whitworth, 1953; Napier and Davis, 1959; Walker and Pickford, 1983; McHenry and Corruccini, 1983; Senut, 1986, 1989; Walker, 1997). Initially attributed to *Proconsul africanus*, it has been identified as a female of *Proconsul nyanzae* (Pickford, 1986) and more recently as *Proconsul heseloni* (Walker *et al.*, 1993). Since the skeleton has been reassembled, it appears clear that anterior and posterior limbs are of similar length. The intermembral and crural indices fall within the range of variation of living anthropoids and suggest that the animal was a quadruped. However, the different traits of the limbs, which compare favourably with platyrrhine monkeys or arboreal cercopithecoids, suggest that it was an arboreal quadruped. Several studies suggest that it had no tail (Ward *et al.*, 1993; Nakatusaka *et al.*, 2004) contra Harrison (1998). These results have been confirmed by the study of a partial skeleton of *Proconsul nyanzae* (Ward *et al.*, 1993). The general morphology of the locomotor apparatus of *Proconsul* is unique among hominoids as it does not show the specialised features seen in later apes such as knuckle-walking or brachiation, for example. This is probably why some authors have excluded *Proconsul* from the hominoid clade. However, the morphology of the elbow joint with its keeled humeral trochlea, and the loss of the tail are hominoid features. From this, we infer that the basal hominoid was an arboreal quadruped.

Middle Miocene

In the Middle Miocene of Africa, large apes were quite diverse; several genera having been recognised: *Afropithecus, Kenyapithecus, Nacholapithecus, Equatorius*, from Kenya, and *Otavipithecus*, from Namibia. The specimens assigned to *Afropithecus* from Moroto (Uganda) are considered under this section, because the Early Miocene age (close to 22 Ma) published in 1997 (Gebo *et al.*, 1997), is in conflict with younger earlier dates (Bishop, 1969) and the palae-ontological data (which suggest an age closer to 17.6 Ma) (Pickford *et al.*, 1986, 1999; Pickford and Mein, 2007). However, new radiometric data accord better with palaeontological data, suggesting a younger age (Sawada *et al.* in prep.).

Afropithecus

Only a few postcranial bones of *Afropithecus turkanensis* are known from Kalodirr and Buluk in Kenya (Leakey *et al.*, 1988; Rose, 1997; Ward, 1998). A single phalanx is known from Buluk, all the other postcranial remains having been found at Kalodirr. The morphology of the limbs of *Afropithecus* has been reported to be similar to those of *Proconsul* (Rose, 1997; Ward 1998). The pub-lication of *Morotopithecus* at Moroto in Uganda (Gebo *et al.*, 1997) does not shed light on the systematics of fossil hominoids of the area. Detailed compari-sons with *Afropithecus* from Kalodirr in Kenya shows that *Morotopithecus* is probably synonymous with *Afropithecus* (Pickford, 2002; Patel and Grossman, 2006). However, study of the dental and postcranial material suggests that two taxa are represented at Moroto: *Ugandapithecus* and *Afropithecus* (Senut, 1998; Pickford *et al.*, 1999, 2009; Gommery *et al.*, 2002).

The left femur questionably assigned to *Morotopithecus* (Gebo *et al.*, 1997), exhibits morphology known in *Ugandapithecus,* and differs from the right femur from the same site (Pickford *et al.*, 1999). The latter has been extensively published (Gebo *et al.*, 1997; MacLatchy *et al.*, 2000; Young and MacLatchy, 2004). Since these publications, additional fragments of the specimen, found in the collections of W.W. Bishop, permit a better reconstruction of the femur (Senut *et al.*, 2001) of which one fragment was incorrectly placed in the original description (Gebo *et al.*, 1997) (Figure 5.2). As a matter of fact the composite reconstruction (Figure 5.3) proposed by MacLatchy on the basis of the two fragmentary femurs do not fit, when the missing parts are glued (Figure 5.4) and the femur appears to be much shorter than previously thought. Three partial lumbar vertebrae are known from the same site. The most complete specimen (Walker and Rose, 1968) has been attributed to *Morotopithecus* (Gebo *et al.*, 1997). According to Ward (1998), *Afropithecus* and *Proconsul nyanzae* are similar in size. In her article, Ward (1998) concluded that for the known parts of the skeleton, *Afropithecus turkanensis* is morphologically and presumably functionally equivalent to *Proconsul nyanzae* and *P. heseloni*. In this case, the vertebral column would have also been closer to that of pronograde quadrupeds (with a sub-horizontal trunk) than to that of African apes. However, consider-ing the morphology of the corpus and the size of the Moroto vertebra (larger

Figure 5.2. Different reconstructions of the femur of *Afropithecus* from Moroto (Uganda). Right: reconstruction by Gebo *et al.*, 1997; left: new reconstruction based on three fragments found in the collections of the Uganda Museum in Kampala by the Uganda Palaeontology Expedition. (Scales represent 1 cm.)

than those of a bonobo) the specimen is too large to belong to *Afropithecus* and can instead be attributed to the large-bodied hominoid represented at Moroto and Napak, *Ugandapithecus* (Senut *et al.*, 2000; Gommery *et al.*, 2002, 2006; Pickford *et al.*, 2009) (*Ugandapithecus gitongai* from Moroto II being smaller

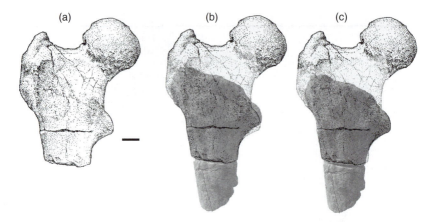

Figure 5.3. Problems in reconstruction of the femur from Moroto II. (a) Composite and erroneous reconstruction based on the right and left femoral specimens (MUZM 80) from Moroto II before the right proximal part of the shaft was recovered; (b) after the missing shaft pieces from the right fragment were glued together, the left proximal femur was fitted according to the base of the greater trochanter and in this case the lesser trochanter shows clearly a different orientation with the one in the composite reconstruction; (c) after the missing shaft pieces from the right fragment were glued together, the left proximal femur was fitted according to the lesser trochanter and in this case the orientation of the greater trochanter does not match the orientation either. (Left side reversed for matching the composite reconstruction.) (Scale = 1 cm.) (Adapted from MacLatchy *et al.*, 2000.)

than *Ugandapithecus major* from Napak). It also appears morphofunctionally more similar to that of extant African apes with an erect trunk. The fragment of scapular glenoid cavity claimed to belong to the Moroto hominoid (Gebo *et al.*, 1997; MacLatchy *et al.*, 2000), is still a matter of debate, but several authors have suggested that it does not belong to a primate (Senut, 1998; Benefit, 1999; Pickford *et al.*, 1999). It is likely to belong to *Morotochoerus*, an anthracothere (Pickford, personal communication). As a matter of fact, a large scapula collected from Napak and attributed to *Ugandapithecus* (Senut *et al.* 2010), shows clear hominoid features and confirms the non-primate status of the specimen found in Moroto. Despite the fact that *Afropithecus*, like *Proconsul*, was primarily a pronograde quadruped (sub-horizontal trunk), climbing would have been an important component of its locomotor repertoire.

Kenyapithecus

Kenyapithecus is the earliest Miocene ape to show marked evidence of terrestriality. Two species are known: *K. africanus* from Maboko and *K. wickeri* from Fort Ternan. The age of Fort Ternan has been refined recently to 13.7 ±

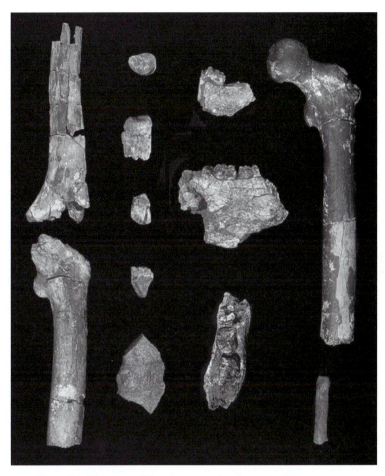

Figure 5.4. Hypodigm of *Orrorin tugenensis* as known in 2001.

0.3 Ma (Pickford *et al.*, 2006). The distal humerus from Fort Ternan shows morphological traits related to climbing, but also bears the classic postero-lateral crest seen in quadrupedal mammals, reflecting its semi-terrestriality (Senut, 1989). Numerous postcranial bones found at Maboko (Kenya) indicate that *Kenyapithecus africanus* was also adapted to arboreal locomotion as shown by the reinforcement of the scapulo-clavicular joint related to the reinforcement of the pectoral girdle in arboreal activities such as climbing. However, the radio-carpal joint bones suggest adaptations to knuckle-walking (McCrossin and Benefit, 1997; McCrossin *et al.*, 1998), which is the earliest evidence for such behaviour in Miocene hominoids.

Nacholapithecus

Nacholapithecus probably represents the best collection for postcranial bones from the Middle Miocene as several almost complete skeletons (associated with skulls and mandibles) have been excavated in Nachola (Kenya) in sediments estimated to be 16.36 ±0.37 Ma to 15.27±0.47 Ma (Sawada *et al.*, 2006). The postcranial elements of *Nacholapithecus kerioi* have been described in several articles (Ishida *et al.*, 2004; Nakatsukasa, 2004; Senut *et al.*, 2004; Nakatsukasa *et al.* 2007). They suggest that this hominoid (half the size of a common chimpanzee) was an arboreal quadruped, but with a stiff back as shown by the increased stability of the lumbar spine (Nakatsukasa *et al.*, 2007). The scapula and clavicle suggest an important mobility of the scapulo-humeral joint, and the general morphology of the scapula resembles that of climbing arboreal primates (such as colobine monkeys) excluding extant apes (Senut *et al.*, 2004). The morphology of the elbow joint confirms arboreal adaptations (Takano *et al.*, 2003). Despite some features that are close to *Proconsul*, *Nacholapithecus* was more specialised for orthograde climbing (with a subvertical trunk), 'hoisting' and bridging (Nakatsukasa, 2004). In particular, the intermembral proportions are very different from *Proconsul*, the upper limb being much longer than the hindlimb.

Equatorius

In 1999, a partial skeleton associated with dental and mandibular fragments of *Equatorius* was published from Kipsaraman in Kenya (Ward *et al.*, 1999). No detailed description of the specimen has been published yet, but in their publication the authors pooled specimens from different sites: Kipsaraman, Nachola, Maboko, Majiwa, Nyakach and Kaloma. In their hypodigm, specimens from different species and even different genera were mixed (Senut, 1999), and it is thus difficult to access the proper features of the genus *Equatorius*. However, the preliminary descriptions suggest that it was a semi-terrestrial animal as shown by the posteriorly orientated olecranon of the ulna. This material is clearly different from *Nacholapithecus*, but could belong to *Kenyapithecus*. However, it is premature to assign the fossils at the specific level.

Otavipithecus

The postcranial morphology of *Otavipithecus namibiensis* is poorly known and represented only by an atlas, a median manual phalanx and a proximal ulna (Conroy *et al.*, 1996; Senut and Gommery, 1997). *Otavipithecus* was adapted to an arboreal life as suggested by the ulnar morphology reminiscent of arboreal quadrupeds such as extant platyrrhine monkeys. The same is true of the manual phalanx as expressed by its curvature and morphology, position and dimensions of the ligamentary insertions. The atlas suggests a balance of the head on the vertebral column close to that of bonobos including orthograde postures (sub-vertical trunk) (Gommery, 2006).

Late Miocene

Several hominoid remains have been found in the Late Miocene of Africa, which are considered as potential hominids, but most of the postcranial elements are fragmentary.

Orrorin tugenensis

From the year 2000 onwards, postcranial bones (three partial femora, a distal humerus and two manual phalanges) were found in the Lukeino Formation in the Tugen Hills, Kenya dated between 6.1 and 5.7 Ma (Senut *et al.*, 2001; Sawada *et al.*, 2002, 2006; Pickford *et al.*, 2002; Galik *et al.*, 2004; Gommery and Senut, 2006)(Figures 5.5 and 5.6). The femora suggest that *Orrorin* was a bipedal creature (as shown by the morphology of the femoral neck, the distribution of cortical bone in the femoral neck and the muscle insertions), but which could also climb trees (as evidenced by the phalanges and the humerus) (Figures 5.3 and 5.6). These results have been later confirmed independently (Richmond and Jungers, 2008). Even if there is still a matter of debate concerning the phylogenetic position of the fossils, it is now accepted that *Orrorin* is a bipedal hominid (*sensu stricto*).

Sahelanthropus tchadensis

Sahelanthropus, found in 2001 in Chadian deposits, is reported to be 6 to 7 Ma old (Brunet *et al.*, 2002; Lebetard *et al.*, 2008) and is represented only by a skull, teeth, mandibles and a possible femoral shaft (Beauvilain and Watté, 2009). On the basis of the position and the orientation of the foramen magnum, the authors suggested that it was a bipedal creature; however, it as been shown that the position (Schaeffer, 1999) (Figure 5.7) and the inclination of the foramen magnum (Pickford, 2005) are variable. Moreover, the enlargement of the braincase during growth plays a role in its position (Biegert, 1963). Several aspects of the skull suggest that it was probably a quadrupedal creature (Wolpoff *et al.*, 2002, 2006; Schwartz, 2004).

Ardipithecus kadabba

Ardipithecus kadabba (Haile-Selassie, 2001) was found in the Middle Awash, Ethiopia, in strata aged between 5.6 to 5.2 Ma (WoldeGabriel *et al.*, 2001). Its

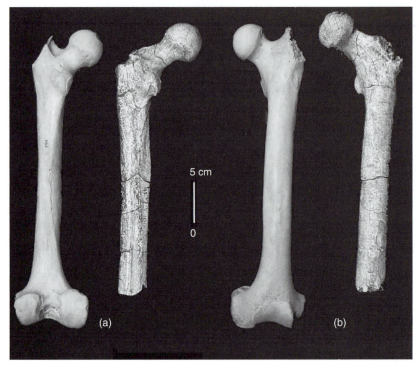

Figure 5.5. Comparisons of the femora of Orrorin tugenensis (BAR 1001'01) (right specimen) and an extant chimpanzee (left specimen); (a) posterior view; (b) anterior view. (From Senut, 2006b.)

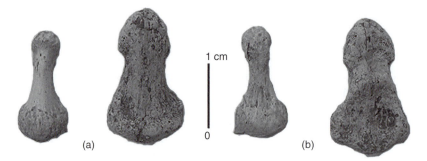

Figure 5.6. The distal thumb phalanx of *Orrorin tugenensis* (right) compared with an extant chimpanzee (left); (a) dorsal view; (b) palmar view. (From Gommery and Senut, 2006.)

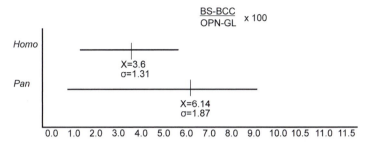

Figure 5.7. Index for estimating the position of the foramen magnum in *Homo* and *Pan* (BS-BCC: distance of basion to bicarotid chord; OPN-GL: cranial length (distance of opisthocranion to glabella). Please note: the horizontal lines represent ranges of variation (from Schaeffer, 1999).

postcranial anatomy is still poorly known. A proximal pedal phalanx resembles the ones from Hadar attributed to the hominid *Australopithecus*, and on the basis of the dorsal orientation of the proximal facet of the bone, it supposedly belongs to a bipedal animal. However, its curvature suggests arboreal adaptations (Stern and Susman, 1983; Susman *et al.*, 1984; Stern, 2000).

Asia

Middle and Upper Miocene

In the Middle Miocene of Eurasia, very few postcranial elements have been found. Whilst the dental remains of *Sivapithecus* or *Lufengpithecus* are well known, the few postcranial specimens known suggest that *Sivapithecus* was adapted to climbing and was partly terrestrial (Rose, 1983, 1997; Senut, 1986).

Europe

Middle Miocene

The available evidence has been discovered in Spain.

Pierolapithecus

In 2004, an almost complete skeleton associated with a skull of a hominoid, *Pierolapithecus catalaunicus* dating to between 12.5 to 13 Ma old from the site of

Barranc de Can Vila 1 in Cataluna, Spain was described. While *Pierolapithecus* exhibits an ape-like morphology of the thorax, the lumbar vertebrae and the wrist suggest an orthograde vertical climbing adaptation, while a few elements are more monkey-like including the short phalanges, which suggest palmigrade (on the palms of the hands) locomotion (Moyà-Solà *et al.*, 2004).

Upper Miocene

In Europe, several skeletons have been described in the past decade including *Dryopithecus* and *Oreopithecus*.

Dryopithecus/Hispanopithecus

The first postcranial bone of *Dryopithecus* (*Dryopithecus fontani*), a humerus, was described by E. Lartet in 1856 from Saint Gaudens, France but an exceptional discovery at Can Llobateres in Spain, a 9.5 Ma old site, provides a lot more information on the locomotion of these early apes from Europe (Moyà-Solà and Köhler, 1993). The complete skeleton of *Hispanopithecus laietanus* is very similar to that of extant hominoids, with adaptations to orthograde postures (shortened lumbar vertebrae, stiff lumbar region and enlarged thorax). The straightness of the humeral shaft, the strongly curved radius, the powerful *brachialis* muscle, very long hand by comparison to body size and enhanced hip mobility, suggest climbing and suspensory behaviours. In comparison with extant great apes, the humerus and the radius are longer, but the femur is shorter suggesting an important elongation of the upper limb and reduction of the leg in *Dryopithecus*.

Oreopithecus

One of the most complete hominoid skeletons known from the European Miocene was discovered in 1958 in the Late Miocene of Tuscany, Italy, *Oreopithecus bambolii* (Hürzeler, 1958). In 1997, additional postcranial elements were described (Köhler and Moyà-Solà, 1997) which suggest orthograde posture and climbing adaptations. Some form of bipedalism was thus inferred to be present in *Oreopithecus*, but it was different from that of hominids, the mechanics of the foot being much different.

Discussion and conclusion

A high diversity of Miocene hominoids is suggested by the wide range of locomotor adaptations, as inferred from the available postcranial elements. As early as the Lower Miocene, *Ugandapithecus* exhibited adaptations to climbing and its lumbar spine recalls that of extant apes and suggests an orthograde posture. In the Lower Miocene, another lineage is represented by *Proconsul*, which exhibits a more flexible vertebral column and adaptations to an arboreal environment. The lighter animals are more arboreal (*P. heseloni*) and the heavier ones (*P. nyanzae* and *Kenyapithecus*) tended to be more terrestrial.

After they diverged from a common ancestor, which was a generalised quadruped, the Asian and African hominoids broadened their locomotor strategies. An erect trunk is known as early as 20 to 19 Ma in *Ugandapithecus,* but its ancestral morphology is still unknown. The evidence probably lies in deposits aged between 30 and 20 million years. In the Middle Miocene, several apes developed an elongation of the upper limb compared to the lower limb, as shown by *Nacholapithecus* and *Dryopithecus,* for example. This tendency might have been retained in Eurasian apes from their African ancestors and further developed in the later hominoids. But, until we fill the gaps in the Upper Miocene fossil record from 13 Ma to 6 Ma, all the proposed scenarios will remain provisional and subject to revision. It seems, however, that our ancestor was probably a tree-dweller, at least for part of the time (Senut, 2006b).

The Asian apes became adapted to slow climbing and suspension and their African relatives added terrestrial quadrupedalism (chimpanzees, bonobos and gorillas) and bipedalism (*Orrorin, Australopithecus* and *Homo*) to their repertoire. It is emphasised here that australopithecines retained arboreal adaptations in their skeleton, as confirmed by the material from Sterkfontein (Clarke and Tobias, 1995) and the recent discovery at Dikika, Ethiopia (Alemseged *et al.*, 2006). Man is the only hominoid that does not exhibit strong climbing adaptations in the skeleton (Senut and Pickford, 2004). Crompton *et al.* (2008) in a study base on biomechanical and ecological data concluded that terrestrial bipedality emerged from an arboreal hand-assisted bipedality, but also rejected a possible knuckle-walking stage in the evolution of bipedalism, which accords with the palaeontological evidence. The fully bipedal characteristics of the locomotor apparatus of *Ardipithecus ramidus* (White *et al.*, 2009; Lovejoy *et al.*, 2009) are debatable. From the available data, it appears that the reconstructions of the skeleton are far too hominid-like. The arm bones are not preserved, nor are the shoulder joint and the vertebral column (except for two vertebrae). The femoral shaft is massive and does not reflect the usual gracility of bipedal hominid creatures; the curvature of the radius implies a strong forearm musculature (as seen in modern chimpanzees). The hominid-like proportions of the skeleton reflecting an elongation of the hindlimb is not convincingly supported by the evidence. The hallux is opposable to the other toes suggesting a grasping foot and the reconstruction of the pelvis has not been widely accepted. And, lastly, the thumb phalanx has not been compared with the available evidence. As a matter of fact, there is a thumb phalanx preserved in *Orrorin* that is clearly different from the one of *Ardipithecus ramidus* as well as of australopithecines and chimpanzees (Gommery and Senut, 2006; Almécija *et al.*, 2010). In this respect, the morphology exhibited by *Ardipithecus* is closer to non-human hominoids than hominids. The evidence of bipedalism in *Ardipithecus ramidus* will be fully debated over the years due to the fact that the data has not been made available to the scientific community. Arboreality in early hominids was also consistent with the humidity of the environment demonstrated in the Late Miocene of Kenya, Ethiopia and Chad (see Senut, 2006c for detailed bibliography). It also suggests that despite the long history and popularity of the 'savanna hypothesis' to explain our origins, it appears that a savanna-like environment was not widespread in the Upper Miocene hominid sites in Africa and that bipedalism did not emerge in a dry climate, but in a much more humid one.

Acknowledgements

I would like to thank the organisers for inviting me to participate in the colloquium 'African Genesis', which led to many dynamic discussions. My sincere thanks go to Professor Tobias for his kindness and attentive ear and readiness to discuss ideas (sometimes 'heretical ones'!) with younger scholars. I would especially like to thank Professor Yves Coppens whose challenging ideas helped to pave the way for a better understanding of the dichotomy between apes and humans and who has never denied the importance of locomotion in our evolution. Finally, special thanks are due to Sally Reynolds for editing this paper and to Dr Martin Pickford for discussions and constructive remarks. He kindly reviewed the English.

References

Alemseged, Z., Spoor, F., Kimbel, W. H. *et al.* (2006). A juvenile early hominid skeleton from Dikika, Ethiopia. *Nature*, **443**: 296–301.

Almécija, S., Moyà-Solà, S. and Alba, D. (2010). Early origin for human-like precision grasping: a comparative study of pollical distal phalanges in fossil hominins. *Plos One*, **5**(7): e11727.

Andrews, P. (1978). A revision of the Miocene Hominoidea of East Africa. *Bulletin of the British Museum (Natural History), Geology*, **30**(2): 85–224.

Beauvilain, A. and Watté, J.-P. (2009). Toumaï (*Sahelanthropus tchadensis*) a-t-il été inhumé? *Bulletin de la Société Géologique de Normandie et des Amis du Muséum du Havre*, **96** (1): 19–26.

Benefit, B. R. (1999). *Victoriapithecus*: the key to Old World monkeys and Catarrhine origins. *Evolutionary Anthropology*, **7**(5): 155–74.

Biegert, J. (1963). The evaluation of characters of the skull, hands and feet for primate taxonomy. In Washburn, S. L. (ed.), *Classification and Human Evolution*. Aldine, Chicago, pp. 116–45.

Bishop, W. W. (1964). Mammalia from the Miocene volcanic rocks of Karamoja, East Africa. *Proceedings of the Geological Society, London*, **1617**: 91–4.

Bishop, W. W., Miller, J. A. and Fitch, F. J. (1969). New potassium–argon age determinations relevant to the Miocene fossil mammal sequence in East Africa. *American Journal of Science*, **267**: 669–99.

Brunet, M., Guy, F., Pilbeam, D. *et al.* (2002). A new hominid from the Upper Miocene of Chad, Central Africa, *Nature*, **418**: 145–51.

Clarke, R. and Tobias, P. V. (1995). Sterkontein Member 2 foot bones of the oldest South African hominid. *Science*, **269**: 521–4.

Conroy, G. C., Senut, B., Gommery, D. *et al.* (1996). Brief communication : new primate remains from the Miocene of Namibia, Southern Africa. *American Journal of Physical Anthropology*, **99**: 487–92.

Coppens, Y. (1983). Les plus anciens fossiles d'Hominidés. In *Recent Advances in the Evolution of Primates*. Rome, Vatican. *Pontificiae Academiae Scientiarium Scripta Varia*, **50**: 1–9.

Coppens, Y. and Senut, B. (eds.) (1991). Origine(s) de la bipédie chez les Hominidés. *Cahiers de Paléoanthropologie*, CNRS, p. 301.

Crompton, R. H., Vereecke, E. E. and Thorpe, K. S. (2008). Locomotion and posture from the common hominoid ancestor to fully modern hominins, with special reference to the last common panin/hominin ancestor. *Journal of Anatomy*, **212**: 501–43.

Galik, K., Senut, B., Pickford, M. *et al.* (2004). External and internal morphology of the BAR 1002'00 *Orrorin tugenensis* femur. *Science*, **305**: 1450–3.

Gebo, D., MacLatchy, L., Kityo, R. *et al.* (1997). A hominoid genus from the Early Miocene of Uganda. *Science*, **276**: 401–4.

Gommery, D. (2006). Evolution of the vertebral column in Miocene hominoids and Plio- Pleistocene hominids. In Ishida, H., Tuttle, R., Pickford, M., Ogihara, N. and Nakatsukasa, M. (eds.), *Human Origins and Environmental Backgrounds*. Series: Developments in Primatology: Progress and Prospects. Springer, University of Chicago, Chicago, pp. 31–43.

Gommery, D. and Senut, B. (2006). La phalange du pouce d'*Orrorin tugenensis*, Miocène supérieur des Tugen Hills, Kenya. *Geobios*, **39**, 372–84.

Gommery, D., Senut, B. and Pickford, M. (1998). Nouveaux restes postcrâniens d'Hominoidea du Miocène inférieur de Napak, Ouganda. Hommage à W.W. Bishop. *Annales de Paléontologie*, **84**(3–4): 287–306.

Gommery, D., Senut, B., Pickford, M. *et al.* (2002). Les nouveaux restes du squelette d'*Ugandapithecus major* (Miocène inférieur de Napak, Ouganda). *Annales de Paléontologie*, **88**: 167–86.

Haile-Selassie, J. (2001). Late Miocene hominids from the Middle Awash, Ethiopia. *Nature*, **412**: 178–81.

Harrison, T. (1998). Evidence for a tail in *Proconsul heseloni*. *American Journal of Physical Anthropology*, **26** (supplement): 93–4.

(2002). Late Oligocene to middle Miocene catarrhines from Afro-Arabia. In Hartwig, H. C. (ed). *The Primate Fossil Record*. Cambridge: Cambridge University Press, pp. 311–38.

Howell, F. C. (1968). *Early Man*. New York: Time Life Books.

Hürzeler, J. (1958). *Oreopithecus bambolii* Gervais. *Verhandlungen Naturforschende Gesellschaft Basel*, **65**(1): 88–95.

Ishida, H., Kunimatsu, Y., Takano, T. *et al.* (2004). *Nacholapithecus* skeleton from the Middle Miocene of Kenya. *Journal of Human Evolution*, **46**: 67–101.

Köhler, M. and Moyà-Solà, S. (1997). Ape-like or hominid-like? The positional behavior of *Oreopithecus bambolii* reconsidered. *Proceedings of the National Academy of Sciences*, **94**: 11747–50.

Leakey, R. E. F., Leakey, M. G. and Walker, A. C. (1988). Morphology of *Afropithecus turkanensis* from Kenya. *American Journal of Physical Anthropology*, **76**: 289–307.

Lebetard, A. E., Bourles, D. L., Duringer, P. *et al.* (2008). Cosmogenic nuclide dating of *Sahelanthropus tchadensis* and *Australopithecus bahrelghazali*: Mio-Pliocene hominids from Chad. *Proceedings of the National Academy of Sciences*, **105**, 3226–31.

Lovejoy, O. C., Simpson, S. C., White, T. D. *et al.* (2009a). Careful climbing in the Miocene: the forelimbs of *Ardipithecus ramidus* and humans are primitive. *Science*, **326**: 70–7.

Lovejoy O. C., Suwa G., Simpson S. C. *et al.* (2009b). The great divides: *Ardipithecus ramidus* reveals the postcrania of our last common ancestors with African apes. *Science*, **326**: 100–6.

MacLatchy, L., Gebo, D., Kityo, R. *et al.* (2000). Postcranial functional morphology of *Morotopithecus bishopi*, with implications for the evolution of modern ape locomotion. *Journal of Human Evolution*, **39**: 159–83.

Martin, L. (1981). New specimens of *Proconsul* from Koru, Kenya. *Journal of Human Evolution*, **10**: 139–50.

McCrossin, M. L. and Benefit, B. R. (1997). On the relationships and adaptations of *Kenyapithecus*, a large bodied hominoid from the Middle Miocene of Eastern Africa. In Begun, D. R., Ward, C. and Rose, M. D. (eds.), *Function, Phylogeny and Fossils: Miocene Hominoid Evolution and Adaptations*. New York: Plenum Press, pp. 241–67.

McCrossin, M. L., Benefit, B. R., Gitau, S. N. *et al.* (1998). Fossil evidence for the origins of terrestriality among Old World higher primates. In Strasser, E., Fleagle, J., Rosenberger, A. and McHenry, H. M. (eds.), *Primate Locomotion: Recent Advances*. New York: Plenum Press, pp. 353–96.

McHenry, H. M. and Corruccini, R. S. (1983). The wrist of *Proconsul africanus* and the origin of hominoid postcranial adaptation. In Ciochon, R. L. and Corruccini,

R. S. (eds.), *New Interpretations of Ape and Human Ancestry*. New York: Plenum Press, pp. 353–67.

Moyà-Solà, S. and Köhler, M. (1993). Recent discoveries of *Dryopithecus* shed new light on evolution of great apes. *Nature*, **365**: 543–5.

Moyà-Solà, S., Köhler, M, Alba, D. M. *et al.* (2004). *Pierolapithecus catalaunicus*, a new Middle Miocene Great Ape from Spain. *Science*, **306**: 1339–44.

Nakatsukasa, M. (2004). Acquisition of bipedalism: the Miocene hominoid record and modern analogues for bipedal protohominids. *Journal of Anatomy*, **204**: 385–402.

Nakatsukasa, M., Ward, C. V., Walker, A. *et al.* (2004). Tail loss in *Proconsul heseloni*. *Journal of Human Evolution*, **46**: 777–84.

Nakatsukasa, M., Kunimatsu, Y., Nakano, Y. *et al.* (2007). Vertebral morphology of *Nacholapithecus kerioi* based on KNM-BG 35250. *Journal of Human Evolution*, **52**: 347–69.

Napier, J. R. and Davis, P. R. (1959). The forelimb skeleton and associated remains of *Proconsul africanus*. *Fossil Mammals of Africa*, **16**: 1–69.

Patel, B. A. and Grossman, A. (2006). Dental metric comparisons of *Morotopithecus* and *Afropithecus*: implications for the validity of the genus *Morotopithecus*. *Journal of Human Evolution*, **51**: 506–12.

Pickford, M. (1986). Sexual dimorphism in *Proconsul*. In Pickford, M. and Chiarelli, B. (eds.), *Sexual Dimorphism in Primates*. Florence: Il Sedicesimo, pp. 133–70.

(2002). New reconstruction of the Moroto hominoid snout and a reassessment of its affinities to *Afropithecus turkanensis*. *Human evolution*, **17**(1–2): 1–19.

(2005). Orientation of the foramen magnum in Late Miocene to extant African apes and hominids. *Anthropologie* (Brno), **43**(2–3): 103–10.

Pickford, M. and Mein, P. (2007). Early Middle Miocene mammals from Moroto II, Uganda. *Beiträge für Paläontologie*, **30**: 361–86.

Pickford, M., Senut, B., Hadoto D. *et al.* (1986). Nouvelles découvertes dans les sites miocènes de Moroto, Ouganda oriental: aspects biostratigraphiques et paléoécologiques. *Comptes Rendus de l'Académie des Sciences de Paris*, II, **302**: 681–6.

Pickford, M., Senut, B. and Gommery, D. (1999). Sexual dimorphism in *Morotopithecus bishopi*, an early Middle Miocene from Uganda and a reassessment of its geological and biological contexts. In Andrews, P. and Banhman, P. (eds.), *Late Cenozoic Environments and Hominid Evolution: a Tribute to Bill Bishop*. London: Geological Society, pp. 27–38.

Pickford, M., Senut, B., Gommery, D. *et al.* (2002). Concise review paper: bipedalism in *Orrorin tugenensis* revealed by its femora. *Comptes Rendus Palevol*, **1**: 191–203.

Pickford, M., Sawada, Y., Tayama, R. *et al.* (2006). Refinement of the age of the Middle Miocene of Fort Ternan, Western Kenya, and its implications for Old World biochronology. *Compte Rendus Geoscience*, **338**: 545–55.

Pickford, M., Senut, B., Gommery, D. *et al.* (2009). Distinctiveness of *Ugandapithecus* from *Proconsul*. *Estudios Geológicos*, **65**(2): 183–241.

Rafferty, K., Walker, A., Ryff, C. *et al.* (1995). Postcranial estimates of body weight in *Proconsul*, with a note on a distal tibia of *P. major* from Napak, Uganda. *American Journal of Physical Anthropology*, **97**: 391–402.

Richmond, B. and Strait D. S. (2000). Evidence that humans evolved from a knuckle-walking ancestor. *Nature*, **404**: 382–5.

Richmond, B. G. and Jungers, W. L. (2008). *Orrorin tugenensis* femoral morphology and the evolution of hominin bipedalism. *Science*, **319**: 1662–5.

Rose, M. D. (1983). Miocene hominoid postcranial anatomy. Monkey-like, ape-like, neither or both? In Ciochon, R. L. and Corruccini, R. S. (eds.), *New Interpretations of Ape and Human Ancestry*. New York: Plenum Press, pp. 405–17.

    (1997). Functional and phylogenetic features of the forelimb in Miocene hominoids. In Begun, D. R., Ward, C. V. and Rose, M. D. (eds.), *Function, Phylogeny, and Fossils: Miocene Hominoid Evolution and Adaptation*. New York: Plenum Press, pp. 79–100.

Sawada, Y., Pickford, M., Senut, B. *et al.* (2002). The age of *Orrorin tugenensis*, an early hominid from the Tugen Hills, Kenya. *Comptes Rendus Palevol*, **1**: 293–303.

Sawada, Y., Saneyoshi, M., Nakayama, K. *et al.* (2006). The ages and geological backgrounds of Miocene hominoids *Nacholapithecus*, *Samburupithecus*, and *Orrorin* from Kenya. In Ishida, H., Tuttle, R., Pickford, M., Ogihara, N. and Nakatsukasa, M. (eds.), *Human Origins and Environmental Backgrounds*. Series: Developments in Primatology: Progress and Prospects. Tokyo: Springer, pp. 71–96.

Schaeffer, M. S. (1999). Brief communication: foramen magnum-carotid foramina relationship: is it useful for species designation? *American Journal of Physical Anthropology*, **110**: 467–71.

Schwartz, J. H. (2004). Issues in hominoid systematics. In *Miscelánea en homenaje a Emiliano Aguirre, Vol. III : Paleoantropologia. Zona Arqueológica* 4, Museo Arqueológico Regional, Madrid, pp. 360–70.

Senut, B. (1986). New data on Miocene humeri from Pakistan and Kenya. In Else, J. G. and Lee, P. C. (eds.), *Primate Evolution*. Cambridge: Cambridge University Press, pp. 151–61.

    (1989). Le coude des primates hominoïdes-anatomie, fonction, taxonomie, évolution. *Cahiers de paléoanthropologie*. Paris: CNRS Editions.

    (1991). Origine(s) de la bipédie humaine : approche paléontologique. In Coppens, Y. and Senut, B. (eds.), *Origines de la bipédie chez les Hominidés. Cahiers de Paléoanthropologie*. Paris: CNRS Editions, pp. 246–57.

    (1998). Les grands singes fossiles et l'origine des Hominidés: mythes et réalités. *Primatologie*, **1**: 93–134.

    (1999). *Equatorius* et *Nacholapithecus*: de nouveaux venus chez les grands singes. *Primatologie*, **2**: 471–4.

    (2003). Palaeontological approach to the evolution of hominid bipedalism: the evidence revisited. *Courier Forschungs-Institut Senckenberg*, **243**: 125–34.

    (2006a). The "East Side Story" twenty years later. *Transactions of the Royal Society of South Africa* (Special Issue, A Festschrift to H.B.S. Cooke, **61**(2):103–9.

(2006b). Arboreal origin of bipedalism. In Ishida, H., Tuttle, R., Pickford, M., Ogihara, N. and Nakatsukasa, M. (eds.), *Human Origins and Environmental Backgrounds*. Series: Developments in Primatology: Progress and Prospects. Springer, pp. 199–208.

(2006c). Bipédie et climat. *Comptes Rendus Palevol*, **5**: 89–98.

Senut, B. and Gommery, D. (1997). Squelette postcrânien d'*Otavipithecus*, Hominoidea du Miocène moyen de Namibie. *Annales de Paléontologie (Vertébrés-Invertébrés)*, **83**(3): 267–84.

Senut, B. and Pickford, M. (2004). La dichotomie grands singes-hommes revisitée. *Comptes Rendus Palevol*, **3**: 265–76.

Senut, B., Pickford, M., Gommery, D. *et al.* (2000). Un nouveau genre d'hominoïde du Miocène inférieur d'Afrique orientale: *Ugandapithecus major* (Le Gros Clark et Leakey, 1950). *Comptes Rendus Palevol*, **331**: 227–33.

Senut, B., Pickford, M., Gommery, D. *et al.* (2001). First hominid from the Miocene (Lukeino Formation, Kenya). *Comptes Rendus de l'Académie des Sciences de Paris*, series IIa, **332**: 137–44.

Senut, B., Nakatsukasa, M., Kunimatsu, Y. *et al.* (2004). Preliminary analysis of *Nacholapithecus* scapula and clavicle from Nachola, Kenya. *Primates*, **45**: 97–104.

Senut, B., Gommery, D., Musiime, E. *et al.* (2010). Postcranial adaptations in the Miocene large apes of Karamoja. Abstract, Symposium *Miocene hominoids: understanding the evolutionary history of apes and humans* XXIIIrd Congress IPS, Kyoto, 12–18 September 2010.

Stern, J. T. (2000). Climbing to the top: a personal memoir of *Australopithecus afarensis*. *Evolutionary Anthropology*, **9**(3): 113–33.

Stern, J. T. and Susman, R. (1983). The locomotor anatomy of *Australopithecus afarensis*. *American Journal of Physical Anthropology*, **60**: 279–317.

Susman, R. L., Stern, J. T. and Jungers, W. L. (1984). Arboreality and bipedality in the Hadar hominids. *Folia primatologica*, **43**: 113–56.

Takano, T., Nakatsukasa, M., Kunimatsu, Y. *et al.* (2003). Functional morphology of the *Nacholapithecus* forelimb long bones. *American Journal of Physical Anthropology*, **36**(supplement): 205–6.

Tuttle, R. H. (1977). Naturalistic positional behaviour of apes and models of hominid evolution, 1929–1976. In *Progress in Ape Research*. New York: Academic Press, pp. 277–296.

Walker, A. and Pickford, M. (1983). Interpretations of newly recognized remains of the hindlimb and forelimb of *Proconsul africanus*. In Ciochon, R. L. and Corruccini, R. S. (eds.), *New Interpretations of Ape and Human Ancestry*. New York: Plenum Press, pp. 325–51.

Walker, A. C. (1997). *Proconsul*. Function and phylogeny. In Begun, D. R., Ward, C.V. and Rose, M. D. (eds.), *Function, Phylogeny and Fossils: Miocene Hominoid Evolution and Adaptations*. New York: Plenum Press, pp. 209–24.

Walker, A. C. and Rose, M. D. (1968). Fossil hominoid vertebra from the Miocene of Uganda. *Nature*, **217**: 980–1.

Walker, A. C., Teaford, M. F., Martin, L. *et al.* (1993). A new species of *Proconsul* from the early Miocene of Rusinga/Mfangano Islands, Kenya. *Journal of Human Evolution*, **25**: 43–56.

Ward, C. V. (1998). *Afropithecus*, *Proconsul*, and the primitive hominoid skeleton. In Strasser, E., Fleagle, J., Rosenberger, A. and McHenry, H. M. (eds.), *Primate Locomotion: Recent Advances*. New York: Plenum Press, pp. 337–52.

Ward, C. V., Walker, A., Teaford, M. F. *et al.* (1993). Partial skeleton of *Proconsul nyanzae* from Mfangano Island, Kenya. *American Journal of Physical Anthropology*, **90**: 77–111.

Ward, S., Brown, B., Hill, A. *et al.* (1999). *Equatorius*, a new hominoid genus from the Middle Miocene of Kenya. *Science*, **285**: 1382–6.

White T. D., Asfaw B., Beyene Y. *et al.* (2009). *Ardipithecus ramidus* and the palebiology of early hominids. *Science*, **326**: 75–86.

Whitworth, T. (1953). A contribution to the geology of Rusinga Island. *Quarterly Journal of the Geological Society, London*, **109**: 75–96.

WoldeGabriel, G., Haile-Selassie, Y., Renne, P. R. *et al.* (2001). Geology and palaeontology of the Late Miocene Middle Awash Valley, Ethiopia, Afar Rift, Ethiopia, *Nature*, **412**: 175–81.

Wolpoff, M. H., Senut, B., Pickford, M. *et al.* (2002). *Sahelanthropus* or *Sahelpithecus*? *Nature*, **419**: 581–2.

Wolpoff, M. H., Hawks, J., Senut, B. *et al.* (2006). An ape or the ape: is the Toumaï cranium TM 266 a hominid? *Paleoanthropology*, **2006**: 36–50.

Young, N. M. and MacLatchy, L. (2004). The phyletic position of *Morotopithecus*. *Journal of Human Evolution*, **46**: 163–84.

6   Orrorin *and the African ape/hominid dichotomy*

MARTIN PICKFORD

Abstract

Prior to the year 2000, the dominant paradigms of hominid origins could be summarised as follows: (a) the African ape/human (AAH) dichotomy occurred about 5 Ma, perhaps 6 Ma for some authors, or as young as 2.5 Ma for others; (b) the precursors of hominids were probably quadrupedal, terrestrial apes; (c) the AAH transition likely took place in the savannah; (d) the last common ancestor (LCA) of African apes and humans looked like a chimpanzee (prolonged face, enlarged canines in males, knuckle-walking locomotion and black body coats); and (e) there was an australopithecine stage between the LCA and the genus *Homo*.

The discovery of the 6 million-year-old bipedal hominid *Orrorin* in the Lukeino Formation, Kenya, in 2000, and in particular its femora, which showed that it was fully bipedal, was bound to pose serious challenges to all these paradigms. Given that *Orrorin* is almost twice as old as Lucy (AL 288–01, *Australopithecus antiquus*, which is possibly a species different from *Australopithecus afarensis* in which it is usually classified) (Ferguson, 1984) and almost 2 million years older than *Ardipithecus ramidus ramidus*, it would be surprising if it didn't upset the apple cart to some extent. Further studies in the Lukeino Formation reveal that most previous ideas concerning remote hominid origins need to be modified or refined. Not only their biological aspects, but also their chronological and environmental aspects require rethinking.

Introduction

The 6 million-year-old Lukeino (Kenya) hominid tooth was discovered in 1974 (Pickford, 1975), the same year that Lucy (AL 288–01, *Australopithecus antiquus*) was found in 3.2 Ma deposits in Ethiopia (Johanson *et al.*, 1982).

African Genesis: Perspectives on Hominin Evolution, eds. Sally C. Reynolds and Andrew Gallagher. Published by Cambridge University Press. © Cambridge University Press 2012.

The Lukeino tooth had a chequered taxonomic history with authors ascribing it variously to Hominidae, *Pan* or *Dryopithecus* (Senut *et al.*, 2001) and gradually, as molecular biology became more influential in palaeoanthropology, its significance waned, because at 6 Ma it was generally perceived to be older than the African ape/human (AAH) dichotomy, mainly because the molecular clock consistently suggested an age of less than 6 Ma for this event (Adachi and Hasegawa, 1995; Gagneux *et al.*, 1999). All this changed in 2000 when additional hominoid material was found in the Lukeino Formation, including three femoral fragments that showed that the Lukeino hominoid was an obligate biped and thus, by definition, a hominid. Enough material was found at Lukeino to show that *Orrorin tugenensis*, as the remains were named, was not only bipedal (Pickford *et al.*, 2002), but was also microdont, had non-chimpanzee-like incisor-molar proportions (Pickford, 2004) and possessed a remarkably human-like terminal thumb phalanx (Gommery and Senut, 2006). It was also endowed with a humerus that is morphologically similar to that of Lucy and chimpanzees, and a curved manual proximal phalanx suggesting that it was probably a climber (Senut *et al.*, 2001). Its femora are characterised by a medially projecting lesser trochanter as in humans and chimpanzees, unlike the posteriorly projecting lesser trochanter of australopithecines, a feature unique among Hominoidea (Pickford *et al.*, 2002). The femoral head in *Orrorin* is slightly anteriorly twisted on the neck whereas those of australopithecines are posteriorly twisted. Considering the iliopsoas musculature, which inserts onto the lesser trochanter of the femur, the main action of which is to lift the leg in front of the body (as in climbing stairs, etc.), the differences in femoral head orientation and lesser trochanter projection indicate that australopithecines may have had externally rotated proximal femora, which would bring the lesser trochanter into a medial position. It is possible that this morphology reflects habitual climbing with the knee joints wide apart (i.e. externally rotated). *Orrorin*, in contrast, possessed a more *Homo*-like orientation of the proximal femur when climbing and walking. In several ways *Orrorin* is more human-like than the australopithecines are, yet the majority of anthropologists consider that *Australopithecus* gave rise to *Homo*. If *Orrorin* is a basal hominid, then interpolating an australopithecine stage (i.e. the genera *Ardipithecus* and *Australopithecus*) between it and *Homo* means that morphological reversions would have occurred, not only in the dentognathic system, but also in the leg and hand. Whilst morphological reversion is possible, it seems unlikely that it would occur so indiscriminately over the body and head, even implicating metabolic relationships such as microdonty and incisor-molar proportions. It is perhaps more likely that *Orrorin* gave rise to *Homo* via a poorly known Pliocene lineage, and that australopithecines represent a lineage that went extinct without issue after enjoying a two to three million year flourishing during the Pliocene. Finally, the discovery of *Orrorin* in a Late Miocene local-ity yielding fauna and flora of forested affinities reveals that the earliest known bipeds are associated with closed environments, a finding that finally lays to rest the savannah hypothesis of hominid origins.

Geochronology

The fact that fully bipedal hominids existed at 6 Ma (Pickford and Senut, 2001a; Sawada *et al.*, 2002) means that the African ape–human transition must have occurred some time prior to this date, perhaps by a substantial amount. Coppens's 'East Side Story' (1994) postulated an African ape/human (AAH) dichotomy at about 9 to 8 Ma, and more recently Janke and Arnason (2001) calculated a dichot-omy at about 12 Ma on the basis of molecular data. The recent announcement of the discovery of ape-like specimens in the same levels as *Orrorin* (Pickford and Senut, 2005a,b) underlines the likelihood that the AAH transition must have taken place a substantial time prior to 6 Ma (Senut and Pickford, 2004).

Palaeoenvironment

The fauna associated with *Orrorin* is varied and abundant. The commonest fos-sils in the Lukeino Formation are hippopotamids, as would be expected for a lakeside depositional environment, but the next most abundant groups are colo-bine monkeys and aepycerotine and tragelaphine bovids. The presence of fruit bats (*Rousettus*), galagids (*Galago*), apes, bunodont suids (*Nyanzachoerus*), tragulids (*Hyaemoschus*), tree hyraxes (*Dendrohyrax*), palm civets (*Nandinia*), cephalophine antelopes, two species of chalicotheres, deinotheres, bunodont proboscideans (*Anancus*), brachyodont elephantids (*Primelephas*), three spe-cies of dendromurines and other murids related to extant arboreal lineages (*Lukeinomys*) (Mein and Pickford, 2006) all indicate the presence of woodland or forest in the vicinity at the time of deposition (Senut and Pickford, 2005). There are some open country mammals, including equids (*Hipparion*), white rhinos (*Ceratotherium*), some murids (*Abudhabia, Saidomys, Petromus*) and lagomorphs (*Serengetilagus*), which indicate the presence of more open habi-tats in the region at the time of deposition.

The discovery of rich leaf floras at various sites within the Lukeino Formation (Senut, 2005) confirms the presence of forest in the basin at the time of depos-ition (Figure 6.1). Preliminary work on part of the assemblage by Marion Bamford indicates that the vegetation consisted of dry evergreen forest, con-taining trees characteristic of this kind of flora including *Hymenaea verrucosa*,

Figure 6.1. A small sample of the abundant and diverse fossil leaf assemblage from the Lukeino Formation, Kenya. Trees yielding these types of leaves typically occur in Kenya today in dry evergreen forest.

Trimeria grandifolia and *Strychnos* cf. *scheffleri* or *mellodora*, among others (Beentje, 1994). Many of the leaves are large (10 cm and above) and a significant proportion of the assemblage have drip points, which are typical of plants that occur in regions with a lot of rain, the drip points functioning to drain water away from the stems of the plants. Mean annual rainfall of about 1200 mm or more is indicated by this flora, probably with two short dry seasons rather than one long one.

There are many palaeosol levels in the Lukeino Formation, but none of them contain carbonate nodules, and many of them are ferruginous, almost laterite-like, although no true laterites have been observed. Laterites form in humid environments, and their incipient formation at Lukeino is probably due to rapid burial of soils, before they could develop into true laterites. Carbonate nodules tend to form in soils that occur in semi-arid climates, like the conditions that prevail today in the region between the Tugen Hills and Lake Baringo. The abundance of carbonate nodules in recent soils of the region, in particular in soils that have developed on the Lukeino Formation, contrasts strongly with their absence in the Lukeino Formation proper, and indicates that because they did not develop in the formation is not due to the composition of the sediments, but to the climatic conditions under which the deposits accumulated.

The presence of large pleiodont bivalves (freshwater clams with a hinge comprising inter-slotting teeth and grooves) in the Lukeino Formation, both in fluvial and lacustrine deposits, indicates that for at least part of the time of deposition, the lake was a freshwater one. The rivers and lakes were inhabited by large otters (*Sivaonyx*) (Morales and Pickford, 2005) and fish. The flora, fauna and palaeopedology are thus concordant in indicating that *Orrorin* was associated with forest.

Interpretation of *Orrorin* fossils

Most of the remains of *Orrorin* have been described and published in detail (Senut *et al.*, 2001; Pickford and Senut, 2001b; Pickford *et al.*, 2002; Galik *et al.*, 2004; Senut and Pickford, 2004, 2005; Senut, 2005; Gommery and Senut, 2006) and while it is evident that more information can be gleaned from the fossils, it is not necessary to repeat or expand on the descriptions here. Comparisons of the remains with Miocene hominoids, extant African apes, australopithecines and *Homo* have been undertaken, and they reveal that *Orrorin* possesses several plesiomorphic characters (thick enamel on the cheek teeth, primitive incisor/molar proportions, relatively short face, deep mandible, relatively low canine crown posed on a long root, arboreal adaptations of the distal humerus, curved proximal manual phalanx, medially projecting lesser trochanter of the femur and platymeric femora). It possesses some features that we take to be apomorphies shared with hominids, including femoral anatomy (elongated femoral neck, antero posteriorly compressed femoral neck, thin cortex in the femoral neck superiorly and thick cortex inferiorly, distally elongated 'false' linea aspera, femoral head large relative to diaphysis diameter, presence of an obturator externus groove) and morphology of the distal thumb phalanx (human-like in many aspects).

The role of sexual dimorphism in *Orrorin* is not currently possible to address on account of the limited quantity of fossil remains of the genus. Thus the reduced canine crown height presently documented, could be due either to all the known specimens being females (with high-crowned male canines not represented in the collections), or to reduction of male canine crown height to resemble those of females, implying decreased dimorphism in canine size. Until more material becomes available we will be unable to resolve this issue in a satisfactory way. It is therefore not possible, at present, to postulate on mating behaviours and social structure in *Orrorin* using sexual dimorphism as a source of information.

The femora and thumb phalanx of *Orrorin* are more similar to those of humans than they are to those of australopithecines. All australopithecines that we have observed show a distally projecting lesser trochanter and a posteriorly twisted femoral head. *Orrorin* in contrast has a medially projecting lesser trochanter (like chimpanzees and humans) and an anteriorly twisted femoral head. The iliopsoas musculature originates in the anterior aspect of the lumbar vertebrae above and inserts onto the lesser trochanter of the femur below. Considering the action of these muscles, which is to lift the leg in front of the body (as in climbing stairs, climbing trees, etc.), the orientation of the lesser trochanter and the twist of the femoral head in *Orrorin* indicate that its femur was not externally rotated during climbing. In australopithecines, in contrast, the posteriorly oriented lesser trochanter and the posteriorly twisted femoral head suggest that their femora were externally rotated during climbing, because it is only by externally rotating the femur (clockwise rotation in the right femur, anticlockwise in the left) that the iliopsoas insertion is lined up with its origin thus maximising its efficiency during its leg lifting action (Figure 6.2).

The distal thumb phalanx of *Orrorin* is remarkably human-like (Gommery and Senut, 2006). It differs from the two known robust australopithecine phalanges by its less spatulate diaphysis and distal tuft. It is remarkably divergent in morphology from the thumb phalanges of chimpanzees, which are small and pointed with narrow diaphyses (Figure 6.3).

Relationships of *Orrorin* to australopithecines

It is almost universally accepted among palaeoanthropologists that a species of *Australopithecus* gave rise to *Homo*. If this is the case, then *Orrorin* at 6 Ma poses certain serious problems. Its femur and thumb phalanx are closer morphologically to those of humans than to those of australopithecines, and its molar size/body size relationships are like those of humans (microdont). The incisor/molar proportions of *Orrorin* and humans fall within the range of variation calculated from Miocene and extant apes excluding chimpanzees and orang-utans, which have considerably enlarged incisors compared to their molar rows (Pickford, 2004). Early australopithecines fall slightly above the regression, indicating the onset of molar enlargement (megadonty), a trend carried to extremes in robust australopithecines, that fall well outside the range of variation (huge molars and small incisors). The difficulty is that if *Orrorin* gave rise to australopithecines, and if australopithecines are human ancestors, then evolutionary reversal would have to have occurred in three separate anatomical systems: the hand, the leg and the dentognathic apparatus (Table 6.1). Reversal would also have to have occurred in the metabolic system (cheek tooth dimensions relative to body size).

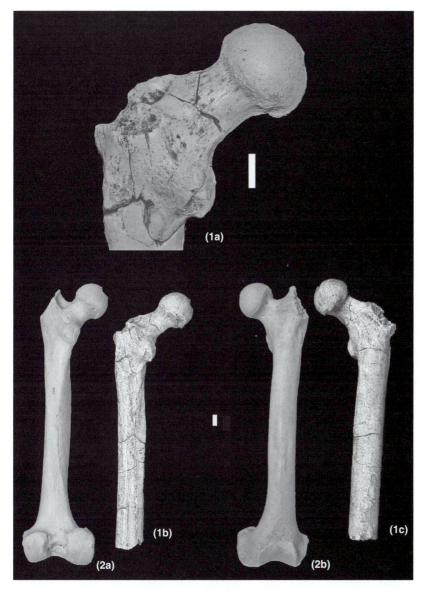

Figure 6.2. Femora of *Orrorin* and chimpanzee (*Pan troglodytes*). (1) *Orrorin tugenensis* cast of left femur: (1a) – posterior view of proximal end highlighting the obturator externus groove, (1b) – posterior view, (1c) – anterior view. (2) *Pan troglodytes* left femur from Mahale, Tanzania: (2a) – posterior view, (2b) – anterior view. Note the damage to the greater trochanters caused by carnivore chewing. (Scale bars 10 mm.)

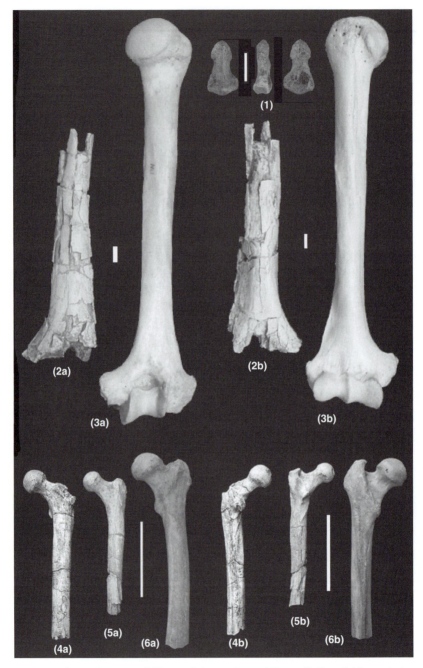

Figure 6.3. Postcranial bones of *Orrorin*, *Pan* and *Homo*. (1) Cast of right terminal thumb phalanx of *Orrorin* (from left to right dorsal, ulnar and palmar views); (2) cast of left humeral diaphysis of *Orrorin*: (2a) – posterior view, (2b) – anterior

Table 6.1. *Summary of evolutionary reversals that arise by inserting australopithecines between* Orrorin *and* Homo.

Morphology	*Orrorin*	*Australopithecus*	*Homo*
Molar/body size proportions	microdont	megadont	microdont
Incisor/molar proportions	on hominoid regression	above hominoid regression	on and slightly below hominoid regression
Thumb terminal phalanx	human-like	extremely spatulate	human-like
Femoral head orientation	anterior twist	posterior twist	anterior twist
Lesser trochanter orientation	medial	posterior	medial

Whilst evolutionary reversal is possible, it is generally viewed not to be indiscriminate, suggesting that its likelihood of occurring together in the hand, leg, dentognathic system and a metabolic relationship is negligible. It is more parsimonious to postulate that *Orrorin* gave rise, sometime during the Pliocene, to humans, without the interposition of an australopithecine stage. The latter group could have evolved from *Orrorin* or a similar early hominid, but once having emerged it diverged more and more from the human lineage, eventually becoming extremely megadont and possessing a different locomotor style from that of humans. Interposing a hominid with thin molar enamel such as *Ardipithecus ramidus ramidus* (White *et al.*, 1994) between *Orrorin* and *Australopithecus* complicates evolutionary scenarios even more, by introducing another character that requires reversal (thick enamel in *Orrorin* to thin in *Ardipithecus*, to thick in *Australopithecus*). Currently available descriptions of *Ardipithecus ramidus ramidus* do not permit resolution of the matter. *Ardipithecus ramidus kadabba* (Haile-Selassie, 2001) is also poorly known, some dental specimens such as the canines resemble *Orrorin*, while others such as the distal humerus diverge markedly from it. It is not impossible that the hypodigm of the latter subspecies contains the remains of two hominoid taxa. The site of Kapsomin (Kenya) where the most comprehensive sample of *Orrorin* was found, yielded two teeth

Figure 6.3 (*cont.*)

view; (3) left humerus of *Pan troglodytes* from Mahale, Tanzania: (3a) – posterior view, (3b) – anterior view; (4) cast of left femur of *Orrorin*: (4a) – anterior view, (4b) – posterior view; (5) cast of left femur of *Australopithecus antiquus* (AL 288–1): (5a) – anterior view, (5b) – posterior view; (6) left femur of *Homo sapiens*: (6a) – anterior view, (6b) – posterior view. Note the position of the lesser trochanter in *Orrorin*, *Australopithecus* and *Homo*. (Scale bars: 10 mm for phalanx and humerus; 10 cm for femora.)

belonging to a larger species of ape (Pickford and Senut, 2005a,b), and a second site has yielded a third specimen. One of these specimens (upper central incisor) was initially included in *Orrorin* because at the time of the discovery it was considered unlikely that there would be two hominoid taxa at the site. With the recovery of the large upper and lower molars with high-relief peripheralised cusps, unlike the smaller, low-relief molars of *Orrorin*, it became evident that the Lukeino Formation contains a second species of hominoid, possibly related to gorillas. This realisation led to a reassessment of the fossils attributed to *Orrorin* and to the removal of the central incisor from the list.

The realisation that, on the basis of the dentognathic remains, there are at least two hominoid taxa at Lukeino complicates the attribution of the postcranial bones. On the grounds that the commonest dentognathic remains are those of *Orrorin,* we provisionally attribute the postcranial bones to this genus, but some doubt must persist until articulated or closely associated specimens are recovered (Figure 6.4).

In summary, the available morphological evidence suggests that there is a more direct evolutionary lineage between *Orrorin* and *Homo*, while the australopithecines represent a side branch that went extinct without issue. The lineage linking Late Miocene *Orrorin* to Late Pliocene *Homo* is possibly represented by several fossils from Kanapoi (humerus and tibia attributed to *Australopithecus anamensis* (Leakey *et al.*, 2001) but probably not belonging to this species), Laetoli (mandible and teeth of *Praeanthropus africanus* generally attributed to *Australopithecus afarensis* (e.g. Leakey, 1987)) and Hadar (Johanson *et al.*, 1982) currently included in australopithecines by many workers. The taxon, *Praeanthropus africanus*, is still poorly known, with a tendency for its fossils to be attributed to *Australopithecus afarensis*. There can be little doubt that australopithecines dominated the Pliocene hominid landscape of Africa, but we consider that a more human-like lineage was present in small numbers, not only in southern Africa (Clarke, 1998), but also in East Africa and Chad (*Australopithecus bahrelghazali*) (Brunet *et al.*, 1996). If this suggestion is correct, then some of the material currently classified in *Australopithecus* should be removed from it.

Relationships of *Orrorin* to chimpanzees

The dentognathic remains of *Orrorin* are similar in many respects to those of Miocene apes (thick enamel in the cheek teeth, bunodont cheek teeth, low canine crowns posed on long roots, lack of diastema, deep mandible, normal incisor/molar proportions and short splanchnocranium). In contrast, in a number of features chimpanzees are remarkably divergent from most Miocene apes (thin enamel in the cheek teeth, deep dentine penetrance into the enamel

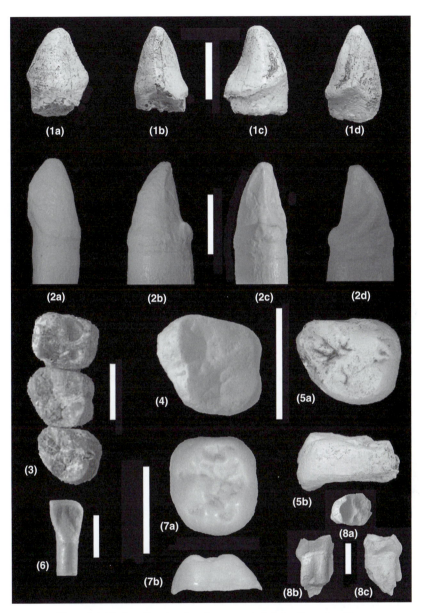

Figure 6.4. Teeth attributed to *Orrorin tugenensis*, Lukeino Formation, Kenya.
(1) Cast of right upper canine: (1a) – labial view, (1b) – distal view, (1c) – slightly
oblique lingual view, (1d) – mesial view; (2) cast of left lower canine: (2a) – labial, (2b) –
slightly oblique distal view, (2c) – distolingual view showing interstitial facet caused by
contact with p3, (2d) – lingual view; (3) right upper tooth row, occlusal view showing
marked wear gradient between upper M1 and M3; (4) enlarged occlusal view of cast of
right M2; (5) enlarged view of cast of right M3: (5a) – occlusal view, (5b) – anterior view
showing low crown height; (6) lingual view of cast of right i1; (7) enlarged view of a cast
of the original Lukeino hominid molar found in 1974, a left m3: (7a) – occlusal view,
(7b) – anterior view to show low crown height; (8) cast of worn right p4: (8a) – occlusal
view, (8b) –anterior view, (8c) – posterior view. (Scale bars 10 mm.)

Table 6.2. *Summary of derived features of chimpanzees (genus* Pan*)*
suggesting that they are not a good model for the last common ancestor of
hominids and African apes.

Morphology	Miocene apes	*Pan*	*Homo*
Splanchnocranium	short	elongated	shortened
Incisor/molar proportions	within general hominoid variation	well outside general hominoid variation	within general hominoid variation
Molar wear gradient	marked	weak	marked
Dentine penetrance in molars	low	high	low
Molar enamel thickness	thick	thin	thick
Molar occlusal basins	small	capacious	small
Canine crowns	low	high (in males)	low
Diastema	absent	present	absent
Femoral platymeria	present	absent	present

cap, large occlusal basins in lower molars, weakly expressed molar wear gradient, enlarged incisors relative to molars, presence of diastema, projecting canine crowns (in males), shallow mandibles, elongated splanchnocranium and absence of femoral platymeria). These differences raise difficulties for the hypothesis that the last common ancestor of African apes and humans looked like a chimpanzee (Zihlman *et al.*, 1978; Wrangham and Pilbeam, 2001), in that interposing a chimp-like ancestor between Miocene apes and humans would mean that several evolutionary reversals would have to occur (Table 6.2).

Relationship of *Orrorin* to Miocene apes

A wide variety of Miocene apes has been described, among which several genera have been claimed, at one time or another, to be early hominids (see Pickford, 1985 for a history of part of this debate). In contrast, there have been few recent claims that any of the Miocene apes gave rise to chimpanzees, save for the European genus *Dryopithecus* (Begun, 1992). This alone informs us that some Miocene apes possessed a suite of morphological characters of the snout, mandible and dentition that are also found in humans and australopithecines, but not in chimpanzees. In their turn, *Kenyapithecus*, *Ramapithecus*, *Oreopithecus*, *Gigantopithecus*, *Sahelanthropus* and others have been interpreted as early hominids based on these features (short face, low canine crown, lack of diastema, thick molar enamel, bunodont molar cusps etc.) (Brunet *et al.*, 2002; Wolpoff *et al.*, 2002, 2006; Schwartz, 2004). Prolonged faces, projecting male canines, diastemata, thin enamelled cheek teeth with capacious occlusal basins and peripheralised molar cusps are rare features in Miocene apes, to such an extent that the only genus in which they have been recorded to occur, *Dryopithecus*, is interpreted by some researchers as representing apomorphic characters shared with chimpanzees (Begun, 2000, 2001). But dryopithecines do not have particularly prolonged faces, indeed they are rather short (Moyà-Solà *et al.*, 2004) reflecting their arboreal lifestyle (Pickford, 2006).

In general, arboreal mammals possess shorter faces than related terrestrial lineages. This appears to be due to a combination of two evolutionary forces. First, arboreal mammals need to see with precision where they are placing their front feet in order to avoid potentially life-threatening falls, and this results in selective forces that favour the evolution of unobstructed fields of view. In terrestrial mammals, in contrast, where falls are not generally life-threatening, selection for shortened faces is relaxed. Second, terrestrial mammals generally require enhanced olfaction compared to related arboreal lineages, not only for predator avoidance, but also for location of food resources. Odour trails are discontinuous in the arboreal environment resulting in a weakened selection for olfaction in arboreal mammals. In terrestrial mammals such as baboons, selection for efficient olfaction results in increase of the surface area of captors for odours (soft tissues within the nasal cavity supported by the turbinates), which require more voluminous nasal cavity. A common evolutionary solution to the requirement to enlarge the volume of the nasal cavity is to increase its length without greatly changing its cross-section.

The only known Miocene ape with an elongated face is *Afropithecus* (and its synonym *Morotopithecus* (Pickford, 2002)) but it is unlikely to be the ancestor of chimpanzees because it has highly divergent dentition with thick enamelled molars, short stubby canine crowns and its facial architecture is different from that of chimpanzees. Also, its postcranial bones are not ape-like. It is more likely that facial prolongation in chimpanzees evolved from a shorter faced ancestor, just as the much elongated faces of extant baboons evolved from shorter faced Pliocene and Pleistocene precursors. The enhancement of the olfactory senses may play a role in the selection of prolonged faces in these terrestrial primates, and it is possible that the moderate prolongation that occurs in chimpanzee faces may likewise be related to positive selection for enhanced olfaction in mammals that spend a lot of time on the ground with their noses not far above the ground surface.

Humans, it could be argued, spend most of their time on the ground, yet their faces are even shorter than in Miocene apes. In upright posture and locomotion, the human head is held well off the ground out of range of all but the most aggressive terrestrial odours. Therefore there would be less selective pressure to enhance olfaction in orthograde hominids than in semi-orthograde apes such as chimps and gorillas whose noses are habitually closer to the ground. I take the shortened faces of australopithecines and humans to mean that they and their immediate ancestors did not go through a quadrupedal semi-orthograde terrestrial phase in their evolution, but that they were fully orthograde from the outset, being upright most of the time in the trees, and remaining upright when they came to the ground.

Relationships of *Orrorin* to humans

Even though *Orrorin* is 6 million years old, it shares several derived features with later hominids. Among these are the presence of an obturator externus groove on the posterior aspect of the proximal femur (Pickford *et al.*, 2002), thin cortex superiorly in the femoral neck and thick cortex inferiorly (Galik *et al.*, 2004), and a distally elongated 'false' linea aspera on the posterior face of the femoral diaphysis. All these features are reported to occur in australopithecines. *Orrorin* also possesses a remarkably human-like distal thumb phalanx (Gommery and Senut, 2006), which is morphologically divergent from that of robust australopithecines. The distal thumb phalanges of the latter group possess more spatulate diaphyses and distal tufts than are observed in *Orrorin* and humans, indicating a different functional adaptation of the thumb. This is possibly related to the style and power of the precision grip between thumb and first finger, although further research is needed to demonstrate this possibility.

Orrorin, like humans, was microdont (small cheek teeth associated with large body size), but overall the dentognathic apparatus of *Orrorin* is not far removed from that of many Miocene apes, including *Kenyapithecus*, *Nacholapithecus* and *Sahelanthropus*. Humans appear to have retained, or even enhanced, microdonty from their Late Miocene precursors, whereas australopithecines diverged more and more towards megadonty (large cheek teeth associated with small body size). *Orrorin* could therefore be ancestral to both australopithecines and to humans, the former diverging away from microdonty towards megadonty, and the latter retaining the microdont condition, perhaps even enhancing it. Alternatively, but perhaps less likely, the australopithecines could have branched off prior to the evolution of *Orrorin*.

Orrorin has a marked wear gradient in the cheek teeth (Figure 6.4), as in humans and several Miocene hominoids, but unlike chimpanzees, which have a lesser degree of differential wear in the molars (Pickford and Senut, 2005a; Figure 6.2). Once linked to prolonged life history variables such as lengthened childhood, the meaning of the enhanced wear gradient in the cheek teeth of fossil hominoids is not so clear today. Enamel thickness and the shape of the dentine–enamel junction (or dentine penetrance into the enamel) may play a significant role in this phenomenon, independent of elongated childhood. Only an increased sample of dentition of *Orrorin* in various stages of wear and eruption will permit clarification of this issue. Suffice to report that the few specimens of *Orrorin* available show a human-like wear gradient (Figure 6.4) that differs markedly from the chimp-like pattern.

The distal humeral diaphysis and curved proximal manual phalanx attributed to *Orrorin* indicate that it was a climber, possessing, as it does, similar morphology to that of chimpanzees and australopithecines. This morphology is likely inherited from the Miocene precursors of hominids and chimpanzees. The distal thumb phalanx, in contrast, is so different from that of chimpanzees, and so similar to that of humans that it is probably highly derived. However, the polarity of the morphology of thumb phalanges is not known, because no specimens from Miocene African ape thumbs are known.

Orrorin and humans thus share a number of primitive and derived features with Miocene apes. Chimpanzees on the one hand, and australopithecines on the other, diverge more from the ancestral Miocene ape condition than *Orrorin* and *Homo* do, in terms of their dentognathic apparatus.

Relationship of *Orrorin* to *Sahelanthropus*

Despite the difficulty of comparing the remains of *Orrorin* and *Sahelanthropus* due to the fact that there are only a few elements in common to the two samples (upper and lower third molars, canines), it is clear that both retain dental morphology similar to that of older apes from the Miocene period. The low canine crowns of *Sahelanthropus* and *Orrorin* are not derived hominid traits, but are inherited from Miocene precursors, where low-crowned canines are common (*Ugandapithecus*, *Afropithecus*, *Nacholapithecus*, *Kenyapithecus*). This is especially obvious when the dimensions of the canine roots are considered, as all these taxa possess elongated canine roots. Australopithecines and humans, in contrast, have reduced canine root dimensions, and eventually reduce the canine crown even more, modifying its morphology. The canine morphology of *Orrorin* (Figure 6.4) and *Sahelanthropus* is thus largely inherited from Miocene precursors, and the tendency to reduce and modify the morphology of this tooth in hominids only started during the Pliocene.

Whereas the evidence for bipedal locomotion in *Orrorin* is now well established, the same cannot be said of *Sahelanthropus* despite interpretations to the contrary on the basis of the morphology of the nuchal area and the angle between the foramen magnum plane and the orbital plane (Zollikofer *et al.*, 2005), both of which have been challenged (Pickford, 2005; Wolpoff *et al.*, 2006). Most of the supposed hominid-like features described for *Sahelanthropus* (short face, low-crowned canine, thick molar enamel, position of foramen magnum, inclination of nuchal plane) are known to occur in older Miocene apes, and they are thus not derived morphology shared with hominids (Schwartz, 2004) but are primitive features retained from their precursors.

Relationship of *Orrorin* to *Ardipithecus*

The dental measurements of *Ardipithecus ramidus* have not been published (White *et al.*, 2009) but close examination of the illustrations and text reveals that, far from representing a basal member of the human lineage, *Ardipithecus ramidus* is probably a derived member of the chimpanzee clade. The authors point out that five of the mandibles in which molar wear can be assessed, show that there is little differential wear on them (meaning that the three molars have almost the same degree of wear). In contrast, most Miocene apes, australopithecines and humans have differential wear in the molars (the first molar is moderately to deeply worn before the third molar has erupted, as in 6 million-year-old *Orrorin* from Kenya). In this respect chimpanzees are like *Ardipithecus ramidus*.

Compared to most known apes, chimpanzees (both bonobos and common chimps) have mesio-distally elongated incisor rows (orang-utans also show this feature, but developed it in parallel to chimpanzees). Most hominoids, both extant and fossil (including humans), have lower incisor cutting edges that are about 60% of the length of the molar row (Figure 6.5; Pickford, 2004). Australopithecines, in contrast, possess lower incisor cutting edges that are much shorter than the length of the molar row. Although it is not possible to provide an accurate assessement of the incisor–molar relationship for *Ardipithecus ramidus*, because the measurements have not been published, examination of the illustrations indicates the likelihood that the lower incisor cutting edge is relatively long compared to the length of the molar row. Proportions estimated from the illustrations indicate that the incisor–molar ratio in *Ardipithecus ramidus* plots closer to the bonobo and the common chimpanzee than to other hominoids, humans included. It plots far from the incisor–molar ratio of australopithecines, making it unlikely that *Ardipithecus* is their ancestor, and even less likely that *Ardipithecus* gave rise to humans via an australopithecine intermediate stage, because such a scenario would require an evolutionary yo-yo, beginning with an elongated incisive edge (*Ardipithecus ramidus*), evolving to a short one (*Australopithecus*), and then returning to a normal one (*Homo*) as in the majority of apes and humans.

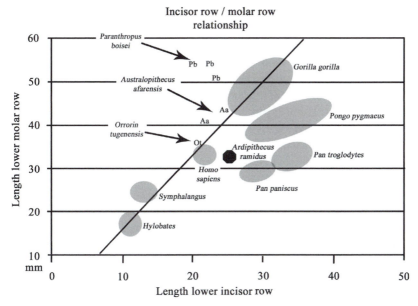

Figure 6.5. Length of cutting edge of lower incisors plotted against length of lower molar row in fossil and extant hominoids. *Pongo* and chimpanzees have elongated lower incisors relative to molar row length, whereas robust australopithecines and *Gigantopithecus* have short incisal edges. The majority of hominoid species, including humans and *Orrorin*, lie about a regression line sloping at *c*. 66%. *Ardipithecus ramidus* is estimated from the published illustrations to plot beneath the regression line, not far from bonobos and common chimps.

The incisor/molar evidence when combined with the chimp-like feet and hands of *Ardipithecus ramidus* (White *et al.*, 2009) (the thumb in particular shows derived chimpanzee-like reduction of the terminal phalanx, in strong contrast to the thumb of 6 Ma *Orrorin* from Kenya, which is human-like), the ape-like skull (assuming that the reconstruction is valid) and dentition, then it seems that *Ardipithecus ramidus* is more likely to represent a proto-chimpanzee than a proto-human, or for that matter, a proto-australopithecine.

The same cannot be concluded of *Ardipithecus kadabba* (5.7 Ma), which in its known parts is more like *Orrorin tugenensis* (the *A. kadabba* hypodigm probably contains remains of two taxa, one like *Orrorin*, the other ape-like).

Discussion and conclusion

The savannah hypothesis of hominid origins was influential for well over a century, but is now generally considered to be invalid for the African ape/hominid divergence. The discovery of *Orrorin* has led to the refutation of the recently resurrected hypothesis that the common ancestor of humans and apes would have looked like a chimpanzee, with thin enamel in the cheek teeth, a long face, large canines (in males) and a knuckle-walking locomotor repertoire among other features (Wrangham and Pilbeam, 2001). The incisor/molar proportions of chimpanzees fall way off the hominoid regression (Pickford, 2004), indicating that the genus *Pan* is highly specialised in this respect and thus not a good model for the common ancestor of extant African apes and humans. The thick molar enamel of *Orrorin* indicates that the common ancestor of African apes and humans probably possessed thick enamel on the cheek teeth, as in many Miocene hominoids. The mandible of *Orrorin* indicates that it had a relatively short face, and the known upper and lower canines have low crowns with predominantly apical wear on a long root as in many Miocene hominoids. The prognathous splanchnocranium of chimpanzees and their enlarged canines (in males) probably represent relatively recent modifications related to their predominantly ground-dwelling quadrupedal habits, and do not represent a stage in the evolution from Miocene apes towards *Homo*. This is because most Miocene apes possessed relatively short faces with low-crowned canines wearing mainly at the apices. The short faces of Miocene apes reflect their predominantly arboreal habits, and the even shorter faces of humans suggest that they did not go through a quadrupedal terrestrial stage in their evolution, but retained a short-faced condition from their arboreal ancestors, eventually accenting facial shortening as a consequence of their fully orthograde bipedal posture and locomotion.

The discovery of *Orrorin* has thus radically modified interpretations of human origins and the environmental context in which the African ape/hominid transition occurred, although it is readily apparent from the recent literature that the less likely hypothesis of derivation of *Homo* from the australopithecines still holds primacy in the minds of most palaeoanthropologists.

Acknowledgements

I would like to thank the organisers of the international symposium *African Genesis* in honour of Professor P.V. Tobias for their invitation to participate in the symposium and to contribute to the proceedings. Particular thanks go to Sally Reynolds, Andrew Gallagher and his co-organisers of the symposium. Thanks also to the Chaire de Paléoanthropologie et de Préhistoire du Collège de France (Professor Yves Coppens) and the Département des Sciences de la Terre, Muséum National d'Histoire Naturelle, Paris, the CNRS (UMR 5143), the Transvaal Museum (Dr Francis Thackeray) and the French Embassy, Pretoria, for support. Thanks to the Orrorin Community Organisation (J. Kipkech, N. Kiptalam) and the Kenya Palaeontology Expedition (Brigitte Senut, Kiptalam Cheboi) who are authorised to carry out reseach in Kenya by the Ministry of Education, Science and Technology. Finally, thanks to Marion Bamford for identifying and interpreting the Lukeino fossil leaves.

References

Adachi, J. and Hasegawa, M. (1995). Improved dating of the human-chimpanzee separation in the mitochondrial DNA tree: heterogeneity among amino acid sites. *Journal of Molecular Evolution*, **40**: 622–8.

Beentje, H. (1994). *Kenya Trees, Shrubs and Lianas*. National Museums of Kenya: Nairobi.

Begun, D. (2000). Middle Miocene hominoid origins. *Science*, **387**: 2375a.
  (2001). European hominoids. In Hartwig, W. C. (ed.), *The Primate Fossil Record*. Cambridge: Cambridge University Press, pp. 339–68.

Begun, D. (1992). Miocene fossil hominids and the chimp-human clade. *Science*, **247**: 1929–33.

Brunet, M., Beauvilain, A., Coppens, Y. *et al.* (1996). *Australopithecus bahrelghazali*, une nouvelle espèce d'Hominidé ancien de la région de Koro Toro (Tchad). *Comptes Rendus de l'Académie des Sciences de Paris*, **322**: 907–13.

Brunet, M., Guy, F., Pilbeam, D. *et al.* (2002). A new hominid from the Upper Miocene of Chad, Central Africa. *Nature*, **418**: 145–51.

Clarke, R. J. (1998). First ever discovery of a well-preserved skull and associated skeleton of *Australopithecus*. *South African Journal of Science*, **94**: 460–3.

Coppens, Y. (1994). East side story: the origin of humankind. *Scientific American*, May 1994, 88–95.

Ferguson, W. W. (1984). Revision of fossil hominid jaws from the Plio-Pleistocene of Hadar, in Ethiopia including a new species of the genus *Homo* (Hominoidea: Homininae). *Primates*, **25**: 519–29.

Gagneux, P., Wills, C., Gerloff, U. *et al.* (1999). Mitochondrial sequences show diverse evolutionary histories of African hominoids. *Proceedings of the National Academy of Sciences*, **96**: 5077–82.

Galik, K., Senut, B., Pickford, M. *et al.* (2004). External and internal morphology of the BAR 1002'00 *Orrorin tugenensis* femur. *Science*, **305**: 1450–3.

Gommery, D. and Senut, B. (2006). The terminal thumb phalanx of *Orrorin tugenensis* (Upper Miocene of Kenya). *Geobios*, **39**: 372–84.

Haile-Selassie, Y. (2001). Late Miocene hominids from the Middle Awash, Ethiopia. *Nature*, **412**: 178–81.

Janke, A. and Arnason, U. (2001). Primate divergence times. In Galdikas, B., Briggs, N., Sheeran, L., Shapiro, G. and Goodall, J. (eds.), *All Apes Great and Small. African Apes*. Volume I. New York: Kluwer/Plenum, pp. 18–25.

Johanson, D. C., Taieb, M. and Coppens, Y. (1982). Pliocene hominids from the Hadar Formation, Ethiopia (1973–1977): stratigraphic, chronologic and palaeoenvironmental contexts, with notes on the morphology and systematics. *American Journal of Physical Anthropology*, **57**: 373–402.

Leakey, M. D. (1987). The Laetoli hominid remains. In Leakey M. D. and Harris J. M. (eds.), *Laetoli: A Pliocene Site in Northern Tanzania*. Oxford: Oxford University Press, pp. 108–17.

Leakey, M. G., Spoor, F., Brown, F. *et al.* (2001). New hominin genus from Eastern Africa shows diverse middle Pliocene lineages. *Nature*, **410**: 433–40.

Mein, P. and Pickford, M. (2006). Late Miocene micromammals from the Lukeino Formation (6.1 to 5.8 Ma), Kenya. *Bulletin mensuel de la Société linnéenne de Lyon*, **75**: 183–223.

Morales, J. and Pickford, M. (2005). Giant bunodont Lutrinae from the Mio-Pliocene of Kenya and Uganda. *Estudios Geologicos*, **61**: 233–46.

Moyà-Solà, S., Köhler, M., Alba, D., Casanovas-Vilar, I. and Galindo, J. (2004). *Pierolapithecus catalaunicus*, a new Middle Miocene great ape from Spain. *Science*, **306**: 1339–44.

Pickford, M. (1975). Late Miocene sediments and fossils from the Northern Kenya Rift Valley. *Nature*, **256**: 279–84.

(1985). *Kenyapithecus*: a review of its status based on newly discovered fossils from Kenya. In Tobias, P. V. (ed.), *Hominid Evolution: Past, Present and Future*. New York: Alan Liss, pp. 107–12.

(2002). New reconstruction of the Moroto hominoid palate and a reassessment of its affinities to *Afropithecus turkanensis*. *Human Evolution*, **17**: 1–19.

(2004). Incisor–molar relationships in chimpanzees and other hominoids: implications for diet and phylogeny. *Primates*, **46**: 21–32.

(2005). Orientation of the foramen magnum in Late Miocene to extant African apes and hominids. Jan Jelinek Commemorative volume. *Anthropologie*, **43**: 103–10.

(2006). Palaeoenvironments, palaeoecology, adaptations and the origins of bipedalism in Hominidae. In Ishida, H., Tuttle, R., Pickford, M., Ogihara, N. and Nakatsukasa, M. (eds.), *Human Origins and Environmental Backgrounds*. Chicago: Springer, pp. 175–98.

Pickford, M. and Senut, B. (2001a). The geological and faunal context of Late Miocene hominid remains from Lukeino, Kenya. *Comptes Rendus de l'Académie des Sciences de Paris*, **332**: 145–52.

(2001b). 'Millenium Ancestor', a 6-million-year-old bipedal hominid from Kenya. *South African Journal of Science*, **97**: 22.

(2005a). Hominoid teeth with chimpanzee- and gorilla-like features from the Miocene of Kenya: implications for the chronology of the ape–human divergence and biogeography of Miocene hominoids. *Anthropological Science*, **113**: 95–102.

(2005b). Implications of the presence of African ape-like teeth in the Miocene of Kenya. In D'Errico, F. and Backwell, L. (eds.), *From Tools to Symbols: From Early Hominids to Modern Humans*. Johannesburg: Witwatersrand University Press, pp. 121–33.

Pickford, M., Senut, B., Gommery, D. *et al.* (2002). Bipedalism in *Orrorin tugenensis* revealed by its femora. *Comptes Rendus Palevol*, **1**: 191–203.

Sawada, Y., Pickford, M., Senut, B. *et al.* (2002). The age of *Orrorin tugenensis*, an early hominid from the Tugen Hills, Kenya. *Comptes Rendus Palevol*, **1**: 293–303.

Schwartz, J. H. (2004). Issues in hominoid systematics. *Zona Arqueologica*, **4**: 360–1.

Senut, B. (2005). Bipédie et climat. *Comptes Rendus Palevol*, **5**: 89–98.

Senut, B. and Pickford, M. (2004). La dichotomie grands singes – homme revisitée. *Comptes Rendus Palevol*, **3**: 265–76.

  (2005). Comment *Orrorin* a changé nos conceptions sur les origines des Hominidés. *Anthropologie*, **43**: 111–19.

Senut, B., Pickford, M., Gommery, D. *et al.* (2001). First hominid from the Miocene (Lukeino Formation, Kenya). *Comptes Rendus de l'Académie des Sciences de Paris*, **332**: 137–44.

White, T., Suwa, G. and Asfaw, B. (1994). *Australopithecus ramidus*, a new species of early hominid from Aramis, Ethiopia. *Nature*, **371**: 306–12.

White, T., Asfaw, B., Beyene, Y. *et al.* (2009). *Ardipithecus ramidus* and the paleobiology of Early Hominids. *Science*, **64**: 75–86.

Wolpoff, M., Senut, B., Pickford, M. *et al.* (2002). Palaeo-anthropology (communication arising): *Sahelanthropus* or *Sahelpithecus*? *Nature*, **419**: 581–2.

Wolpoff, M., Hawks, J., Senut, B. *et al.* (2006). An ape or *the* ape: is the Toumaï cranium TM 266 a hominid? *PaleoAnthropology*, **2006**: 36–50.

Wrangham, R. and Pilbeam, D. R. (2001). African apes as time machines. In Galdikas, B., Briggs, N., Sheeran, L., Shapiro, G. and Goodall, J. (eds.), *All Apes Great and Small. African Apes*. Volume I. New York: Kluwer/Plenum, pp. 5–17.

Zihlman, A., Cronin, J., Cramer, D. *et al.* (1978). Pygmy chimpanzee as a possible prototype from the common ancestor of humans, chimpanzees and gorillas. *Nature*, **275**: 744–6.

Zollikofer, C., Ponce de León, M., Lieberman, D. *et al.* (2005). Virtual reconstruction of *Sahelanthropus tchadensis*. *Nature*, **434**: 755–9.

7 A brief review of history and results of 40 years of Sterkfontein excavations

RONALD J. CLARKE

Abstract

Although the palaeoanthropological significance of the Sterkfontein Caves was first highlighted in 1936 with Robert Broom's discovery of the first adult *Australopithecus* (Broom, 1936), 30 years were to pass before a programme of continuous systematic excavation would be initiated by Phillip.V. Tobias and Alun R. Hughes. The year 2006 marked the 70th anniversary of Broom's important discovery and also the 40th year of full-time excavation at Sterkfontein. The past 40 years of work at Sterkfontein have opened many doors to research opportunities in the fields of cave and site formation, stratigraphy, dating, faunal analysis, taphonomy, palaeoecology, hominid evolution and cultural evolution. In addition to the numerous scientific publications that have appeared on these topics, there is also an invaluable record of this work in the annual reports produced by Tobias and his team in the School of Anatomical Sciences. The results bear testimony to the old Biblical adage 'seek and ye shall find' (Book of Luke, Chapter 11 verse 9). Tobias and Hughes sought to understand the extent of the breccias, to recover more fossils and artefacts, and to find methods of dating the deposits. They did indeed find what they were seeking. Furthermore we sought deeper deposits in Member 5 and recovered Oldowan artefacts, we sought early hominids in Silberberg Grotto and found the world's only near-complete skeleton of *Australopithecus*, and we sought hominids in the Jacovec Cavern and found them. There is still much more to seek and to find at Sterkfontein and the next 40 years of research are full of promise.

Introduction

Although the palaeoanthropological significance of the Sterkfontein Caves was first highlighted in 1936 with Robert Broom's discovery of the first adult

African Genesis: Perspectives on Hominin Evolution, eds. Sally C. Reynolds and Andrew Gallagher. Published by Cambridge University Press. © Cambridge University Press 2012.

120

Australopithecus (Broom, 1936), 30 years were to pass before a programme of continuous systematic excavation would be initiated by P.V. Tobias and A.R. Hughes. They had anticipated a 20-year duration for the project (Tobias and Hughes, 1969) but the success of the operation in terms of discovery and stratigraphic understanding ensured that it continued for another 20 years.

Tobias and Hughes (1969) stated what had been their objectives when they reopened Sterkfontein excavations in 1966.

These were:

- a vegetation survey conducted and published by A.O.D. Mogg (1975)
- a topographic survey conducted by I. Watt, who also established a grid system of numbered and lettered three-feet squares over the surface of the fossil site
- an archaeological excavation of the overburden to determine the outline and extent of the cave and to understand the relationships between the type site (where *Australopithecus* fossils had been found) and the Extension site (where early stone tools had been found)
- systematic excavation into the *in situ* breccia with the aim of determining the validity of the division into lower, middle and upper breccias, and to recover fossil fauna and stone tools as well as samples for climatological and ecological analysis
- it was hoped that a method of absolute dating of the breccias might be found.

Progress over the last 40 years

The major research results of the past 40 years can be listed as follows.

(1)   A greatly increased sample of *Australopithecus* fossils from lime miners' dumps and from *in situ* breccia, as well as a greatly increased faunal sample from the Sterkfontein Members (Turner, 1987, 1997; Pickering, 1999; Kibii, 2000, 2004).

(2)   Claims for the recognition of a 'second species' of *Australopithecus* contemporary with *A. africanus* (Clarke, 1988).

(3)   The discovery of fossil wood associated with *Australopithecus* (Bamford, 1999).

(4)   Stratigraphic studies leading to a better understanding of the relationships of the breccias (Partridge, 1978; Partridge and Watt, 1991; Clarke, 1994, 2006; Kuman and Clarke, 2000).

(5)   An increased sample of early stone tools from lime miners' dumps and from *in situ* breccia leading to confirmation that previously

recovered tools were early Acheulean in age (Kuman, 1994, 1998; Kuman and Clarke, 2000).

(6) The discovery of *Homo ergaster* in association with Early Acheulean artefacts (Kuman and Clarke, 2000).

(7) The discovery of even older artefacts belonging to the Oldowan industry (Kuman, 1994, 1998, 2007; Kuman and Field, 2009).

(8) The location of a collapsed breccia connection between the stone tool-bearing Member 5 and the underground Name Chamber (Clarke, 1994).

(9) The discovery of an ancient connection between the stone tool-bearing Member 5 and the adjacent Lincoln Cave (Kuman and Clarke, 2000; Reynolds *et al.*, 2003, 2007).

(10) The discovery of an *Australopithecus* skeleton in a lower breccia (Member 2 of the Silberberg Grotto) (Clarke and Tobias, 1995; Clarke, 1998, 1999, 2002a; Deloison, 2003).

(11) The discovery of *Australopithecus* fossils and fauna in an adjacent cavern (Jacovec Cavern) (Partridge *et al.*, 2003; Kibii, 2004).

(12) Dating of the deposits (Partridge *et al.*, 1999, 2003; Partridge, 2005; Schwarcz *et al.*, 1994).

(13) Taphonomic studies, which have helped to elucidate the agents responsible for the accumulation of fossils in the various Sterkfontein Members (Pickering, 1999; Pickering *et al.*, 2004a,b; Clarke, 2007).

The excavations

A meeting had been held at the site on 14 October 1966 between Phillip Tobias, Alun Hughes, Bob Brain and Revil Mason, and the recommendations of Mason concerning excavation procedure were adopted. For the first few years of excavation, the yield in terms of further hominid fossils, was very small. By 10 June 1968, only one hominid tooth was discovered (from lime miners' dump 13), but Tobias and Hughes (1969:167) made it clear that 'from the beginning the deliberate search for more specimens of hominids has not been given a high priority'. Their aim was rather to develop a clear understanding of the extent of the site and of how the various breccia deposits related to each other (Figure 7.1). Their patience and methodological approach were to bring rich rewards. With the exception of a cranium, StW 13, and mandible StW 14, all hominid discoveries during the first ten years came from lime miners' dumps. These dumps were located, numbered, excavated and processed. This resulted in the recovery of large quantities of fossils and stone tools, which could be related to adjacent bodies of breccia. A map of these dumps is published in Tobias and Hughes (1969:164). In 1973 Hughes located a lime miners'

Sterkfontein 1967

Figure 7.1. Views of Sterkfontein excavations in 1967.

dump in a cavern at the back of the type site, where Broom and Robinson had recovered so many *Australopithecus* fossils. This dump, D18, when processed, was to yield not only an abundance of fossil fauna, but also over 50 hominid fossils, some of which fitted onto specimens previously recovered by Broom and Robinson (Clarke, 1990). This dump is still being processed and on 29 August 2002 a very significant discovery was made: Clarke (2006) recognised a tooth, just cleaned out of one block of breccia, as being the missing left third molar from Broom's first adult *Australopithecus* cranium found in 1936. It was thus found 66 years after Broom's discovery, and well exemplifies the need for continued, systematic processing of the breccia. On 2 September 2002, Clarke (2006) then checked the teeth that had previously been recovered from Dump 18, and found the missing right third premolar (numbered as StW 91) from the same cranium (Figure 7.2).

After clearing the surface dumps Hughes, with his team of ten labourers, began to excavate decalcified breccia out of solution pockets in the breccia, starting at the western end of the site. This led to the discovery, in August 1976, of fragments of a hominid cranium, StW 53, occurring in both the decalcified breccia and the hard breccia in the wall of the solution pocket (Hughes and Tobias, 1977). For the next few years excavation at the western end yielded only a few hominid fossils, but many early Acheulean stone tools. One important discovery was that of a crushed mandible (StW 80) of *Homo ergaster* in association with these Acheulean artefacts (Figure 7.3).

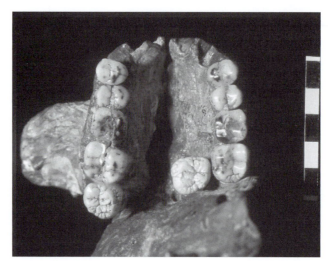

Figure 7.2. TM 1511, palate of the first adult *Australopithecus*, discovered in 1936, with newly added upper left third molar and upper right third premolar.

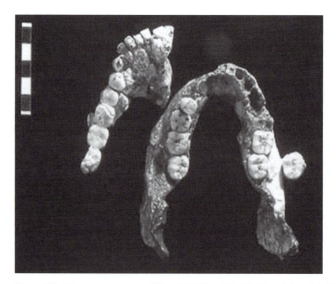

Figure 7.3. *Homo ergaster* mandibles, StW 80 at left, SK 15 at right, with StW 80 third molar at far right.

Sterkfontein stratigraphy

Although various assessments of the structure and ancient infills of the Sterk-fontein caves were published (Cooke, 1938; Brain, 1958; Robinson, 1962; Wilkinson, 1973) it was to be Partridge (1978) who would provide the first analysis of the total depth of breccia in what he termed the Sterkfontein Formation. He divided the breccias into six stratigraphic Members with the oldest and deepest being Member 1. The lower breccia of Robinson (1962) that contained the *Australopithecus* fossils was termed Member 4. Robinson's stone tool-bearing Middle Breccia became Member 5 and his Upper Breccia became Member 6. Beneath Member 4 and exposed in the Silberberg Grotto leading off of the tourist cave, were Members 1, 2 and 3, which had not previously been recorded as separate deposits. Members 2 and 3 were rich in fossil bone, as could be seen where they were exposed by lime miners, but they had not been excavated by researchers. In 1991, Partridge and Watt published a further analysis of the Sterkfontein breccias based on core drilling samples. Further interpretations on stratigraphy were made by Clarke (1994, 2006) and Kuman and Clarke (2000) based on observations resulting from their continued excavations (Figures 7.4 and 7.5).

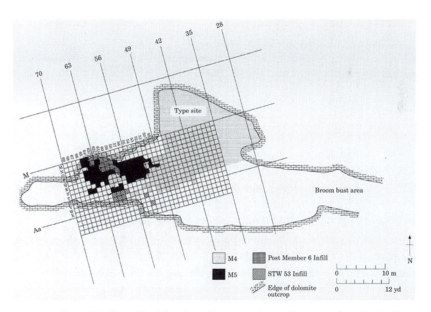

Figure 7.4. Plan of Sterkfontein surface excavations, with new stratigraphic details (from Kuman and Clarke, 2000).

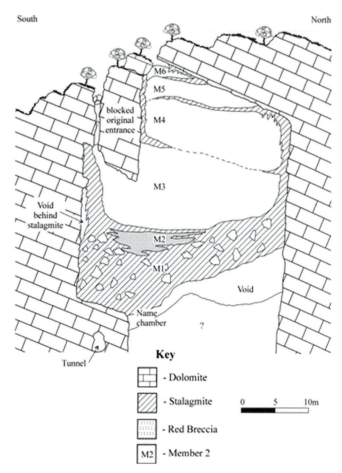

Figure 7.5. Schematic profile of Sterkfontein deposits (from Clarke, 2006).

Excavation of Member 4

By June 1982, Hughes had turned his attention to the excavation of the eastern end of the Sterkfontein site (an area consisting of Member 4 breccia) and
the pace of discovery of hominid fossils increased dramatically. The area consisted of a large body of decalcified breccia that could be excavated with pick
and shovel and the excavated material sieved. For the next nine years, until
his retirement in 1991, Hughes was to concentrate on that eastern Member 4
area, excavating to a depth of 33 feet below datum, and producing another 276
hominid specimens. These individual specimens ranged from isolated teeth
through mandibles, crania and isolated post-cranial bones, to a partial skeleton,

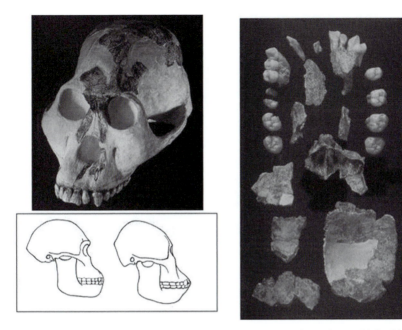

Figure 7.6. The second species, StW 252 cranium (top left and right), with Sts 36 mandible (bottom centre), compared to *A. africanus* (bottom left), based on the Sts 5 cranium and Sts 52 mandible.

StW 431, found in 1987. This was only the second partial *Australopithecus* skeleton from Sterkfontein, the other being Sts 14, recovered from solid Member 4 breccia by Broom and Robinson in 1947 (Toussaint *et al.* 2003; Kibii and Clarke 2003; Clarke 2007).

Several of the *Australopithecus* jaws recovered by Hughes (e.g. those of StW 183, StW 252, StW 384 and StW 498) had enormous and rather bulbous-cusped teeth compared to *Australopithecus africanus*. This, together with the flatter faced, thin-browed crania of StW 252 and Sts 71 led Clarke (1988) to suggest there was a second larger toothed species of *Australopithecus* living at the same time as *A. africanus* (Figure 7.6).

From the excavation of the Member 4 decalcified breccia, Hughes recovered not only a large faunal sample (Turner, 1986, 1987, 1997; Kibii, 2004; Pickering *et al.*, 2004a), but also about 300 fragments of fossil wood. These were later sectioned and identified by Dr Marion Bamford (1999) as belonging mainly to the liana *Dichapetalum mombuttense*, which now grows only in tropical forests of West and Central Africa (Figure 7.7). This fact, together with the presence of another shrub genus (*Anastrabe*), that now occurs in more tropical climates, indicated that *Australopithecus* inhabited areas of tropical forest. This accorded with the fauna, which included numerous large monkeys

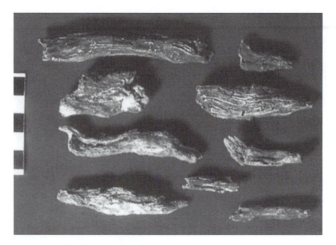

Figure 7.7. Fossil wood from Sterkfontein Member 4.

of the genus *Parapapio*, as well as some large colobus monkeys of the genus *Cercopithecoides*.

Further excavation of Member 5

In 1991, following the retirement of Alun Hughes, I was appointed to direct the excavations and I decided to excavate more of the Member 5 breccia, as well as to excavate previously unexplored areas of the caves. The Member 5 excavations produced a much larger sample of stone tools of the Early Acheulean period (*c.* 1.6 to 1.7 Ma) including two excellent cleavers.

At a deeper level, Oldowan stone tools were discovered for this first time (Figure 7.8), dating to *c.* 2 Ma (the oldest in southern Africa) and associated with three teeth of *Paranthropus* (Kuman and Clarke, 2000). Details of the Sterkfontein archaeology are published in Kuman (1994, 1998, 2007) and in Field (1999) and Kuman and Field (2009).

During the excavation into the Oldowan deposits, a large cavity was uncovered leading downwards through the breccia. A hosepipe was passed through the cavity and emerged into the Name Chamber of the tourist cave below, on top of a massive talus slope of breccia (Clarke, 1994). Subsequently, excavations were started in parts of this talus slope and they are continuing at present. It appears that this breccia had collapsed into the lower cavern from the western end of the main excavation site. It was found to contain early stone tools (three cores of either Oldowan or early Acheulean industries) by Robinson (1962). The recent excavations have also produced small artefacts that are suggestive

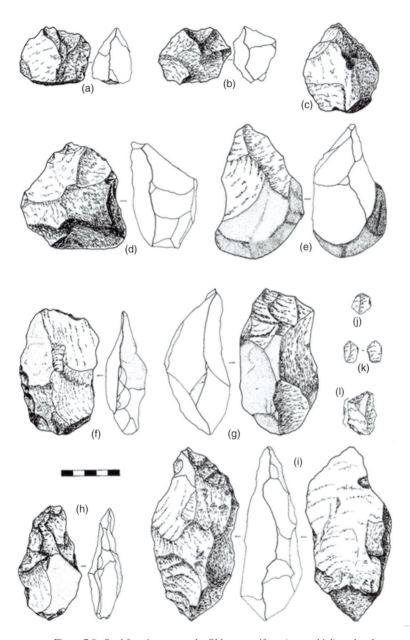

Figure 7.8. Sterkfontein stone tools: Oldowan artifacts (a–e and j–l), and early Acheulean artifacts (f–i).

of an Oldowan industry and show that the surface of this talus slope consists of collapsed Member 5 breccia. Deeper portions of the talus might prove to contain collapsed Member 4 breccia. Only continued excavation will determine whether this is the case.

Excavations in the Silberberg Grotto

In 1978, inspired by the discoveries of an older species of *Australopithecus* (*A. afarensis*) at Hadar in Ethiopia, Tobias and Hughes decided to investigate the lowermost breccias in the Silberberg Grotto in the hope of finding a similar early *Australopithecus* (Tobias, 1979). The Randfontein Estates Gold Mine assisted by installing a flight of wooden steps descending into the Grotto, together with a wooden platform and winch bucket, so that all the rubble left on the cavern floor by lime miners could be taken to the surface and processed. A great number of fossils were recovered, consisting mainly of *Parapapio* monkeys and several carnivores, but very few bovids and, so it seemed, no hominids.

In 1992, Tobias and I enlisted the help of mining engineer John Cruise and his explosives assistant Dusty van Rooyen to blast out some of the *in situ* Member 2 breccia at the eastern end of the cavern. Again many primates and carnivores were recovered, but no hominids. On 6 September 1994, a remarkable series of events was set in motion that was to lead to the discovery of the world's first near-complete *Australopithecus* skeleton in the Member 2 breccia of the Silberberg Grotto. First I discovered four conjoining *Australopithecus* left foot bones in a bag of animal fossils that had been cleaned out of the lime miners' breccia blocks in 1980 (Clarke and Tobias, 1995). Then, between 19 and 27 May 1997, I found more of the same foot and leg and also of the right foot and lower leg bones, making a total of twelve bones (Clarke, 1998). These twelve foot and leg bones are described in Deloison (2003). I gave a cast of the broken-off tibia shaft to Stephen Motsumi and Nkwane Molefe and instructed them to search the Silberberg Grotto breccia for a matching section of bone. Remarkably, after only one-and-a-half days of searching with hand-held lamps, they found a matching section with perfect contact. Subsequent excavation has uncovered a near-complete skeleton on the steep talus slope of Member 2 (Figure 7.9; Clarke, 1998, 1999, 2002a,b). The skeleton was dated by palaeomagnetic dating of the surrounding flowstones to 3.3 million years (Partridge *et al.*, 1999) and later by cosmogenic nuclide burial dating of the breccia to about 4 million years (Partridge *et al.*, 2003). This latter date, however, seems a little old for both the fossil and the stratigraphic situation whilst the 3.3 Ma date fits well

Figure 7.9. Stages in uncovering the StW 573 skull.

with both. The skull is distinct from all known *A. africanus* and has similarities to the second *Australopithecus* species mentioned on page 127, found in Member 4 and at Makapansgat.

Excavations in the Jacovec Cavern

The Jacovec Cavern is situated to the east of the Silberberg Grotto and the main Sterkfontein breccia bodies. It is also at a lower level and Wilkinson (1983) had suggested that the breccias contained within it were older than those previously known. In 1995, whilst Mr Dusty van Rooyen was blasting breccia at the eastern end of the Silberberg Grotto, two of the charges exploded but did not break away the breccia, which indicated to Dusty that there must be a big cavity to the east into which the force of the blast was released. As the Jacovec Cavern lay to the east of that end of the Silberberg Grotto, I concluded that there may be a connection between the breccias of Silberberg Grotto and those of Jacovec Cavern. Accordingly, on 8 August 1995, I asked Meshaka Makgothokgo, Stephen Motsumi and Nkwane Molefe to search the breccia deposits exposed in the walls and ceiling of the Jacovec Cavern to see if they

Figure 7.10. Jacovec Cavern *Australopithecus* fossils, with Meshaka Makgothokgo
pointing to position of cranium *in situ*.

could locate diagnostic fossils, particularly primates, carnivores and, hopefully,
hominids. On 9 August they located a sectioned-through *Australopithecus* brain
case, high up in the ceiling. Further parts of this cranium, as well as several
other *Australopithecus* fossils (Figure 7.10) and much other fauna were located
in the subsequent excavation of the massive debris heap of collapsed breccia
on the floor beneath. The importance of this deposit is that it is separate from
the main body of breccia in the main Sterkfontein sequence and appears to be
of an age equal to Member 2 of the Silberberg Grotto. It was dated by buried
cosmogenic nuclide dating to around 4 million years (Partridge *et al.*, 2003)
and although this date seems older than we would have expected, there is an
Australopithecus clavicle, which suggests it is very ancient (Clarke, in Partridge
et al., 2003). The clavicle is similar to that of a chimpanzee, whereas all other
known clavicles from Sterkfontein Member 4, as well as from Hadar, Ethiopia
are like those of humans. Futhermore, the temporal bone of the Jacovec cranium has a tympanic region more ape-like than those of *A. africanus* (Clarke,
in Partridge *et al.*, 2003). The top half of an *Australopithecus* femur from this
cavern is to date the best preserved *Australopithecus* femur from Sterkfontein.

The fauna of the Jacovec Cavern included some well preserved limb bones
of the long-legged hunting hyaena genus *Chasmaporthetes*. A complete tibia of
this hyaena well illustrates the considerable length, when compared with those
of the spotted, striped and brown hyaenas. The fauna as a whole was studied
by J. M. Kibii for his Masters thesis (Kibii, 2000) and partly for his PhD thesis
(Kibii, 2004). The excellent preservation of some of these fossils and the great
depth of deposit remaining show that it is a part of the cave system well worth
further intensive excavation.

Excavations in Lincoln Cave

Immediately to the north of the main Sterkfontein excavation is a cavern system known as the Lincoln Cave – Fault Cave system, and in the Lincoln Cave are several exposures of breccia that had been extensively excavated and removed by lime miners. In 1997, Sally Reynolds elected to excavate one of these breccia bodies as a research project for her Honours, and then later for her Masters thesis (Reynolds, 2002). The deposit yielded a mixture of Middle Stone Age and Early Acheulean elements, including some teeth of *Homo ergaster*, and was sandwiched between two flowstones dated by John C. Vogel by uranium–thorium dating methods to 115 300 ± 7000 years for the upper and 252 600 ± 35 600 for the lower (Reynolds *et al.*, 2003). A decalcified portion of the deposit extends southward toward the Member 5 area of the main Sterkfontein excavation site. In that area of the site, excavation revealed that there had been ancient erosion forming a cavity northward through the early Acheulean breccia of Member 5 and that it undoubtedly connected with the Lincoln Cave deposits. The eroded cavity had then been filled with more recent, probably Middle Stone Age, deposit that we termed Post-Member 6 (Kuman and Clarke, 2000). The conclusion was that this deposit in the Lincoln Cave had incorporated the early Acheulean artefacts and *Homo ergaster* teeth eroded out of Member 5 (Reynolds *et al.*, 2007).

Taphonomic studies

Systematic excavations at both Sterkfontein and Swartkrans and taxonomic analysis of the fossil faunal accumulations has coincided with an increased interest in the taphonomic history of those fossils. A general overview of such taphonomic studies was provided by Brain (1981), and more recent taphonomic analyses of accumulations from various Sterkfontein breccias have been conducted on Member 2 by Pickering *et al.* (2004b), on Member 4 hominids by Pickering *et al.* (2004a), on Member 4 and Jacovec Cavern by Kibii (2000, 2004), Member 5 by Pickering (1999), and on Member 6 and Post-Member 6 by Ogola (2007). There was also an intriguing study of cut marks, which I (Clarke, in press) argue to be natural, on the hominin cranium StW 53 by Pickering *et al.* (2000), suggesting that this particular hominin cranium was apparently de-fleshed by another hominin using a stone tool. This raises the question of whether toolmaking early *Homo* was perhaps killing and eating individuals of other hominin species such as *Australopithecus*. The earliest known stone tools from Ethiopia date to 2.6 Ma (Semaw, 2000, 2006), a time when *Australopithecus* was very much in existence in South Africa. But so perhaps was early *Homo* or a *Homo* ancestor. It is known that chimpanzees hunt, kill and eat monkeys, and humans hunt, kill and eat chimpanzees (Himmelheber and Himmelheber, 1958). Thus it would not be unexpected primate behaviour for early *Homo* to have killed and eaten *Australopithecus*, or for *Australopithecus* to have killed and eaten monkeys. This introduces an interesting possible explanation for the presence of a complete *Australopithecus* skeleton, StW 573, deep in the Silberberg Grotto. Abundant fossils of monkeys (*Parapapio*, *Papio* and *Cercopithecoides*) have been recovered from Member 2 at the eastern end of the Silberberg Grotto, together with many fossils of big cats and hyaenas. They apparently fell into a natural trap and one can suppose that some carnivores may have on occasion been attacking the monkeys when they fell to their death in the shaft.

Dating of the deposits

Tobias and Hughes (1969:167) stated that they 'wished to explore the possibilities of absolute dating on the site, since no single South African australopithecine site has been so dated – in contrast with East African sites, which have been well dated by the potassium–argon and fission-track methods'. During the past 40 years, the added information and increased understanding of the Sterkfontein stratigraphy and the faunal, hominid and artefact contents have made it possible to give some relative dates through comparison with absolutely dated East African sites (Clarke, 2002b). At different times, various attempts have been made to obtain absolute dates on the flowstones and breccias of Sterkfontein. Some have not proved helpful, e.g. electron spin resonance (ESR) dating of Member 4 (Schwarcz *et al.*, 1994), whilst others, e.g. the uranium–thorium dates mentioned above for the Lincoln Cave, seem close to what would have been expected in terms of contents and stratigraphic position of the breccia.

There have, however, been two recent attempts at absolute dating of the Member 2 *Australopithecus*, which have raised some questions. First, buried cosmogenic nuclide dating of the breccia around the StW 573 skeleton gave an age of around 4 million years (Partridge *et al.*, 2003), which is much older than we had estimated based on stratigraphic position and content, and much older than the 3.3 million years provided by the relative dating method of palaeomagnetism (Partridge *et al.*, 1999). Second, and most recently, uranium–lead dating of the flowstones above and below the skeleton has provided an age of about 2.2 million years (Walker *et al.*, 2006). This is much younger than we estimated based on the stratigraphic position and content and on the palaeomagnetic age. Walker *et al.* (2006:1594) claimed that their younger geological age for the skeleton is preferable to older dates, because, among other reasons, the uranium–lead dating 'requires no assumptions about depositional history or about overall stratigraphy'. Such statements imply that the absolute date must necessarily be preferable due to the fact that they are unbiased, while the stratigraphic sequence plays no role in providing an assessment of the geological age of the material contained within the breccia. In reality, however, the stratigraphic sequence is crucial to an understanding of the age of any deposit, and absolute dates, to be acceptable, should correlate with the known facts about stratigraphy and relative dating. Another problem with the date of 2.2 Ma for the Member 2 StW 573 *Australopithecus* is that the top of Member 4 has been given a date of 2.14 Ma (Partridge, 2005) by palaeomagnetism, and therefore if one accepts these dates, one would have to accept a 16-metre accumulation of deposit in the space of 60 000 years. Although this is not impossible, it is highly improbable.

So-called 'absolute' dates and dating methods can produce incorrect dating information, even in East Africa where there are radioactive volcanic deposits that lend themselves readily to absolute dating methods, such as potassium–argon and argon–argon isotopic methods. There have sometimes been mistakes due to sampling error, contamination and other factors such as incorrect reading of stratigraphy (Gathogo and Brown, 2006), which have affected the end result. Whilst in most cases nowadays, the controls over dating of East African sites are very stringent and based on long experience, the same cannot be said of southern African cave sites where a variety of absolute dating methods are only in their infancy and trial phases. Complex depositional scenarios within these caves compound the difficulties of interpreting dates in isolation. Cave infilling with externally derived sediment and rock was not a continuous, uninterrupted process. There would undoubtedly have been periods when there was no infilling, as demonstrated by the periodic build-up of flowstones that occurred in sealed caverns. This could have occurred after small entrances became choked with rocks and debris, preventing further ingress, or when changes in surface topography and vegetation cover limited or stopped the ingress of surface sediments and rocks into the cavern. Thus there would have been short and long periods of quiescence, during which there was no accumulation of infill. Similarly there would have been dry periods with no development of flowstone. These factors have to be considered when estimating the amount of time taken to form any one deposit. For example, in the Sterkfontein caves there are apparently no deposits that can be attributed to the past 100 000 years, and yet we know that at least that amount of time has passed since the formation of the Lincoln Cave deposits, dated to about 115 000 years ago. Thus in South Africa, 'absolute' dates should be reviewed in the context of the stratigraphy and faunal and cultural content, before they can be accepted as reasonable.

In any discussion of dating of the Sterkfontein deposits, certain key facts should be kept in mind. These are that the upper part of Member 5 is rich in Early Acheulean artefacts, which are associated with a *Homo ergaster* mandible (StW 80). By comparison with dated Early Acheulean and *Homo ergaster* fossil localities in East Africa, upper Member 5 therefore can be said to date to between 1.7 and 1.4 Ma. Second, the lower part of Member 5 contains Oldowan artefacts and some *Paranthropus* teeth, which by comparison with East Africa can be said to date to about 1.9 to 1.8 Ma. The underlying Member 4 does not contain a single stone tool nor any hominids assigned to early *Homo* or *Paranthropus*. By comparison with dated sites in East Africa, and in conjunction with its stratigraphic position, Member 2 is therefore undoubtedly older than 2 Ma and the possibility exists that it could be considerably older. Member 4, which is about eight metres in thickness, is rich in *Australopithecus* fossils (about 500 specimens), which together with other fauna show signs of having been accumulated by predators (Pickering *et al.*, 2004a).

Member 3, which is situated beneath Member 4 and contains abundant fossil bones, is at least eight metres thick and is exposed in the Silberberg Grotto. Member 3 was partly blasted by lime miners who left the breccia mixed with that of Member 2 blasted material on the floor of the Silberberg Grotto. All of this breccia has been processed and it is clear that Member 3 has so far not yielded a single stone tool or *Homo* or *Paranthropus* or *Australopithecus* fossil. Thus one can say that Member 3 is stratigraphically older than Members 4 and 5, and that all three Members differ in content from each other. Member 3 is separated from the underlying Member 2 by a thick flowstone. Member 2, like Member 3, does not contain a single stone tool, or *Homo* or *Paranthropus* fossil or any *Australopithecus* fossil apart from the StW 573 skeleton. This individual, like many other fossils of primates and carnivores within Member 2, apparently fell into a natural death trap (Pickering *et al.*, 2004b). This fossil assemblage thus differs radically from that of Member 4 in terms of content and mode of accumulation and is consistent with having accumulated early in the history of the cave when entrances were still small.

Member 1 consists of large dolomite and chert blocks that fell from the cavern ceiling before any opening had formed to the surface. These blocks were cemented with stalagmite that eventually formed as a massive stalagmite boss against the southern wall of the cavern. This stalagmite continued to be formed at intervals during the deposition of Member 2 and thus layers of flowstone are interleaved with the breccia of Member 2. Parts of Member 2 were deposited under water when the water table was very high. Such deposition of Member 1 and Member 2 in conjunction with a high water table is consistent with processes early in the history of a cave infill. These are breakdown of the cavern ceiling with eventual breakthrough to the surface, and formation of stalagmite and stalactite first in a sealed cavern, followed by ingress of external material through small openings.

This sequence of events given above, beginning with Member 1 and ending with Member 5, provides a framework into which dates, both absolute and relative, can be fitted. The relative dating of the Sterkfontein deposits still provides us with a good assessment of the ages of the hominids and artefacts. In the future it is possible that absolute dating methods that have been applied to the flowstones and breccias will be refined and will provide dates that correspond with the stratigraphic and relative dating framework.

A date of 2.2 Ma for the breccia containing the StW 573 hominid might be argued to indicate that it represents a younger intrusion beneath older deposits. Whilst it is true that younger deposits can, through collapse, come to rest at very low levels in the cave, such deposits (e.g. in the Name Chamber) are jumbled, the contained bones are scattered, and are not sealed in by more ancient flowstone. By contrast, the StW 573 skeleton is intact and is stratified within deposits of flowstone and breccia and sealed in by an ancient flowstone that began forming within the sealed cavern during Member 1 times (Clarke, 2006). The stratigraphic sequence of events presented by Partridge and Watt (1991) and elaborated by Clarke (2006) is logical in terms of what is known about dolomite cave formation and infill.

In contrast, if one accepts the date suggested by Walker *et al.* (2006) of 2.2 Ma for the StW 573 skeleton, then the stratigraphic sequence becomes illogical and very difficult to explain. Thus, one is led to conclude that the StW 573 skeleton is highly unlikely to represent a more recent intrusion beneath older deposits, and that it would be difficult to propose a meaningful stratigraphic scenario to explain how the flowstone that sealed in Member 2 and is beneath Member 3 could be nearly as young as the flowstone capping Member 4. The most logical explanation stratigraphically, anatomically and taphonomically is that the StW 573 skeleton fell into a deep shaft early in the history of the cave opening and infilling and that the Member 4 *Australopithecus* fossils accumulated much later as a result of predator activity around bigger openings to the cave. StW 573 *Australopithecus* was not alone in falling into the cavern because from the eastern end of Member 2 came mainly monkey fossils, followed by cats, and then a few antelope and hyaenas. The fact that articulating parts of skeletons of both monkeys and cats are represented and that there is very little sign of carnivore damage in the total assemblage suggests that these animals and the one hominid fell into a natural death trap (Pickering *et al.*, 2004a).

It was shown (Clarke, 2002a) that there had been an ancient collapse disrupting the StW 573 skeleton and leaving spaces that were later filled with flowstone. This is indisputable proof that the flowstone is younger than the skeleton and cannot be used to date it.

Conclusion

The past 40 years of work at Sterkfontein have opened many doors to research opportunities in the fields of cave and site formation, stratigraphy, dating, faunal analysis, taphonomy, palaeoecology, hominid evolution and cultural evolution. In addition to the numerous scientific publications that have appeared on these topics, there is also an invaluable record of this work in the annual reports produced by Tobias and his team in the School of Anatomical Sciences. The results bear testimony to the old Biblical adage 'seek and ye shall find' (Book of Luke, Chapter 11, verse 9). Tobias and Hughes sought to understand the extent of the breccias, to recover more fossils and artefacts, and to find methods of dating the deposits. They did indeed find what they were seeking. Furthermore we sought deeper deposits in Member 5 and recovered Oldowan artifacts, we sought early hominids in Silberberg Grotto and found the world's only near-complete skeleton of *Australopithecus*, and we sought hominids in the Jacovec Cavern and found them. There is still much more to seek and to find at Sterkfontein and the next 40 years of research are full of promise.

References

Bamford, M. (1999). Pliocene fossil woods from an early hominid cave deposit, Sterkfontein, South Africa. *South African Journal of Science*, **95**: 231–7.

Brain, C. K. (1958). The Transvaal Ape-Man Bearing Cave Deposits. Memoirs of the Transvaal Museum, No. 11, Pretoria.

(1981). *The Hunters or the Hunted? An Introduction to African Cave Taphonomy*. Chicago: University of Chicago Press.

Broom, R. (1936). A new fossil anthropoid skull from South Africa. *Nature*, **138**: 486–8.

Clarke, R. J. (1988). A new *Australopithecus* cranium from Sterkfontein and its bearing on the ancestry of *Paranthropus*. In Grine, F. (ed.), *Evolutionary History of the 'Robust' Australopithecines*. New York: Aldine de Gruyter, pp. 285–92.

(1990). Observations on some restored hominid specimens in the Transvaal Museum, Pretoria. In Sperber, G. H. (ed.), *From Apes to Angels, Essays in Anthropology in Honor of Phillip V. Tobias*. New York: Wiley-Liss.

(1994). On some new interpretations of Sterkfontein stratigraphy. *South African Journal of Science*, **90**: 211–14.

(1998). First ever discovery of a well-preserved skull and associated skeleton of *Australopithecus*. *South African Journal of Science*, **94**: 460–3.

(1999). Discovery of complete arm and hand of the 3.3 million-year-old *Australopithecus* skeleton from Sterkfontein. *South African Journal of Science*, **95**: 477–80.

(2002a). Newly revealed information on the Sterkfontein Member 2 *Australopithecus* skeleton. *South African Journal of Science*, **98**: 523–6.

(2002b). On the unrealistic 'Revised age estimates' for Sterkfontein. *South African Journal of Science*, **98**: 415–18.

(2006). A deeper understanding of the stratigraphy of Sterkfontein fossil hominid site. *Transactions of the Royal Society of South Africa*, **61**(2): 111–20.

(2007). Taphonomy of Sterkfontein *Australopithecus* skeletons. In Pickering, T. R., Schick, K. and Toth, N. (eds.), *Breathing Life into Fossils: Taphonomic Studies in Honor of C.K. (Bob) Brain*. Bloomington (Indiana): Stone Age Institute Press, pp. 167–73.

(In press). *Australopithecus* from Sterkfontein Caves South Africa. In Reed, K., Fleagle, J. and Leakey, R. (eds.), *The Paleobiology of* Australopithecus. New York: Springer.

Clarke, R. J. and Tobias, P. V. (1995). Sterkfontein Member 2 foot-bones of the oldest South African hominid. *Science*, **269**: 521–4.

Cooke, H. B. S. (1938). The Sterkfontein bone breccia: a geological note. *South African Journal of Science*, **35**: 204–8.

Deloison, Y. (2003). Fossil footbones anatomy from South Africa between 2.4 and 3.5 MY old. Interpretation in relation to the kind of locomotion [in French]. *Biometrie Humaine et Anthropologie*, **21**: 189–230.

Field, A. S. (1999). An analytical and comparative study of the Earlier Stone Age archaeology of the Sterkfontein Valley. MSc dissertation, Departments of Archaeology and Anatomical Sciences, University of the Witwatersrand, Johannesburg.

Gathogo, P. N. and Brown, F. H. (2006). Revised stratigraphy of Area 123, Koobi Fora, Kenya, and new age estimates of its fossil mammals, including hominins. *Journal of Human Evolution*, **51**: 471–9.

Himmelheber, H. and Himmelheber, U. (1958). *Die Dan*. Stuttgart: W. Kohlhammer Verlag.

Hughes, A. R. and Tobias, P. V. (1977). A fossil skull probably of the genus *Homo* from Sterkfontein, Transvaal. *Nature*, **265**: 310–12.

Kibii, J. M. (2000). The macrofauna from Jacovec Cavern, Sterkfontein. MSc dissertation, University of the Witwatersrand, Johannesburg.

(2004). Comparative taxonomic, taphonomic and palaeoenvironmental analysis of 4–2.3 million year old Australopithecine cave infills at Sterkfontein. PhD thesis, University of the Witwatersrand.

Kibii, J. M. and Clarke, R. J. (2003). A reconstruction of the StW 431 *Australopithecus* pelvis based on newly discovered fragments. *South African Journal of Science*, **99**: 225–6.

Kuman, K. (1994). The archaeology of Sterkfontein: past and present. *Journal of Human Evolution*, **27**: 471–95.

(1998). The earliest South African industries. In Petraglia, M. and Korisettar, R. (eds.), *Early Human Behavior in Global Context: The Rise and Diversity of the Lower Palaeolithic Record*. London: Routledge Press, pp. 151–86.

(2007). The Earlier Stone Age in South Africa: site context and the influence of cave studies. In Pickering, T. R., Schick, K. and Toth, N. (eds.), *Breathing Life into*

Fossils: Taphonomic Studies in Honor of C.K. (Bob) Brain. Bloomington (Indiana): Stone Age Institute Press, pp. 181–98.

Kuman, K. and Clarke, R. J. (2000). Stratigraphy, artefact industries and hominid associations for Sterkfontein, Member 5. *Journal of Human Evolution*, **38**: 827–47.

Kuman, K. and Field, A. S. (2009). The Oldowan Industry from Sterkfontein Caves, South Africa. In Schick, K. and Toth, N. (eds.), *Approaches to the Earliest Stone Age*. Bloomington, Indiana: Stone Age Institute Press, pp. 151–70.

Mogg, A. O. D. (1975). *Important Plants of Sterkfontein, An Illustrated Guide.* Johannesburg: Bernard Price Institute, University of the Witwatersrand.

Ogola, C. (2007). The Sterkfontein western breccias: stratigraphy, fauna and artefacts. PhD thesis, University of the Witwatersrand.

Partridge, T. C. (1978). Re-appraisal of lithostratigraphy of Sterkfontein hominid site. *Nature*, **275**: 282–7.

  (2005). Dating of the Sterkfontein hominids: progress and possibilities. *Transactions of the Royal Society of South Africa*, **60**: 107–9.

Partridge, T. C. and Watt, I. B. (1991). The stratigraphy of the Sterkfontein hominid deposit and its relationship to the underground cave system. *Palaeontologia Africana*, **28**: 35–40.

Partridge, T. C., Shaw, J., Heslop, D. *et al.* (1999). The new hominid skeleton from Sterkfontein, South Africa: age and preliminary assessment. *Journal of Quaternary Science*, **14**(4): 293–8.

Partridge, T. C., Granger, D. E., Caffee, M. W. *et al.* (2003). Lower Pliocene hominid remains from Sterkfontein. *Science*, **300**: 607–12.

Pickering, T. R. (1999). Taphonomic interpretations of the Sterkfontein early hominid site (Gauteng, South Africa) reconsidered in light of recent evidence. PhD thesis, University of Wisconsin, Madison. University Microfilms, Ann Arbor, Michigan.

Pickering, T. R., White, T. D. and Toth, N. (2000). Cutmarks on a Plio-Pleistocene hominid from Sterkfontein, South Africa. *American Journal of Physical Anthropology*, **111**: 579–84.

Pickering, T. R., Clarke, R. J. and Moggi-Cecchi, J. (2004a). The role of carnivores in the accumulation of the Sterkfontein Member 4 hominid fossil assemblage: a taphonomic reassessment of the complete hominid fossil sample (1936–1999). *American Journal of Physical Anthropology*, **125**: 1–15.

Pickering, T. R., Clarke, R. J. and Heaton, J. L. (2004b). The context of StW 573, an early hominid skull and skeleton from Sterkfontein Member 2: taphonomy and paleoenvironment. *Journal of Human Evolution*, **46**: 277–95.

Reynolds, S. C. (2002). Sterkfontein: exploration of some lesser known archaeological and fossil deposits. MSc thesis, University of the Witwatersrand, Johannesburg.

Reynolds, S. C., Vogel, J. C., Clarke, R. J. and Kuman, K. A. (2003). Preliminary results of excavations at Lincoln Cave, Sterkfontein, South Africa. *South African Journal of Science*, **99**: 286–8.

Reynolds, S. C., Clarke, R. J. and Kuman, K. (2007). The view from the Lincoln Cave: mid- to late Pleistocene fossil deposits from Sterkfontein hominid site, South Africa. *Journal of Human Evolution*, **53**(3): 260–71.

Robinson, J. T. (1962). Sterkfontein stratigraphy and the significance of the extension site. *South African Archaeological Bulletin*, **17**: 87–107.

Schwarcz, H. P., Grün, R. and Tobias, P. V. (1994). ESR dating studies of the australopithecine site of Sterkfontein, South Africa. *Journal of Human Evolution*, **26**: 175–81.

Semaw, S. (2000).The world's oldest stone artefacts from Gona, Ethiopia: their implications for understanding stone technology and patterns of human evolution between 2.6–1.5 million years ago. *Journal of Archaeological Science*, **27**: 1197–214.

   (2006). The oldest stone artefacts from Gona (2.6–2.5 Ma), Afar, Ethiopia: implications for understanding the earliest stages of stone knapping. In Toth, N. and Schick, K. (eds.), *The Oldowan: Case Studies into the Earliest Stone Age*. Gosport, Indiana: Stone Age Institute Press, pp. 43–75.

Tobias, P. V. (1979). The Silberberg Grotto, Sterkfontein, Transvaal, and its importance in palaeo-anthropological research. *South African Journal of Science*, **75**: 161–4.

Tobias, P. V. and Hughes, A. R. (1969). The new Witwatersrand University excavation at Sterkfontein. *South African Archaeological Bulletin*, **24**: 158–69.

Toussaint, M., Macho, G. A., Tobias, P. V. *et al.* (2003). The third partial skeleton of a late Pliocene hominid (StW 431) from Sterkfontein, South Africa. *South African Journal of Science*, **99**: 215–23.

Turner, A. (1986). Miscellaneous carnivore remains from Plio-Pleistocene deposits in the Sterkfontein Valley (Mammalia Carnivora). *Annals of the Transvaal Museum*, **34**: 203–26.

   (1987). New fossil carnivore remains from the Sterkfontein hominid site (Mammalia Carnivora). *Annals of the Transvaal Museum*, **34**: 319–47.

   (1997). Further remains of Carnivora (Mammalia) from the Sterkfontein hominid site. *Palaeontologia Africana*, **34**: 115–26.

Walker, J., Cliff, R. A. and Latham, A. G. (2006). U-Pb isotopic age of the StW 573 hominid from Sterkfontein, South Africa. *Science*, **314**: 1592–4.

Wilkinson, M. J. (1973). Sterkfontein Cave System: evolution of a karst form. Unpublished MA thesis, University of the Witwatersrand, Johannesburg.

   (1983). Geomorphic perspectives on the Sterkfontein australopithecine breccias. *Journal of Archaeological Science*, **10**: 515–29.

Part II

Hominin morphology through time: brains, bodies and teeth

8 Hominin brain evolution, 1925–2011: an emerging overview

DEAN FALK

Abstract

Since Raymond Dart named *Australopithecus africanus* in 1925, palaeoanthropology has been advanced by the discovery of numerous additional australopithecine and other fossil hominins, as well as applications of medical imaging technology for reconstructing and measuring their remains. Although improved dates for some fossils and a better understanding of their developmental trajectories have helped to modify some earlier beliefs about hominin evolution, the now much-enlarged fossil record of South African australopithecines is of key importance for understanding human evolution. This chapter details how the accumulated advances in palaeoanthropology, in general, and the South African record of endocasts, in particular, impact on our understanding of the nature and timing of hominin brain evolution. Three-dimensional computed tomography (3D-CT) of certain South African australopithecines has led to new reconstructions in the form of virtual endocasts as well as revised cranial capacity estimates that impact the overview of the tempo and mode of hominin brain evolution during the Plio-Pleistocene. The recent discovery and reaction to *Homo floresiensis* is discussed and compared with the earlier reception of Taung's discovery by scientists and the public. The endocasts of Taung and LB1 are briefly reviewed within the context of the ongoing debate about the respective evolutionary roles of brain size and neurological reorganisation during human evolution.

Introduction

On 7 February 1925, a new era in palaeoanthropology began with the publication in *Nature* of the discovery of *Australopithecus africanus* from the site of Taungs (now Taung), South Africa, by the Australian anatomist Raymond

African Genesis: Perspectives on Hominin Evolution, eds. Sally C. Reynolds and Andrew Gallagher. Published by Cambridge University Press. © Cambridge University Press 2012.

145

Arthur Dart. As is well known, Dart's claim of having discovered a 'man-ape' that was transitional between apes and humans met with controversy from the scientific community as well as the public. Piltdown had not yet been disclosed as fraudulent and, because of this forgery, scientists expected human ancestors to be large-brained and to hail from Asia. With a few exceptions (notably Robert Broom), they were therefore skeptical of Dart's 'baby', which was small-brained and from Africa. In addition to most of the leading scientists at that time who criticised Dart's description of Taung and his evolutionary conclusions (Washburn, 1985), the public's reception to Dart's discovery was, at best, cool: 'The skull had been the subject of jests both in parliament ('The Hon. Member from Taungs') and on the vaudeville stage ('Who was that girl I saw you with last night – is she from Taungs?')' (Findlay, 1972). Negative public opinion, including that expressed abroad, seems to have been due, at least partly, to religious conviction. Five months after Dart's paper appeared, John Scopes was convicted of teaching evolution to high school students in Dayton, Tennessee in the 'Scopes monkey trial'.

Taung was bipedal, said Dart, and although its brain was small like that of an ape, he described its organisation as advanced toward a human condition based on the hypothetical location of the lunate sulcus. As has become palaeoanthropological lore, eventually Dart's discovery was vindicated and bipedalism became recognised as the most important trait that defines hominins. Dart's observations of Taung's endocast, although controversial (Keith, 1931), opened up a discussion that still goes on about the relative evolutionary importance of brain size versus neurological reorganisation (Gould, 2001; Preuss, 2001). Despite the fact that numerous hominin taxa have been recognised only to be 'sunk', *Australopithecus africanus* is still with us. In short, Dart had the satisfaction during his long life of witnessing Taung's acceptance and the subsequent accumulation of a burgeoning fossil record of australopithecines and the rest, as they say, is history.

Or is it? Since Dart's day, various australopithecines have been (and continue to be) discovered in south (Clarke, 2008; Berger *et al.*, 2010), east (Walker *et al.*, 1986; Brown *et al.*, 1993; Alemseged *et al.*, 2006; Spoor *et al.*, 2007) and central Africa (Brunet *et al.*, 1995). A fossil record for numerous species of the genus *Homo* has also accumulated in Africa and elsewhere, including the surprisingly tall lad from Nariokotome in Kenya (Walker and Leakey, 1993) and an equally surprising (if not more so) small 'hobbit' from the island of Flores in Indonesia (Brown *et al.*, 2004; Morwood *et al.*, 2004). Important *Homo erectus* fossils from Java have been redated (Swisher *et al.*, 1994), and early *Homo* fossils have been discovered at Dmanisi, Republic of Georgia (Gabunia *et al.*, 2000; Balter and Gibbons, 2002; Vekua *et al.*, 2002). Significantly, applications of medical imaging technology to skulls and endocasts have contributed to a revolution in our abilities to observe and quantify palaeoneurological information (Conroy and Vannier, 1985; Conroy *et al.*, 1990, 1998; Spoor *et al.*, 2000; Semendeferi, 2001; Falk, 2004b; Falk and Clarke, 2007; Carlson, *et al.*, 2011). In my view, all of these discoveries have important implications for the nature and timing of hominin brain evolution. And, as discussed below, South Africa has continued to play a central role in our developing understanding about human brain evolution.

Virtual anthropology: implications for palaeoneurology

Because cranial capacity is only slightly larger than the volume of the brain, it has traditionally been used as a surrogate for brain mass, with one cubic centimetre of cranial capacity approximating one gram of brain tissue. The advantage of using cranial capacities to estimate brain size is that, unlike actual brains, they may be collected from fossilised as well as extant crania. Crania also preserve details about the brain's surface that remain impressed on the walls of the braincase. Endocasts of hominin braincases reproduce these details to greater or lesser degrees depending on the state of the skull, age of the individual at death and luck. Endocasts may include information about brain shape, sulcal pattern, the pathways for major nerves, blood vessels, venous sinuses and details of the cerebellum. The hominin endocasts from South Africa are nicely detailed, perhaps partly because they formed naturally as fine lime sediment replaced brain tissue during the fossilisation process. Another factor is that smaller brained species within mammalian lineages tend to produce good details compared with their larger brained relatives (Radinsky, 1972).

The field of palaeoneurology is currently being advanced by the application of computed tomography (CT) to the gathering of data, visualisation and modelling of 'virtual endocasts' from fossilised skulls, and much of this work was pioneered on South African australopithecine fossil material. In medical CT scanners, an X-ray source and an array of detectors rotate around a skull and collect data that may be visualised in a grayscale image in which white represents the highest density and black the lowest. This process is particularly good for visualising density differences between fossilised bone and attached matrix (Spoor *et al.*, 2000). A series of contiguous or overlapping scans is used in 3D-CT, which has become state-of-the-art for reconstructing missing portions of virtual endocasts by mirror imaging and for obtaining highly accurate cranial capacities by flood-filling braincases (Conroy and Vannier, 1985; Zollikoffer *et al.*, 1995; Conroy *et al.*, 1998). For example, Spoor and colleagues (2000) used 3D-CT to electronically remove matrix from the cranial cavity of a robust australopithecine, SK 47 (*Paranthropus robustus*), from

Swartkrans, South Africa, which revealed an enlarged occipital/marginal (O/M) sinus that, to date, appears in twelve of twelve scorable *Paranthropus* specimens (Tobias and Falk, 1988; Falk *et al.*, 1995; de Ruiter *et al.*, 2006). On the other hand, Conroy and colleagues (1990) used 3D-CT to document the absence of an enlarged O/M sinus in a partial skull from a gracile australopithecine that was filled with solid matrix, MLD 37/38 (*Australopithecus africanus*) from Makapansgat, South Africa. They also obtained a cranial capacity of 425 cubic centimetres (cm^3) for the specimen, which was very close to the published estimate in the literature.

The application of 3D-CT methods to another South African specimen, StW 505 ('Mr. Ples') from Sterkfontein (Conroy *et al.*, 1998) is particularly interesting. Conroy and colleagues reconstructed its virtual skull (which is distorted in the fossil) and endocast, the volume of which was electronically determined to be 515 cm^3. Because visual inspection of the actual fossil suggests that the volume of StW 505's braincase is relatively large compared with other South African australopithecines, some experts expected that, when finally measured with advanced imaging technology, its cranial capacity would turn out to be considerably larger than it did (perhaps over 600 cm^3). Conroy and his colleagues suggested that the inflated expectations for StW 505 might be due to inflated estimates for other hominins such as Sts 71 in the literature. I, too, had expected a larger volume for StW 505's reconstructed braincase for the simple reason that my hard copies of its skull and endocast *looked* much larger than comparable australopithecine specimens in my collection. Because of the findings of Conroy *et al.* (Falk, 1998), my colleagues and I wondered about the accuracy of the cranial capacities and morphological descriptions that had been published for other australopithecine endocasts and, therefore, undertook a study of those in my collection (Falk *et al.*, 2000).

What we found was that endocasts of gracile and robust australopithecines are characterised by striking shape differences in the orbital surfaces of their frontal lobes and in their temporal poles (Falk *et al.*, 2000). In lateral view, endocasts of *Paranthropus* have a beak-shaped profile on their orbital surfaces in the region that contains their olfactory bulbs, which is similar to the profiles of chimpanzee and gorilla endocasts. When viewed dorsally (or ventrally), the rostral contours of their frontal lobes are pointed, which contributes to a generally pear-shaped outline (Figure 8.1). Ventrally, the temporal poles of robust australopithecines are rounded and stubby, i.e. they do not project very far forward relative to sella turcica (Figure 8.2). The shape of endocasts of gracile australopithecines is another story. When oriented along the frontal pole–occipital pole (fp–op) axis that is the convention for endocasts (Connolly, 1950), the lateral profile of the orbital surfaces of the frontal lobes is more massive and extends further caudally than the smaller, beak-shaped region in *Paranthropus*. From

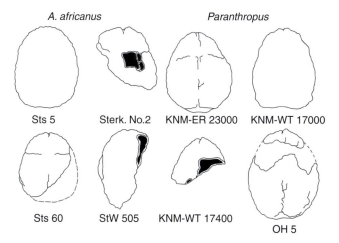

Figure 8.1. Outlines of dorsal views of endocasts from *A. africanus* on left
(Sts 5, Sterk No. 2, Sts 60, StW 505), and *Paranthropus* on right (KNM-ER 23000,
KNM-WT 17000, KNM-WT 17400, OH 5). Frontal lobes are at the top of each
image. The frontal lobes of *A. africanus* are wider while those of *Paranthropus*
are more pointed, which gives the overall outline of the latter a teardrop shape.
Reproduced from Falk *et al.* (2000).

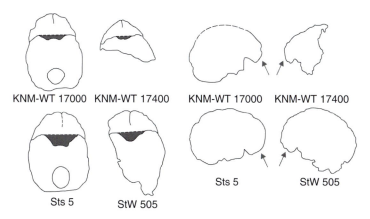

Figure 8.2. Outlines of basal views (on left) and lateral views (on right) from
Paranthropus (KNM-WT 17000, KNM-WT 17400) and *A. africanus* (Sts 5, StW
505) endocasts. The temporal poles of *Paranthropus* are rounded and do not project
very far forward relative to the anterior border of sella turcica (area indicated by
grey fill), compared to the more pointed and anteriorly projecting temporal poles
of *A. africanus*. Lateral views on the right are positioned 'nose-to-nose'. Note that
the orbital surfaces of *Paranthropus* are beak shaped and smaller than those of *A.
africanus*, which are more expanded underneath the frontal lobes (indicated by
arrows).

the basal view, a greater amount of cerebral cortex separates the cribriform plate (upon which the olfactory bulbs rest) from the rostral edge of the frontal lobes in gracile australopithecines. Rather than being pointed, the rostral contours of their frontal lobes are more filled-out laterally, which gives them a bit of a squared-off appearance. Compared with *Paranthropus*, the temporal poles of *Australopithecus* protrude rostrally and laterally relative to sella turcica, which gives them a more pointed and less stubby appearance, similar to extant *Homo* (Figure 8.2). Further details and measurements pertaining to these differences are published elsewhere (Falk *et al.*, 2000).

Falk *et al.* noted that the area that is expanded at the rostral ends of the frontal lobes on endocasts of gracile australopithecines in basal view (Falk *et al.*, 2000: 711–12):

> corresponds to Brodmann's area 10 in both apes and humans, which has been shown experimentally to be involved in abstract thinking, planning of future actions, and undertaking initiatives (Semendeferi, 1994). Because the relative size of human area 10 is twice that of both bonobos and chimpanzees, Semendeferi (1994) suggested that this area of the cerebral cortex increased in relative size at some point along the line from the first hominids to the early representatives of the genus *Homo*. Our results support her suggestion, and further suggest that area 10 had begun to increase in size in *Australopithecus*.

Semendeferi and her colleagues have recently shown that human brain evolution was probably characterised by an increase in the number and width of minicolumns and in the space for interconnections between neurons in layer III of the frontal polar part of BA 10, which is important because this layer gives rise to connections with other regions of cortex (Semendeferi *et al.*, 2011). As discussed below, Semendeferi's findings as they pertain to *Australopithecus africanus* take on added significance in light of the discovery of *Homo floresiensis* and morphology of its endocast (Falk *et al.*, 2005, 2007, 2009b).

An important implication of Falk and colleagues' (2000) findings is that gracile and robust australopithecine endocasts are very different in the shape and, presumably, also in the organisation of their orbitofrontal cortices and temporal poles. These are not subtle shape differences and, indeed, are easily discerned by visual inspection. As noted, the caudal end of endocasts of these two groups also differ dramatically in their venous drainage patterns, with fixation of a derived enlarged O/M sinus in twelve out of twelve scorable robust australopithecines, versus a very low frequency of this trait in *Australopithecus africanus*, in which, of six scorable specimens, only Taung manifests the trait (Tobias and Falk, 1988; Falk *et al.*, 1995; Falk and Clarke, 2007). Because the beautifully complete skull of Sts 5 was discovered early on, numerous workers have naturally used its endocast as a model for reconstructing the missing parts of other australopithecine endocasts, including those from *Paranthropus* skulls. However, our re-analysis of the South African endocasts made it clear that one should not use a gracile australopithecine endocast, no matter how complete, to recreate the missing portions of endocasts of *Paranthropus*.

My colleagues and I therefore re-reconstructed the endocasts of four robust australopithecines (SK 1585, OH 5, KNM-ER 407 and KNM-ER 732) using available *Paranthropus* endocasts from my collection (see Falk *et al.*, 2000: appendix, for details). Our new reconstructions were water-displaced to obtain new cranial capacities, and in all four cases the cranial capacities were smaller than earlier estimates. Because the orbital surfaces and temporal poles of *Paranthropus* are now known to be relatively smaller than comparable regions in *A. africanus*, it is not surprising that we obtained a mean cranial capacity of robust australopithecines that is smaller than previous estimates. When the four new cranial capacities for *Paranthropus* are combined with estimates for other specimens, the mean for that genus decreases from approximately 480 cm^3 to 450 cm^3, which equals rather than exceeds the mean for *A. africanus* (Falk *et al.*, 2000). The brains of gracile and robust australopithecines, thus, seem to have averaged about the same mass, but their shapes and inferred neurological organisation were very different. Of the two groups, the brain morphology of *Australopithecus africanus* appears more human-like than that of *Paranthropus*, at least in terms of overall frontal lobe and temporal pole shape (Falk *et al.*, 2000).

Rethinking the tempo and mode of hominin brain evolution

Certain other basic assumptions about the evolution of hominin brain size are now in need of re-evaluation. For example, received wisdom has it that, compared with australopithecines, cranial capacity 'took off' rather abruptly in *Homo* around two million years ago and eventually doubled in size from an initial value of around 700 cm^3 to roughly 1400 cm^3 (Falk, 1998, 2004b). However, specimens from the approximately 1.75 million-year-old Eurasian site of Dmanisi, Republic of Georgia (Gabunia *et al.* 2000; Vekua *et al.*, 2002) cast doubt on this hypothesis. Several skulls from Dmanisi share features with both *Australopithecus* and African early *Homo erectus*, and are associated with Oldowan-like stone tools found with the former (Balter and Gibbons, 2002). Analysis by 3D-CT of one skull (D 2700) reveals features that are transitional between the two genera including a cranial capacity of about 600 cm^3 (Vekua *et al.*, 2002). If one adds these Dmanisi specimens to a graph plotting cranial capacity over time, they remove the hypothetical 'take off' that was supposed to have characterised brain size evolution in early *Homo* compared with australopithecines (Figure 8.3; Table 8.1), whether or not one attributes them

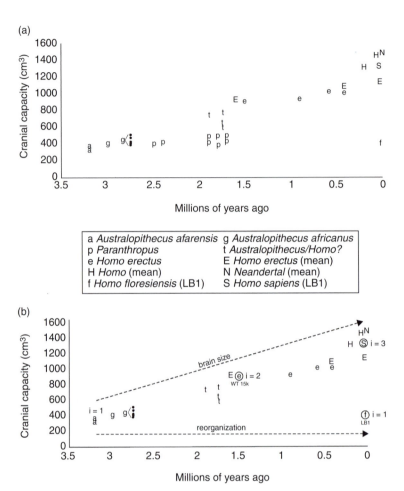

Figure 8.3. Cranial capacities of select hominins plotted against time; data from Table 8.1. (a) plot includes capacities for robust australopithecines (*Paranthropus*). The trend for brain size increase appears flat until around 2.0 Ma, and then begins to increase in *Homo*. (b) the same plot, but without the *Paranthropus* specimens (generally thought not to be ancestral to *Homo*). The trend towards brain size increase now appears to increase from before 3.0 Ma. Part of the reason for this is the recently described 'transitional' specimens from Dmanisi, Republic of Georgia (listed under *Australopithecus/Homo* in Table 8.1). The earliest australopithecines and relatively recent LB1 (*Homo floresiensis*) have brain sizes expected for apes of equivalent body sizes (i = 1); *Homo erectus* from Nariokotome (KNM-WT 15000) has a brain that is twice the size expected for an ape or australopithecine (i = 2), although its adult body weight is in the range for modern men; and contemporary *Homo sapiens'* mean brain size is three times that expected for apes of equivalent body size (i = 3). This figure illustrates the trends for increasing brain size (vertical axis) and ongoing neurological reorganisation (horizontal axis). Reproduced from Falk (2007).

Table 8.1. *Following Holloway* et al. *(2004), the chronological data are approximate middle values for estimated dates (see also Falk* et al.*, 2000). See Figure 8.3 for plots of data. Table reproduced from Falk (2007).*

Species	Date (Ma)	Specimen	Adult, cm³	Reference
Australopithecus				
A. *afarensis*	~3.2	AL 333–105	343	Falk, 1987
–	~3.2	AL 162–28	375	Falk, 1985
A. *africanus*	~3.0	MLD 37/38	425	Conroy *et al.*, 1990
–	~2.75	Sts 60	400	Holloway *et al.*, 2004
–	–	Sts 71	428	Holloway *et al.*, 2004
–	–	Sts 5	485	Holloway *et al.*, 2004
–	–	Sts 19	436	Holloway *et al.*, 2004
–	–	StW 505	515	Conroy *et al.*, 1998
Paranthropus				
P. *aethiopicus*	~2.5	KNM-WT 17000	410	Walker *et al.*, 1986
P. *boisei*	~2.4	Omo L339y-6	427	Holloway *et al.*, 2004
–	~1.9	KNM-ER 23000	491	Brown *et al.*, 1993
–	~1.8	KNM-WT 17400	400	Holloway *et al.*, 2004
–	~1.8	OH 5	500	Falk *et al.*, 2000
–	~1.9	KNM-ER 407	438	Falk *et al.*, 2000
–	~1.7	KNM-ER 732	466	Falk *et al.*, 2000
P. *robustus*	~1.7	SK 1585	476	Falk *et al.*, 2000
Australopithecus/ Homo?				
–	~1.9	KNM-ER 1470	752	Holloway *et al.*, 2004
–	~1.75	D2700	600	Vekua *et al.*, 2002
–	–	D2282	650	Gabunia *et al.*, 2000
–	–	D2280	780	Gabunia *et al.*, 2000
Homo erectus				
Java (Sangiran)	~1.6	*n* = 6	mean = 932	Holloway *et al.*, 2004
Africa	~1.5	KNM-WT 15000	909	Walker and Leakey, 1993
Java (Trinil)	~0.9	Trinil 2	940	Holloway *et al.*, 2004
China (Beijing)	~0.585	Skull D1	1020	Weidenreich, 1943
China (Beijing)	~0.423	*n* = 3	mean = 1090	Weidenreich, 1943
Hexian	~0.412	–	1025	Wu *et al.*, 2005
Java (Solo)	~0.027	*n* = 6	mean = 1149	Holloway *et al.*, 2004
Homo				
European	~0.2	–	mean = 1314	Hofman, 1983
Neandertals	~0.07	–	mean = 1487	Hofman, 1983
European	~0.04	–	mean = 1460	Hofman, 1983
H. *sapiens*	~0.01	–	mean = 1330	Holloway *et al.*, 2004
Homo floresiensis	~0.018	LB1	417	Falk *et al.*, 2005

to *Australopithecus* (despite their Eurasian location) or to early *Homo* (Wood and Collard, 1999). This is all the more apparent if one removes *Paranthropus* specimens that are generally thought not to have been ancestral to *Homo* from the graph (Figure 8.3).

The oldest dates for *Homo erectus* from Java are now believed to be closer to two million years ago (Swisher *et al.*, 1994) rather than one million years ago as previously believed (Figure 8.3; Table 8.1), and adjusting the placement of these specimens on the cranial capacity versus time graph (Figure 8.3) also dampens the impression that a sharp increase in brain size began in the middle Pleistocene, which may have contributed to the assumption that brain size evolution was subject to punctuated equilibrium (Leigh, 1992; Hofman, 2001; Lee and Wolpoff, 2003). As suggested by Figure 8.3, cranial capacity remained relatively conservative in *Paranthropus*, did not 'take off' around 2.0 million years ago in early *Homo* or its direct ancestors as was previously thought, and continued to increase fairly steadily until it peaked in Neandertals, after which it decreased somewhat and then may have levelled off. (Interestingly, according to models of Hofman (2001) further increase is still possible.) Furthermore, cranial capacity may have begun to increase by 3.0 million years ago in the *Australopithecus* ancestors of *Homo*, which is considerably earlier than the hypothesised jump in our lineage at around 2.0 million years ago.

Of course, the discussion so far refers only to trends over time for absolute cranial capacity as a surrogate for brain size and has not taken the important variable of body size into account. I am reluctant to estimate brain size/body size ratios (or relative brain size, RBS) for fossils that lack either a relatively complete braincase or enough postcranial material to be reasonably confident of estimating an accurate body mass. What one can be sure of, however, is that with a mean cranial capacity of approximately 450 cm^3 and generally ape-sized dimensions (and proportions) of their collected postcrania, australopithecines had mean RBSs that were generally in the ape range. In Figure 8.3 and elsewhere (Falk *et al.*, 2005, supporting online material), their ape-like RBS is indicated with an index (i) equal to 1.

The Nariokotome *Homo erectus* skeleton (KNM-WT 15000) from Kenya, on the other hand, has an estimated adult body weight (68 kg) that falls comfortably within the range for extant men, but an estimated adult cranial capacity (909 cm^3) that is only about two-thirds of the mean for modern men (Walker and Leakey, 1993). Nevertheless, Nariokotome's cranial capacity is twice the mean for australopithecines or, roughly speaking, twice that expected for an ape of equivalent body size, which accounts for its index of i = 2 in Figure 8.3. As is well known, humans have brains that are approximately three times the mass one would expect for an ape of equivalent body weight (Passingham, 1975), and this is indicated in Figure 8.3 with the label i = 3.

Homo floresiensis: new species on the block

In some ways, history has repeated itself with the announcement of the new species, *Homo floresiensis* in the 28 October 2004 issue of *Nature*. Just four months shy of the 80th anniversary of the announcement of Taung in that same journal, the designation of another new species of hominin by a team led by another Australian scientist, Michael Morwood, caused a stir that rivals the one set off by Raymond Dart in 1925. As was the case for *Australopithecus africanus* (Falk, 2009), the naming of *Homo floresiensis* as a new hominin species has met with controversy in worldwide scientific and public arenas (Falk, 2011). With respect to the latter, the 1925 'monkey trial' in Tennessee has been replaced with contemporary 'creation science' trials in Kansas, Pennsylvania, and elsewhere. Instead of being ridiculed on the vaudeville stage the way that Taung was, LB1 has been relegated by some scientists to a group of individuals who were once familiar carnival 'sideshow' attractions – namely humans afflicted with the pathological condition of microcephaly. In response, Falk *et al.* conducted research on ten virtual endocasts from microcephalics, which led them to reject the suggestion that LB1 was a microcephalic (Falk *et al.*, 2007, 2009b). Additional research raises serious questions about other suggestions that LB1 had suffered from Laron syndrome (Falk *et al.*, 2009a) or some unspecified pathological asymmetry of the skull and body (Falk *et al.*, 2010).

The parallels do not stop there. Like Taung, LB1 has a small cranial capacity (404 cm^3 for Taung and 417 cm^3 for LB1, Table 8.1). Taung is now thought to have died at the age of around 3.5 years instead of 5 to 6 years as originally believed (Bromage, 1985; Bromage and Dean, 1985) and to have developed dentally at a rate that was more similar to apes than humans (Smith, 1986), which fits with the current consensus that australopithecines probably matured like apes rather than people. Since chimpanzees are our closest non-human relatives, one may use associated dental and cranial capacity data from chimpanzees to estimate the adult cranial capacity of an australopithecine with erupting first permanent molars, such as Taung. Thus, a large sample of chimpanzees surveyed by Ashton and Spence (1958) suggests that Taung's cranial capacity of 404 cm^3 would have achieved 94% of its adult value, or 430 cm^3, if sex is unknown, which is not much larger than LB1's 417 cm^3. If Taung were female, then the adult estimate based on Ashton and Spence's data would be 421 cm^3, making it virtually identical to the value for LB1. Elsewhere, Falk and Clarke (2007) estimate an adult value of 406 cm^3, based on a new reconstruction of the endocast. Because most of LB1's skeleton is available, it is associated with sufficient body size data (Brown *et al.*, 2004) that permits the calculation of RBS (Falk *et al.*, 2005). Similar to australopithecines, i = 1 for LB1 (Figure 8.3), which raises interesting questions about whether *Homo floresiensis* is a dwarfed descendant of *Homo erectus* or some other species (Brown *et al.*, 2004; Morwood *et al.*, 2004; Falk *et al.*, 2005; Falk, 2011).

Taung and LB1 are both associated with detailed endocasts that have implications for the important question of the relative roles of brain size and neurological reorganisation during hominin evolution (Gould, 2001). Whether or not australopithecines were neurologically reorganised in a mosaic fashion that focused on the caudal (posterior) end of the cerebral cortex despite their ape-sized brains has been a subject of intense debate that has focused on the lunate sulcus (LS), which approximates the anterolateral boundary of the primary visual cortex in monkeys and apes (Falk, 1980, 2004a; Holloway *et al.*, 2004) but not humans (Allen *et al.*, 2006). Holloway and I agree that a lunate sulcus cannot be identified on the Taung endocast with certainty, although we continue to have different views about some of the other early hominin endocasts (Holloway *et al.*, 2004; Falk, 2009, 2011):

> The problem with the Taung endocast…is that the LS cannot be unambiguously identified on the endocast, in part because the relevant region is occupied by the lambdoid suture which possibly masks the LS.
>
> (Holloway *et al.*, 2004: 290)

Important research by John Allen and colleagues (2006) show that, for all practical purposes, humans lack lunate sulci. The rare occurrence of sulci in, or near, the occipital lobes of humans that are superficially shaped like lunate sulci of apes are not homologous to ape lunate sulci because they are usually discontinuous beneath the surface and do not approximate the border of primary visual cortex (Allen *et al.*, 2006). As is well known, occasional sulci of humans that appear similar to ape lunate sulci because of their superficial crescent shape are located much more posteriorly (caudally) than is normal for lunate sulci of monkeys or apes. Without clear reproductions of lunate sulci in intermediary locations on endocasts of fossil hominins that bridge australopithecines and extant *Homo*, one can only speculate about whether or not lunate sulci migrated caudally during the course of hominin brain evolution (as Dart and others had assumed) prior to disappearing. Unfortunately, sulci in this part of the brain do not reproduce well on endocasts (Connolly, 1950), which accounts for some of the confusion about the lunate sulcus in the literature.

Meanwhile, the endocast of LB1 offers new insight into the size versus neurological reorganisation question because it suggests that global, rather than mosaic, cortical reorganisation had occurred in at least one hominin species that had a small, ape-sized brain (Falk *et al.*, 2005, 2009b). Thus, LB1's highly convoluted endocast reveals a cerebral cortex with derived features that span the entire surface. Beginning at the back, the cerebellum is underslung beneath the occipital cortex. A small crescent-shaped sulcus appears in a very caudal position on the left occipital lobe, behind the lambdoid suture and medial to the inferior occipital sulcus. Because this sulcus would be identified as the lunate sulcus in modern humans (Connolly, 1950), it has been so identified by Falk *et al.* (2005), although one cannot know if it bordered primary visual cortex or just superficially resembled the shape of an ape lunate sulcus (Allen *et al.*, 2006). Further, no signs of crescent-shaped sulci are found in the primitive (rostral) ape-like location. The temporal lobes of LB1 are extremely wide, which gives the entire endocast a brachycephalic appearance. Enlarged temporal lobes are another derived feature of human compared with ape brains (Semendeferi, 2001; Rilling and Seligman, 2002). Moving to the front end of LB1's endocast, the orbital surface has an expanded shape that appears in the fossil record in *Australopithecus africanus* and (as discussed above) differs from the primitive ape-like shape of *Paranthropus* (Falk *et al.*, 2000). Even more dramatic, LB1 has two large convolutions at the tip of the frontal lobes that represent expansions of Brodman's area 10. As illustrated by the No. 2 endocast from Sterkfontein (Figure 8.1), the trend for an expanded area 10 had begun by the time of *Australopithecus africanus*, although the extent of the expansion did not approach that of LB1. This part of the human prefrontal cortex is differentially enlarged in humans compared with apes and is involved in higher cognitive processes such as the undertaking of initiatives and planning of future activities (Semendeferi *et al.*, 2001, 2002). Significantly, Brodmann's area 10 also seems to be important for internal dialogue (silent thought) and keeping track of responses to external versus internal stimuli (Burgess *et al.*, 2005). In sum, these numerous derived features that are seen in the endocast of LB1 are consistent with the cognitive abilities that have been attributed to *Homo floresiensis* pertaining to hunting, use of fire and tool production (Brown *et al.*, 2004; Morwood *et al.*, 2004).

The endocast of LB1 has important implications for bracketing the parameters of hominin brain evolution (Figure 8.3). Although the RBS of LB1 is ape-like (i = 1), its endocast indicates that *Homo floresiensis* is a relatively recent species that evolved a highly reorganised cerebral cortex despite its small brain size. Figure 8.3 therefore illustrates that brain size *and* neurological reorganisation were both important variables during hominin evolution (Gould, 2001). The lower graph in Figure 8.3 has two variables, cranial capacity (as a surrogate for brain size) on the vertical axis and neurological reorganisation on the horizontal axis. These may be thought of as two vectors that 'tugged' on hominin populations through time. With the addition of LB1, Figure 8.3 defines a much broader space that, potentially, can encompass extensive variation in the relative expressions of brain size and reorganisation in hominins. Who knows what other surprising hominin species are out there, just waiting to be discovered?

Acknowledgements

Many of the ideas in this chapter were discussed at the African Genesis Symposium in honour of the 80th birthday of Professor Phillip V. Tobias and the 80th anniversary of the discovery of Taung, held in Johannesburg, South Africa in January 2006. I have benefited greatly from Professor Tobias's encouragement as well as his seminal work on hominin brain evolution, and have been honoured to collaborate with him on a project involving the Taung endocast. I have also been extremely fortunate to collaborate with Michael Morwood and his colleagues and with my dear colleagues at Mallinckrodt Institute of Radiology on the LB1 endocast, and more recently on investigating endocasts of microcephalics. Some of the research discussed in this chapter has been supported by the National Geographic Society (grants 7769–04, 7897–05). Colette Berbesque is acknowledged for help with the manuscript. Finally, I thank the organisers of the African Genesis Symposium for inviting me to participate.

References

Alemseged, Z., Spoor, F., Kimbel, W. H. *et al.* (2006). A juvenile early hominin skeleton from Dikika, Ethiopia. *Nature*, **443**: 296–301.

Allen, J. S., Bruss, J. and Damasio, H. (2006). Looking for the lunate sulcus: a magnetic resonance imaging study in modern humans. *The Anatomical Record Part A*, **288A**(8): 867–76.

Ashton, E. H. and Spence, T. F. (1958). Age changes in the cranial capacity and foramen magnum of hominoids. *Proceedings of the Zoological Society of London*, **130**: 169–81.

Balter, M. A. and Gibbons, A. (2002). Were 'little people' the first to venture out of Africa? *Science*, **297**: 26–7.

Berger, L. R., de Ruiter, D. J., Churchill, S. E. *et al.* (2010). *Australopithecus sediba*: a new species of *Homo*-like australopith from South Africa. *Science*, **328**: 195–204.

Bromage, T. G. (1985). Taung facial remodeling: a growth and development study in hominid evolution. In Tobias, P. V. (ed.), *Hominid Evolution: Past, Present and Future*. New York: Alan R. Liss, pp. 239–45.

Bromage, T. G. and Dean M. C. (1985). Re-evaluation of the age at death of immature fossil hominids. *Nature*, **317**: 525–7.

Brown, B., Walker, A., Ward, C. V. *et al.* (1993). New *Australopithecus boisei* calvaria from east Lake Turkana. *American Journal of Physical Anthropology*, **91**: 137–59.

Brown, P., Sutikna, T., Morwood, M. J. *et al.* (2004). A new small-bodied hominin from the late Pleistocene of Flores, Indonesia. *Nature*, **431**: 1055–61.

Brunet, M., Beauvilant, A., Coppens, Y. *et al.* (1995). The first australopithecine 2,500 kilometres west of the Rift Valley (Chad). *Nature*, **378**: 273–5.

Burgess, P. W., Simons, J. S., Dumontheil, I. *et al.* (2005). The gateway hypothesis of rostral prefrontal cortex (area 10) function. In Duncan, J., Mcleod, P. and Phillips, L. (eds.), *Measuring the Mind: Speed, Control, and Age.* Oxford: Oxford University Press, pp. 215–46.

Carlson, K. J., Stout, D., Jashashvili, T. *et al.* (2011). The endocast of MH1, *Australopithecus sediba. Science*, **333**: 1402–7.

Clarke, R. J. (2008). Latest information on Sterkfontein's *Australopithecus* skeleton and a new look at *Australopithecus. South African Journal of Science*, **104**: 443–9.

Connolly, C. J. (1950). *External Morphology of the Primate Brain.* Springfield, Illinois: Charles C. Thomas.

Conroy, G. C. and Vannier, M. W. (1985). Endocranial volume determination of matrix-filled fossil skulls using high-resolution computed tomography. In Tobias, P. V. (ed.), *Hominid Evolution: Past, Present and Future.* New York: Alan R. Liss, pp 419–26.

Conroy, G. C., Vannier, M. W. and Tobias, P. V. (1990). Endocranial features of *Australopithecus africanus* revealed by 2- and 3-D computed tomography. *Science*, **247**: 838–41.

Conroy, G. C., Weber, G. W., Seidler, H. *et al.* (1998). Endocranial capacity in an early hominid cranium from Sterkfontein, South Africa. *Science*, **280**: 1730–1.

Dart, R. A. (1925). *Australopithecus africanus*: the man-ape of South Africa. *Nature*, **2884**: 195–9.

de Ruiter, D. J., Steininger, C. M. and Berger, L. R. (2006). A cranial base of *Australopithecus robustus* from the hanging remnant of Swartkrans, South Africa. *American Journal of Physical Anthropology*, **130**: 435–44.

Falk, D. (1980). A reanalysis of the South African australopithecine natural endocasts. *American Journal of Physical Anthropology*, **53**: 525–39.

(1985). Hadar AL 162–28 endocast as evidence that brain enlargement preceded cortical reorganization in hominid evolution. *Nature*, **313**: 45–7.

(1987). Hominid paleoneurology. *Annual Review of Physical Anthropology*, **16**: 13–30.

(1998). Hominid brain evolution: looks can be deceiving. *Science*, **280**: 1714.

(2004a). *Braindance* (revised and expanded edition). Gainesville: University Press of Florida.

(2004b). Hominin brain evolution: new century, new directions. *Collegium Antropologicum*, **28**: 59–64.

(2007). Evolution of the primate brain. In Henke, W., Rothe, H. and Tattersall, I. (eds.), *Handbook of Palaeoanthropology. Volume 2: Primate Evolution and Human Origin.* Heidelberg: Springer-Verlag.

(2009). The natural endocast of Taung (*Australopithecus africanus*): insights from the unpublished papers of Raymond Arthur Dart. *Yearbook of Physical Anthropology*, **52**: 49–65.

(2011). *The Fossil Chronicles: How Two Controversial Discoveries Changed our View of Human Evolution.* University of California Press.

Falk, D. and Clarke, R. (2007). Brief communication: new reconstruction of the Taung endocast. *American Journal of Physical Anthropology*, **134**: 529–34.

Falk, D., Gage, T., Dudek, B. *et al.* (1995). Did more than one species of hominid coexist before 3.0 Myr? Evidence from blood and teeth. *Journal of Human Evolution*, **29**: 591–600.

Falk, D., Redmond Jr., J. C., Guyer, J. *et al.* (2000). Early hominid brain evolution: a new look at old endocasts. *Journal of Human Evolution*, **38**: 695–717.

Falk, D., Hildebolt, C., Smith, K. *et al.* (2005). The brain of 'Hobbit' (LB1, *Homo floresiensis*). *Science*, **308**: 242–5.

   (2007). Brain shape in human microcephalics and *Homo floresiensis*. *Proceedings of the National Academy of Sciences of the USA*, **104**: 2513–18.

   (2009a). The type specimen (LB1) of *Homo floresiensis* did not have Laron syndrome. *American Journal of Physical Anthropology*, **140**: 52–63.

   (2009b). LB1's virtual endocast, microcephaly, and hominin brain evolution. *Journal of Human Evolution*, **57**: 597–607.

   (2010). Nonpathological asymmetry in LB1 (*Homo floresiensis*): a reply to Eckhardt and Henneberg. *American Journal of Physical Anthropology*, **143**: 340–2.

Findlay, G. H. (1972). *Dr Robert Broom, F.R.S. Palaeontologist and Physician 1866– 1951*. Cape Town: A. A. Balkema.

Gabunia, L., Vekua, A., Lordkipanidze, D. *et al.* (2000). Earliest Pleistocene hominid cranial remains from Dmanisi, Republic of Georgia: taxonomy, geological setting, and age. *Science*, **288**: 1019–25.

Gould, S. J. (2001). Size matters and function counts. In Falk, D. and Gibson, K. R. (eds.), *Evolutionary Anatomy of the Primate Cerebral Cortex*. Cambridge: Cambridge University Press, pp. xiii–xvii.

Hofman, M. A. (1983). Encephalization in hominids: evidence for the model of punctuationalism. *Brain Behavior and Evolution*, **22**: 102–17.

   (2001). Brain evolution in hominids: are we at the end of the road? In Falk, D. and Gibson, K. R. (eds.), *Evolutionary Anatomy of the Primate Cerebral Cortex*. Cambridge: Cambridge University Press, pp. 113–27.

Holloway, R. L. (1970). Australopithecine endocast (Taung specimen, 1924): a new volume determination. *Science*, **168**: 966–8.

Holloway, R. L., Broadfield, D. C. and Yuan, M. S. (2004). *The Human Fossil Record. Volume Three. Brain Endocasts the Paleoneurological Evidence*. New York: Wiley-Liss.

Holloway, R. L., Clarke, R. J. and Tobias, P. V. (2004). Posterior lunate sulcus in *Australopithecus africanus*: was Dart right? *Comptes Rendus Palevol*, **3**: 287–93.

Keith, A. (1931). *New Discoveries Relating to the Antiquity of Man*. New York: W. W. Norton and Company.

Lee, S.-H. and Wolpoff, M. (2003). The pattern of evolution in Pleistocene human brain size. *Paleobiology*, **29**: 186–96.

Leigh, S. R. (1992). Cranial capacity evolution in *Homo erectus* and early *Homo sapiens*. *American Journal of Physical Anthropology*, **87**: 1–13.

Morwood, M. J., Soejono, R. P., Roberts, R. G. *et al.* (2004). Archaeology and age of a new hominin from Flores in eastern Indonesia. *Nature*, **431**: 1087–91.

Passingham, R. E. (1975). Changes in the size and organization of the brain in man and his ancestors. *Brain Behavior and Evolution*, **11**: 73–90.

Preuss, T. M. (2001). The discovery of cerebral diversity: an unwelcome scientific revolution. In Falk, D. and Gibson, K. R. (eds.), *Evolutionary Anatomy of the Primate Cerebral Cortex*. Cambridge: Cambridge University Press, pp. 138–64.

Radinsky, L. B. (1972). Endocasts and studies of primate brain evolution. In Tuttle, R. (ed.), *The Functional and Evolutionary Biology of Primates*. Chicago: Aldine, pp. 175–84.

Rilling, J. K. and Seligman, R. A. (2002). A quantitative morphometric comparative analysis of the primate temporal lobe. *Journal of Human Evolution*, **42**: 505–33.

Semendeferi, K. (1994). Evolution of the hominoid prefrontal cortex: a quantitative and image analysis of area 13 and 10. Unpublished PhD dissertation, Department of Anthropology, Iowa City University of Iowa.

  (2001). Advances in the study of hominoid rain evolution: magnetic resonance imaging (MRI) and 3-D reconstruction. In Falk, D. and Gibson, K. R. (eds.), *Evolutionary Anatomy of the Primate Cerebral Cortex*. Cambridge: Cambridge University Press, pp. 257–89.

Semendeferi, K., Armstrong, E., Schleicher, A. *et al.* (2001). Prefrontal cortex in humans and apes: a comparative study of Area 10. *American Journal of Physical Anthropology*, **114**: 224–41.

Semendeferi, K., Lu, A., Schenker, N. *et al.* (2002). Humans and great apes share a large frontal cortex. *Nature Neuroscience*, **5**: 272–6.

Semendeferi, K., Teffer, K., Buxhoeveden, D. P. *et al.* (2011). Spatial organization of neurons in the frontal pole sets humans apart from great apes. *Cerebral Cortex*, **21**: 1485–97.

Smith, B. H. (1986). Dental development in *Australopithecus* and early *Homo*. *Nature*, **323**: 327–30.

Spoor, F., Jeffery, N. and Zonneveld, F. (2000). Using diagnostic radiology in human evolutionary studies. *Journal of Anatomy*, **197**: 61–76.

Spoor, F., Leakey, M. G., Gathogo, P. N. *et al.* (2007). Implications of new early *Homo* fossils from Ileret, east of Lake Turkana, Kenya. *Nature*, **448**: 688–91.

Swisher III, C. C., Curtis, G. H., Jacob, T. *et al.* (1994). Age of the earliest known hominids in Java, Indonesia. *Science*, **263**: 1118–21.

Tobias, P. V. and Falk, D. (1988). Evidence for a dual pattern of cranial venous sinuses on the endocranial cast of Taung (*Australopithecus africanus*). *American Journal of Physical Anthropology*, **76**: 309–12.

Vekua, A., Lordkipanidze, D., Rightmire, G. P. *et al.* (2002). A new skull of early *Homo* from Dmanisi, Georgia. *Science*, **297**: 85–9.

Walker, A. and Leakey, R. (1993). *The Nariokotome* Homo erectus *Skeleton*. Cambridge: Harvard University Press.

Walker, A. C., Leakey, R. E., Harris, J. M. *et al.* (1986). 2.5-myr *Australopithecus boisei* from west of Lake Turkana, Kenya. *Nature*, **322**: 517–22.

Washburn, S. L. (1985). Human evolution after Raymond Dart. In Tobias, P. V. (ed.), *Hominid Evolution Past, Present and Future*. New York: Alan R. Liss, pp. 3–18.

Weidenreich, F. (1943). The skull of *Sinanthropus pekinensis*: a comparative study on a primitive hominid skull. *Paleontologia Sinica*, new series D, **10**: 1–485.

Wood, B. and Collard, M. (1999). The human genus. *Science*, **284**: 65–71.

Wu, X., Schepartz, L. A., Falk, D. and Liu, W. (2005). Endocranial cast of Hexian *Homo erectus* from South China. *American Journal of Physical Anthropology*, **130**: 445–54.

Zollikoffer, C. P. E., Ponce de León, M. S., Martin, R. D. *et al.* (1995). Neanderthal computer skulls. *Nature*, **375**: 283–5.

9 The issue of brain reorganisation in Australopithecus and early hominids: Dart had it right

RALPH L. HOLLOWAY

Abstract

In commemoration of P. V. Tobias's 80th birthday, and the 80th year since Dart published his paper on Taung, newer studies on chimpanzee brains and newer fossil discoveries (e.g. Hadar 162–28, StW 505) make it appropriate to re-assess Dart's original contribution. The matter of where to place the lunate sulcus has been a controversial issue, but the contrast between the Taung child's endocast morphology, and that of pongids, particularly the chimpanzee, as well as the clear-cut lunate sulcus in a posterior position of StW 505 indicate that Dart was indeed right, and that the brain of australopithecines was reorganised prior to any size increase in endocranial volume. This reorganisation involved a relative increase in posterior parietal association cortex, the flip-side, as it were, of a relative reduction in primary visual striate cortex. It is most probable that the changes in cerebral organisation were an adaptive response to changing and expanding ecological opportunities for these early hominids. The latter development of any major size increase of the whole brain had to await the evolution of *Homo* lineages. Clearly, from at least three million years ago, the evolution of the hominid brain has been a mosaic process of both size increases, allometric and non-allometric, as well as critical reorganisational changes, of which the posterior placement of the lunate sulcus is proof of that change, which Dart had already appreciated in 1924–5.

Introduction

If one examines most of the textbooks on physical anthropology, human evolution or biological anthropology, one often only finds a very short chapter

African Genesis: Perspectives on Hominin Evolution, eds. Sally C. Reynolds and Andrew Gallagher. Published by Cambridge University Press. © Cambridge University Press 2012.

163

on a topic of central importance to understanding our own species' evolution. Indeed, aside from the increase of size from roughly 400 ml to about 1400 ml, one will find little in the way of descriptions of how the organisation of the brain changed through time, or what evolutionary selection pressures might have accounted for the obvious mosaic of intercalated size and organisational changes. The basic fact is that most that is written about hominid brain evolution is almost completely speculative, and one of the major reasons for this is that paleoneurology is often ignored and, unfortunately, for a legitimate reason: the data it provides, aside from endocranial volumes, is meagre.

Three areas of research are essential if we wish to have a fuller understanding of how our brain evolved: (1) the study of paleoneurology provides the only direct evidence for this evolution, as it is based on a data-poor recovery from endocast surface details and accompanying volume estimates; (2) the study of comparative neuroanatomy provides the data-rich understanding of how neural variation relates to behavioural variability both within and between different animal species. An essential weakness of this approach is seldom appreciated, which is that comparative neurology uses currently extant animal species for its study, and these are not an evolutionary sequence (but see the excellent reviews by Tiller Edinger, 1949). One still sees the usual sequence of rat–macaque–chimpanzee–human comparisons of neural structures, as if any of these animals (except human) were an evolutionary sequence. A third area, molecular neurogenomics, is beginning to emerge, which in time promises to identify those genes and genetic and epigenetic interactions that have been under selective pressures during the past, and further, to hopefully identify how these genes and their 'evo-devo' expression relate to behaviour, for as important as 'constraints' might be (Finlay *et al.*, 2001), it remains a fact that it is the departures from the constraints that will best define a species' behavioural evolutionary adaptations (Holloway, 2001).

The issues of reorganisation have come a long way since the days of Jerison's (1973) dismissal of the concept as 'misplaced' (p. 81; see Holloway, 1967, 1974, 1979, 2003; Holloway *et al.*, 2004b; Rilling 2006; Broadfield *et al.*, 2010, and papers therein for comments regarding reorganisation, species-specific behaviour, and instances of reorganisation of hominid brains from the evidence of paleoneurology). Species-specific patterns of behaviour cannot be understood in any evolutionary context without also understanding the species-specific changes that have taken place in the nervous systems of all species. In *that* sense, perhaps, 'reorganisation' might be regarded as 'trivial' (Jerison, 1973), but surely when we wish to understand hominid evolution in particular (or any other animal lineage) endocranial volume is a necessary part of the picture; but ignoring reorganisation involving enlargements of and decreases in volume of various cortical lobes, the progressive increase in cerebral asymmetries, including Broca's caps, then speculations based entirely on brain mass are not viable explanations for the complexity that was involved in human brain evolution.

The goal of the remainder of this chapter is to show some specific examples of hominid brain reorganisation based on newer paleoneurological evidence. To do so, however, requires a return to the contentious area of the Taung child's endocast, and the issue of the now infamous lunate sulcus.

The lunate sulcus and yet another look at Taung

The lunate sulcus is usually a crescentic-shaped sulcus, with a concave-posterior orientation, that most frequently defines the anterior extent of primary visual cortex (PVC), or what has been known traditionally as Brodmann's area 17, or visual striate cortex, also referred to as V1. As Allen *et al.* (2006) show, it is often present in modern humans, but in a fragmented condition, rarely whole, as in apes and monkeys. We know from applying residual analysis to Stephan and colleagues (1981) data that the human volume of PVC falls some 121% below the expected value of PVC if the human brain were allometrically scaled as in other primates (see Figure 9.1). The history of this feature was described in Holloway (1985), particularly in relationship to Dart's belief that he saw an un-pongid like anterior position for this sulcus in the Taung child's natural endocast, which he published in 1925, 1926 and made explicit reference to again in 1956, particularly regarding the concept of reorganisation, and in his book (1967). Keith (1931) and, much later, Falk (1980) tried to show positions for the lunate sulcus in Taung that suggested a more anthropoid-like morphology. Indeed, Falk's 'dimple' was so far anterior as to place Taung within the *Cercopithecoidea*, although she did not explicitly suggest this taxonomic designation. Assuming that *Pan* (either *troglodytes, paniscus,* or *Gorilla)* and hominids split between 5 to 7 million years ago (Ma), and that Taung would be most close to *Pan*, I tried to show that when the coordinates of the lunate sulcus (stereoplotting, Holloway 1981, 1988), were compared with chimpanzees (as in Figure 9.2), or when a large sample of chimpanzees were measured for the metrical distances of arcs and chords from the occipital pole to either the dorsal or lateral margin the of lunate sulcus, that this distance was almost three standard deviations (s.d.) greater than the distance of the putative lunate sulcus on Taung, or the evident lunate sulcus (by Falk's 1983 own declaration see Figures 9.3 and 9.4) on the *A. afarensis* 162–28 endocast (Figure 9.5a, Holloway *et al.*, 2003). In 1985, I pointed out that Dart had, after all, taken his degree under G. E. Smith, the person most responsible for defining and delineating the lunate sulcus in primates and humans, and that Dart wrote a dissertation on the evolution

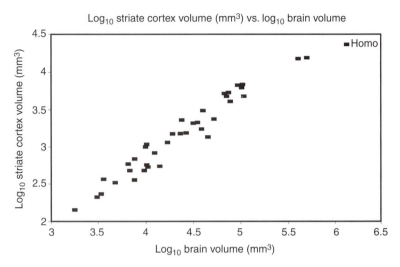

Figure 9.1. A log-log plot of volume of primary visual cortex against brain volume. The point for *Homo* in upper right-hand part of graph is 121% less than expected. Data are from Stephan *et al.* (1981).

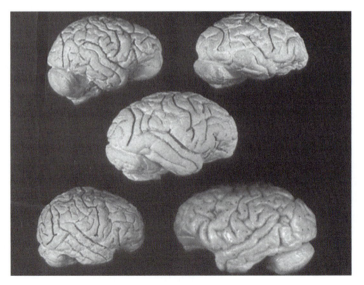

Figure 9.2. A sample of five chimpanzee (*Pan troglodytes*) brain casts, with the lunate sulcus strongly marked, showing the anterior position of this sulcus as it normally appears in all apes.

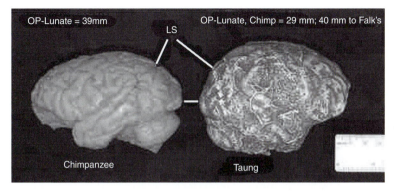

Figure 9.3. A lateral view of a chimpanzee brain cast (right) and the Taung australopithecine endocast. The white dots on the Taung endocast indicate where the lunate sulcus would be found *if* the lunate sulcus were in a typical pongid (chimpanzee) position. LS: lunate sulcus; OP: occipital pole. The line anterior to the dots is where Falk (1980) placed the LS.

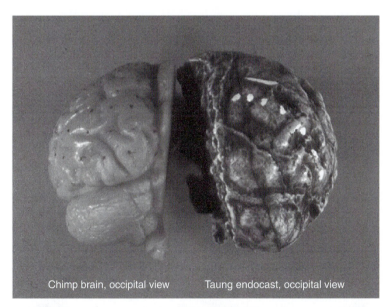

Figure 9.4. An occipital view of chimpanzee and the Taung endocast. Note how the chimpanzee LS placement violates the sulcal and gyral morphology on the Taung endocast.

of the turtle brain, giving him some reason to claim some expertise on brain evolution. Indeed, as I showed several times, placing a chimpanzee-like position of the lunate sulcus on the Taung natural endocast simply violated the available convolutional morphology on that endocast. The anterior position suggested by Falk, and by Keith earlier, would resemble the position of the lunate sulcus on a macaque or baboon, and certainly not a hominid, recently split from a pongid line. As we know, the Taung endocast shows a strong lambdoid suture in the region that Dart believed a lunate sulcus existed. The suggestion that Dart actually confused the lunate sulcus with the lambdoid suture is simply poppycock.

Let Dart speak for himself here:

> I must emphasize here the particular reason for my excitement. The most impressive feature of this endocast…was the marked distance separating the two well-defined furrows at the back of its outer surface.

And:

> In the Taung's cast, so much of this expansion had occurred between the lunate and parallel [superior temporal] sulci that they were separated by a distance *three times as great* as in any existing endocast of a living ape's skull.

(Dart, 1967: 6)

Part of the problem, of course, is that the illustrations for the Taung endocast only show two-dimensional aspects of the lateral and occipital views. If the Taung endocast is held so one sights along an axis following the lambdoid suture, one can clearly see a groove or depression in that region that could be the lunate sulcus and I here emphasise the word 'could'.

The recent uncovering of Dart's archived correspondence by Falk (2009, 2011) is quite valuable and interesting, but whether or not Smith actually agreed with Dart on his placement of a lunate sulcus is unclear, and basically irrelevant, unless Smith independently studied this issue in detail, and even then is as much subject to error as Dart, Falk and myself! The bottom line here, however, is that Falk (2009, 2011) simply does not agree that Dart had it right (a sort of reverse *ad verecundiam*). It is doubtful that the Taung lunate sulcus question will ever be resolved, given that both of our respective arguments lack clear-cut evidence of a completely visible lunate sulcus. Falk (2011) now questions whether there was any 'mosaic' brain evolution. Let us then move on to other australopithecines.

Back to Hadar and the AL 162–28 endocast

The Hadar *A. afarensis* 162–28 parietal and occipital fragments, completely undistorted show cortical morphology that we (Holloway, 1983; Holloway and Kimbel, 1986) interpreted as a possible posterior position for a lunate sulcus.

This was done on the basis of a posterior placement of the interparietal sulcus, the posterior end of which usually abuts the lunate sulcus in most anthropoids, and this is certainly so in chimpanzee and gorilla. We were circumspect in interpreting the obvious depression just anterior to the lambdoidal sutural fragment as a true lunate, but Falk did so interpret that depression as a lunate. From the more than 100 chimpanzee, gorilla and bonobo endocasts from my collection of endocasts, it is very often the case that one finds a depression just anterior to the lambdoid suture, which represents a depression caused by the posterior inferior lip of the parietal bone. This has been known since Clark *et al.*'s (1936) paper. If indeed it is the lunate sulcus as Falk (1983) suggested, then the distance from occipital pole to lambdoid suture remnant (i.e. lunate sulcus, or posterior end of interparietal sulcus) on the AL 162–28 endocast measures about 15 mm, about half of the distance that one normally finds on chimpanzee

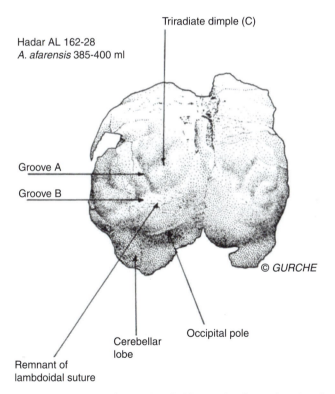

Figure 9.5a. Diagram of the Hadar 162–28 *Australopithecus afarensis* endocast, adapted from Holloway 1983, in *Nature*, and drawn by J. Gurche. Most importantly, the distance from the occipital pole to the posterior end of IP (interparietal sulcus) is about 15.5 mm, or roughly half of what the distance would be on a chimpanzee endocast of roughly the same volume, i.e. 385 to 400 ml.

brains of similar brain volume, e.g. 385 to 400 ml. This clearly suggests a diminution of PVC in *A. afarensis*, some 3 Ma ago, and perhaps thus even earlier than Taung. We are not talking about simply one chimpanzee brain here, but a large sample of some 78 hemispheres (Holloway *et al.*, 2001a,b, 2003), and in which the distance from occipital pole (OP) to the most lateral edge of the lunate sulcus averages between 30 and 40 mm. In essence, a reduced volume of PVC would be a derived character state, and even an autapomorphy, as it appears unique to the hominid lineage right up to modern *Homo sapiens*.

SK 1585 natural endocast from Swartkrans

Another robust australopithecine specimen, SK 1585, from Swartkrans, has a well preserved natural endocast of the right side, and part of the left occipital, which I described (Figure 9.5b; Holloway, 1972). Upon re-examining this endocast, I am convinced that a good case can be made for a posteriorly placed lunate sulcus on the both right and left occipital lobes, particularly in the inferior-medial aspect, well separated from any lambdoidal sutural complication, as is the case with the Taung specimen. I described the possible lunate this way:

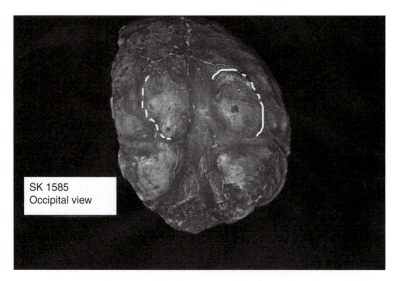

SK 1585
Occipital view

Figure 9.5b. Occipital view of the cast of SK 1585, showing smallish occipital lobes, and in particular both right and left medial outlines just inferior to the lambdoid suture show a highly probable lunate sulcus in a posterior position. These are shown in white lines, broken under the lambdoid suture, continuous elsewhere.

The occipital lobes, posterior to the lambdoid suture, are 'puckered' and asymmetrical...The gyral configuration immediately anterior to the lambdoid suture does not provide an unequivocal lunate sulcus...The constriction caused by the lambdoid suture probably occurs over the lunate sulcus, for anterior there is no indication of a sulcus which could be interpreted as a lunate. Indeed the gyri anterior to the suture all appear to bend and retroflex somewhat anterior to the suture, and immediately behind the suture in the upper portion of the occipital lobe is a small lipping, the most superior ridge of which may represent the lunate.

(Holloway, 1972:176–7)

Lucy, or the AL 288–1 occipital fragment

An extremely faint depression can be seen on the endocranial surface of the right occipital lobe, just in the vicinity of the lambdoid suture, but the depression is towards the mid sagittal plane. Consequently, while a lunate sulcus could have been present in 'Lucy', it cannot be demonstrated unequivocally.

The smoking gun is StW 505

I refer the interested reader to our 2004 paper in *Comptes Rendus, Palvol* 3, (Holloway *et al.*, 2004a), which provides a detailed description and illustrated

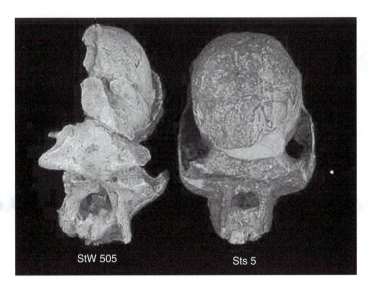

Figure 9.6. Dorsal views of both the new StW 505 cranium, and that of 'Mrs. Ples', Sts 5.

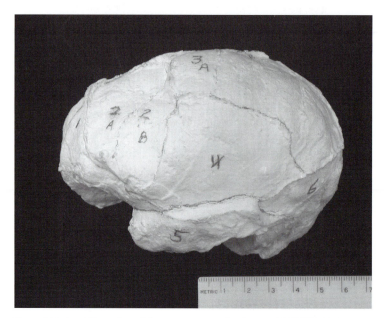

Figure 9.7. An oblique view of the unreconstructed endocast of StW 505. Each
number (1 to 6) is a region that is either somewhat distorted or misaligned with
neighbouring areas.

view of the StW 505 endocast, kindly provided to this author by Ronald J.
Clarke. This cranium was described most fully (Lockwood and Tobias, 1999) as
discussed earlier (Conroy *et al*., 1998; Hawks and Wolpoff, 1999; Figure 9.6).
As far as this author can tell, these discussions only dealt with the problematic
issue of endocranial volume, and no mention was ever made of the fact that
StW 505 showed a singularly strong crescentic sulcus, concave posterior, in
exactly the region where a more human-like lunate sulcus would be expected
to occur. The currently calculated volume of 515 ml (Hawks and Wolpoff,
1999) is clearly too small, and does not correct for the distortions and shifts of
cranial bony elements in the cranium, which also has some plastic deformation
(see Figure 9.7.) Fortunately, the frontal midline was not distorted, thus permitting reconstruction of a midsagittal plane, and thence a reconstruction with
plasticine of the missing posterior portion medial to where the lunate sulcus
appears (Figure 9.8) The distance from the lateral edge of the LS to the midline
is about 25 to 30 mm, but the distance to that midsagittal plane to an occipital
pole would be roughly 10 mm less, thus placing the lateral displacement of
the lunate sulcus outside of the chimpanzee range (see Figure 9.9a,b). Indeed,
the ratio between hemisphere volume and lateral lunate sulcus is about 0.5 to
0.6 for chimpanzee, and an estimated distance for the lunate sulcus, if StW

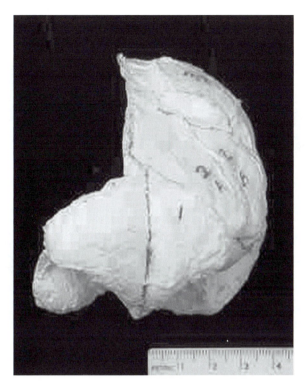

Figure 9.8. A frontal view of the endocast showing that there are undistorted frontal and prefrontal regions, which help in reconstructing a midsagittal plane.

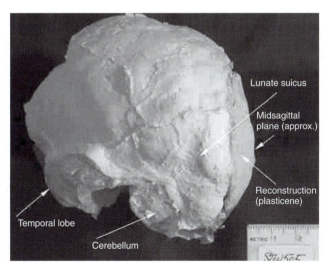

Figure 9.9a. An oblique view of the reconstructed StW 505 endocast, showing the presence of the crescentic concave-posterior lunate sulcus in sharp relief.

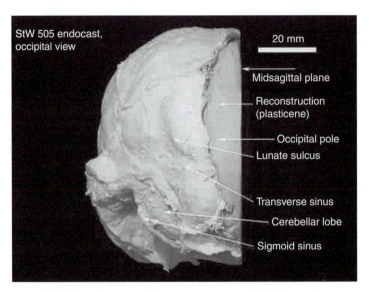

StW 505 endocast,
occipital view

20 mm

Midsagittal plane

Reconstruction
(plasticene)

Occipital pole
Lunate sulcus

Transverse sinus

Cerebellar lobe

Sigmoid sinus

Figure 9.9b. An occipital view of the reconstructed StW 505 endocast. It is important to note that the distance from where the occipital pole would be and the midsagittal plane is only about 10 mm, the OP–LS distance is only 10 to 15 mm.

505 were following a chimpanzee LS organisation would be closer to 45 to 50 mm. Indeed, I believe the endocranial volume of StW 505 is most likely to be slightly above 575 ml, thus again underlining the relatively posterior position of the lunate sulcus, and its departure from a *Pan*-like more anterior location. In our 2004 paper, we said:

> No other sulcus normally found in the occipital lobe, including the lateral calcarine, inferior and lateral occipital sulci, matches the position or strong crescentic concavity of this sulcus on the StW 505 brain endocast, either in chimpanzee or *Homo*.
>
> (Holloway *et al.*, 2004a: 290)

To date, we have not seen any attempt to refute this observation or the measurements supporting our conclusion, Falk's (2009) recent descriptions and assertions notwithstanding.

We concluded in our 2004 paper the following:

> The StW 505 specimen indicates that at least this early hominid brain was indeed reorganized toward a more human-like pattern despite its small brain volume, and prior to any significant cortical enlargement as seen in the genus Homo. In sum, this endocast strongly suggests that cortical reorganization preceded brain enlargement in hominid evolution as argued elsewhere…We repeat, that in brains with strongly developed lunate sulci, the sulci are the anterior limit to PVC. We have not found evidence that this finding is violated in either humans or apes…
>
> (Holloway *et al.*, 2004a: 290)

In fact, we may have to temper this last sentence somewhat as Allen *et al.* (2006) have convincingly shown that in modern humans, the lunate is most often fragmented, and PVC is not always delimited by the fragments, although it is agreed that the primary visual cortex is diminished in *Homo* compared to *Pan*, relative to cortical size.

Why is the lunate sulcus important to hominid brain evolution?

A relative reduction in PVC also means that something else is relatively expanded, and that something else was whatever was adjacent to PVC, which in Brodmann's terms, would be para- and peri-striate cortex, areas 18 and 19 respectively, and part of the posterior parietal lobe, suggesting, of course, some expanded degree of cognitive abilities. It would prove that by australopithecine times (at least for *A. afarensis* and *A. africanus,* and perhaps *A. robustus*, as per SK 1585) the cerebral cortex had already undergone some reorganisation, where natural selection most probably favoured cognitive behaviours that were advanced beyond those known for chimpanzees in an expanded ecological niche, and this occurring prior to any significant brain enlargement as found in the *Homo* hominids.

We put it this way in 2004:

> RLH has speculated that reorganization of the *Australopithecus* brain indicates an expanded posterior cerebral cortex, and was most likely associated with enhanced social behavior including communication: (1) this region involves multimodal processing involving visual, auditory, and sensorimotor integration; (2) visuospatial integration related to tool use and making, throwing objects with force and accuracy, as well as more sophisticated longer-term memory of spatial locations and qualities of self, others (i.e., facial recognition), prey and predators, including objects and resources (stone, digging sticks, trees, waterholes, etc.). All of these were possibly adding to a more advanced cognitive adaptation within a changing and expanding ecological zone, and formed the basis for additional cognitive changes, such as patterned toolmaking, and possibly more advanced communicative skills that accompanied the evolution of the genus *Homo*.
>
> (Holloway *et al.*, 2004a: 292)

It is also important, in my humble opinion, because it vindicates Dart's prescient discovery some 80-plus years ago, and eliminates older arguments that first the brain had to expand before it underwent reorganisation (see Falk, 1983; Holloway *et al.*, 2003). In addition, it demonstrates (or at least I hope) that palaeoneurology, while difficult to interpret and prone to controversy, can offer some important glimpses into the complexities of hominid brain evolution, which clearly involved more than brain enlargement, whether allometric or not. This evidence clearly shows that reorganisation and brain enlargement were intercalated affairs in hominid brain evolution, a true mosaic that comparative neurology cannot fully address, and for which

Table 9.1. *A chart showing the regions of the cerebral cortex that are relevant to looking for reorganisation of the hominid brain (after Holloway et al., 2004a).*

Major cortical regions in early hominid evolution

Cortical regions	Brodmann's areas	Functions
primary visual striate cortex	17	primary visual
posterior parietal and anterior occipital	18, 19	secondary and tertiary visual
(peri- and parastriate cortex)		integration with area 17
posterior parietal, superior lobule	5, 7	secondary somatosensory
posterior parietal, inferior lobule (mostly right side. Left side processes symbolic–analytical)	39	angular gyrus perception of spatial relations among objects, face recognition
posterior parietal, inferior lobule (mostly right side. See above)	40	supramarginal gyrus spatial ability
posterior superior temporal cortex	22	Wernicke's area, posterior superior temporal gyrus. Comprehension of language.
posterior inferior temporal	37	polymodal integration, visual, auditory. Perception and memory of objects' qualities.
lateral prefrontal cortex	44, 45, 47	Broca's area (Broca's cap) motor control of vocalisation, language
	(also 8, 9, 10, 13, 46)	complex cognitive functioning memory, inhibiton of impulse, foresight, etc.

palaeoneurology must play a primary role, although it would appear that Falk (2009, 2011) would not agree. Indeed, Falk now claims that the Taung endocast shows reorganisation in parietal, temporal and frontal lobes (in agreement with Dart, a truly *ad verecundiam* argument), which she believes invalidates any 'mosaic' brain evolution concept in early hominid evolution, but she does not offer a single quantitative fact to substantiate such a claim. Even if demonstrated, such changes would be prior to any major brain size enlargement as I have argued above.

Of course, the cerebral cortex includes much more than the occipital and parietal lobes. Other reorganisational changes included enlargement of the prefrontal lobe and the formation of human-like Broca's regions (areas 44, 45 and 47) so important to the motor aspects of language in *Homo sapiens*, and the development of hemispheric specialisations into analytic and gestalt-style reasoning, as well as handedness. These developments, however, are not unequivocally present in any of the australopithecine endocasts

Table 9.2. *Chart showing the two basic reorganisational changes (lunate sulcus, and Broca's regions) in the fossil record (after Holloway* et al.*, 2004a).*

Reorganisational changes in the evolution of the human brain

Brain changes (reorganisation)	Taxa	Time (Ma ago)	Evidence
(1) Reduction of primary visual striate cortex, area 17, and relative increase in posterior parietal cortex	*A. afarensis* *A. africanus*	3.5 to 3.0 3.0 to 2.0	AL 162–28 endocast Taung child, StW 505 endocast SK 1585 endocast
(2) Reorganisation of frontal lobe (third inferior frontal convolution, Broca's area, widening prefrontal)	*Homo rudolphensis* *H. habilis, H. erectus*	2.0 to 1.8	KNM-ER 1470 endocast Indonesian endocasts
(3) Cerebral asymmetries, left-occipital, right-frontal petalias	*Homo rudolphensis* *H. habilis, H. erectus*	2.0 to 1.8	KNM-ER 1470 endocast Indonesian endocasts
(4) Refinements in cortical organisation to a modern *Homo* pattern	*? Homo erectus* to Present?	1.5 to 0.1	*Homo* endocasts (*erectus, neanderthalensis, sapiens*)

thus far discovered, but must await the evolution of *Homo* lineages, and that is at present best shown by the KNM-ER 1470 endocast of *Homo rudolfensis*, as the endocasts of OH 7, OH 13, OH 16 and OH 24 are either lacking frontal portions, both sides or, as in OH 24, have unfortunate distortion and lack of true anatomical detail in the frontal lobes. Hopefully, the newer discoveries of *Homo georgicus* may shed light on these and other possible changes that occurred during early *Homo* evolution (see Grimaud-Herve and Lordikipanidze, 2010), where it would appear that clear-cut asymmetries cannot be fully assessed, except for D2280). Tables 9.1, 9.2 and 9.3 reflect my view as to how brain size and reorganisation were part of the 'mosaic' evolution of the hominin brain.

Of course, palaeoneurology is but one window where one can hope to observe how the human brain evolved over the last 4 to 5 million years, and the lunate sulcus is but one morphological component that may shed some light on how the hominin brain changed through time. Absolute and relative brain size changes through time, maturation schedules, behavioural repertoires wrested from the archaeological record, insights from comparative neurology of structure/function relationships and, increasingly, neurogenomics are also important ingredients in the making of the bouillabaisse that we call hominin brain

Table 9.3. *Chart summarising the possible allometric and non-allometric changes that have accompanied hominid brain evolution, and which have been integrated with reorganisational changes (Table 9.2). (After Holloway et al., 2004a).*

Summary of size changes in human brain evolution

Brain changes (brain-size related)	Taxa	Time (Ma)	Evidence
(1) Small increase, allometric[a]	*A. afarensis to A. africanus*	3.0 to 2.5	Brain size increases from 400 ml to 450 ml, 500+ ml
(2) Major increase, rapid, both allometric and non-allometric	*A.africanus to Homo habilis*	2.5 to 1.8	KNM-1470, 752 ml (*c.* 300 ml)
(3) Small allometric increase in brain size to 800 ml to 1000 ml (assumes habilis was KNM 1470-like)	*Homo habilis to Homo erectus*	1.8 to 0.5	*Homo erectus* brain endocasts and postcranial bones, e.g. KNM-ER 17000
(4) Gradual and modest size increase to archaic *Homo sapiens* mostly non-allometric	*Homo erectus to Homo sapiens, Homo neanderthalensis*	0.5 to 0.10	Archaic *Homo* and Neandertal endocasts 1200 to 1700+ ml
(5) Small reduction in brain size among modern *Homo sapiens*, which was allometric	*Homo sapiens*	0.015 to present	modern endocranial capacities

[a] Allometric means related to body size increase or decrease, while non-allometric refers to brain size increase without a concomitant body-size increase.

evolution, but heavily dependent on sampling, and completeness of specimens. Hopefully, with more discoveries, and a better understanding of the roles of organisation and size (see papers in Broadfield *et al.*, 2010), we will find more to argue about than the lunate sulcus!

Acknowledgements

My sincerest appreciation to the organisers of this Conference, for the hospitality and for their patience in bringing its contents to publication. I am grateful to all my colleagues who have made the discoveries, allowed me access to study these precious fossils and have contributed to my understanding of human evolution.

References

Allen, J. S., Bruss, J. and Damasio, H. (2006). Looking for the lunate sulcus: a magnetic resonance imaging study in modern humans. *Anatomical Record A*, **288**: 867–76.

Broadfield, D. C., Yuan, M., Schick, K. *et al.* (eds.) (2010). *The Human Brain Evolving: Paleoneurological Studies in Honor of Ralph L. Holloway.* Stone Age Institute Publication Series #4. Indiana: Stone Age Institute Press.

Conroy, G. C., Weber, G., Seidler, H. *et al.* (1998). Endocranial capacity in an early hominid cranium from Sterkfontein, South Africa. *Science*, **280**:1730–1.

Dart, R. A. (1925). *Australopithecus africanus*: the man-ape of South Africa. *Nature*, **115**: 195–9.

(1926). Taungs and its significance. *Natural History*, **26**: 315–27.

(1956). The relationship of brain size and brain pattern to human status. *South African Journal of Medical Science*, **21**: 23–45.

(1967). *Adventures with the Missing Link*. Philadelphia: The Institute Press.

Edinger, T. (1949). Paleoneurology versus comparative brain anatomy. *Confina Neurologica Separatum*, **9**: 5–24.

Falk, D. (1980). A reanalysis of South African Australopithecine natural endocasts. *American Journal of Physical Anthropology*, **53**: 525–39.

(1983). Hadar AL 162–28 endocast as evidence that brain enlargement preceded cortical reorganization in hominid evolution. *Nature*, **313**: 45–7.

(1985). Apples, oranges, and the lunate sulcus. *American Journal of Physical Anthropology*, **67**: 313–15.

(2009). The natural endocast of Taung (*Australopithecus africanus*): insights from the unpublished papers of Raymond Arthur Dart. *Yearbook of Physical Anthropology*, **52**: 49–65.

(2011). *The Fossil Chronicles: How Two Controversial Discoveries Changed Our View of Human Evolution*. Berkeley, California: University of California Press.

Finlay, B. L., Darlington, R. B. and Nicastro, N. (2001). Developmental structure in brain evolution. *Behavioral Brain Science*, **24**: 283–308.

Grimaud-Herve, D. and Lordikipanidze, D. (2010). The fossil hominid brains of Dmanisi: D 2280 and D 2282. In Broadfield, D. C., Yuan, M., Schick, K. and Toth, N (eds.), *The Human Brain Evolving: Paleoneurological Studies in Honor of Ralph L. Holloway*. Stone Age Institute Publication Series #4. Indiana: Stone Age Institute Press, pp. 59–82.

Hawks, J. and Wolpoff, M. H. (1999). Endocranial capacity of early hominids. *Science*, **283**: 9b (in technical comments).

Holloway, R. L. (1967). The evolution of the human brain: some notes toward a synthesis between neural structure and the evolution of complex behavior. *General Systems*, **12**: 1–19.

(1972). New Australopithecine endocast, SK1585 from Swartkrans, S. Africa. *American Journal of Physical Anthropology*, **37**(2): 173–86.

(1974). On the meaning of brain size. *Science*, **184**: 677–9.

(1979). Brain size, allometry, and reorganization: toward a synthesis. In Hahn, M. E., Jensen, C. and Dudek, BC. (eds.), *Development and Evolution of Brain Size. Behavioral Implications*. New York: Academic Press, pp. 59–88.

(1981). Exploring the dorsal surface of hominoid brain endocasts by stereoplotter and discriminant analysis. *Philosophical Transactions Royal Society, London, B Biological Sciences*, **292**:155–66.

(1983). Cerebral brain endocast pattern of *Australopithecus afarensis*. *Nature*, **303**: 420–2.

(1985). The past, present, and future significance of the lunate sulcus in early hominid evolution. In Tobias, P. V. (ed.), *Hominid Evolution: Past, Present, and Future*. New York: Alan R. Liss. pp. 47–62.

(1988). Some additional morphological and metrical observations on *Pan* brain casts and their relevance to the Taung endocast. *American Journal of Physical Anthropology*, **77**: 27–33.

(2001). Does allometry mask important brain structure residuals relevant to species-specific behavioral evolution? *Behavioral Brain Sciences*, **24**: 286–7.

Holloway, R. L. and Kimbel, W. H. (1986). Endocast morphology of Hadar hominid AL 162–28. *Nature*, **321**: 536.

Holloway, R. L., Broadfield, D. C. and Yuan, M. S. (2001a). Revisiting australopithecine visual striate cortex: newer data from chimpanzees suggest it could have been reduced during australopithecine times. In Falk, D. and Gibson, K. R (eds.), *Evolutionary Anatomy of Primate Cerebral Cortex*. New York: Cambridge University Press, pp. 177–86.

(2001b). The parietal lobe in early hominid evolution: newer evidence from chimpanzee brains. In Tobias, P. V., Raath, M. A., Moggi-Cecchi, J. and Doyle, G. A. (eds.), *Humanity from African Naissance to Coming Millennia*. Florence: Florence University Press, pp. 365–71.

(2003). Morphology and histology of the chimpanzee visual striate cortex indicate brain reorganization predated brain expansion in early hominid evolution. *Anatomical Record*, **273A**: 594–602.

Holloway, R. L., Clarke, R. J. and Tobias, P. V. (2004a). Posterior lunate sulcus in *Australopithecus africanus*: was Dart right? *Comptes Rendus Palevol*, **3**: 287–93.

Holloway, R. L., Broadfield, D. C. and Yuan, M. S. (2004b). *The Human Fossil Record. Volume 3: Brain Endocasts: the Paleoneurological Evidence*. New York: Wiley-Liss.

Jerison, H. J. (1973). *Evolution of the Brain and Intelligence*. New York: Academic Press.

Keith, A. (1931). *New Discoveries Relating to the Antiquity of Man*. New York: WW Norton.

Lockwood, C. A. and Tobias, P. V. (1999). A large male cranium from Sterkfontein, South Africa, and the status of *Australopithecus africanus*. *Journal of Human Evolution*, **36**: 637–85.

Rilling, J. K. (2006). Human and nonhuman primate brains: are they allometrically scaled versions of the same design? *Evolutionary Anthropology*, **15**: 65–77.

Stephan, H., Frahm, H. D. and Baron, G. (1981). New and revised data on volumes of brain structures in Insectivores and Primates. *Folia Primatologia*, **35**: 1–29.

10 *The mass of the human brain: is it a spandrel?*

PAUL R. MANGER, JASON HEMINGWAY,

MUHAMMAD A. SPOCTER AND

ANDREW GALLAGHER

Abstract

The current chapter examines allometric exponents as they apply to the evolution of the size, or mass, of the modern human brain relative to the mass of the body. The mass of the brain is considered as a single level of organisation of the nervous system and is treated separately to other levels of organisation. A comprehensive dataset is used to examine the relationship between brain and body mass in primates and hominids. This analysis allows us to postulate that the evolution of the size of the human brain can, for the most part, be accounted for by scaling with body size. There appears to be a minimum of two potential adaptive events that have led to alterations in the scaling laws that help explain the actual mass of the human brain. These two events occur at the origin of primates and the origin of the hominid lineage. These scaling laws appear to obviate much of the need for adaptationist explanations in terms of the evolution of the mass of the human brain.

Introduction

> A trend in one specially favoured character...may result in trends in various correlated characters. In other words, a particular trend may be nothing but the by-product of a trend in a different character, *such as body size*.
>
> (Ernst Mayr, 2002: 240, our italics)

The human brain, at an average mass of approximately 1355 g (e.g. Ruff *et al.*, 1997; Wood and Collard, 1999), is potentially the most complex biological structure to have evolved. This brain is composed of 100 billion

African Genesis: Perspectives on Hominin Evolution, eds. Sally C. Reynolds and Andrew Gallagher. Published by Cambridge University Press. © Cambridge University Press 2012.

neurons, each neuron being connected to between 1000 and 10 000 other neurons, up to 5000 billion glial cells and approximately 20 billion neurons in the human cerebral cortex, with a total of 60 trillion synapses (Blinkov and Glezer, 1968). Yet this structure, as with everything to do with the anatomy, biochemistry, physiology and behaviour of *Homo sapiens*, has evolved over time. This process may be the result of a number of factors, including: (a) natural selection responding to potential adaptations; (b) phylogenetic contingencies and constraints; and (c) structural laws of form (Gould, 2002). Of all the features of modern humans it is the brain and the cognitive power of this organ that distinguishes *Homo sapiens* most clearly from the rest of the Kingdom Animalia. Few studies to date have examined in sufficient detail the internal architecture and structure of the human brain to allow extensive theorising or analysis of changes at the various levels of organisation within the brain in an evolutionary setting (i.e. not enough data is available to analyse sufficiently all potential evolutionary explanations relating to the genesis of the form of the various levels of organisation of the human brain). In contrast, significant effort has been directed towards establishing the changes in the mass of the brain during the evolution of the Family Hominidae (e.g. Ruff *et al.*, 1997; Henneberg, 1998; Wood and Collard, 1999; amongst many others), as cranial capacity is one parameter that can be determined with a reasonable degree of accuracy from the fossil record (although the exact data is often debated).

The brain of *Homo sapiens* is not the largest brain in existence, this is found in some of the larger cetaceans (Manger, 2006), but the human brain is the largest brain relative to body mass of all animals (e.g. Jerison, 1973). This large relative brain mass has been proposed to be, most prominently by Jerison but also by many others, the major factor in the biological determination of human intelligence. While mass is a readily quantifiable character, has too much emphasis been placed on mass and relative mass in the determination of the capabilities of any individual brain? A recent analysis of the evolution of the cetacean brain suggests that mass and/or relative mass alone may not be the most reliable indicator of intelligence (Manger, 2006). Rather, all levels of organisation of the brain must be examined and explained in order to understand the complexity of information processing of any given brain – the brain is undoubtedly hierarchically organised (Manger, 2005).

Despite this, mass is a specific feature of organisation of the brain and mass does play a major role in overall functioning, as many other features of the brain at various levels of organisation are related to overall mass (e.g. Finlay and Darlington, 1995). Thus how the mass of the human brain evolved is an important focal point of study. The potential effect of mass on other features of brain organisation at various levels is encapsulated by Gould:

The spandrels of the human brain must greatly outnumber the immediately *adaptive* reasons for increase in size…

(Gould, 2002: 87, our italics)

The present contribution examines the evolution of the mass of the human brain as a single level of neural organisation, and as indicated in the title, puts forward the possibility that the mass of the brain is a spandrel, thus extending even Gould's (2002) evolutionary explanations of human brain mass evolution. While allometric relationships are well known for brain and body mass amongst mammals, these have not been the central focus of explanation of total brain mass in hominid evolution, with adaptationist explanations, and more recently gene mutational studies, dominating this debate. In contrast, we explore the allometric relationships in the present analysis. We first examine the allometric data available for brain and body mass in mammalian, primate and hominid evolution. We then discuss the potential 'chicken and egg' conundrum that may result from a strong allometric relationship between brain and body mass (specifically stated, did a larger brain mass evolve as a correlation to a selection for larger body mass, or did selection for a larger brain mass lead to an increase in body mass?). We hypothesise that body mass was most likely selected for in hominid evolution, leaving us with the conclusion that the mass of the human brain 'may be nothing but the by-product of a trend in a different character' (Mayr, 2002).

Structural laws of form and human brain mass

Generalised mammalian brain and body mass scaling

When examining mammals in a general framework, a distinct, highly predictable and strongly statistically significant scaling of body mass to brain mass is found. This relationship has been known since the early 1800s (Dubois, 1897), but was brought to the fore by the publication of Jerison's 1973 monograph. The relationship between mammalian body mass (Mb) and brain mass (Mbr) is seen as a negative allometric scaling that can be described by the equation (from Manger, 2006):

$$M_{br} = 0.069 M_b^{0.718} \ (r^2 = 0.950; P = 2.4 \times 10^{-178})$$

The above equation is derived from a regression plot for all mammals (those with known brain and body masses), but excludes the primates, hominids, cetaceans and pinnipeds due to the fact that these groups exhibit a form of scaling between brain and body mass that differs to the remainder of mammals

(Manger, 2006). Using this function we can see that for every doubling in body mass of a mammal, the mass of the brain will increase 1.65 times ($2^{0.718}$). Thus, as mammals get larger the brain will get larger, but the percentage of the entire body mass that is brain mass will decrease, both occurring in a highly predictable fashion (95% of the variability in brain mass can be accounted for by variability in body mass).

What, in terms of evolution in brain mass, can be concluded from this statistical analysis? We can conclude that increases in body mass and brain mass in mammals are so strongly interconnected that they should not be treated separately a priori. This scaling law of form can be considered a class-level allometric phylogenetic constraint upon brain mass evolution in mammals. If one were to imagine a colossal mammal, say five times the body mass of the modern African elephant (*Loxodonta africana*), one could predict with a relatively high degree of certainty, the brain mass this mega-mammal would have. We can also conclude that if a group of mammals exhibits a brain–body mass allometric scaling that differs from, or falls outside of the range of, this generalised scaling law of form for mammals that something different has occurred in the evolution of this group of mammals (see analysis of primates and hominids below).

It is this basic allometric phylogenetic constraint that serves as the strongest predictor of the evolution of brain mass amongst the mammals, and it is against this basis that any specific differences in groups of mammals, or individual species, must be compared (see for example the analysis of cetaceans by Manger, 2006).

Primate brain and body mass scaling

Primates, as an order, have larger brains than would be expected for their body mass when compared to the generalised mammalian pattern of scaling (e.g. Martin, 1981, 1983; Manger, 2006). Interestingly, the components of the brain, in terms of subdivisions such as neocortex, diencephalon, cerebellum etc., are very close to what one would predict for a mammal with a brain of the mass found in primates (e.g. Finlay and Darlington, 1995). This means that the larger brain mass in primates is not due to selective expansion of one particular structure, for example the neocortex (as often asserted in the literature as neocorticalisation), but is due to an overall allometric increase in the mass of all components of the brain, summing to an increase in total brain mass relative to body mass. We undertook an analysis of non-hominin simian primates (Figure 10.1) and found that the relationship between brain and body mass was highly significant and can be described by the equation:

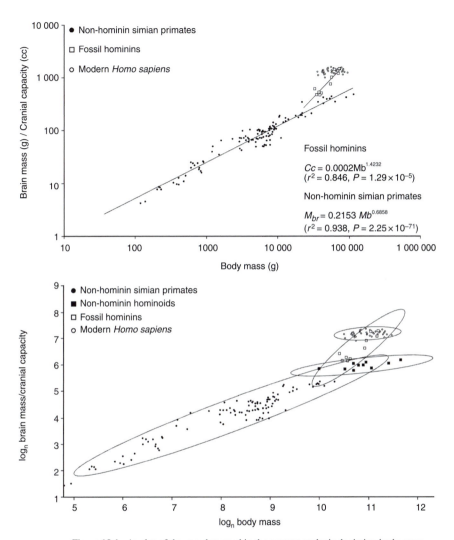

Figure 10.1. A: plot of the raw data used in the current analysis depicting body mass plotted against brain mass or cranial capacity. B: more restricted plot of the raw data with 95th percentile ellipses drawn around the different groups.

$$M_{br} = 0.2153 M_b^{0.6858} \ (r^2 = 0.938; P = 2.25 \times 10^{-71})$$

This equation suggests several points of interest. First, for every doubling in the body mass of the non-hominin simian primates the brain increases in mass by 1.61 times ($2^{0.6858}$, a negative allometry) which closely parallels that of the general mammalian trend (see above); thus, the manner in which brains and bodies scale in the mammals and the non-hominin simian primates is similar. This indicates that whatever processes are controlling the relationship of brain mass to body mass are likely to be similar in the non-hominin simian primates and mammals in general. Second, the high correlation coefficient tells us that 93.8% of the variability in brain mass in the non-hominin simian primates can be accounted for by variations in body mass. Thus, this relationship is highly predictable for this primate subgroup, as seen in mammals in general. Lastly, the *y* intercept, at 0.2153 is larger than that seen for mammals in general (0.069), indicating that the brain mass of this group is generally larger in relation to body mass than that found for mammals in general. All primates (including prosimians) exhibit brains that are larger than would be expected for mammals of their body mass, with encephalisation quotients (EQ) ranging from around 1.25 through to that for humans, which falls between 7 and 8 – the average EQ for mammals is 1 (Manger, 2006).

We subdivided this group, into non-hominoid simian primates and non-hominin hominoids, and determined the 95% confidence intervals for these two groups (Figure 10.1). Only two species of the latter group (*Gorilla gorilla* and *Pongo pygmaeus*) could be distinguished from the non-hominoid simian primates as the data for these two species fell outside of the 95% confidence intervals. These two species exhibited larger body masses than would be expected for a non-hominoid simian primate and this may be the result of secondary somatic growth, or evolutionary adaptation for increased somatic mass in these two species.

Despite this data the remaining eight species of non-hominin hominoids fell within the 95% confidence intervals of the non-hominoid simian primates. From this we can conclude that it is highly likely that no specific change in the allometric relationship between these two groups has occurred and can thus be treated together. This is an important distinction to make, as it indicates that there are no features of the brain–body mass relationship evident in the closest extant relatives of modern humans that indicate variation from the pattern seen across a large cohort of the order primates in the direction of the hominin lineage. Thus, we may conclude that it is likely that no features of the mass of the brain relative to the body in non-hominin primates is indicative of the well documented changes seen in the hominin lineage.

Fossil hominin brain and body mass scaling

We analysed the manner in which brains and bodies scaled in the fossil hominin species (extinct genera *Australopithecus* and *Homo*, including fossil *H. sapiens*) using as many records as we could find in the literature (see Tables 10.1

and 10.2). We have treated these species as one group, as they all exhibit habitual bipedalism as a locomotory feature that distinguishes them from the remaining primates. Alternative scenarios may indeed subdivide this group in relation to the differing locomotory repertoires, but for the purposes of the present analysis we do not deal with these other possibilities. As absolute brain mass cannot be measured in these species, we used the published estimates of cranial capacity as a substitute for brain mass. While this is a good indicator of changes in the mass of the brain over time, there is one major disadvantage, this being that the brain occupies only between 80 to 85% of the endocranial cavity in modern humans (Tobias, 1994). Thus, the proxies of brain mass that we have used in the analysis of these species may overestimate fossil brain masses, but at present are the best indicators of total brain mass in the fossil hominin species. A second drawback is that estimates of body mass are also used, with all the inherent difficulties involved (Spocter and Manger, 2007). However, with these potential problems and grouping limitations in mind, the analysis indicates an interesting trend in the relationship between the endocranial capacity and the estimates of body mass (Figure 10.1). We found that the relationship between endocranial capacity (Cc) and body mass (M_b) estimates was highly significant and can be described by the equation:

$$Cc = 0.0002M_b^{1.4232} \ (r^2 = 0.846; P = 1.29 \times 10^{-5})$$

Several points of interest emerge from this analysis. The first point is that the relationship is highly significant, and the derived equation indicates that 84.6% of the variability in endocranial capacity can be accounted for by variation in body mass estimates in the fossil hominins. Second, the slope of the derived equation indicates that this relationship forms a positive allometry; thus for every doubling in body mass estimate in the fossil hominins, the endocranial capacity increases by 2.68 times ($2^{1.4232}$). This positive allometry is significantly different from that found for the non-hominin simian primates ($P = 0.0058$, using the mean squares within and between slopes), indicating that the manner in which the brain and body scales in the two groups is very different.

If we examine the 95% confidence intervals generated for the various groups used in the current analysis (Figure 10.1), we see that all of the fossil hominins lie outside of the range of the non-hominoid simian primates. Second, we see that only two of the smallest fossil hominins lie with the 95% confidence intervals of the non-hominin hominoids (*Australopithecus afarensis and A. africanus*). Thus, on statistical grounds, the brain and body mass of the fossil hominins is completely different to that of the non-hominoid simian primates. While the two smallest fossil hominins lie within the 95% confidence intervals of the non-hominin hominoids, they are on the very outer limits of this interval, and the remaining fossil hominins are clearly segregated. Thus, for the

Table 10.1. *Published body mass estimates for Miocene, Pliocene and Pleistocene hominins.*
(Data taken from: Aiello and Dean, 1990; McHenry, 1992; Ruff et al., 1997; Abbate et al., 1998;
Asfaw et al., 1999, 2002; Senut et al., 2001; Zollikofer et al., 2005; Rightmire et al., 2006).

Specimen	Element	Sex	Taxon	Age (million years)	Mass
BAR 1002'00	Proximal femur	?	*Orrorin tugenensis*	6.000	35.96
KNM-KP 29285	Proximal fibia	M	*Australopithecus anamensis*	4.300	55.00
MAK-VP-1/1	Proximal femur	M	*Australopithecus afarensis*	3.800	47.50
A.L. 333–3	Proximal femur	M	*Australopithecus afarensis*	3.600	50.10
A.L. 333–4	Distal femur	M	*Australopithecus afarensis*	3.600	41.40
A.L. 333–7	Distal tibia	M	*Australopithecus afarensis*	3.600	42.60
A.L. 33w-56	Distal femur	M	*Australopithecus afarensis*	3.600	40.30
A.L. 333x-26	Proximal tibia	M	*Australopithecus afarensis*	3.600	48.20
A.L. 333–42	Proximal tibia	M	*Australopithecus afarensis*	3.600	45.00
A.L. 333–6	Distal tibia	F	*Australopithecus afarensis*	3.600	33.50
A.L. 288–1	Proximal femur	F	*Australopithecus afarensis*	3.200	28.00
A.L. 129–1a	Distal femur	F	*Australopithecus afarensis*	3.200	28.20
A.L. 129–1b	Proximal tibia	F	*Australopithecus afarensis*	3.200	27.20
Sts 14	Proximal femur	F	*Australopithecus africanus*	2.300	30.00
Sts 392	Femoral head	F	*Australopithecus africanus*	2.300	32.70
StW 25	Femoral head	F	*Australopithecus africanus*	2.300	34.40
StW 102	Talus	F	*Australopithecus africanus*	2.300	30.60
StW 347	Talus	F	*Australopithecus africanus*	2.300	27.60
StW 358	Distal tibia	F	*Australopithecus africanus*	2.300	23.40
TM 1513	Distal femur	F	*Australopithecus africanus*	2.300	32.60
Sts 34	Distal femur	M	*Australopithecus africanus*	2.300	38.50
StW 311	Femoral head	M	*Australopithecus africanus*	2.300	40.70

Table 10.1. (*cont.*)

Specimen	Element	Sex	Taxon	Age (million years)	Mass
StW 389	Distal tibia	M	*Australopithecus africanus*	2.300	38.00
StW 99	Proximal Femur	M	*Australopithecus africanus*	2.300	45.40
StW 431	Femoral head	M	*Australopithecus africanus*	2.300	49.25
TM 1517	Talus	F	*Paranthropus robustus*	1.800	33.80
SK 82	Proximal femur	M	*Paranthropus robustus*	1.800	37.40
SK 97	Proximal femur	M	*Paranthropus robustus*	1.800	42.90
KNM-ER 1500	Partial skeleton	F	*Paranthropus boisei*	1.800	34.00
KNM-ER 1464	Talus	M	*Paranthropus boisei*	1.800	48.60
KNM-ER 3735	Partial skeleton	M	*Homo habilis sensu stricto*	1.800	37.00
OH 8	Talus	F	*Homo habilis sensu stricto*	1.800	31.00
OH 35	Distal tibia	F	*Homo habilis sensu stricto*	1.800	31.90
KNM-ER 3228	Femoral head	M	*Homo sp. indet*	1.950	62.00
KNM-ER 1481	Femoral head	M	*Homo sp. indet*	1.800	57.20
KNM-ER 813	Femoral diaphysis	?	*Homo sp. indet*	1.800	51.80
KNM-ER 1472	Femoral head	?	*Homo sp. indet*	1.800	49.70
KNM-ER 737	Femoral diaphysis	?	*Homo erectus*	1.800	52.80
KNM-ER 736	Femoral diaphysis	M	*Homo erectus*	1.800	59.00
KNM-ER 1808	Femoral diaphysis	M	*Homo erectus*	1.800	59.00
KNM-ER 803	Femoral diaphysis	F	*Homo erectus*	1.800	49.90
OH 28	Acetabulum	F	*Homo erectus*	1.800	54.00
OH 34	Tibial diaphysis	F	*Homo erectus*	1.800	51.00
Arago 44	Femoral head	M	*Homo erectus*	0.400	79.20
Zhoukoudian FeIV	Femoral head	?	*Homo erectus*	0.440	58.30
Gesher-Benot-Ya'acov	Femoral head	?	*Homo erectus*	0.500	53.40
KNM-BK 66	Femoral head	?	*Homo erectus*	0.500	62.10
Ain Maarouf1	Femoral head	?	*Homo erectus*	0.600	54.50
Ngandong B	Femoral head	F	*Homo erectus*	0.120	54.10
Broken Hill 689	Femoral head	?	*Homo heidelbergensis*	0.300	73.80
Broken Hill 690	Femoral head	?	*Homo heidelbergensis*	0.300	48.90
Broken Hill 691	Femoral head	?	*Homo heidelbergensis*	0.300	62.40
Broken Hill 719	Femoral head	M	*Homo heidelbergensis*	0.300	73.60

Table 10.1. (*cont.*)

Specimen	Element	Sex	Taxon	Age (million years)	Mass
Broken Hill 907	Femoral head	?	*Homo heidelbergensis*	0.300	80.60
Boxgrove 1	Femoral head	M	*Homo heidelbergensis*	0.500	86.70
Amud 1	Femoral head	M	*Homo neanderthalensis*	0.045	70.30
La Chapelle- aux-Saints	Femoral head	M	*Homo neanderthalensis*	0.052	77.30
La Ferrassie 1	Femoral head	M	*Homo neanderthalensis*	0.072	85.00
La Ferrassie 2	Femoral head	F	*Homo neanderthalensis*	0.072	67.00
Fond-de-Foret 1	Femoral head	M	*Homo neanderthalensis*	0.050	83.90
Kebara 2	Femoral head	M	*Homo neanderthalensis*	0.060	75.60
Kiik-Koba 1	Femoral head	M	*Homo neanderthalensis*	0.050	78.10
Lezetxiki 1	Proximal tibia	?	*Homo neanderthalensis*	0.075	73.90
Neandertal 1	Femoral head	M	*Homo neanderthalensis*	0.050	78.90
La Quina 5	Femoral head	?	*Homo neanderthalensis*	0.050	71.20
Regourdou 1	Femoral head	?	*Homo neanderthalensis*	0.075	72.10
Saint-Cesaire 1	Femoral head	M	*Homo neanderthalensis*	0.036	78.90
Spy 1	Femoral head	F	*Homo neanderthalensis*	0.050	67.50
Spy 2	Femoral head	M	*Homo neanderthalensis*	0.050	83.60
Shanidar 1	Femoral head	M	*Homo neanderthalensis*	0.050	80.50
Shanidar 3	Femoral head	M	*Homo neanderthalensis*	0.050	79.90
Shanidar 5	Femoral head	M	*Homo neanderthalensis*	0.050	68.50
Krapina 207	Femoral head	M	*Homo neanderthalensis*	0.130	57.10
Krapina 208	Femoral head	F	*Homo neanderthalensis*	0.130	68.40
Krapina 209	Femoral head	F	*Homo neanderthalensis*	0.130	63.70
Krapina 213	Femoral head	M	*Homo neanderthalensis*	0.130	80.60
Krapina 214	Femoral head	F	*Homo neanderthalensis*	0.130	62.60
Grotte du Prince	Femoral head	F	*Homo neanderthalensis*	0.100	74.80
Shanidar 2	Femoral head	M	*Homo neanderthalensis*	0.100	75.20
Shanidar 4	Femoral head	M	*Homo neanderthalensis*	0.100	72.00
Shanidar 6	Femoral head	F	*Homo neanderthalensis*	0.100	59.40
Tabun C1	Femoral head	F	*Homo neanderthalensis*	0.150	63.20
Qafzeh 3	Femoral head	F	*Homo sapiens*	0.090	57.30
Qafzeh 7	Femoral head	M	*Homo sapiens*	0.090	67.60
Qafzeh 8	Femoral head	M	*Homo sapiens*	0.090	77.40
Qafzeh 9	Femoral head	F	*Homo sapiens*	0.090	63.20
Skhul 4	Femoral head	M	*Homo sapiens*	0.090	70.30
Skhul 5	Femoral head	M	*Homo sapiens*	0.090	67.60
Skhul 6	Femoral head	M	*Homo sapiens*	0.090	71.30
Skhul 7	Femoral Head	M	*Homo sapiens*	0.090	65.30
Skhul 7a	Femoral head	F	*Homo sapiens*	0.090	54.70
Skhul 9	Femoral head	M	*Homo sapiens*	0.090	71.30
Baousse de Torre 2	Femoral head	M	*Homo sapiens*	0.025	75.40
Caviglione 1	Femoral head	M	*Homo sapiens*	0.025	65.20
Cro-Magnon 1	Femoral head	M	*Homo sapiens*	0.030	67.60
Cro-Magnon 4293	Femoral head	?	*Homo sapiens*	0.030	67.00
Cro-Magnon 4297	Femoral head	?	*Homo sapiens*	0.030	73.10
Cro-Magnon 4315	Femoral head	M	*Homo sapiens*	0.030	70.80
Cro-Magnon 4317	Femoral head	?	*Homo sapiens*	0.030	59.60

Table 10.1. (*cont.*)

Specimen	Element	Sex	Taxon	Age (million years)	Mass
Cro-Magnon 4321	Femoral head	?	*Homo sapiens*	0.030	59.20
Cro-Magnon 4322	Femoral head	?	*Homo sapiens*	0.030	70.50
Cro-Magnon 4330	Femoral head	?	*Homo sapiens*	0.030	65.30
Dolni Vestonice 3	Femoral head	F	*Homo sapiens*	0.026	54.80
Dolni Vestonice 13	Femoral head	M	*Homo sapiens*	0.026	68.00
Dolni Vestonice 14	Femoral head	M	*Homo sapiens*	0.027	72.00
Dolni Vestonice 16	Femoral head	M	*Homo sapiens*	0.026	71.00
Grotte des Enfants 4	Femoral head	M	*Homo sapiens*	0.028	83.80
Grotte des Enfants 5	Femoral head	F	*Homo sapiens*	0.028	52.80
Mladec 24	Femoral head	?	*Homo sapiens*	0.035	76.80
Mladec 22	Femoral head	?	*Homo sapiens*	0.035	76.50
Mladec 21	Femoral head	M	*Homo sapiens*	0.035	62.70
Paglicci 25	Femoral head	F	*Homo sapiens*	0.024	60.60
Pataud 4	Femoral head	?	*Homo sapiens*	0.021	63.00
Pataud 5	Femoral head	?	*Homo sapiens*	0.021	60.90
Paviland	Femoral head	M	*Homo sapiens*	0.026	72.90
Pavlov 1	Femoral head	M	*Homo sapiens*	0.026	79.00
Predmosti 1	Femoral head	F	*Homo sapiens*	0.027	55.40
Predmosti 3	Femoral head	M	*Homo sapiens*	0.027	70.80
Predmosti 4	Femoral head	F	*Homo sapiens*	0.027	65.10
Predmosti 9	Femoral head	F	*Homo sapiens*	0.027	57.70
Predmosti 10	Femoral head	F	*Homo sapiens*	0.027	70.60
Predmosti 14	Femoral head	M	*Homo sapiens*	0.027	65.90
La Rochette 1	Femoral head	?	*Homo sapiens*	0.030	64.70
Stetten 1	Femoral head	?	*Homo sapiens*	0.032	65.90
Nazlet Khater 1	Femoral head	M	*Homo sapiens*	0.032	52.20
Arene Candide 1-IP	Femoral head	M	*Homo sapiens*	0.019	66.40
Barma Grande 2	Femoral head	M	*Homo sapiens*	0.019	80.70
Barma Grande 3	Femoral head	F	*Homo sapiens*	0.019	58.50
Barma Grande 4	Femoral head	M	*Homo sapiens*	0.019	66.40
Bichon 1	Femoral head	M	*Homo sapiens*	0.012	58.40
Bruniquel 2	Femoral head	F	*Homo sapiens*	0.012	60.10
Cap Blanc 1	Femoral head	F	*Homo sapiens*	0.012	57.80
Chancelade 1	Femoral head	M	*Homo sapiens*	0.012	64.50
Arene Candide 1a	Femoral head	?	*Homo sapiens*	0.011	75.40
Arene Candide 1	Femoral head	M	*Homo sapiens*	0.011	56.30
Arene Candide 2	Femoral head	M	*Homo sapiens*	0.011	67.70
Arene Candide 4	Femoral head	M	*Homo sapiens*	0.011	71.60
Arene Candide 5	Femoral head	M	*Homo sapiens*	0.011	68.70
Arene Candide 10	Femoral head	M	*Homo sapiens*	0.011	68.70
Arene Candide 12	Femoral head	M	*Homo sapiens*	0.011	68.30
Arene Candide 13	Femoral head	F	*Homo sapiens*	0.011	51.00
Arene Candide 14	Femoral head	F	*Homo sapiens*	0.011	53.40
Farincourt 1	Femoral head	F	*Homo sapiens*	0.010	54.20

Table 10.1. (*cont.*)

Specimen	Element	Sex	Taxon	Age (million years)	Mass
Continenza 1	Femoral head	M	*Homo sapiens*	0.010	68.10
Grotte des Enfants 3	Femoral head	M	*Homo sapiens*	0.010	51.50
Laugerie Basse 54298a	Femoral head	?	*Homo sapiens*	0.012	81.70
Laugerie Basse 54298b	Femoral head	?	*Homo sapiens*	0.012	63.60
Laugerie Basse 9	Femoral head	?	*Homo sapiens*	0.012	60.10
Laugerie Basse 54298c	Femoral head	?	*Homo sapiens*	0.012	67.20
La Madeleine 1	Femoral head	?	*Homo sapiens*	0.012	66.70
Neussing 2	Femoral head	M	*Homo sapiens*	0.018	70.80
Oberkassel 1	Femoral head	M	*Homo sapiens*	0.012	72.40
Oberkassel 2	Femoral head	F	*Homo sapiens*	0.012	56.80
Parabita 1	Femoral head	M	*Homo sapiens*	0.010	73.30
Parabita 2	Femoral head	F	*Homo sapiens*	0.010	69.70
Le Placard 15	Femoral head	?	*Homo sapiens*	0.013	58.60
Le Placard 16	Femoral head	?	*Homo sapiens*	0.013	66.50
Romito 3	Femoral head	M	*Homo sapiens*	0.011	72.70
Romito 4	Femoral head	F	*Homo sapiens*	0.011	60.40
Saint Germain-la-Riviere 1	Femoral head	F	*Homo sapiens*	0.015	61.50
San Teodoro 1	Femoral head	F	*Homo sapiens*	0.011	64.60
San Teodoro 3	Femoral head	?	*Homo sapiens*	0.011	61.90
San Teodoro 4	Femoral head	F	*Homo sapiens*	0.011	68.20
Veryier 1	Femoral head	M	*Homo sapiens*	0.010	56.20
Nahal Ein Gev 1	Femoral head	F	*Homo sapiens*	0.021	51.70
Kubbaniya 1	Femoral head	M	*Homo sapiens*	0.020	69.60
Ohalo 2	Femoral head	M	*Homo sapiens*	0.019	73.50
Minatogawa 1	Femoral head	M	*Homo sapiens*	0.018	60.30
Minatogawa 2	Femoral head	F	*Homo sapiens*	0.018	45.90
Minatogawa 3	Femoral head	F	*Homo sapiens*	0.018	50.20
Minatogawa 4	Femoral head	F	*Homo sapiens*	0.018	47.40
Ein Gev 1	Femoral head	F	*Homo sapiens*	0.016	54.30
Neve David 1	Femoral head	?	*Homo sapiens*	0.013	61.50
Jebel Sahaba 117–1	Femoral head	?	*Homo sapiens*	0.013	66.50
Jebel Sahaba 117–4	Femoral head	F	*Homo sapiens*	0.013	57.60
Jebel Sahaba 117–5	Femoral head	M	*Homo sapiens*	0.013	65.20
Jebel Sahaba 117–6	Femoral head	F	*Homo sapiens*	0.013	65.30
Jebel Sahaba 117–7	Femoral head	F	*Homo sapiens*	0.013	54.50
Jebel Sahaba 117–10	Femoral head	F	*Homo sapiens*	0.013	63.10

Table 10.1. (*cont.*)

Specimen	Element	Sex	Taxon	Age (million years)	Mass
Jebel Sahaba 117–11	Femoral head	M	*Homo sapiens*	0.013	62.10
Jebel Sahaba 117–15	Femoral head	F	*Homo sapiens*	0.013	50.30
Jebel Sahaba 117–17	Femoral head	M	*Homo sapiens*	0.013	62.20
Jebel Sahaba 117–18	Femoral head	M	*Homo sapiens*	0.013	70.80
Jebel Sahaba 117–19	Femoral head	M	*Homo sapiens*	0.013	61.70
Jebel Sahaba 117–20	Femoral head	M	*Homo sapiens*	0.013	60.80
Jebel Sahaba 117–21	Femoral head	M	*Homo sapiens*	0.013	59.30
Jebel Sahaba 117–22	Femoral head	F	*Homo sapiens*	0.013	60.10
Jebel Sahaba 117–26	Femoral head	F	*Homo sapiens*	0.013	53.60
Jebel Sahaba 117–28	Femoral head	F	*Homo sapiens*	0.013	54.50
Jebel Sahaba 117–29	Femoral head	M	*Homo sapiens*	0.013	73.10
Jebel Sahaba 117–33	Femoral head	F	*Homo sapiens*	0.013	61.00
Jebel Sahaba 117–39	Femoral head	M	*Homo sapiens*	0.013	65.70
Jebel Sahaba 117–38	Femoral head	M	*Homo sapiens*	0.013	65.90
Jebel Sahaba 117–40	Femoral head	M	*Homo sapiens*	0.013	65.00
Jebel Sahaba 117–42	Femoral head	M	*Homo sapiens*	0.013	67.80
Jebel Sahaba 117–102	Femoral head	M	*Homo sapiens*	0.013	63.90
Pecos	Femoral head	F	*Homo sapiens*	0.001	52.00
Pecos	Femoral head	F	*Homo sapiens*	0.001	52.00
Pecos	Femoral head	F	*Homo sapiens*	0.001	48.30
Pecos	Femoral head	M	*Homo sapiens*	0.001	63.50
Pecos	Femoral head	F	*Homo sapiens*	0.001	51.40
Pecos	Femoral head	F	*Homo sapiens*	0.001	52.20
Pecos	Femoral head	M	*Homo sapiens*	0.001	66.40
Pecos	Femoral head	M	*Homo sapiens*	0.001	61.00
Pecos	Femoral head	F	*Homo sapiens*	0.001	49.20
Pecos	Femoral head	M	*Homo sapiens*	0.001	67.80
Pecos	Femoral head	M	*Homo sapiens*	0.001	62.90
Pecos	Femoral head	F	*Homo sapiens*	0.001	48.10
Pecos	Femoral head	M	*Homo sapiens*	0.001	60.20

Table 10.1. (*cont.*)

Specimen	Element	Sex	Taxon	Age (million years)	Mass
Pecos	Femoral head	M	*Homo sapiens*	0.001	51.00
Pecos	Femoral head	M	*Homo sapiens*	0.001	55.20
Pecos	Femoral head	F	*Homo sapiens*	0.001	43.20
Pecos	Femoral head	F	*Homo sapiens*	0.001	43.20
Pecos	Femoral head	M	*Homo sapiens*	0.001	65.50
Pecos	Femoral head	F	*Homo sapiens*	0.001	53.90
Pecos	Femoral head	F	*Homo sapiens*	0.001	54.30
Pecos	Femoral head	F	*Homo sapiens*	0.001	52.50
Pecos	Femoral head	F	*Homo sapiens*	0.001	54.90
Pecos	Femoral head	F	*Homo sapiens*	0.001	52.70
Pecos	Femoral head	M	*Homo sapiens*	0.001	61.00
Pecos	Femoral head	M	*Homo sapiens*	0.001	58.40
Pecos	Femoral head	M	*Homo sapiens*	0.001	57.10
Pecos	Femoral head	M	*Homo sapiens*	0.001	54.30
Pecos	Femoral head	M	*Homo sapiens*	0.001	59.70
Pecos	Femoral head	F	*Homo sapiens*	0.001	57.90

most part, the fossil hominins are reliably segregated from the non-hominin hominoids. This latter segregation must be tempered slightly by the potential overestimate of brain mass using endocranial volume in the fossil hominins – the exact estimate may change somewhat but the overall pattern identified in this analysis is unlikely to change.

Thus, we propose the following conclusions: (1) fossil hominins show a pattern of brain mass to body mass scaling that is different from other simian primates; (2) this pattern exhibits a positive allometry, indicating that brain mass will increase at a faster rate than body mass when there are increases in body mass; (3) the fossil hominins, including fossil *H. sapiens*, form a distinct grouping within the primates when examining the brain–body mass relationship; and (4) a unique evolutionary event leading to a phenotypically unusual positive allometry of the brain to body relationship in the primates occurred at the genesis of the hominin clade.

The modern human brain body mass

On average, *Homo sapiens* has the largest brain mass relative to body mass of all known animal species (Jerison, 1973) and this distinguishes modern humans from our closest extant counterparts, and from our closest extinct relatives. Despite this, our statistical analysis indicates that this gap based on

Table 10.2. *Published cranial capacities for Miocene, Pliocene and Pleistocene hominins.*
(Data taken from: Aiello and Dean, 1990; McHenry, 1992; Ruff et al., 1997; Abbate et al., 1998;
Asfaw et al., 1999, 2002; Senut et al., 2001; Zollikofer et al., 2005; Rightmire et al., 2006).

Specimen	Sex	Taxon	Age (million years)	Cranial capacity (cm³)
TM 266–01–60–1	?	*Sahelanthropus tchadensis*	6.000	365.00
A.L. 333–45	M	*Australopithecus afarensis*	3.400	500.00
A.L. 162–28	F	*Australopithecus afarensis*	3.400	400.00
A.L. 444–2	M	*Australopithecus afarensis*	2.900	500.00
ARA-VP-12/130	M	*Australopithecus garhi*	2.600	400.00
KNM-WT 17000	M	*Paranthropus aethiopicus*	2.500	410.00
MLD 1	M	*Australopithecus africanus*	2.600	500.00
MLD 37/38	?	*Australopithecus africanus*	2.600	435.00
Sts 5	M	*Australopithecus africanus*	2.250	485.00
Sts 19/58	?	*Australopithecus africanus*	2.250	436.00
Sts 60	?	*Australopithecus africanus*	2.250	428.00
Sts 71	?	*Australopithecus africanus*	2.250	428.00
StW 505	M	*Australopithecus africanus*	2.250	585.00
KNM-ER 406	M	*Paranthropus boisei*	1.800	510.00
KNM-ER 732	F	*Paranthropus boisei*	1.800	500.00
KNM-ER 13750	?	*Paranthropus boisei*	1.800	475.00
KNM-ER 407	?	*Paranthropus boisei*	1.800	506.00
OH 5	M	*Paranthropus boisei*	1.810	530.00
SK 1585	M	*Paranthropus robustus*	1.810	530.00
OH 7	?	*Homo habilis*	1.810	674.00
OH 13	?	*Homo habilis*	1.810	673.00
OH 16	?	*Homo habilis*	1.810	638.00
OH 24	?	*Homo habilis*	1.810	594.00
KNM-ER 1805	?	*Homo habilis*	1.810	582.00
KNM-ER 1813	?	*Homo habilis*	1.810	509.00
KNM-ER 1470	M	*Homo rudolfensis*	1.810	752.00
D2700	F	*Homo georgicus*	1.700	600.00
D2280	M	*Homo georgicus*	1.700	775.00
D2282	M	*Homo georgicus*	1.700	655.00
KNM-ER 3733	M	*Homo erectus*	1.780	804.00
KNM-ER 3883	M	*Homo erectus*	1.580	848.00
OH 9	M	*Homo erectus*	1.200	1067.00
UA 31	M	*Homo erectus*	1.000	775.00
BOU-VP-2/66	M	*Homo erectus*	1.000	995.00
Gongwangling 1	?	*Homo erectus*	1.150	780.00
Sangiran 2	?	*Homo erectus*	1.000	813.00
Sangiran 10	?	*Homo erectus*	0.800	700.00
Sangiran 12	M	*Homo erectus*	0.800	1059.00
Sangiran 17	M	*Homo erectus*	0.800	1004.00
Zhoukoudian D1	M	*Homo erectus*	0.440	1030.00
Zhoukoudian E1	?	*Homo erectus*	0.440	915.00
Zhoukoudian H3	M	*Homo erectus*	0.440	1140.00
Zhoukoudian L1	M	*Homo erectus*	0.440	1225.00
Zhoukoudian L2	?	*Homo erectus*	0.440	1015.00

Table 10.2. (*cont.*)

Specimen	Sex	Taxon	Age (million years)	Cranial capacity (cm³)
Zhoukoudian L3	?	*Homo erectus*	0.440	1030.00
Sambungmacan 1	M	*Homo erectus*	0.400	1035.00
Hexian 1	?	*Homo erectus*	0.200	1025.00
Ngandong 1	?	*Homo erectus*	0.200	1172.00
Ngandong 5	M	*Homo erectus*	0.200	1251.00
Ngandong 6	F	*Homo erectus*	0.200	1013.00
Ngandong 9	M	*Homo erectus*	0.200	1135.00
Ngandong 10	M	*Homo erectus*	0.200	1231.00
Ngandong 11	F	*Homo erectus*	0.200	1090.00
Saldanha 1	M	*Homo heidelbergensis*	0.500	1225.00
Swanscombe 1	M	*Homo heidelbergensis*	0.400	1325.00
Arago 21	M	*Homo heidelbergensis*	0.400	1166.00
Steinheim 1	F	*Homo heidelbergensis*	0.300	950.00
Petralona 1	M	*Homo heidelbergensis*	0.300	1230.00
Ndutu 1	M	*Homo heidelbergensis*	0.400	1100.00
Atapuerca 4	M	*Homo heidelbergensis*	0.300	1390.00
Atapuerca 5	M	*Homo heidelbergensis*	0.300	1125.00
Atapuerca 6	M	*Homo heidelbergensis*	0.300	1140.00
Broken Hill 1	M	*Homo heidelbergensis*	0.300	1280.00
Dali 1	M	*Homo heidelbergensis*	0.300	1120.00
Ehringsdorf 9	M	*Homo heidelbergensis*	0.200	1450.00
Jinnu Shan 1	F	Archaic *Homo*	0.200	1300.00
Narmada 1	M	Archaic *Homo*	0.300	1260.00
Singa 1	M	Archaic *Homo*	0.150	1550.00
Laetoli 18	M	Archaic *Homo*	0.130	1367.00
Omo-Kibish 2	M	Archaic *Homo*	0.130	1435.00
Krapina 3	F	*Homo neanderthalensis*	0.130	1200.00
Saccopastore 1	F	*Homo neanderthalensis*	0.100	1258.00
Tabun C1	F	*Homo neanderthalensis*	0.150	1271.00
Amud 1	M	*Homo neanderthalensis*	0.045	1750.00
La Chapelle-aux-Saints	M	*Homo neanderthalensis*	0.052	1626.00
La Ferrassie 1	M	*Homo neanderthalensis*	0.072	1681.00
Forbes' Quarry	F	*Homo neanderthalensis*	0.050	1200.00
Ganovce 1	F	*Homo neanderthalensis*	0.050	1320.00
Guattari 1	M	*Homo neanderthalensis*	0.057	1550.00
Le Moustier 1	M	*Homo neanderthalensis*	0.040	1600.00
La Quina 5	F	*Homo neanderthalensis*	0.050	1350.00
La Quina 18	F	*Homo neanderthalensis*	0.050	1310.00
Spy 1	F	*Homo neanderthalensis*	0.050	1305.00
Spy 2	M	*Homo neanderthalensis*	0.050	1553.00
Shanidar 1	M	*Homo neanderthalensis*	0.050	1600.00
Shanidar 5	M	*Homo neanderthalensis*	0.050	1550.00
Teshik-Tash 1	M	*Homo neanderthalensis*	0.050	1578.00
Qafzeh 6	M	*Homo sapiens*	0.090	1535.00
Qafzeh 9	M	*Homo sapiens*	0.090	1531.00
Qafzeh 11	F	*Homo sapiens*	0.090	1280.00

Table 10.2. (*cont.*)

Specimen	Sex	Taxon	Age (million years)	Cranial capacity (cm^3)
Skhul 4	M	*Homo sapiens*	0.090	1554.00
Skhul 5	M	*Homo sapiens*	0.090	1518.00
Skhul 9	M	*Homo sapiens*	0.090	1587.00
Cro-Magnon 1	M	*Homo sapiens*	0.030	1600.00
Dolni Vestonice 3	F	*Homo sapiens*	0.026	1322.00
Grotte des Enfants 4	M	*Homo sapiens*	0.028	1775.00
Grotte des Enfants 5	F	*Homo sapiens*	0.028	1375.00
Grotte des Enfants 6	M	*Homo sapiens*	0.028	1580.00
Mladec 1	M	*Homo sapiens*	0.035	1620.00
Mladec 5	M	*Homo sapiens*	0.035	1500.00
Paderbourne	M	*Homo sapiens*	0.027	1531.00
Pataud 1	F	*Homo sapiens*	0.021	1380.00
Pavlov 1	M	*Homo sapiens*	0.026	1522.00
Predmosti 3	M	*Homo sapiens*	0.027	1608.00
Predmosti 4	M	*Homo sapiens*	0.027	1518.00
Predmosti 9	M	*Homo sapiens*	0.027	1555.00
Predmosti 10	F	*Homo sapiens*	0.027	1452.00
Nazlet Khater 1	M	*Homo sapiens*	0.033	1420.00
Minatogawa 1	M	*Homo sapiens*	0.018	1390.00
Minatogawa 2	F	*Homo sapiens*	0.018	1170.00
Minatogawa 4	F	*Homo sapiens*	0.018	1090.00
Zhoukoudian Up. Cave 1	M	*Homo sapiens*	0.018	1500.00
Zhoukoudian Up. Cave 2	F	*Homo sapiens*	0.018	1380.00
Zhoukoudian Up. Cave 3	F	*Homo sapiens*	0.018	1290.00
Arene Candide 1-IP	M	*Homo sapiens*	0.018	1490.00
Arene Candide 1	F	*Homo sapiens*	0.011	1414.00
Arene Candide 2	F	*Homo sapiens*	0.011	1424.00
Arene Candide 4	M	*Homo sapiens*	0.011	1520.00
Arene Candide 5	M	*Homo sapiens*	0.011	1661.00
Barma Grande 2	M	*Homo sapiens*	0.019	1880.00
Bruniquel 2	M	*Homo sapiens*	0.012	1555.00
Cap Blanc 1	F	*Homo sapiens*	0.012	1434.00
Chancelade 1	M	*Homo sapiens*	0.012	1700.00
Oberkassel 1	M	*Homo sapiens*	0.012	1500.00
Oberkassel 2	F	*Homo sapiens*	0.012	1370.00
Saint Germain-la-Riviere 1 F		*Homo sapiens*	0.015	1354.00
San Teodoro 1	F	*Homo sapiens*	0.011	1565.00
San Teodoro 2	M	*Homo sapiens*	0.011	1569.00
San Teodoro 3	M	*Homo sapiens*	0.011	1560.00
San Teodoro 5	F	*Homo sapiens*	0.011	1484.00
Veryier 1	M	*Homo sapiens*	0.010	1430.00
Pecos	F	*Homo sapiens*	0.001	1300.00
Pecos	F	*Homo sapiens*	0.001	1030.00

Table 10.2 (*cont.*)

Specimen	Sex	Taxon	Age (million years)	Cranial capacity (cm^3)
Pecos	F	*Homo sapiens*	0.001	1275.00
Pecos	M	*Homo sapiens*	0.001	1300.00
Pecos	F	*Homo sapiens*	0.001	1120.00
Pecos	F	*Homo sapiens*	0.001	1380.00
Pecos	M	*Homo sapiens*	0.001	1380.00
Pecos	M	*Homo sapiens*	0.001	1270.00
Pecos	F	*Homo sapiens*	0.001	1100.00
Pecos	M	*Homo sapiens*	0.001	1465.00
Pecos	M	*Homo sapiens*	0.001	1320.00
Pecos	F	*Homo sapiens*	0.001	1285.00
Pecos	M	*Homo sapiens*	0.001	1350.00
Pecos	M	*Homo sapiens*	0.001	1440.00
Pecos	M	*Homo sapiens*	0.001	1410.00
Pecos	F	*Homo sapiens*	0.001	1350.00
Pecos	F	*Homo sapiens*	0.001	1190.00
Pecos	M	*Homo sapiens*	0.001	1300.00
Pecos	F	*Homo sapiens*	0.001	1390.00
Pecos	F	*Homo sapiens*	0.001	1350.00
Pecos	F	*Homo sapiens*	0.001	1140.00
Pecos	F	*Homo sapiens*	0.001	1155.00
Pecos	F	*Homo sapiens*	0.001	1178.00
Pecos	M	*Homo sapiens*	0.001	1340.00
Pecos	M	*Homo sapiens*	0.001	1500.00
Pecos	M	*Homo sapiens*	0.001	1550.00
Pecos	M	*Homo sapiens*	0.001	1400.00
Pecos	M	*Homo sapiens*	0.001	1350.00
Pecos	F	*Homo sapiens*	0.001	1325.00

averages may not be as huge a chasm as previously thought. The normal adult human brain can vary in mass from around 850 g through to 1900 g, with body mass varying from 40 to 140 kg. We plotted the data on brain and body mass from a range of individuals of modern humans and compared these with the data from the fossil hominins (Figure 10.1). One interesting aspect of the plots with the 95% confidence intervals depicted is that for the most part, the brain and body masses of modern humans are statistically indistinguishable from the range predicted statistically for the fossil hominins, and in fact the averaged data we have for the largest fossil hominins (*H. sapiens, H. neanderthalensis* and *H. heidelbergensis*) fall well within the 95% confidence intervals for modern humans, with *H. erectus* lying just outside these intervals. Only the smallest or the very largest modern humans were found to have combined brain and body masses that fell outside the 95% confidence intervals of the fossil hominins.

Moreover, the data point for fossil *H. sapiens* (which includes individuals up to 90 ka before present) lies almost directly in the centre of the 95% confidence interval ellipse for the modern *H. sapiens*. Given that we have used species averages for both endocranial capacity and body mass estimates in our analysis of the fossil hominins (with their inherent drawbacks), it is still very striking that modern humans are not completely segregated. Modern humans fall outside of the range found for extant non-hominin hominoids. What we can conclude from this comparison, is that the relationship between brain mass and body mass in modern humans is not different from that seen for the fossil hominins – an important point that we will come back to later.

Two potential evolutionary events in brain mass evolution

The current analysis points to two important events in the evolution of human brain mass that must be considered in more detail. At this point it is important to emphasise that we are discussing species averages – i.e. we are not discussing in detail the great amount of variation that should be found in most species and that we have highlighted in part for modern humans. Moreover, we are not discussing variation, or residuals, around the regressions that indicate the variability that species averages exhibit. Both of these factors are important points, but in terms of the current chapter are peripheral to our central argument. Variation within a species is clearly the material upon which natural selection can select positively to give rise to change, or indeed select negatively to preclude change. The residuals of individual species, whether it is the brain–body mass ratio or any other biological feature, are the material of species specificity, and by examining residuals one may be able to understand the life history or phenotype of that particular species. However, in this one must also be cognisant of the fact that the residuals may be constituted of the innate error of the regression model on which they are based. What we are attempting to outline in the present analysis is the manner in which the actual average mass of the human brain may have evolved. To this end, we first discuss the advent of scaling of the primate brain, then look more specifically at the scaling of the hominin brain.

The genesis of the primate brain–body scaling

The analysis done in the present study for primates, and in many previous studies (e.g. Jerison, 1973; Manger, 2006) indicate that all primates, including prosimians, have larger brains than would be expected for their body mass for a mammal. These studies have also indicated that the non-hominin primates show a strong scaling law of form linking body mass and brain mass. This scaling law of form tells us, with a high and predictable reliability, with which changes in body mass there will be accompanying changes in brain mass. What is also interesting is that the manner in which primate brains and bodies scale runs parallel to that seen for mammals in general, indicating a similar mechanism governing the changes – the only difference being that the brain will be around twice the mass expected for a mammal of similar body mass. Thus, we have an order-specific phylogenetically constrained scaling law of form in the non-hominin primates regulating the mass of the brain relative to the mass of the body. From this it is possible to extrapolate that this scaling law of form regulating the relative mass of the brain and body was founded at the genesis of the primate order. A possible scenario is the uncoupling of the scaling law between these two variables in the very earliest primates, and after a period of intense, but non-lethal mutational changes in the genotype, the law regulating these two variables was recoupled in a manner not dissimilar to that found in other mammals. It is presently unknowable if there were a small population through which a mutational change of this scaling law of form was rapidly spread, whether it was positively selected for through a specific environmental selection pressure, or whether a different mechanism was responsible. The exact mechanism is peripheral to the arguments of this essay – the fact that it occurred and persisted in all subsequent primate descendants is the key point.

The genesis of hominin brain–body scaling

Given the fact that primates have larger brains for their body mass than other mammals and that this is consistent for all primate species, how might the difference in the hominins have arisen? It is important to reiterate here that there is a strong and highly predictable structural law of form that appears to be regulating the relationship between brain and body mass in the hominins. This relationship is evidenced as a positive allometry, meaning that changes in the mass of the brain will occur at a faster rate than changes in the mass of the body. It is possible that the scaling law of form that couples the mass of the brain to the mass of the body in primates may have been uncoupled very early in hominin evolution. Once the hominin lineage stabilised, this scaling law may have recoupled, but in a manner different to that found in the primates, producing the observed positive allometry. It is quite possible that the genetic changes associated with bipedality in the hominins may have had a pleiotropic effect on the genes involved in the regulation of the brain and body mass relationship.

The earliest hominins were not large creatures, with body masses in the range of 25 to 50 kg; thus, they would not have had changes in the mass of the brain relative to those in primates that would require major changes in their ecological niche. As the body mass of the hominins increased, we see concomitant increases in the mass of the brain. At first, this is not so marked in the australopithecines, where body mass may have only increased by a few kilograms relative to the earliest hominids such as *Orrorin tugenesis* (recovered from Kenya, Senut *et al.*, 2001). Later in hominin evolution there was a marked increase in body mass and an even more marked increase in brain mass, occurring simultaneously in early *Homo*, where body mass increased by between 15 to 20 kg and cranial capacity by 100 to 200 ml. The greater proportional increase in cranial capacity could be attributed to the positive allometry in the brain–body mass scaling relationship. The remaining evolution of the *Homo* lineage shows increases in body mass, with allometrically rapid increases in cranial capacity until modern times. We are thus left with the conclusion that the positive allometric relationship between brain and body mass in the hominin lineage is likely to be the reason that the brain of modern *Homo sapiens* is the mass we can readily observe. This combined with the initial allometrically constrained increase in the brain–body mass relationship of primates provides a substantial evolutionary explanation as to why the modern human brain is far larger that would be expected for our body mass in comparison to other mammals.

Conclusion

Given that it is possible that the majority of the evolution of the mass of the modern human brain can be explained by allometric laws of scaling, there are still several areas that cannot yet be addressed with our current state of knowledge. The first is the reason why the scaling laws changed during the early evolution of primates, endowing the primates with larger brains for their body mass than would be expected for mammals. The second is the manner in which the scaling laws changed at the origin of the hominin lineage. We feel it is likely to be related to pleiotropic effects of the genes responsible for bipedalism, but further experimentation is required to determine if this may be true. Third, there is very little information available on the evolution of the microstructure of the human brain. Features such as the complexity of the single neuron (Elston *et al.*, 2006), the number of areas in the cerebral cortex (Manger, 2005), the molecular functionality of intra- and extracellular components of receptor complexes, and so on – all need to be studied in detail across extant primates to determine where modern humans differ and how these difference might have evolved, what effect they will have on the function of the brain, and whether these changes are related to overall mass of the brain (Gould may have called these 'spandrels upon spandrels').

Another factor that must be understood is whether, with the allometric scalings that are known, there was selection for increased body mass, or increased brain mass in hominin evolution. At this point we may create a chicken-and-egg argument – was increased brain mass selected for resulting in increased body mass, or vice versa? The African elephant (*Loxodonta africana*) has a brain that weighs approximately 6 kg, and a body that is very large; however, it has an encephalisation quotient (EQ) of approximately 1.12, or just slightly larger (1.12 times) than that expected for a mammal of its mass. In explaining the mass of the elephant brain, should we postulate that this mammal required a large brain and the selection pressures providing the impetus for a large brain resulted in a de facto large body? On the other end of the mass scale, if we examine the Proboscis bat (*Rhynchonycteris nasa*) that has a body mass of 3.8 g and a brain mass of 0.118 g, giving an EQ of 0.9 (slightly smaller than expected for a mammal of its body mass), do we propose that selection pressures requiring a small brain and a concomitantly small body produced this phenotype? In both cases, it is more parsimonious to propose that pressures selecting for the differing body masses produced the mass of the brain – but along the trajectory determined by the mammalian class level allometric scaling law of form.

Given the phylogenetic occurrence of allometric scaling between brain and body mass across all vertebrates, and the clear relationship between environmental factors and body mass across all vertebrates (e.g. Pearson, 2000), should we single out the hominin lineage as a special case? This of course has been done when seeking adaptationist rationale for the evolution of the brain mass of modern humans. If, however, we take the more parsimonious approach and argue that the mass of the human brain evolved as a by-product of increasing body mass in hominins, we then must conclude that human brain mass is in fact a spandrel – a functionally useful one to be sure, probably not something to be selected against, but the by-product of a change in the scaling relationship of brain and body mass that occurred at the genesis of the hominin lineage. Further studies into the evolution of hominin body mass and the relationship of this to environmental or other factors will potentially shed more light on the evolution of human brain (Pearson, 2000).

References

Abbate, E., Albianelli, A., Azzaroli, A. *et al.* (1998). A one-million-year old *Homo* cranium from the Danakil (Afar) Depression of Eritrea. *Nature*, **393**: 458–60.

Aiello, L. C. and Dean, M. C. (1990). *An Introduction to Human Evolutionary Anatomy.* London. Academic Press.

Asfaw, B., White, T., Lovejoy, C. O. *et al.* (1999). *Australopithecus garhi*: a new species of early hominid from Ethiopia. *Science*, **284**:629–35.

Asfaw, B., Gilbert, W. H., Beyene, J. *et al.* (2002). Remains of *Homo erectus* from Bouri, Middle Awash, Ethiopia. *Nature*, **416**: 317–20.

Blinkov, S. M. and Glezer, I. I. (1968). *The Human Brain in Figures and Tables. A Quantitative Handbook.* New York: Plenum Press.

Dubois, E. (1897). Sur le rapport de l'encéphale avec la grandeur du corps chez les Mammifères. *Bulletin de la Societe Anthropologie Paris, 4e série*, **8**: 337–74.

Elston, G. N., Benavides-Piccione, R., Elston, A. *et al.* (2006). Specializations of the granular prefrontal cortex of primates: implications for cognitive processing. Anatomical Record A. *Discoveries in Molecular Cellular and Evolutionary Biology*, **288**: 26–35.

Finlay, B. L. and Darlington, R. B. (1995). Linked regularities in the development and evolution of mammalian brains. *Science*, **268**:1578–84.

Gould, S. J. (2002). *The Structure of Evolutionary Theory.* Cambridge, MA: Belknap Press.

Henneberg, M. (1998). Evolution of the human brain: is bigger better? *Clinical and Experimental Pharmacology and Physiology*, **25**: 745–9.

Jerison, H. J. (1973). *Evolution of the Brain and Intelligence.* New York: Academic Press.

Manger, P. R. (2005). Establishing order at the systems level in mammalian brain evolution. *Brain Research Bulletin*, **66**: 282–9.

(2006). An examination of cetacean brain structure with a novel hypothesis correlating thermogenesis to the evolution of a big brain. *Biological Reviews of the Cambridge Philosophical Society*, **81**: 293–338.

Martin, R. D. (1981). Relative brain size and basal metabolic rate in terrestrial vertebrates. *Nature*, **293**: 57–60.

(1983). Human brain evolution in an ecological context. *52nd James Arthus Lecture on the Evolution of the Human Brain.* New York: American Museum of Natural History.

Mayr, E. (2002). *What Evolution Is.* London: Phoenix.

McHenry, H. M. (1992). Body size and proportions in early hominids. *American Journal of Physical Anthropology*, **87**: 407–431.

Pearson, O. M. (2000). Activity, climate, and postcranial robusticity: implications for modern human origins and scenarios of adaptive change. *Current Anthropology*, **41**: 569–607.

Rightmire, G. P., Lordkipanidze, D. and Vekua, A. (2006). Anatomical descriptions, comparative studies and evolutionary significance of the hominin skulls from Dmanisi, Republic of Georgia. *Journal of Human Evolution*, **50**: 115–41.

Ruff, C. B., Trinkaus, E. and Holliday, T. W. (1997). Body size and encephalisation in Pleistocene *Homo. Nature*, **387**: 173–6.

Senut, B., Pickford, M., Gommery, D. *et al.* (2001). First hominid from the Miocene (Lukeino Formation, Kenya). *Compte Rendus Academie des Sciences, Paris*, **337**: 137–44.

Spocter, M. A. and Manger, P. R. (2007). The use of cranial variables for the estimation of body weight in fossil hominids. *American Journal of Physical Anthropology*, **134**: 92–105.

Tobias, P. V. (1994). The craniocerebral interface in early hominids. In Corruccini, R. S. and Ciochon, R. L. (eds.), *Integrative Paths to the Past: Paleoanthropological Advances in Honor of F. Clark-Howell*. Englewood Cliffs, New Jersey: Prentice Hall, pp. 185–203.

Wood, B. and Collard, M. (1999). The human genus. *Science*, **284**: 65–71.

Zollikofer, C. P. E., Ponce de León, M. S., Lieberman, D. E. *et al.* (2005). Virtual reconstruction of *Sahelanthropus tchadensis*. *Nature*, **434**: 755–9.

11 Origin and diversity of early hominin bipedalism

HENRY M. MCHENRY

Abstract

The causes and conditions that lead to the expansion of knowledge are multiple, but sometimes there arises a singular and powerful force. For more than a half a century, Phillip Tobias has exerted such an influence on our understanding of human evolution. His influence has been profound not only from his prolific scholarship, but in his generous gift of inspiring a generation of students and colleagues. It is auspicious indeed that Taung and Tobias entered our world in the same year.

What more have we learned in the 80 years that followed? First and foremost is that Dart was right: *Australopithecus africanus* was on the uniquely human branch of the tree of life (despite its ape-sized brain), was bipedal, and that Africa is truly the cradle of humankind as abundantly shown by discovery teams led by Tobias, Clarke, Broom, Robinson, the Leakeys, Howell, Johanson, Kimbel, White, Brunet, Hill, Senut, Pickford, Asfaw, Haile-Selassie and many others.

In the rich literature on why our ancestors became bipedal appear advocates of single hypotheses and those who take a more ecumenical approach. The beginning place has to be an appreciation of historical constraints. Our last common ancestor with the animal world was constrained by the fact that it had a body of a hominoid without typical mammalian quadrupedal specialisations. Terrestrially, chimps walk quadrupedally and bipedally with equal energetic expenditure, which is about 50% more expensive than the average mammal. This fact is based on studies of two young chimps, but ongoing studies at University of California, Davis of the bioenergetics of three adult female and two male chimps confirm this finding.

Does our current published sample of early hominins document the intermediate steps between ape-like and human-like gaits? There is a rich series of craniodental transformations through time from ape-like to human-like, but

African Genesis: Perspectives on Hominin Evolution, eds. Sally C. Reynolds and Andrew Gallagher. Published by Cambridge University Press. © Cambridge University Press 2012.

so far the intermediate steps between ape and human gaits are undocumented. All of the candidates for earliest hominin show signs of upright walking. The head balance of *Sahelanthropus*, the human-like thighs of *Orrorin*, the dorsally canted toes of *Ardipithecus kadabba* suggest the adoption of bipedality came before 6 to 5 million years ago. Between 4 and 2 million years there is abundant fossil evidence of bipedally adapted hominins, but analyses of this material often reveal surprisingly different complexes of locomotor traits that appear to indicate considerable diversity of adaptations.

Introduction

The African Genesis Symposium celebrated the year 1925 that saw the announcement of the discovery of the Taung child and the birth of Phillip V. Tobias. Both events have had a profound effect on our understanding of human evolution. The Taung child was cradled by hands that knew what it meant: Dart recognised its odd combination of human and ape characteristics (Dart, 1925). What it meant was clarified by discoveries at Sterkfontein, Kromdraai, Swartkrans and especially by Tobias's and others' work at Makapansgat. *Australopithecus africanus* is a key link to the origin of *Homo* and it is wonderful that he provided the definitive description and interpretation of the origin of the genus *Homo* in his majestic volumes on *Homo habilis* (Tobias, 1991). This chapter will raise three topics for discussion: (1) bipedal origins; (2) fossil evidence for intermediate steps between ape-like and human-like gaits; and (3) diversity and uniqueness in the postcranium of early hominins.

Bipedalism

Darwin was certainly ecumenical and cautious: bipedalism arose when our ancestors began 'to live somewhat less on trees and more on the ground', which was due to 'a change in its manner of procuring subsistence, or to a change in the conditions of its native country' (Darwin, 1872: 135). In the century and a half that followed the publication of these words arose numerous clarifications.

One was the appreciation of historical constraints. The body plan of the last common ancestor of African apes and humans was constrained by the fact that it had a body of a hominoid without typical mammalian quadrupedal specialisations. Apes and people have peculiar trunks and forelimbs, a fact particularly emphasised by Keith (1923), Gregory (1928) and many others. Our ancestors did not give up the powerful and efficient running ability of the typical quadrupedal mammal – they never had such ability. They shared the distinctive characteristics of all living members of the superfamily Hominoidea – short lower backs, flat chests, and highly mobile shoulders, elbows, and wrists – suitable for climbing, hanging, swinging in trees, but not ideal for terrestrial quadrupedalism.

In a classic study published in 1973, Taylor and Rowntree (1973) showed that terrestrially, chimps walk quadrupedally and bipedally with equal energetic expenditure, which is about 50% more expensive than the average mammal (Rodman and McHenry, 1980). This finding has been doubted because it is based on studies of two very young (two-year-old) chimps (Steudel-Numbers, 2003). A major reason that this study has not been replicated with more subjects is that adult chimps are notoriously difficult to control. There have been studies of the energetics of other non-human primates walking bipedally especially using *Macaca fuscata* subjects (Nakatsukasa *et al.*, 2006), but not of chimps until now.

Results from ongoing studies at the University of California, Davis, of the bioenergetics of three adult female and two adult male chimps trained for four months to walk on a treadmill appear to confirm some of Taylor and Rowntree's (1973) findings. Michael Sockol's efforts reveal that adult chimps are also inefficient quadrupeds (by mammalian standards) and equally inefficient bipeds (Figure 11.1; Sockol, 2006; Sockol *et al.*, 2007). Perhaps the most significant finding is the presence of considerable variability among individual chimps in their quadrupedal and bipedal energetics. Although most of the subjects used less energy while walking on all fours, one chimp expended considerably less energy while walking bipedally than she did quadrupedally. It is reasonable to assume that such variability existed in the Miocene common ancestors of

Figure 11.1. The bioenergetics of bipedal and quadrupedal walking in *Pan troglodytes* determined by Michael Sockol of the University of California, Davis. (See plate section for colour version.)

human and chimps. Phenotypic variability is the fuel that allows natural selection to operate when conditions change.

What do these energetic findings mean to the origin of human bipedality? First and foremost it means that there is no energetic Rubicon to cross – our ancestor was not giving up a terrestrial locomotor skill that was anything like that of a typical quadrupedal mammal (Rodman and McHenry, 1980). Second, it confirms what has long been known from comparative anatomy – species of Hominoidea have trunks and forelimbs poorly suited to typical mammalian quadrupedalism (Richmond *et al.*, 2001). Third, it fits very well within the framework of evolutionary ecology. From this point of view the trigger for bipedality can be multiple. With no energetic Rubicon, our common ancestor may have adopted bipedality for a number of reasons. There is certainly a variety of ideas to advocate. Some of the favourite explanations for the origin of human bipedality include carrying (Bartholomew Jr. and Birdsell, 1953; Hewes, 1961, 1964; Lovejoy, 1981; Marzke and Shackley, 1986), display or warning (Livingstone, 1962; Wescott, 1967; Ravey, 1978; Jablonski and Chaplin, 1992, 1993, 2004), new feeding adaptations (DuBrul, 1962; Jolly, 1970; Hunt, 1994; Stanford, 2003; Kingdon, 2003), tools (Washburn, 1960, 1963) or a combination of these (Napier, 1963; Sigmon, 1971; Rose, 1976, 1982, 1989). Habitat changes probably played an important role in the adoption of bipedalism in our hominoid ancestor as Darwin (1872) noted long ago and many others have supported (Romer, 1959; Hockett and Ascher, 1964; Ishida, 2006). Particularly important may have been the feeding-site fragmentation that occurred during the later part of the Miocene when our ancestors witnessed the back and forth shrinking and expanding of the forest resources (Vrba *et al.*, 1995; Andrews, 1996; Andrews *et al.*, 1997; Pilbeam and Young, 2004; Trauth *et al.*, 2005; Behrensmeyer, 2006). For some populations, terrestrial travel distance between feeding sites became greater and greater. Some knuckle-walked, but some, like all lesser apes today, preferred to walk bipedally. Here is where multiple causes can be invoked – there is no energetic threshold – all hominoids are awkward terrestrially except for modern humans. Feeding from the ground as chimps do today, carrying food, infants, weapons, all the many advantages of having hands free, can be cited as reasons for bipedality in our hominoid ancestor.

According to those who have done the first descriptions and analyses of *Ardipithecus ramidus*, that 4.4 million-year-old species shares derived traits uniquely with later hominins relative to apes and it provides a basis for reconstructing the last common ancestor of the ape and human lineages (Lovejoy *et al.*, 2009). An alternative interpretation that needs to be explored by independent observers who now will be allowed access to the original fossils is the possibility that *Ar. ramidus* has little to do with the origin of human bipedalism. Its crushed ilium may be reconstructed as shorter than the equivalent bone in

Figure 11.1. The bioenergetics of bipedal and quadrupedal walking in *Pan troglo-dytes* determined by Michael Sockol of the University of California, Davis.

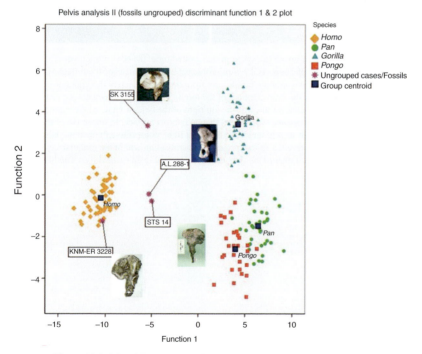

Figure 11.5. Plot of functions 1 and 2 (accounting for 97% of the total variance) of a multiple discriminant analysis of 16 shape variables. Note the very human-like projection of the 1.9 million-year-old KNM-ER 3228, the intermediate positions and close proximity of the *Australopithecus afarensis* (A.L. 288–1; 3.2 Ma) and *A. africanus* (Sts 14; *c.* 2.7 Ma) specimens, and the unique position of the *Paranthropus robustus* pelvis (SK 3155; *c.* 1.7 Ma).

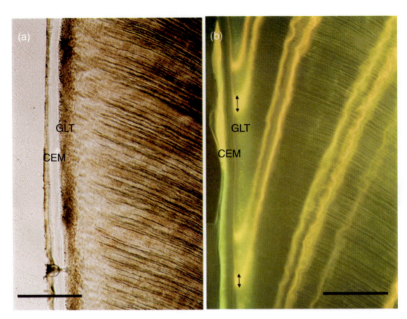

Figure 14.2. In image (a), taken in transmitted light, the cementum layer (CEM) and granular layer of Tomes (GLT) are visible each approximately 50 μm thick. Deep to these layers, many dentine tubules run from the region deep to the granular layer of Tomes towards the pulp chamber of the tooth. Some daily increments are just visible in the dentine, clearest towards the top right of the field of view, where rates are much faster (and increments wider apart) than at the root surface. In image (b) of the same root surface, but seen in incident ultraviolet light, consecutive fluorescing label-lines of tetracycline reveal a faster spread of mineralisation within the granular layer of Tomes (arrowed) than in the thinner label-lines just deep to this layer. The black scale bars = 200 μm.

Figure 14.3. Ground section of the mesial M₃ root in polarised transmitted light showing coarse accentuated incremental markings in the more complete lingual root. The buccal root is eroded at the surface and preserves only the inner portion and that part adjoining the lingual root at the bifurcation. Between the trabeculae in the alveolar bone, crystals, probably calcite, have formed in some of the marrow spaces. Field width 6.75 mm.

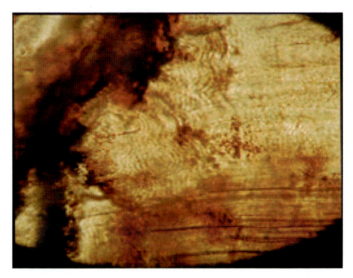

Figure 14.4. Daily incremental markings in the dentine of the canine root apex. In this position the increments are spaced approximately 2.5 μm apart and are characteristically calcospheritic.

Figure 16.1. The digital fossil (blue – Mrs. Ples alias Sts 5 from South Africa; yellow inside – its virtual endocast shining through the transparent cranium; orange in the background – coronal, sagittal and transversal projection views) can be visualised, manipulated and measured in a computer environment using 3D software (here Amira© 5.3.3).

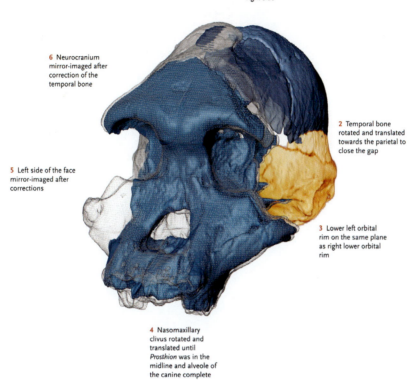

1 Supraorbital torus
mirror-imaged from
right side

6 Neurocranium
mirror-imaged after
correction of the
temporal bone

2 Temporal bone
rotated and translated
towards the parietal to
close the gap

5 Left side of the face
mirror-imaged after
corrections

3 Lower left orbital
rim on the same plane
as right lower orbital
rim

4 Nasomaxillary
clivus rotated and
translated until
Prosthion was in the
midline and alveole of
the canine complete

Figure 16.2. The anatomical reconstruction of StW 505 (South Africa). (From Gunz, 2005.)

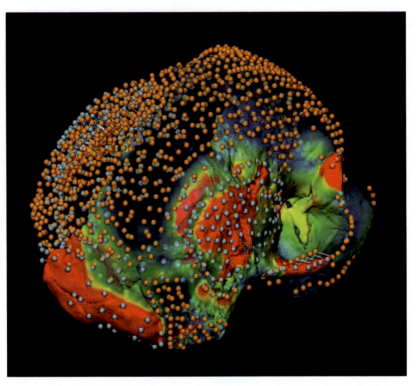

Figure 16.3. The geometric reconstruction of Sts 71 (South Africa) using hundreds of landmarks and semi-landmarks, including points on the internal braincase (orange spheres: before reconstruction; blue spheres: after reconstruction based on Sts 5). Red areas indicate large differences between the original and the reconstruction, blue indicates small differences. (From Gunz, 2005.)

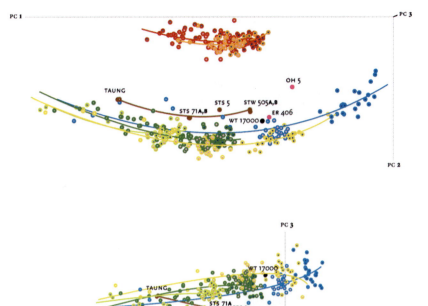

Figure 16.4. Growth trajectories of extant hominoids and australopiths based on several hundred 3D landmarks and semi-landmarks on the entire cranium. *Pan paniscus* in light green, *Pan troglodytes* in dark green, *Gorilla gorilla* in blue, *Pongo pygmaeus* in yellow, *Homo sapiens* (Khoi San) in orange, *Homo sapiens* (Europe) in red, *Australopithecus africanus* in brown, *A./P. boisei in* magenta, WT 17000 in black. (From Gunz, 2005.)

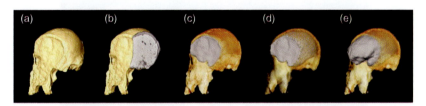

Figure 16.5. 3D reconstruction (yellow) and virtual endocast (grey) of MLD 37/38: (a) displays the virtual specimen as it is; (b) shows a parasagittal cut and the composition of the embedded matrix along this CT slice; (c) the virtual endocast results in 378 cm³ for the preserved endocranial cavity; (d) virtual endocast and semi-landmarks in the transparent cranium; (e) the reconstructed virtual endocast based on TPS warping using Sts 5 as reference specimen gives 450 cm³ as the estimate for the cranial capacity of MLD 37/38.

Figure 26.2. Sibudu Cave excavations.

Figure 27.8. Marine shells modified by Middle Palaeolithic humans (Ronen *et al.*, 2007).

Figure 27.10. Engraved ochre 70 ka old from Blombos Cave, South Africa.

modern apes, but its very long ischium and divergent hallux place it squarely among the non-hominins. For those who are familiar with the radiation of Miocene Hominoidea, its hominin status is subject to doubt (Harrison, 2010).

Fossil record of transition?

Does the fossil record document the transition between non-bipedal prehominins and human bipedalism? A major clue is the StW 573 skeleton. Its discovery was a great triumph for the Sterkfontein Research Unit under the direction of Phillip Tobias and a well deserved reward for the skillful and persistent work of Ron Clarke (Clarke and Tobias, 1995; Tobias, 1998; Clarke, 1998,1999a,b, 2002; Tobias *et al.*, 1999–2001; Partridge *et al.*, 2003; Pickering *et al.*, 2004).

The first reports after Ron Clarke's discovery of Little Foot emphasised its adaptation to bipedalism, but also its abducted and mobile hallux (Clarke and Tobias, 1995). In their 1995 *Science* article, Clarke and Tobias noted features of the navicular and especially of the medial cuneiform that supported their view that the big toe was divergent. The facet for the first metatarsal on the medial cuneiform is strongly convex and wraps more medially than is true of modern humans. When this paper was published, I happened to be travelling among museums collecting comparative data on ape and human postcranial variability. So I began collecting information on the medial cuneiform to compare with StW 573. In particular I measured the area projected on the medial plane of the hallucial facet and of the total medial surface of the medial cuneiform.

The results (McHenry and Jones, 2006) showed that humans and apes contrast sharply (Figure 11.2). The average per cent of the total medial surface area that is taken up by the hallucial facet is 8% in humans with an observed range of 3 to 14%. Chimps have an average of 36% (24 to 45% range), StW 573 is 13% – at the upper end of the human range but below *Pan* (Table 11.1).

In this one trait, 'Little Foot' (StW 573) appears to have a convergent big toe, but the original describers (Clarke and Tobias, 1995) point out many other characters that seem to show that the Sterkfontein Member 2 hominin had a divergent big toe. It does make one wonder, however, about our current early hominin sample of postcranial elements. Does it document the transition between non-bipedal prehominins and human bipedalism? Certainly fossil hominin postcrania show many traits unlike modern humans and presumably left over from the last common ancestor (Stern, 2000; Ward, 2002). 'Lucy' and her kin from the Pliocene beds of Hadar had curved fingers and toes, relatively short femora and a whole host of other primitive features. So in some sense *Australopithecus afarensis* is transitional in its body plan. But there is wisdom in what the original describers emphasised about the postcranium of this

Table 11.1. *Relative size of metatarsal one facet on the medial surface of the medial cuneiform expressed as a percentage of total medial surface area of the medial cuneiform. McHenry and Jones (2006) describe the comparative sample and measurement techniques.*

Specimens	Sample size	Relative size of MT I facet (%)	Observed range (%)
Homo sapiens	33	8.2	3.1–13.7
Pan	18	35.7	24.3–44.8
Gorilla	12	30.1	16.0–37.7
Pongo	15	25.7	16.0–34.8
StW 573	1	13.0	–
OH 8	1	16.1	–

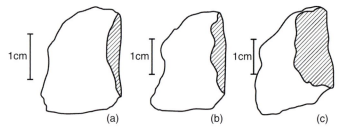

Figure 11.2. Medial side of the medial cuneiform of *Homo sapiens* (a), StW 573c (b) and *Pan paniscus* (c) with the facet for the first metatarsal shaded.

species (Johanson *et al.*, 1982a,b; Lovejoy, 2005a,b). Its body plan was altered in significant ways to adapt it to bipedality. No other primate has such a relatively short iliac blade, strong lumbar curve, medial convergence of the knees and adducted hallux. These changes imply a profound alteration of the genetic template controlling the growth of the locomotor skeleton away from the normal primate pattern to something novel.

From 3.5 to 1.5 million years ago there is a rich fossil record of postcranial elements that appears to belong to bipedal hominins, but does it show a steady transformation through time from the primitive last common ancestor to *Homo sapiens*? Do postcranial changes track time the way some aspects of the craniodental traits appear to do? A case can be made for craniodental transformations that vaguely track time (McHenry, 2002). The earliest specimens are remarkably primitive in many craniodental features. For example, the first deciduous lower molar is ape-like in *Ardipithecus*, slightly less so in *Australopithecus anamensis*, and more human-like in later species of *Australopithecus*

(Leakey *et al.*, 1998). The basicranium looks rather ape-like in the earliest species, more human-like in *A. africanus*, and *Homo*-like in the late species of robust australopithecines and *Homo* (Dean and Wood, 1981, 1982; Strait *et al.*, 1997; Strait, 2001). Brains expand through time from apes-sized to the larger early members of the genus *Homo* and then expand explosively over the last 2 million years (McHenry and Coffing, 2000; Delson *et al.*, 2000).

Does postcranial morphology follow a similar pattern? In some traits it does, perhaps. For example, the capitate of the 4.1 million-year-old *Australopithecus anamensis* has more ape-like orientation of the MC II facet relative to the MC III facet than is true of that of *A. afarensis* and *A. africanus* (McHenry, 1983; Leakey *et al.*, 1998; Ward *et al.*, 2001). The capitates of these later australopithecine species still exhibit more ape-like shapes relative to *Homo*. Another example is the relative length of the femur – at 3.2 million years ago, it is short relative to the length of the humerus; by 2.5 million years ago it is intermediate; and by 1.54 million years ago it is relatively long like modern humans (Jungers, 1982; Ruff and Walker, 1993; Richmond *et al.*, 2002; Haeusler and McHenry, 2004; Reno *et al.*, 2005). But in most respects, our current fossil record does not reveal an obvious pattern of primitive to derived traits through time. In fact, sometimes what appear to be primitive features re-appear through time despite the accumulation of

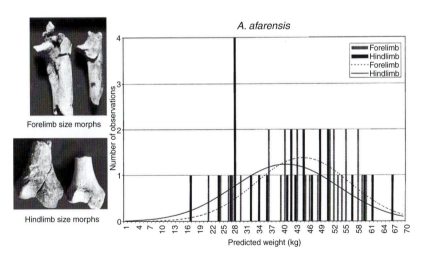

Figure 11.3. Fore- and hindlimb proportions in *Australopithecus afarensis* using body mass predicting formulae derived from a modern human sample (McHenry and Berger, 1998). Both large and small morphs are represented in the forelimb skeleton (e.g. the proximal ulnae A.L. 333x-5 on the left and A.L. 333w-36 on the right) and the hindlimb skeleton (e.g. the distal femora A.L. 333–4 on the left and A.L. 129–1A on the right).

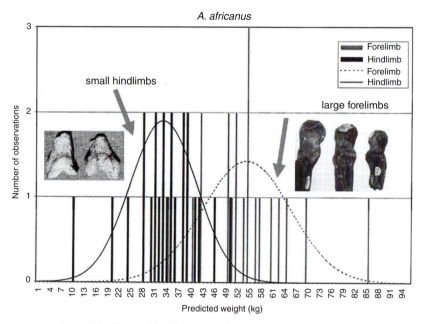

Figure 11.4. Fore- and hindlimb proportions in *Australopithecus africanus* using body mass predicting formulae derived from a modern human sample (McHenry and Berger, 1998). Although large and small morphs are represented in the forelimb skeleton (e.g. StW 431 on the left versus StW 398 on the right), large morph hindlimb specimens are rarely represented in the sample (e.g. StW 34, on the left, is the largest distal femur specimen and TM 1513, on the right, is the smallest).

craniodental synapomorphies in geologically later species. A case in point is relative limb-joint size. In the more ancient and craniodentally more primitive species of *A. afarensis*, fore-to-hindlimb joint sizes are like those seen in *Homo* (there are small and big fore- and hindlimb elements) (Figure 11.3; McHenry and Berger, 1998). But in *A. africanus*, which is later in time and craniodentally more like *Homo*, forelimb joints are bigger and hindlimb joints are smaller in size (Figure 11.4). This same pattern can be seen in the two associated partial skeletons of *A. afarensis* (A.L. 288–1) and *A. africanus* (StW 431). The size of the forelimb relative to the lower body is more human-like in *A. afarensis* and more ape-like in *A. africanus*.

Diverse styles of bipedalism?

Living models, or analogues, are important to accurately reconstruct the functional meaning of morphological traits. For human evolutionary studies, the closest extant species are highly specialised bipeds and knuckle-walking quad-rupeds. It is to be expected that ancient hominins had postures and locomotor repertoires that were not exactly like these living models. Unfortunately, many studies of early hominid postcranial specimens have been unnecessarily lim-ited by attempts to interpret the functional morphology of fossils without fully appreciating the uniqueness of extinct species. Often the question asked in these studies is too simple: is the specimen from a biped or not? When traits or combinations of features are found that do not occur in modern humans or apes, functional interpretation is more difficult to establish and therefore less reliable in the reconstruction of posture and locomotion. They can be dis-missed as noise that provides little information about the functional anatomy of the fossil species. But the noise has become deafening.

Perhaps the loudest bell rang when Kamoya Kimeu discovered the early *Homo* skeleton KNM-WT 15000 in 1984 and the whole of this specimen emerged by the skillful work of the Leakey–Walker team (Walker and Leakey, 1993). Its body contrasted so sharply with what was known for *Australopithecus* that it made some previous interpretations of early hominin postcrania sus-pect. According to the original describers, *Australopithecus afarensis* had an 'adaptation to full and complete bipedality' (Johanson *et al.*, 1982b: 386) and a forelimb 'not primarily involved in locomotor behavior' (Johanson *et al.*, 1982b: 385). That interpretation contrasted strongly with descriptions empha-sising the apparent arboreal adaptations of *A. afarensis* (Tuttle, 1981; Stern and Susman, 1983; Susman *et al.*, 1984, 1985). When 'Lucy' (*A. afarensis*) lies next to the Turkana Boy (*H. erectus*), the contrast becomes overwhelming and the uniqueness and diversity of the australopithecine body-plan become undeniable. The simple dichotomy of bipedal human versus quadrupedal ape remains important but oversimplified. Many have pointed this out long ago when the sample of fossils was small. For example, it is the theme of Charles Oxnard's 1975 book *Uniqueness and Diversity in Human Evolution* (Oxnard, 1975), but there has always been resistance to accepting uniqueness because, by definition, there are no living analogues. The relationship between acet-abulum size and iliac blade size and shape in the *Paranthropus robustus* hip fragment, SK 3155, for example, is outside that seen in modern apes and humans (Figure 11.5; McHenry, 1975b). One can analyse it biomechanically so it fits with human expectations (McHenry, 1975a), but it is still unlike any-thing alive today.

The sample of fossil hominin ulnae shows remarkably diverse morphologies that do not spread neatly between early specimens that are more ape-like and later specimens that are more human-like. Instead, the 3.4 million-year-old spe-cimen of *A. afarensis*, A.L. 438–1a, is remarkably human-like (Drapeau *et al.*, 2005) relative to the geologically more recent and unusual specimens from

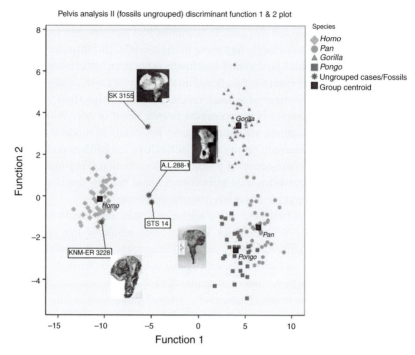

Figure 11.5. Plot of functions 1 and 2 (accounting for 97% of the total variance) of a multiple discriminant analysis of 16 shape variables. Note the very human-like projection of the 1.9 million-year-old KNM-ER 3228, the intermediate positions and close proximity of the *Australopithecus afarensis* (A.L. 288–1; 3.2 Ma) and *A. africanus* (Sts 14; *c.* 2.7 Ma) specimens, and the unique position of the *Paranthropus robustus* pelvis (SK 3155; *c.* 1.7 Ma). (See plate section for colour version.)

Olduvai Bed IV, OH 36, (Aiello *et al.*, 1999) and Omo, L40–19 (McHenry *et al.*, 1976). The postcranial specimens attributed to *Ardipithecus* (White *et al.*, 1994; Haile-Selassie, 2001; Lovejoy *et al.*, 2009), have morphologies unlike *A. afarensis* or any other hominoid species. Those charged with the duty of describing *Ardipithecus* have published important papers on the embryogenesis of postcranial elements that are directed at understanding the way in which adult morphologies form developmentally and, by inference, evolutionarily (Lovejoy *et al.*, 1999, 2000, 2002, 2003; Lovejoy, 2005a,b). One needs to understand the genetic and developmental processes involved in the formation of adult morphologies, of course, but it is still a challenge to understand what unique fossil morphologies mean in terms of adaptation.

Once the process of transformation from ape-like posture and locomotion to human-like bipedalism is explained in a way that seems reasonable, it will become apparent that there may have been many hominoid species that adopted bipedalism. The possibility of several bipedal apes is a common theme in the literature on human evolution (e.g. Kingdon, 2003). It is entirely possible that bipedal hominoids do not form a monophyletic group. Such an idea stirs actively in many minds involved in interpreting human evolution. Only one bipedal hominid lineage survived (*Homo*), but the ancestry of that lineage may have included many bipedal hominoids. *Sahelanthropus* may be a bipedal ape with a reduced canine that evolved because it had free hands for sticks and stones to replace the function of threatening and damaging male canines (Darwin, 1872). The same might be true of *Orrorin* and *Ardipithecus*. The mosaic of human-like, ape-like and unique features of the postcranium of *Au. sediba* are further evidence of the complexity in the evolution of hominin bipedality (Berger *et al.*, 2010; Kibii *et al.*, 2011; Kivell *et al.*, 2011; Zipfel *et al.*, 2011). The 'robust' australopithecines might be an entirely different lineage to the one leading to *Homo*, but the fact that the later species share so many characteristics with *Homo* makes that unlikely from the point of view of parsimony (McHenry, 1996; Strait and Grine, 2004).

One might despair at the apparent difficulties of interpreting the hominin fossil record. An honest view can hardly be arrogant. Certainty in human evolution studies it is a sure sign of self-deception. We work in a branch of science that generates extraordinary interest by all who are curious, but we must accept that we will always be living with working hypotheses that are alive and ready for revision as new evidence arrives.

Conclusions

New data and analyses on the bioenergetics of adult chimpanzee locomotion show that the cost of bipedalism is actually lower than that of quadrupedalism in one out of five subjects. It is reasonable to infer that variability in locomotor efficiency was present in populations of the last common ancestor of chimps and humans. There was no energetic barrier to the adoption of bipedalism and many advantages to having free hands (e.g. carrying, display, new feeding adaptations, tools). Unfortunately, at present there are no published fossils that clearly document the intermediate stages between quadrupedalism and bipedalism. Even the very early remains from Sterkfontein Member 2 have bipedal specialisations, although they and other early fossils retain many primitive features. The fossil record does document a surprising amount of diversity among hominid species in their postcranial morphology that surely relates to differences in posture and locomotion. There is no linear accumulation of human-like traits through time, but diversity that reflects adaptations to local environments.

We are so fortunate to live at this exciting time when we are discovering so much about the roots of our biological family. We celebrate these discoveries and particularly we pay tribute to key players in the study of human evolution. Raymond Dart recognised the Taung child as part of our lineage and Phillip Tobias has carried the torch of Dart's wisdom throughout the stormy waves of political upheavals and collegial disagreements to a place where we can truly appreciate the magnificent unfolding of our lineage's origin.

Acknowledgements

I thank Professor Phillip V. Tobias for his support, encouragement, mentorship and wisdom over more than three-and-a-half decades of friendship. I am grateful to Sally Reynolds, Andrew Gallagher, Heather White, Colin Menter and all their colleagues, staff, donors and students who made the African Genesis Symposium possible. I am particularly grateful to Ron Clarke for more than three-and-a-half decades of friendship, good advice and generosity in allowing me to study the precious fossils that he has discovered. I thank R. E. Leakey, M. G. Leakey, the late M. D. Leakey and the staff of the National Museum of Kenya; D. C. Johanson, B. Latimer, W. Kimbel, and the staff of the Cleveland Museum of Natural History and the Institute of Human Origins; Solomon Wordekal, Alemu Ademasu, Berhane Asfaw, T. D. White and the staff of the National Museum of Ethiopia; C. K. Brain, F. Thackeray and the staff of the Transvaal Museum; and P. V. Tobias, the late A. R. Hughes, R. J. Clarke, the staff of the Department of Anatomy and Human Biology, University of Witwatersrand, and L. R. Berger for permission to study the original fossil material in their charge and for numerous kindnesses. The author also thanks the late L. Barton, D. R. Howlett, C. Powell-Cotton and the staff of the Powell-Cotton Museum; M. Rutzmoser and the staff of the Museum of Comparative Zoology, Harvard University; R. Thorington and the staff of the Division of Mammology, Smithsonian Institution; D. H. Ubelaker and the staff of the Department of Anthropology, Smithsonian Institution; P. Andrews and the staff of Natural History Museum London; the staff of the Musée d'Afrique Centrale, Tervuren; R. D. Martin and the staff of the Anthropologische Institut, Zurich; the late W. W. Howells and the staff of the Peabody Museum, Harvard University for many kindnesses and for the permission to study the comparative material in their charge; B. Richmond, M. Drapeau and S. Reynolds for exceptionally helpful comments on an earlier draft; and L. J. McHenry and C. C. Brown for their invaluable good advice and help on this project. Partial funding was provided by the Committee on Research, University of California, Davis.

References

Aiello, L. C., Wood, B., Key, C. *et al.* (1999). Morphological and taxonomic affinities of the Olduvai Ulna (OH 36). *American Journal of Physical Anthropology*, **109**: 89–110.

Andrews, P. (1996). Palaeoecology and hominoid palaeoenvironments. *Biological Reviews of the Cambridge Philosophical Society*, **71**: 257–300.

Andrews, P., Begun, D. R. and Zylstra, M. (1997). Interrelationships between functional morphology and paleoenvironments in Miocene hominoids. In Begun, D. R., Ward, C. V. and Rose, M. D. (eds.), *Function, Phylogeny, and Fossils: Miocene Hominoid Evolution and Adaptations*. New York: Plenum Press, pp. 29–58.

Bartholomew Jr., G. A. and Birdsell, J. B. (1953). Ecology and the protohominids. *American Anthropology*, **55**: 481–98.

Behrensmeyer, A. K. (2006). Climate change and human evolution. *Science*, **311**: 476–8.

Berger, L. R., de Ruiter, D. J., Churchill, S. E. *et al.* (2010). *Australopithecus sediba*: A new species of *Homo*-like australopith from South Africa. *Science*, **238**: 195–204.

Clarke, R. J. (1998). First ever discovery of a well-preserved skull and associated skeleton of *Australopithecus*. *South African Journal of Science*, **94**: 460–3.

(1999a). Bipedalism and arboreality in *Australopithecus*. In Franzen, J. L., Köhler, M. and Moyà-Solà, S. (eds.), *13th International Senckenberg Conference*. Werner Reimers Foundation, Bad Homburg v. d. H., and at the Senckenberg Research Institute, Frankfurt am Main: Forschungsinstitut Senckenberg, pp. 79–83.

(1999b). Discovery of complete arm and hand of the 3.3 million-year-old *Australopithecus* skeleton from Sterkfontein. *South African Journal of Science*, **96**: 477–80.

(2002). Newly revealed information on the Sterkfontein Member 2 *Australopithecus* skeleton. *South African Journal of Science*, **98**: 523–6.

Clarke, R. J. and Tobias, P. V. (1995). Sterkfontein Member 2 foot bones of the oldest South African hominid. *Science*, **269**: 521–4.

Dart, R. A. (1925). *Australopithecus africanus*: the man-ape of South Africa. *Nature*, **115**: 195–9.

Darwin, C. (1872). *The Descent of Man and Selection in Relation to Sex*. New York: D. Appleton and Co.

Dean, M. C. and Wood, B. A. (1981). Metrical analysis of the basicranium of extant hominoids and *Australopithecus*. *American Journal of Physical Anthropology*, **54**: 63–72.

(1982). Basicranial anatomy of Plio-Pleistocene hominids from East and South Africa. *American Journal of Physical Anthropology*, **59**: 157–74.

Delson, E., Tattersall, I., Van Couvering, J. A. *et al.* (2000). *Encyclopedia of Human Evolution and Prehistory*. New York: Garland Publishing, Inc., pp. 753.

Drapeau, M. S. M., Ward, C. V., Kimbel, W. H. *et al.* (2005). Associated cranial and forelimb remains attributed to *Australopithecus afarensis* from Hadar, Ethiopia. *Journal of Human Evolution*, **48**: 593–642.

DuBrul, E. L. (1962). The general phenomenon of bipedalism. *American Zoologist*, **2**: 205–8.

Gregory, W. K. (1928). The upright posture of man: a review of its origin and evolution. *Processes of the American Philosophical Society*, **67**: 339–76.

Haeusler, M. and McHenry, H. M. (2004). Body proportions of *Homo habilis* reviewed. *Journal of Human Evolution*, **46**: 433–67.

Haile-Selassie, Y. (2001). Late Miocene hominids from the Middle Awash, Ethiopia. *Nature*, **412**: 178–81.

Harrison, T. (2010). Review of *Ardipithecus kadabba*. In Haile-Selassie, Y. and WoldeGabriel, G. (eds.), Ardipithecus kadabba: *Late Miocene Evidence from the Middle Awash*. Berkeley: University of Califorania Press.

Hewes, G. W. (1961). Food transport and the origin of hominid bipedalism. *American Anthropologist*, **63**: 687–710.

(1964). Hominid bipedalism: independent evidence for the food-carrying theory. *Science*, **146**: 416–18.

Hockett, C. F. and Ascher, R. (1964). The human revolution. *Current Anthropology*, **5**: 135–47.

Hunt, K. D. (1994). The evolution of human bipedality: ecology and functional morphology. *Journal of Human Evolution*, **26**: 183–202.

Ishida, H. (2006). Current thought on terrestrialization in African apes and the origin of human bipedalism. In Ishida, H., Tuttle, R., Pickford, M., Ogihara, N. and Nakatsukasa, M. (eds.), *Human Origins and Environmental Backgrounds*. New York: Springer, pp. 259–67.

Jablonski, N. G. and Chaplin, G. (1992). The origin of hominid bipedalism re-examined. *Perspectives in Human Biology 2, Archaeology in Oceania*, **27**: 113–19.

(1993). Origin of habitual terrestrial bipedalism in the ancestor of the Hominidae. *Journal of Human Evolution*, **24**: 259–80.

(2004). Becoming bipedal: how do theories of bipedalization stand up to anatomical scrutiny? In Anapol, F., German, R. Z. and Jablonski, N. G. (eds.), *Shaping Primate Evolution: Form, Function, and Behavior*. Cambridge: Cambridge University Press, pp. 281–96.

Johanson, D. C., Lovejoy, C. O., Kimbel, W. H. *et al.* (1982a). Morphology of the Pliocene partial hominid skeleton (A.L. 288–1) from the Hadar Formation, Ethiopia. *American Journal of Physical Anthropology*, **57**: 403–52.

Johanson, D. C., Taieb, M. and Coppens, Y. (1982b). Pliocene hominids from the Hadar Formation, Ethiopia (1973–1977): stratigraphic, chronologic, and paleoenvironmental contexts, with notes on hominid morphology and systematics. *American Journal of Physical Anthropology*, **57**: 373–402.

Jolly, C. J. (1970). The seed-eaters: a new model of hominid differentiation based on a baboon analogy. *Man*, **5**: 5–26.

Jungers, W. L. (1982). Lucy's limbs: skeletal allometry and locomotion in *Australopithecus afarensis*. *Nature*, **297**: 676–8.

Keith, A. (1923). Man's posture: its evolution and disorders. *The British Medical Journal*. March 17–April 21: 451–454, 499–502, 545–548, 587–590, 624–626, 669–672, 687.

Kibii, J. M., Churchill, S. E., Schmid, P. *et al.* (2011). A partial pelvis of *Au. sediba*. *Science*, **333**: 1407–11.

Kingdon, J. (2003). *Lowly Origins: Where, When, and Why Our Ancestors First Stood Up*. Princeton, NJ: Princeton University Press.

Kivell, T. L., Kibii, J. M., Churchill, S. E. *et al.* (2011). *Australopithecus sediba* hand demonstrates mosaic evolution of locomotor and manipulative abilities. *Science, 333: 1411–17.*

Leakey, M. G., Feibel, C. S., McDougall, I. *et al.* (1998). New specimens and confirmation of an early age for *Australopithecus anamensis. Nature*, **393**: 62–6.

Livingstone, F. B. (1962). Reconstructing man's Pliocene pongid ancestor. *American Anthropologist*, **64**: 301–5.

Lovejoy, C. O. (1981). The origin of man. *Science.* 211: 341–350.

(2005a). The natural history of human gait and posture Part 1. Spine and pelvis. *Gait & Posture*, **21**: 95–112.

(2005b). The natural history of human gait and posture Part 2. Hip and thigh. *Gait & Posture*, **21**: 113–24.

Lovejoy, C. O., Cohn, M. J. and White, T. D. (1999). Morphological analysis of the mammalian postcranium: a developmental perspective. *Proceedings of the National Academy of Sciences*, **96**: 13247–52.

(2000). The evolution of mammalian morphology: a developmental perspective. In O'Higgins, P. and Cohn, M. J. (eds.), *Development, Growth, and Evolution: Implications for the Study of the Hominid Skeleton*. The Linnean Society of London, pp. 41–55.

Lovejoy, C. O., Meindl, R. S., Ohman, J. C. *et al.* (2002). The Maka femur and its bearing on the antiquity of human walking: applying contemporary concepts of morphogenesis to the human fossil record. *American Journal of Physical Anthropology*, **119**: 97–133.

Lovejoy, C. O., McCollum, M. A., Reno, P. L. *et al.* (2003). Developmental biology and human evolution. *Annual Reviews in Anthropology*, **32**: 85–109.

Lovejoy, C. O., Suwa, G., Simpson, S. W. *et al.* (2009). The great divides: *Ardipithecus ramidus* reveals the postcrania of our last common ancestors with African Apes. *Science*, **326**: 100–6.

Marzke, M. W. and Shackley, M. S. (1986). Hominid hand use in the Pleistocene: evidence from experimental archaeology and comparative morphology. *Journal of Human Evolution*, **15**: 439–60.

McHenry, H. M. (1975a). Biomechanical interpretation of the early hominid hip. *Journal of Human Evolution*, **4**: 343–56.

(1975b). A new pelvic fragment from Swartkrans and the relationship between the robust and gracile australopithecines. *American Journal of Physical Anthropology*, **43**: 245–62.

(1983). The capitate of *Australopithecus afarensis* and *Australopithecus africanus*. *American Journal of Physical Anthropology*, **62**: 187–98.

(1996). Homoplasy, clades and hominid phylogeny. In Meikle, W. E., Howell, F. C. and Jablonski, N. G. (eds.), *Contemporary Issues in Human Evolution*. San Francisco: California Academy of Sciences, pp. 77–92.

(2002). Introduction to the fossil record of human ancestry. In Hartwig, W. C. (ed.), *The Primate Fossil Record*. Cambridge: University of Cambridge Press, pp. 401–6.

McHenry, H. M. and Berger, L. R. (1998). Body proportions in *Australopithecus afarensis* and *A. africanus* and the origin of the genus *Homo. Journal of Human Evolution*, **35**: 1–22.

McHenry, H. M. and Coffing, K. (2000). *Australopithecus* to *Homo*: transformations in body and mind. *Annual Review of Anthropology*, **29**: 129–46.

McHenry, H. M. and Jones, A. L. (2006). Hallucial convergence in early hominids. *Journal of Human Evolution*, **50**: 534–9.

McHenry, H. M., Corruccini, R. S. and Howell, F. C. (1976). Analysis of an early hominid ulna from the Omo Basin, Ethiopia. *American Journal of Physical Anthropology*, **44**: 295–304.

Nakatsukasa, M., Hirasaki, E. and Ogihara, N. (2006). Locomotor energetics in non-human primates: a review of recent studies on bipedal performing macaques. In Ishida, H., Tuttle, R., Pickford, M., Ogihara, N. and Nakatsukasa, M. (eds.), *Human Origins and Environmental Backgrounds*. New York: Springer, pp. 149–57.

Napier, J. R. (1963). The locomotor functions of hominids. In Washburn, S. L. (ed.), *Classification and Human Evolution*. Chicago: Aldine de Gruyter, pp. 178–89.

Oxnard, C. E. (1975). *Uniqueness and Diversity in Human Evolution*. Chicago: University of Chicago Press.

Partridge, T. C., Granger, D. E., Caffee, M. W. *et al.* (2003). Lower Pliocene hominid remains from Sterkfontein. *Science*, **300**: 607–12.

Pickering, T. R., Clarke, R. J. and Heaton, J. L. (2004). The context of StW 573, an early hominid skull and skeleton from Sterkfontein Member 2: taphonomy and paleo-environment. *Journal of Human Evolution*, **46**: 279–99.

Pilbeam, D. and Young, N. (2004). Hominoid evolution: synthesizing disparate data. *Comptes Rendus Palevol*, **3**: 305–21.

Ravey, M. (1978). Bipedalism: an early warning system for Miocene hominoids. *Science*, **199**: 372.

Reno, P. L., De Gusta, D., Serrat, M. A. *et al.* (2005). Plio-Pleistocene hominid limb proportions: evolutionary reversals or estimation errors? *Current Anthropology*, **46**: 575–88.

Richmond, B., Aiello, L. and Wood, B. (2002). Early hominin limb proportions. *Journal of Human Evolution*, **43**: 529–48.

Richmond, B. G., Begun, D. R. and Strait, D. S. (2001). Origin of human bipedalism: the knuckle-walking hypothesis revisited. *Yearbook of Physical Anthropology*, **44**: 70–105.

Rodman, P. S. and McHenry, H. M. (1980). Bioenergetics and the origin of hominid bipedalism. *American Journal of Physical Anthropology*, **52**: 103–6.

Romer, A. S. (1959). *The Vertebrate Story*, 4th edition. Chicago: University of Chicago Press.

Rose, M. D. (1976). Bipedal behavior of olive baboons (*Papio anubis*) and its relevance to an understanding of the evolution of human bipedalism. *American Journal of Physical Anthropology*, **44**: 247–62.

(1982). Food acquisition and the evolution of positional behavior: the case of bipedalism. In Chivers, D. J., Wood, B. A. and Bilsborough, A. (eds.), *Food Acquisition and Processing in Primates*. New York: Plenum Press, pp. 509–24.

(1989). The evolution of human bipedalism: general considerations. *OSSA, International Journal of Skeletal Research*, **14**: 33–4.

Ruff, C. B. and Walker, A. (1993). Body size and body shape. In Walker, A. and Leakey, R. (eds.), *The Nariokotome* Homo erectus *Skeleton*. Cambridge: Harvard University Press, pp. 234–65.

Sigmon, B. A. (1971). Bipedal behavior and the emergence of erect posture in man. *American Journal of Physical Anthropology*, **34**: 55–60.

Sockol, M. D. (2006). Origin of hominid bipedalism: the energetics of chimpanzee locomotion. *American Journal of Physical Anthropology*, **129**: 168.

Sockol, M. D., Raichlen, D. A. and Pontzer, H. (2007). Chimpanzee locomoter energetics and the origin of human bipedalism. *Proceedings of the National Academy of Sciences of the USA*, **104**: 12265–9.

Stanford, C. (2003). *The Evolutionary Key to Becoming Human*. Boston: Houghton Mifflin Company.

Stern, J. T. (2000). Climbing to the top: a personal memoir of *Australopithecus afarensis*. *Evolutionary Anthropology*, **9**: 113–33.

Stern, J. T. and Susman, R. L. (1983). The locomotor anatomy of *Australopithecus afarensis*. *American Journal of Physical Anthropology*, **60**: 279–318.

Steudel-Numbers, K. L. (2003). The energetic cost of locomotion: humans and primates compared to generalized endotherms. *Journal of Human Evolution*, **44**: 255–62.

Strait, D. S. (2001). Integration, phylogeny, and the hominid cranial base. *American Journal of Physical Anthropology*, **114**: 243–97.

Strait, D. S. and Grine, F. E. (2004). Inferring hominoid and early hominid phylogeny using craniodental characters: the role of fossil taxa. *Journal of Human Evolution*, **47**: 399–452.

Strait, D. S., Grine, F. E. and Moniz, M. A. (1997). A reappraisal of early hominid phylogeny. *Journal of Human Evolution*, **32**: 17–82.

Susman, R. L., Stern, J. T. and Jungers, W. L. (1984). Arboreality and bipedality in the Hadar hominids. *Folia Primatologica*, **43**: 113–56.

(1985). Locomotor adaptations in the Hadar hominids. In Delson, E. (ed.), *Ancestors: the Hard Evidence*. New York: Alan R. Liss, pp. 184–92.

Taylor, R. C. and Rowntree, V. J. (1973). Running on two or four legs: which consumes more energy? *Science*, **179**: 186–7.

Tobias, P. V. (1991). *Olduvai Gorge Volume 4: The Skulls, Endocasts and Teeth of* Homo habilis. Cambridge: Cambridge University Press.

(1998). History of the discovery of a fossilised Little Foot at Sterkfontein, South Africa, and the light it sheds on the origins of hominin bipedalism. *Mitteliungen de Berliner Gesellschaft fur Anthropologie*, **19**: 47–56.

Tobias, P. V., Clarke, R. J., Kuman, K. *et al.* (1999–2001). *Sterkfontein Research Unit*. Johannesburg: Sterkfontein Research Unit: School of Anatomical Sciences.

Trauth, M. H., Maslin, M. A., Deino, A. *et al.* (2005). Late cenozoic moisture history of east Africa. *Science*, **309**: 2051–3.

Tuttle, R. H. (1981). Evolution of hominid bipedalism and prehensile capabilities. *Philosophical Transactions of the Royal Society B*, **292**: 89–94.

Vrba, E. S., Denton, G. H., Partridge, T. C. *et al.* (1995). *Paleoclimate and Evolution, with Emphasis on Human Origins*. New Haven: Yale University Press.

Walker, A. and Leakey, R. (eds.) (1993). *The Nariokotome* Homo erectus *Skeleton*. Cambridge: Harvard University Press.

Ward, C. V. (2002). Interpreting the posture and locomotion of *Australopithecus afarensis*: where do we stand? *Yearbook of Physical Anthropology*, **45**: 185–215.

Ward, C. V., Leakey, M. G. and Walker, A. (2001). Morphology of *Australopithecus anamensis* from Kanapoi and Allia Bay, Kenya. *Journal of Human Evolution*, **41**: 255–368.

Washburn, S. L. (1960). Tools and human evolution. *Scientific American*, **203**: 3–15.

  (1963). Behavior and human evolution. In Washburn, S. L. (ed.), *Classification and Human Evolution*. Chicago: Aldine, pp. 190–203.

Wescott, R. W. (1967). The exhibitionistic origin of human bipedalism. *Man*, **2**: 630.

White, T. D., Suwa, G. and Asfaw, B. (1994). *Australopithecus ramidus*, a new species of early hominid from Aramis, Ethiopia. *Nature*, **371**: 306–12.

Zipfel, B., DeSilva, J. M., Kidd, R. S. *et al.* (2011). The foot and ankle of *Au. sediba*. *Science*, **333**: 1417–20.

12 *Forelimb adaptations in* Australopithecus afarensis

MICHELLE S. M. DRAPEAU

Abstract

This chapter explores upper limb adaptation in *Australopithecus afarensis* in order to identify possible adaptations to behaviours other than arboreality. Limb length proportions and elbow articular morphology suggest that the upper limb of *A. afarensis* does not display a morphology that implies strong directional, or even stabilising selection, for arboreality. On the other hand, many traits suggest that *A. afarensis* adapted to use of the upper limbs for manipulation. The species had no carpometacarpal ligament between the second metacarpal and the capitate, a curved and more proximally oriented second metacarpal-capitate articular surface, and a more coronally and transversally oriented tra-pezio-second metacarpal facet. All these traits allow for rotation of the second metacarpal during manipulation. In addition, the second and third metacarpal heads of *A. afarensis* are tapered with a marked asymmetry in distal view. In palmar view, the articular facet of the *A. afarensis* second metacarpal is also asymmetrical, with the radial size projecting more proximally and palmarly than the ulnar side. This results in pronation of the second finger during flex-ion, which allows the finger to conform to the shape of the manipulated object. Again, this list of traits is found only in humans among extant hominoids. Other traits such as a relatively longer thumb and a proximally oriented olecra-non also suggest that *A. afarensis* had adapted to manipulatory activities. The absence of archaeological sites contemporaneous with *A. afarensis* may be due to various factors, such as the use of perishable material, the absence of a home base or of foraging route standardisation, and so forth. In conclusion, it is not possible to positively demonstrate that *A. afarensis* made or used tools without finding fossil remains in association with tools, but their morphology is con-sistent with the finger dexterity and the positioning of hands close to the body that are part of toolmaking and tool-using activities, a novel behaviour for hom-inins. If *A. afarensis* was still indeed a habitual arboreal animal, its upper limbs

African Genesis: Perspectives on Hominin Evolution, eds. Sally C. Reynolds and Andrew Gallagher. Published by Cambridge University Press. © Cambridge University Press 2012.

223

show a compromise for this novel behaviour that was extremely important and that, perhaps, was made possible by the adoption of bipedal stance.

Introduction

Much has been learned about the postcranial adaptations of *Australopithecus afarensis* since its discovery almost 40 years ago. Many analyses have centred on the locomotion of the species, showing clear adaptations to bipedality (e.g. Stern and Susman, 1983; Lovejoy, 1988). However, other type of behaviours can be inferred from the postcrania. This chapter focuses on the upper limb, which is important for understanding the aspects of early hominin behaviour that are not necessarily related to locomotion, such as tool-use and manufacture.

When trying to functionally interpret the upper-limb morphology of *A. afarensis*, researchers usually compare them to extant hominoid species. For many traits, these early hominins present a morphology that is chimp-like, gorilla-like, human-like or somewhat intermediate between these taxa. Some traits observed in *Pan* and *Gorilla*, such as dorsal ridges on metacarpal heads and on the capitate dorsum, a dorsal projection of the distal radial articulation, a fused os centrale and the relatively short proximal phalanges, have been identified as terrestrial adaptations (Tuttle, 1970; Marzke, 1971; Corruccini, 1978; Begun, 1993, 1994; Richmond and Strait, 2000; Corruccini and McHenry, 2001; Richmond *et al.*, 2001). When such traits are absent in *A. afarensis*, as is the case for the dorsal ridge of the metacarpal heads, it underscores the widely accepted interpretation that the species was not knuckle-walking. Other traits that are present in *A. afarensis*, like a fused os centrale, are interpreted as retained primitive morphologies inherited from the last common ancestor of *Pan* and humans, possibly a knuckle-walker itself (Washburn, 1967; Marzke, 1971; Corruccini, 1978; Begun, 1993, 1994; Richmond and Strait, 2000; Corruccini and McHenry, 2001; Richmond *et al.*, 2001). When *A. afarensis* shares traits with African apes that are adaptations to arboreality, such as a relatively great intermembral index (ratio of forelimb length to hindlimb length), it is interpreted as evidence of retention of an arboreal locomotor component in the fossil species (e.g. Stern and Susman, 1983; Susman *et al.*, 1984; Senut and Tardieu, 1985). However, African apes are not predominantly arboreal animals. Within extant hominioids, only orang-utans (*Pongo*) and gibbons (*Hylobates*) are mostly arboreal[1]. Chimpanzees (*Pan*) and gorillas (*Gorilla*)

[1] Only male orang-utans from Borneo are documented as spending a significant amount of time on the ground, generally when travelling (Sugardjito and Cant, 1994). It appears to be an energetically more efficient mode of locomotion than strict arboreality for these large animals. It is hypothesised that males from Sumatra to avoid tigers do not travel on the ground, their only natural

are predominantly terrestrial animals with a mixed arboreal and terrestrial locomotion, and their upper limb is a compromise between these two loco-motor modes (e.g. Tuttle, 1970). As a consequence, the upper-limb morph-ology of *Pan* and *Gorilla*, instead of representing an upper limb optimised for arboreality, is a compromise between arboreal locomotion and knuckle-walking. The differences in locomotion between African and Asian apes are reflected in disparities in upper-limb morphology. For example, in comparison to *Pongo* and *Hylobates*, *Pan* and *Gorilla* have shorter forearms, hands and fin-gers. The morphology of African apes probably reflects a compromise between the advantage of long upper limbs and hands for arboreal locomotion and the need to reduce bending strain in the forearm and hand generated by compres-sive forces during terrestrial locomotion. In contrast, Asian apes load their upper limbs mostly in tension, substantially reducing bending strains (Swartz *et al.*, 1989). Early hominins, by becoming bipedal, were relieved of the mech-anical constraints related to terrestrial quadrupedalism and their upper limbs were not under selective pressure to maintain adaptations specific to terrestrial locomotion (Latimer, 1991).

Although there is still debate on the importance of the retention of an arbor-eal component in the locomotor repertoire of *A. afarensis* (see Stern, 2000; Ward, 2002), it is generally agreed that *A. afarensis* was completely bipedal when terrestrial. Some lower-limb adaptations for terrestriality, such as shorter toes (relative to apes), reduced or no halluxal abduction, shortening of the pel-vis, realignment of the knee and ankle joints (see Lovejoy, 1988; Stern and Susman, 1983) and eversion of the anterior foot as reflected by metatarsal head torsion (Drapeau and Harmon, 2008), certainly reduced the arboreal compe-tence of the lower limbs relative to apes (Latimer and Lovejoy, 1989; Latimer 1991). If these early hominins were still habitually arboreal, their upper limbs were unconstrained by terrestriality and were free to improve or at least main-tain their adaptations to arboreality, assuming that it improved their probabil-ities of survival. For example, one might expect to observe a lengthening of the forearm, hand and fingers or, at the very least, maintenance of the length hypothesised to be inherited from the last common ancestor of humans and chimpanzees. One may also expect to observe an increase, or at least preserva-tion, of upper-limb muscularity. We certainly would not expect to see a conver-gence towards the human form, which is characterised by relatively short arms, hands and fingers, and reduced upper-body muscularity.

This chapter explores upper-limb adaptation in *A. afarensis* in order to iden-tify possible adaptations to behaviours other than arboreality. First I show that

predator (Sugardjito and Cant, 1994). Tigers are absent from Borneo, but this absence may be due to a fairly recent extinction on the island (Hooijer, 1963; Kitchener, 1999). As a consequence, the terrestrial locomotion of male orang-utans may be a fairly recent behavioural novelty.

Table 12.1. *Descriptive statistics of the comparative sample and fossil specimens included in metric analyses.*

Species	Size surrogate[1] Mean (st. dev.) / n	Ulna length[1] Mean (st. dev.) / n	Metacarpal 3 length[1] Mean (st. dev.) / n	Keeling angle distal[2] Mean (st. dev.) / n	Keeling angle proximal[2] Mean (st. dev.) / n	Olecranon orientation[2] Mean (st. dev.) / n
H. sapiens	16.9 (1.7) / 89	232 (20) / 89	66.2 (5.4) / 66	139 (4) / 28	121 (9) / 28	111 (8) / 11
P. paniscus	15.1 (0.9) / 19	254 (14) / 19	87.5 (3.1) / 17	129 (8) / 17	109 (9) / 17	105 (6) / 20
P. troglodytes	17.1 (1.6) / 50	266 (18) / 50	88.9 (5.5) / 48	124 (5) / 27	107 (7) / 28	102 (7) / 28
G. gorilla	23.5 (3.4) / 64	312 (31) / 64	90.0 (9.6) / 61	134 (6) / 34	115 (9) / 34	96 (7) / 20
P. pygmaeus	17.4 (2.6) / 24	343 (25) / 24	99.8 (10.4) / 24	124 (8) / 24	110 (8) / 23	97 (9) / 25
Hylobates	8.5 (1.3) / 22	260 (29) / 22	58.4 (6.7) / 7			
A.L. 288–1				134	127	118
A.L. 333w–36				131		
A.L. 438–1	18.8	252	64.8	130	132	125
StW 113				133	127	
StW 431					127	

[1] Measurement in mm
[2] Measurement in degrees

the upper limb of *A. afarensis* does not display a morphology that suggests strong directional or even stabilising selection for arboreality. I then focus on adaptations that suggest that the upper limb was used for manipulation, consequently suggesting that reliance on an arboreal component in the habitual locomotor repertoire was reduced or had become relatively less important than more human-like behaviours.

All ape metric data are from a sample of wild shot animals housed in the Cleveland Museum of Natural History, the National Museum of Natural History and the Musée Royal de l'Afrique Centrale (Table 12.1). The human sample is of Euro-American, Afro-American and Native American origin, dates from the latter part of the eighteenth to the early part of the twentieth century, and is housed in the Cleveland Museum of Natural History and the Canadian Museum of Civilization. All samples have approximately equivalent numbers of males and females. All measures and observations of *A. afarensis* are made on the original specimens. In addition to the fossils listed in Table 12.1, visual observation of metacarpal base and heads and capitates were made on the following fossils attributed to *A. afarensis* and *A. africanus*: MC3, A.L. 333–16, A.L. 333–65, A.L. 333–144, A.L. 333–153, A.L. 333w-6, A.L. 438–1, StW 27, StW 64, StW 68; MC2, A.L. 333–15, A.L. 333–48, A.L. 333w-23, A.L. 438–1, StW 382; Capitate, A.L. 288–1, A.L. 333–40, TM 1526. All measurements and methods are described in Drapeau (2004, 2008) and Drapeau *et al.* (2005).

The size surrogate is calculated as the geometric mean of three measurements on the ulna (maximum mediolateral width of the proximal trochlear notch, midshaft mediolateral and anteroposterior widths). Regression of that variable to species- and sex-specific published body mass (Smith and Jungers, 1997) of hominoid species and subspecies in a natural logarithm space gave a coefficient of correlation (r^2) of 0.99 (slope = 2.71). Per cent predicted errors (% PE; [observed values – predicted value]/predicted value × 100) calculated from the regression were all below 5% except for female *H. sapiens* (6.7%) and female *Hylobates muelleri* (5.4%), which may have their body mass underestimated, and for male *Hylobates agilis* (–7.8%) and female *Hylobates leucogenys* (–9.5%), which may have the body mass overestimated.

Is there evidence of maintenance of arboreal competence in *A. afarensis*?

Upper-limb segment length proportions

In general, arboreal apes have longer upper limbs relative to lower limbs and longer forearms relative to arm. Relative length of the hand and fingers is also

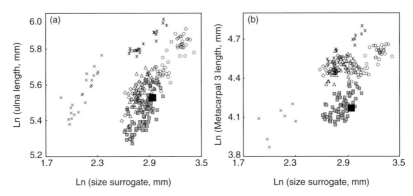

Figure 12.1. Ulna and third metacarpal length relative to body size. (a) Ulna length to size. (b) Third metacarpal to size (humans, grey squares; bonobos, diamonds; chimpanzees, triangles; gorillas, circles; orang-utans, stars; gibbons, crosses; A.L. 438–1 (*A. afarensis*), black square). Body size is estimated as the geometric mean of three measurements of the ulna (see text for details).

indicative of locomotor preferences in hominoids. Ulna length, relative to the size surrogate value, shows that African apes have much shorter forearms than their Asian counterparts (Figure 12.1a). In humans, forearms are even shorter, although relatively not much more than that of gorillas (Figure 12.1a). *A. afarensis* falls within the distribution of *Pan* and humans, but resembles humans the most.

The same pattern is observed with the second and third metacarpal lengths, although, in this case, chimpanzees are more similar to Asian apes (Figure 12.1b). Only gorillas, the most terrestrial of extant apes, have relative values that resemble that of humans. *Australopithecus afarensis* has metacarpal lengths that are very human-like in both absolute and relative terms. Finger to metacarpal lengths have a constant proportion among all great apes and humans (Schultz, 1969), so length of the *A. afarensis* hand can be assumed to be very human-like. Similarly, Latimer (1991) has shown that the A.L. 288–1x finger phalanx is relatively shorter than what is observed in *Pan* and much more similar to human lengths.

The humerofemoral index of *A. afarensis* is reported to be intermediate between that of *Pan* (chimpanzees and bonobos) and humans (Jungers and Stern, 1983; Susman *et al.*, 1984; Richmond *et al.*, 2002; Haeusler and McHenry, 2004). Although, this index appears to reflect differences between taxa that are mostly in the lower limb length rather than in the upper limb (Jungers, 1994), it indicates that *A. afarensis* did not maintain inter-limb proportions (i.e. relatively much longer upper- than lower-limbs) that are hypothesised to favour climbing abilities in extant great apes (Cartmill, 1974), but instead has approached the human proportion of relatively longer legs.

In short, *A. afarensis* has proportions that are either intermediate between humans and *Pan* or clearly human-like. Overall, these proportions in *A. afarensis* suggest no lengthening in any forelimb segments despite the absence of terrestrial constraints in its upper limbs and lower limbs that were proportionally longer. Instead, *A. afarensis* shows evidence of shortening of its ulna, metacarpals and fingers.

Ulnar keeling

The high ulnar keel of hominoids is hypothesised to increase resistance of transverse loads generated by strong muscle contractions from the superficial finger and wrist flexors (Preuschoft, 1973). Morphology of the keel seems to indicate forearm muscularity in conjunction with arboreality in the hominoids. Distally and proximally, humans have the least keeled trochlear notches and orang-utans (*P. pygmaeus*), chimpanzees (*P. troglodytes*) and bonobos (*P. paniscus*) have the most keeled (Figure 12.2). Gorillas are intermediate.

Distally, all *A. afarensis* specimens have a notch that is relatively keeled, comparable to what is observed in apes (Figure 12.2a). Proximally, they have notches that are more similar to what is observed in humans (Figure 12.2b). The same is observed on *A. africanus* specimens. The morphology of *A. afarensis* and *A. africanus* suggest a somewhat reduced muscularity of the superficial finger and wrist flexors relative to orang-utans and, to a lesser degree, relative to chimpanzees (*P. troglodytes*), bonobos (*P. paniscus*) and gorillas.

Other forelimb traits have been suggested to suggest an arboreal component in the locomotor repertoire of *A. afarensis*, such as the orientation of the glenoid fossa, and the form of the pisiform (Stern and Susman, 1983; Susman *et al.*, 1984; Stern, 2000; Alemseged *et al.*, 2006). *Pan* have glenoid surfaces that are oriented more proximally, reflecting use of the forelimb in a position above the head, while humans have a more lateral orientation, reflecting use of the arms predominantly in an adducted position. The orientation of the glenoid surface of the scapula in *A. afarensis* is intermediate between that of *Pan* and humans and similar to that of gorillas (Bush *et al.*, 1982; Alemseged *et al.*, 2006, supp. info.). The intermediate position of *A. afarensis* suggests less use of the arm in an above-head position than what is observed in chimpanzees and bonobos.

The *A. afarensis* pisiform is described as being rod-like (Bush *et al.*, 1982; Susman *et al.*, 1984; Stern, 2000), a form more similar to that of chimpanzees than to the much shorter human pisiform. However, in absolute length, the unassociated pisiform of *A. afarensis* is intermediate in length between humans and *Pan* (see Stern, 2000; pers. obs.).

(a)

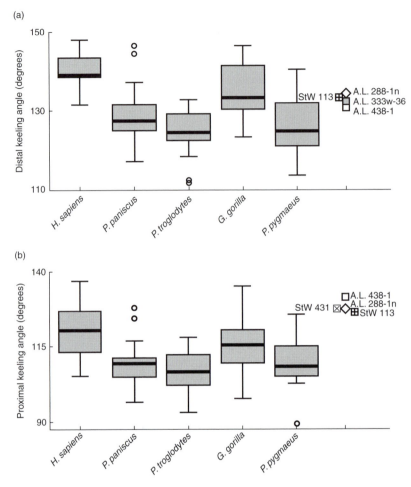

(b)

Figure 12.2. Box-plot of (a) distal and (b) proximal keeling angle. The box represents the 25–75 percentile, the horizontal bar represents the mean, whiskers represent the range excluding outliers (defined as exceeding ±1.5 the interquartile range), which are represented as circles.

The last common ancestor of hominins and chimpanzees was probably habitually arboreal, and the forelimbs of *A. afarensis* display some characteristics clearly more chimp-like, such as curved phalanges with strong expression of muscle attachments and with trochleae displaying large subtended angles and deep grooves (Stern and Susman, 1983; Susman *et al.*, 1984; Stern, 2000). However, as discussed above, numerous other traits of the fossil species' forelimb have a morphology that can be characterised as intermediate between modern humans and *Pan*. Although this review of the upper limb in *A. afarensis*

is limited, it shows that several adaptations important for arboreality in hominoids were not enhanced or even maintained by natural selection in this species.
Given the changes towards a more human form, the morphology of *A. afarensis* suggests that other behaviours than arboreality must have been important
in modelling *A. afarensis* forearms and hands. Some have suggested that some
forelimb traits of *A. afarensis* point to an adaptation to increase manipulatory
abilities (Marzke, 1983, 1986, 1997, 2005; Marzke and Shackley, 1986; Alba
et al., 2003).

Adaptation to a novel behaviour

The human hand presents adaptations that facilitate manipulation. For example,
the second metacarpal axially rotates while the hand is cupped, while manipulating objects in the three-jaw chuck, or nesting objects in the palm of the hand
(Lewis, 1977; Marzke, 1986). In humans, axial rotation of the second metacarpal is facilitated by a series of specific adaptations. First, humans have a
trapezio-second metacarpal articular surface that is oriented in a more coronal
and transverse plane than African apes, which have a surface that is more sagittally oriented (Marzke and Shackley, 1986; Tocheri *et al.*, 2003, 2005; Drapeau
et al., 2005; Marzke, 2005). Unlike apes, the human hand also has a continuous
articular facet between the second metacarpals and the capitate (Figure 12.3a;
Lewis, 1973, 1977, 1989; McHenry, 1983; Marzke, 1986). Finally, in humans,
the articular facet of the second metacarpal is convex while the articular facets
of the third metacarpal and capitate are concave (Figure 12.3b; Lewis, 1973).
In contrast, all extant apes have a carpometacarpal ligament or fibres that tran-
sect the second metacarpal articulation with the capitate (Figure 12.3a; Lewis,
1977, 1989; Marzke, 1986, 1997; Drapeau *et al.*, 2005). In addition, their dual
second metacarpal-capitate facets are aligned in the sagittal plane (Figure
12.3b; Lewis, 1973). The presence of a carpometacarpal ligament between the
second metacarpal and capitate and the uncurved articulation limit the rotation
of the second metacarpal in apes.

   All *A. afarensis* specimens have a coronally and transversally oriented tra-
pezio-metacarpal facet and a continuous second metacarpal-capitate facet that
is concavo-convex (Figure 12.3c, e; Bush *et al.*, 1982; McHenry, 1983; Marzke
and Shackley, 1986; Marzke, 1986, 2005; Tocheri *et al.*, 2003; Drapeau *et al.*,
2005). Although discontinuous second metacarpal-capitate facets observed
on dry bones do not necessarily imply that a ligament was present, continuous facets necessarily imply that it was absent. These observations indicate
that *A. afarensis* had no carpometacarpal ligament between the capitate and
second metacarpal, an apomorphy for the hominin clade, and it suggests that

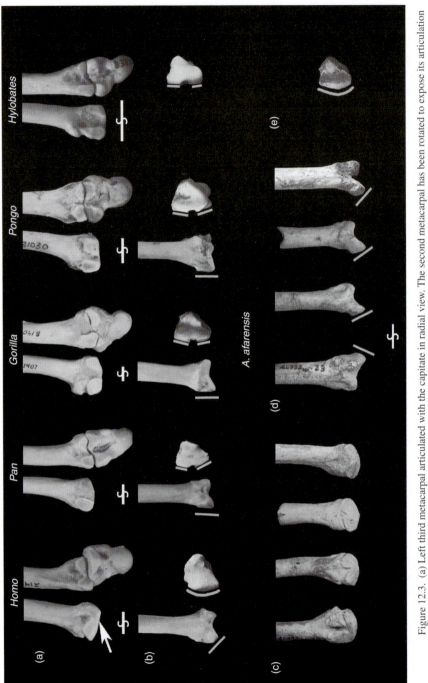

Figure 12.3. (a) Left third metacarpal articulated with the capitate in radial view. The second metacarpal has been rotated to expose its articulation with the third metacarpal and capitate (scale, white line marked with an S, equals 1 cm). The white arrow shows the continuous second

its metacarpal basal morphology permitted second metacarpal axial rotation comparable to what is observed in humans.

The orientation of the capitate-second metacarpal facet has also been suggested to reflect axial rotation capacities of the metacarpal (Marzke, 1986). In the human hand, it is oriented somewhat proximally, while in apes it is oriented sagittally (Figure 12.3b; McHenry, 1983; Marzke, 1986). Although there is not consensus on the functional significance of the orientation of the second metacarpal-capitate articulation in hominins (see Susman, 1998; Lovejoy *et al.*, 2009), Marzke and Shackley (1986) suggested that, in addition to facilitate rotation of the second metacarpal, a proximal orientation of that articulation allows for load transfer from the metacarpal to the capitate in axial loading during the 'thumb to side' and 'three-jaw chuck' grips. *Australopithecus afarensis* specimens have a facet that is generally proximally oriented although somewhat less than in humans (Figure 12.3d; Bush *et al.*, 1982; McHenry, 1983; Drapeau *et al.*, 2005).

Non-hominoid primates are sometimes characterised by a continuous and/or a proximal orientation of the second metacarpal-capitate articulation (Lewis, 1989; Susman, 2005), but extant apes, including gibbons (*Hylobates*), are not variable and always have a discontinuous articulation and a capitate facet oriented sagittally. The Miocene hominoid *Sivapithecus* from the Chinji Formation, Pakistan, has a capitate (specimen number GSP 17119) with a discontinuous palmar-dorsal second metacarpal facet (Rose, 1984). The *Dryopithecus* capitates (RUD 167 and RUD 203) from Rudabanya, Hungary, also displays dual facets, with a predominantly sagittal orientation (Kivell and Begun, 2009). The hand of *Oreopithecus* has been argued by Moyà-Solà and colleagues (1999, 2005) to display traits that reflect some precision grip capabilities including a more proximally oriented capitate facet on the second metacarpal. However, it does not have a continuous second metacarpal-capitate articulation (pers. obs.). The discontinuous facet, found in all extant apes and in *Sivapithecus*,

Figure 12.3. (*cont.*)

metacarpal-capitate articulation in humans compared to apes that are characterised by a discontinuous articulation. (b) The second metacarpal in dorsal and proximal view (scale is as in (a); dorsal view is missing in *Hylobates*). In the dorsal view, the grey line shows the orientation of the capitate facet on the second metacarpal. In the proximal view, the grey line(s) shows the profile of the same articulation. (c) and (d) Second metacarpal of *A. afarensis* in (c) ulnar and (d) dorsal view (from left to right: A.L. 333w-23, A.L. 333–48, A.L. 333–15, A.L. 438–1e; all left except A.L. 333w-23). All specimens have a continuous and a more proximally oriented capitate facet. (e) Proximal view of A.L. 438–1e showing the curved capitate facet. Proximal views are not available for the other three specimens, but the same morphology was observed on all of them as well as on the two *A. afarensis* capitates (A.L. 333–40 and A.L. 288–1w).

Dryopithecus and *Oreopithecus* may be an adaptation to forelimb-dominated climbing or below-branch suspension. These locomotor behaviours may have required improved stability of the carpo-metacarpal joints. Among euhominoids (the clade that includes all living hominoids and related extinct species, usually typified by an orthograde posture), only hominins (fossil and extant) have modified their morphology, improving rotational capacity of the second metacarpal at the expense of greater hand joint stability.

In a recent description of the *Ardipithecus ramidus* hand by Lovejoy and colleagues (2009), these authors propose that numerous traits observed in extant great apes, such as the carpometacarpal ligament between capitate and the second and third metacarpals, the long metacarpals, a relatively gracile and short thumb with a small head, and a stiff fourth and fifth carpometacarpal joint would be instead independently derived relative to a more primitive hand with a robust and long thumb and relatively mobile carpometacarpal joints (including the hypothenar region). This hypothesis would imply very little changes from the hominin primitive condition to obtain the dexterous human hand, but also requires substantial homoplasy of the ape and human upper limbs that would have evolved for strikingly different functions (vertical climbing and suspension in apes, manipulation in humans). Although this hypothesis deserves further consideration and analyses, it appears equally parsimonious to suggest that some aspect of the unique morphology of *Ardipithecus* (for a Pliocene hominoid) is independently adapted to palmigrady.

The morphology of *A. afarensis* suggests that it was not impeded by a ligament stabilising the carpo-metacarpal articulation, but instead had a certain potential for axial rotation of the second metacarpal (Marzke and Shackley, 1986; Marzke, 1986, 2005; Drapeau *et al.*, 2005). This morphology is not identical to modern humans, but shows a clear human-like derived morphology unlike that of all hominoids, extent or fossil, observed or believed to have practised some form of vertical climbing and/or below-branch suspension. It is interesting to note, in passing, that all specimens from the Member 4 of Sterkfontein attributed to *A. africanus* have similar capitate and second and third metacarpal morphology as described above for *A. afarensis* (McHenry, 1983; pers. obs.).

While studying the human hands, some have noted the tapering and marked asymmetry of the second metacarpal heads in distal view (Figure 12.4b; Lewis, 1977, 1989; Susman, 1979). The distal articular facet narrows dorsally. The third metacarpal head is similar in morphology to the second, but is less marked in asymmetry and in tapering (Figure 12.4c). The metacarpal head of orang-utans also narrows dorsally, but it is not characterised by the marked asymmetry typical of humans. Hylobatids (gibbons) do not have asymmetric or even tapering second and third metacarpal heads (Lewis, 1989; pers. obs.). Knuckle-walkers

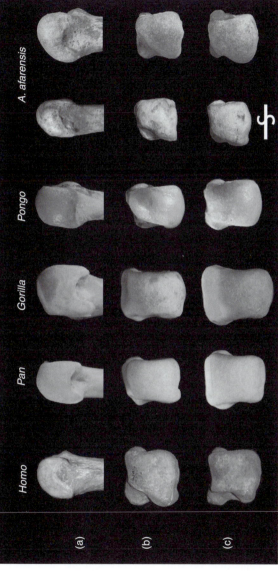

Figure 12.4. (a) Second metacarpal head in palmar view. (b) Second metacarpal head in distal view. (c) Third metacarpal head in distal view. All are from the left side. The A. *afarensis* specimens are: (from top to bottom in the first row) A.L. 333–48, palmar and distal, and A.L. 333–16, (in the second row) A.L. 438–1e, palmar and distal, and A.L. 438–1d. All views show the greater articular asymmetry of the human and A. *afarensis* metacarpal heads. (Scale, white line marked with an S, equals 1 cm.)

have heads that are wide palmarly and dorsally and, in some cases, present dorsal ridges (Figure 12.4b, c). Lewis (1989) has argued that dorsal tapering may be primitive for primates. He suggests that the radiodorsal tapering forces supination of the proximal phalanx during full extension, which allows for the volar surface of the phalanx to be in full contact to the substrate during palmar quadrupedal locomotion (Lewis, 1989). However, given that no extant apes have both tapering and asymmetrical heads, it is most parsimonious to assume that the last common ancestor of hominins and *Pan* also did not exhibit these morphologies, and that the morphology of humans reflects a different use of the hand than is observed in extant apes. *Australopithecus afarensis* is clearly human-like, in having asymmetrical dorsally tapering second and third metacarpal head (Figure 12.4b, c; Drapeau *et al.*, 2005).

In palmar view, the articular facet of the human second metacarpal is also asymmetrical, with the radial side projecting more proximally and palmarly than the ulnar side, a condition not found or less obvious in apes (Figure 12.4a; Lewis, 1989). This asymmetry results in pronation of the second finger during flexion (Susman, 1979; Lewis, 1989; Marzke and Shackley, 1986; Marzke, 2005), which allows for the palmar aspect of the finger to conform to the shape of the manipulated object. All specimens of *A. afarensis* have second metacarpal heads that are human-like (Figure 12.4a). The heads have a marked asymmetry in distal and palmar view. It suggests adaptations for finger rotation and is consistent with improved manipulatory capabilities in these hominins. Again, *A. africanus* presents a metacarpal head morphology that is very similar to *A. afarensis*.

The capacity of humans to make pad-to-pad grips is mostly due to a long thumb relative to the other fingers (e.g. Napier, 1960, 1962; Marzke, 1986; Susman, 1998). It was shown above that the second and third metacarpals of *A. afarensis* are relatively short, particularly when compared to gibbons, orang-utans, chimpanzees and bonobos. There is no certain association of the thumb with any other digit in *A. afarensis*, but Alba and colleagues (2003) have shown that the assemblage of hand bones of the 'First Family' (A.L. 333) from Hadar, Ethiopia, whether it belongs to one or many individuals, comes from a population with short fingers and relatively long thumbs (see also Marzke, 1986; Latimer, 1991; Watkins *et al.*, 1993; and see Green and Gordon, 2008 for similar results in *A. africanus*), comparable to what is observed in modern humans. These relative proportions suggest that *A. afarensis* had a hand well adapted to pad-to-pad, pad-to-side and three-jaw chuck grips, resulting in more refined manipulatory movements than possible with a typical ape hand (Marzke and Shackley, 1986; Alba *et al.*, 2003).

In addition to the traits discussed above, Marzke (2005) also observes a relatively well marked first dorsal interosseous muscle origin on the first

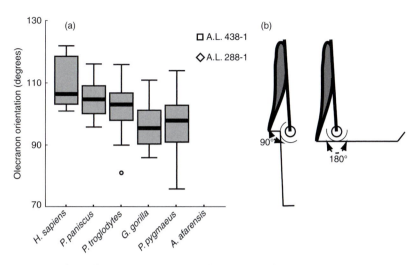

Figure 12.5. (a) Box-plot showing the olecranon orientation measured as the angle between two lines drawn from the axis of flexion of the ulna to the tip of the olecranon and to the ulnar head (in lateral view). Legend is as in Figure 12.2. (b) Schematic forelimbs representing the ulna, with its olecranon, articulating with the humerus. In this figure, the *triceps brachii* muscle, in grey, originates on the humerus and inserts on the olecranon.

metacarpal of *A. afarensis*, suggesting increased loading of the thumb relative to apes. Marzke and Marzke (1987) noted the presence of a transverse groove between the hook of the hamate and the carpometacarpal joint surfaces, which, they suggest, may indicate the possible presence of a pisometacarpal ligament to the third metacarpal that stabilises the base of the third metacarpal.

Moving away from the hand, other traits suggest increased manipulation in early hominins. At the elbow, humans are characterised by a proximally oriented olecranon (Figure 12.5a; Senut, 1981; Aiello *et al.*, 1999; Drapeau, 2004). The olecranon is the bony lever for the *triceps brachii* muscle, the main extensor of the forearm. A proximally orientated olecranon gives best leverage to the *triceps brachii* when the forearm is flexed, while a posteriorly oriented olecranon gives best leverage when the forearm is extended (Figure 12.5b). In orang-utans and knuckle-walkers, the bony lever for the triceps is more posteriorly oriented (Drapeau, 2004). This orientation in apes provides best leverage when the forearm is in full extension. In knuckle-walkers, for example, the triceps is active during terrestrial locomotion and the posterior orientation of the lever reflects use of the triceps when walking with an extended forearm to keep the elbow from collapsing (Tuttle, 1970; Tuttle and Basmanjian, 1974; Drapeau, 2004). The proximally orientated olecranon of humans provides best leverage for the *triceps brachii* muscle when the forearm is in a flexed position. Activities in which that muscle may be recruited include scraping motions away from the body and rapid extension as in hammering motions. *Australopithecus afarensis*, like humans, has a proximal orientation of the lever for the triceps (Figure 12.5a; Drapeau, 2004). This proximal orientation suggests use of the triceps when the forearm is flexed and the hands are closer to the body.

The humeral head torsion of *A. afarensis*, although rather low (Larson, 1996), falls within the 95% confidence intervals of many human populations (Larson *et al.*, 2007). Humans have forearms operating in a sagittal plane, facilitating manipulation of objects in front of the body. The morphology of *A. afarensis* implies similar capacities.

Overall, the upper limbs of *A. afarensis* display numerous traits suggesting that this species was under selective pressure to adapt to a novel behaviour that involved greater finger axial rotation, the possibility of three-jaw and pad-to-pad grips, and use of the hands when close to the body. These behaviours are associated with tool-use and tool-manufacture in humans (Marzke and Sackley, 1986).

Presently, there are no tools or any archaeological material attributed to *A. afarensis* or found in similar time horizons. This does not necessarily mean that tool-manufacture or tool-use was not important. The current oldest archaeological site dates to 2.6 Ma (Semaw *et al.*, 2003), and many are identified by 2.3 million years (Chavaillon, 1976; Merrick and Merrick, 1976; Roche et Tiercelin, 1980; Howell *et al.*, 1987; Kibunjia *et al.*, 1992; Kimbel *et al.*, 1996; de Heinzelin *et al.*, 1999; Roche *et al.*, 1999). Some of these very old sites, such as Lokalalei 2C (West Turkana, Kenya) and the Gona (Afar, Ethiopia) suggest well developed knapping skills and a certain understanding of flake-producing processes (Roche *et al.*, 1999; Delagnes and Roche, 2005), including the selection of raw materials with higher flaking qualities (Semaw, 2000; Semaw *et al.*, 2003). These oldest occurrences are not likely to represent early hominins' first attempts at stone-tool making. Given the skills exhibited, it appears to be an activity that was practised and already improved from an earlier, less sophisticated production.

A few hypotheses can be proposed to explain the absence of archaeological sites older than 2.6 Ma despite possible important tool-related activities by hominins (Potts, 1991; Panger *et al.*, 2002). For any archaeological site to be found, it must consist of a minimal density of recognisable debitage, or flaking debris. Such accumulations are more likely only if hominins use sites repeatedly. A few behavioural hypotheses have been proposed to explain the sudden appearance of Oldowan sites (see Potts, 1991 and Panger *et al.*, 2002 for reviews). They include the use of a home base in which tools are processed and used and other activities are performed, routed foraging, the establishment of tool caches to facilitate the processing of animal carcasses, changes in the way hominins used the landscape (possibly due to climate-related habitat alteration) and the exploitation of resources that are found repeatedly in the same locality (Potts, 1991; Panger *et al.*, 2002; Brooks and Laden, n.d. (cited in Panger *et al.*, 2002)). Any of these activities may constitute a behavioural novelty and may explain the sudden 'appearance' of sites with already fairly sophisticated tool-knapping skills, while earlier, tool-use and tool-manufacture may have been opportunistic, sporadic or conducted in contexts not related to home bases.

Archaeological sites can be identified only if the modified material preserves and remains relatively undisturbed until discovery. Behavioural studies of wild chimpanzees have revealed that they make and use tools mostly made of organic materials (see Boesch and Boesch, 1990; Whiten *et al.*, 1999). Early hominins may have relied increasingly on these behaviours but such tool-use and tool-manufacture would remain invisible archaeologically, even if it were extremely important to the survival of the species (Marzke, 1997; Alba *et al.*, 2003). The first appearance of recognisable stone tools around 2.6 million years ago would really just be the 'discovery' and mastery of a new type of raw material, utilising motor skills already previously developed.

Also, early hominin hand dexterity could reflect an increased need for manipulation but not necessarily to make tools. Improved finger dexterity in *A. afarensis* may simply reflect the use or manipulation of unmodified objects in a particular fashion, for example, peeling of fruits or tubers, picking up of small objects. Jolly (1970) has proposed a model of hominin differentiation based on a seed-eating adaptation similar to that observed in *Theropithecus gelada*. This model underscored the manual dexterity of gelada baboons, particularly the use of the thumb and index in a precision-grip to pick up grass blades. However, despite the observation of continuous use of the particular kind of grip, the gelada baboons are not characterised by all the morphological apomorphies observed in *A. afarensis*. Although their second metacarpal heads taper dorsoradially, they have second-third metacarpal and second metacarpal-capitate articulations that are discontinuous and clearly separated in dorsal and ventral sections (Jablonski, 1986; pers. obs.). The second metacarpal-capitate articulation, when viewed dorsally, lies in the sagittal plane (pers. obs.). These morphological traits do not suggest axial rotational capacities of the second metacarpal in that species. The derived morphology of *A. afarensis* suggest that their behaviour required more hand dexterity than what is required of the hand of the gelada baboon, or that its importance was such that it overcame other form of selection possibly favouring metacarpal articular stability. The discovery of possible hominin-made marks on bones from Dikika, dated at more than 3.39 Ma, supports the hypothesis that *A. afarensis* did use its hands for manipulation of objects used as tools (McPherron *et al.*, 2010).

Despite clear adaptations to better finger mobility, the hand of *A. afarensis* has not developed all the traits associated to dexterous manipulation in modern humans (Marzke, 1986, 1997, 2005; Tocheri *et al.*, 2008). Compared to humans, *A. afarensis* probably lacked rotational capacities of the fifth digit (Marzke *et al.*, 1992; Marzke, 1997, 2005), had a thumb that was less mobile, less robust and less strong (Susman, 1994; Marzke, 2005; Tocheri *et al.*, 2008), had a third metacarpal lacking a styloid process, which is interpreted to help resist dislocation of the third metacarpal base (Marzke and Marzke, 1987; Marzke, 2005), and did not have a capitate-trapezoid articulation that extended palmarly (Tocheri *et al.*, 2005, 2008). Nonetheless, the hand of *A. afarensis* displays traits that were modified by the processes of natural selection beyond what is observed in any extant apes or monkeys. This change in morphology towards an unmistakeably human form implies that the manipulatory behaviours to which the *A. afarensis* hand was adapted needed to be important for the survival of these early hominins, but they may not have any specific modern equivalent in extant species or human populations.

The 'appearance' of a human-like trait reflecting hand dexterity is osteologically obvious only in species that have become bipedal. It may be that bipedality, by freeing the hands from terrestrial locomotion, allowed for the hands to develop novel adaptations (e.g. Washburn, 1960). Recent work by Corbetta (2005) reveals an inverse relationship between use of the upper limb in locomotion in developing humans and the expression of handedness and hand specialisation. Quadrupedalism in humans, as in the crawling stage, seem to impede the hand preference that is observed before crawling and re-appear following the acquisition of bipedal locomotion (Corbetta, 2005). Since finger and hand specialisation is an important aspect of manipulation and of hand coordination as required in more complex tasks (Corbetta, 2005), it may not be a coincidence that osteologically visible improved hand dexterity occurs only in species that are known to be bipedal.

Very little is known about the hand morphology of species preceding *A. afarensis*, but one eroded capitate attributed to *Australopithecus anamensis* appears to have a sagitally oriented articular facet with the capitate, a morphology that is more ape-like (Ward *et al.*, 2001). Unfortunately, the capitate is too damaged to determine whether the articular facet with the capitate was discontinuous or not (Ward *et al.*, 2001), so it is unclear whether *A. anamensis* displayed manipulation adaptations. The *Ardipithecus* hand is characterised by a continuous capitate-MC2 surface (Lovejoy *et al.*, 2009), suggesting that it is a trait that has evolved prior to the origin of the *Australopithecus* genus. The discovery of more hand bones associated to species older than *A. afarensis*, but demonstrably bipedal, would serve to determine how close the association is between locomotion and hand adaptations. With *Ardipithecus*, the hypothesis that adaptations of the hand to manipulation are concurrent with bipedality is not yet falsified.

In conclusion, it is not possible to positively demonstrate that *A. afarensis* made or used tools without finding fossil remains in association with tools, but their morphology is consistent with the finger dexterity and the positioning of hands close to the body that are part of toolmaking and tool-using activities. This is a morphology that is novel in the taxon and must reflect adaptations to novel behaviours.

Although this morphology in early hominins suggests selection for traits favouring finger dexterity, it is not necessarily incompatible with arboreal locomotion. *Australopithecus afarensis* had a greater humero-femoral index than modern humans (Jungers, 1982), longer and more curved toes and fingers (Stern and Susman, 1983; Susman *et al.*, 1984; Stern, 2000), and appeared to be relatively more muscular (Drapeau, 2008). They were certainly much better climbers than any humans, and arboreality may have been important for the survival of the individual as well. But the *A. afarensis* upper limbs show synapomorphies shared with humans that clearly indicate that manipulatory activities were very important, and some of these traits, such as more mobile metacarpals and relatively shorter forearms and hands, were selected at the expense of arboreal adaptations. If, as argued by Corbetta (2005), the freeing of the upper limb from locomotion is a prerequisite of complex hand manipulation, the presence of derived, manipulatory enhancing traits in the hand of *A. afarensis* could be used to suggest little or no use of its upper limb in locomotion, whether terrestrial or arboreal. However, this chapter does not solve the debate about the possibility of an arboreal component to the locomotor repertoire of *A. afarensis*. It simply stresses that hand use for other purposes than locomotion was an important selective force that shaped the upper limb of these hominins. If *A. afarensis* were still indeed a habitual arboreal animal, its upper limbs show a compromise for a novel behaviour that was extremely important in the taxon. The archaeological record may still be silent, but the morphology of these early hominins provides strong support for a different, more human-like use of their hands. Although tool manufacture has long being rejected as a trait characterising hominins from their beginning, the evidence of hand dexterity in *A. afarensis* suggest that the uniquely human adaptations to behaviours of precise manipulation takes root at the dawn of the hominin lineage. It can be hypothesised that this novel behaviour, coupled with a bipedal stance while on the ground and, possibly, maintenance of an arboreal component in the locomotor repertoire of the species, provided a competitive advantage over other animals. This unique combination of behaviours may have been an important precursor step in the adaptive success of subsequent species clearly associated to lithic technologies. Although reasons for the colonisation success of the genus *Homo* in the Pleistocene may be numerous, it is difficult to argue that the capacity to make tools and modify materials did not play an important part in that success. The evidence of manipulatory behaviour in *Australopithecus* suggests that this trait was central to the nature of the lineage earlier than generally agreed. The importance it had in the success of the lineage early on may be difficult to assess, but given its importance at a later period, we could argue that it was an essential aspect for most of the hominin's history. For a good part of the past century, tools were believed to be one of the hallmarks of the human lineage. Discoveries of more ancient species to which no tools were associated forced a re-evaluation of what characterised the hominin lineage from its beginnings. The evidence of manipulatory adaptations in *A. afarensis* suggests that the earliest interpretations may not have been so wrong after all; manipulation, if not tool-use, may have been an important adaptive shift for early hominins.

We can only hope that further discoveries of hominin fossils from the early Pliocene in addition to the enigmatic *Ardipithecus* will help us resolve whether *Australopithecus afarensis* was the first hominin with a clearly derived hand morphology suggesting human-like manipulatory capacities or if that behaviour may have appeared earlier, possibly closer to the origin of bipedality, and may help provide some possible cause or consequence to that novel and unique mode of locomotion within the primate order.

Acknowledgements

I wish to thank the organisers of the African Genesis Symposium for the invitation to participate in this event celebrating the 80th birthday of Dr Phillip Tobias and of the discovery of the Taung child. I would also like to thank Drs William Kimbel and Donald Johanson for granting me access to the *A. afarensis* material, Dr Lorenzo Rook, for access to the *Oreopithecus* material, and Dr David Begun for providing a morphological description of an unpublished *Drypithecus* capitate specimen for an earlier version of this manuscript. I would also like to thank Mamitu Yilma from the National Museum of Ethiopia, Drs Jerome Cybulski, from the Canadian Museum of Civilization, Bruce Latimer and Yohannes Haile-Selassie, from the Cleveland Museum of Natural History, Richard Thorington, from the National Museum of Natural History, and Wim Van Neer, from the Musée Royal de l'Afrique Centrale, for access to the fossil and osteological collections in their care. I am grateful to Drs Sarah Elton, Elizabeth Harmon, Henry McHenry and Sally Reynolds for constructive comments on an earlier version of this manuscript and to Jeffrey Spate for editorial corrections.

References

Aiello, L. C., Wood, B., Key, C. *et al.* (1999). Morphological and taxonomic affinities of the Olduvai ulna (OH 36). *American Journal of Physical Anthropology*, **109**: 89–110.

Alba, D. M., Moyà-Solà, S. and Köhler, M. (2003). Morphological affinities of the *Australopithecus afarensis* hand on the basis of manual proportions and relative thumb length. *Journal of Human Evolution*, **44**: 225–54.

Alemseged, Z., Spoor, F., Kimbel, W. H. *et al.* (2006). A juvenile early hominin skeleton from Dikika, Ethiopia. *Nature*, **443**: 296–301.

Begun, D. (1993). Knuckle-walking ancestors. *Science*, **259**: 294.

  (1994). Relations among the great apes and humans: new interpretations based on the fossil great ape *Dryopithecus*. *Yearbook of Physical Anthropology*, **37**: 11–63.

Boesch, C. and Boesch, H. (1990). Tool use and tool making in wild chimpanzees. *Folia Primatologica*, **54**: 86–99.

Brooks, A. S. and Laden, G. (n.d.). Environmental determinants of site visibility: comparative ethnoarchaeology in the Kalahari Desert and Ituri Forest with implications for the 'emergence' of human culture.

Bush, M. E., Lovejoy, C. O., Johanson, D. C. *et al.* (1982). Hominid carpal, metacarpal, and phalangeal bones recovered from the Hadar Formation: 1974–1977 Collections. *American Journal of Physical Anthropology*, **57**: 651–77.

Cartmill, M. (1974). Pads and claws in arboreal locomotion. In Jenkins, F. A. (ed.), *Primate Locomotion*. New York: Academic Press, pp. 45–83.

Chavaillon, J. (1976). Evidence for the technical practices of early Pleistocene hominids, Shungura Formation, Lower Omo Valley, Ethiopia. In Coppens, Y., Howell, F. C., Isaac, G. L. and Leakey, R. E. (eds.), *Earliest Man and Environments in the Lake Rudolf Basin*. Chicago: University of Chicago Press, pp. 565–573.

Corbetta, D. (2005). Dynamic interactions between posture, handedness, bimanual coordination in human infants: why stone knapping might be a uniquely hominin behaviour. In Roux, V. and Bril, B. (eds.), *Stone Knapping. The Necessary Conditions for a Uniquely Hominin Behaviour*. Cambridge: McDonald Institute for Archaeological Research, pp. 187–204.

Corruccini, R. S. (1978). Comparative osteometrics of the hominoid wrist joint, with special reference to knuckle-walking. *Journal of Human Evolution*, **7**: 307–21.

Corruccini, R. S. and McHenry, H. M. (2001). Knuckle walking hominid ancestors. *Journal of Human Evolution*, **40**: 507–11.

de Heinzelin, J., Clark, J. D., White, T. *et al.* (1999). Environment and behavior of 2.5-million-year-old Bouri hominids. *Science*, **284**: 625–9.

Delagnes, A. and Roche, H. (2005). Late Pliocene hominid knapping skills: the case of Lokalalei 2C, West Turkana, Kenya. *Journal of Human Evolution*, **48**: 435–72.

Drapeau, M. S. M. (2004). Functional anatomy of the olecranon process in hominoids and Plio-Pleistocene hominins. *American Journal of Physical Anthropology*, **124**: 297–314.

  (2008). Articular morphology of the proximal ulna in extant and fossil hominoids and hominins. *Journal of Human Evolution*, **55**: 86–102.

Drapeau, M. S. M. and Harmon, E. H. (2008). Metatarsal head torsion in apes, humans and *A. afarensis*. *American Journal of Physical Anthropology*, Supp. **46**: 92.

Drapeau, M. S. M., Ward, C. V., Kimbel, W. H. *et al.* (2005). Associated cranial and forelimb remains attributed to *Australopithecus afarensis* from Hadar, Ethiopia. *Journal of Human Evolution*, **48**: 593–642.

Green, D. J. and Gordon, A. D. (2008). Metacarpal proportions in *Australopithecus africanus*. *Journal of Human Evolution*, **54**: 705–19.

Haeusler, H. M. and McHenry, H. M. (2004). Body proportions of *Homo habilis* reviewed. *Journal of Human Evolution*, **46**: 433–65.

Hooijer, D. A. (1963). Further 'hell' mammals from Niah. *The Sarawak Museum Journal*, **11**: 196–200.

Howell, F. C., Haesaerts, P. and de Heinzelin, J. (1987). Depositional environments, archeological occurrences and hominids from Members E and F of the Shungura Formation (Omo Basin, Ethiopia). *Journal of Human Evolution*, **16**: 665–700.

Jablonski, N. G. (1986). The hand of *Theropithecus brumpti*. In Else, J. G. and Lee P. C. (eds.), *Proceedings of the Tenth Congress of the International Primatology Society. Volume 1. Primate Evolution*. Cambridge: Cambridge University Press, pp. 173–82.

Jolly, C. J. (1970). The seed-eaters: a new model of hominid differentiation based on a baboon analogy. *Man*, **5**: 5–26.

Jungers, W. L. (1982). Lucy's limbs: skeletal allometry and locomotion in *Australopithecus afarensis*. *Nature*, **297**: 676–8.

(1994). Ape and hominid limb length. *Nature*, **369**: 194.

Jungers, W. L. and Stern, J. T. (1983). Body proportions, skeletal allometry and locomotion in the Hadar hominids: a reply to Wolpoff. *Journal of Human Evolution*, **12**: 673–84.

Kibunjia, M., Roche, H., Brown, F. H. *et al.* (1992). Pliocene and Pleistocene archeological sites west of Lake Turkana, Kenya. *Journal of Human Evolution*, **23**: 431–8.

Kimbel, W. H., Walter, R. C., Johanson, D. C. *et al.* (1996). Late Pliocene *Homo* and Oldowan tools from the Hadar Formation (Kada Hadar Member), Ethiopia. *Journal of Human Evolution*, **31**: 549–61.

Kitchener, A. C. (1999). The evolution of the tiger. In Seidensticker, J., Christie, S. and Jackson, P. (eds.), *Tiger Distribution, Phenotypic Variation and Conservation Issues*. Cambridge: Cambridge University Press, pp. 19–39.

Kivell, T. L. and Begun, D. R. (2009). New primate carpal bones from Rudabánya (late Miocene, Hungary): taxonomic and functional implications. *Journal of Human Evolution*, **57**: 697–709.

Larson, S. G. (1996). Estimating humeral torsion on incomplete fossil anthropoid humeri. *Journal of Human Evolution*, **31**: 239–57.

Larson, S. G., Jungers, W. L., Morwood, M. J. *et al.* (2007). *Homo floresiensis* and the evolution of the hominin shoulder. *Journal of Human Evolution*, **53**: 718–31.

Latimer, B. (1991). Locomotor adaptations in *Australopithecus afarensis*: the issue of arboreality. In Coppens, Y. and Senut, B. (eds.), *Origine(s) de la Bipédie chez les Hominidés*. Paris: Centre National de la Recherche Scientifique, pp. 169–76.

Latimer, B. and Lovejoy, C. O. (1989). The calcaneus of *Australopithecus afarensis* and its implications for the evolution of bipedality. *American Journal of Physical Anthropology*, **78**: 369–86.

Lewis, O. J. (1973). The hominoid os capitatum, with special reference to the fossil bones from Sterkfontein and Olduvai Gorge. *Journal of Human Evolution*, **2**: 1–12.

(1977). Joint remodeling and the evolution of the human hand. *Journal of Anatomy*, **123**: 157–201.

(1989). *Functional Morphology of the Evolving Hand and Foot.* Oxford: Oxford University Press.

Lovejoy, C. O. (1988). Evolution of human walking. *Scientific American*, **259**: 118–25.

Lovejoy, C. O., Simpson, S. W., White, T. D., Asfaw, B. and Suwa, G. (2009). Careful climbing in the Miocene: the forelimbs of *Ardipithecus ramidus* and humans are primitive. *Science*, **326**: 70e71–70e78.

Marzke, M. W. (1971). Origin of the human hand. *American Journal of Physical Anthropology*, **34**: 61–84.

(1983). Joint function and grips of the *Australopithecus afarensis* hand, with special reference to the region of the capitate. *Journal of Human Evolution*, **12**: 197–211.

(1986). Tool use and the evolution of hominid hands and bipedality. In Else, J. G. and Lee, P. C. (eds.), *Proceedings of the 10th Congress of the International Primatology Society.* Volume 1. New York: Cambridge University Press, pp. 203–9.

(1997). Precision grips, hand morphology, and tools. *American Journal of Physical Anthropology*, **102**: 91–110.

(2005). Who made stone tools? In Roux, V. and Bril, B. (eds.), *Stone Knapping. The Necessary Conditions for a Uniquely Hominin Behaviour.* Cambridge: McDonald Institute for Archaeological Research, pp. 243–55.

Marzke, M. W. and Shackley, M. S. (1986). Hominid hand use in the Pliocene and Pleistocene: evidence from experimental archaeology and comparative morphology. *Journal of Human Evolution*, **15**: 439–60.

Marzke, M. W. and Marzke, R. F. (1987). The third metacarpal styloid process in humans: origin and functions. *American Journal of Physical Anthropology*, **73**: 415–531.

Marzke, M. W., Wullstein, K. L. and Viegas, S. F. (1992). Evolution of the power ('squeeze') grip and its morphological correlates in hominids. *American Journal of Physical Anthropology*, **89**: 283–98.

McHenry, H. M. (1983). The capitate of *Australopithecus afarensis* and *A. africanus*. *American Journal of Physical Anthropology*, **62**: 187–98.

McPherron, S. P., Alemseged, Z., Marean, C. W. *et al.* (2010). Evidence for stone-tool-assisted consumption of animal tissues before 3.39 million years ago at Dikika, Ethiopia. *Nature*, **466**: 857–60.

Merrick, H. V. and Merrick, J. P. S. (1976). Archeological occurrences of earlier Pleistocene age from the Shungura Formation. In Coppens, Y., Howell, F. C., Isaac, G. L. and Leakey, R. E. (eds.), *Earliest Man and Environments in the Lake Rudolf Basin.* Chicago: University of Chicago Press, pp. 574–84.

Moyà-Solà, S., Köhler, M. and Rook, L. (1999). Evidence of hominid-like precision grip capability in the hand of the Miocene ape *Oreopithecus*. *Proceedings of the National Academy of Sciences of the United States of America*, **96**: 313–17.

246 *Michelle S. M. Drapeau*

Moyà-Solà, S., Kohler, M., Alba, D. M. *et al.* (2005). Response to Comment on 'Pierolapithecus catalaunicus, a new middle Miocene great ape from Spain'. *Science*, **308**: 203d.

Napier, J. R. (1960). Studies of the hands of living primates. *Proceedings of the Zoological Society of London*, **134**: 647–57.

Napier, J. (1962). The evolution of the hand. *Scientific American*, **207**: 56–62.

Panger, M. A., Brooks, A. S., Richmond, B. G. *et al.* (2002). Older than the Oldowan? Rethinking the emergence of hominin tool use. *Evolutionary Anthropology*, **11**: 235–45.

Potts, R. (1991). Why the Oldowan? Plio-Pleistocene toolmaking and the transport of resources. *Journal of Anthropological Research*, **47**: 153–76.

Preuschoft, H. (1973). Functional anatomy of the upper extremity. In Bourne, G. H. (ed.), *The Chimpanzee*. Basel: Karger, pp. 34–120.

Richmond, B. G. and Strait, D. S. (2000). Evidence that humans evolved from a knuckle-walking ancestor. *Nature*, **404**: 382–5.

Richmond, B. G., Begun, D. R. and Strait, D. S. (2001). Origin of human bipdalism: the knuckle-walking hypothesis revisited. *Yearbook of Physical Anthropology*, **44**: 70–105.

Richmond, B. G., Aiello, L. C. and Wood B. (2002). Early hominin limb proportions. *Journal of Human Evolution*, **43**: 529–48.

Roche, H. and Tiercelin, J.-J. (1980). Industries lithiques de la formation plio-pléistocène d'Hadar Ethiopie (campagne 1976). In Leakey, R. E. and Ogot, B. A. (eds.), *Proceedings of the 8th Pan-African Congress of Prehistory and Quaternary Studies, Nairobi, 5 to 10 September 1977*. Nairobi: The International Louis Leakey Memorial Institute for African Prehistory. pp. 194–9.

Roche, H., Delagnes, A., Brugal, J.-P. *et al.* (1999). Early hominid stone tool production and technical skill 2.34 Myr ago in West Turkana, Kenya. *Nature*, **399**: 57–60.

Rose, M. D. (1984). Hominoid postcranial specimens from the middle Miocene Chinji Formation, Pakistan. *Journal of Human Evolution*, **13**: 503–16.

Schultz, A. H. (1969). The skeleton of the chimpanzee. In Bourne, G. H. (ed.), *The Chimpanzee*. Basel, New York: Karger, pp. 50–103.

Semaw, S. (2000). The world's oldest stone artefacts from Gona, Ethiopia: their implications for understanding stone technology and patterns of human evolution between 2.6–1.5 million years ago. *Journal of Archaeological Science*, **27**: 1197–214.

Semaw, S., Rogers, M. J., Quade, J. *et al.* (2003). 2.6-million-year-old stone tools and associated bones from OGS-6 and OGS-7, Gona, Afar, Ethiopia. *Journal of Human Evolution*, **45**: 169–77.

Senut, B. (1981). *L'humérus et ses articulations chez les hominidés plio-pléistocènes*. Paris: Centre National de la Recherche Scientifique.

Senut, B. and Tardieu, C. (1985). Functional aspects of Plio-Pleistocene hominid limb bones: implications for taxonomy and phylogeny. In Delson, E. (ed.), *Ancestors: The Hard Evidence*. New York: Alan R. Liss, Inc., pp. 193–201.

Smith, R. J. and Jungers, W. L. (1997). Body mass in comparative primatology. *Journal of Human Evolution*, **32**: 523–59.

Stern, J. T. (2000). Climbing to the top: a personal memoir of *Australopithecus afarensis*. *Evolutionary Anthropology*, **9**: 113–33.

Stern, J. T. and Susman, R. L. (1983). The locomotor anatomy of *Australopithecus afarensis*. *American Journal of Physical Anthropology*, **60**: 279–317.

Sugardjito, J. and Cant, J. G. (1994). Geographic and sex differences in positional behavior of orang-utans. *Treubia*, **31**: 31–41.

Susman, R. L. (1979). Comparative and functional morphology of Hominoid fingers. *American Journal of Physical Anthropology*, **50**: 215–36.

   (1994). Fossil evidence for early hominid tool use. *Science*, **265**: 1570–3.

   (1998). Hand function and tool behavior in early hominids. *Journal of Human Evolution*, **35**: 23–46.

   (2005). *Oreopithecus*: still apelike after all these years. *Journal of Human Evolution*, **49**: 405–11.

Susman, R. L., Stern, J. T. and Jungers, W. L. (1984). Arboreality and bipedality in the Hadar hominids. *Folia Primatologica*, **43**: 113–56.

Swartz, S. M., Bertram, J. E. A. and Biewener, A. A. (1989). Telemetered *in vivo* strain analysis of locomotor mechanics of brachiating gibbons. *Nature*, **342**: 270–2.

Tocheri, M. W., Marzke, M. W., Liu, D. *et al.* (2003). Functional capabilities of modern and fossil hominid hands: three-dimensional analysis of trapezia. *American Journal of Physical Anthropology*, **122**: 101–12.

Tocheri, M. W., Razdan, A., Williams, R. C. *et al.* (2005). A 3D quantitative comparison of trapezium and trapezoid relative articular and nonarticular surface areas in modern humans and great apes. *Journal of Human Evolution*, **49**: 570–86.

Tocheri, M. W., Orr, C. M., Jacofsky, M. C. *et al.* (2008). The evolutionary history of the hominin hand since the last common ancestor of *Pan* and *Homo*. *Journal of Anatomy*, **212**: 544–62.

Tuttle, R. and Basmajian, J. V. (1974). Electromyography of brachial muscle in *Pan gorilla* and hominoid evolution. *American Journal of Physical Anthropology*, **41**: 71–90.

Tuttle, R. H. (1970). Postural, propulsive, and prehensile capabilities in the cheiridia of chimpanzees and other great apes. In Bourne, G. H. (ed.), *The Chimpanzee*. Basel/New York: Karger. pp. 167–253.

Ward, C. V. (2002). Interpreting the posture and locomotion of *Australopithecus afarensis*: where do we stand? *Yearbook of Physical Anthropology*, **45**: 185–215.

Ward, C. V., Leakey, M. G. and Walker, A. (2001). Morphology of *Australopithecus anamensis* from Kanapoi and Allia Bay, Kenya. *Journal of Human Evolution*, **41**: 255–368.

Washburn, S. L. (1960). Tools and human evolution. *Scientific American*, **203**: 63–75.

   (1967). Behaviour and the origin of man. *Proceedings of the Royal Anthropological Institute of Great Britain and Ireland*, **3**: 21–7.

Watkins, B., Parkinson, D. and Mensforth, R. (1993). Morphological evidence for the abandonment of forelimb dominance in *Australopithecus afarensis*. *American Journal of Physical Anthropology*, Supp. **16**: 205.

Whiten, A., Goodall, J., McGrew, W. C. *et al.* (1999). Cultures in chimpanzees. *Nature*, **399**: 52–66.

13 Hominin proximal femur morphology from the Tugen Hills to Flores

BRIAN G. RICHMOND AND
WILLIAM L. JUNGERS

Abstract

The proximal femur has played a prominent role in our understanding of the origin and evolution of human gait because of its functional importance and relatively good representation in the fossil record. This study examines the morphology of femora from the fossil record, including those attributed to *Orrorin tugenensis* (BAR 1002'00) and *Homo floresiensis* (LB1/9). Considerable debate surrounds both of these taxa, focusing primarily on the evidence that the former is a hominin and shows convincing adaptations for bipedalism, and over whether or not the latter is a pathological diminutive modern human or a distinct species (and what the anatomy suggests regarding the evolutionary history of *H. floresiensis*). This study addresses the questions of whether *Orrorin* femoral morphology more closely resembles femora of humans and fossil hominins than apes, and whether it is more similar to the femora of *Homo* among the hominins. Our study also tests the hypothesis that the femoral morphology of LB1/9 is consistent with that of a small-bodied modern human, or more closely resembles fossil hominins. To test these questions, we compare the proximal femoral morphology of BAR 1002'00 and LB1/9 to a large sample of adult humans, chimpanzees, bonobos, gorillas, orang-utans and most available early hominin taxa. Importantly, the human sample includes individuals from large- and small-bodied populations that overlap with the small sizes of BAR 1002'00 and LB1/9.

   The results show that the external morphology of the *Orrorin* femur more closely resembles the femora of *Australopithecus* and *Paranthropus* than those of great apes, or fossil and modern *Homo*. Its morphology is not consistent with it being characterised as more like human than australopith femora, or a phylogenetic hypothesis that *Orrorin* is ancestral to *Homo* to the exclusion of the australopithecines. However, its morphology is consistent with its 6

African Genesis: Perspectives on Hominin Evolution, eds. Sally C. Reynolds and Andrew Gallagher. Published by Cambridge University Press. © Cambridge University Press 2012.

million-year-old age and its taxonomic assignment as a basal, bipedal hominin. The external morphology of the *Orrorin* femora shares similarities with those of gracile and robust australopiths despite some evidence suggesting more primitive cortical structure, raising potential questions about hip function in *Orrorin*. The proximal femoral anatomy of LB1/9 shows that it is not a small modern human, and instead supports evidence from other anatomical regions that it represents a distinct species, *Homo floresiensis*, with strikingly primitive femoral morphology resembling early hominins.

Introduction

In studies of the origin and evolution of human gait, the proximal femur has played a prominent role because of its functional importance and relatively good preservation in the hominin fossil record. While there is broad agreement that femoral anatomy varies over the course of human evolutionary history, some disagreements continue over what morphology characterises certain taxa, and major debates persist over the mechanical and behavioural implications of this morphological variation.

Numerous researchers have studied the femoral anatomy of gracile and robust australopiths (e.g. Napier, 1964; Day, 1969, 1973; Robinson, 1972; Lovejoy *et al.*, 1973; Walker, 1973; McHenry, 1975; Wood, 1976; McHenry and Corruccini, 1976a, 1978; Stern and Susman, 1983; Lovejoy, 1988; Jungers, 1991; Ruff, 1995, 1998; Lovejoy *et al.*, 2002; Richmond and Jungers, 2008; Harmon, 2007, 2009a,b). Perhaps the most important functional characteristic is femoral length, which in *Australopithecus afarensis* is intermediate between African apes and humans (Jungers, 1982). Compared with modern humans, the proximal femur of *Australopithecus* and *Paranthropus* is characterised by a long and anteroposteriorly-narrow neck, small head, superiorly projecting and laterally flat greater trochanter, and a robust femoral shaft (see references above). Some have debated whether *Australopithecus* had a relatively small femoral head (e.g. McHenry and Corruccini, 1976a,b; Jungers, 1988, 1991) or not (e.g. Wolpoff, 1976; Ruff, 1998). Researchers mainly disagree over the choice of the most appropriate size variable against which to compare the size of the femoral head (see below).

The femoral anatomy of early *Homo* is unique, differing from that of australopiths and modern humans. Relative femur length is similar to modern humans in early *H. erectus* (Ruff and Walker, 1993; Lordkipanidze *et al.*, 2007) and differs significantly from that of *A. afarensis* (Richmond *et al.*, 2002). However, proximal femur shape is unique in early *Homo*, with a large femoral head, long femoral neck (primitive) and wide mediolateral (ML) shaft, with its narrowest point occurring more distally than in modern humans. Ruff (1995) makes a convincing argument that the great mediolateral shaft width and low position of minimum breadth are biomechanically related to elevated bending moments that would result from the long femoral neck, and potentially laterally flaring ilia, retained in early *Homo*.

It was relatively late in human evolution that we find evidence of a short femoral neck and reduction in the breadth of the femoral shaft (Ruff, 1995). By the Middle Pleistocene, femora (e.g. Gesher Benot Ya'acov 1, Israel) no longer have the ML-broad and relatively AP-narrow proximal shaft shape seen in *H. erectus*. Thus, archaic *Homo* has a more human-like proximal femur shape with large femoral heads, short femoral necks and more rounded proximal shafts (Ruff, 1995).

As noted above, where researchers have debated over how to characterise fossil hominin proximal femur morphology, the main source of discrepancy has been the choice of size variable used to standardise the sizes of other variables (e.g. McHenry and Corruccini, 1976b; Wolpoff, 1976; Jungers, 1988, 1991; Ruff, 1998). Femoral head size has functional implications because large joint sizes are related to high joint loads and/or high levels of joint mobility (Godfrey *et al.*, 1995; Ruff, 2002). Some who argue that *Australopithecus* had a modern human-like relative joint size interpret the gait of *Australopithecus* as being essentially modern human-like. Some who argue that femoral head size is small in *Australopithecus* interpret the small joint size as indicating relatively low levels of loading; this in turn suggests that while bipedal, *Australopithecus* was not adapted for running or walking long distances (e.g. Stern and Susman, 1983; Jungers, 1988; Bramble and Lieberman, 2004). Others point out that the small femoral head is part of a biomechanical complex including a long femoral neck and therefore more effective moment arm for the gluteal muscle action during gait (Lovejoy *et al.*, 1973; Ruff, 1998), leading some to interpret *Australopithecus* as having the 'expected' head size (Lovejoy *et al.*, 1973) or a head size still smaller than expected within its biomechanical environment (Jungers, 1991; Ruff, 1998). These differences of opinion can be traced in part back to phrasing the question in different terms of 'relative size', shape per se versus mass-adjusted size of the femoral head.

In this study, we use the geometric mean of proximal femur measurements because the geometric mean is a size surrogate that has proven to reliably preserve shape information in scaling studies (Jungers *et al.*, 1995), and allows us to assess whether anatomical features such as the femoral head are small relative to the rest of the proximal femur. Restricting our variables to those preserved on the proximal femur also allows us to include a relatively large sample of fossils (e.g. compared to methods requiring other associated elements or known/estimated body mass; Auerbach and Ruff, 2004).

We evaluate the pattern of shape variation in a sample of Miocene-Pleistocene hominin femora against a large sample of extant great apes and samples of six modern human populations spanning the human size range. To this sample, we add the proximal femora belonging to two recently described taxa from the very earliest and latest periods of the hominin fossil record, *Orrorin tugenensis* (*c*. 6 Ma) and *H. floresiensis* (Late Pleistocene), in order to examine how they compare with the femora of other hominins.

Since its initial discovery, researchers have debated whether or not the femoral morphology of *Orrorin* indicates that it was adapted to bipedality. Although numerous qualitative traits (e.g. obturator externus groove, relative femoral head size, relatively long neck) are consistent with bipedalism, each of them occur to some extent in other primates and therefore do not conclusively indicate that *Orrorin* was bipedal. For example, the obturator externus groove is often cited as a bipedal trait, but it is not unique to humans. As various authors have noted, the obturator externus groove occurs in other primates such as *Ateles* and *Papio* as well as humans. Its presence therefore indicates 'frequent bipedalism', including bipedalism practised by monkeys and apes (Stern and Larson 1990; Stern and Susman 1991; Pickford *et al.*, 2002). Other features of the *Orrorin* femoral anatomy would benefit from an analysis using quantitative statistical methods. For example, Senut *et al.* (2001) and Pickford *et al.* (2002) note that the femoral head in *Orrorin* is larger relative to its shaft than it is in A.L. 288–1 (the *A. afarensis* specimen from Hadar commonly known as 'Lucy'). However, in this measure, A.L. 288–1 has a femoral head size comparable to those of great apes, and it is unclear whether or not the *Orrorin* femoral head (BAR 1002'00) is significantly larger than those of apes. Similarly, *Orrorin* is described as having a long femoral neck (Senut *et al.*, 2001; Pickford *et al.*, 2002; Galik *et al.*, 2004), but quantitative analyses are needed (Richmond and Jungers, 2008).

Analyses of CT images of BAR 1002'00 have led to conflicting interpretations. An initial study (Galik *et al.*, 2004) of femoral neck cortical distribution concluded that the ratio of the inferior to superior cortical bone thickness in BAR 1002'00 is high as in modern human femora. More recent analyses of those CT scans concluded that the skewness of femoral neck cortical distribution more closely resembled chimpanzee than modern human femora (Kuperavage *et al.*, 2010), although the data showed considerable overlap among the samples. Others have argued that the CT scans are unfortunately too coarse to reliably characterise the internal morphology (Ohman *et al.*, 2005). At present, the cortical geometry evidence has not resolved debates about bipedalism in *Orrorin*.

Senut *et al.* (2001) also argue that BAR 1002'00 is morphologically more human-like than *Australopithecus* femora, and propose that *Orrorin* is ancestral to *Homo* while *Ardipithecus* and *Australopithecus* are not. These authors subscribe to the relatively uncommon view that the Hadar hominins represent two taxa – *Australopithecus afarensis* and *Praeanthropus afarensis*, in which they argue the former comprises a clade with other *Australopithecus* species and with *Paranthropus*, and the latter they argue to be ancestral to *Homo*.

This study builds on recent work (Richmond and Jungers, 2008) to address the questions about how *Orrorin* femoral morphology compares with femora of humans, fossil hominins and apes, and whether the morphology is more similar to the femora of *Homo* compared to those of other early hominin taxa.

At the other end of the temporal spectrum, the recent discovery of skeletal elements attributed to *H. floresiensis* on the Indonesian island of Flores (Brown *et al.*, 2004; Morwood *et al.*, 2005) has raised many questions about the nature of these remains, especially whether the remains represent pathological modern humans, or a dwarfed taxon with a long evolutionary history. Much of the debate has focused on brain and skull size and shape, with some arguing that LB1/9 displays the morphology consistent with microcephally and/or other pathologies in modern humans (Weber *et al.*, 2005; Jacob *et al.*, 2006; Martin *et al.*, 2006a,b; Richards, 2006; Hershkovitz *et al.*, 2007) and others refuting this conclusion and demonstrating similarities in cranial and endocranial shape with early hominins, including early *Homo* and even *Australopithecus* (Falk *et al.*, 2005, 2007, 2009; Argue *et al.*, 2006; Gordon *et al.*, 2008). Evidence from the postcranium suggests that the Liang Bua skeletal remains come from a hominin with primitive morphology, notably limb proportions including a relatively short femur and long forearm (Morwood *et al.*, 2005), robust limb bones (Jungers *et al.*, 2009a), a carpal complex resembling *Australopithecus* and *H. habilis* (Tocheri *et al.*, 2007), foot with primitive and unique attributes (Jungers *et al.*, 2009b) and a primitive shoulder complex, including a short clavicle and humerus with little torsion (Larson *et al.*, 2007, 2009). We investigate the proximal femoral anatomy of LB1/9 in the context of this debate to assess whether the morphology is consistent with that of a small-bodied modern human, or more closely resembles those of other fossil hominins.

Methods

In order to account for size-related variation in proximal femur morphology, we measured a large sample of great apes and humans. We sampled a wide range of human populations including, from smallest to largest, Andaman Islanders, African Pygmies, Pre-Dynastic Egyptians, European Americans, Inuit and African Americans, with a total of 130 individuals (Table 13.1). The

Table 13.1. *Extant and fossil samples.*

Extant and fossil taxa	Population/specimen #s	*n*
Homo sapiens		130
	Andaman Islanders	31
	African Pygmies	18
	Pre-Dynastic Egyptians	20
	Inuit	20
	African Americans	20
	European Americans	21
Pan troglodytes		49
Pan paniscus		14
Gorilla gorilla		59
Pongo pygmaeus		32
Orrorin tugenensis	BAR 1002'00	1
Australopithecus afarensis	A.L. 288–1ap, A.L. 333–3	2
Paranthropus robustus	SK 82, SK 97	2
?Paranthropus boisei	KNM-ER 1503	1
early *Homo*	KNM-ER 1472, 1481	2
Homo heidelbergensis	Berg Aukas	1
Homo floresiensis	LB 1/9	1

great ape sample (*n* = 154) also includes a wide size range, from *Pongo* and *Pan paniscus* to *Gorilla*, that encompasses the fossil size range.

In addition to extant samples, the *Orrorin tugenensis* and *H. floresiensis* femora (BAR 1002'00 and LB1/9, respectively) were compared to the femora of a number of extinct hominin taxa, including *A. afarensis* from Hadar (Ethiopia), *P. robustus* from Swartkrans (South Africa), femora from Koobi Fora (Kenya) attributed to *P. boisei* and early *Homo*, and the large femur from Berg Aukas (Namibia) attributed to archaic *Homo* (Grine *et al.*, 1995; Table 13.1). Measurements were collected on original specimens of all but the Hadar femora, in which case measurements were taken on casts at Stony Brook University and verified against comparable measurements in the literature.

The variables are as follows (see also McHenry and Corruccini, 1978):

(1) Femoral head SI: the supero-inferior diameter of the femoral head.
(2) Femoral head AP: the anteroposterior diameter of the femoral head.
(3) Lesser troch–head: the minimum distance from the lesser trochanter to the rim of the head.
(4) Neck height: the supero-inferior height of the femoral neck.
(5) Neck breadth: the anteroposterior breadth of the femoral neck.
(6) Biomechanical neck length: the distance from the lateral aspect of the greater trochanter to the medial aspect of the femoral head, minus half of femoral head SI (measurement 1, above).

(7) Subtrochanteric AP: the anteroposterior diameter of the shaft just below the lesser trochanter.
(8) Subtrochanteric ML: the medio-lateral diameter of the shaft just below the lesser trochanter.

The lateral edge of the greater trochanter of BAR 1002'00 (*Orrorin*) is unfortunately broken. We conservatively estimate that 2 mm is missing and add it to the minimum measured value (72 mm) in which neck length is taken directly to the broken lateral edge of the greater trochanter. Analyses that include the minimum value do not differ qualitatively (i.e. BAR 1002'00 retains the same nearest-neighbour relationships) from the analysis with the reconstructed biomechanical neck length.

The geometric mean (GM, the *n*th root of the product of *n* measurements) was selected because it faithfully preserves shape information when variables (e.g. femoral head size) are assessed relative to the GM (Jungers *et al.*, 1995). Proximal femur size was represented by the GM of all eight measurements. Size is therefore based on the femoral measurements themselves rather than an independent substitute for size that would be unavailable for most of the fossils or have to be estimated for all with attendant confidence intervals (e.g. body mass). Each variable was divided by the GM to create size-adjusted, scale-free 'shape' variables, which then reflect the relative size of each anatomical feature. Each shape variable was logged prior to entry into the multivariate analyses (Darroch and Mosimann, 1985).

Multivariate and bivariate analyses were conducted. A canonical variates analysis (CVA) was performed using seven of the shape variables (relative femoral head SI was omitted because it was identified in the analysis as being redundant with relative femoral head AP in that they co-vary so closely). Each of the modern and fossil species were treated as separate groups, resulting in 12 groups (5 extant and 7 fossil species). Canonical variates analysis makes the assumption that groups share equivalent variance/covariance structure, and therefore assumes that the fossil hominin taxa (represented by small sample sizes) have the dispersion structures comparable to those of the modern great ape and human taxa. Fortunately, CVA is relatively robust to violations of these underlying assumptions. Canonical variates analysis differs from principal components analysis in maximising between-group differences instead of maximising variation among individuals (regardless of group membership) in the entire sample. It also adjusts the between-groups distances relative to the within-group variation, and plots individuals in this adjusted, Mahalanobis distance space.

Bivariate analyses are performed with raw variables plotted against the GM. Fossils are examined in scatter plots relative to reduced major axis (RMA) regression lines through pooled, raw data as the relationships are expected to be symmetric between variables (Smith, 2009).

Results

The results show that proximal femoral shape is distinct among various modern and fossil taxa, including early hominins. The CVA of proximal femur shape completely separates modern humans from the great apes along the first axis, which accounts for 74.8% of the variation (Figure 13.1a). A principal components analysis (not shown) produced very similar results. The key variables influencing CVA1 are a relatively large lesser trochanter-to-head distance and small femoral head towards the right (great ape side) of the axis (Table 13.2). To a lesser extent, small neck height and breadth are correlated with the axis as well. Thus, human femora are characterised by relatively small lesser trochanter-to-head distances, large femoral heads and, to a lesser degree, relatively large neck diameters (Figures 13.1, 13.4).

Along axis one, the fossil hominin femora all fall towards the human direction relative to the great apes and, with a few exceptions (the Hadar and Swartkrans specimens) fall outside the great ape range on this axis. Axis two accounts for 16.2% of the variation and primarily separates orang-utan femora from those of other taxa; it is most strongly influenced by relatively large femoral heads and small subtrochanteric shaft anteroposterior depths (Figure 13.1a, Table 13.2), a combination that characterises orang-utan femora.

The femora of extinct hominins cluster together, mainly in the lower middle portion of the plot (Figure 13.1a). The Turkana Basin (Kenya) femora attributed to early *Homo* lie in the modern human shape space. There is some disparity in shape between KNM-ER 1481 and KNM-ER 1472, but the difference is consistent with the variation seen in modern taxa. While most authors interpret these femora as representing the same taxon, some have interpreted the morphological differences between these specimens as indicating that they belong to separate taxa. Some of the apparent morphological difference (e.g. smaller head size of KNM-ER 1472) is influenced by how one reconstructs damage to the specimen. In light of this uncertainty, and the fact that the morphological difference can be accommodated with intra-specific variation in modern taxa, we have no grounds for rejecting the hypothesis that they belong to the same genus, early *Homo*.

Of particular note in the CVA analysis is the result that all the non-*Homo* femora cluster together in a unique space outside of the range of human and, with the exception of Swartkrans specimen SK97, great ape variation (Figure 13.1a). The *Orrorin* and *H. floresiensis* femora cluster with these early hominin femora attributed to *Australopithecus* and *Paranthropus*.

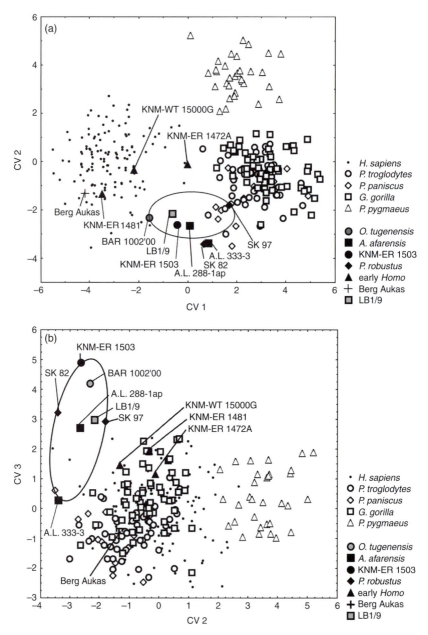

Figure 13.1. Canonical variates analysis (CVA) based on seven proximal femur shape variables. The first two axes (a) show that humans, African apes and orang-utans are distinct from one another in proximal femur shape. All the non-*Homo* femora cluster together in a unique space outside the human and, with the exception of SK97, great ape variation. The *Orrorin* and *H. floresiensis* femora cluster with these early hominin femora. The third axis (b) further separates these early hominins (except A.L. 333–3) from the modern taxa. Note that the *Orrorin* and *H. floresiensis* femora cluster with these early hominin femora, and away from other fossil and modern *Homo* along this axis, underscoring the primitive morphology in these taxa.

Table 13.2. *Factor structure matrix of canonical variates analysis, with the most influential variables on the first three roots shown in bold.*

Shape variables	Root 1	Root 2	Root 3
Femoral head AP	**–0.5209**	**0.7226**	–0.0311
Lesser troch–head	**0.6489**	0.3259	–0.0887
Neck height	–0.4420	–0.1299	0.2108
Neck breadth	–0.3899	–0.2852	**–0.6987**
Subtrochanteric AP	0.2272	**–0.5352**	–0.1825
Subtrochanteric ML	0.2241	–0.2700	**0.4879**
Biomechanical neck length	–0.2383	–0.3113	**0.6179**
% Variance explained	74.8	16.2	5.5
% Variance (cumulative)	74.8	91.0	96.5

Table 13.3. *Mahalanobis D^2 distances.*

Taxon/specimen	BAR 1002'00	LB1
Homo sapiens	31.97	25.62
Pan troglodytes	50.82	32.12
Pan paniscus	49.45	29.77
Gorilla gorilla	47.66	29.95
Pongo pygmaeus	67.92	51.31
BAR 1002'00	0	17.56
Australopithecus afarensis	16.64	12.06
Paranthropus robustus	18.04	10.89
KNM-ER 1503	13.04	8.65
early *Homo*	33.49	27.55
Berg Aukas	49.74	38.16
LB1	17.56	0

The third CVA axis (5.5% of variation) separates most of this early hominin group from the remaining fossil and extant taxa, and is most strongly influenced (towards the top) by narrow neck breadth (AP), long biomechanical neck length and large subtrochanteric ML diameter (Figure 13.1b, Table 13.2). The distinct femora (towards the top) include those attributed to *Paranthropus* (SK 82, SK 97 and KNM-ER 1503) and *A. afarensis* (A.L. 288–1, but not A.L. 333–3) (Figure 13.4). Once again, the *Orrorin* and *H. floresiensis* femora cluster with this primitive, australopith group (Figures 13.1b, 13.4).

The Mahalanobis D^2 distances further illustrate how much more similar the *Orrorin* and *H. floresiensis* femora are to the australopith femora than they are to any of the extant or other fossil femora (Table 13.3). Distances between all the extant taxa, and between extant and fossil taxa, differ significantly

(F-statistic, $p < 0.01$) from one another. With respect to these shape variables, BAR 1002'00 is most similar to KNM-ER 1503, the Hadar femora, LB1/9, and the Swartkrans femora, followed distantly by modern humans and the early *Homo* femora. LB1/9 similarly clusters most closely to KNM-ER 1503, the Swartkrans femora, the Hadar femora, BAR 1002'00, followed more distantly by modern humans and the remaining non-human groups (Table 13.3).

Femoral head size is of special interest because it has been described as relatively large in BAR 1002'00 (Pickford *et al.*, 2002), and there has been some debate about allometric patterns in human femoral head size. When compared against proximal femur size (the geometric mean of all eight measurements), femoral head size in humans and orang-utans is greater than those of African apes (Figure 13.2). This is true even at the smallest overall proximal femoral sizes, meaning that femoral size alone does not explain the relatively small head size observed in *Australopithecus*, *Paranthropus* and *H. floresiensis* femora (or the large ones in orang-utans). The *Orrorin* femur has an intermediate head size, greater than the typical size of African apes or australopiths, but less

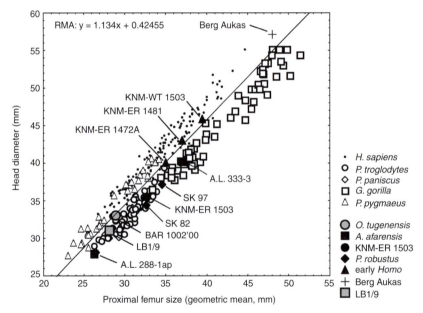

Figure 13.2. Bivariate plot of head diameter and proximal femur size, with RMA line fit through all data. Femoral head size in humans and orang-utans is relatively greater than those of African apes, even at the smallest sizes. *Australopithecus*, *Paranthropus* and *H. floresiensis* femora have smaller heads than modern humans of comparable size. The *Orrorin* femur (BAR 1002'00) has an intermediate head size, greater than the typical size of African apes or australopiths, and less than most humans and orang-utans. The *H. floresiensis* femur (LB1/9) has a relatively small head.

than most humans and orang-utans. However, its head size is within the intra-specific range of either. The head sizes of KNM-ER 1472, KNM-ER 1481 and KNM-WT 15000 are also intermediate, relatively larger than those of austra-lopiths and within the range of comparably sized modern humans. The slightly low positions of the early *Homo* femoral head sizes are influenced to some extent by other variables (e.g. biomechanical neck length, shaft breadth) that contribute to large proximal femur sizes for these specimens. The Berg Aukas femoral head is larger than any in our extensive modern human sample, but has a relative size expected for such a large femur.

Biomechanical neck length is one of the most influential variables separating the early hominin femora from extant and other fossil femora in the multivari-ate analysis (Table 13.2). The proximal femur size adjustment in this analysis yields similar results to previous studies that have noted the long femoral necks of the femora from Hadar, Swartkrans and East Turkana specimen KNM-ER 1503 (e.g. Napier, 1964; Day, 1969; Lovejoy *et al.*, 1973). When plotted against proximal femur size (Figure 13.3), it is apparent that the most of the fossil

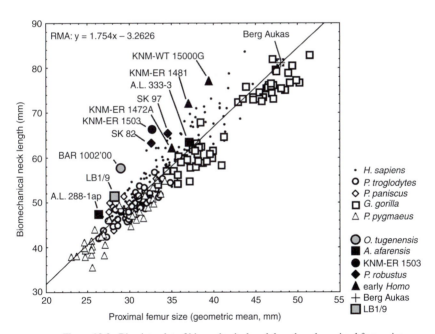

Figure 13.3. Bivariate plot of biomechanical neck length and proximal femur size, with RMA line fit through all data. Most of the fossil hominin femora have long necks, with some (e.g. KNM-ER 1503) exceeding the range of modern human variation. The *Orrorin* femur has an unusually long neck, greater than that seen in the two Hadar femora. Like A.L. 288–1, LB1/9 has a longer neck than expected for a comparably sized modern human.

hominin femora have long necks, with some (e.g. KNM-ER 1503) exceeding the range of modern human variation. In this regard, the *Orrorin* femur has an unusually long neck, greater than that seen in the two Hadar femora. Like A.L. 288–1 (but not A.L. 333–3), LB1/9 has a longer neck than expected for a comparably sized modern human. KNM-ER 1481 and KNM-WT 15000G also have unusually long necks, longer than that of KNM-ER 1472 and beyond the modern human range. Berg Aukas has a neck length consistent with its massive size.

Biomechanical neck length, as measured in this and previous studies (e.g. McHenry and Corruccini, 1978) from the lateral extent of the greater trochanter, is influenced by the morphology of the greater trochanter. Modern human and early *Homo* femora tend to have laterally projecting greater trochanters (Figure 13.4; Harmon, 2009a), but considerable variability exists. The lateral extent of the greater trochanter increases the mechanical lever arm of the gluteal musculature, and this increased leverage is reflected in the biomechanical neck length measurement. In this regard, the lateral projection of the greater trochanter in the Flores specimen LB1/9 contributes to its long neck in a manner resembling femora of early *Homo* (Figure 13.4), including KNM-ER 1481, KNM-ER 1472 and KNM-WT 15000 from the Turkana Basin, and D4167 from Dmanisi, Georgia (Lordkipanidze *et al.*, 2007). The adaptive significance, if any, of the laterally-projecting greater trochanter is unknown, but could be related to changes in the gluteal insertions (Harmon, 2009a) or as a means of maintaining a long gluteal lever arm without further lengthening the femoral neck and subjecting it to more elevated bending moments. The long biomechanical neck (i.e. including trochanter projection) is associated with laterally-flaring ilia in australopiths (Lovejoy *et al.*, 1973) and *H. floresiensis* specimen LB1 (Jungers *et al.*, 2009a). Modern human femora have short biomechanical neck lengths despite the lateral projection of the greater trochanter, likely associated with relatively narrow iliac breadth (Ruff, 1995).

Discussion

The questions posed in this study concern what the femora of two new hominin taxa, *O. tugenensis* and *H. floresiensis*, tell us about the evolution of the hip and bipedal gait. The results clearly show that the *Orrorin* femur does not resemble those of great apes, but rather resembles those of fossil hominins, supporting the conclusions reached by Senut *et al.* (2001), Pickford *et al.* (2002) and Galik *et al.* (2004). Results also show that the *Orrorin* femur resembles those of the early hominins *A. afarensis* and *Paranthropus* more closely than femora of fossil or modern *Homo*. Although BAR 1002'00 has a slightly larger femoral head than in most early hominin femora, it shares the long, narrow (AP) neck and broad (ML) shaft distinctive of *Australopithecus* and *Paranthropus* femora (Figure 13.4). Therefore, its overall morphological similarity to the femora of gracile and robust australopiths contrasts with Pickford *et al.*'s (2002) characterisation of the *Orrorin* femur as being more human-like than australopithecines. This, in turn, conflicts with the phylogenetic hypothesis that *Orrorin* is ancestral to *Homo* to the exclusion of the australopithecines (Senut *et al.*, 2001). Instead, the overall primitive hominin morphology of the *Orrorin* femur is consistent with a phylogenetic hypothesis that it is a basal member of the hominin clade, namely a sister taxon to a clade consisting of *Australopithecus* and later hominins (*Ardipithecus* and *Sahelanthropus* are not being considered here owing to a lack of comparable data). We believe this hypothesis to be the most likely one, given current anatomical and geochronological evidence. While the femora of *Orrorin* and gracile and robust australopiths are not identical, and the possibility of homoplasy cannot yet be ruled out (Wood and Harrison, 2011), the similarities among them point to phylogenetic and functional affinities (Richmond and Jungers, 2008).

Regarding the continuing debate over whether or not australopiths have relative small femoral heads, the results here suggest that they do, supporting conclusions reached by some (e.g. McHenry and Corruccini, 1976a,b; Jungers, 1988, 1991) but not others (e.g. Wolpoff, 1976; Ruff, 1998). Wolpoff (1976) criticised McHenry and Corruccini (1976a) for assessing head size relative to neck length and shaft breadth because the latter variables are large in australopiths and therefore are not suitable variables for size adjustment. However, McHenry and Corruccini (1976a) did include a multivariate analysis, in which the australopiths were characterised by small femoral heads when all variables were considered together. In our study, all the variables were used to construct a proximal femur size measure that minimises the influence of any single variable. Because size here incorporates all the variables, it is not surprising that our results comparing femoral head size to proximal femur size concur with those of McHenry and Corruccini (1976b) in showing that australopiths have relatively small femoral heads. While some have implied that small femoral heads in the small-bodied australopiths relative to modern humans is a consequence of positive allometry in femoral head size coupled with biomechanical factors (Lovejoy *et al.*, 1973), others found positive allometry in human females but not males (Corruccini and McHenry, 1978) and no evidence of positive allometry in some human populations (Wood and Wilson, 1986). Using a narrow allometric approach with small-bodied humans as comparative specimens, femoral head size in *Australopithecus* was smaller than expected (Jungers, 1988, 1991). In his biomechanical analysis of Hadar specimen A.L. 288–1, Ruff's (1998) body mass estimate derived from estimates of bi-iliac breadth and stature led to the conclusion that A.L. 288–1's femoral head may not be unexpectedly small. However, this conclusion will remain a tentative hypothesis until the effects of extrapolation, choice of line-fitting techniques and broad prediction intervals for estimated body mass are known. To be fair, we also note that the aim of Ruff's study was to assess the biomechanics of the early hominin hip, not to address relative femoral head size in the context of overall proximal femoral size and shape (as we do here). To help resolve the issue of whether or not the femoral head size in A.L. 288–1 meets biomechanical expectations, it would be interesting to see a comparable analysis to Ruff's with a larger sample of small-bodied humans that overlap in size with A.L. 288–1. Our analysis does not explicitly include body mass, but shows that relative to the proximal femur as a whole, femoral head size in *Australopithecus* and *Paranthropus* is small relative to comparably sized humans (Figure 13.3).

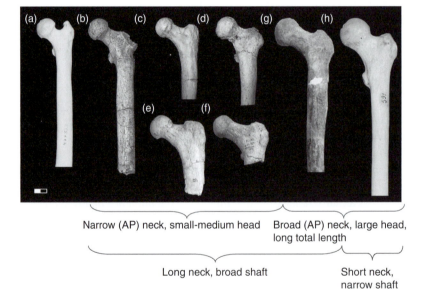

Figure 13.4. Femora of (a) *P. troglodytes*, (b) BAR 1002'00 (cast), (c) A.L. 288–1ap (cast), (d) LB1/9, (e) KNM-ER 1503 (reversed), (f) SK 97 (reversed), (g) KNM-ER 1481 and (h) *H. sapiens*. The *Orrorin* and *H. floresiensis* femora are similar to the femora attributed to *Australopithecus* and *Paranthropus* in having very narrow (AP) necks, and relatively small-intermediate heads. These and the femora attributed to early *Homo* (KNM-ER 1472, 1481) also have a relatively long neck and broad (ML) shaft. The early *Homo* femora share with modern humans a broader neck, larger head and (where known) a longer total length. Modern human femora have a short neck and narrow shaft. In proximal femoral anatomy, neither *Orrorin* nor *H. floresiensis* resemble fossil or modern *Homo* more closely than they resemble australopiths.

The results also show that the femoral anatomy of *H. floresiensis* is not consistent with that of a modern human at small size. For example, some of the Andaman Islanders and Pygmies have a comparable (a few even smaller) proximal femur size to that of LB1/9, but LB1/9 has a smaller femoral head and longer femoral neck (Figures 13.2 and 13.3). In these respects, the Flores specimen LB1/9 resembles Hadar specimen A.L. 288–1, Turkana specimen KNM-ER 1481 and other early hominins (Figures 13.2 to 13.4). The primitive morphology of the proximal femur is therefore not explained by the small size of LB1/9. Researchers who argue that LB1 represents a diseased modern human (Weber *et al.*, 2005; Jacob *et al.*, 2006; Martin *et al.*, 2006a, 2006b; Richards, 2006; Hershkovitz *et al.*, 2007) need to present evidence that the disease results in the development of primitive hip anatomy in conjunction with a relatively small brain, and primitive anatomy of the brain, cranium (Argue *et al.*, 2006; Gordon *et al.*, 2008), wrist (Tocheri *et al.*, 2007), shoulder (Larson *et al.*, 2007), foot (Jungers *et al.*, 2009b), limb proportions (Morwood *et al.*, 2005; Jungers, 2009) and limb bone robusticity (Jungers *et al.*, 2009a). Our results instead support findings based on the morphology of these anatomical regions that LB1/9 and other Liang Bua skeletal remains represent a distinct species likely separated from the modern human lineage by a considerable amount of time. If australopiths or early *Homo* had a unique pattern of bipedal gait (e.g. Stern and Susman, 1983; Susman *et al.*, 1984), then the femoral anatomy and limb robusticity and proportions suggest that *H. floresiensis* retained (or independently evolved) a gait distinct from that of modern humans, including the smallest people on Earth.

Conclusion

The results of this study show that the *Orrorin* femur more closely resembles the femora of *Australopithecus* and *Paranthropus* than those of extant great apes, or fossil or modern *Homo*. Its morphology is therefore not consistent with it being characterised as more like human than australopith femora (Pickford *et al.*, 2002) or a phylogenetic hypothesis that *Orrorin* is ancestral to *Homo* to the exclusion of the australopithecines (Senut *et al.*, 2001). However, its morphology is consistent with its age of 6 Ma, its taxonomic assignment as a hominin and the functional conclusion that it was adapted for bipedalism (Senut *et al.*, 2001; Pickford *et al.*, 2002). However, some aspects of femoral neck cortical geometry (Kuperavage *et al.*, 2010), if confirmed with more reliable, higher resolution CT imaging (Ohman *et al.*, 2005; Richmond and Jungers, 2008), may raise questions about hip function.

The proximal femoral anatomy of LB1/9 shows that it is not a small modern human, and instead supports evidence from other anatomical regions that it represents a distinct species, *H. floresiensis*, with strikingly primitive femoral morphology.

Acknowledgements

We thank Sally Reynolds, Andrew Gallagher and Colin Menter for inviting us and for their efforts and patience in organising the conference and edited volume; Brigitte Senut and Martin Pickford for encouraging us to examine the *Orrorin* fossils; and the curators of the museums housing the modern and fossil specimens used in this study for their permission and hospitality. We also thank Mike Morwood, Thomans Sutikna and numerous Indonesian colleagues for their support and access to the *Homo floresiensis* fossils. We also thank Henry McHenry, Osbjorn Pearson and the editors for valuable comments, and acknowledge funding support from the George Washington University, Stony Brook University, NSF-BCS 0521835 and the Australian Research Council.

References

Argue, D., Donlon, D., Groves, C. *et al.* (2006). *Homo floresiensis*: microcephalic, pygmoid, *Australopithecus*, or *Homo*? *Journal of Human Evolution*, **51**: 360–74.

Auerbach, B. M. and Ruff, C.B. (2004). Human body mass estimation: a comparison of 'morphometric' and 'mechanical' methods. *American Journal of Physical Anthropology*, **125**: 331–42.

Bramble, D. M. and Lieberman, D. E. (2004). Endurance running and the evolution of *Homo*. *Nature*, **432**: 345–52.

Brown, P., Sutikna, T., Morwood, M. J. *et al.* (2004). A new small-bodied hominin from the Late Pleistocene of Flores, Indonesia. *Nature*, **431**: 1055–61.

Corruccini, R. S. and McHenry, H. M. (1978). Relative femoral head size in early hominids. *American Journal of Physical Anthropology*, **49**: 145–8.

Darroch, J. N. and Mosimann, J. E. (1985). Canonical and principal components of shape. *Biometrika*, **72**: 241–52.

Day, M. H. (1969). Femoral fragment of a robust australopithecine from Olduvai Gorge, Tanzania. *Nature*, **221**: 230–3.

  (1973). Locomotor features of the lower limb in hominids. *Symposia of the Zoological Society of London*, **33**: 29–51.

Falk, D., Hildebolt, C., Smith, K. *et al.* (2005). The brain of LB1, *Homo floresiensis*. *Science*, **308**: 242–5.

  (2007). Brain shape in human microcephalics and *Homo floresiensis*. *Proceedings of the National Academy of Sciences of the USA*, **104**: 2513–8.

(2009). LB1's virtual endocast, microcephaly, and hominin brain evolution. *Journal of Human Evolution*, **57**: 597–607.

Galik, K., Senut, B., Pickford, M. *et al.* (2004). External and internal morphology of the BAR 1002'00 Orrorin tugenensis femur. *Science*, **305**: 1450–3.

Godfrey, L. R., Sutherland, M. R., Paine, R. R. *et al.* (1995). Limb joint surface areas and their ratios in Malagasy lemurs and other mammals. *American Journal of Physical Anthropology*, **97**: 11–36.

Gordon, A. D., Nevell, L. and Wood, B. (2008). The *Homo floresiensis* cranium (LB1): size, scaling, and early *Homo* affinities. *Proceedings of the National Academy of Sciences of the USA*, **105**: 4650–5.

Grine, F. E., Jungers, W. L., Tobias, P. V. *et al.* (1995). Fossil *Homo* femur from Berg Aukas, northern Namibia. *American Journal of Physical Anthropology*, **97**: 151–85.

Harmon, E. H. (2007). The shape of the hominoid proximal femur: a geometric morphometric analysis. *Journal of Anatomy*, **210**: 170–85.

(2009a). The shape of the early hominin proximal femur. *American Journal of Physical Anthropology*, **139**: 154–71.

(2009b). Size and shape variation in the proximal femur of *Australopithecus africanus*. *Journal of Human Evolution*, **56**: 551–9.

Hershkovitz, I., Kornreich, L. and Laron, Z. (2007). Comparative skeletal features between *Homo floresiensis* and patients with primary growth hormone insensitivity (Laron syndrome). *American Journal of Physical Anthropology*, **134**: 198–208.

Jacob, T., Indriati, E., Soejono, R. P. *et al.* (2006). Pygmoid Australomelanesian *Homo sapiens* skeletal remains from Liang Bua, Flores: population affinities and pathological abnormalities. *Proceedings of the National Academy of Sciences of the USA*, **103**: 13421–6.

Jungers, W. L. (1982). Lucy's limbs: skeletal allometry and locomotion in *Australopithecus* afarensis. *Nature*, **297**: 676–8.

(1988). Relative joint size and hominoid locomotor adaptations with implications for the evolution of hominid bipedalism. *Journal of Human Evolution*, **17**: 247–65.

(1991). A pygmy perspective on body size and shape in *Australopithecus afarensis* (AL 288–1, 'Lucy'). In Senut, B. and Coppens, Y. (eds.), *Origine(s) de la Bipédie Chez les Hominidés*. Paris: Cahiers de Paleoanthropologie, pp. 215–24.

(2009). Interlimb proportions in humans and fossil hominins: variability and scaling. In Grine, F. E., Fleagle, J.G. and Leakey, R. E. (eds.), *The First Humans: Origin and Early Evolution of the Genus* Homo. Springer Science and Business Media BV, pp. 93–8.

Jungers, W. L., Falsetti, A. B. and Wall, C. E. (1995). Shape, relative size, and size-adjustments in morphometrics. *Yearbook of Physical Anthropology*, **38**: 137–61.

Jungers, W. L., Larson, S. G., Harcourt-Smith, W. *et al.* (2009a). Descriptions of the lower limb skeleton of *Homo floresiensis*. *Journal of Human Evolution*, **57**: 538–54.

Jungers, W. L., Harcourt-Smith, W. E., Wunderlich, R. E. *et al.* (2009b). The foot of *Homo floresiensis*. *Nature*, **459**: 81–4.

Kuperavage, A. J., Sommer, H. J. and Eckhardt, R. B. (2010). Moment coefficients of skewness in the femoral neck cortical bone distribution of BAR 1002'00. *Journal of Comparative Human Biology*, **61**(4): 244–52.

Larson, S. G., Jungers, W. L., Morwood, M. J. *et al.* (2007). *Homo floresiensis* and the evolution of the hominin shoulder. *Journal of Human Evolution*, **53**: 718–31.

Larson, S. G., Jungers, W. L., Tocheri, M. W. *et al.* (2009). Descriptions of the upper limb skeleton of *Homo floresiensis*. *Journal of Human Evolution*, **57**, 555–70.

Lordkipanidze, D., Jashashvili, T., Vekua, A. *et al.* (2007). Postcranial evidence from early *Homo* from Dmanisi, Georgia. *Nature*, **449**: 305–10.

Lovejoy, C. O. (1988). Evolution of human walking. *Scientific American*, **259**: 118–25.

Lovejoy, C. O., Heiple, K. G. and Burstein, A. H. (1973). The gait of *Australopithecus*. *American Journal of Physical Anthropology*, **38**: 757–79.

Lovejoy, C. O., Meindl, R. S., Ohman, J. C. *et al.* (2002). The Maka femur and its bearing on the antiquity of human walking: applying contemporary concepts of morphogenesis to the human fossil record. *American Journal of Physical Anthropology*, **119**: 97–133.

Martin, R. D., Maclarnon, A. M., Phillips, J. L. *et al.* (2006a). Flores hominid: new species or microcephalic dwarf? *Anatomical Record A: Discoveries in Molecular, Cellular, and Evolutionary Biology*, **288**: 1123–45.

Martin, R. D., Maclarnon, A. M., Phillips, J. L. *et al.* (2006b). Comment on 'The Brain of LB1, *Homo floresiensis*'. *Science*, **312**: 999.

McHenry, H. M. (1975). Biomechanical interpretation of the early hominid hip. *Journal of Human Evolution*, **4**: 343–55.

McHenry, H. M. and Corruccini, R. S. (1976a). Fossil hominid femora and the evolution of walking. *Nature*, **259**: 657–8.

(1976b). Fossil hominid femora. *Nature*, **264**: 813.

(1978). The femur in early human evolution. *American Journal of Physical Anthropology*, **49**: 473–88.

Morwood, M. J., Brown, P., Jatmiko *et al.* (2005). Further evidence for small-bodied hominins from the Late Pleistocene of Flores, Indonesia. *Nature* **437**: 1012–7.

Napier, J. R. (1964). The evolution of bipedal walking in the hominids. *Archives de Biologie (Liege)*, **75**: 673–708.

Ohman, J. C., Lovejoy, C. O. and White, T. D. (2005). Questions about *Orrorin* femur. *Science*, **307**: 845.

Pickford, M., Senut, B., Gommery, D. *et al.* (2002). Bipedalism in *Orrorin tugenensis* revealed by its femora. *Comptes Rendus Palevol*, **1**: 1–13.

Richards, G. D. (2006). Genetic, physiologic and ecogeographic factors contributing to variation in *Homo sapiens*: *Homo floresiensis* reconsidered. *Journal of Evolutionary Biology*, **19**: 1744–67.

Richmond, B. G., Aiello, L. C. and Wood, B. A. (2002). Early hominin limb proportions. *Journal of Human Evolution*, **43**: 529.

Richmond, B. G. and Jungers, W. L. (2008). *Orrorin tugenensis* femoral morphology and the evolution of hominin bipedalism. *Science*, **319**: 1662–5.

Robinson, J. T. (1972). *Early Hominid Posture and Locomotion*. Chicago: University of Chicago Press.

Ruff, C. B. (1995). Biomechanics of the hip and birth in early *Homo*. *American Journal of Physical Anthropology*, **98**: 527–74.

  (1998). Evolution of the hominid hip. In Strasser, E., Fleagle, J. G., Rosenberger, A. and McHenry, H. M. (eds.), *Primate Locomotion: Recent Advances*. New York: Plenum Press. pp. 449–69.

  (2002). Long bone articular and diaphyseal structure in old world monkeys and apes. I: locomotor effects. *American Journal of Physical Anthropology*, **119**: 305–42.

Ruff, C. B. and Walker, A. C. (1993). Body size and body shape. In Walker, A. C. and Leakey, R. E. (eds.), *The Nariokotome* Homo erectus *Skeleton*. Cambridge: Harvard University Press, pp. 234–65.

Senut, B., Pickford, M., Gommery, D. *et al.* (2001). First hominid from the Miocene (Lukeino Formation, Kenya). *Comptes Rendus de l'Académie des Sciences, série IIa*, **332**: 137–44.

Smith, R. J. (2009). Use and misuse of the reduced major axis for line-fitting. *American Journal of Physical Anthropology*, **140**, 476–86.

Stern, J. T. and Susman, R. L. (1991). 'Total morphological pattern' versus the 'magic trait': conflicting approaches to the study of early hominid bipedalism. In Coppens, Y. and Senut, B. (eds.), *Origine(s) de la Bipedie chez les Hominidés*. Paris: Cahiers de Paleoanthropologie, CNRS, pp. 99–112.

Stern, J. T. J. and Larson, S. G. (1990). Electromyographic studies of the obturator muscle in non-human primates: implications for interpreting the obturator externus groove. *American Journal of Physical Anthropology*, **24**: 403–27.

Stern, J. T. J. and Susman, R. L. (1983). The locomotor anatomy of *Australopithecus afarensis*. *American Journal of Physical Anthropology*, **60**: 279–317.

Susman, R. L., Stern, J. T. and Jungers, W. L. (1984). Arboreality and bipedality in the Hadar hominids. *Folia Primatologica*, **43**: 283–306.

Tocheri, M. W., Orr, C. M., Larson, S. G. *et al.* (2007). The primitive wrist of *Homo floresiensis* and its implications for hominin evolution. *Science*, **317**: 1743–5.

Walker, A. C. (1973). New *Australopithecus* femora from East Rudolf, Kenya. *Journal of Human Evolution*, **2**: 545–55.

Weber, J., Czarnetzki, A. and Pusch, C. M. (2005). Comment on 'The brain of LB1, *Homo floresiensis*'. *Science*, **310**: 236.

Wolpoff, M. H. (1976). Fossil hominid femora. *Nature*, **264**: 812–13.

Wood, B. A. (1976). Remains attributable to *Homo* in the East Rudolph Succession. In Coppens, Y., Howell, F. C., Isaac, G. L. and Leakey, R. E. (eds.), *Earliest Man and Environments in the Lake Rudolph Basin*. Chicago: University of Chicago Press. pp. 490–506.

Wood, B. A. and Harrison, T. (2011). The evolutionary context of the first hominins. *Nature*, **470**: 347–52.

Wood, B. A. and Wilson, G. B. (1986). Patterns of allometry in modern human femora. In Singer, R. and Lundy, J. K. (eds.), *Variation, Culture, and Evolution in African Populations*. Johannesburg: Witwatersrand University Press, pp. 101–8.

14 Daily rates of dentine formation and root extension rates in Paranthropus boisei, *KNM-ER 1817*, from Koobi Fora, Kenya

M. CHRISTOPHER DEAN

Abstract

Ground sections were prepared of the seven root apices of five teeth preserved in the fossil hemi-mandible specimen, KNM-ER 1817, from Koobi Fora, Kenya. The sections were studied with transmitted polarised light microscopy. Despite the poor gross macroscopic preservation of the mandibular bone, the dentine microstructure was well preserved. Good details of typical dentine structure were observed in many of the sections including both short-period daily incremental lines and long-period lines. The spacing between consecutive daily incremental lines were compared with those published for dentine in modern humans and other primates. Close to the root surface, there appears to be a consistent rate of ~2.5 μm (micrometres) per day. Coarser accentuated lines (Owen's lines) together with long-period lines were also clearly visible in the largest apical root section of the M_3. These were used to reconstruct the slowing rates of root extension in the last 4 mm of the mesial M_3 apex of KNM-ER 1817, which were then compared with those known for a sample of modern human molars.

Introduction

A poorly preserved hemi-mandibular fragment was discovered at Koobi Fora during the 1973 field season by Bwana A. Kilonzo. Wood (1991) has previously reported that KNM-ER 1817 was found within the Okote Member of the Koobi Fora Formation, below the Black Pumice Tuff and that it dates to between 1.55 and 1.65 Ma. KNM-ER 1817 is a badly weathered left mandibular corpus

African Genesis: Perspectives on Hominin Evolution, eds. Sally C. Reynolds and Andrew Gallagher. Published by Cambridge University Press. © Cambridge University Press 2012.

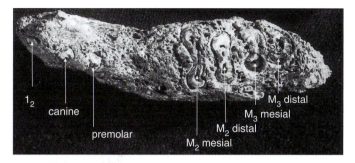

Figure 14.1. Hominin hemi-mandible (KMN-ER 1817) containing seven root apices belonging to five permanent teeth (I_2, C, P_3, M_2 mesial, M_2 distal, M_3 mesial and M_3 distal). The specimen is shown here viewed occlusally.

(Figure 14.1) and contained seven root apices belonging to five permanent teeth embedded in the alveolar bone (Furseth Klinge, *et al.*, 2005). The specimen measures 91 mm long and 23 mm buccolingually at it widest point. Wood (1991) cautioned that no useful gross morphological or metrical data could, or should, be recorded from this specimen. While the official taxonomic designation of this specimen is Hominidae gen. et sp. indet. (Leakey, 1974; Wood, 1991), from its size and the morphology of the root apices, it seems likely this specimen is a robust australopith, and is most typical of *Paranthropus boisei*. The M_2 mesial root measured 17 mm wide and the M_2 distal root 15 mm wide buccolingually at the level of the surrounding alveolar bone. Because of its obviously limited morphological value, KNM-ER 1817 was considered an appropriate fossil for histological examination. One aim of this study was to record the spacing of short-period daily incremental markings in root dentine and to compare these at different positions and different depths between each of the root apices that preserved them. Data from certain primate and non-primate species (such as pig, *Sus scrofa*) as well as modern human dentine (Dean, 1998) and fossil hominin dentine (Dean, *et al.*, 2001) are available for comparison with those from KNM-ER 1817. A second aim was to estimate rates of root extension in a portion of one of the better preserved roots of this robust australopith. The majority of the roots were no more than apical fragments and/or showed no evidence of incremental markings in the dentine. For just one root, the mesial M_3 root apex, it was possible to reconstruct successive root extension rates in KNM-ER 1817 at regular intervals for 4 mm just prior to apex closure. This was possible by combining the known daily rates of dentine formation in this root fragment with the orientation of the long-period and accentuated markings in the root dentine.

Two kinds of normal physiological incremental markings exist in dentine. Short-period or daily lines are spaced a few micrometres apart (rarely more than 5 µm apart in root dentine) and resemble watermarks of the kind that, when present, are visible if paper is held against the light. In dentine these daily lines are sometimes referred to as von Ebner's lines. Slow-forming dentine often mineralises as tiny spheres (called calcospherites), which then coalesce. In sections made through calcospherites close to the root surface daily lines often appear circular or 'ring-like'. This represents the typical pattern of mineralisation in root dentine close to the cement–dentine junction. A few micrometres deep to the root surface, and along a strip of dentine immediately deep to the cementum, the most minute of all these spheres, or calcospherites, of mineralising dentine fail to coalesce completely for reasons unknown. Here, the spaces of unmineralised matrix between adjacent calcospherites take on the appearance of small, dark granules in transmitted light microscopy. Thus, this so-called granular layer of Tomes is a clear marker for the outermost edge of mineralising root dentine (Figure 14.2) and is only covered with a thin layer of translucent dentine (the hyaline layer) and an outer layer of cementum.

When growing teeth are labelled with dyes that bind (or chelate) with the calcium ions laid down as the tooth forms (Figure 14.2) it becomes clear that mineralisation spreads more quickly within the granular layer of Tomes at the edge of the root than it does in the predentine just deep to this region (see Figure 14.2). However, mineralising daily incremental rings within each calcospherite indicate that the rate of mineralisation is slowest in this part of the root surface. This apparent paradox may be explained because of the fast rate at which new calcospherites seed down the root edge. This appears to exceed the rate of mineralisation within each of the individual calcospherites, which also persists over a longer period of time.

Long-period lines in dentine (sometimes called Andresen lines) are coarser and more widely spaced markings (anything between 15 and 20 µm apart) and have the same periodicity as long-period lines (or striae of Retzius) in enamel. They can be seen in deeper dentine beneath the granular layer of Tomes but do not usually pass to the root surface through this layer. Superimposed on all these lines, but without any physiological regularity, are other accentuated increments (sometimes called Owen's lines). These result from disturbances or alternations in dentine growth, which are often caused by stress or illness during the period of tooth formation. Both long-period lines (Andresen lines) and irregular accentuated lines (Owen's lines) follow the contour of the forming odontoblast sheet as it was during root formation. Successive lines of either kind mark successive positions of the secretory front in the root as it grew in length. In longitudinal ground sections of tooth roots they represent a record of the inclination of the former odontoblast cell sheet to the root surface during development. This in turn is a reflection of the rate of proliferation of newly

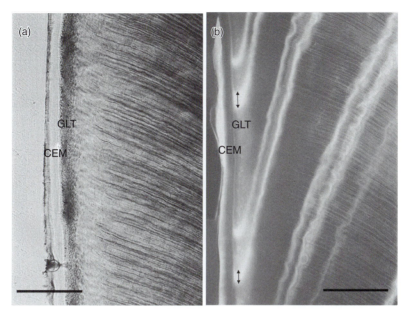

Figure 14.2. In image (a), taken in transmitted light, the cementum layer (CEM) and granular layer of Tomes (GLT) are visible each approximately 50 μm thick. Deep to these layers, many dentine tubules run from the region deep to the granular layer of Tomes towards the pulp chamber of the tooth. Some daily increments are just visible in the dentine, clearest towards the top right of the field of view, where rates are much faster (and increments wider apart) than at the root surface. In image (b) of the same root surface, but seen in incident ultraviolet light, consecutive fluorescing label-lines of tetracycline reveal a faster spread of mineralisation within the granular layer of Tomes (arrowed) than in the thinner label-lines just deep to this layer. The black scale bars = 200 μm. (See plate section for colour version.)

differentiated odontoblasts starting to secrete predentine close to the developing root sheath. This determines the rate of increase in root length, referred to more correctly as the root extension rate (Shellis, 1984).

Either long-period or accentuated lines or both were visible in a number of the sections of root apices from KNM-ER 1817 at lower magnification in transmitted polarised light (Figure 14.3). These lines made it possible to calculate the root extension rate in the terminal phase of M_3 root apex closure of KNM-ER 1817. Previous studies (Dean, 1998, together with the data collected in the first part of this study – see below) show that daily incremental lines in dentine, close to the root surface, mineralise at rates that average about 2.5 μm per day over an initial thickness of 200 μm. The data presented in Dean (1998) show that there is a gradient of increasing dentine mineralisation rates that starts close to 1.5 μm per day close to the granular layer of Tomes and rises to

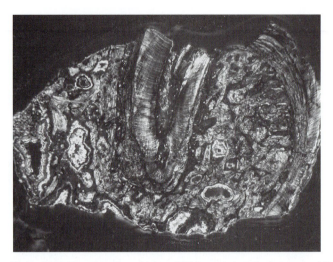

Figure 14.3. Ground section of the mesial M_3 root in polarised transmitted light showing coarse accentuated incremental markings in the more complete lingual root. The buccal root is eroded at the surface and preserves only the inner portion and that part adjoining the lingual root at the bifurcation. Between the trabeculae in the alveolar bone, crystals, probably calcite, have formed in some of the marrow spaces. Field width 6.75 mm. (See plate section for colour version.)

about 3.0 μm per day when dentine 200 to 300 μm deep to the root surface is forming. However, beyond 200 μm deep to the root surface, the rates of dentine mineralisation start to vary considerably between taxa (Dean, 1998). If the average rate over a 200 μm thickness is 2.5 μm per day, then it follows that this thickness of dentine takes approximately 80 days to form from the root surface. Thus a time scale can be retrieved from histological sections of teeth, which, together with the orientation of prominent accentuated lines in dentine, can be used to estimate rates of root extension along the length of a tooth root (Macchiarelli, *et al.*, 2006). This calculation does not, however, take account of the possibly faster rates of apical extension of mineralisation in the granular layer of Tomes that may exceed that within each individual calcospherite (Figure 14.2) but which here has been presumed to be close to the rate of pre-dentine secretion at the root surface.

Material and methods

The tooth apices present in the mandible were I_1, C, P_3, M_2 mesial, M_2 distal, M_3 mesial and M_3 distal (Figure 14.1). Each of the tooth apices were removed from the alveolar bone using a long, coarse, diamond-fissure bur in a dental

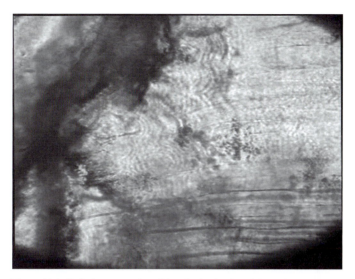

Figure 14.4. Daily incremental markings in the dentine of the canine root apex. In this position the increments are spaced approximately 2.5 μm apart and are characteristically calcospheritic. (See plate section for colour version.)

air-rotor with integral water spray-irrigation designed to cool the bur and bone during cutting. An 'inkwell' slot was cut into the bone around the perimeter of each root apex and a cylindrical block containing the root cracked free from its base and extracted. Each block was then sectioned axially through the original buccolingual longitudinal plane of the root apex with a diamond-wafering blade in a Buehler IsoMet® saw. Eight ground sections were made of seven root apices (two sections were cut from the M_2 distal apex). One aspect of the block was polished and then fixed with epoxy resin to a glass slide and a thin section cut from it. This was lapped and polished to ~100 μm thickness and mounted for light microscopy. Sections were examined in polarised transmitted light and photomontages constructed using ×25 and ×12.5 objectives. The hemi-mandible was then reconstructed with wax using silicone moulds made at the start of the study to restore the original occlusal surface contour. The blocks and sections were returned to the National Museums of Kenya in anticipation of future histological or isotopic analysis.

Each longitudinal section of root dentine was divided into zones of increasing depth from the root surface. The zones were defined 0 to 100 μm, 100 to 200 μm and 200 to 300 μm deep to the granular layer of Tomes. Daily incremental markings within these zones (Figure 14.4) were then identified on the photomontages according to the criteria set out in Dean (1998, 1999). In some roots, notably the canine root apex, it was possible to identify incremental markings at several levels between the cervical and apical limits of the

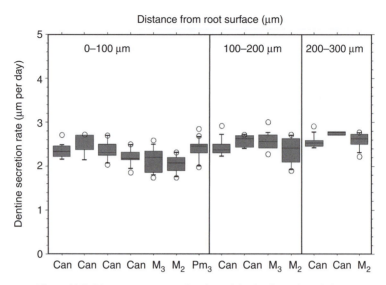

Figure 14.5. Measurements across five days of dentine formation (six incremental lines) were averaged. Each box plot represents between 10 and 15 such sets of measurements. More than one set was possible in some roots at different positions between the more cervical and apical regions of the root. In the case of KNM-ER 1817, sets of measurements were grouped into three zones of increasing depth from the root surface (0–100 μm, 100–200 μm and 200–300 μm). Too few well preserved increments exist to split these into 50 μm zones.

section. In all cases the incremental lines initially had a calcospheritic pattern adjacent to the granular layer of Tomes that gradually became more laminar in their contour through the first few hundred micrometres of root dentine and which subsequently aligned to the contour of the growing root dentine front. In order to reduce measurement error across small increments, a series of six lines was identified on the high-power montages and one measurement of the distance across them measured with digital callipers. This measurement was then divided by five to give an average spacing for one day over five days' dentine growth. The same procedure was repeated between 10 and 15 times in any one zone of root dentine to produce a set or group of measurements representative of a region. The results are compared as box plots split by 100 μm zones up to 300 μm for the various roots in KNM-ER 1817 (Figure 14.5). The grand means for zones in all root apices of KNM-ER 1817 are compared with similar data for zones in other hominins (including modern humans) and hominoids in Figure 14.6. In this plot, the first two zones are for 50 μm thickness up to 100 μm, since good data exist to this resolution for some taxa, and the last zone is for 100 to 200 μm only, data beyond this thickness having been omitted here.

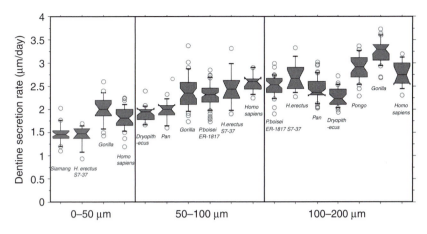

Distance from the granular layer of Tomes at the root surface

Figure 14.6. The grand means for rates of daily root dentine formation for all the root apices in KNM-ER 1817 combined are shown in the context of similar comparative data for the M^1 and P^4 of S7–37, a *Homo erectus* specimen from Java (Dean *et al.*, 2001) together with data for modern human root dentine, data from siamang (*Hylobates [Symphalangus] syndactylus*) root dentine, and some data for chimpanzee (*Pan*), orang-utan (*Pongo*) and gorilla (*Gorilla*) root dentine as well as for *Dryopithecus laietanus* (Kelley *et al.*, 2001). In this plot the zones are for 0 to 50 µm, 50 to 100 µm and 100 to 200 µm since better data exist for some taxa than for KNM-ER 1817 close to the granular layer of Tomes. The notches on the boxes represent the upper (95%) and lower (5%) confidence intervals; the open circles are outlier measurements.

The lower power montages (×12.5 objective) were then used to track accentuated lines identified 200 µm deep in the dentine back to the root surface (Macchiarelli *et al.*, 2006). The length of root from the start point to the end point represents the length of root formed in ~80 days. Consecutive measurements of root extension rate (calculated in micrometres per day) made in this way were then plotted against data collected in an identical way for a sample of 20 modern human molar roots. Since the length of the M_3 root in KNM-ER 1817 is unknown, an estimate of 14 mm (based on descriptions and radiographs of similar specimens in Wood, 1991) was used for apex closure on the *x* axis.

Results

Average, or median, values for daily rates of dentine formation close to the root surface in all of the root apices of KNM-ER 1817 fell close to 2.5 µm per day (Figure 14.5). This was despite measurements being made at different

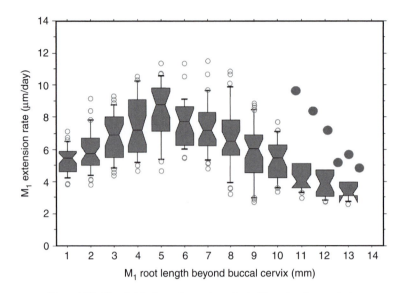

Figure 14.7. The distribution of extension rates in 20 modern human first permanent molars are shown as box plots for each mm of root length between the buccal cervix and the root apex. The notches on the boxes represent the upper (95%) and lower (5%) confidence intervals; the open circles are outlier measurements. Extension rates for the mesial M_3 apex shown in Figures 14.1 and 14.2 are plotted here as solid circles. The assumption here, for the sake of the plot, was that the root was ~14 mm long but this is obviously unknown. The impression is that extension rates are falling from higher values earlier in root formation but this is speculative.

heights within the roots of the teeth preserved. Furthermore, little difference in rate appeared to exist between the zones defined in this study, although the comparative data for modern humans and some non-human primate material (Dean, 1998; Kelley, *et al.*, 2001) showed greater rates in some of the deeper zones than in the more superficial zones.

Extension rates in the modern human molars began at rates around 4 µm per day and then rose to a peak with average rates of around 8 or 9 µm per day before declining again over the last half of root growth (Figure 14.7). Extension rates are very variable but seem to show a clear spurt around the time of root bifurcation formation in modern human molars. Extension rates over the terminal 4 mm of root formation in the M_3 of KNM-ER 1817 fell from ~10 µm per day to ~4 µm per day. It is obviously not possible to place these measurements into the context of root growth as a whole or, for example, to tell if there were a similar spurt in root extension rate earlier in root development as in modern human molars. These data do suggest, however, there were higher rates of root extension earlier in root development than in the terminal portion of root growth, and that these might have exceeded those in modern humans.

Discussion

Short-period daily incremental markings typical of those described and defined by Dean (1998, 1999) were observed in many of the high-power micrographs of root dentine in the specimen KNM-ER 1817. While these clearly resemble those found in modern human dentine, for some unknown reason they often appear better preserved in fossil material than in most modern material.

Daily dentine lines are also well described in several Miocene fossil hominoids including *Proconsul* (Beynon *et al.*, 1998) and *Dryopithecus* (Kelley *et al.*, 2001). The only data for daily rates of dentine formation in fossil hominins so far come from the root dentine of a specimen from Java, S7–37, attributed to *Homo erectus* (Dean *et al.*, 2001) and which are presented in Figure 14.5 for comparison. In the S7–37 specimen, daily rates in the root dentine also averaged ~2.5 µm per day during the first 200 µm of dentine formation (Dean *et al.*, 2001). The data presented here for daily rates of dentine formation are important because they suggest some constancy, at least among hominins, close to the root surface that can be utilised to measure root extension rates in other fossil specimens where only long-period lines are clearly visible (Dean, 1995; Macchiarelli *et al.*, 2006).

Conclusions

A great deal is now known about the timing of enamel formation in early fossil hominins and fossil hominoids. However, the timing of dentine formation, and root growth in particular, remains less well documented and less well understood. The data presented here for rates of dentine formation and root extension rates are among the first for any fossil hominin and they provide clues as to how we can now begin to predict the rates of root extension and the time taken to grown any given length of tooth root during the eruptive and post-eruptive phases of root development. Among the crucial questions for the future are (i) how fast do roots extend in length, as they are forming between the end of enamel formation and gingival eruption; and (ii) how much root length is formed at gingival emergence in the various living and fossil hominoid taxa and by how much does this vary? The suggestion from this study is that molar roots in *Paranthropus boisei* may have had faster rates of root extension towards the end of root formation than those of modern human molars at this stage of development. While this first glimpse of root development in *Paranthropus boisei* is both preliminary and speculative, it was only made possible because of the poor gross preservational state of the specimen that presented no barrier for this kind of histological analysis.

Acknowledgements

I thank the organisers of the African Genesis Symposium for inviting me to present this study and for their hospitality and kindness during the meeting. I am grateful to Sam Cobb, Bernard Wood, Anthony Kegley and Sally Reynolds for their comments and suggestions on this chapter. I thank the Government of Kenya and the trustees of the National Museums of Kenya for permission to study valuable fossil material in their care. I thank Meave Leakey and Alan Walker for their support with this project. The project was funded by a grant to MCD from the Leverhulme Trust to study rates of dentine formation in primates. I thank the Royal Society for providing funding to attend this Symposium.

References

Beynon, A. D., Dean, M. C., Leakey, M. G. *et al.* (1998). Comparative dental development and microstructure of *Proconsul* teeth from Rusinga Island, Kenya. *Journal of Human Evolution*, **35**, 163–209.

Dean, C., Leakey, M. G., Reid, D. *et al.* (2001). Growth processes in teeth distinguish modern humans from *Homo erectus* and earlier hominins. *Nature*, **414**, 628–31.

Dean, M. C. (1995). The nature and periodicity of incremental lines in primate dentine and their relationship to periradicular bands in OH 16 (*Homo habilis*). In Moggi-Cecchi, J (ed.), *Structure, Function and Evolution of Teeth. Ninth International Symposium on Dental Morphology*. Florence: International Institute for the Study of Man, pp. 239–65.

  (1998). Comparative observations on the spacing of short-period (von Ebner's) lines in dentine. *Archives of Oral Biology*, **32**, 1009–21.

  (1999). Hominoid tooth growth; using incremental lines in dentine as markers of growth in modern human and fossil primate teeth. In Hoppa, R. and FitzGerald, C. (eds.), *Human Growth in the Past. Studies from Bones and Teeth*. Cambridge: Cambridge University Press, pp. 11–127.

Furseth Klinge, R., Dean, M. C., Gunnæs, A. *et al.* (2005). Microscopic structure and mineral distribution in tooth and periodontal tissues in a robust australopithecine fossil hominid from Koobi Fora, Kenya. In Żądzińska, E. (ed.), *Current Trends in Dental Morphology Research. 13th International Symposium on Dental Morphology*. Wydawnictwo Uniwersytetu Lodzkiego Lodz, Poland, pp. 233–42.

Kelley, J., Dean, M. C. and Reid, D. J. (2001). Molar growth in the late Miocene hominoid, *Dryopithecus laietanus*. In Brook, A (ed.), *Dental Morphology*. Sheffield Academic Press, pp.123–34.

Leakey, R. E. F. (1974). Further evidence of Lower Pleistocene hominids from East Rudolf, North Kenya. *Nature*, **248**, 653–6.

Macchiarelli, R., Bondioli, L., Debénath, A. *et al.* (2006). How Neanderthal molar teeth grew. *Nature*, **444**,748–51.

Shellis R. P. (1984). Variations in growth of the enamel crown in human teeth and a possible relationship between growth and enamel structure. *Archives of Oral Biology*, **29**, 697–705.

Wood, B. A. (1991) *Koobi Fora Research Project. Volume 4. Hominid Cranial Remains*. Oxford: Clarendon Press, p. 466.

15   *On the evolutionary development of early hominid molar teeth and the Gondolin* Paranthropus *molar*

KEVIN L. KUYKENDALL

Abstract

In 1997 two isolated hominid molars were recovered from the Plio-Pleistocene site named Gondolin, in the North West Province, South Africa. One of these teeth (GDA-2) is a left mandibular M_2 that was characterised as *Paranthropus* sp. indet. (Menter *et al.*, 1999). A more specific taxonomic affiliation was not considered because a number of enigmatic morphological features of GDA-2 are normally attributed to 'hyper-robust' east African *Paranthropus* taxa, in particular its large crown size and the presence of two distal accessory (C6) cusps. This chapter presents a discussion of research in the evolutionary development of teeth, focusing on developmental processes relating to molar tooth crown size and cusp morphology. Details of the GDA-2 crown and cusp morphology are discussed in the context of enamel–dentine junction (EDJ) formation, enamel knots and related aspects of a tooth's developmental biology. This approach is useful in furthering our understanding of early hominid variation, adaptation and development.

Introduction

Two hominid molar teeth were recovered in 1997 from the Plio-Pleistocene site at Gondolin, South Africa (Menter *et al.*, 1999; Kuykendall and Conroy, 1999). The morphology of the *Paranthropus* lower left M_2 (GDA-2) is of particular interest because it demonstrates traits (extremely large crown, presence of two distal accessory cusps) normally associated with the east African 'hyper-robust' taxon *P. boisei* (Wood and Abbott, 1983; Wood, 1991; Suwa *et al.*, 1994, 1996). Despite these differences, and accenting the specimen's geographic provenance, it seems most reasonable to assign this isolated molar

African Genesis: Perspectives on Hominin Evolution, eds. Sally C. Reynolds and Andrew Gallagher. Published by Cambridge University Press. © Cambridge University Press 2012.

tooth to the taxon *P. robustus* – it would require additional and substantially more complete craniodental fossil material to convincingly identify the taxon *P. boisei* in a southern African assemblage. Consequently, it is possible to (albeit speculatively) account for the occurrence of such unexpected molar tooth morphology at a South African site in terms of sampling biases, predator selection or other factors (see below). Future fossil finds from Gondolin and other sites, and particularly those of more complete craniodental specimens, may clarify the taxonomic interpretation of this tooth.

The equivocal features of the GDA-2 molar tooth can also be discussed in the context of the recent research advances in developmental biology, and this may eventually be relevant to its morphological and taxonomic interpretation. Evolutionary developmental biology, sometimes referred to as 'evo-devo' biology, seeks to understand the developmental basis for evolutionary change. Ultimately, morphological shifts that we recognise in the fossil record, and by which we define species, are the product of alterations in the timing and pattern of developmental processes by which juveniles of a species become adults (Fabian, 1985; Goodman and Coughlin, 2000; Jernvall, 2000). Thus different species should be characterised by differences in development, as well as in morphology, and both are important components of a species' unique adaptive strategy (see discussions in Smith and Tompkins, 1995; Wood, 1996). One significant question is whether such differences would be detectable (particularly from isolated dental fossils) in closely related and thus morphologically similar species, such as different members of the genus *Paranthropus*.

Research into the developmental biology of tooth morphology has received extensive attention in recent years (e.g. Thesleff and Jernvall, 1997; Jernvall, 2000; Jernvall *et al.*, 2000; McCollum and Sharpe, 2001), and it is thus possible to reconstruct a general model for molar tooth development that is applicable to extinct hominids (McCollum and Sharpe, 2001). With the view that formulation of useful and testable models is crucial to furthering our interpretations of fossils, the aim of this chapter is to discuss current models describing the developmental biology of teeth as they relate to the distinctive morphology of the Gondolin molar GDA-2 compared to other *Paranthropus* mandibular second molars from southern and eastern Africa.

Morphology of GDA-2

As described initially (Menter *et al.*, 1999), the GDA-2 *Paranthropus* molar is an isolated complete left mandibular M_2 including the roots. This determination is based on two basic observations: GDA-2 displays both mesial and distal interproximal wear facets, like M_1s and M_2s (barring the occurrence of

Table 15.1. *Descriptive statistical comparisons of MD and BL diameters and calculated crown area for early hominid mandibular M2 teeth. Data from Wood (1991), Grine (1993), Keyser et al. (2000), Moggi-Cecchi et al. (2005). Measurements in mm, abbreviations as in Figure 15.1.*

Taxon ID		MD (cor) mm	BL (max) mm	MD × BL crown area (mm²)
AH	Maximum	14.1	14.3	201.63
	Mean	**12.8**	**12.5**	**160.26**
	Minimum	11.3	11.1	129.95
	Standard deviation	0.8	0.8	18.91
EAH	Maximum	17.5	15.4	269.50
	Mean	**14.7**	**13.0**	**191.74**
	Minimum	12.2	10.9	140.30
	Standard deviation	1.4	1.3	36.88
SAH	Maximum	14.6	13.0	189.80
	Mean	**14.4**	**12.7**	**182.23**
	Minimum	14.2	12.3	174.66
	Standard deviation	0.3	0.5	10.71
SAG	Maximum	17.7	16.8	285.60
	Mean	**15.7**	**14.5**	**227.85**
	Minimum	14.2	12.7	182.88
	Standard deviation	1.0	1.0	28.78
SAR	Maximum	18.0	16.5	295.20
	Mean	**16.1**	**14.4**	**239.30**
	Minimum	13.4	13.0	180.90
	Standard deviation	1.1	2.5	29.87
EAR	Maximum	20.8	19.0	386.88
	Mean	**18.2**	**16.8**	**310.07**
	Minimum	15.0	14.5	232.00
	Standard deviation	1.7	1.2	46.18
GDA		*18.8*	*18.1*	*340.28*

supernumerary molars, which are known to occur in both humans and apes (Lavelle and Moore, 1973)), but is too large for any known hominid M_1 tooth, given known metrical variation (Wood and Abbott, 1983; Suwa *et al.*, 1994, 1996) and the trend for increasing tooth dimensions through the molar row in *Paranthropus* (Robinson, 1956). For a South African specimen it is of exceptional size, measuring 18.80 mm (uncorrected MD) and 18.10 mm (BL) in diameter, with a calculated crown base area of 340.3 mm². Table 15.1 and Figure 15.1 compare this tooth metrically to other early hominid M_2s, demonstrating that it completely exceeds the size range defined by other South African *Paranthropus* M_2s, but that it falls comfortably within the size range for the east African *Paranthropus* sample. In fact, GDA-2 dimensions are

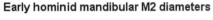

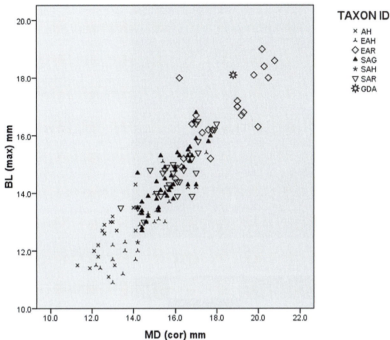

Figure 15.1. Scatterplot of MD and BL diameters of African early hominid mandibular M2 teeth. Measurements in mm, data from Wood (1991), Grine (1993), Keyser *et al.* (2000) and Moggi-Cecchi *et al.* (2005). Abbreviations: AH (Asian *Homo erectus*); EAH (East African *Homo*); EAR (East African robust); GDA (Gondolin); SAG (South African gracile); SAH (South African *Homo*); SAR (South African robust).

in excess of three standard deviations above the mean for both MD and BL diameters of the South African sample, but are approximately one standard deviation above the mean of both measurements for east African *Paranthropus* M$_2$s (Menter *et al.*, 1999).

Size alone is not usually considered to have much taxonomic utility for hominids (Suwa *et al.*, 1996), but the GDA-2 molar also differs in crown and cusp morphology compared to the known sample of South African mandibular M$_2$s (Kuykendall and Conroy, 1999). As shown in Figure 15.2, GDA-2 demonstrates the typical hominoid Y5 molar cusp pattern, but additionally has two distal accessory cusps, which have been identified as the tuberculum sextum (C6) and a distoconulid (Grine, 1984); the latter is also referred to as a second C6 cusp (Wood, 1991; Wood and Abbott, 1983).

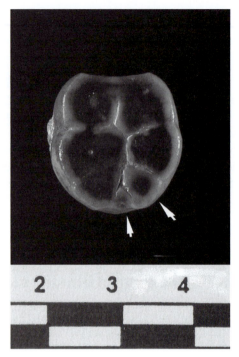

Figure 15.2. The *Paranthropus* mandibular M2 tooth (GDA-2) from Gondolin in occlusal view. The arrows indicate the position of the two C6 accessory cusps.

The notable morphological distinction of the GDA-2 crown is that no other South African *Paranthropus* M_2 (or any other molar) has been identified with two distal accessory (C6) cusps, and it is also rare among east African *Paranthropus* specimens (e.g. only one was reported by Wood, 1991). This feature is, however, more common in east African *Paranthropus* M_3s (Wood and Abbott, 1983; Wood, 1991).

In summary, the GDA-2 left mandibular M_2 is unique among South African *Paranthropus* specimens in its exceptional size, and in the possession of two distal accessory cusps. The addition of such accessory cusps serves to expand the (absolute and relative) size of the distal molar crown as part of a general masticatory and dietary adaptation in this genus, but this adaptive complex is most strongly expressed among the east African 'hyper-robust' *Paranthropus* species and involves other craniodental features (Rak, 1988). Thus based on the detail of the available tooth crown morphology, this isolated specimen is taxonomically ambiguous. Similarly, Skinner and colleagues (2008a) concluded that the GDA-2 molar is ambiguous in both taxonomy and tooth position (M_2 or M_3) based on virtual reconstructions of EDJ morphology from micro-CT scan data.

Obviously, these features of the tooth crown and EDJ represent comparably minor morphological distinctions, and the GDA-2 molar is but a single tooth – morphological definitions of taxa clearly involve more than just tooth morphology. Additional material from Gondolin and other South African sites will hopefully come to light with future fieldwork, and may clarify the interpretation and eventual taxonomic assessment of this isolated tooth. Meanwhile, the unexpected morphology of this specimen could perhaps be explained through various hypothetical scenarios. For example, it should be noted that the majority of available South African *Paranthropus* fossils were recovered from Swartkrans (Grine, 1988, 1993; Brain, 1993) – a single locality – and relatively few others from nearby Kromdraai. Only recently has new material been recovered and described from Drimolen (Keyser 2000; Keyser *et al.*, 2000). Thus despite several decades of South African fieldwork, it is possible that the 'unique' features of Gondolin can be explained as a sampling artefact since only a small number of sites have been excavated – new finds may (but so far have not) produce additional similar specimens.

Another possibility is that there was some difference in predator presence or selection between eastern and southern Africa, so that larger male hominids (of a sexually dimorphic species) were rarely prey victims and thus were not incorporated into the predator accumulations represented by South African fossil cave sites (Grine, pers. comm.; see also Lockwood and Tobias, 1999; but see Pickering *et al.*, 2004 regarding other modes of accumulation in cave sites). These ideas may become testable in future with additional fieldwork and analyses, but at present they are not easily tested and remain hypothetical.

While also hypothetical, the relatively new field of developmental biology provides a useful context for asking novel questions that may provide information allowing a fuller interpretation of this specimen and of *Paranthropus* palaeobiology generally. The remainder of this chapter will focus on aspects of developmental biology of teeth as they relate to understanding the apparently unique morphology of the GDA-2 *Paranthropus* molar.

Evidence from developmental biology of teeth

Evolutionary developmental biology offers a relatively new approach that has recently been applied to questions of early hominid morphology and variation (e.g. McCollum, 1999; Lovejoy *et al.*, 1999, 2002, 2003; McCollum and Sharpe, 2001; Hlusko, 2004), and may provide useful insight for interpreting the unexpected morphology of the GDA-2 tooth. Experimental research in evolutionary developmental biology aims to understand how modifications in gene expression and function effect changes in morphology through alterations to the developmental process (Goodman and Coughlin, 2000). The experimental approach involves experimental manipulation of cellular and tissue interactions, and the identification of signalling pathways, cell products and genetic controls on embryogenic and organogenic processes. At least in a preliminary sense, it is possible to apply the results of experimental studies in extant taxa to problems presented by the hominid (dental) fossil record (McCollum and Sharpe, 2001; Hlusko, 2004).

McCollum and Sharpe (2001) clearly summarised the complex background information from recent studies in 'dental evo-devo' (see below), and applied it to an assessment of phylogenetic patterns of the early hominid dentition, focusing primarily on modifications along the tooth row. Thus it is possible to explore the nature of the (reconstructed) developmental patterns of the GDA-2 molar in comparison to 'typical' *P. robustus* molars in an effort to identify developmental features that may have taxonomic, phylogenetic or more general biological significance.

Although teeth are morphologically complex, dental evolution may involve only subtle changes in gene expression and 'gene expression differences should be linkable to corresponding morphological differences' (Jernvall *et al.*, 2000:14444). Using this approach to assess the Gondolin molar morphology, the 'default model' might be that the GDA-2 molar is more likely to represent *P. robustus*, on the basis of geographical provenance. We can hypothesise that tooth development (and other aspects of maturity) in east African *P. boisei* differed from South African *P. robustus* in significant, yet perhaps subtle, ways to produce the morphological distinctions between the two taxa. Thus we could ask whether the observed morphological differences between the GDA-2 molar and other SA robust australopith M_2s could plausibly result from 'normal' developmental variation (gene expression and its effects) within the taxonomic population of *P. robustus*. Alternately, we could consider the nature and magnitude of developmental modifications required to produce a tooth like the GDA-2 M_2 from the developmental 'template' for a typical *Paranthropus robustus* M_2.

Tooth development: gene expression and molecular signalling

The complex process of tooth development has been described in detail elsewhere (Ten Cate, 1994; see also Thesleff and Jernvall, 1997; Thesleff and Sharpe, 1997; Jernvall *et al.*, 1998, 2000; Ferguson *et al.*, 2000; Jernvall 2000; McCollum and Sharpe, 2001; Pispa and Thesleff, 2003), and its understanding requires some knowledge of microstructural features of tooth development (see e.g. Dean 1987, 2000; Schwartz and Dean, 2000). Briefly, the development and morphogenesis of teeth involves a number of molecular signalling networks between epithelium and mesenchyme (i.e. aggregates of cells derived variously from the three embryonic germ layers, and which interact to form functioning structures), which control the proliferation and differentiation of cells during the developmental period (Jernvall *et al.*, 1998) and result in species-specific patterns of tooth position, type and shape (Tucker *et al.*, 1998; Ferguson *et al.*, 2000). Early stages of mammalian tooth morphogenesis are evident (at about six weeks in humans) by a thickening of the oral epithelium, followed by epithelial cell proliferation under the influence of the *Sonic hedgehog (Shh)* signalling pathway (Hardcastle *et al.*, 1998), and invagination into underlying mesenchymal cells to form the tooth bud. The presence of bone morphogenic protein (BMP) and fibroblast growth factor (FGF) signalling molecules are associated with subsequent folding of the dental epithelium to form the EDJ in the cap stage, and formation of the primary and secondary enamel knots that control the size, number and arrangement of cusps across the tooth's occlusal surface. Fibroblast growth factor in particular seems to control for the differentiation of cells to become odontoblasts and ameloblasts (cells forming tooth dentine and enamel, respectively), though comparatively little is known of the processes of dentine or enamel formation. Jernvall (1995; see also Salazar-Ciudad and Jernvall, 2004) elaborated on the manner in which such processes may act during evolution in conjunction with historical and functional constraints to produce the observed patterns of molar cusp diversity among mammals. Further consideration of these developmental events is relevant to clarifying the adaptive and evolutionary modifications to robust australopith molar morphology, in particular, increases in tooth size, variation in cusp number, and the concomitant modifications to cusp arrangements and crown proportions.

Tooth size

Tooth size ultimately results from the combined processes of epithelial cell proliferation at the bud stage, folding of the dental epithelium at the cap stage, and the position and spacing of the secondary enamel knots. Finally, events during amelogenesis (the process of enamel formation) determine enamel thickness and may also have an effect on crown size. Bromage *et al.* (2004) examined the relationship between microstructural features in tooth enamel of (taxonomically unspecified) molar teeth from the Shungura Formation (Omo basin, Ethiopia), and found that features such as the number of appositional and imbricational striae, incremental rate and extension rate, and the shape of the strial contour were contributing factors to large crown base areas (tooth size) in this sample of fossil hominid teeth. In an earlier study of a larger sample of Omo hominid teeth (including both robust and non-robust taxa), Ramirez-Rozzi *et al.* (1999) found that a similar set of microstructural traits were associated with differences in enamel thickness among teeth, and that these morphological trends reflected climatic changes through time for the Shungura sequence.

While tooth size itself is not considered to be a distinctive taxonomic indicator in hominids (see discussions in Suwa *et al.*, 1994; Suwa *et al.*, 1996; McCollum and Sharpe, 2001), it would be useful to obtain a better understanding of the complex developmental basis for overall increases in tooth crown dimensions, as well as the effect of changes to different internal components of a tooth: the size and morphology of the EDJ, enamel thickness variation in different parts of the crown, and structure of the roots and pulp cavity. In particular, it would be useful to examine the developmental relationship between factors such as tooth crown size, cusp number, and enamel formation – do larger molar tooth crowns exclusively possess larger cusps, more (accessory) cusps, thicker enamel, etc.? Answers to such questions would lead to better understanding of the adaptive and developmental factors involved in tooth size increase in the robust australopith lineage (as well as to tooth size decrease in the genus *Homo*).

Cusp number

After formation of the EDJ, the critical process of enamel-knot signalling during the cap stage of development induces formation of secondary enamel knots (Butler, 1995; Thesleff and Jernvall, 1997; McCollum and Sharpe, 2001) and thus controls the spacing of cusps across the crown, and helps to determine the size and layout of the occlusal surface of the tooth. The enamel knots are therefore critical in establishing the size and shape relationships of the final crown (cuspal) morphology.

Addition of new cusps might seem to constitute novelty in morphology, but Jernvall (2000) found that variations in molar complexity in Russian seal teeth did not require major changes in developmental complexity. In his model, variations of between three to five molar cusps were explained by the normal patterning cascade of signalling processes between the primary enamel knot and a variable number of secondary enamel knots. While absolute tooth size itself was not found to be related to increased variation (number) in the smaller and more peripheral cusps, the relative height and spacing of the prominent cusps in seal molars (which are aligned linearly along the mesial-distal axis) did play a role in predicting variation in cusp number. Thus '[d]evelopmentally, the sequential activation of the secondary enamel knots requires only small developmental changes to produce large morphological changes' (Jernvall, 2000: 2645). At the population level, variations in tooth crown and cusp morphology can involve the generation of novel cusp arrangements without major disruptions to common developmental processes.

However, additional research suggests that mammalian teeth in general are highly 'evolvable', and that evolutionary (morphological) changes at higher taxonomic levels (i.e. relating to adaptive radiations within lineages) involve the same developmental processes to generate diversity in dental morphology (Jernvall *et al.*, 1996, 2000). This interplay between development, morphology and systematics appears to be a central issue for resolving taxonomic and phylogenetic relationships, but our current understanding is far from complete. For example, Skinner and Gunz (2010) reported that the presence of a C6 cusp in a sample of *Pan* lower molars was predicted by both tooth crown size, and the relative size and spacing of the distal crown cusps. These results are consistent with Jernvall's patterning cascade model, but this does not fully explain variation in hominid molar crown morphology, or the variable prevalence of different accessory cusps either within or between species.

The enamel–dentine junction, enamel knots and cusp formation

The results of enamel knot research suggest that new cusps require formation of a novel secondary enamel knot (Jernvall, 1995; Jernvall and Thesleff, 2000), which would indicate that there should be a high correspondence between EDJ and crown (cusp) morphology in completely formed teeth. Thus the presence of extra accessory cusps should theoretically be reflected in the morphology of the EDJ. Figure 15.3 shows 0.8 mm CT slices approximating the EDJ of the GDA-2 molar in transverse (occlusal) orientation, demonstrating that there is at least a general correspondence between EDJ and occlusal cuspal morphology. The slice resolution shown is not refined enough to determine the exact level of correspondence, especially in the critical region of the second C6 cusp. However, recent micro-CT research (Skinner *et al.*, 2008a,b, 2009: Figure 5) has demonstrated the general correspondence of EDJ and OES morphology of this specimen.

Previous CT research on the Carabelli feature in australopith maxillary molars suggests that some aspects of occlusal morphology are not represented at the EDJ. The Carabelli cusp is a common feature in *A. africanus*, but rare or absent in *Paranthropus*, and this difference has both taxonomic and

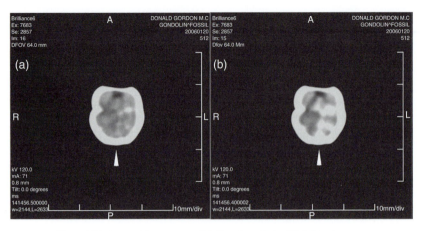

Figure 15.3. Image (a) transverse CT slice through the GDA-2 molar at approximately the position of the EDJ. Enamel is white; dentine is grey. The distal accessory (second C6) cusp is indicated by the white arrow (compare to Figure 15.2). Image (b) is of a more occlusal slice.

developmental significance. Schwartz and colleagues (1998) found that there was little correspondence between the expression of the Carabelli cusp, EDJ topography, and the linear thickness of the enamel in the adjacent region of the tooth crown: 'Different combinations of EDJ and crown surface topography are therefore possible in these two early hominid species making phylogenetic and/or ontogenetic inferences…difficult based solely on data concerning the internal architecture of hominid teeth' (Schwartz *et al.* 1998: 539). Is it possible for a Carabelli (or other) cusp to be produced by processes acting *after* secondary enamel knot formation? In any event, it appears that the Carabelli features can be strongly expressed in the absence of comparable topography at the EDJ.

Skinner and colleagues (2008b) studied the correspondence of dental trait expression at the enamel surface and at the EDJ, including that of the C6 cusp, in a small sample of extant and extinct hominoids. While the degree of expression of such dental traits at the enamel surface is largely determined at the EDJ (i.e. by the presence of a dentine horn) it was concluded that expression of the C6 was markedly influenced by enamel distribution in thick enamelled taxa such as *A. africanus* and *P. robustus*, and thus a small dentine horn at the EDJ was represented by a relatively large C6 cusp at the enamel surface in (only) those taxa. This suggests that cusp morphology in at least some taxa may be influenced during amelogenesis, i.e. well after enamel knot formation is completed (see also Skinner *et al.*, 2010).

Summary and conclusions

The GDA-2 molar is interesting because the details of its size, number and arrangement of cusps present do not neatly fit into the existing descriptions of the South African *Paranthropus* dentition. This tooth is significantly larger than any other South African 'robust' molar; and it possesses two distal accessory cusps and relative cusp proportions reflecting the observed morphology of east African 'hyper-robust' specimens. Notably, these features of crown morphology were identified by Suwa and colleagues (1994) as the primary traits distinguishing east African from South African *Paranthropus* molars. However, the best evidence for resolution of these taxonomic questions will be found in more complete craniodental fossil material from Gondolin and other sites. At the very least, the GDA-2 *Paranthropus* molar, due to its distinctive morphology, suggests that the previously-known South African *Paranthropus* assemblage does not adequately sample the variation in tooth size and morphology for this taxon, and that individuals demonstrating *P. boisei*-like molars were present, even if very rare, in South Africa.

The essential view emphasised this discussion is that differences in dental morphological pattern result from variation in dental developmental processes ultimately under genetic control (Goodman and Coughlin, 2000; Jernvall *et al.*, 2000). Thus interspecific variation in morphology reflects phylogenetically significant differences in those developmental processes. The aim of this chapter has been to seek a better understanding of the developmental history of the GDA-2 tooth crown in an effort to shed some light on its evolutionary significance. While these issues presently provoke many questions, their continued pursuit should prove important for understanding robust australopith palaeobiology, adaptation and systematics.

Much of the research conducted so far on the developmental mechanisms of teeth has been either descriptive to work out the basic processes (see e.g. Thesleff and Sharpe, 1997; Jernvall *et al.*, 1998; Salazar-Cuidad and Jernvall, 2004), or comparative between species with distinctively different tooth crown morphology (Jernvall, 1995; Jernvall *et al.*, 2000) and separated taxonomically above the genus level. Thus it is not yet known how these developmental processes might vary, and be expressed on the tooth crown, within populations of the same species, or between closely related species such as southern and east African *Paranthropus*. At this stage, it is somewhat paradoxical that the high degree of variation in mammalian molar tooth morphology appears to be due to subtle differences in common, general processes of tooth development. At the same time, there must be a threshold in developmental variation at the population or demic level that is relevant to questions about systematics, as well as adaptation, of closely related species. Given that development 'produces' morphology, how much developmental variability is needed to translate into interspecific morphological variation? Can the same patterning cascade model explain all the observed intra- *and* interspecific variation in hominid molar morphology equally well?

The ultimate aim of such research is not to answer questions about taxonomy, though this may become relevant with the recovery of additional fossils and with development of techniques to non-invasively record variation in micro-structural details of tooth crowns that reflect developmental processes (see Smith, *et al.*, 2007). The really interesting questions, and perhaps the more important ones in terms of understanding evolutionary biology of early hominids, have to do with the biological interface between development and adaptive or evolutionary change. Though GDA-2 is only an isolated tooth, why is it so large, and why is the cusp pattern and EDJ morphology distinctive from other South African robusts? These questions can be approached through consideration of the controls on and effect of different aspects of developmental variation producing tooth crown morphology. In addition, the geographic and taphonomic uniqueness of the Gondolin site raise new questions about the environmental context in which this individual – and whichever taxon it represents – lived and died. This information is also informative in constructing adaptive, developmental and life-history models for early hominids (e.g. Smith and Thompkins, 1995; Bogin, 1997, 1999; Kuykendall, 2003).

The developmental reconstruction provided here in relation to the GDA-2 molar tooth relies on general and common processes that are responsible for producing variation in tooth morphology among all mammals. This might suggest that there is no obvious feature of the GDA-2-crown and cusp morphology that requires a distinctive developmental explanation compared to other South African *Paranthropus* specimens. However, the specimen remains an unexpected variant among South African *Paranthropus* molars, and its unique morphology is difficult to account for in terms of the known morphological (and underlying developmental) variation for the taxon *P. robustus*. The size and morphology of this tooth might lead one to a reasonable speculation that it represents an individual whose craniodental and masticatory complex were also atypical compared to other South African *Paranthropus* individuals – and more similar to east African specimens. This speculation can only be addressed with the recovery of new fossils.

Acknowledgements

I would like to thank the initial excavation team at Gondolin, whose efforts made these fossils available for further study. In addition, my appreciation goes to Peter Fleming and his family for allowing us to carry out research on his property, and for continued support of this research. I thank Bill Kimbel for editorial comments on a related manuscript from which this chapter is derived; Chris Dean, Beverly Kramer, Andrew Gallagher and Sally Reynolds reviewed and provided valuable comments and advice on earlier versions of this manuscript. I would also like to thank the organising committee of the African Genesis Conference for the invitation to participate in the conference in Johannesburg, South Africa.

References

Bogin, B. (1997). Evolutionary hypotheses for human childhood. *Yearbook of Physical Anthropology*, **40**: 63–89.

(1999). Evolutionary perspective on human growth. *Annual Review of Anthropology*, **28**: 109–53.

Brain, C. K. (ed.) (1993). *Swartkrans: a Cave's Chronicle of Early Man*. Transvaal Museum Monograph 8. Pretoria: Transvaal Museum.

Bromage, T. G., Rozzi, F. R. and Walker, C. (2004). Shape of the enamel forming front influences crown size in molars from the Shungura Formation, Ethiopia. In Baquendano, E. (ed.), *Homenaje a Emiliano Aguirre*. Madrid: Museo Arqueologico Regional, pp. 82–7.

Butler, P. M. (1995). Ontogenetic aspects of dental evolution. *International Journal of Developmental Biology*, **39**: 25–34.

Dean, M. C. (1987). Growth layers and incremental markings in hard tissues: a review of the literature and some preliminary observations about enamel structure in *Paranthropus boisei*. *Journal of Human Evolution*, **16**: 157–72.

(2000). Progress in understanding hominoid dental development. *Journal of Anatomy*, **197**: 77–102.

Fabian, B. (1985). Ontogenetic explorations into the nature of evolutionary change. In Vrba, E. S. (ed.), *Species and Speciation*. Transvaal Museum Monograph No. 4. Transvaal Museum, Pretoria, pp. 77–85.

Ferguson, C. A., Hardcastle, Z. and Sharpe, P. T. (2000). Development and patterning of the dentition. In O'Higgins, P. and Cohn, M. (eds.), *Development, Growth and Evolution: Implications for the Study of the Hominid Skeleton*. Linnean Society Symposium Series, No. 20. San Diego: Academic Press, pp. 187–205.

Goodman, C. S. and Coughlin, B.C. (2000). The evolution of evo-devo biology. *Proceedings of the National Academy of Sciences*, **97**: 4424–5.

Grine, F. E. (1984). The deciduous dentition of the Kalahari San, the South African Negro and the South African Plio-Pleistocene hominids. PhD dissertation, University of the Witwatersrand.

(1988). New craniodental fossils of *Paranthropus* from the Swartkrans Formation and their significance in 'Robust' Australopithecine evolution. In Grine, F. E.

(ed.), *Evolutionary History of the 'Robust' Australopithecines*. New York: Aldine de Gruyter, pp. 223–43.

(1993). Description and preliminary analysis of new hominid craniodental fossils from the Swartkrans Formation. In Brain, C.K. (ed.), *Swartkrans: a Cave's Chronicle of Early Man*. Transvaal Museum Monograph 8. Pretoria: Transvaal Museum, pp. 75–116.

Hardcastle, Z., Mo, R., Hui, C. C. and Sharpe, P. T. (1998). The Shh signalling pathway in tooth development: defects in Gli2 and Gli3 mutants. *Development*, **125**: 2803–11.

Hlusko, L. J. (2004). Integrating the genotype and phenotype in hominid paleontology. *Proceedings of the National Academy of Sciences*, **101**: 2653–7.

Jernvall, J. (1995). Mammalian molar cusp patterns: developmental mechanisms of diversity. *Acta Zoologica Fennica*, **198**: 1–61.

(2000). Linking development with generation of novelty in mammalian teeth. *Proceedings of the National Academy of Sciences*, **97**: 2641–5.

Jernvall, J. and Thesleff, I. (2000). Return of lost structure in the developmental control of tooth shape. In Teaford, M., Smith, M. M., Ferguson, M. (eds.), *Development, Function and Evolution of Teeth*. Cambridge: Cambridge University Press, pp. 13–21.

Jernvall, J., Hunter, J. P. and Fortelius, M. (1996). Molar tooth diversity, disparity, and ecology in Cenozoic ungulate radiations. *Science*, **274**: 1489–91.

Jernvall, J., Aberg, T., Kettunen, P. *et al.* (1998). The life history of an embryonic signalling center: BMP-4 induces *p21* and is associated with apoptosis in the mouse tooth enamel knot. *Development*, **125**: 161–9.

Jernvall, J., Keranen, S. V. E. and Thesleff, I. (2000). Evolutionary modification of development in mammalian teeth: quantifying gene expression patterns and topography. *Proceedings of the National Academy of Sciences*, **97**: 14444–8.

Keyser, A. W. (2000). The Drimolen skull: the most complete australopithecine cranium and mandible to date. *South African Journal of Science*, **96**: 189–93.

Keyser A. W., Menter C. G., Moggi-Cecchi J. *et al.* (2000). Drimolen: a new hominid-bearing site in Gauteng, South Africa. *South African Journal of Science*, **96**, 193–7.

Kuykendall, K. L. (2003). Reconstructing australopithecine growth and development: what do we think we know? In Thompson, J. L., Krovitz, G. E. and Nelson, A. J. (eds.), *Patterns of Growth and Development in the Genus* Homo, Cambridge: Cambridge University Press, pp. 191–218.

Kuykendall, K. L. and Conroy, G. C. (1999). Description of the Gondolin teeth: hyper-robust hominids in South Africa? 68th Annual Meeting of the American Association of Physical Anthropologists, Columbus, Ohio. Abstracted in *American Journal of Physical Anthropology*, **108**, S28:176–7.

Lavelle, C. L. B., and Moore, W. J. (1973). The incidence of agenesis and polygenesis in the primate dentition. *American Journal of Physical Anthropology*, **38**:671–80.

Lockwood, C. A. and Tobias, P. V. (1999). A large male hominin cranium from Sterkfontein, South Arica, and the status of *Australopithecus africanus*. *Journal of Human Evolution*, **36**: 637–85.

Lovejoy, C. O., Cohn, M. J. and White, T. D. (1999). Morphological analysis of the mammalian postcranium: a developmental perspective. *Proceedings of the National Academy of Sciences*, **96**:13247–52.

Lovejoy, C. O., Meindl, R. S., Ohman, J. C. *et al.* (2002). The Maka femur and its bearing on the antiquity of human walking: applying contemporary concepts of morphogenesis to the human fossil record. *American Journal of Physical Anthropology*, **119**: 97–188.

Lovejoy, C. O., McCollum, M. A., Reno, P. L. *et al.* (2003). Developmental biology and human evolution. *Annual Review of Anthropology*, **32**: 85–109.

Menter, C., Kuykendall, K. L., Keyser, A. W. *et al.* (1999). First record of hominid teeth from the Plio-Pleistocene site of Gondolin, South Africa. *Journal of Human Evolution*, **37**: 299–307.

McCollum, M. A. (1999). The robust australopithecine face: a morphogenetic perspective. *Science*, **284**: 301–5.

McCollum, M. A. and Sharpe, P. T. (2001). Developmental genetics and early hominid craniodental evolution. *BioEssays*, **32**: 481–93.

Moggi-Cecchi, J., Grine, F. E. and Tobias, P. V. (2005). Early hominid dental remains from Members 4 and 5 of the Sterkfontein Formation (1966–1996 excavations): Catalogue, individual associations, morphological descriptions and initial metrical analysis. *Journal of Human Evolution*, **50**: 239–328.

Pickering, T. R., Clarke, R. J. and Heaton, J. L. (2004). The context of StW 573, and early hominid skull and skeleton from Sterkfontein Member 2: taphonomy and paleoenvironment. *Journal of Human Evolution*, **46**: 279–97.

Pispa, J. and Thesleff, I. (2003). Mechanisms of ectodermal organogenesis. *Developmental Biology*, **262**: 195–205.

Rak, Y. (1988). On variation in the masticatory system of *Australopithecus boisei*, In Grine, F. E. (ed.), *Evolutionary History of the 'Robust' Australopithecines*. New York: Aldine de Gruyter, pp. 193–8.

Ramirez Rozzi, F. V., Walker, C. and Bromage, T. (1999). Early hominid dental development and climate change. In Bromage, T. G. and Schrenk, R. (eds.), *African Biogeography, Climate Change, and Early Hominid Evolution*. Oxford University Press, pp. 349–63.

Robinson, J. T. (1956). *The Dentition of the Australopithecinae*. Transvaal Museum Memoir No. 9. Transvaal Museum, Pretoria.

Salazar-Cuidad, I. and Jernvall, J. (2004). How different types of pattern formation mechanisms affect the evolution of form and development. *Evolution & Development*, **6**: 1, 6–16.

Schwartz, G. T. and Dean, M. C. (2000). Interpreting the hominid dentition: ontogenetic and phylogenetic aspects. In O'Higgins, P. and Cohen, M. (eds.), *Development, Growth and Evolution: Implications for the Study of Hominid Skeleton*. London: Academic Press, pp. 207–33.

Schwartz, G. T., Thackeray, J. F., Reid, C. *et al.* (1998). Enamel thickness and the topography of the enamel-dentine junction in South African Plio-Pleistocene hominids with special reference to the Carabelli trait. *Journal of Human Evolution*, **35**: 523–42.

Skinner, M. M., Gunz, P., Wood, B. A. *et al.* (2008a). Enamel–dentine junction (EDJ) morphology distinguishes the lower molars of *Australopithecus africanus* and *Paranthropus robustus*. *Journal of Human Evolution*, **55**: 979–88.

Skinner, M. M., Wood, B. A., Boesch, C. *et al.* (2008b). Dental trait expression at the enamel–dentine junction of lower molars in extant and fossil hominoids. *Journal of Human Evolution*, **54**: 173–86.

Skinner, M. M., Wood, B. A. and Hublin, J. J. (2009). Protostylid expression at the enamel–dentine junction and enamel surface of mandibular molars of *Paranthropus robustus* and *Australopithecus africanus*. *Journal of Human Evolution*, **56**: 76–85.

Skinner, M. M. and Gunz, P. (2010). The presence of accessory cusps in chimpanzee lower molars is consistent with a patterning cascade model of development. *Journal of Anatomy*, **217**: 245–53.

Skinner, M. M., Evans, A., Smith, T. *et al.* (2010). Brief communication: contributions of enamel–dentine junction shape and enamel deposition to primate molar crown complexity. *American Journal of Physical Anthropology*, **142**: 157–63.

Smith, B. H. and Thompkins, R. L. (1995). Toward a life history of the Hominidae. *Annual Review of Anthropology*, **24**: 257–79.

Smith, T. M., Tafforeau, P., Reid, D. J. *et al.* (2007). Earliest evidence of modern human life history in North African early *Homo sapiens*. *Proceedings of the National Academy of Sciences*, **104**: 6128–33.

Suwa, G., Wood, B. A. and White, T. D. (1994). Further analysis of mandibular molar crown and cusp areas on Pliocene and Pleistocene hominids. *American Journal of Physical Anthropology*, **93**: 407–26.

Suwa, G., White, T. D. and Howell, F. C. (1996). Mandibular postcanine dentition from the Shungura Formation, Ethiopia: crown morphology, taxonomic allocations, and Plio-Pleistocene hominid evolution. *American Journal of Physical Anthropology*, **101**: 247–82.

Ten Cate, A. R. (1994). *Oral Histology: Development, Structure and Function*, 4th edn. St. Louis: Mosby.

Thesleff, I. and Jernvall, J. (1997). The enamel knot: a putative signalling center regulating tooth development. In *Pattern Formation During Development. Cold Spring Harbor Laboratory Symposium 62*, pp. 257–67.

Thesleff, I. and Sharpe, P. (1997). Signalling networks regulating dental development. *Mechanisms of Development*, **67**: 111–23.

Tucker, A. S., Matthews, K. L. and Sharpe, P. T. (1998). Transformation of tooth type induced by inhibition of BMP signalling. *Science*, **282**: 1136–8.

Wood, B. A. (1991). *Koobi Fora Research Project, Volume 4. Hominid Cranial Remains*. Oxford: Claredon Press.

(1996). Hominid palaeobiology: have studies of comparative development come of age? *American Journal of Physical Anthropology*, **99**: 9–15.

Wood, B. A. and Abbott, S. A. (1983). Analysis of the dental morphology of Plio-Pleistocene hominids. I. Mandibular molars: crown area measurements and morphological traits. *Journal of Anatomy*, **136**: 197–219.

16 Digital South African fossils: morphological studies using reference-based reconstruction and electronic preparation

GERHARD W. WEBER, PHILIPP
GUNZ, SIMON NEUBAUER, PHILIPP
MITTEROECKER AND FRED L. BOOKSTEIN

Abstract

Virtual anthropology (VA) is a multidisciplinary approach to studying anatomical data in three spatial dimensions, or in space through time, particularly for humans, their ancestors and their closest relatives (www.virtual-anthropology. com). The quantitative analysis of biological structures in varying detail is a key element, as is the availability of digital data. This fusion of anthropology, mathematics, physics, computer science, medicine and industrial design incorporates know-how for applications spanning evolutionary biology, hominoid development and growth, forensics, biometric identification, medical diagnosis and teaching (Figure 16.1). In this chapter, we demonstrate the VA toolkit by reviewing some recent results based on high-resolution CT data from South African fossil hominids. We show examples of electronic preparation (MLD 37/38) and anatomical and geometric reconstruction (Taung, Sts 71, StW 505, SK 48, MLD 37/38), and we explain the outcomes or findings regarding endocranial measurements, venous drainage systems, sexual dimorphism in *A. africanus*, growth trajectories of hominoids, and the allometric scaling of robust australopithecines. Digital specimens, available independent of time or location, allow us to capture novel and more reproducible data of traits and form, as from inaccessible or hitherto unformalised regions. Delicate specimens can be protected from damage when digital fossils are used to make

African Genesis: Perspectives on Hominin Evolution, eds. Sally C. Reynolds and Andrew Gallagher. Published by Cambridge University Press. © Cambridge University Press 2012.

casts, to share data among scientists and to underlie alternative measurement schemes. We argue that these themes represent one substantial area of development for contemporary fossil-based palaeoanthropology.

Introduction

Physical anthropology is a reflexive science: humans investigate their own natural history. For thousands of years, this self-investigation was bound to the avenues of physical accessibility and the availability of real objects. Although measurements such as skull width or arm length can describe organisms or parts of organisms, characterisation in this way is severely limited; as is the information available from two-dimensional photographs. Not until the introduction of digital technology did object representation became visually realistic. 'Virtual anthropology' (VA) is in fact the continuation of one of the oldest scientific disciplines using the possibilities provided by twenty-first century instrumentation (Weber *et al.*, 1998, 2001; Weber and Bookstein, 2011). This new technology has paved the way for new approaches that were unfeasible in the actual anthropology lab.

Virtual anthropology depends on the fast processing of vast amounts of data, and so, naturally, methodology is one of its main foci. Compared with the classical approach, it introduces a new level of abstraction to anthropology: instead of real objects, imaginary objects are investigated. The virtual space in which they reside makes novel manipulations and analyses possible – the barriers of the physical world and of human memory do not apply. Hidden structures can be measured almost as easily as the outer surface of a biological structure, and high-resolution quantitative descriptors enable comparisons that far exceed the capabilities of the scientist's own brain. The geometrical aspects of structures can be compared as a whole – not distance by distance, or angle by angle, only, as in traditional methods – and mean configuration and variation can be assessed at once. Furthermore, the usage of virtual specimens helps to protect the originals from physical manipulations.

We characterise VA as an interdisciplinary approach to studying anatomical data, particularly that of humans, their ancestors and their closest relatives (www.virtual-anthropology.com), in three or four dimensions (space or space-time). The quantitative analysis of biological structures in varying detail is a key element, as is the presence of digital data. This fusion of anthropology, mathematics, physics, computer science, medicine and industrial design incorporates know-how for applications spanning evolutionary biology, hominoid development and growth, forensics, biometric identification, medical diagnosis and teaching.

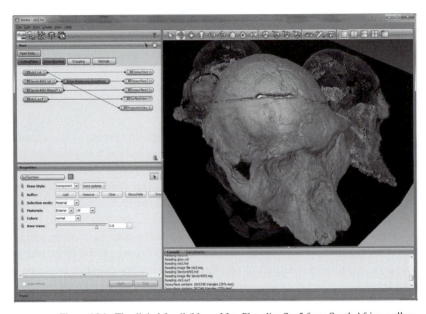

Figure 16.1. The digital fossil (blue – Mrs. Ples alias Sts 5 from South Africa; yellow inside – its virtual endocast shining through the transparent cranium; orange in the background – coronal, sagittal and transversal projection views) can be visualised, manipulated and measured in a computer environment using 3D software (here Amira© 5.3.3). (See plate section for colour version.)

We divide VA into six operational areas (Weber and Bookstein, 2011), each of which relates to different tasks, technologies and interactions with other fields of research:

(1) Digitise – mapping the physical world
(2) Expose – looking inside
(3) Compare – using numbers
(4) Reconstruct – dealing with missing data
(5) Materialise – back to the real world
(6) Share – collaboration at the speed of light

These tasks all involve collaboration with other fields of techno-science. These fields overlap in their language with those of other biological disciplines such as palaeontology, zoology or anatomy. The generation of digitised volume datasets exploits technologies developed principally for purposes of medical diagnosis, and so VA is closely connected to diagnostic radiology (Spoor *et al.*, 2000). But the relationship between anthropology and the medical sciences is reciprocal, as the knowledge of anthropology's new methods and procedures may return to the clinical environment, like for functional lung diagnosis (Recheis *et al.*, 2004) or surgical planning for implants and prostheses (Heuze *et al.*, 2008). Mathematical and statistical sciences provide the methodological basis for the actual information content of the individual images and the composite datasets to which they contribute. Of equal importance is the domain of computer science that expedites the implementation of the associated complex computations in software and occasionally even in hardware. Physics is involved not only in the acquisition of data for VA but also in data analysis whenever that rests on physical models or analogues.

Morphological studies on South African hominins

We review here some recent Vienna projects on South African specimens. One project, the statistical and geometric reconstruction of certain fossil crania, became the doctoral dissertation of Philipp Gunz; the other, concerned with the endocranium of *Australopithecus africanus* MLD 37/38, turned into Simon Neubauer's Masters thesis. Both are good demonstrations of manipulations of digital specimens in a computer environment to produce scientific insights.

Anatomical and geometric reconstruction of fossil crania

Because fossils are often discovered in a broken or distorted condition, reconstruction is almost inevitably the first step towards an analysis of their form. We use computed tomography (CT) to gain data from precious fossils without harming the originals. These digital data resources combine with landmark-based statistics in new procedures for handling fossil specimens that go beyond the mere assembly of fragments (Weber *et al.*, 2002; Weber *et al.* 2003). Whenever warranted by anatomical cues, deformations are corrected by mirror-imaging or translation and reorientation of parts (anatomical reconstruction) obtained through segmentation. We then measure the three-dimensional coordinates of anatomical landmarks and hundreds of semi-landmarks on the surfaces of the fossil specimen and large samples of crania from extant hominoids. The positions of the (semi)landmark points that would lie on missing or deformed portions of the fossils are estimated using multivariate methods (geometric reconstruction).

Semi-landmarks are points along curves or on surfaces that are used to capture morphology in areas where no explicit point-locations are defined using the traditional landmark definitions, for instance large areas along the neurocranial surface (Gunz *et al.*, 2005). The same number of points is measured in approximately the same location on each specimen in the dataset. Subsequently, a thin-plate spline interpolation (a coordinate transformation based on minimal bending energy criterion) is used to make these points geometrically homologous within the sample: the semi-landmarks are allowed to slide along the curvature so as to minimise the thin-plate spline bending energy between each specimen (Bookstein, 1997) and the Procrustes average form (the average computed from the Procrustes coordinates of several specimens). The Procrustes coordinates are computed by a Procrustes superimposition that rotates, translates and scales the specimens in the sample according to a least-squares criterion, thus removing information about orientation, position and scale of the configurations.

Any reconstruction requires assumptions about functional constraints, integration and symmetry, and sometimes about gender, species affinity and taphonomy. When such assumptions are stated explicitly, their validity can become subject to evaluation and discussion (Zollikofer *et al.*, 2005; Gorder, 2005; Gunz *et al.*, 2009; Weber and Bookstein, 2011). As different assumptions and algorithms lead to different estimations there is no 'all-purpose' reconstruction; instead one creates multiple reconstructions and examines their variation.

Implicitly formalising biological knowledge about integration, symmetry and curvature-smoothness, Gunz (2005) presented two iterative approaches to reference-based reconstruction (see also Gunz *et al.*, 2009): (1) geometric reconstruction, using the thin-plate-spline bending energy based on a single reference specimen; and (2) statistical reconstruction, exploiting the covariance matrix of a reference sample.

The reconstruction of Sterkfontein Member 4 specimen StW 505 is based on the assumption that the cranium was symmetric before distortion occurred, and that it belongs to the same group as the crania Sts 71 and Sts 5. Figure 16.2 shows the steps of anatomical reconstruction that were performed on a CT scan of StW 505 (Lockwood and Tobias, 1999). At first the volume was cut into four parts; the temporal bone was translated and rotated so as to remove the gap between the parietal and the squamosal part of the temporal bone. Then the nasoalveolar clivus was cut from the facial part and realigned so that prosthion lies in the local midplane of the face and the two parts of the right alveolus of the canine were joined. Using landmark-based warping of the CT volume the inferior margin of the left orbit was forced upward so as to lie in the same transverse plane as the inferior margin on the right

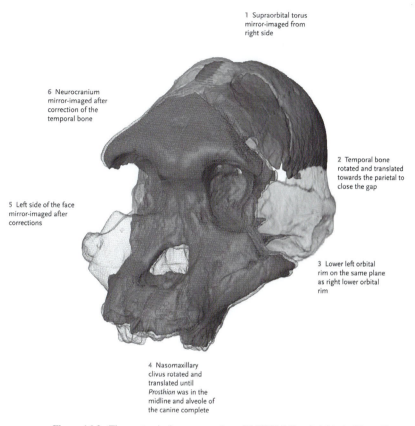

1 Supraorbital torus mirror-imaged from right side

6 Neurocranium mirror-imaged after correction of the temporal bone

2 Temporal bone rotated and translated towards the parietal to close the gap

5 Left side of the face mirror-imaged after corrections

3 Lower left orbital rim on the same plane as right lower orbital rim

4 Nasomaxillary clivus rotated and translated until *Prosthion* was in the midline and alveole of the canine complete

Figure 16.2. The anatomical reconstruction of StW 505 (South Africa). (From Gunz, 2005.) (See plate section for colour version.)

side; the root of the right zygomatic arch was allowed to move accordingly, while the rest of the face was held constant. Note that this does not fully correct for the distortion of the temporal process of the zygomatic bone. The right supraorbital torus was then mirrored to the left along the local midplane of the upper face. Finally, the now-corrected left side was mirrored to the right, creating a symmetric cranium with a reoriented temporal bone, a realigned nasoalveolar clivus, an almost complete supraorbital torus and corrected orbits.

This reconstruction protocol does not correct for the slight distortion of the neurocranium described by Lockwood and Tobias (1999). Whereas the rotation of the temporal is incontestable, evidence of a rotation of the complete parietal bone is less clear. It proved to be impossible to correct for such a possible

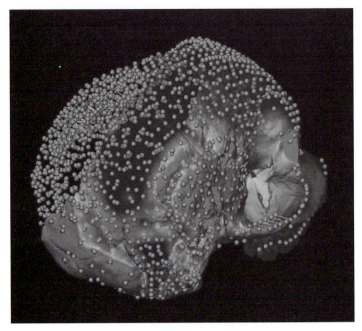

Figure 16.3. The geometric reconstruction of Sts 71 (South Africa) using hundreds
of landmarks and semi-landmarks, including points on the internal braincase (orange
spheres: before reconstruction; blue spheres: after reconstruction based on Sts 5).
Red areas indicate large differences between the original and the reconstruction, blue
indicates small differences. (From Gunz, 2005.) (See plate section for colour version.)

rotation of the parietal in a principled way. This was not due to 'technical limitations' – it is possible to rotate the parietal by several degrees clockwise and
produce perfectly reasonable morphologies; but we do not see any algorithmic
possibility of determining the axis and amount of rotation arithmetically. This
process would involve too many subjective assumptions. Therefore, the parietal was treated as if it were in its original position (acknowledging that to
tolerate the slight possible distortion was considered less misinformative than
to introduce an arbitrary, and subjective, bias).

Figure 16.3 visualises the correction of the neurocranial deformation in
Sterkfontein cranial specimen Sts 71. The orange spheres show the semi-
landmarks before correction, the blue ones the same points after correction.
The same 3D coordinates were measured on a reference cranium (in this case
Sts 5). The colours code the amount of correction applied to the original surface of Sts 71 – ranging from blue (no correction) to red. Naturally, the choice
of the reference specimen will lead to different reconstructions, so we always
use more than one reference cranium and treat the resulting reconstructions

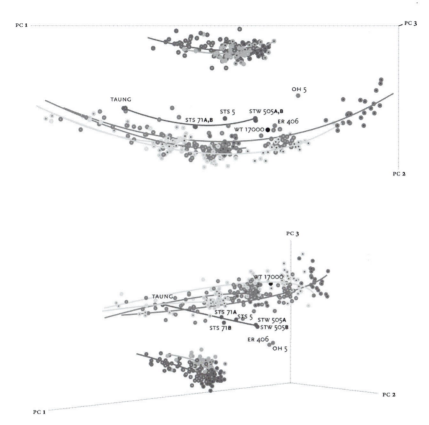

Figure 16.4. Growth trajectories of extant hominoids and australopiths based on several hundred 3D landmarks and semi-landmarks on the entire cranium. *Pan paniscus* in light green, *Pan troglodytes* in dark green, *Gorilla gorilla* in blue, *Pongo pygmaeus* in yellow, *Homo sapiens* (Khoi San) in orange, *Homo sapiens* (Europe) in red, *Australopithecus africanus* in brown, *A./P. boisei in* magenta, WT 17000 in black. (From Gunz, 2005.) (See plate section for colour version.)

as if they were separate specimens in the analyses. This makes it possible to evaluate the impact of the choice of reference on the results.

In Figure 16.4 we show an analysis of post-natal growth trajectories of extant hominoids and australopithecines based on several hundred 3D landmarks and semi-landmarks on the cranium. We performed this analysis in Procrustes form space ('size-shape space' cf. Mitteroecker *et al.*, 2004), which is a variant of principal component analysis (PCA) in geometric morphometrics. PCA can be computed in shape space from the Procrustes shape variables. It is possible to retain the size information in 'Procrustes form space', by computing the PCA from the Procrustes variables along with an additional column for log centroid size. Because log centroid size typically will have the largest variation, the first PC axis in form space is usually highly correlated with size.

In this PCA of Procrustes form space the *Australopithecus africanus* specimens from Taung (Taung child skull) and Sterkfontein Sts 71 and StW 505 are each represented by two reconstructions, which plot so closely together that they are hard to distinguish. Clearly the choice of the reference for the reconstruction has no significant impact on this particular analysis: the shape differences of the reconstructions, resulting from different assumptions, are not large enough to alter any conclusion drawn from the analysis.

The two panels show two projections of the first three principal components (PCs) of form space of a dataset that comprises an ontogenetic series of all great apes and two human populations. In the upper panel the growth trajectories (all groups grow from left to right) seem to be almost parallel; the bottom figure, however, reveals that the ontogenetic trajectories diverge. The ontogenetic trajectories, drawn as quadratic regressions of shape against the logarithm of centroid size, appear very similar in the first two PCs of form space. However, in the third principal component *Homo sapiens* and australopithecines differ from the apes.

Postnatal trajectories of the apes are approximately parallel but stop at different adult values for the first PC score. Note that the sexes are separated along this growth trajectory, which is particularly apparent in orang-utans (*Pongo pygmaeus*: yellow) and gorillas (*Gorilla gorilla*: blue). The separation of male and female chimpanzees (*Pan troglodytes*: dark green), and bonobos (*Pan paniscus*: light green) and humans of both populations (red and orange) along this allometric trajectory is less pronounced and there is considerable overlap. The growth trajectory of the gracile hominin *A. africanus* lies between that of apes and humans, differing from the former in the third component. The robust australopithecines *Australopithecus/ Paranthropus boisei* specimens lie on the extension of this trajectory with respect to the first two dimensions but in a different 'plane' of the third component. The results of this comparative geometric morphometric analysis show that many cranial differences among extant and fossil hominins can be explained by allometric scaling. Species-specific morphologies, however, develop early during individual development and are already established in the youngest specimens of our sample (eruption of the first permanent molar).

In this way, careful attention to the details of reconstructing incomplete and distorted fossils can sometimes permit them to participate fully in analyses that contrast them with extant forms or complete fossils.

The endocranium of *Australopithecus africanus* MLD 37/38

MLD 37/38 is an incomplete but well-preserved *Australopithecus africanus* cranium, found embedded in two blocks of pink breccia mined in the Limeworks cave at Makapansgat, South Africa (Dart, 1959, 1962). Most of the face and parts of the frontal neurocranium are missing. Furthermore, the endocranial cavity is filled with stone matrix, a so-called natural endocast.

Using CT scans of MLD 37/38, the first step was to segment the CT images so that fossilised bone and natural endocast could be analysed separately. A semi-automated segmentation approach, called region-growing, was used on the stack of CT images to delimit the stone matrix region. In this approach, a seed point is set within the stone matrix region on every single CT image and allowed to grow according to the greyscale-bounded border of the endocast by stating a range of grey values (threshold). After segmentation, an (incomplete) endocast and also a matrix-free endocranium are available for description and measurements.

The preserved endocast that was segmented comprises the calvarial surface up to approximately the coronal suture (left of endobregma missing small portions and on the right side enclosing also parts of the frontal lobe), both occipital and cerebellar lobes, the entire right temporal lobe and also most of the left temporal lobe. It is missing only the most anterior parts. The missing frontal endocast part of MLD 37/38 was subsequently reconstructed using Sts 5 as a reference specimen. The geometric reconstruction used here is similar to that introduced above but relies on a deformation of the reference specimen's *endocranial* surface by thin-plate spline warping. The endocranial surface of Sts 5 was warped to that of MLD 37/38 (Neubauer, 2005) using 8 homologous ectocranial landmarks and 455 endocranial semi-landmarks (a total of 463 points) to match them exactly. The complete endocranial surface of Sts 5 was deformed accordingly so that the missing endocranial surface of MLD 37/38 is estimated by the warped frontal part of Sts 5.

The volume of the preserved natural endocast is 378 cm³ and the total endocranial capacity (after geometric reconstruction using Sts 5 as reference specimen) is 440 cm³ (Figure 16.5). This estimate is considerably smaller than the first estimate by Dart (1962, 480 cm³) and slightly larger than the more recent estimates of Holloway (1972, 435 cm³) and Conroy *et al.* (1990, 425 cm³). The sample mean of endocranial capacity for *Australopithecus africanus* (Neubauer *et al.*, 2004) thus increases to 454 ± 32 cm³ (std. dev) ($n = 7$).

In general, the endocast of MLD 37/38 is lower and wider than that of Sts 5, StW 505, Sts 71 and the Taung specimen. Only Sterkfontein specimen Sts 60 is lower and wider than the endocast of MLD 37/38. While other natural and artificial endocasts, whether real or virtual, sometimes show detailed convolutions,

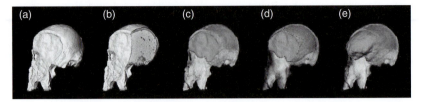

Figure 16.5. 3D reconstruction (yellow) and virtual endocast (grey) of MLD 37/38: (a) displays the virtual specimen as it is; (b) shows a parasagittal cut and the composition of the embedded matrix along this CT slice; (c) the virtual endocast results in 378 cm^3 for the preserved endocranial cavity; (d) virtual endocast and semi-landmarks in the transparent cranium; (e) the reconstructed virtual endocast based on TPS warping using Sts 5 as reference specimen gives 450 cm^3 as the estimate for the cranial capacity of MLD 37/38. (See plate section for colour version.)

no such details could be found on the endocranial surface of MLD 37/38. Also, the controversially debated lunate sulcus is not detectable on this specimen. We assume that the absence of detail is due not to the methodology used here but to the circumstance that in this particular specimen the brain left no detailed imprints on the internal table. The slight displacement of the right parietal bone over the left causes small asymmetries of the endocast. Additionally, a small right occipital petalia can be seen.

Endocasts give evidence of venous drainage from the brain and arterial supply to the internal table of bone and the dura mater. MLD 37/38 shows a well developed lateral venous drainage system (transverse and sigmoid sinuses) on both sides, while there is no evidence for an enlarged occipital-marginal sinus system. Except for the juvenile Taung fossil, all known *Australopithecus africanus* specimens exhibit this pattern of cranial venous drainage. But assuming that the ontogenetic development of the venous sinus pattern in *A. africanus* resembles that of modern humans, the occipital-marginal pattern in the juvenile Taung specimen could have been replaced by a lateral transverse-sigmoid pattern if the Taung juvenile had reached adulthood. In contrast to the condition in *A. africanus*, enlarged occipital-marginal sinus systems are frequent in *A./P. robustus*, *A./P. boisei* and *A. afarensis* and have been used as a claim to robust australopithecine membership (Tobias, 1968; Falk and Conroy, 1983; Kimbel, 1984; Falk, 1986; White and Falk, 1999; Falk *et al.*, 2000; Holloway *et al.*, 2002).

Internal blood supply of the brain is not detectable on an endocast but meningeal vessels frequently leave imprints on the internal table of cranial bone. Several branches of meningeal vessels could be detected on the left side of the endocast of MLD 37/38. On the right side, only rudimentary branches can be seen because the cranium broke apart on the boundary between fossilised bone and the natural endocast in this region. While one branch on the left side gives evidence that the middle third of the braincase was supplied by the external carotid artery through the foramen spinosum, another branch on the right side stems from the orbit and therefore originates from the internal carotid artery. Statistical analysis showed that Falk's pattern A (blood supply by meningeal vessels originating from the internal carotid artery with an increasing extent of supply by the middle meningeal artery from A1 to A4) or E (blood supply alone by the middle meningeal artery originating from the external artery) in one hemisphere strongly predicts the same pattern in the other (Falk, 1993). We can thus assume that there was blood supply from both the internal and external carotid artery to the middle third of the braincase (pattern A2, A3 or A4 of Falk, 1993).

The stone matrix was removed from some apertures and foramina so that they could be traced from the outside inwards. Parts of the right orbit were preserved within the stone matrix. The superior orbital fissure was found to be round in shape and therefore should be called 'superior orbital foramen' instead. This feature in MLD 37/38 conforms to the character state in African apes, *A. afarensis* and *A. africanus*, the latter being in contrast with humans and robust australopithecines that show elongated, comma-shaped superior orbital fissures (Rak *et al.*, 1996). The crescent of foramina (superior orbital fissure/foramen, foramen rotundum, foramen ovale, foramen spinosum) in MLD 37/38 has the same morphological condition as the other *A. africanus* and *A. afarensis* specimens.

Relevance of the virtual anthropology approach in comparative morphology

From these examples of successfully reconstructed individual fossils we now turn to a more general critique of the underlying methodology as it might sustain better comparative inferences about form across palaeoanthropology. Three criteria might characterise comparison of form: (1) the forms to be compared should be captured comprehensively and accurately; (2) comparisons between groups should rely on the largest practicable number of specimens; and (3) comparisons of form should always be interpreted in the context of the process that governed them (such as evolution, growth or disease). Virtual anthropology offers approaches that are beneficial according to all three of these criteria.

First, measurements based on digital data can be taken accurately, and on every spot of the volume. They can be taken in regions not accessible on real specimens (Tobias, 2001) and, as demonstrated above, previously unformalised regions can be captured using another type of landmark, the semi-landmark. Second, a large number of specimens can be compared at once. In most applications, groups have to be compared with other groups or a new specimen assigned to an existing group. The number of two-specimen comparisons can be very large. For purposes like comparison, estimation of missing data and classification, VA permits the computation of a generalised configuration for a whole group of specimens, a formalised 'reference model' that includes information on mean configuration, variability and probability distributions (e.g. Weber *et al.*, 2006). Third, the particular formal technique of landmark/semi-landmark points enforces one particular rule for keeping comparisons under the control of biological theory: the rule of homology (comparing like to like). In VA, with its emphasis on digital data and configurations of landmarks, geometric morphometrics (GM) is a core technology. Geometric morphometrics is a subdiscipline of statistics that is concerned with the analysis of shape and shape changes of geometrical objects (Bookstein, 1991; Rohlf and Marcus, 1993; Bookstein, 1996; Dryden and Mardia, 1998). Central to the GM approach are some key elements (e.g. Procrustes superimposition, thin-plate spline), which we describe at length elsewhere (Bookstein, 1989, 1991; Slice, 2005; Weber and Bookstein, 2011): the representation of forms by size along with shape coordinates, the reliance on the full mathematical machinery of the statistical theory of shape, and the visualisation not only of single forms but also of comparisons, via the deformation grids that illustrate and formalise shape differences between geometrical objects. Moreover the way data are represented in VA allows the scientist to compute means and variances of groups at the same time that differences between two specimens or mean configurations are visualised as deformation grids. As we saw in the australopithecine example, the resulting quantitative reference model may be used to reconstruct shape or form. Even though the choice of the reference specimen or group requires justification, the reconstruction process itself is transparent and reproducible, two elementary prerequisites for scientific discussion.

To expose hidden structures was the driving force at the beginning of VA, and it still lies at its core. As shown in the work on the Makapansgat specimen, MLD 37/38, the exposed structures may be treated qualitatively or quantitatively, or both. Of course segmentation per se is not remotely novel, but we showed (in the endocast example) how this newly revealed structure could in turn be brought into the process of reference-based reconstruction: the estimate of endocranial capacity thus became an objective, reproducible one (Neubauer *et al.*, 2004).

Although there is a price to be paid (expensive equipment, training of highly qualified staff), in our view there are overwhelming advantages to combine classic and virtual anthropology techniques in a laboratory:

- 3D data is available on the desktop at all times
- there are no physical barriers to hamper research

- quantitative analyses of spatial structures are feasible in arbitrary detail
- results are easier to reproduce
- different teams can work on the same object.

Spreading the technology

One of the main aims of VA is that our science needs more people trained to get information out, not just to put data in. Electronic archives will inevitably grow (see below) and fill the storage of computer systems. To convert this accumulation of data into useful information is the next step. Virtual anthropology is still not so widespread; a background of course in biology, but also in mathematics or computer science, is required. Young researchers have to be trained in more than one of these domains to fully exploit the possibilities. The European Commission therefore funded a large research training network (European Virtual Anthropology Network – EVAN, Weber *et al.*, 2005) from 2006 to 2009 to implement the new interdisciplinary approach and to provide better infrastructure regarding digital archives and, importantly, tools. As EVAN (www.evan.at) included 15 partners from diverse sectors (academia, clinics, museums and industry), 28 doctoral and post-doctoral fellows could be trained in all kinds of different technologies (Figure 16.6). One milestone was the development of a new software (EVAN-Toolbox) that saves its users from

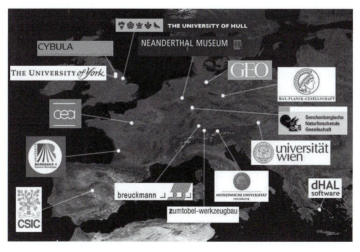

Figure 16.6. The European Virtual Anthropology Network (EVAN) consisted of 15 partners from six countries to train young researchers in the new techniques and to foster collaborations between academia, medicine, museums and industry.

312   *Gerhard W. Weber* et al.

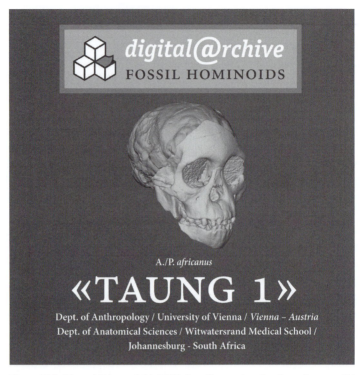

Figure 16.7. The publicly available DVD (http://www.virtual-anthropology.com/3d_
data/3d-archive) of 'Taung 1', the type specimen of *A. africanus* (South Africa).

programming the usual routines such as Procrustes superimposition, principal
component analysis or partial least squares analysis, which are fundamental to
the GM analysis of shape and form. The software is now further developed and
maintained by the EVAN-Society (www.evan-society.org) and includes tools
for semi-landmarking as well.

The South African institutions, in particular the University of the
Witwatersrand and Transvaal Museum, have always been open minded and
offered generous access to the original specimens, not always a matter of
course in our field (Weber, 2001; Gibbons, 2002). Some of the most important
South African specimens such as Mrs. Ples (Sts 5), Sts 60, Sk 48 or Sts 71 are
accessible in the 'digital@rchive of Fossil Hominoids' (Figure 16.7).

It was on the occasion of the African Genesis Symposium 2006, that Phillip V.
Tobias and his distinguished colleagues gave permission to include one of the most
valuable fossils of man's heritage in this digital archive. Some 80 years after its
discovery, the Taung child is now available for a broad community of researchers

and the interested public (www.virtual-anthropology.com/Members/3d_data/3d-archive). It is fitting to close this survey of our recent work by repeating, again, how grateful we are to Professor Tobias for his generous sharing of data and theories with us, which exemplifies the collaborations that will drive the usefulness of our emerging VA toolkit for many decades to come.

Acknowledgements

It is a privilege to be invited to contribute to the African Genesis Symposium volume in honour of our much-valued colleague Phillip V. Tobias, whom we thank for his invaluable support and collaboration over the last decade. Our workgroup 'Virtual Anthropology' at Vienna represents part of a new approach to palaeoanthropological research for the twenty-first century, a new approach to which Phillip Tobias himself, despite his busy life and long experience, contributes as enthusiastically as the rest of us here, using the full power of his intellectuality, vitality, openness and even his sense of humour. So we also thank you, Phillip, for setting such a wonderful example. The work presented here was done in collaboration with Horst Seidler, Katrin Schäfer, Bence Viola, Markus Bernhard, Andrea Stadlmayr and Christian Huber, and with technical support from Nora Dibowski and Roman Ginner. We like to thank the following colleagues for support: Phillip V. Tobias, the late Heather White, Francis Thackeray, Mike Raath, Ron Clarke, Kevin Kuykendall, Stephanie Potze, Beverly Kramer, L. H. Labuscagne, Lee Berger, Jeffrey Schwartz, Glenn Conroy, Dean Falk, George Koufos, Zumtobel Staff, Bernhard Illerhaus, Maria Teschler-Nicola, Wolfgang Recheis and Dieter zur Nedden. Projects were funded by the Austrian Science Foundation Project No. P14738 and the Austrian Federal Ministry of Education, Science and Culture Project No. GZ 200.093/I-VI/2004, and EU FP6 Marie Curie Actions MRTN-CT-2005–019564.

References

Bookstein, F. L. (1989). Principal warps: thin plate splines and the decomposition of deformations. *IEEE Transactions on Pattern Analysis and Machine Intelligence*, **1**: 567–85.

(1991). *Morphometric Tools for Landmark Data: Geometry and Biology*. Cambridge, New York: Cambridge University Press.

(1996). Combining the tools of geometric morphometrics. In Marcus, L. F. (ed.), *Advances in Morphometrics*. New York: Plenum Press, pp. 131–52.

(1997). Analyzing shape data from multiple sources: the role of the bending energy matrix. Proceedings of Leeds Applied Statistics Workshop. Leeds.

Conroy, G. C., Vannier M. W. and Tobias P. V. (1990). Endocranial features of *Australopithecus africanus* revealed by 2- and 3-D computed tomography. *Science*, **247**: 838–41.

Dart, R. A. (1959). The first *Australopithecus* cranium from the pink breccia at Makapansgat. *American Journal of Physical Anthropology*, **17**: 77–82.

(1962). The Makapansgat pink breccia australopithecine skull. *American Journal of Physical Anthropology*, **20**: 119–26.

Dryden, I. L. and Mardia, K. V. (1998). *Statistical Shape Analysis*. New York: John Wiley and Sons.

Falk, D. (1986). Evolution of cranial blood drainage in hominids: enlarged occipital/marginal sinuses and emissary foramina. *American Journal of Physical Anthropology*, **80**: 335–9.

(1993). Meningeal arterial patterns in great apes: implications for hominid vascular evolution. *American Journal of Physical Anthropology*, **92**: 81–97.

Falk, D. and Conroy, G. C. (1983). The cranial venous sinus system in *Australopithecus afarensis*. *Nature*, **306**: 779–81.

Falk, D., Redmond, J. C., Guyer, J. *et al.* (2000). Early hominid brain evolution: a new look at old endocasts. *Journal of Human Evolution*, **38**: 695–717.

Gibbons, A. (2002). Glasnost for hominids: seeking access to fossils. *Science* **297**: 1464–8.

Gorder, P. F. (2005). Toumai: reverse-engineering a human ancestor. *Computing in Science & Engineering (IEEE CS & AIP)*, **7**(4): 10–13.

Gunz, P. (2005). Statistical and geometric reconstruction of hominid crania. Reconstructing australopithecine ontogeny. Dissertation, Vienna: Department of Anthropology, University of Vienna.

Gunz, P., Mitteroecker, P. and Bookstein, F. L. (2005). Semilandmarks in three dimensions. In Slice, D. E. (ed.), *Modern Morphometrics in Physical Anthropology*, New York: Kluwer Press.

Gunz, P., Mitteroecker, P., Neubauer, S. *et al.* (2009). Principles for the virtual reconstruction of hominin crania. *Journal of Human Evolution*, **57**(1): 48–62.

Heuzé, Y., Marreiros, F., Verius, M. *et al.* (2008). The use of Procrustes average shape in the design of custom implant surface for large skull defects. *International Journal for Computer Assisted Radiology and Surgery*, **3**(Suppl 1): S283–S284.

Holloway, R. L. (1972). Australopithecine endocasts, brain evolution in the Hominoidea, and a model of hominid evolution. In Tuttle, R. (ed.), *The Functional and Evolutionary Biology of Primates*. Chicago: Aldine, pp. 185–204.

Holloway, R. L., Yuan, M. S., Broadfield, D. C. *et al.* (2002). Missing Omo L338y-6 occipital-marginal sinus drainage pattern: ground sectioning, computer tomography scanning, and the original fossil fail to show it. *Anatomical Record*, **266**: 249–57.

Kendall, D. (1984). Shape manifolds. Procrustean metrics and complex projective spaces. *Bulletin of the London Mathematical Society*, **16**: 81–121.

Kimbel, W. H. (1984). Variation in the pattern of cranial venous sinuses and hominid phylogeny. *American Journal of Physical Anthropology*, **63**: 243–63.

Lockwood, C. A. and Tobias, P. V. (1999). A large male hominin cranium from Sterkfontein, South Africa, and the status of *Australopithecus africanus*. *Journal of Human Evolution*,**36**: 637–85.

Mitteroecker, P., Gunz, P., Bernhard, M. *et al.* (2004). Comparison of cranial ontogenetic trajectories among great apes and humans. *Journal of Human Evolution*, **46**: 679–97.

Neubauer, S. (2005). The endocranium of *Australopithecus africanus* MLD 37/38: new insights using virtual anthropology. Diploma thesis, Vienna: Department of Anthropology, University of Vienna.

Neubauer, S., Gunz, P., Mitteroecker, P. *et al.* (2004). Three-dimensional digital imaging of the partial *Australopithecus africanus* endocranium MLD 37/38. *Canadian Association of Radiologists Journal*, **55**: 271–8.

Rak, Y., Kimbel, W. H. and Johanson, D. C. (1996). The crescent of foramina in *Australopithecus afarensis* and other early hominids. *American Journal of Physical Anthropology*, **101**: 93–9.

Recheis, W., Straub, M., Tschirren, J. *et al.* (2004). Matching lung volume data sets: a novel approach. *Collegium Antropologicum*, **28**(suppl. 2): 103–11.

Rohlf, F. J. and Slice, D. E. (1990). Extensions of the Procrustes method for the optimal superimposition of landmarks. *Systematic Zoology*, **39**: 40–59.

Rohlf, F. J. and Marcus, L. F. (1993). A revolution in morphometrics. *TREE*, **8**: 129–32.

Slice, D. E. (2005). *Modern Morphometrics in Physical Anthropology*. New York: Kluwer Press.

Spoor, F., Jeffery, N. and Zonneveld, F. (2000). Using diagnostic radiology in human evolutionary studies. *Journal of Anatomy*, **197**: 61–76.

Tobias, P. V. (1968). The pattern of venous sinus grooves in the robust australopithecines and other fossils and modern hominoids. In Peter, R., Schwartzfischer, F., Glowatzki, G. and Ziegelmayer, G. (eds.), *Anthropologie und Humangenetik*. Stuttgart: Gustav Fischer, pp. 1–10.

(2001). Re-creating ancient hominid virtual endocasts by CT-scanning. *Clinical Anatomy*, **14**: 134–41.

Weber, G. W. (2001). Virtual anthropology (VA): a call for glasnost in paleoanthropology. *Anatomical Record*, **265**: 193–201.

Weber, G. W. and Bookstein, F. L. (2011). *Virtual Anthropology: a Guide to a New Interdisciplinary Field*. Wien Springer Verlag.

Weber, G. W., Recheis, W., Scholze, T. and Seidler, H. (1998). Virtual anthropology (VA): methodological aspects of linear and volume measurements – first results. *Collegium Antropologicum*, **22**: 575–84.

Weber, G. W., Schäfer, K., Prossinger, H. *et al.* (2001). Virtual anthropology: the digital evolution in anthropological sciences. *Journal of Physiological Anthropology and Applied Human Sciences*, **20**: 69–80.

Weber, G. W., Neumaier, A. and Bookstein, F. L. (2002). Shape analysis and reconstruction using parameterised Skull Reference Models. *Collegium Antropologicum*, **26** (Suppl): 237.

Weber, G. W., Gunz, P., Mitteroecker, P. *et al.* (2003). Skull Reference Models (SRM) and the ontogeny of *A. africanus*. *American Journal of Physical Anthropology*. Suppl. **36**: 221–2.

Weber, G. W., Bookstein, F. L., Austin, J. *et al.* (2005). *European Virtual Anthropology Network – EVAN: EU FP6 Marie Curie Actions MRTN-CT-2005–019564*. Brussels: European Commission FP6.

Weber, G. W., Gunz, P., Mitteroecker, P. *et al.* (2006). External geometry of Mladec neurocrania compared with anatomically modern humans and Neandertals. In Teschler-Nicola, M. (ed.), *Early Modern Humans at the Moravian Gate*. Vienna, New York: Springer Verlag, pp. 453–71.

White, D. D. and Falk, D. (1999). A quantitative and qualitative reanalysis of the endocast from the juvenile *Paranthropus* specimen L338y-6 from Omo, Ethiopia. *American Journal of Physical Anthropology*, **110**: 399–406.

Zollikofer, C. P., Ponce de León, M. S., Lieberman, D. E. *et al.* (2005) Virtual cranial reconstruction of *Sahelanthropus tchadensis*. *Nature*, **434**: 755–9.

Part III

Modern human origins: patterns and processes

17   Body size in African Middle Pleistocene Homo

STEVEN E. CHURCHILL, LEE R. BERGER,

ADAM HARTSTONE-ROSE AND

B. HEADMAN ZONDO

Abstract

It is generally accepted that archaic humans of the African later Early and early Middle Pleistocene constituted the source population for anatomically modern humans. Due to limited fossil and archaeological records, however, relatively little is known about the morphology, behaviour and ecology of these presumed ancestors of modern humans. Fragmentary fossils (variously attributed to *Homo heidelbergensis*, *H. rhodesiensis* and *H. helmei*) from across Africa suggest that these archaic humans were both taller and more massive than their extant modern human descendants in this region, and perhaps had a body shape that was stockier and less 'nilotic' than seen among extant sub-Saharan Africans. Fragmentary fossils attributed to *Homo sapiens*, on the other hand, appear to represent individuals closer in body size to the means of recent sub-Saharan Africans. Since body size and shape are critical to the ecology, energetics and thermoregulatory adaptations of early humans, these differences in morphology may signal important adaptive changes at the time of the origins of modern humans. Comparative analyses of femoral and orbital dimensions support the claim that Middle Pleistocene Africans were of greater body size (both stature and mass) and had greater mass/stature ratios than modern Africans, and support the claim that early African *H. sapiens* were of smaller body size than their Middle Pleistocene ancestors.

Introduction

Body size is perhaps the single most important determinant of an organism's biology, affecting both physiological processes (McNab, 1983, 1990) and

African Genesis: Perspectives on Hominin Evolution, eds. Sally C. Reynolds and Andrew Gallagher. Published by Cambridge University Press. © Cambridge University Press 2012.

ecological relationships (Calder, 1984; Eisenberg, 1990). On the physiological side, body size and body shape are key determinants of the absolute and relative metabolic rates of organisms, and thus dictate caloric needs and dietary quality, as well as life history variables such as growth rate, fecundity and life span. Size is also central to thermoregulation, with smaller (in terms of mass) being better when it comes to maintaining thermal constancy in hot tropical or subtropical environments (see McNab, 1990; Ruff, 1994; Katzmarzyk and Leonard, 1998). Ecologically, body size is related to trophic strategies, substrate choice, and day range and home range sizes (Eisenberg, 1990). For Middle Stone Age humans engaged in at least some degree of carnivory, and who likely had to capture prey using close-range hunting tactics, body size (and strength) was likely related to prey size selection and hunting success rates with different sizes and types of prey (see Churchill and Rhodes, 2006). From a palaeoanthropological perspective, estimations of mass in extinct hominins, or the use of some skeletal proxy that reliably reflects mass, is requisite to studies of encephalisation or megadonty (Aiello and Wood, 1994; Kappelman, 1996; Ruff *et al.*, 1997), while knowledge of stature, mass and body proportions are critical to studies of locomotor kinematics and bioenergetics (Steudel-Numbers and Tilkens, 2004; Weaver and Steudel-Numbers, 2005; Churchill, 2006; Steudel-Numbers and Weaver, 2006).

The estimation of hominin body size has thus always been central to studies of adaptive evolution in paleoanthropology. Adaptive shifts attending the emergence of the genus *Homo*, which involved changes in dietary quality, brain size, tool use, ranging behaviour, thermoregulatory systems and life history variables, are thought to be intimately associated with the increase in body size (a *c.* 60% increase in mass in early African *Homo erectus* [*H. ergaster*] relative to gracile australopiths) reflected in the fossil record of early *Homo* (McHenry and Coffing, 2000; Aiello and Wells, 2002; Pontzer *et al.*, 2010). However, the recent recovery at Ileret (Kenya) of a 1.55 million-year-old partial cranium of a very small individual attributed to *H. erectus* (Spoor *et al.*, 2007), along with the attribution of a taxonomically uncertain pelvis from 1.4 to 0.9 million–year-old deposits at Gona (Ethiopia) to *H. erectus* (Simpson *et al.*, 2008), has raised uncertainty about the overall body size of early *Homo* and its degree of sexual dimorphism, and intensified debate on this issue (Ruff, 2007, 2010; Graves *et al.*, 2010). Similar uncertainty surrounds our knowledge of body size in the immediate ancestors of modern humans.

Archaic humans of the African Middle Pleistocene (AMP) variously attributed to *Homo heidelbergensis*, *H. rhodesiensis* and *H. helmei* appear, on the basis of a rather limited fossil record, to have been of great stature and body mass relative to humans living in sub-Saharan Africa today (Kappelman, 1996, 1997; Ruff *et al.*, 1997). The available fossil evidence suggests that large body size was the norm in Middle Pleistocene Africa, as well as in Europe (e.g. at the Sima de los Huesos site in Spain: Arsuaga *et al.*, 1999) and Asia (e.g. at Jinnushan, China: Rosenberg *et al.*, 2006). Human body size may have reached its apogee in Middle to early Late Pleistocene times, with a pan-Old World sample of 550 000 to 400 000-year-old fossils having a mean estimated mass some 16.7% larger than the worldwide mean of living humans (Ruff *et al.*, 1997).

There is, however, some evidence to suggest intrapopulational variation in body size, shape and robusticity in Africa during both the Middle Pleistocene and the preceding terminal Early Pleistocene: this evidence includes a small distal humerus from 600 000-year-old contexts at Bodo, Ethiopia (Conroy *et al.*, 2000), a relatively gracile ulna and other postcranial elements from 550 000 to 500 000-year-old deposits at Kapthurin, Kenya (Solan and Day, 1992; Fisher and McBrearty, 2002), and a very small 970 000 to 900 000-year-old partial cranium from Olorgesailie, Kenya (Potts *et al.*, 2004).

The fossil record for the earliest anatomically modern humans (*H. sapiens*) is likewise sparse, but sufficient to suggest that there was a reduction in mean body size in this group relative to earlier humans (with some degree of establishment of patterns of regional variation seen among recent African populations: see Grine *et al.*, 1998; Pfeiffer, 1998; Pearson, 2000). It is generally accepted that archaic humans of the African later Early and early Middle Pleistocene constituted the source population for *H. sapiens*, which suggests that a reduction in body mass and stature was a part of the morphological transition to anatomically modern humans. Since body size and shape are critical to the ecology, energetics and thermoregulatory adaptations of early humans, these differences in morphology may signal important adaptive changes at the time of the origins of modern humans.

We review here the AMP fossil evidence for body size and shape with the following objectives: (1) to test the hypothesis that Middle Pleistocene archaic humans were large relative to recent sub-Saharan Africans (Kappelman, 1996, 1997; Ruff *et al.*, 1997); (2) to test for possible differences in body proportions between AMP archaic humans and sub-Saharan African modern humans; and (3) to test the hypothesis that AMP early modern humans were similar in body size to recent sub-Saharan Africans.

Materials and methods

The estimation of body size parameters (mass and stature) in fossil hominins is fraught with difficulties: the choice of the appropriate methods and references samples are often unclear (and highly contested), and the error associated with such estimates is often large or, worse, unknowable (see Feldesman and Lundy, 1988; Feldesman *et al.*, 1990; McHenry, 1992; Hartwig-Scherer, 1993; Aiello and Wood, 1994; Feldesman and Fountain, 1996; Kappelman, 1996; Smith, 1996; Holliday and Ruff, 1997; Ruff *et al.*, 1997; Ruff, 2000; Pearson *et al.*, 2001; Auerbach and Ruff, 2004). To make matters worse, we are usually dealing with fragmentary remains whose original dimensions must be estimated before they can in turn be used to estimate body size parameters, compounding greatly the error inherent in the exercise. To avoid these difficulties, we use here direct comparisons of aspects of the skeleton that have been shown to be reasonably well correlated with body size in modern humans.

Our choice of variables was largely constrained by the vagaries of preservation in the AMP hominin fossil record. Reasonable estimates of femoral maximum length (FML: measurement M1 in Martin, 1928) can be made for a small number of individuals in this sample, and we used this measure as a proxy for stature in fossil hominins. Between-group variation in body proportions (femoral length to stature ratios) may make the comparison of fossil and recent human femoral lengths questionable (see Holliday and Ruff, 1997 vs. Feldesman and Fountain, 1996), given that body proportions of AMP hominins are currently unknown. In the absence of associated skeletal elements that will allow us to assess body proportions in hominins of the AMP, we must work under the assumption that between-group variation in FML is a reasonable indicator of between-group variation in stature. The lengths of other long bones are measurable or can be reasonably estimated in a few individuals, but do not provide a sufficient number of specimens to construct sample means: we simply report these long bone lengths, in relation to mean values from African modern human samples taken from the literature, where appropriate.

Femoral head anteroposterior diameter (FHAP: M19, Martin, 1928) can also be measured in a few of the AMP fossils, and we took this dimension as a reflection of body mass in our samples (since weight-bearing joints are expected, for mechanical reasons, to be proportional to mass: McHenry, 1992; Ruff *et al.*, 1997; Auerbach and Ruff, 2004). Because many of the AMP fossil specimens consist of isolated crania, we also used orbital area as a proxy for body mass. Orbital area (ORBA) has been shown to be perhaps the best single predictor among craniofacial variables of hominin body mass (Aiello and Wood, 1994; Kappelman, 1996). Following Aiello and Wood (1994) we calculated orbital area as the product of orbital height (distance between the upper and lower borders of the orbit, perpendicular to the long axis of the orbit and bisecting it: Howells, 1973) and breadth (distance from ectoconchion to dacryon, approximating the longitudinal axis that bisects the orbit into equal upper and lower parts: Howells, 1973), taken on the left orbit as possible given preservation. To explore between-group variation in body proportions, we used

Table 17.1. *Middle Pleistocene specimens.*

Specimen	Date (ka BP)	Dating references
Archaic humans (*Homo heidelbergensis, H. rhodesiensis, H. helmei*)		
Berg Aukas (Namibia)	Presumed Middle Pleistocene	Conroy *et al.*, 1993; Grine *et al.*, 1995
Bodo (Ethiopia)	640–550	Clark *et al.*, 1994
Cave of Hearths (South Africa)	Terminal Middle Pleistocene or early Late Pleistocene	Howell, 1978; Pearson and Grine, 1997
Eliye Springs (Kenya)	none	Brauer and Leakey, 1986a,b
Ileret [ER 999] (Kenya)	300	Brauer *et al.*, 1997
Florisbad (South Africa)	260	Grun *et al.*, 1996
Hoedjiespunt (South Africa)	350–200	Berger and Parkington, 1995; Churchill *et al.*, 2000
Kabwe [Broken Hill] (Zambia)	700–400	Klein, 1994; Rightmire, 1998
Kapthurin [Baringo] (Kenya)	550–500	Deino and McBrearty, 2002
Modern humans (*Homo sapiens*)		
Border Cave (South Africa)	115–90	see McBrearty and Brooks, 2000
Herto (Ethiopia)	160–154	Clark *et al.*, 2003
Jebel Irhoud (Morocco)	190–90	see McBrearty and Brooks, 2000
Klasies River Mouth (South Africa)	118–94	see McBrearty and Brooks, 2000
Ngaloba (Tanzania)	490–200	see McBrearty and Brooks, 2000
Omo I (Ethiopia)	195 (198–104)	McDougall *et al.*, 2005

the ratio of femoral head anteroposterior diameter to femoral maximum length (FHAP/FML). Since FHAP diameter is proportional to body mass and FML is proportional to stature, individuals with the 'nilotic' body builds characteristic of many sub-Saharan Africans (Roberts and Bainbridge, 1963) should have low ratios relative to individuals with more stocky builds.

Our sample includes every published Middle Pleistocene African specimen preserving measurable skeletal features reflective of body size (Table 17.1). The temporal period spanned by this sample is roughly *c.* 730 to 115 thousand years before present (ka BP): corresponding to Oxygen Isotope Stages 18–5e. The sample also includes specimens that are undated, such as those from Kabwe (Zambia) and Berg Aukas (Namibia), but which are widely presumed to derive from Middle Pleistocene contexts. The sample is divided into an archaic group, including fossils that have been attributed to *Homo heidelbergensis, H. rhodesiensis* and *H. helmei* and deriving from deposits roughly 700 to 190 ka, and a modern group, composed of specimens attributed to *H. sapiens* and dating roughly between 195 to 115 ka (with some specimens perhaps being as young as 90 ka). Following Day *et al.* (1980) and Hublin (1991, 1992), we include the material from Ngaloba (Tanzania) and Jebel Irhoud (Morocco) in the early modern human group. A number of relevant Middle Pleistocene craniofacial specimens – including Eyasi 1 (Tanzania), Ileret (ER 3884: Kenya), Ndutu (Tanzania), Omo II (Ethiopia), Saldanha (South Africa), Salé (Morocco), Singa (Sudan) and Thomas Quarries (Morocco) – are too incomplete to allow reliable estimation of orbital dimensions. We have purposefully limited the modern human sample to specimens of terminal Middle Pleistocene (and early last interglacial) age, as our intent was to examine possible body size changes at the time of the emergence of anatomically modern humans. In the interest of space, we have omitted discussion of the geochronological context, archaeological associations and taxonomic attributions of the specimens, and instead refer the reader to the review provided by McBrearty and Brooks (2000).

For comparative purposes, we also collected FML, FHAP and ORBA data on 100 Nguni South-African specimens (50 male, 50 female) from the Raymond Dart Collection of the University of the Witwatersrand, and 105 African-Americans (all male) from the Terry Collection at the National Museum of Natural History (Smithsonian Institution). Our choice of comparative samples was based in part on availability of skeletal material, and one might reasonably wonder how representative these samples are of the body size and shape of modern sub-Saharan Africans generally. Ruff (1994) provides mean mass and stature values for 17 non-pygmy, sex-specific samples of sub-Saharan Africans, which produce grand means for mass and stature of 55.8 ± 4.6 kg and 163.5 ± 6.3 cm, respectively. The mean mass and stature values can be used to derive an average mass/stature (M/S) ratio for each group (0.341 ± 0.020, n = 17). Mean mass and stature values for a mixed-sex sample of Zulu, who represent northern Nguni peoples, are provided by Hiernaux (1968). The Zulu population is on average both taller (166.1 ± 1.2 cm, n = 106) and more massive (66.8 ± 0.6 kg, n = 106) than the average sub-Saharan African sample (based on the grand means above), but this population does still fall within the range of mean values for both dimensions reported by Ruff (1994). In terms of M/S, the Nguni (at 0.402) appear to be considerably more stocky (less nilotic) than the groups reported by Ruff (1994), which might be a function of their greater distance from the equator (all of the groups reported by Ruff are tropical in origin, the Zulu are subtropical), and this should be borne in mind in the comparisons that follow. The African-American sample (n = 105) has a mean stature (based on cadaveric measurements) of 174.8 ± 7.8 cm and a mean cadaveric mass of 56.3 ± 8.3 kg. However, mass measurements on cadavers are notoriously unreliable (because of dehydration during storage, as well as high proportions in cadaver samples of individuals who were underweight at the time of death due to advanced age or long-term illness), and accordingly the mean mass reported here is likely to underestimate the mean body size of this population. This can be appreciated when one notes that the mean stature of the African-American sample falls at the high end of the range of means of male, non-pygmy, sub-Saharan Africans reported by Ruff (1994), while their mean mass falls at the low end of the reported means. Because of uncertainty about the appropriateness of the African-American sample as representatives of sub-Saharan African body size and shape, we limit all statistical tests to the Nguni comparative sample (and merely report the African-American values to enrich the comparative context).

Small fossil sample sizes (three to four specimens) make it difficult to detect potentially biologically significant differences between AMP and modern human samples (since non-significant statistical test results may simply be a function of a lack of statistical power). To overcome this limitation, we used the bootstrapped mean procedure in Resampling Procedures version 1.3 (Howell, 2001) to generate from the pooled-sex Nguni sample 5000 means of the same sample size as the fossil sample under consideration. This procedure allowed us to evaluate the probability of drawing at random (with replacement) a sample with a mean equal to that observed in the fossils from a population with the same mean and variance as our Nguni sample. Bootstrapped-t intervals were used to determine the 95% confidence intervals for the distribution of bootstrapped means, and we considered a fossil sample to be significantly different ($p \leq 0.05$) from the Nguni sample if it fell outside of the 95% confidence distribution of the bootstrapped means.

African Middle Pleistocene archaic humans

Berg Aukas (Namibia)

A single individual is represented by a single fossil element – the proximal half of a right femur – from the site of Berg Aukas in northern Namibia (Grine *et al.*, 1995). Based on the large size of the specimen, the individual is presumed to have been male. Grine and colleagues (1995) estimated the interarticular length of the femur, based on a multiple regression of six measures of the femoral head and neck on femoral length in a sample of African-Americans, to be 518 ± 16 mm. However, Trinkaus and colleagues (1999) argued, based on the morphology of the medial buttress, that Grine *et al.* (1995) had overestimated the length of the bone, and that FML would have been about 480 mm. Even at 480 mm, the Berg Aukas femur is large relative to extant Africans, falling more than 1.5 standard deviations above the mean FML in a large sample of males from the Dart Collection (448.5 ± 20.1 mm, $n = 175$: Feldesman and Lundy, 1988). The femoral head is large in this specimen (FHAP = 57.6 mm: Grine *et al.*, 1995), and from its dimensions Grine *et al.* (1995) estimated the mass of the Berg Aukas specimen to be *c.* 93 kg. Trinkaus *et al.* (1999) interpreted the exceedingly low neck shaft angle in Berg Aukas as reflecting exceptionally high levels of activity in this individual prior to maturity (see Trinkaus, 1993a), and argued that high levels of joint reaction forces at the hip prior to skeletal maturity had resulted in a femoral head that was large for the individual's mass. If this is correct, then the mass of Berg Aukas would have been less than predicted, perhaps considerably so, and not determinable based on the size of the femoral head. Trinkaus *et al.* (1999) also note that the mass predicted by Grine and colleagues (1995) would suggest body proportions that would be unusual for a human living in the hot and arid conditions of the Namib desert during the Middle Pleistocene. A number of observations militate against this interpretation. First, experimental studies indicate that joint sizes are largely developmentally irresponsive to their loading environment, and are 'ontogenetically constrained, and related to locomotor behavior at the species level and to body mass at the individual level' (Lieberman *et al.*, 2001: 266), as reflected in the relatively low levels of bilateral asymmetry seen in joint dimensions (Trinkaus *et al.*, 1994). Second, even in highly active populations (such as Neandertals: *Homo neanderthalensis*), body estimates derived from femoral head dimensions are largely concordant with 'morphometric' estimates using stature and body breadth (see supplementary data in Ruff *et al.*, 1997; Auerbach and Ruff 2004). Finally, consideration of other Middle Pleistocene archaic humans (see Kabwe, and discussion, below) tentatively suggest that body mass relative to stature may have been greater in AMP archaic humans, calling into question the assumption that they should correspond to body shape patterns seen in recent sub-Saharan Africans. Based on current evidence, we see little reason to suspect that the femoral head of Berg Aukas was disproportionately large relative to his mass.

Given an estimated FML of 480 mm, Berg Aukas would have a FHAP/FML ratio of 0.120, which is large in comparison to the ratios derived from the femora of two individuals from Kabwe (see below). If one accepts a femoral length estimate between 502 and 534 mm (the 68% confidence interval surrounding the bone length estimated by Grine *et al.*, 1995), the resultant FHAP/FML ratios are similar to those seen in the femora from Kabwe. Accordingly, we provisionally accept the femoral length estimate by Grine and colleagues as best representing the actual size and proportions of Berg Aukas.

Bodo (Ethiopia)

The remains from the Bodo localities in the Middle Awash region of Ethiopia include a partial cranium, a left parietal and a distal humeral fragment (Conroy *et al.*, 1978; Rightmire, 1996). The partial cranium (likely that of a male, based on the size and robusticity of the preserved cranial vault superstructures) preserves much of a facial skeleton, and allows measurement of orbital dimensions. Rightmire (1996) reported an orbital height of 39 mm and an orbital breadth of 47.5 mm, which produces an orbital area of 1852.5 mm^2.

Cave of Hearths (South Africa)

Remains from Cave of Hearths include a partial mandible and the proximal end of a right radius (Tobias, 1971; Pearson and Grine, 1997). The radius does not preserve enough of its length to provide a reasonable estimate of the total length of the bone, but we mention it here as it contributes to our understanding of body size and shape variation in the Middle Pleistocene. The radial head is relatively large (estimated to be 24 to 25 mm by Tobias, 1971), and is well above the means of recent African males. The radial tuberosity also has an area that is large relative to recent humans overall (Pearson and Grine, 1997). However, the neck of the specimen is short even when compared to recent African females (Tobias, 1971: Table 12), which implies a shorter bone and hence a relatively short individual. Taken together, the morphology of the Cave of Hearths' radius suggests a short but massive (robust and muscular) individual.

Eliye Springs (Kenya)

The cranium from Eliye Springs (ES-11693: Brauer and Leakey, 1986a,b) on western Lake Turkana preserves a portion of the facial skeleton, which, although heavily eroded, allows for estimated measures of the orbital dimensions. The sex of the specimen is not known. After checking facial dimensions taken from a cast of the specimen with those reported by Brauer and Leakey (1986b), we estimated orbital height at 36 mm and orbital breadth at 44 mm, producing an orbital area of 1584 mm^2.

Ileret (Kenya)

While the partial cranium (KNM-ER 3884) from Ileret does not preserve sufficient portions of the face to derive orbital dimensions, a partial left femur (KNM-ER 999: Day and Leakey, 1974) from the area does provide data pertinent to human body size. The sex of the individual represented by KNM-ER 999 is indeterminate. The specimen has an estimated bicondylar length of 470 to 500 mm (Trinkaus, 1993b), corresponding to a maximum length of roughly 490 to 520 mm.

Florisbad (South Africa)

A partial cranium from Florisbad (Dreyer, 1935; Rightmire, 1978; Clarke, 1985), of indeterminate sex, preserves portions of the right orbit sufficient to determine orbital dimensions. According to Rightmire (1978) the specimen has an orbital height of 36 mm and an orbital breadth of 51 mm, for an estimated ORBA of 1836 mm^2.

Hoedjiespunt (South Africa)

Middle Pleistocene human remains from Hoedjiespunt include isolated teeth and cranial vault fragments from a juvenile of about 12 years old (Berger and Parkington, 1995) and a right tibial diaphysis, likely deriving from the same individual (Churchill *et al.*, 2000). The bone lacks both its articular ends, but based on estimates following Steele and McKern (1969), supported by morphological comparisons with recent human tibiae, the complete bone had a maximum length of *c.* 367 ± 14 mm. Note, however, that had he or she survived to adulthood, the Hoedjiespunt juvenile would have experienced another 19 to 25% growth in tibial length (and stature generally: see Cameron *et al.*, 1982; Ruff and Walker, 1993; Humphrey, 1998), which with even the most conservative values (19% elongation of a tibia that was 353 mm long) suggests an adult tibial length (*c.* 420 mm) that would have been comparable to that of the specimen from Kabwe (see below). Even this conservative estimate is large relative to the mean tibial length of a large sample of South-African adult males (381 ± 23 mm, *n* = 175: Feldesman and Lundy, 1988), yet falls within the range of means reported on small samples of Ugandan adult males (397 to 433 mm; Allbrook, 1961).

Kabwe [Broken Hill] (Zambia)

Ten hominin fossils were discovered by miners in Middle Pleistocene deposits in the Broken Hill lead and zinc mine. The fossils were thought by Pycraft (1928) to derive from three individuals: a male represented by a cranium, a right distal humerus (E.898), a sacrum (E.688), a left partial os coxa (E.720), the proximal and distal ends of a left femur (E.689) and a complete left tibia

(E.691); a larger and presumably male individual represented by a partial right os coxa (E.719) and a right proximal femur (E.907); and a smaller, possibly female, individual represented by a fragment of maxilla. The associations suggested by Pycraft are supported by careful consideration of articular congruence, and by an overall concordance in size and robusticity of the elements (Churchill, pers. obs.), but cannot be definitively confirmed with present evidence.

The left femur (E.689) was estimated by Pycraft (1928), on the basis of overall size similarity to a single 'Bantu' specimen, to be 477 mm in total length. We obtained similar results using the equation for predicting femoral length from dimensions of the proximal femur as developed by Grine *et al.* (1995), using dimensions from Pycraft (1928) and measurements obtained from a high-quality epoxy cast of the specimen (after checking the dimensions of the cast against published values). The regression, which is based on 53 African-American femora and has a mean absolute prediction error of *c.* 16 mm, produces an estimated maximum length of 476 mm. Thus we can say (assuming similar proximal femoral to total femoral length dimensions in the reference sample and the Kabwe femur) that there is a 68% probability that the femur was between 460 and 492 mm in length. The specimen has an antero-posterior head diameter of 50 mm (Pycraft, 1928).

The dimensions of the larger right proximal femur (E.907) of the second individual predict a somewhat shorter maximum femoral length (470 ± 16 mm: using the equation of Grine *et al.*, 1995 and again using published dimensions along with measures taken on a cast) than that of the first individual. The larger femoral head (52 mm: Pycraft, 1928) in this individual suggests a body build that was somewhat more stocky than that of the first individual.

Using the FML values that fall at the 68% confidence limits of the estimated bone lengths, along with the published FHAP values, the taller but less massive individual represented at Kabwe had FHAP/FML ratios in the range of 0.102 to 0.109, while the shorter but more massive individual produces a range from 0.107 to 0.115, which are close to those observed in the Berg Aukas femur.

The Kabwe cranium, presumably belonging to the first individual, has an orbital height of 38 mm and an orbital breadth of 48 mm (Rightmire, 1978), for an estimated orbital area of 1824 mm^2.

Kapthurin [Baringo] (Kenya)

Solan and Day (1992) provide a description of the largely complete right ulna from deposits along the Kapthurin River west of Lake Baringo. The sex of the specimen is not known. The ulna lacks only the head and styloid process distally, and has a length from the proximal surface of the olecranon process to the pronator quadratus crest of 245 mm (Aiello *et al.*, 1999). Solan and Day (1992) estimated the maximum length at 272.8 mm, based on the minimum shaft diameter. Aiello and coworkers (1999) used four ulnar dimensions in a sample of modern humans to predict the length of the missing distal end of the specimen (pronator quadratus crest to distal articular surface) at 39 ± 5.56 mm, which gives an overall length (proximal olecranon process to distal articular surface) of 284 ± 5.6 mm. This falls at the low end of the range of mean values of ulnar length reported for males of various eastern African tribes (284 to 306 mm: Allbrook, 1961), and might suggest that the specimen represents a female.

Body size in AMP archaic humans

Based on femoral and orbital osteometric proxies for body mass and stature, we are unable to reject the hypothesis that AMP archaic humans were, on average, larger than recent sub-Saharan Africans. In terms of femoral dimensions (Table 17.2), mean values of both FHAP (as a proxy for body mass) and FML (as a proxy for stature) fall well above the mean values for Nguni and African-American males. The AMP archaic sample comprises only three specimens, one of which (Berg Aukas) has an unusually large femoral head; however, the FHAP values in the two specimens from Kabwe still exceed the FHAP means in the male Nguni and African-American samples. Comparison of AMP archaic human fossil means with the bootstrapped means derived from the pooled-sex Nguni sample show the fossils to be significantly larger than the recent Africans at $p \leq 0.05$ (Table 17.3). A possible caveat in accepting these results concerns the possibility that the AMP archaic sample may be composed entirely of males, which were compared to bootstrapped means drawn from a pooled-sex sample. However, given equal numbers of males and females in the Nguni sample, roughly 12.5% of the bootstrapped means represent subsamples composed only of Nguni males, and these means entered into the estimation of the 95% confidence intervals. Accordingly, we can reject the null hypothesis (size parity between AMP archaic and recent sub-Saharan African humans) within the reported confidence bounds.

The same pattern appears to hold for isolated long bones (for which sample sizes were too small to derive reasonable means). The single AMP archaic human upper limb element from which a reasonable measure of length can be derived (the ulna from Kapthurin) has a length that also exceeds the mean value in Nguni males (Table 17.4). It is important to note that the Nguni are tall relative to the grand mean for stature in sub-Saharan Africans (see discussion

Table 17.2. *Femoral dimensions in AMP hominins and modern humans.*

	FHAP (mm)	FML (mm)	FHAP/FML
AMP archaic humans			
Berg Aukas	57.6	502[a]	0.115
		518[b]	0.111
		534[c]	0.108
		480[d]	0.120
Ileret (KNM-ER 999)	–	490[e]	–
		505[e]	
		520[e]	
Kabwe E.689	50	460[a]	0.109
		476[b]	0.105
		492[c]	0.102
Kabwe E.907	52	454[a]	0.115
		470[b]	0.111
		486[c]	0.107
mean	53.2 ± 3.9	492.3 ± 23.0[f]	0.109 ± 0.003[g]
	–3	–4	–3
Nguni males	44.7 ± 2.4	457.3 ± 23.0	0.098 ± 0.005
	–50	–50	–50
Nguni females	39.9 ± 1.9	426.6 ± 18.2	0.093 ± 0.004
	–49	–50	–49
Nguni, pooled sexes	42.3 ± 3.2	441.9 ± 25.8 (100)	0.096 ± 0.005
	–99		–99
African American males	48.1 ± 2.6	477.6 ± 28.4	0.101 ± 0.006
	–105	–105	–105

[a] Lower 68% confidence limit value based on the regression in Grine *et al.*, 1995.
[b] Predicted femoral length based on the regression in Grine *et al.*, 1995.
[c] Upper 68% confidence limit value based on the regression in Grine *et al.*, 1995.
[d] Femoral length estimate of Trinkaus *et al.*, 1999.
[e] Low, midpoint and high end of range of maximum length estimates based on bicondylar length estimates in Trinkaus, 1993b.
[f] Mean of the predicted lengths of Berg Aukas, Kabwe E.689 and E.907 and the midpoint of the range of estimated values for Ileret.
[g] Mean of the ratios based on the predicted femoral lengths.

under 'Materials and methods'), and that the Kapthurin ulna is long (even using the lowest estimate of its length: see Table 17.4) relative even to males in the Nguni sample. However, some tropical Africans are also tall, and it is interesting to note that the length of Kapthurin ulna (even using the maximum estimate obtained) falls below most of the mean ulnar length values reported by Allbrook (1961) for Ugandan males. Thus while the Kapthurin ulna is long relative to those of sub-Saharan Africans generally, it is short relative to males from eastern equatorial Africa. The length of the tibia from Kabwe and the

Table 17.3. *Comparison of mean body size proxies in AMP archaic human samples with bootstrapped means from pooled-sex Nguni sample.*

Variable	AMP archaic humans[a]	Pooled-sex Nguni	Bootstrapped mean[b]	Lower 95% CI	Upper 95% CI
FHAP	53.2 ± 3.9[c] −3	42.3 ± 3.2 −99	41.0 [0.328]	40.0	41.9
FML	492.3 ± 23.0[c] −3	441.9 ± 25.8 −100	420.5 [4.038]	411.8	435.1
FHAP/FML	0.109 ± 0.003[c] −3	0.096 ± 0.005 −99	0.098 [0.001]	0.090	0.102
ORBA	1774 ± 127[c] −4	1411 ± 119 −98	1398 [37.9]	1209	1470

[a] Means as determined in Table 17.2.
[b] Based on 5000 means of a sample size equal to that of the fossil sample, drawn (with replacement) from the pooled-sex Nguni sample. The number in brackets denotes the standard error of the bootstrap distribution.
[c] Fossil sample significantly different from bootstrapped mean at $p \leq 0.05$.

Table 17.4. *Humeral and ulnar length in AMP hominins and modern humans.*

	Humeral maximum length (mm)	Ulnar maximum length (mm)
AMP archaic humans		
Kapthurin (KNM-BK 66)	–	278.4[a] 284.0[b] 289.6[c]
Early modern humans		
Klasies River Mouth	–	237.8[a] 248.6[b] 259.4[c]
Border Cave	333[b]	–
Omo 1	368[b]	
Nguni males	328.0 ± 14.8 (40)[d]	274.3 ± 16.8 (25)[e]
Nguni females	294.7 ± 15.0 (43)[d]	249.2 ± 10.8 (25)[e]

[a] Lower 68% confidence limit value of the estimated length (see text for details).
[b] Estimated length (see text for details).
[c] Upper 68% confidence limit value of the estimated length (see text for details).
[d] Data from Steyn and İşcan, 1999.
[e] Data from Churchill *et al.*, 1996.

Table 17.5. *Orbital area in AMP hominins and modern humans.*

	Orbital area (mm^2)
AMP archaic humans	
Bodo	1852.5
Eliye Springs	1584
Florisbad	1836
Kabwe	1824
mean (*n* = 4)	1774 ± 127
AMP modern humans	
Herto	1428
Jebel Irhoud 1	1615
Ngaloba (LH 18)	1353
mean (*n* = 3)	1465 ± 135
Nguni males (*n* = 50)	1448 ± 122
Nguni females (*n* = 48)	1373 ± 104
Nguni, sexes pooled (*n* = 98)	1411 ± 119
African-American males (*n* = 102)	1399 ± 127

projected adult length of the tibia from Hoedjiespunt also exceed (consider-ably) the mean value reported for South-African males (Feldesman and Lundy, 1988). While there may be a degree of sexual dimorphism or regional variation in body size that complicates the interpretation of some of these isolated elem-ents, they do not negate the observation of overall greater size (both mass and stature) in AMP archaic humans relative to recent sub-Saharan Africans.

Orbital dimensions, and by inference body mass, are also large in the AMP archaic human sample. The mean ORBA derived from four specimens far exceeds the mean male values in the Nguni and African-American samples (Table 17.5). Again, bootstrapped confidence intervals (Table 17.3) support the hypothesis of greater size in Middle Pleistocene archaic Africans.

Individual fossil and mean ratios of FHAP to FML can be found in Table 17.2. Despite their generally greater length, the available AMP archaic human femora have FHAP/FML ratios that are high relative to the Nguni and African-American samples, and bootstrap results (Table 17.3) show the archaic humans to be significantly larger in this ratio than the Nguni. Thus we cannot reject the hypothesis that AMP archaic humans had mass/stat-ure ratios that were larger than those generally seen in recent sub-Saharan Africans. Again, it is important to note that the Nguni are relatively stocky (high mass/stature ratios) compared to most sub-Saharan Africans (see dis-cussion above under 'Materials and methods'). Archaic humans of the AMP were stockier still. The short yet robust radius from Cave of Hearths also lends support to the observation of AMP archaic humans who had large M/S ratios relative to living sub-Saharan populations.

African Middle Pleistocene modern humans

Border Cave (South Africa)

Border Cave has produced remains of several individuals presumably from a Middle Stone Age context. These remains include a partial adult cranium, two adult fragmentary mandibles, the fragmentary postcranial skeleton of a child, and assorted adult and juvenile postcranial elements (De Villiers, 1973; Morris, 1992). The postcranial remains include the diaphysis of a right humerus and the proximal end of a right ulna (Morris, 1992; Pearson and Grine, 1996; Pfeiffer and Zehr, 1996). The ulna preserves only the proximal articulation and its complete length cannot be determined. However, in size it is a match for the proximal ulna from the SAS member of Klasies River Mouth (see below), suggesting that it derives from a small individual (see Pearson and Grine, 1996). The humerus lacks both articular ends, but its length has been estimated at 333 mm (Pfeiffer and Zehr, 1996). Given the poor preservation of the specimen, this estimate should be seen as highly tentative. If one accepts the estimate, the length of the Border Cave humerus would fall well above (more than two standard deviations) the mean length obtained in a small sample of Later Stone Age males from South Africa (Pfeiffer and Zehr, 1996).

Herto (Ethiopia)

The cranium of an adult male (BOU-VP-16/1) from Herto preserves the facial skeleton, and has an orbital height of 34 mm and an orbital breadth of 42 mm (White *et al.*, 2003: supplementary materials), producing an estimated orbital area of 1428 mm^2.

Jebel Irhoud (Morocco)

The site of Jebel Irhoud has produced the remains of at least four individuals, including cranial remains of two adults and a mandible and humerus from two juveniles (Hublin, 1991). The most intact cranium – Jebel Irhoud 1 (an individual of indeterminate sex) – retains complete orbits. Cohen (1996) provides orbital height and breadth dimensions of 33.0 mm and 23.0 mm, respectively, for Jebel Irhoud 1. We note that these values are 22 to 39% smaller than the dimensions suggested by our own cast of the specimen (42.5 mm and 38.0 mm). An error in the reported orbital dimensions is apparent when one considers the values for bi-orbital breadth (EKB) and interorbital breadth (DKB) obtained by Cohen (1996) on the same specimen. Since orbital breadth (OBB) is taken as the distance from dacryon to ectoconchion on the left orbit, EKB is the ectoconchion to ectoconchion distance, and DKB is the distance from dacryon to dacryon, then:

$$OBB \cong (EKB - DKB)/2$$

Based on Cohen's measures of EKB (115.0 mm) and DKB (30.5 mm), OBB should be about 42.3 mm. We thus feel justified in using the dimensions obtained from the cast in place of the values published by Cohen (1996). Use of these dimensions produces an estimated orbital area of 1615 mm^2.

Klasies River Mouth (South Africa)

Klasies River Main Site has produced numerous fragmentary human remains from Middle Stone Age contexts (Singer and Wymer, 1982; Rightmire and Deacon, 1991; Grine *et al.*, 1998). While the incomplete nature of most of this material precludes estimating body size, the cranial and postcranial material generally denotes individuals of relatively small body size (i.e. within the range of Later Stone Age Cape coastal peoples and historically known Khoisan: Grine *et al.*, 1998; Pfeiffer, 1998). A relatively small proximal right ulna from the SAS member supports this inference. The ulna has a maximum length, estimated from the dimensions of the proximal end using a regression based on recent African ulnae, of 248.6 ± 10.8 mm (Churchill *et al.*, 1996).

Ngaloba (Tanzania)

A partial cranium (LH 18) from Laetoli (Day *et al.*, 1980) preserves portions of the facial skeleton, which, following reconstruction (Cohen, 1996), allow estimation of orbital dimensions. The facial skeleton is relatively small, and Cohen provides an orbital height of 22.5 mm and a breadth of 31.5 mm based on the reconstruction. As was the case with Jebel Irhoud 1, the orbital dimensions reported by Cohen appear to be too small in light of dimensions from a cast of the specimen and measurements taken from scaled photos (Cohen, 1996). Also, as was the case with Jebel Irhoud, the bi-orbital and interorbital breadths reported by Cohen indicate an error in the reported orbital breadth (EKB =

109.0 mm, DKB = 30.0 mm, suggesting an OBB $\cong$ 39.5 mm: see rationale under the discussion of Jebel Irhoud, above). Based on casts and photos, we estimate orbital height and breadth to be 33 mm and 41 mm, respectively. This produces an estimated orbital area of 1353 mm².

Omo (Ethiopia)

The Kibish Formation at Omo has produced the remains of two adults, one of which (Omo 1) preserves a partial postcranial skeleton (Day, 1969; Day *et al.*, 1991). While the skeleton is highly fragmentary, Pearson (2000) estimates humeral length at 368 mm for Omo 1, and reports an estimated stature (using regressions from Trotter and Gleser, 1952) of 182 cm.

Body size in AMP modern humans

As with the AMP archaic human fossil record, the AMP modern human fossil sample is small, and provides even less information overall about body size (for example, not a single specimen preserves a measurable femoral head). Postcranial proxies for body mass are not preserved in this sample, but a small sample ($n = 3$) of crania with preserved orbits gives us some idea of the relative mass of these early modern Africans. Mean ORBA is large relative to the values obtained for both Nguni and African-American male samples (Table 17.5). However, bootstrapped confidence limits (based on 5000 samples of $n = 3$ drawn at random, with replacement, from the pooled-sex Nguni sample) do not allow us to reject the null hypothesis of mean size equivalence in the AMP modern human and Nguni samples (AMP mean ORBA: 1465 ± 135 mm², $n = 3$; pooled-sex Nguni mean: 1411 ± 119 mm², $n = 98$; bootstrapped mean, standard error and confidence intervals: 1397 mm², 44.2 mm², 1047–1491 mm²).

Isolated postcranial elements suggest that early modern human stature may have been quite variable across sub-Saharan Africa. Based on estimated humeral lengths, the eastern African specimen from Omo appears to have been tall relative to the Nguni (but likely within the range of humeral lengths of recent equatorial eastern Africans), while the individual from Border Cave appears to have had a stature comparable to (and perhaps slightly taller than) the average Nguni male (Table 17.4). The ulna from Klasies River Mouth, on the other hand, is relatively small, but is still close to the mean ulnar length for Nguni females (Table 17.4). The greater inferred stature of the eastern African individual from Omo, combined with the similarity in bone lengths between the southern African specimens and Nguni, may indicate the establishment of the recent human pattern of regional variation in stature by the early Late Pleistocene – a possibility whose testing which must await a richer AMP and early Late Pleistocene modern human fossil sample.

Discussion

The overall pattern suggests that there was a reduction in mean body size between archaic and early modern humans in Africa. African archaic humans appear to have been large (on average) relative to extant Africans, and this difference in size appears to have been associated with a difference in body shape. African Middle Pleistocene archaic humans appear to have been both more massive and to have had greater mass per unit stature (as reflected in FHAP to FML ratios: Table 17.2) than seen in extant sub-Saharan Africans. This suggests a shift away from the 'nilotic' body proportions seen in the Early Pleistocene *Homo ergaster* skeleton from Nariokotome (Ruff and Walker, 1993) and that characterise equatorial Africans today (Roberts and Bainbridge, 1963). Although on average taller, the African archaic humans are most similar in body build to Neandertals (and most likely other European and Asian archaic humans), which is surprising given that the wide bodies of Neandertals are generally interpreted as a reflection of thermoregulatory adaptation to cold climates (Ruff, 1991, 1993, 1994; Churchill, 2006).

While it is clear that mean annual temperatures dropped across Africa during glacial periods (Hostetler and Clark, 2000) and that upland areas may even have seen glacier formation (see review in Goudie, 1999), it is unlikely that Middle Pleistocene Africans experienced the extremes of cold endured by their European and Asian contemporaries. It is more likely that the stocky build inferred for archaic Middle Pleistocene Africans is a reflection of the combined effects of foraging ecology and thermoregulation. Archaic humans across the Old World were part of a large-bodied fauna (and can themselves be seen as the large-bodied versions of humans), which in Africa included a number of now extinct giant herbivores, such as the giant buffalo (*Pelorovis antiquus*), giant hartebeest (*Megalotragus priscus*), giant Cape zebra (*Equus capensis*) and various large-bodied warthogs (*Metrideochoerus andrewsi* and *M. compactus*) (Klein, 1984). The Middle Pleistocene ancestors of extant taxa were also larger than modern forms by 20% or more (Anderson, 1984; Peters *et al.*, 1994; Brink, 1993). Larger body size was likely selectively advantageous in cooler and drier Pleistocene environments with lower productivity, as larger animals have greater day-journey lengths and can better utilise lower quality food sources, and thus they monopolise a disproportionate amount of the energy in local ecosystems (Brown and Maurer, 1986). Perhaps more importantly, increased aridity and seasonality during glacial cycles (deMenocal, 2004) may have favoured larger individuals, since within species individuals with larger body sizes have greater fasting endurance (see review in Reynolds, 2007). During periods of reduced productivity, carnivore size would also be expected to increase due to thermo-regulatory factors, increased prey size, intensified aggressive interactions within the carnivore guild, and demands for both greater mobility and greater fasting endurance as carrying capacity diminished and secondary biomass was reduced. Carnivore body size is a key variable in prey body size selection and in success rates with prey of varying size, and for humans who were most likely engaged in close-range hunting of large-bodied herbivores (see Churchill, 1993, 2002; Schmitt *et al.*, 2003), body size – especially mass and muscularity – was no doubt critical to hunting success (Churchill and Rhodes, 2006). Thus to the extent that AMP archaic humans were predatory, they would have experienced selection pressures for larger size similar to those experienced by other members of the carnivore guild (see discussion in Churchill and Rhodes, 2006). Archaic humans may then have been patterning as do non-human herbivores and carnivores, such that body mass change was a response to the combined effects of temperature and productivity.

The terminal Pleistocene was marked by a global reduction in mamma-lian body sizes, which was in part due to the extinction of the megaher-bivores on most continents (Owen-Smith, 1987; Johnson, 2002; Brook and Bowman, 2004) and partly owing to reduction in average body size in taxa that remained extant (Anderson, 1984; Brink, 1993; Peters *et al.*, 1994). Global reduction in mammalian body size was likely a consequence of Holocene warming trends and attendant increases in ecological productivity across biomes, with perhaps some anthropogenic contribution to the extinc-tion of some megaherbivores (Owen-Smith, 1987; Johnson, 2002; Brook and Bowman, 2004). Within both herbivore and carnivore families, the greatest reductions in body size are centred on the interval between about 26 000 and 10 000 years ago (Owen-Smith, 1987; Estévez, 2004; Leonard *et al.*, 2007). What is interesting – and here the acquisition of better quality data for early modern humans is essential – is the hint that humans reduced in body size in the late Middle or early Late Pleistocene, some 200 000 to 100 000 years ahead of the mammalian curve. It is tempting to think that technological innovations – especially with respect to the development of projectile weap-ons that may have changed the dynamics of body-size ecology (Brooks *et al.*, 2005; Shea, 2006; Churchill and Rhodes, 2006) – or other behavioural/cul-tural innovations (such as changes in subsistence organisation or information networks: see McBrearty and Brooks, 2000) at the time of or shortly after the origins of modern humans was implicated in body-size reduction. Attempts to address this possibility, however, must await the recovery of a larger sample of archaic and early modern Africans.

Acknowledgements

We thank Andrew Gallagher, Colin Menter and Sally Reynolds for the invitation to participate in the African Genesis conference in celebration of Phillip V. Tobias's 80th birthday, and to contribute to this volume. Leslie Aiello, Andrew Gallagher, Fred Grine and Sally Reynolds provided comments that greatly improved the quality of this chapter, and Damiano Marchi provided help with the statistical analysis: to all of them we are very thankful. For access to skeletal material in the Raymond Dart Collection at the University of the Witwatersrand, we thank Kevin Kuykendall. Dave Hunt at the National Museum of Natural History, Smithsonian Institution, kindly allowed us access to skeletal material in the Terry Collection.

References

Aiello, L. C. and Wells, C. K. (2002). Energetics and the evolution of the genus *Homo*. *Annual Review of Anthropology*, **31**: 323–38.

Aiello, L. C. and Wood, B. A. (1994). Cranial variables as predictors of hominine body mass. *American Journal of Physical Anthropology*, **95**: 409–26.

Aiello, L. C., Wood, B., Key, C. *et al.* (1999). Morphological and taxonomic affinities of the Olduvai ulna (OH 36). *American Journal of Physical Anthropology*, **109**: 89–110.

Allbrook, D. (1961). The estimation of stature in British and East African Males. *Journal of Forensic Medicine*, **8**: 15–28.

Anderson, E. (1984). Who's who in the Pleistocene: a mammalian bestiary. In Martin, P. S. and Klein, R. G. (eds.), *Quaternary Extinctions: a Prehistoric Revolution*. Tucson, AZ: University of Arizona Press, pp. 40–89.

Arsuaga, J.-L., Lorenzo, C., Carretero, J.-M. *et al.* (1999). A complete human pelvis from the Middle Pleistocene of Spain. *Nature*, **399**: 255–8.

Auerbach, B. M. and Ruff, C. B. (2004). Human body mass estimation: a comparison of 'morphometric' and 'mechanical' methods. *American Journal of Physical Anthropology*, **125**: 331–42.

Berger, L. R. and Parkington, J. E. (1995). Brief communication: a new Pleistocene hominid-bearing locality at Hoedjiespunt, South Africa. *American Journal of Physical Anthropology*, **98**: 601–9.

Brauer, G. and Leakey, R. E. (1986a). A new archaic *Homo sapiens* cranium from Eliye Springs, West Turkana, Kenya. *Zeitschrift für Morphologie und Anthropologie*, **76**: 245–52.

(1986b). The ES-11693 cranium from Eliye Springs, west Turkana, Kenya (Hominidae). *Journal of Human Evolution*, **15**: 289–312.

Brauer, G., Yokoyama, Y., Falgueres, C. *et al.* (1997). Modern human origins back-dated. *Nature*, **386**: 337–8.

Brink, J. S. (1993). Postcranial evidence for the evolution of the black wildebeest, *Connochaetes gnou*: an exploratory study. *Palaeontologica Africana*, **30**: 61–9.

Brook, B. W. and Bowman, D. M. J. S. (2004). The uncertain blitzkrieg of Pleistocene megafauna. *Journal of Biogeography*, **31**: 517–23.

Brooks, A. S., Yellen, J. E., Nevell, L. *et al.* (2005). Projectile technologies of the African MSA: implications for modern human origins. In Hovers, E. and Kuhn, S. (eds.), *Transitions Before the Transition: Evolution and Stability in the Middle Paleolithic and Middle Stone Age*. New York: Kluwer, pp. 233–55.

Brown, J. H. and Maurer, B. A. (1986). Body size, ecological dominance and Cope's rule. *Nature*, **324**: 248–50.

Calder, W. A. (1984). *Size, Function, and Life History*. Cambridge, MA: Harvard University Press.

Cameron, N., Tanner, J. M. and Whitehouse, R. H. (1982). A longitudinal analysis of the growth of limb segments in adolescence. *Annals of Human Biology*, **9**: 211–20.

Churchill, S. E. (1993). Weapon technology, prey size selection, and hunting methods in modern hunter-gatherers: implications for hunting in the Palaeolithic and Mesolithic. In Peterkin, G. L., Bricker, H. M. and Mellars, P. A. (eds.), *Hunting and Animal Exploitation in the Later Palaeolithic and Mesolithic of Europe*. Volume 4. American Anthropological Association Archaeological Paper. pp. 11–24.

(2002). Of assegais and bayonets: reconstructing prehistoric spear use. *Evolutionary Anthropology*, **11**: 185–6.

(2006). Bioenergetic perspectives on Neandertal thermoregulatory and activity budgets. In Havarti, K. and Harrison, T. (eds.), *Neanderthals Revisited: New Approaches and Perspectives*. New York: Springer, pp. 113–33.

Churchill, S. E. and Rhodes, J. A. (2006). How strong were the Neandertals? Leverage and muscularity at the shoulder and elbow in Mousterian foragers. *Periodicum Biologorum*, **108**: 457–70.

Churchill, S. E., Pearson, O. M., Grine, F. E. *et al.* (1996). Morphological affinities of the proximal ulna from Klasies River Main Site: archaic or modern? *Journal of Human Evolution*, **31**: 213–37.

Churchill, S. E., Berger, L. R. and Parkington, J. (2000). A Middle Pleistocene human tibia from Hoedjiespunt, Western Cape, South Africa. *South African Journal of Science*, **96**: 367–8.

Clark, J. D., De Heinzelin, J., Schick, K. D. *et al.* (1994). African *Homo erectus*: old radiometric ages and young Oldowan assemblages in the Middle Awash Valley, Ethiopia. *Science*, **264**: 1907–10.

Clark, J. D., Beyene, Y., WoldeGabriel, G. *et al.* (2003). Stratigraphic, chronological and behavioral contexts of Pleistocene *Homo sapiens* from Middle Awash, Ethiopia. *Nature*, **423**: 747–52.

Clarke, R. J. (1985). A new reconstruction of the Florisbad cranium, with notes on the site. In Delson, E. (ed.), *Ancestors: the Hard Evidence*. New York: Alan R. Liss, Inc. pp. 301–5.

Cohen, P. (1996). Fitting a face to Ngaloba. *Journal of Human Evolution*, **30**: 373–9.

Conroy, G. C., Jolly, C. J., Cramer, D. *et al.* (1978). Newly discovered fossil hominid skull from the Afar depression, Ethiopia. *Nature*, **276**: 67–70.

Conroy, G. C., Pickford, M., Senut, B. *et al.* (1993). Diamonds in the desert: the discovery of *Otavipithecus namibiensis*. *Evolutionary Anthropology*, **2**: 46–52.

Conroy, G. C., Weber, G. W., Seidler, H. *et al.* (2000). Endocranial capacity of the Bodo cranium determined from three-dimensional computed tomography. *American Journal of Physical Anthropology*, **113**: 111–18.

Day, M. H. (1969). Omo human skeletal remains. *Nature*, **222**, 1135–8.

Day, M. H. and Leakey, R. E. F. (1974). New evidence of the genus *Homo* from East Rudolf, Kenya (III). *American Journal of Physical Anthropology*, **41**: 367–80.

Day, M. H., Leakey, M. D. and Magori, C. (1980). A new hominid fossil skull (L.H.18) from the Ngaloba Beds, Laetoli, northern Tanzania. *Nature*, **284**: 55–6.

Day, M. H., Twist, M. H. C. and Ward, S. (1991). Les vestiges post-craniens d'Omo I (Kibish). *L'Anthropologie*, **95**: 595–610.

deMenocal, P. B. (2004). African climate change and faunal evolution during the Plio-Pleistocene. *Earth and Planetary Science Letters*, **220**: 3–24.

De Villiers, H. (1973). Human skeletal remains from border cave, Ingwavuma District, KwaZulu. *Annals of the Transvaal Museum*, **28**: 229–56.

Deino, A. and McBrearty, S. (2002). 40Ar/(39)Ar dating of the Kapthurin Formation, Baringo, Kenya. *Journal of Human Evolution*, **42**: 185–210.

Dreyer, T. F. (1935). A hominid skull from Florisbad, Orange Free State, with a note on the endocranial cast by C.U. Ariens Kappers. *Proceedings of the Amsterdam Academy of Sciences*, **38**: 119–28.

Eisenberg, J. F. (1990). The behavioral/ecological significance of body size in the Mammalia. In Damuth, J. and MacFadden, B. J. (eds.), *Body Size in Mammalian Paleobiology: Estimation and Biological Implications*. Cambridge: Cambridge University Press, pp. 25–37.

Estévez, J. (2004). Vanishing carnivores: what can the disappearance of large carnivores tell us about the Neanderthal world? *International Journal of Osteoarchaeology*, **14**: 190–200.

Feldesman, M. R. and Fountain, R. L. (1996). 'Race' specificity and the femur/stature ratio. *American Journal of Physical Anthropology*, **100**: 207–24.

Feldesman, M. R. and Lundy, J. K. (1988). Stature estimates for some African Plio-Pleistocene fossil hominids. *Journal of Human Evolution*, **17**: 583–96.

Feldesman, M. R., Kleckner, J. G. and Lundy, J. K. (1990). The femur/stature ratio and estimates of stature in mid- and late-Pleistocene fossil hominids. *American Journal of Physical Anthropology*, **83**: 359–72.

Fisher, R. and McBrearty, S. (2002). The comparative morphology of hominin postcranial remains from the Kapthurin Formation, Baringo District, Kenya. *American Journal of Physical Anthropology*, **117**: 70.

Goudie, A. S. (1999). The Ice Age in the tropics and its human implications. In Slack, P. (ed.), *Environments and Historical Change*. Oxford: Oxford University Press, pp. 10–32.

Graves, R. R., Lupo, A. C., McCarthy, R. C. *et al.* (2010). Just how strapping was KNM-WT 15000? *Journal of Human Evolution*, **59**: 542–54.

Grine, F. E., Jungers, W. L., Tobias, P. V. *et al.* (1995). Fossil *Homo* femur from Berg Aukas, Northern Namibia. *American Journal of Physical Anthropology*, **97**: 151–85.

Grine, F. E., Pearson, O. M., Klein, R. G. *et al.* (1998). Additional human fossils from Klasies River Mouth, South Africa. *Journal of Human Evolution*, **35**: 95–107.

Grun, R., Brink, J. S., Spooner, N. A. *et al.* (1996). Direct dating of Florisbad hominid. *Nature*, **382**: 500–1.

Hartwig-Scherer, S. (1993). Body weight prediction in early fossil hominids: towards a taxon-'independent' approach. *American Journal of Physical Anthropology*, **92**: 17–36.

Hiernaux, J. (1968). *La Diversité Humaine en Afrique Subsaharienne: Recherches Biologiques*. Bruxelles: Institut de Sociologie, Université Libre de Bruxelles.

Holliday, T. W. and Ruff, C. B. (1997). Ecogeographical patterning and stature prediction in fossil hominids: comment on M. R. Feldesman and R. L. Fountain, *American Journal of Physical Anthropology* (1996) 100:207–224. *American Journal of Physical Anthropology*, **103**: 137–40.

Hostetler, S. W. and Clark, P. U. (2000). Tropical climate at the last glacial maximum inferred from glacier mass-balance modeling. *Science*, **290**: 1747–50.

Howell, D. C. (2001). Resampling Procedures v. 1.3. Freeware available at www.uvm.edu/~dhowell/StatPages.

Howell, F. C. (1978). Hominidae. In Maglio, V. and Cooke, H. B. S. (eds.), *Evolution of African Mammals*. Cambridge, MA: Harvard University Press, pp. 154–248.

Howells, W. W. (1973). *Cranial Variation in Man*. Cambridge, MA: Peabody Museum.

Hublin, J. J. (1991). L'Emergence Des Homo Sapiens Archaiques: Afrique du Nord-Ouest et Europe occidentale. These d'Etat, Université de Bordeaux 1, Bordeaux.

(1992). Recent human evolution in Northern Africa. *Philosophical Transactions of the Royal Society of London*, B, **337**: 185–192.

Humphrey, L. T. (1998). Growth patterns in the modern human skeleton. *American Journal of Physical Anthropology*, **105**: 57–72.

Johnson, C. N. (2002). Determinants of loss of mammal species during the Late Quaternary 'megafauna' extinctions: life history and ecology, but not body size. *Proceedings of the Royal Society of London*, B, **269**: 2221–7.

Kappelman, J. (1996). Evolution of body mass and relative brain size in fossil hominids. *Journal of Human Evolution*, **30**: 243–76.

(1997). They might be giants. *Nature*, **387**: 126–7.

Katzmarzyk, P. T. and Leonard, W. R. (1998). Climatic influences on human body size and proportions: ecological adaptations and secular trends. *American Journal of Physical Anthropology*, **106**: 483–503.

Klein, R. G. (ed.) (1984a). *The Large Mammals of Southern Africa: Late Pliocene to Recent*. Rotterdam: Balkema.

(ed.) (1994b) *Southern Africa before the Iron Age*. Englewood Cliffs, NJ: Prentice Hall.

Leonard, J. A., Vilà, C., Fox-Dobbs, K. *et al.* (2007). Megafaunal extinctions and the disappearance of a specialized wolf ecomorph. *Current Biology*, **17**: 1146–50.

Lieberman, D. E., Devlin, M. J. and Pearson, O. M. (2001). Articular area responses to mechanical loading: effects of exercise, age, and skeletal location. *American Journal of Physical Anthropology*, **116**: 266 – 77.

Martin, R. (1928). *Lehrbuch der Anthropologie*, 2nd edition. Jena: Verlag von Gustav Fischer.

McBrearty, S. and Brooks, A. S. (2000). The revolution that wasn't: a new interpretation of the origin of modern human behavior. *Journal of Human Evolution*, **39**: 453–563.

McDougall, I., Brown, F. H. and Fleagle, J. G. (2005). Stratigraphic placement and age of modern humans from Kibish, Ethiopia. *Nature*, **433**: 733–6.

McHenry, H. M. (1992). Body size and proportions in early hominids. *American Journal of Physical Anthropology*, **87**: 407–31.

McHenry, H. M. and Coffing, K. (2000). *Australopithecus* to *Homo*: transformations in body and mind. *Annual Review of Anthropology*, **29**: 125–46.

McNab, B. K. (1983). Energetics, body size, and the limits to endothermy. *Journal of Zoology*, **199**: 1–29.

(1990). The physiological significance of the body size. In Damuth, J. and MacFadden, B. J. (eds.), *Body Size in Mammalian Paleobiology: Estimation and Biological Implications*. Cambridge: Cambridge University Press, pp. 11–23.

Morris, A. G. (1992). Biological relationships between Upper Pleistocene and Holocene populations in southern Africa. In Brauer, G and Smith, F. H. (eds.), *Continuity or Replacement. Controversies in* Homo sapiens *Evolution*. Rotterdam: Balkema, pp. 131–43.

Owen-Smith, N. (1987). Pleistocene extinctions: the pivotal role of megaherbivores. *Paleobiology*, **13**: 351–62.

Pearson, O. M. (2000). Postcranial remains and the origin of modern humans. *Evolutionary Anthropology*, **9**: 229–47.

Pearson, O. M. and Grine, F. E. (1996). Morphology of the Border Cave hominid ulna and humerus. *South African Journal of Science*, **92**: 231–6.

(1997). Re-analysis of the hominid radii from Cave of Hearths and Klasies river mouth, South Africa. *Journal of Human Evolution*, **32**: 577–92.

Pearson, O., Jungers, W., Grine, F. *et al.* (2001). The reliability of estimates of hominin body mass derived from bi-iliac breadth and stature. *American Journal of Physical Anthropology*, suppl. **32**: 118.

Peters, J., Gautier, A., Brink, J. S. *et al.* (1994). Late Quaternary extinction of ungulates in sub-Saharan Africa: a reductionist's approach. *Journal of Archaeological Science*, **21**: 17–28.

Pfeiffer, S. (1998). Klasies River Mouth post-cranial comparisons. *Journal of Human Evolution*, **34**: A17.

Pfeiffer, S. and Zehr, M. K. (1996). A morphological and histological study of the human humerus from Border Cave. *Journal of Human Evolution*, **31**: 49–59.

Pontzer, H., Rolian, C., Rightmire, G. P. *et al.* (2010). Locomotor anatomy and biomechanics of the Dmanisi hominins. *Journal of Human Evolution*, **58**: 492–504.

Potts, R., Behrensmeyer, A. K., Deino, A. *et al.* (2004). Small mid-Pleistocene hominin associated with east African Acheulean technology. *Science*, **305**: 75–8.

Pycraft, W. P. (1928). Rhodesian Man: description of the skull and other human remains from Broken Hill. In Pycraft, W. P., Elliot Smith, G., Yearsley, M. *et al.* (eds.), *Rhodesian Man and Associated Remains*. London: British Museum, pp. 1–51.

Reynolds, S. C. (2007). Mammalian body size changes and Plio-Pleistocene environmental shifts: implications for understanding hominin evolution in eastern and southern Africa. *Journal of Human Evolution*, **53**: 528–48.

Rightmire, G. P. (1978). Florisbad and human population succession in Southern Africa. *American Journal of Physical Anthropology*, **48**: 475–86.

(1996). The human cranium from Bodo, Ethiopia: evidence for speciation in the Middle Pleistocene? *Journal of Human Evolution*, **31**: 21–39.

(1998). Human evolution in the Middle Pleistocene: the role of *H. heidelbergensis*. *Evolutionary Anthropology*, **6**: 218–27.

Rightmire, G. P. and Deacon, H. J. (1991). Comparative studies of Late Pleistocene human remains from Klasies River Mouth, South Africa. *Journal of Human Evolution*, **20**: 131–56.

Roberts, D. F. and Bainbridge, D. R. (1963). Nilotic physique. *American Journal of Physical Anthropology*, **21**: 341–70.

Rosenberg, K. R., Lu, Z. and Ruff, C. B. (2006). Body size, body proportions, and encephalization in a Middle Pleistocene archaic human from northern China. *Proceedings of the National Academy of Science*, **103**: 3552–6.

Ruff, C. and Walker, A. C. (1993). Body size and shape. In Walker, A. C. and Leakey, R. E. (eds.), *The Nariokotome Skeleton*. Cambridge: Harvard University Press, pp. 234–65.

Ruff, C. B. (1991). Climate and body shape in hominid evolution. *Journal of Human Evolution*, **21**: 81–105.

(1993). Climatic adaptation and hominid evolution: the thermoregulatory imperative. *Evolutionary Anthropology*, **2**: 53–9.

(1994). Morphological adaptation to climate in modern and fossil hominids. *Yearbook of Physical Anthropology*, **37**: 65–107.

(2000). Body mass prediction from skeletal frame size in elite athletes. *American Journal of Physical Anthropology*, **113**: 507–17.

(2007). Body size prediction from juvenile skeletal remains. *American Journal of Physical Anthropology*, **133**: 698–716.

(2010). Body size and body shape in early hominins: implications of the Gona pelvis. *Journal of Human Evolution*, **58**: 166–78.

Ruff, C. B., Trinkaus, E. and Holliday, T. W. (1997). Body mass and encephalization in Pleistocene *Homo*. *Nature*, **387**: 173–6.

Schmitt, D. O., Churchill, S. E. and Hylander, W. L. (2003). Experimental evidence concerning spear use in Neandertals and early modern humans. *Journal of Archaeological Science*, **30**: 103–14.

Shea, J. J. (2006). The origins of lithic projectile point technology: evidence from Africa, the Levant, and Europe. *Journal of Archaeological Science*, **33**: 823–46.

Simpson, S. W., Quade, J., Levin, N. E. *et al.* (2008). A female *Homo erectus* pelvis from Gona, Ethiopia. *Science*, **322**: 1089–92.

Singer, R. and Wymer, J. J. (1982). *The Middle Stone Age at Klasies River Mouth in South Africa*. Chicago: University of Chicago Press.

Smith, R. J. (1996). Biology and body size in human evolution: statistical inference misapplied. *Current Anthropology*, **37**: 451–81.

Solan, M. and Day, M. H. (1992). The Baringo (Kapthurin) ulna. *Journal of Human Evolution*, **22**: 307–13.

Spoor, F., Leakey, M. G., Gathogo, P. N. *et al.* (2007). Implications of new early *Homo* fossils from Ileret, east of Lake Turkana, Kenya. *Nature*, **448**: 688–91.

Steele, D. G. and McKern, T. W. (1969). A method for assessment of maximum long bone length and living stature from fragmentary long bones. *American Journal of Physical Anthropology*, **31**: 215–27.

Steudel-Numbers, K. and Weaver, T. D. (2006). Froude number corrections in anthropological studies. *American Journal of Physical Anthropology*, **131**: 27–32.

Steudel-Numbers, K. L. and Tilkens, M. J. (2004). The effect of lower limb length on the energetic cost of locomotion: implications for fossil hominins. *Journal of Human Evolution*, **47**: 95–109.

Steyn, M. and İşcan, M. Y. (1999). Osteometric variation in the humerus: sexual dimorphism in South Africans. *Forensic Science International*, **106**: 77–85.

Tobias, P. V. (1971). Human skeletal remains from the Cave of Hearths, Makapansgat, Northern Transvaal. *American Journal of Physical Anthropology*, **34**: 335–67.

Trinkaus, E. (1993a). Femoral neck-shaft angles of the Qafzeh-Skhul early modern humans, and activity levels among immature Near Eastern Paleolithic hominids. *Journal of Human Evolution*, **25**: 393–416.

(1993b). A note on the KNM-ER 999 hominid femur. *Journal of Human Evolution*, **24**: 493–504.

Trinkaus, E., Churchill, S. E. and Ruff, C. B. (1994). Postcranial robusticity in *Homo*. II: Humeral bilateral asymmetry and bone plasticity. *American Journal of Physical Anthropology*, **93**: 1–34.

Trinkaus, E., Ruff, C. B. and Conroy, G. C. (1999). The anomalous archaic *Homo* femur from Berg Aukas, Namibia: a biomechanical assessment. *American Journal of Physical Anthropology*, **110**: 379–91.

Trotter, M. and Gleser, G. C. (1952). Estimation of stature from long bones of American whites and Negroes. *American Journal of Physical Anthropology*, **10**: 463–514.

Weaver, T. D. and Steudel-Numbers, K. (2005). Does climate or mobility explain the differences in body proportions between Neandertals and their Upper Paleolithic successors? *Evolutionary Anthropology*, **14**: 218–23.

White, T. D., Asfaw, B., DeGusta, D. *et al.* (2003). Pleistocene *Homo sapiens* from Middle Awash, Ethiopia. *Nature*, **423**: 742–7.

18 *The African origin of recent humanity*

MILFORD H. WOLPOFF AND

SANG-HEE LEE

Abstract

It is broadly agreed that all recent/living human populations ultimately descend
from Africans. In this chapter we examine new anatomical and genetic evidence
that addresses one way this could be the case, a unique recent African origin for
living humanity (meaning that all living humans descend from recent Africans
and only descend from recent Africans, by species replacement). The male cranium from Herto (BOU-VP-16/1) is useful for examining this issue. Its description (White *et al.*, 2003) raised questions about both the origin of recent humans
and the fate of the Neandertals. Together, these two questions address the pattern of recent population evolution because if the ancestry of recent populations
is uniquely African, Neandertals can have played no significant role in their
evolution. The hypothesis we examine here is whether Neandertals were the
end point of a species-lineage that was distinct from a different African species-
lineage, including Herto, leading to recent humans. We examine the possibility
of unique African origins by assuming this hypothesis is correct, and testing for
the presence of evidence addressing its consequences. Specimens on a distinct
Neandertal species-lineage are expected to be more different from Herto than
they are from the common ancestors of Herto and Neandertals because there is
more genetic distance from Herto to the Neandertals than there is from either
Herto or the Neandertals to their common ancestor. We quantify the similarity
of the large Herto male to 12 other mostly or fully complete Middle and Late
Pleistocene male crania from Africa and other regions of the world, to test for
this pattern of similarity. We also examine whether similarities between Herto
and other Pleistocene Africans reveal a distinct African palaeo-deme.[1] We show
that comparisons of other crania to Herto indicate that the penecontemporary
Europeans are not evolving in a different direction than the Africans. This result

[1] A palaeo-deme as used here is a 'designation, reflecting inclusive genealogically related
geographic group(s)' (Howell, 1999: 203).

African Genesis: Perspectives on Hominin Evolution, eds. Sally C. Reynolds and Andrew
Gallagher. Published by Cambridge University Press. © Cambridge University Press 2012.

is supported by direct evidence of interbreeding between members of this Herto-descendent palaeo-deme and Neandertals, found in the analysis of Neandertal nuclear DNA. There is demonstrable, significant influence of the Neandertal genome on human genetic variation today (Green *et al.*, 2010; Yotova *et al.*, 2011). The Neandertal influence involves genes that evolved in Neandertals and other archaic populations and spread through non-African populations under selection. These data refute the hypothesis of a Neandertal species-lineage and support the interpretation of an African palaeo-deme in the Pleistocene that is one of the ancestors of living humans; hence, the African origin of recent humanity is one of several sources. The African palaeo-deme is not a species-lineage, and Neandertals are also among the ancestors of living Europeans and other non-African populations. Their influence is such that our ancestors would not have become modern without them.

> The claim may be advanced that in the Afro-Asian land-mass, the true placement of the Garden of Eden, in the sense of the cradle of recent humanity, was in Africa, but it is far more likely to have been in ancient, 1 mya Africa, than in recent, 200,000 year-old Africa.
>
> (Tobias, 1995: 164)

Introduction: Africa and human evolution

Africa has played a key role in the evolution of recent humanity, as it has throughout human evolution. For the most part this understanding was not appreciated in the earlier half of the twentieth century, when it was quite rare to focus on the origin of recent humanity as a particular question of interest (but see Dart, 1940). Modern thinking on the subject began with a seminal paper by Protsch (1975), summarising his dissertation. Protsch's argument was that people resembling recent humans were found in Africa earlier than anywhere else, and therefore 'modern humans' must have originated there. While not all of Protsch's work has held up over the years, this paper has done so and many, perhaps most, of the dates he proposed have withstood the test of time. This fundamental point was accepted and repeated by some of Protsch's German colleagues; for instance Bräuer (1978, 1981, 1984), who came to argue that Europeans must be of African descent, much as Dart (1940) had proposed earlier, but armed with evidence from the dates Protsch published.

In arguing for African origins, neither Protsch nor Bräuer contended that early humans of modern form in Africa implied unique African origins; theories of modern human origins had not yet diverged on this point. Multiregional evolution (Wolpoff *et al.*, 1984; Wolpoff, 1989), in its centre-and-edge contention, also proposed that Africa was a significant source of new genetic variation during human evolution, because for most of the Pleistocene the predominant direction of gene flow was from the more densely occupied African centre to the more sparsely occupied peripheries of the human range. The dominance of African population size for most of the Pleistocene has widely discussed consequences (Harpending, 1996; Eller, 2001; Relethford, 2001, 2003; Hawks and Wolpoff, 2003).

There was an older, alternative hypothesis about modern human origins, interpreting recent and living humans as representing a distinct species with great antiquity (Hawks and Wolpoff, 2003 and references therein). The idea of a unique evolutionary origin for a modern human species (*Homo sapiens sapiens*) also originated in the German-speaking world, and there is a strong intellectual thread from Haeckel (1883) and his theory of human origins on the 'lost continent' of Lemuria, to Howells (1942), and then to Tattersall (1995). The central contention in this thread is that recent humans are the latest populations of an ancient species evolving in parallel with other hominid species, now extinct.

What brought African origins and human origins together was the contention of recency (Proctor, 2003) – the theory of an African origin for a recently evolved modern human species. The most important basis for this synthesis was the interpretation of mitochondrial DNA studies (reviewed by Tobias, 1995) that the ancestors of recent humans first appeared in Africa and replaced other populations because they were a new species that could not, and did not, interbreed (Stoneking and Cann, 1989). The subsequent explanation that replacement without mixture accounted for recent populational origins was quickly accepted by some palaeoanthropologists, beginning with Stringer and Andrews (1988). In this chapter we examine new anatomical and genetic evidence that addresses the issue of a unique recent African origin for living humanity.

Herto

The human remains from the Ethiopian site of Herto Bouri (Clark *et al.*, 2003; White *et al.*, 2003) provide important new information about the pattern of Late Pleistocene evolution that addresses the issue of how recent human populations evolved. The Herto Bouri remains were placed in a new subspecies of *Homo sapiens* and described both as 'on the verge of anatomical modernity but not yet fully modern' (White *et al.*, 2003), or alternatively as 'anatomically modern *Homo sapiens*' (Clark *et al.*, 2003).[2] One new specimen, BOU-VP-16/1, is

---

[2] 'Anatomical modernity' has proven to be difficult and problematic to define or describe (Wolpoff, 1986; Kidder *et al.*, 1992; Tobias, 1995; Wolpoff and Caspari, 1997) and was not defined or described in these works.

a large, robust male of an age comparable to the European Neandertals (most complete Neandertal crania are also male). Because of this antiquity, Herto was said to 'exclud[e] Neandertals from a significant contribution to the ancestry of modern humans' (White *et al.*, 2003) since Herto looks more like modern humans than Neandertals do. We believe this phenetic interpretation is logically incorrect and does not address questions of Neandertal ancestry.

Here is why: this interpretation of Herto phylogeny requires an implicit assumption about whether recent humans are a distinct phylogenetic entity. In order for similarities between Herto and recent humans to validly address Neandertal evolution there would have to be a monophyletic group composed of Herto and all recent and living humans, but excluding Neandertals and their European ancestors (and by inference also excluding Middle Pleistocene Asians). Otherwise, the contributions of Neandertals to later Europeans could not be identified by examining the character states in populations penecon-temporaneous with Neandertals or older in Africa: a 'pre-*sapiens* hypothesis' sensu Vallois (1954). This is, no doubt, what White and colleagues assume, and it is the conclusion of their research.

Our intent is to test the hypothesis of a Neandertal species-lineage, because this directly addresses the issue of single versus multiple ancestries for recent humans. We will examine the hypothesis that there was a distinct and genetically isolated lineage of Neandertals and determine whether data refute the predictions that follow from this assumption. This hypothesis follows from the conclusions of the initial descriptions of the Herto BOU-VP-16/1 remains (Clark *et al.*, 2003; White *et al.*, 2003); that the adult male is a part of an African

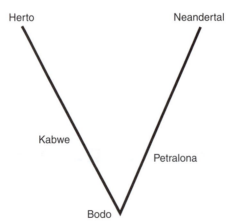

Figure 18.1. The hypothesis of separate African and European lineages, with the assumption that Bodo, or specimens in a population like it, are similar to the last common ancestor.

lineage uniquely related to living humans, and that the European Neandertals comprise a separately evolving lineage. If this interpretation is valid, we expect that the branches of these two diverging lineages (Figure 18.1) will be more distinct from each other than either is from their common ancestor, and that the branches continue to diverge over time. This is the fundamental expectation that we test for. We also examine the question of whether the adult Herto male BOU-VP-16/1 is part of a discernable African palaeo-deme, and the relation of this deme to other populations

Materials and methods

A significant consequence of two independently evolving species-lineages is the expectation of their continued divergence over time. If Bodo is considered to represent the common ancestor of Herto BOU-VP-16/1 and Neandertals (Figure 18.2), we might expect the descendents, either Herto or Neandertals, to be more similar to Bodo than they are to each other. This is because the differences between Herto and the Neandertals are the sum of differences between Herto and Bodo, and Bodo and the Neandertals, under the assumption of separate lineages. In these and all other comparisons, the specimens are male.

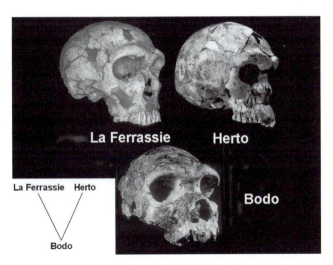

Figure 18.2. Comparison of Herto (BOU-VP-16/1) with a male Neandertal from La Ferrassie and cranium from Bodo, a potential common male ancestor. The Neandertal lineage hypothesis requires that La Ferrassie and Herto each be more similar to Bodo than they are to each other. Visual inspection suggests this is not the case. Bodo and Herto are from White and colleagues (2003).

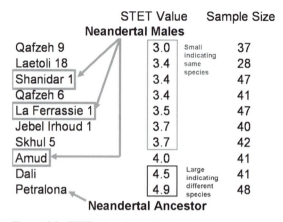

Figure 18.3. STET values for the Herto cranium BOU-VP-16/1 compared with other mostly complete male crania from the Middle and earlier Late Pleistocene. The number of cranial measurements common to Herto and each specimen compared was limited by completeness of the specimen and the measurements reported for Herto. Neandertals are shown in boxes – the hypothesis that they are a separate lineage predicts that the Neandertal specimens should be most different from Herto.

Direct comparison of Neandertals and BOU-VP-16/1 with Bodo is not possible in detail because Bodo is not as well preserved as Herto (Rightmire, 1996). However, the same relationships pertain to comparisons with early male members of the African lineage (we use Kabwe) and with early male members of the European lineage (we use Petralona), shown in Figure 18.1, and are possible because both Kabwe and Petralona are very well preserved. Under the separate lineage hypothesis, the similarity of Neandertals to the early European, or Herto to the early African, is expected to be greater than the similarity of Herto to Neandertals (Figure 18.1). These and other comparisons, detailed in Figure 18.3, are with the most complete male crania from Africa and Eurasia spanning the Middle and earlier Late Pleistocene that preserve anatomical regions comparable to Herto.

Our comparisons require a measure of phenetic rather than phylogenetic similarity. The phylogenetic method for establishing similarity is widely used, but we do not believe it is appropriate for the questions we examine, because they are about very closely related populations, whether or not they differ at the species level. The closeness of relationship of these lineages or palaeo-demes (which description is valid is a question that this work addresses) assures that no phylogenetic hypothesis could be adequately tested with the limited amount of information available to us (Hawks, 2004; Wood and Harrison, 2011).

Our phenetic approach to the question of similarity is detailed in Wolpoff and Lee (2001). This approach is based on a methodology to establish similarity that was first suggested by Lovejoy (1979), and subsequently was developed by Thackeray and colleagues (Thackeray *et al.*, 1995, 1997). These quantified the relationship of pairs of specimens by examining similarities shown in comparisons of homologous measurements. Their key insight is that the dispersion of variables around the regression line for homologous measurements is important for examining similarity hypotheses, not the slope of the line itself. This dispersion was found to effectively reflect taxonomic differences for a wide range of hominid crania (Aiello *et al.*, 2000) when pairs of crania were compared.

We modified the dispersion statistic proposed by Thackeray and colleagues (Wolpoff and Lee, 2001), and the procedure for using it, and call our modified approach the STandard Error Test of the null hypothesis – STET. In STET we regress all of the homologous measurement pairs available in each comparison. Moreover, we address the cases where the bivariate sample is not symmetric around a linear regression line; when the regression of X on Y differs from the regression of Y on X, and the standard errors of the regression slopes differ as well. Since we have no *a priori* reason to choose independent and dependent variables, we calculate standard errors of the mean for both comparisons (s.e.$_{mx}$ for the linear regression of X on Y and s.e.$_{my}$ for Y on X), and report a combined value as the square root of the sum of the squares of the two. One could think of STET as a hypotenuse joining the sides of a triangle determined by the two orthogonal standard errors.

$$STET = [(s.e._{mx})^2 + (s.e._{my})^2]^{1/2}$$

Values of STET reflect a measure of differences between pairs of specimens. Two specimens with a larger STET value are more different from each other than two with a smaller STET value (e.g. Figure 18.4), in that there is greater dispersion around the linear regression line.

Finally, although the bivariate comparisons have different sample sizes, we found no significant relation between the STET value and sample size for comparisons made over the range of sample sizes in this chapter (Figure 18.5).

The predictions of the hypothesis of separate species-lineages were tested by comparing pairs of similarities, as measured by STET. We used as many observations as possible in the pairings, the largest limitation being the number of observations available for Herto. We were able to identify a subset of 51 variables, out of the published measurements for Herto BOU-VP-16/1 that we found corresponded to measurements we have on hand from earlier studies of the specimens in Figure 18.3. Because these measurements reflect variation in almost all aspects of the entire vault, as well as in specific regions of it, we are confident that they provide a sufficient basis for our STET analysis.

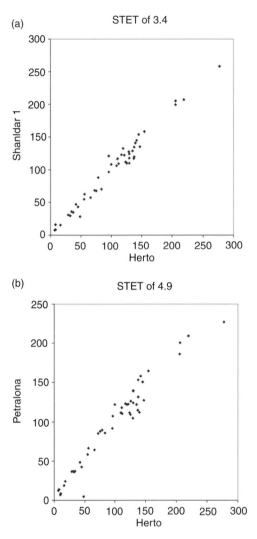

Figure 18.4. Bivariate plots of Herto (BOU-VP-16/1) and two male specimens from the European deme: (a) Shanidar 1 (later) and (b) Petralona (earlier). These plots are created by plotting all of the linear measurements both specimens share. Lower STET values mean less dispersion around the common regression and imply a closer phenetic relationship. In a European species-lineage divergence from Herto should increase for its more recent members such as Shanidar. This is not the case.

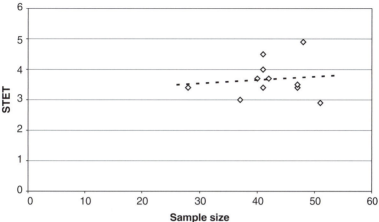

Figure 18.5. STET is not significantly related to sample size for the comparisons in Figure 18.3. The slight positive slope shown in this figure is not significant.

Comparisons

The Herto BOU-VP-16/1 comparisons (Figure 18.3) directly address the question of a distinct Neandertal lineage. If the Neandertals are at the end of a species-lineage different from the Herto lineage leading to modern humans, as noted we might expect them to be the most different from Herto. Neandertal STET values should lie at the distant end of the STET value range shown in Figure 18.3, if this is the case, because they should be furthest removed from Herto BOU-VP-16/1. The mean Neandertal (Amud, La Ferrassie, Shanidar) STET is 3.6; however, this is less, not more, than the mean STET for the comparison of Herto BOU-VP-16/1 with the ancestral condition for the two putative lineages; the mean STET with Kabwe and Petralona is 3.9. The mean Neandertal STET of 3.6 is much less that the European ancestral (Petralona) STET of 4.9. None of these comparisons support the contention of a diverging Neandertal lineage relative to Herto BOU-VP-16/1.

Another way of addressing the question of whether Neandertals are more different from Herto BOU-VP-16/1 than are the other hominids is to examine their distribution in the sample of STET values. Do the Neandertals cluster at the high end of the range of STET values, as expected under the separate lineage hypothesis? A sample runs test for the order of STET values shows the pattern of ordering is not significantly different from random at $p = 0.05$.

We also examine the issue of whether there is support for an African palaeo-deme[3] based on these comparisons. In this case, the specimens with least STET values are African, regardless of age. Kabwe, Laetoli 18 and Jebel Irhoud 1, as a group, are the most similar specimens to the BOU-VP-16/1 male. If we consider the Skhul/Qafzeh remains as an additional part of the African sample, as some have suggested (Klein, 1999), the mean STET value for all the African comparisons with BOU-VP-16/1 (Jebel Irhoud, Kabwe, Laetoli, Qafzeh, Skhul) is 3.4, notably smaller than the 4.3 mean STET value for the non-African comparisons (the Neandertal specimens, Dali and Petralona). These results support the notion of an African palaeo-deme, with BOU-VP-16/1 part of it, and a Mann-Whitney U test for these central tendencies rejects the hypothesis that the African and non-African STET samples were drawn from the same population, at $p = 0.01$. They also confirm White *et al.*'s (2003) contention that BOU-VP-16/1 is closely related to (in the sense of being similar) and could be directly intermediate between these two (their Figure 4 illustrates the sequence of Kabwe→Herto→Qafzeh 9).

The similarities and differences reflected in the STET values are widespread across the cranium and involve different functional regions reacting to different biomechanical and growth histories. The bivariate comparisons include far too many features to reasonably be explained by evolutionary parallelism (independent evolution of similar morphological features in two lineages descending from a different anatomy in the common ancestor). The results indicate that the hypothesis of different species-lineages for the African populations ancestral to Herto and the European populations ancestral to Neandertals is incorrect. These different sets of ancestral-descendent populations are palaeo-demes.[4]

The greater than expected similarity of BOU-VP-16/1 and Neandertals compared with the ancestral condition is far too much to be a result of independent evolution. The most likely explanation of the pattern of similarities is that genes underlying the similarities of BOU-VP-16/1 and Neandertals, relative to the ancestral condition (Figure 18.2), spread throughout the subdivided human species under selection (more than 10% of the human genome is demonstrably under recent selection, according to Wang *et al.*, 2006, and this is most probably an under-estimation). The obvious question is whether there is other evidence of gene flow under selection during the Late Pleistocene.

[3] The Africans would have to be described as a palaeo-deme and not a lineage, in the absence of evidence demonstrating their reproductive isolation.
[4] Features showing sufficient geographic variation to be useful in forensic analysis are often found in the midface (Gill and Gilbert, 1990).

Direct evidence of significant ancient gene flow

There are two sources of information directly addressing the issue of mixture between the Neandertal palaeo-deme and the African palaeo-deme that encountered Neandertals. These are (1) post-Neandertal anatomical variation in Europe; and (2) direct evidence of gene flow with Neandertals. Combined, they clearly show that there was significant mixture.

First, post-Neandertal anatomical variation in Europe includes specifically and in some cases otherwise uniquely Neandertal features (Figure 18.6). Evidence for this conclusion has been in the literature for some time, and continues to accumulate (Frayer, 1992, 1997; Wolpoff and Caspari, 1996; Duarte *et al.*, 1999; Wolpoff *et al.*, 2001, 2006; Trinkaus *et al.*, 2003; Frayer *et al.*, 2006; Soficaru *et al.*, 2006; Rougier *et al.*, 2007).

Second, studies of nuclear variation in modern populations provide information about Neandertal alleles and alleles of other archaic populations that can now be found in the modern gene pool, where they have become established for the most part by selection. This is direct evidence of intermixture, and the anatomical observations of Neandertal features found in post-Neandertal Europeans indicate that the gene flow was reciprocal. Archaeological evidence suggests that there were significant contacts (Zilhão, 2001; D'Errico, 2003; D'Errico *et al.*, 2003; Zilhão *et al.*, 2006) and the fact that different anatomical features are found on different specimens also indicates that the contacts were numerous. The importance of the genetic interchanges is not related to their number, it is related to selection acting on the genes that are interchanged. Even before the sequencing of Neandertal and Denisovan nDNA, Plagnol and Wall (2006) conservatively estimated about 5% nuclear gene ancestry from archaic humans.

Following on earlier studies where the inheritance of human genetic variation from Neandertals was inferred from the pattern of distribution (Morral *et al.*, 1993; Deeb *et al.*, 1994; Harding *et al.*, 2000), there is now direct evidence of alleles in the gene pool today that appear to be Neandertal derived. Many have been under recent selection. This evidence is primarily from the draft sequence of the Neandertal genome based on the analysis of three specimens from Vindija Cave, Croatia (Burbano *et al.*, 2010; Green *et al.*, 2010; Yotova *et al.*, 2011). Additional genomic data from ancient DNA extracted from three other Neandertal sites and, significantly, from a non-Neandertal specimen from Denisova Cave in Siberia (Reich *et al.*, 2010), also provide evidence of gene flow between archaic hominids and other ancestors of modern humans. These ancient populations account for some 8% of the ancestry of living humans according to Reich and colleagues (2010), which is a substantial percentage, given that these peripheral populations (Neandertals and Denisovans) at the northern margin of the Eurasian range may not have been as much as 8% of the world population at that time.

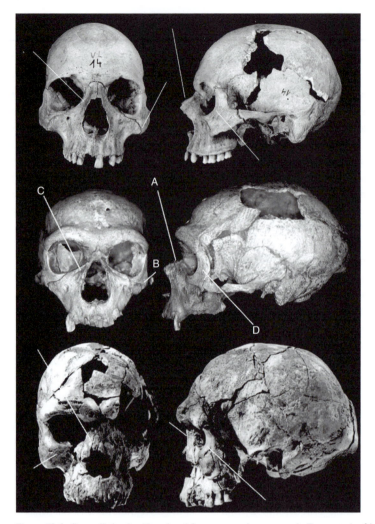

Figure 18.6. Some distinctive Neandertal features remain common in Europe today.[3,4]
Here we show four features of the midface in La Chapelle (centre), with similar
anatomy in the modern specimen (above), a Copper Age male from a 8–10 century
Croatian site – Lijeva Bara (Vukovar, Croatia) – and contrasting with anatomy in
the Herto Ethiopian (below) (from White *et al.*, 2003). Crania are shown to the same
approximate size. The European regional characteristics marked are:

(A) the high nasal angle defined by the slope of the lofty nasal bridge as it rises up
between the orbits and incorporates the frontal processes of the maxillae as well as
the nasal bones themselves (not preserved in La Chapelle, the view shows the nasal
process of the maxilla)
(B) the course of the zygomaxillary suture (enhanced) that turns inward at its most
inferior aspect
(C) the maxillary expansion at the lateral nasal borders, resulting in a 'pinching' of
the region so that these borders are laterally oriented
(D) the lateral orientation of the zygomatic bone.

Conclusions

We examine new anatomical and genetic evidence that addresses the issue of a unique recent African origin for living humanity. Herto BOU-VP-16/1 is a large, robust male cranium that affords the first opportunity to compare the Europeans to an African specimen of Neandertal age, clearly related to modern populations. Comparisons of Herto and Neandertals to common ancestors allow us to examine the evolutionary direction in two different regions and evaluate whether the two samples are evolving away from each other. We know the African is from a population ancestral to recent human populations, and can evaluate whether the Europeans fit the model of a species lineage distinct from it, evolving in a different direction, without confusing the evaluation with issues of size and robustness.

The Europeans are not evolving in a different direction, away from the rest of humanity. The European palaeo-deme, including Neandertals, evolved to be more similar to the descendents of Herto over time, not less similar. The convergence of African and European palaeo-demes demonstrates the presence of gene flow between them, and we agree with the description of these palaeo-demes as 'varieties in a single metapopulation' (Hawks and Cochran, 2006). Moreover, later than the Neandertals, post-Neandertal anatomical variation in Europe includes Neandertal features, even features that evolved locally to be characteristic of most or all Neandertals and were rare or absent in other regions.

Direct evidence on genetic interconnections, interbreeding if you will, now exists between this Herto-descendent palaeo-deme and Neandertals, found in the first analysis of Neandertal nDNA. The influence of the Neandertal genome on human genetic variation today is also evident and, significantly, involves genes that evolved in Neandertals and other archaic populations and spread through the rest of humanity under selection.

These results significantly undermine attempts to demonstrate the human species was any less widespread and geographically dispersed at the beginning of the Late Pleistocene than we know it to have been at its end. The descent of recent populations is from many ancestors; here we minimally show African descent and a second ancestral region, and recognise there are more regions involved in human ancestry (Weidenreich, 1943; Thorne and Wolpoff, 1981; Jelínek, 1982; Kramer, 1991; Kennedy, 1994; Wu, 1997, 1998). Recent human origins are multiregional.

Acknowledgements

We thank the African Genesis organising committee, for the invitation to present this research and for the support to attend the African Genesis conference in honour of Phillip Tobias's 80th birthday. Measurements of all comparative specimens but two were taken on the original materials by one of the authors (MHW). We thank the curators of these remains for access and permission to study them. Dali was also studied in the original, the Dali and Shanidar 1 measurements were taken on accurate casts and compared with published measurements; we use these whenever possible. We thank Rachel Caspari, John Hawks, Tom Roček, Karen Rosenberg, Adam Van Arsdale and members of the 2006 seminar on African Origins at the University of Michigan for their valuable insights and comments. This research was supported by several grants from the National Science Foundation, the National Academy of Sciences, and the University of Michigan. We cannot adequately thank the Professor for his many contributions to public anthropology, his many innovations and discoveries in human evolution, past and present, and of course his influence on our research and analysis. Happy birthday, PVT, and many more to come.

References

Aiello, L. C., Collard, M., Thackeray, J. F. *et al.* (2000). Assessing exact randomization-based methods of determining the taxonomic significance of variability in the human fossil record. *South African Journal of Science*, **96**: 179–83.

Bräuer, G. (1978). The morphological differentiation of anatomically modern man in Africa, with special regard to recent finds from East Africa. *Zeitschrift für Morphologie und Anthropologie*, **69**(3): 266–92.

(1981). Current problems and research on the origin of *Homo sapiens* in Africa. *Human biologia Budapestinensis*, **9**: 69–78.

(1984). The 'Afro-European *sapiens* hypothesis' and hominid evolution in East Asia during the late middle and upper Pleistocene. In Andrews, P. and Franzen, J. L. (eds.), The early evolution of man, with special emphasis on Southeast Asia and Africa. *Courier Forschungsinstitut Senckenberg*, **69**: 145–65.

Burbano, H. A., Hodges, E., Green, R. E. *et al.* (2010). Targeted investigation of the Neandertal genome by array-based sequence capture. *Science*, **328**(5979): 723–5.

Clark, J. D., Beyene, Y., Woldegabriel, G. *et al.* (2003). Stratigraphic, chronological and behavioural contexts of Pleistocene *Homo sapiens* from Middle Awash, Ethiopia. *Nature*, **423**: 747–51.

Dart, R. A. (1940). Recent discoveries bearing on human history in southern Africa. *Journal of the Royal Anthropological Institute of Great Britain and Ireland*, **70**: 13–27.

Deeb, S. S., Jørgensen, A. L., Battisi, L. *et al.* (1994). Sequence divergence of the red and green visual pigments in the great apes and man. *Proceedings of the National Academy of Sciences USA*, **91**: 7262–6.

D'Errico, F. (2003). The invisible frontier: a multiple species model for the origin of behavioral modernity. *Evolutionary Anthropology*, **12**: 188–202.

D'Errico, F., Julien, M., Liolios, D. *et al.* (2003). Many awls in our argument. Bone tool manufacture and use in the Châtelperronian and Aurignacian levels of the Grotte de Renne at Arcy-sur-Cure. In Zilhão, J. and D'Errico, F. (eds.), *The chronology of the Aurignacian and of the transitional technocomplexes. Dating, stratigraphies, cultural implications.* Proceedings of Symposium 6.1 of the XIVth Congress of the UISPP. Lisbon: Instituto Português de Arqueologia, pp. 247–70.

Duarte, C., Maurício, J., Pettitt, P. B. *et al.* (1999). The early Upper Paleolithic human skeleton from the Abrigo do Lagar Velho (Portugal) and modern human emergence in Iberia. *Proceedings of the National Academy of Sciences of the USA*, **96**: 7604–9.

Eller, E. (2001). Estimating relative population sizes from simulated data sets and the question of greater African effective size. *American Journal of Physical Anthropology*, **116**(1): 1–12.

Frayer, D. W. (1992). Evolution at the European edge: Neanderthal and the Upper Paleolithic relationships. *Préhistoire Européene/European Prehistory*, **2**: 9–69.

(1997). Perspectives on Neanderthals as ancestors. In Clark, G. A. and Willermet, C. M. (eds.), *Conceptual Issues in Modern Human Origins Research*. Aldine de Gruyter, pp. 220–35.

Frayer, D. W., Jelínek, J., Oliva, M. *et al.* (2006). Aurignacian male crania, jaws, and teeth from the Mladeč Caves, Moravia, Czech Republic. In Teschler-Nicola, M. (ed.), *Early Modern Humans at the Moravian Gate: the Mladeč Caves and their Remains*. Wien: Springer, pp. 185–272.

Green, R. E., Krause, J., Briggs, A. W. *et al.* (2010). A draft sequence of the Neandertal genome. *Science*, **328**(5979): 710–22.

Gill, G. W. and Gilbert, B. M. (1990). Race identification from the midfacial skeleton: American Blacks and Whites. In Gill, G. W. and Rhine, S. (eds), Skeletal attribution of race: methods for forensic anthropology. *Anthropological papers of the Maxwell Museum of Anthropology*, **4**: 47–53.

Haeckel, E. (1883). *The History of Creation, or the Development of the Earth and its Inhabitants by Natural Causes. A Popular Exposition of the Doctrine of Evolution in General, and that of Darwin, Goethe, and Lamark in Particular.* New York: Appleton.

Harding, R. M., Healy, E., Ray, A.J. *et al.* (2000). Evidence for variable selective pressures at MC1R. *American Journal of Human Genetics*, **66**(4): 1351–61.

Harpending, H. C. (1996). Genetic evidence about the origins of modern humans. In Bar-Yosef, O., Cavalli-Sforza, L. L., March, R. J. and Piperno, M. (eds.), *The Lower and Middle Paleolithic*. Colloquium X: The origin of modern man. International Congress of Prehistoric and Protohistoric Sciences. Forlì: A.B.A.C.O., pp. 127–31.

Hawks, J. (2004). How much can cladistics tell us about early hominid relationships? *American Journal of Physical Anthropology*, **125**: 207–19.

Hawks, J. and Cochran, G. (2006). Dynamics of adaptive introgression from archaic to modern humans. *PaleoAnthropology*, **2006**: 101–15.

Hawks, J. and Wolpoff, M. H. (2003). Sixty years of modern human origins in the American Anthropological Association. *American Anthropologist*, **105**(1): 87–98.

Howell, F. C. (1999). Paleo-demes, species clades, and extinctions in the Pleistocene hominin record. *Journal of Anthropological Research*, **55**: 191–244.

Howells, W. W. (1942). Fossil man and the origin of races. *American Anthropologist*, **44**: 182–93.

Jelínek, J. (1982). The east and southeast Asian way of regional evolution. *Anthropologie (Brno)*, **20**: 195–212.

Kennedy, K. A. R. (1994). Evolution of South Asian Pleistocene hominids: demic displacement or regional continuity? In Parpola, A. and Koskikallio, P. (eds.), *South Asian Archaeology*. Helsinki: Suomalainen Tiedeakatemia, pp. 337–44.

Kidder, J. H., Jantz, R. L. and Smith, F. H. (1992). Defining modern humans: a multivariate approach. In Bräuer, G. and Smith, F. H. (eds.), *Continuity or Replacement? Controversies in* Homo sapiens *Evolution*. Rotterdam: Balkema, pp. 157–77.

Klein, R. G. (1999). *The Human Career*, 2nd edn. Chicago: University of Chicago Press.

Kramer, A. (1991). Modern human origins in Australasia: replacement or evolution? *American Journal of Physical Anthropology*, **86**(4): 455–73.

Lovejoy, C. O. (1979). Contemporary methodological approaches to individual primate fossil analysis. In Morbeck, M. E., Preuschoft, H. and Gomberg, N. (eds.), *Environment, Behavior, and Morphology*. New York: Gustav Fischer, pp. 229–43.

Morral, N., Nunes, V., Casals, T. *et al.* (1993). Microsattelite haplotypes for cystic fibrosis: mutation frameworks and evolutionary tracers. *Human Molecular Genetics*, **2**(7): 1015–22.

Plagnol, V. and Wall, J. D. (2006). Possible ancestral structure in human populations. *PLoS Genetics*, **2**(7): e105.

Proctor, R. N. (2003). Three roots of human recency. *Current Anthropology*, **44**(2): 213–39.

Protsch, R. (1975). The absolute dating of Upper Pleistocene sub-Saharan fossil hominids and their place in human evolution. *Journal of Human Evolution*, **4**: 297–322.

Reich, D., Green, R. E., Kircher, M. *et al.* (2010). Genetic history of an archaic hominin group from Denisova Cave in Siberia. *Nature* **468**(7327): 1053–60.

Relethford, J. H. (2001). *Genetics and the Search for Modern Human Origins*. New York: Wiley-Liss.

  (2003). *Reflections of the Past*. Boulder: Westview.

Rightmire, G. P. (1996). The human cranium from Bodo, Ethiopia: evidence for speciation in the Middle Pleistocene? *Journal of Human Evolution*, **31**(1): 21–39.

Rougier, H., Milota, S., Rodrigo, R. *et al.* (2007). Petera cu Oase 2 and the cranial morphology of early modern Europeans. *Proceedings of the National Academy of Sciences of the USA*, **104**(4): 1165–70

Soficaru, A., Dobos, S. and Trinkaus, E. (2006). Early modern humans from the Petera Muierii, Baia de Fier, Romania. *Proceedings of the National Academy of Sciences of the USA*, **103**: 17196–201

Stoneking, M. and Cann, R. L. (1989). African origins of human mitochondrial DNA. In Mellars, P. and Stringer, C. B. (eds.), *The Human Revolution: Behavioural and Biological Perspectives on the Origins of Modern Humans*. Edinburgh: Edinburgh University Press, pp. 17–30.

Stringer, C. B. and Andrews, P. (1988). Genetic and fossil evidence for the origin of modern humans. *Science*, **239**: 1263–8.

Tattersall, I. (1995). *The Fossil Trail: How we Know What we Think we Know about Human Evolution*. New York: Oxford University Press.

Thackeray, J. F., Bellamy, C. L., Bellars, D. *et al.* (1997). Probabilities of conspecificity: application of a morphometric technique to modern taxa and fossil specimens attributed to *Australopithecus* and *Homo*. *South African Journal of Science*, **93**(4): 195–6.

Thackeray, J. F., Helbig, J. and Moss, S. (1995). Quantifying morphological variability within extant mammalian species. *Palaeontologia Africana*, **31**: 23–5.

Thorne, A. G. and Wolpoff, M. H. (1981). Regional continuity in Australasian Pleistocene hominid evolution. *American Journal of Physical Anthropology*, **55**: 337–49.

Tobias, P. V. (1995). The bearing of fossils and mitochondria DNA on the evolution of modern humans, with a critique of the 'Mitochondrial Eve' hypothesis. *South African Archaeological Bulletin*, **50**: 155–67.

Trinkaus, E., Milota, Ş., Rodrigo, R. *et al.* (2003). Early modern human cranial remains from the Peştera cu Oase, Romania. *Journal of Human Evolution*, **45**: 245–53.

Vallois, H. V. (1954). Neanderthals and presapiens. *Journal of the Royal Anthropological Institute*, **84**: 111–30.

Wang, E. T., Kodama, G., Baldi, P. *et al.* (2006). Global landscape of recent inferred Darwinian selection for *Homo sapiens*. *Proceedings of the National Academy of Sciences of the USA*, **103**: 135–40.

Weidenreich, F. (1943) The skull of *Sinanthropus pekinensis*: a comparative study of a primitive hominid skull. *Palaeontologia Sinica, New Series D*, **10**, 1–484.

White, T. D., Asfaw, B., Degusta, D. *et al.* (2003) Pleistocene *Homo sapiens* from Middle Awash, Ethiopia. *Nature*, **423**: 742–7.

Wolpoff, M. H. (1986). Describing anatomically modern *Homo sapiens*: a distinction without a definable difference. *Anthropos (Brno)*, **23**: 41–53.

(1989). Multiregional evolution: the fossil alternative to Eden. In Mellars, P. and Stringer, C. B. (eds.), *The Human Revolution: Behavioural and Biological Perspectives on the Origins of Modern Humans*. Edinburgh: Edinburgh University Press, pp. 62–108.

Wolpoff, M. H. and Caspari, R. (1996). An unparalleled parallelism. *Anthropologie (Brno)*, **34**(3): 215–23.

(1997). What does it mean to be modern? In Clark, G. A. and Willermet, C. M. (eds.), *Conceptual Issues in Modern Human Origins Research*. New York: Aldine de Gruyter. pp. 28–44, and combined bibliography on pp. 437–92.

Wolpoff, M. H. and Lee, S-H. (2001). The late Pleistocene human species of Israel. *Bulletins et Mémoires de la Société d'Anthropologie de Paris*, **13**: 291–310.

Wolpoff, M. H., Wu Xinzhi and Thorne, A. G. (1984). Modern *Homo sapiens* origins: a general theory of hominid evolution involving the fossil evidence from east Asia. In Smith, F. H. and Spencer, F. (eds.), *The Origins of Modern Humans: a World Survey of the Fossil Evidence*. New York: Alan R. Liss, pp. 411–83.

Wolpoff, M. H., Hawks, J. D., Frayer, D. W. *et al.* (2001). Modern human ancestry at the peripheries: a test of the replacement theory. *Science*, **291**: 293–7.

Wolpoff, M. H., Frayer, D. W. and Jelínek, J. (2006). Aurignacian female crania and teeth from the Mladeč Caves, Moravia, Czech Republic. In M. Teschler-Nicola (ed.), *Early Modern Humans at the Moravian Gate: The Mladeč Caves and their Remains*. Wien: Springer, pp. 273–340.

Wood, B. and Harrison, T. (2011). The evolutionary context of the first hominins. *Nature*, **470**: 347–52.

Wu Xinzhi (1997). On the descent of modern humans in East Asia. In Clark, G. A. and Willermet, C. M. (eds.), *Conceptual Issues in Modern Human Origins Research*. New York: Aldine de Gruyter, pp. 283–93, and combined bibliography on pp. 437–92.

  (1998). Continuity or replacement: viewed from the source of certain features of modern humans in China. In Omoto, K. and Tobias, P. V. (eds.), *Origins and Past of Modern Humans: Towards Reconciliation*. Singapore: World Scientific, pp. 139–44.

Yotova, V., Lefebvre, J.-F., Moreau, C. *et al.* (2011). An X-linked haplotype of Neandertal origin is present among all non-African populations. *Molecular Biology and Evolution*, **28**(7): 1957–62.

Zilhão, J. (2001). Neandertal/modern human interaction in Europe. In Thacker, P. and Hays, M. (eds.), Questioning the answers: resolving fundamental problems of the early Upper Paleolithic. *British Archaeological Reports International Series*, **1005**: 13–19.

Zilhão, J., d'Errico, F., Bordes, J-G. *et al.* (2006). Analysis of Aurignacian interstratification at the Châtelperronian-type site and implications for the behavioral modernity of Neandertals. *Proceedings of the National Academy of Sciences of the USA*, **103**(33): 12643–8.

19 Assimilation and modern human origins in the African peripheries

FRED H. SMITH, VANCE T. HUTCHINSON
AND IVOR JANKOVIĆ

Abstract

The vast majority of pertinent genetic and human palaeontological evidence indicates that an early transition from archaic to modern humans occurs in Africa. Interestingly, the earliest well dated modern human fossils all derive from eastern Africa: Omo Kibish KHS (196 ka to 172 ka) and Herto (160 ka to 154 ka), both in Ethiopia (ka = thousand years ago). This suggests that modern humans may have originated in, and ultimately radiated out of, eastern Africa into the 'peripheral' regions of Africa, defined here as northern Africa and southern Africa, as well as into Eurasia. Evidence of the earliest presence of purported modern humans from both African 'peripheral' regions is assessed in this study. These include the Klasies River Mouth (KRM) sample from southern Africa and the Aterian-associated remains from North Africa, particularly the fragmentary subadult maxilla from Mugharet el 'Aliya (High Cave) near Tangier, Morocco. Both samples are maximally dated to ~130 ka and thus are significantly younger than the earliest eastern African modern humans. The KRM sample exhibits a significant amount of size and morphological variation, the latter reflecting a mosaic of archaic/modern anatomy. We interpret this morphological pattern as reflecting an admixed sample. The northern African evidence is less clear, but the morphology of the Tangier maxilla demonstrates archaic elements in the Aterian population, and this may well reflect the same pattern of admixture. We conclude that the evidence from the African 'peripheries' is consistent with admixture and that this broadly supports the assimilation model of modern human origins.

African Genesis: Perspectives on Hominin Evolution, eds. Sally C. Reynolds and Andrew Gallagher. Published by Cambridge University Press. © Cambridge University Press 2012.

Introduction

Evidence accumulated over the past two decades or so has consistently pointed to Africa as the homeland of modern humans, based on morphology (e.g. Rightmire, 1984; Bräuer, 1984, 2004, 2008; Stringer, 2002; Trinkaus, 2005; Klein, 2009; Schwartz and Tattersall, 2010), genetic evidence (Relethford, 2001; Templeton, 2002, 2005; Pearson, 2004; Weaver and Roseman, 2008) and some would assert behavioural evidence as well (McBrearty and Brooks, 2000; Willoughby, 2007; Klein, 2009). There is, of course, continuing debate on the nature of modern human origins, with advocates of the multiregional evolution (MRE) model arguing against a strictly 'out of Africa' origin for modern humans. However, supporters of the MRE model have more recently accepted the possibility that the majority of the modern human gene pool could have an African origin (Wolpoff *et al.*, 2000, 2001, 2004), based primarily on the argument by Relethford (1999) that until recently more people lived in Africa than elsewhere. Supporters of the recent African origin (RAO) model hold that not only is Africa the homeland of modern humans, but also that the spread of modern people into Eurasia was accompanied by an essentially complete replacement of archaic Eurasian populations (Klein, 2009; Schwartz and Tattersall, 2010). Although many advocates of the RAO model are willing to accept the possibility of some contributions by local Eurasian archaic peoples (e.g. Neandertals) to initial modern populations (Stringer, 2002; Bräuer, 2004, 2008) it seems clear that these contributions are considered to be fundamentally insignificant (Bräuer and Stringer, 1997; Bräuer *et al.*, 2004). In our opinion (see Smith, 2002, 2010; Smith *et al.*, 2005), the data are not as consistent in support of either of these models as their advocates assert. In other words, it is possible that either the RAO or the MRE model might be correct. It is also possible that both are, at least in part, wrong.

While some uncertainty concerning aspects of the process that led to our species must be acknowledged, the currently available fossil hominin record and its chronometric framework demonstrate two things quite clearly. First, there is an early transition towards the modern human morphological pattern in Africa, a transition that is clearly underway by 250 ka (Rightmire, 1984; Bräuer, 1984, 1992, 2004; Stringer and Andrews, 1988; Smith, 1993; Hublin, 1993, 2000; Stringer, 2002). Second, the earliest specimens that can be considered morphologically modern are also found in Africa (White *et al.*, 2003; MacDougall *et al.*, 2005). On the surface, these facts lend support to the RAO model, but the reality may be more complex. For example, recent analyses demonstrate that both mitochondrial and nuclear DNA support a 'mostly out of Africa' (MOA) model. The MOA model recognises that while a substantial majority of recent human genetic variation derives from Africa, it is not likely that all human genetic variation did (Relethford, 2001; Templeton, 2002, 2005; Green *et al.*, 2010). These perspectives on the genetic evidence do not support either the total replacement of the RAO model, or the original MRE model implication that Africa might not be the predominant source of modern humans. Additionally, archaeological markers of behavioural modernity may have an African origin as well. Regardless, whether one accepts the gradual accretion model of McBrearty and Brooks (2000) or the language revolution model of Klein (2000, 2003), the fact is that these behavioural changes occur long after modern humans have appeared morphologically and thus are not directly relevant to that emergence.

New fossil hominin discoveries at Herto, Ethiopia (White *et al.*, 2003); establishment of a firmer chronological position for the Omo-Kibish 1 specimen, also from Ethiopia (MacDougall *et al.*, 2005); and some genetic evidence (Passarino *et al.*, 1998; Quintana-Murci, 1999; Underhill *et al.*, 2000; Semino *et al.*, 2002) strongly suggest that the earliest appearance of modern humans is likely to be specifically located in the eastern African region. If this turns out to be true, modern human populations would have spread within, as well as out of, Africa. Here we discuss the perspective that samples of fossil hominins in southern and northern Africa, which post-date the earliest eastern African evidence for the appearance of modern humans, reflect the admixture of expanding modern and indigenous archaic peoples in these parts of the continent. Of particular interest are the hominin remains from the Klasies River Mouth (KRM) caves in southern Africa, which have been described as 'fully anatomically modern' (Bräuer, 1984; Rightmire and Deacon, 1991) and the remains associated with the Aterian lithic industry of Morocco and other regions of northern Africa (Table 19.1).

The African transitional group and the earliest modern Africans

From our perspective, the most convincing evidence for an African, or mostly African, biological origin of modern humans is found in the fossil record. Particularly compelling is the anatomical pattern of a series of remains, found throughout Africa – from Morocco to South Africa, that is referred to here as the African transitional group or ATG. This is not a large sample of specimens (see Table 19.2); and while many of these are rather incomplete, their morphological pattern is basically consistent across the sample. Much of the work that

Table 19.1. *Selected early modern human sites and specimens from South and North Africa.*

Site, country	Human remains	Date	Dating references
Border Cave (South Africa)	Adult cranium, infant skeleton, 2 adult mandibles, humerus, ulna, 2 metatarsals	>49 ka (^{14}C) 80–55 ka (ESR) 121–47 ka[a] 74 ± 5 ka	Beaumont *et al.* (1978) Grün and Stringer (1991) Miller *et al.* (1993) Grün *et al.* (2003)
Dar-es-Soltane II (Morocco)	Adult anterior skull (Dar-es-Soltane 5), child's skull, adolescent mandible	127–34 ka[b]	Debénath *et al.* (1986); Hublin (1993)
Equus Cave (South Africa)	Mandibular fragment, 10 unassociated teeth	71–>27 ka[c]	Grine and Klein (1985); Klein (2009)
Haua Fteah (Libya)	Two mandible fragments	>47 ka (^{14}C) 150–30 ka[d]	McBurney (1967)
Hoedjiespunt (South Africa)	Cranial fragments, teeth, postcranial fragments	300–71 ka[e]	Berger and Parkington (1995); Stynder *et al.* (2001)
Die Kelders Cave 1 (South Africa)	Isolated teeth (>20), 2 hand phalanges	71–45 ka[c]	Grine *et al.* (1991)
Klasies River Mouth Caves (South Africa)	Five partial mandibles; zygomatic; fragments of 2 maxillae, temporal, supraorbital region, and other cranial bones; isolated teeth; several postcranial pieces, including a radius and ulna.	115–60 ka[c]	Grün and Stringer (1991); Deacon and Shuurman (1992); Feathers (2002)
Mugharet el 'Aliya (Morocco)	Subadult maxillary fragment	127–34 ka[b]	Debénath *et al.* (1986)
Nazlet Khater (Egypt)	Two partial skeletons	37.6 + 0.35/ −0.31 ka[f]	Vermeersch (2002)
Sea Harvest (South Africa)	Premolar and phalanx	127–>40 ka[g]	Grine and Klein (1993)
Taramsa Hill (Egypt)	Juvenile partial skeleton	80–~50 ka[h]	Vermeersch *et al.* (1998)
Témara (Smuggler's Cave) (Morocco)	Frontal, parietal, occipital and mandible fragments	127–34 ka[b]	Debénath *et al.* (1986); Hublin (1993)
Zouhrah Cave (Morocco)	Partial mandible, canine	127–34 ka[b]	Hublin (1993)

[a] These dates are isolucine epimerisation of ostrich egg shell. The dates from two lower levels are 106 ka and 145 ka. Miller and colleagues believe the actual age lies between these extremes, so the average is used here.

Table 19.1. (*cont.*)

[b] These dates are based on association with the Aterian industry (Klein, 2009). There are no chronometric dates from this site. It is not possible to determine where in this time range the human skeletal material falls, and the upper end of the range may be too old.
[c] Dated by ESR, faunal associations and geology.
[d] Dated by association with the North African Levalloiso-Mousterian industry (Klein, 2009).
[e] Dated by uranium series, faunal association and geology.
[f] AMS ^{14}C.
[g] Dated by ^{14}C and geology.
[h] OSL (optically stimulated luminescence).

has established this morphological pattern has been contributed by Rightmire (1976, 1978, 1983, 1984), Bräuer (1984, 1989, 1992) and Hublin (1985, 1993), while others have emphasised the importance of the pattern (Stringer and Andrews, 1988; Smith *et al.*, 1989; Smith, 1997a).

The ATG morphological pattern combines a relatively archaic cranial vault, moderately low with receding frontal squamae and prominent supraorbital tori (Figure 19.1), with faces that are more modern-like in that they are generally smaller, less prognathic, and exhibit canine fossae and angled zygomaticoalveolar margins (Figure 19.2).

Until relatively recently, the dating of some of these specimens was very problematic, and it could be previously argued some were relatively recent in geological age (see discussion in Smith, 1985 and Smith *et al.*, 1989). In some cases these dates were simply erroneous. For example, the Florisbad specimen, now directly dated by ESR to 259 ka (see Table 19.2) was long claimed to have a collagen radiocarbon date of 39 ka (Protsch, 1974). However, most dates were simply unclear, and some remain so. For example, Eliye Springs and Omo Kibish 2 are surface finds, and the exact stratigraphic contexts of Jebel Irhoud 1–3 are equivocal. Omo Kibish 2 likely eroded out of Kibish Member 1 (Butzer, 1969), and recent re-analysis continues to assert its contemporaneity with Omo Kibish 1 (cf. McDougall *et al.*, 2008). Unfortunately, due to the nature of its context, there will always be uncertainty regarding the age of Omo Kibish 2 (see Smith *et al.*, 1989). Similarly, the Jebel Irhoud 1–3 specimens are likely to derive from the Mousterian deposits that definitely yielded specimen JH 4, but some uncertainty remains. Still, a strong case can be made that the ATG sample falls chronologically between about 260 ka and 130 ka (Table 19.2). In fact, we assert the most influential factor resulting in the acceptance of an African origin of the modern human morphological pattern has been the ability to secure reliable chronometric dating for fossil specimens between roughly 30 000 ka and 400 ka in Africa and Eurasia (Smith, 1994, 1997b, 2002). We consider this chronological revolution critical to the argument for an

(a)

(b)

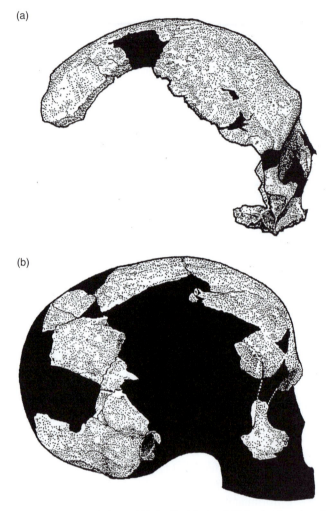

Figure 19.1. Lateral views of (a) the Florisbad and (b) Border Cave 1 partial crania. Note the obvious modern contours of the Border Cave frontal compared to that of Florisbad. Also note the presence of a pronounced supraorbital projection and the relatively slight prognathism of Florisbad. Drawing by M. Cartmill (from Cartmill and Smith, 2009).

African biological homeland for modern humans and the subsequent spread of modern humans within and out of Africa.

In addition to the ATG, the earliest well dated evidence of hominins with a fundamentally modern morphological gestalt derives from Africa, and this

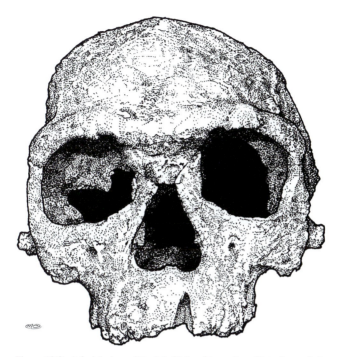

Figure 19.2. A facial view of the Jebel Irhoud 1 cranium. Note the angled zygomatico-alveolar margin and the relatively small overall face. Drawing by M. Cartmill (from Cartmill and Smith, 2009).

fact has been solidly established since the early twenty-first century (Clark *et al.*, 2003; White *et al.*, 2003; Stringer, 2003; MacDougall *et al.*, 2005). The Omo Kibish 1 partial skeleton from Member 1 at site KHS at Omo in southern Ethiopia is fragmentary but certainly modern in form (Day and Stringer, 1982; Pearson *et al.*, 2008). In addition to modern vault contours, Omo 1 preserves evidence of a putative canine fossa and a chin structure (Figure 19.3). The dating of Omo 1 was rather contentious for years (see discussion in Smith *et al.*, 1989) but, in 2005, McDougall and colleagues provided new evidence of an age in excess of 104 ka for the specimen. Specifically, they report an Argon-Argon date of 196 ka in Member 1 below the level where the Omo 1 specimen was recovered and another Argon-Argon date of 104 ka from the overlying Member 3. MacDougall *et al.* (2005) argue that these deposits accumulated quickly and that the date of 196 ka is close to the age of the Omo 1 specimen, because the dated tuff is just below the level of this specimen. Estimates based on relative speed of accumulation of sediments are notoriously imprecise, but

Table 19.2. *Fossil human remains assigned to the African Transitional Group (ATG). All specimens are adults unless otherwise indicated.*

Site	Human remains – brief description	Date (reference)
Florisbad (S. Africa)	Fragmentary facial skeleton with third molar. Anterior cranial vault.	259 + 35 ka[a] (Grün *et al.*, 1996)
Ngaloba (Tanzania) [Laetolil hominid 18]	Complete cranial vault except lacking most of the cranial base. Complete but unattached face.	>200 ka[b] (Manega, 1993)
Eliye Springs (Kenya) [KNM-ES-11693]	Complete cranium with a damaged, eroded face.	undated surface find (Bräuer and Leakey, 1986)
Guomde (Kenya) [KNM-ER 3884]	Posterior cranial vault, supraorbital torus, and maxilla with dentition.	272 ka + ∞, – 113 ka[c] (Bräuer *et al.*, 1997)
Omo Kibish PHS [Omo Kibish2]	Cranial vault with supraorbital torus, lacking the face and cranial base.	undated surface find[d] (Butzer, 1969)
Jebel Irhoud (Morocco)	JI 1 – Complete cranium and face, lacking most of cranial base. JI 2 – Cranial vault, lacking the face and most of the cranial base. JI 3 – Mandible of an eight year old. JI 4 – Right juvenile humerus shaft.	190–130 ka[e] (Grün and Stringer, 1991)

Notes:
[a] ESR date
[b] amino acid racemisation dating of ostrich egg shells from the Ngaloba Beds
[c] gamma ray spectrometry date
[d] Butzer provides a convincing case that the specimen eroded out of Member 1, which would date it to between 196 ka and 104 ka (McDougall *et al.*, 2005, 2008)
[e] Grün and Stringer correlate the deposits to OIS 6, thus giving this age range.

recent tuff correlations imply an age of >172 ka for Omo Kibish 1 (McDougall *et al.*, 2008). Clearly this specimen dates well in excess of 104 ka and may indeed approach an age of 196 ka.

In 2003, White and colleagues provided additional evidence of early modern Africans at the site of Herto, also from Ethiopia. The adult Herto 1 specimen is slightly distorted but exhibits the full suite of modern human cranial morphology (Figure 19.4). As is the case for Omo 1, the most primitive aspect of Herto 1 is a prominent supraorbital torus, but the face is not prognathic, and it exhibits an angled zygomaticoalveolar margin and presence of a canine fossa. Herto 2 is both more fragmentary and more robust than Herto 1, but its morphology also does not deviate from the modern human pattern. The juvenile Herto 5 (6 to 7 years old at death) cranium also highlights the modern anatomical pattern of these specimens. This specimen lacks the cranial

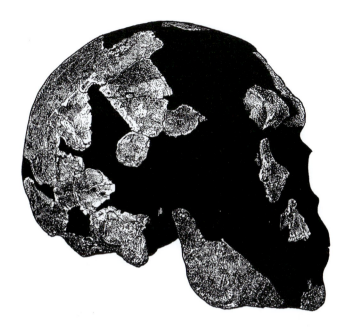

Figure 19.3. Lateral view of the Omo Kibish 1 cranium and mandible. Although fragmentary, the modern contours of the vault are evident, as are the presence of at least a mental trigone and an indication of a canine fossa. Drawing by M. Cartmill (from Cartmill and Smith, 2009).

superstructures seen in the adults, as would be expected for a subadult of this age. It shows a globular vault with a high forehead, rounded sagittal occipital contour and exhibits a modern profile from the rear. These specimens, from the Upper Herto Formation, date to between 160 ka and 154 ka, based on Argon-Argon dating results (Clark *et al.*, 2003).

There are other specimens from eastern Africa that might have bearing on the initial origin of the modern human anatomical pattern. A partial mandible from Diré Dawa (Port Epic) in Ethiopia is dated to >60 ka based on results obtained from obsidian hydration dating, as well as its association with Middle Stone Age lithic material (Clark, 1988). The specimen itself is small and badly eroded. It has been described as a mosaic of modern (vertical symphysis) and archaic (lacking a chin) morphology (Bräuer, 1984). From the Mumba rock shelter in Tanzania, three isolated molars were recovered, dating to between 130 ka and 109 ka by uranium series methods and described as modern in size and morphology (Bräuer and Mehlman, 1988). In addition, cranial vault bones from Bouri and Aduma (both from Ethiopia) are morphologically modern and appear to date between 105 ka and 79 ka

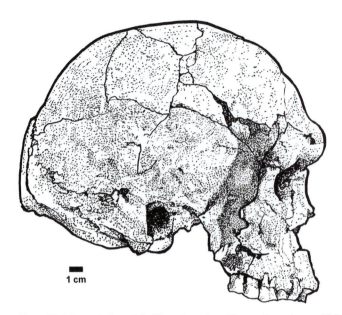

1 cm

Figure 19.4. Lateral view of the Herto 1 cranium. The specimen shows a high frontal squama, a high and rounded vault, and an orthognathic face. Like most other early modern African and Near Eastern adults, Herto 1 retains a prominent supraorbital torus. Drawing by M. Cartmill (from Cartmill and Smith, 2009).

(Haile-Selassie *et al.*, 2004), considerably later than the Herto and Omo Kibish specimens.

Most interesting, however, is an enigmatic cranium from the Sudan, found in 1924. Singa is a complete calvarium with some damage to the base, most recently studied by Stringer (1979; Stringer *et al.*, 1985). The specimen has been dated using electron spin resonance (ESR) analysis of two animal teeth from the site that produced estimates of 97 ka (early uptake) and 160 ka (linear uptake) (Grün and Stringer, 1991). There is also a uranium-thorium date of 133 ± 2 ka based on analysis of the matrix adhering to the specimen (McDermott *et al.*, 1996), which is considered a minimum age for the skull. Like the Herto and Omo Kibish 1 skulls, Singa exhibits a modern-shaped vault with large mastoid processes. It also has particularly prominent parietal bossing. Like the Ethiopian specimens, the most archaic aspect of Singa is its relatively thick, prominent supraorbital torus. However, one complicating factor with Singa is the long-held view that some aspects of the specimen's form might relate to pathology (Brothwell, 1974). Spoor *et al.* (1998) have identified a rare pathology in Singa, absence of the bony labyrinth in the right temporal bone, probably the result of an acoustic neuroma.

It is not clear to what extent the pathology of the specimen influences its modern appearance, but the presence of modern crania at Herto and Omo Kibish from the same time frame suggests that this specimen could well be modern in form regardless of the impact of the individual pathology of the Singa specimen.

The dating and morphological pattern of the Omo and Herto specimens, perhaps supported by that of the Singa skull, establish that early modern humans are present in Africa by at least 154 ka ago, and possibly even earlier. Interestingly, while the ATG is spread throughout Africa, this evidence suggests that the earliest modern specimens from Africa are in fact geographically restricted to the eastern African region. Although admittedly a small sample, the Herto and Omo early modern specimens are several tens of thousands of years older than any other reliably dated specimens in Africa or Eurasia that have been considered 'anatomically modern'. Thus, in addition to focusing on the dispersal pattern of modern humans out of Africa, we should also consider that modern morphology also probably spread within Africa from a more regionally circumscribed initial area of origin, in this case from East Africa.

Early modern humans in southern Africa

This possibility casts a different light on some pertinent southern African hominin specimens, particularly the fragmentary human remains from the Klasies River Mouth Caves, located on the southern Cape coast of South Africa. Although the Klasies River Mouth (KRM) sample has been described as fully anatomically modern (Singer and Wymer, 1982; Bräuer, 1984, 1989, 1992; Rightmire and Deacon, 1991), it has also been interpreted as exhibiting a mosaic of archaic and modern morphologies, as opposed to a fully modern one (Smith, 1985, 1993, 1994; Smith, *et al.*, 1989; Wolpoff and Caspari, 1990; Lam *et al.*, 1996). This is interesting since the vast majority of the KRM hominin fragments derive from the SAS Member at the site and thus are located stratigraphically above uranium disequilibrium dates of 98 ka and 110 ka for the upper part of the older LBS Member (Deacon, 1989). This would bracket the age of the diagnostic KRM hominins between 110 ka and 60 ka, with only the two maxilla fragments coming from deposits stratigraphically below, and thus older than, this age range (Deacon and Shuurman, 1992). Optically stimulated luminescence dating (OSL) by Feathers (2002) indicates an age of <130 ka for the LBS Member and thus as a maximum age for the SAS Member and all of its hominin remains. This chronological evidence demonstrates that the KRM hominins are considerably younger than the Herto and probably the Omo 1 remains.

The KRM human fossil remains are quite fragmentary; in fact, there are no complete skeletal elements. Despite the fragmentation, some elements exhibit clear diagnostic morphology. For example, the most diagnostic postcranial element from KRM is a well preserved proximal ulna, described as exhibiting an archaic total morphological pattern (Churchill *et al.*, 1996). According to Churchill and colleagues, this pattern includes an anterior-facing trochlear notch (like Neandertals and the Border Cave ulna) and archaic cross-sectional geometry of the shaft, although both features do overlap with some modern humans.

The Klasies River cranial fossils are particularly fragmentary and are mostly not very informative. However, a small supraorbital fragment (from just above the nose and medial orbits), a virtually complete left zygomatic bone and a temporal bone fragment do give some insight into the KRM craniofacial form. The zygomatic arch (KRM 16651) has been described as modern (Singer and Wymer, 1982, Rightmire and Deacon, 1991, Bräuer and Singer, 1996), and its inferior margin does suggest a horizontal zygomaticoalveolar margin (ZAM), like in modern humans (Figure 19.5). However, this feature is already found in the ATG (Figure 19.2). Several studies (Smith, 1993, 1994; Janković and Smith, 2005) show that the frontal process (lateral orbital margin) is columnar, as in archaic specimens (Figure 19.5). This morphology can be found in early modern humans as well, but the KRM zygomatic measurements fall solidly within the range of Neandertal samples. Table 19.3 gives the results of an analysis using the frontal process index (FPI), which quantifies the form of the frontal process of the zygomatic. The FPI compares the breath of the facial plate of the process with its minimum breadth (Figure 19.5). A lower value indicates a more columnar form, and the KRM specimen lies well below the archaic mean. Z-scores, which show the divergence of a specimen from the mean in standard deviation units, also indicate a higher probability that the KRM specimen is derived from an archaic population, because the Z-score for the KRM–archaic comparison (–1.25) is smaller that that for the KRM–modern comparison (–1.96).

Additionally, the KRM zygomatic is quite large in overall size, comparable in size to archaic African specimens like Kabwe 1 and Bodo (Smith, 1993). Size, however, does not affect the form of the frontal process of the zygomatic (Janković and Smith, 2005). Furthermore, there is some expansion of the maxillary sinus into the zygomatic body, a feature that is present in all observed Neandertal specimens, but not seen in any of the specimens from the modern human sample. Clearly KRM 16651 is no Neandertal, but its morphology does show distinctively archaic aspects in the form of the columnar lateral orbital margin and its enormous size. This one specimen, then, reflects the mosaic of features that characterises the KRM sample as a whole.

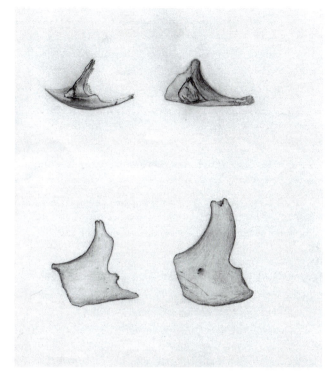

Figure 19.5. Comparison of a recent left zygomatic bone (left) with the KRM 16651 left zygomatic (right), viewed from above (top) and frontally (bottom). Note the columnar nature of the KRM frontal process, which results in increasing the surface area of the zygomatic-frontal articular surface. This is accomplished by essentially 'filling in' the area between the zygomatic frontal process's facial and orbital plates. (Drawing by M. O. Smith.)

The supraorbital specimen (KRM 16425) has the broad interorbital region characteristic of African late Pleistocene specimens, and does not exhibit a supraorbital torus like earlier African archaics (Smith, 1993). This is the basis of the specimen's presumed modernity (Rightmire and Deacon, 1991), and it contrasts sharply with the early modern African adults Herto 1 and Omo Kibish 1, both of which exhibit tori. However, it is not certain that KRM 16425 is fully adult. Ahern and Smith (2004) show that the KRM specimen has frontal sinus development commensurate with a mid-aged subadult rather than an adult. This is important because even older subadult Neandertals lack a strongly developed supraorbital torus, as the Le Moustier 1 specimen demonstrates (Ahern and Smith, 2004). Perhaps the KRM frontal is a specimen at the same ontogenetic level as the Le Moustier Neandertal. If that is the case, the

Table 19.3 *Metric data on the frontal process of the zygomatic in recent modern humans, Neandertals and KRM 16651. The frontal process index (FPI) is calculated by dividing the facial plate breadth by minimum breadth of the frontal process (see Figure 19.5).*

Sample/specimen	Mean FPI	Range	S.D.	*n*
Neandertals[a]	1.19	1.06–1.27	0.08	7
Moderns[b]	1.64	1.22–2.32	0.28	50
KRM 16651	1.09			

Neandertal and modern human sample means differ significantly (p = <0.0001).
Notes:
[a] Specimens from Krapina and Vindija (Croatia) and the Neander Valley (Germany).
[b] Sample composed of robust individuals from Bronze Age through Medieval Croatia.

adult version of KRM 16425 might well have a developed torus as is the case for earlier modern African crania. Like Le Moustier 1, KRM 16425 exhibits a swelling that could be seen as an incipient stage in torus development. Another specimen, this one a fragmentary temporal bone, is mainly modern in form (Grine *et al.*, 1998), but the medial wall of the glenoid (mandibular) fossa is formed entirely from the temporal bone, which is common in some archaic humans (Smith, 1976).

The key elements in the KRM sample are the mandibles. There are five mandibles, four of which preserve the symphysis. The most striking thing about all of them is their relatively small size, particularly given the size and morphology of the KRM zygomatic specimen. Like the cranial pieces, the mandibles have been described as fully modern (Rightmire and Deacon, 1991). The KRM 16424 mandible, the only one lacking a symphysis, is unusually small (Lam *et al.*, 1996). The most commonly pictured KRM mandible is 41815, and it has a distinct mental trigone and a symphyseal morphology that is clearly modern. However, the other three (KNM 21776, 13400, 14695) have relatively vertical symphyses, and only 21776 shows any clear indication of a mental trigone. In fact, the symphyseal profiles of these specimens do not differ much from some late Neandertals (Smith, 1993, 1994). As was the case with the cranial bones, these mandibles are certainly not Neandertals; but as one of us has previously argued (Smith, 1994), it would be difficult to find a recent modern African sample with 75% of its individuals lacking a chin structure. Lam and colleagues (1996) note that the morphological pattern of the KRM mandibles is different from both Neandertals and recent humans. Further, a recent study of lower second molar and mandibular corpus metrics show that KRM exhibits more variability than do recent modern human samples and Neandertals, but not more than samples from Skhūl, Dolní Věstonice or Sima del los Huesos (Royer *et al.*, 2009).

Emergence of modern humans in southern Africa:
an explanation

There are several possible explanations for the KRM morphology. Previously, it has been suggested that the archaic features of the KRM sample reflected their status as early modern humans, for which a mixture of archaic and modern features might be expected (Smith, *et al.*, 1989), and this may still be the case (Bräuer, 1992). Royer and colleagues (2009) explain the marked size variation at KRM compared to recent modern humans as the result of greater sexual dimorphism at KRM. Overall, however, the KRM sample appears more archaic than the earlier modern specimens from Ethiopia, as well as exhibiting high degrees of metric variability. This requires some further discussion.

We believe that the KRM sample reflects the intermixture of early modern populations radiating out of the eastern African region, with local late archaic Africans (likely members of the ATG) in southern Africa. Ackermann *et al.* (2006) have shown that 'hybridity' in baboons is reflected in a higher frequency of skeletal abnormalities (e.g. supernumerary teeth and unusual suture configurations) and unusual degrees of morphological variation. The KRM sample provides no comparable examples of the former, but the extreme small size of the 16424 mandible and teeth might be interpreted as anomalous (but see Royer *et al.*, 2009). We also hold that the high degree of morphological variability seen in the KRM sample reflects its 'hybrid' status. In other words, the mosaic of modern and archaic features in the sample results from admixture between expanding modern people from eastern Africa and indigenous late archaics in southern Africa.

In addition, the rather marked size variation present in the KRM sample also likely reflects admixture. As discussed above, the KRM zygomatic is from a very large individual, but many of the KRM people are substantially smaller. For example, the KRM 16424 mandible is smaller in corpus and dental measurements than any individual drawn from a large sample of more recent, prehistoric Bushmen specimens housed in the South African Museum, and the difference in molar size between this specimen and one of the larger mandible (KRM 13400) exceeds that in the museum sample (Smith, pers. obs.). Royer and colleagues (2009) note that the KRM metric variability, while greater than for living humans and Neandertals, is not unusual for other Pleistocene hominin samples. They find metric variability, comparable to that of KRM, in three fossil samples: Skhūl, Dolní Věstonice and Sima del los Huesos. They attribute all of these cases to increased amounts of sexual dimorphism. Indeed that is likely the explanation for the Middle Pleistocene Sima del los Huesos sample, as higher degrees of sexual dimorphism are likely to characterise human samples of this antiquity (Frayer and Wolpoff, 1985) and a case for such higher degrees of sexual dimorphism has been made previously for this sample (Rosas *et al.*, 2002). However, the Skhūl sample may also demonstrate some admixture of archaic and modern humans (see discussion in Cartmill and Smith, 2009), and Dolní Věstonice, dated at 27 ka, may also reflect residual impact of admixture. To be clear, there are other explanations for the variability in these samples, but admixture cannot be rejected. The demonstration of Neandertal genetic contributions to modern Eurasians (Green *et al.*, 2010) enhances the possibility of such an explanation for both the Dolní Věstonice and Skhūl samples.

Previously, dates for the Border Cave remains from South Africa suggested an age for these hominins of as much as 195 ka (Butzer *et al.*, 1978). The Border Cave cranial and mandibular remains are fully modern (Rightmire, 1979; Bräuer, 1984) as is shown by the fragmentary Border Cave 1 skull (Figure 19.1). Similarly the postcranial remains from the site appear modern (Morris, 1992), except for the ulna, which is similar to the KRM and Neandertal specimens (Churchill *et al.*, 1996). If these specimens were really 195 ka in age, southern African modern humans would be chronologically as early as those from eastern Africa. However, while the dates may be sound indicators of the age of the Border Cave strata, the derivation of the human skeletal remains from those levels has been broadly doubted (Klein, 1983; 2009; Smith *et al.*, 1989). Recently, however, direct ESR dating of the Border Cave 5 mandible indicates an age of ~74 ka for the Border Cave remains (Grün *et al.*, 2003). Thus it would appear that Border Cave and other modern South African remains (Table 19.1) post-date the KRM sample and early East African samples. By this time, the traces of the archaic/modern mosaic and extreme size variation seen in the KRM sample are no more, and there are no longer distinct traces of admixture in southern Africa.

The explanation for the pattern of human evolution outlined above is likely the same as that described by Levin (2002) as extinction by hybridisation. In this process, a species with larger numbers simply overwhelms one with fewer numbers; and over a period of time the rarer species is, according to Levin, first 'mongrelised' and then fully assimilated into the numerically dominant species. We are not convinced that there are different species among late Pleistocene hominins, but the same basic process could result in demographic and genetic swamping of one population, particularly one much smaller in numbers, by a larger one. Although there is evidence that populations were larger in Africa during the late Pleistocene than in Eurasia (see discussion in Relethford, 2001), we do not know whether such a distinction characterises the eastern African region compared with the southern Africa region during this period. However, there are some indications, albeit very imprecise ones (Hassan, 1981), that archaic human populations were generally smaller than modern ones (see also Smith, 2010). We believe that 'extinction' via assimilation of archaic peoples is the type of process that is likely responsible for modern human origins throughout Eurasia and in the southern African 'periphery'.

Early modern humans in North Africa

In North Africa, early modern, or possibly modern, specimens have been recovered from a number of sites (Table 19.1), but problems of chronology make it challenging to identify morphological patterns during the early part of the North African Late Pleistocene. It is difficult to establish the maximum age of any of these specimens, but archaeological associations with the Middle Paleolithic Aterian could mean an age of up to ~130 ka for them (Klein, 2009; Cartmill and Smith, 2009), while the Middle Paleolithic Levalloiso-Mousterian could extend back to ~190 ka (Grün and Stringer, 1991). We can at least be relatively certain that all of these specimens are older than 30 or 40 ka.

The only human remains associated with the Mousterian, other than the Jebel Irhoud specimens, are the two posterior mandible pieces from Haua Fteah, Libya (McBurney, 1967). It is possible that these mandibles are from the same time range as Jebel Irhoud, but it is not possible to establish this based on currently available information. Initial description of the specimens indicated a relatively archaic morphology (Tobias, 1967). However, both specimens have the coronoid/mandibular notch morphology characteristic of modern humans as defined by Rak (1998; but see Jabbour *et al.*, 2002). Additionally, neither specimen exhibits a horizontal-oval mandibular foramen, and the more complete specimen lacks a retromolar space. Thus like the Jebel Irhoud 3 subadult mandible (Hublin and Tillier, 1981), the Haua Fteah specimens do not morphologically correspond to a 'typical' Neandertal form; but they are too fragmentary to provide a complete picture of the overall morphology of their owners.

The Aterian, an interesting Middle Paleolithic variant that dates roughly from ~130 ka to ~40 ka, has some human fossils associated with it. The most complete of the Aterian-associated hominins is an anterior cranial vault and mandible from the Dar-es-Soultane II cave in Morocco, which has been described by Ferembach (1976a; see also Hublin, 1993, 2000). The specimen, Dar-es-Soultane 5, is relatively robust and quite broad, but it exhibits a basically modern form. This is reflected in its relatively high forehead, angled zygomaticoalveolar margin, large and robust mastoid process, and orthognathic face. According to Hublin, the mandible is robust, but modern. However, like many late Pleistocene African crania, Dar-es-Soultane 5 exhibits a moderately developed supraorbital torus. The Aterian-associated specimens from Témara, also from Morocco, are more fragmentary, but the frontal and occipital are described as modern (Ferembach, 1976b). The Témara mandible does not exhibit strong development of a chin, but the overall form of the specimen is modern (Hublin, 1993). The age of these specimens within the Aterian time span is unknown.

The final significant specimen associated with the Aterian is the left side of an approximately nine-year-old child's maxilla from the Mugharet el 'Aliya (High cave) near Tangier, Morocco (Figure 19.6). The specimen, also called the Tangier maxilla, is fragmentary, preserving just the alveolar process of the maxilla originally from the distal I^2 at the front to the extreme mesial part of the crypt for the developing permanent M^2 at the rear. The anterior portion of the specimen (the area around the nasospinale and the incisor sockets) was broken off during its original study. The permanent canine and premolars were present in their crypts, but the canine and P^3 were removed for detailed examination. Discovered by Carleton Coon in 1939, the maxilla was first described by Şenyürek (1940) as a North African representative of the Neandertals. The Neandertal, or at least archaic, affinity of this specimen was reaffirmed by a subsequent study (Myster and Smith, 1990) but questioned by Minugh-Purvis (1993). Minugh-Purvis argued that the Neandertal-like (or archaic) features of the specimen were due to its young age and that the dental metrics overlapped between early moderns and Neandertals. However, a detailed comparative analysis of the Tangier maxilla (Hutchinson, 2000) shows that the dimensions of the alveolar process and dentition tend to fall more than two standard deviations above an age-appropriate sample of modern humans (Table 19.4). In addition, although fragmentary, the specimen lacks a canine fossa and has an orientation of the infraorbital region that approaches the Neandertal condition. These two features were also questioned by Minugh-Purvis, but again when more age-appropriate samples are used (Hutchinson, 2000), the Tangier specimen clearly reflects an archaic, although perhaps not necessarily Neandertal, form.

While this specimen is too fragmentary to allow its unequivocal classification as a Neandertal, its strong similarity to these people cannot be easily dismissed. Given the Neandertal similarities of the Jebel Irhoud hominins discussed elsewhere (Smith *et al.*, 1995), the morphology of the Tangier maxilla becomes all the more interesting. It certainly seems to exhibit a different morphological pattern from the other Aterian-associated specimens, and this raises some intriguing questions. Could the Tangier child's maxilla be evidence of

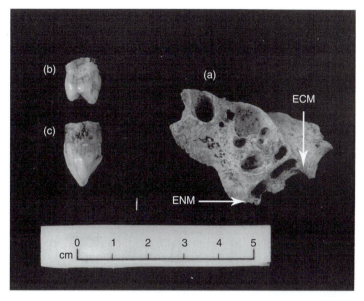

Figure 19.6. An occlusal view of (a) the Tangier subadult maxilla and (b, c) the two permanent teeth removed during its initial analysis: (b) third premolar; (c) canine. (ECM: ectomolare; ENM: entomolare.) Photo: Hillel Burger © President and Fellows of Harvard College, Peabody Museum, Harvard.

Neandertal encroachment into North Africa across the Strait of Gibraltar, which was narrowed during Pleistocene glacial periods? Does it reflect Neandertal biological influence on the morphological makeup of early Late Pleistocene northern African populations? Both of these ideas are generally dismissed, but added to the evidence from Jebel Irhoud, this connection is logical and quite possible given the reduced width of the Strait during Pleistocene glacial events (see Smith *et al.*, 1995). Whatever the source, the Tangier maxilla is more archaic morphologically than other Aterian-associated northern African specimens. This fact, in turn, suggests that early Late Pleistocene North African populations exhibited a morphological mosaic that may well reflect mixing of moderns expanding from eastern Africa and an archaic element already present in North Africa. Whether that archaic element reflects some influence from Neandertals is possible but not definite.

Even if they are from the older end of the complex's temporal range of ~130 ka, these Aterian remains from Mugharet el 'Aliya, Témara and Dar-es-Soultane would still be younger than the early modern sample from East Africa. Thus the North African evidence is also commensurate with possible assimilation, similar to that proposed above for southern Africa.

Table 19.4. *Comparison of the Tangier maxilla with an age-appropriate sample from the S. R. Atkinson Collection, School of Dentistry, University of the Pacific (Hutchinson, 2000).*

	Tangier	Modern mean (*n*, S.D.)	Range	Z-score
Subnasal height	(18.8)[a]	14.3 (88, 2.25)	10.5–19.8	2.0
I² Socket buccolingual width	8.4	6.4 (26, 0.94)	4.5–8.4	2.1
I² Alveolar width	11.0	7.88 (33, 1.3)	4.9–10.7	2.5
C (Upper) buccolingual diameter	10.7	8.2 (87, 1.19)	5.9–11.0	2.1
P³ Buccolingual diameter	10.3	9.1 (84, .5)	7.9–10.1	2.2
P⁴ Socket buccolingual width	14.1	11.8 (54, 1.19)	10.3–12.4	1.9
M¹ Socket buccolingual width	17.8	13.2 (73, 1.21)	10.7–15.9	3.8
M¹ Alveolar width	18.2	14.4 (73, 1.4)	11.3–17.6	2.6
I² Socket/ P⁴ socket	0.6	0.54 (26, 0.028)	0.47–0.62	2.1
I² Alveolus/ M¹ alveolus	0.6	0.55 (33, .021)	0.48–0.61	2.3
C (Upper) B-L diameter/ P³ B-L diameter	1.05	0.85 (84, 0.062)	0.71–1.01	3.2

The modern comparative sample ranges from 7.1 to 11.9 years of age.
Note:
[a] The position of prosthion must be estimated.

A number of other clearly anatomically modern specimens are associated with Upper Paleolithic cultural complexes in North Africa, but most date to <30 ka (Klein, 2009). Probably the oldest is a partial skeleton from Taramsa Hill in Egypt, which according to Vermeersch and colleagues (1998) is likely to date to between 80 ka and 50 ka. This specimen is not yet fully studied but appears to be morphologically similar to the Skhūl/Qafzeh hominins from Israel. Next oldest are the partial skeletons from Nazlet Khater in Egypt, which have been dated to ~37 ka (Vermeersch, 2002). The postcranial anatomy of the more complete specimen, Nazlet Khater 2, is robust but clearly modern. Analyses of this specimen's cranium (Crevecoeur *et al.*, 2009) and mandible (Crevecoeur and Trinkaus, 2004) reaffirm its modern morphology.

It is not clear when archaic features disappear from human populations in North Africa, due to the imprecise chronology in this region. For example, the Tangier maxilla is dated only by its association with the Aterian lithic industry. Thus we do not know whether it is early or late within this sequence. The same is true for essentially all of the Mousterian- or Aterian-associated hominins. But certainly by at least 40 ka, only fully modern populations characterise North Africa, and traces of archaic or admixed samples are gone.

The assimilation model and modern human origins

The assimilation model (AM) was formally articulated in 1989 (Smith *et al.*, 1989); however, elements of it were present earlier. The AM has always asserted that modern humans likely arose in Africa; however, the move towards accepting that Africa may have exerted a recent, significant impact on modern human origins by supporters of the MRE model is a more recent shift in perspective. It now appears likely that modern humans evolved specifically in East Africa, and then spread, with their distinct morphological makeup from this homeland to other parts of the Old World and ultimately beyond. In these points the AM does not differ from the RAO model. However, whereas the RAO model theoretically accepts the possibility of admixture, this is viewed as being inconsequential in the emergence of modern humans outside Africa. The AM agrees with the MRE model that gene flow occurs between regional populations of archaic and early modern humans outside the African homeland of the latter. However, the AM differs with the MRE model in terms of the likely extent of that gene flow. For example, a recent paper by Wolpoff and colleagues (2004) indicates that the degree of Neandertal contribution to early modern Europeans could be as much as 50%. In contrast, the AM holds that evidence of local morphological continuity across the archaic/modern human 'boundary' is much less extensive, being reflected only in limited details of anatomy superimposed on the modern morphological pattern originally derived from Africa (Smith *et al.*, 1989, 2005, 2010; Smith, 2002; Trinkaus and Zilhão, 2002; Trinkaus, 2005; Cartmill and Smith, 2009). This level of morphological continuity is more commensurate with the evidence for relatively small non-African contributions to extant human genetic variation, reflected in the aptly-named 'mostly out of Africa' genetic perspective (see discussions in Relethford, 2001; Templeton, 2002, 2005). The AM is also reasonable given the conclusion that currently-available ancient mito-chondrial DNA for early modern Europeans statistically cannot preclude a Neandertal contribution of <25% (Serre *et al.*, 2004). The AM would expect that contribution to be far less than 25%. If the recent estimate of 1 to 4% Neandertal contribution to extant Eurasian populations is correct (Green *et al.*, 2010), such a level of non-African contribution also fits well with AM predictions. Thus, while there are definitely uncertainties with the model, we believe that the AM is a robust model for conceptualising the emergence of modern people in general.

The evidence from the early modern populations of the African 'peripheries' is also consistent with the AM. This is particularly true in the southern African KRM sample. Considering this sample to be the result of assimilation provides a more satisfying explanation for the fact that its morphology reflects more of an archaic/modern mosaic than the geologically earlier samples of eastern African early modern humans. North Africa is far less compelling a case but, with the Tangier maxilla, there is evidence of an archaic presence in an other-wise largely modern series of Aterian-associated remains. Whatever the ultim-ate process was, there is reason to believe that modern humans radiated within Africa in addition to out of Africa and that the population dynamics leading to modern humans were as complex within those areas as in other regions of the Old World.

Acknowledgements

We thank Andrew Gallagher, Sally Reynolds and Colin Menter for the invi-tation to participate in this tribute to Phillip Tobias; we thank Professor Tobias for all he has done to promote our science and the dignity of the human condition; and we thank Maria Smith and Matt Cartmill for drawing certain of the figures. We are grateful to the many individuals and institu-tions who/that have granted access to the specimens and samples discussed here, and we thank the many colleagues for discussions that influenced our thinking. In particular we are grateful to: A. Morris (Cape Town), G. Avery (Cape Town), B. Asfaw (Addis-Ababa), G. Bräuer (Hamburg), J. Relethford (Oneonta), E. Trinkaus (St. Louis), C. Mulligan (Gainesville), R. Ackermann (Cape Town), F. Grine (Stony Brook), J. Ahern (Laramie), D. Pilbeam (Cambridge), S. Myster (St. Paul), N. Minugh-Purvis (Philadelphia), A. Kramer (Knoxville), D. Serre (Montreal), J-J. Hublin (Leipzig), the Spencer R. Atkinson Library of Applied Anatomy Skull Collection, and the Peabody Museum (Harvard University). Any error in fact or interpretation remains, of course, our responsibility.

References

Ackermann, R., Rogers, J., and Cheverud, J. (2006). Identifying the morphological signatures of hybridization in primate and human evolution. *Journal of Human Evolution*, **51**: 632–45.

Ahern, J. and Smith, F. (2004). Adolescent archaics or adult moderns? Le Moustier 1 as a model for estimating age at death of fragmentary supraorbital fossils in the modern human origins debate. *Homo*, **55**: 1–19.

Beaumont, P., de Villiers, H. and J. Vogel (1978). Modern man in sub-Saharan Africa prior to 49,000 years BP: a review and evaluation with particular reference to Border cave. *South African Journal of Science*, **74**: 409–14.

Berger, L. and Parkington, J. (1995). A new Pleistocene hominid-bearing locality at Hoedjiespunt, South Africa. *American Journal of Physical Anthropology*, **98**: 601–9.

Bräuer, G. (1984). A craniological approach to the origin of anatomically modern *Homo sapiens* in Africa and implications for the appearance of modern Europeans. In Smith, F. and Spencer, F. (eds.), *The Origins of Modern Humans. A World Survey of the Fossil Evidence*. New York: Liss, pp. 327–410.

(1989). The evolution of modern humans: a comparison of the African and non-African evidence. In Mellars, P. and Stringer, C. (eds.), *The Human Revolution: Behavioral and Biological Perspectives on the Origins of Modern Humans*. Edinburgh: University of Edinburgh Press, pp. 123–54.

(1992). Africa's place in the evolution of *Homo sapiens*. In Bräuer, G. and Smith, F. (eds.), *Continuity or Replacement? Controversies in* Homo sapiens *Evolution*. Rotterdam: Balkema, pp. 83–98.

(2004). Das Out-of-Africa-Modell und die Kontroverse um den Ursprung des modernen Menschen. In Conard, N. (ed.), *Woher kommt der Mensch*. Tübingen: Atempo, pp. 164–87.

(2008). The origin of modern anatomy: by speciation or intraspecific evolution? *Evolutionary Anthropology*, **17**: 22–37.

Bräuer, G. and Leakey, R. (1986). The ES-11693 cranium from Eliye Springs, West Turkana, Kenya. *Journal of Human Evolution*, **15**: 289–312.

Bräuer, G. and Mehlman, M. (1988). Hominid molars from a Middle Stone Age level at Mumba Rock shelter, Tanzania. *American Journal of Physical Anthropology*, **75**: 69–76.

Bräuer, G. and Singer, R. (1996). The Klasies zygomatic bone: archaic or modern? *Journal of Human Evolution*, **30**: 161–5.

Bräuer, G. and Stringer, C. (1997). Models, polarization and perspectives on modern human origins. In Clark, G. and Willermet, K. (eds). *Conceptual Issues in Modern Human Origins Research*. New York: Aldine De Gruyter, pp. 191–201.

Bräuer, G., Yokoyama, Y., Falguères, C. *et al.* (1997). Modern human origins back-dated. *Nature*, **386**: 337–8.

Bräuer, G., Collard, M. and Stringer, C. (2004). On the reliability of recent tests of the Out of Africa hypothesis for modern human origins. *Anatomical Record*, **279A**: 701–7.

Brothwell, D. (1974). The Upper Pleistocene Singa skull: a problem in paleontological interpretation. In Bernhard, W. and Kandler, A. (eds.), *Bevölkerungsbiologie*. Stuttgart: Fischer, pp. 534–45.

Butzer, K. (1969). Geological interpretation of two Pleistocene hominid sites in the Lower Omo Basin. *Nature*, **222**: 1133–5.

Butzer, K., Beaumont, P. and Vogel, J. (1978). Lithostratigraphy of Border Cave, KwaZulu, South Africa: a Middle Stone Age sequence beginning c. 195,000 B.P. *Journal of Archaeological Science*, **5**: 317–41.

Cartmill, M. and Smith, F. (2009). *The Human Lineage*. Hoboken: Wiley-Blackwell.

Churchill, S. E., Pearson, O. M., Grine, F. E. *et al.* (1996). Morphological affinities of the proximal ulna from Klasies River Mouth Main Site: archaic or modern? *Journal of Human Evolution*, **3**: 213–37.

Clark, J. (1988). The Middle Stone Age of East Africa and the beginnings of regional identity. *Journal of World Prehistory*, **2**: 235–305.

Clark, J., Beyenne, Y., WoldeGabriel, G. *et al.* (2003). Stratigraphic, chronological and behavioural context of Pleistocene *Homo sapiens* from Middle Awash, Ethiopia. *Nature*, **423**: 747–52.

Crevecoeur, I. and Trinkaus, E. (2004). From the Nile to the Danube: a comparison of the Nazlet Khater 2 and Oase 1 early modern human mandibles. *Anthropologie*, **42**: 229–39.

Crevecoeur, I., Rougier, H., Grine, F. *et al.* (2009). Modern human cranial diversity in the late Pleistocene of Africa and Eurasia: evidence from Nazlet Khater, Peştera cu Oase, and Hofmeyr. *American Journal of Physical Anthropology*, **140**: 347–58.

Day, M. and Stringer, C. (1982). A reconsideration of the Omo-Kibish remains and the *erectus–sapiens* transition. In deLumley, M. (ed.), *L'Homo erectus et la place de l'homme de Tautavel parmi les hominids*. Nice: CNRS, pp. 814–46.

Deacon, H. (1989). Late Pleistocene paleoecology and archaeology in the southern Cape, South Africa. In Mellars, P. and Stringer, C. (eds.), *The Human Revolution: Behavioral and Biological Perspectives on the Origins of Modern Humans*. Edinburgh: University of Edinburgh Press, pp. 547–64.

Deacon, H. and R. Shuurman (1992). The origins of modern people: the evidence from Klasies River. In Bräuer, G. and Smith, F. (eds.), *Continuity or Replacement? Controversies in* Homo sapiens *Evolution*. Rotterdam: Balkema, pp. 121–9.

Debénath, A., Raynal, J.-P., Roche, J. *et al.* (1986). Stratigraphie, habitat, typologie, et devenir de l'Atérien marocain: données récentes. *L'Anthropologie*, **90**: 233–46.

Feathers, J. (2002). Luminescence dating in less than ideal conditions: case studies from Klasies River main site and Duinefontein, South Africa. *Journal of Archaeological Science*, **29**: 177–94.

Ferembach, D. (1976a). Les restes humains de la grotte de Dar-es-Soultane 2 (Maroc). *Bulletin et mémoire de la Société de l'Anthropologie de Paris*, **3**: 183–93.

(1976b). Les restes humains de Témara (Campagne 1975). *Bulletin et mémoire de la Société de l'Anthropologie de Paris*, **3**: 175–80.

Frayer, D. and Wolpoff, M. (1985). Sexual dimorphism. *Annual Review of Anthropology*, **14**: 429–73.

Green, R., Krause, J., Briggs, A. *et al.* (2010). A draft sequence of the Neandertal genome. *Science*, **238**: 710–22.

Grine, F. and Klein, R. (1985). Pleistocene and Holocene human remains from Equus Cave, South Africa. *Anthropology*, **8**: 55–98.

(1993). Late Pleistocene human remains from the Sea Harvest site, Saldanha Bay, South Africa. *South African Journal of Science*, **89**: 145–52.

Grine, F., Klein, R. and Volman, T. (1991). Dating, archaeology, and human fossil remains from the Middle Stone Age levels of Die Kelders, South Africa. *Journal of Human Evolution*, **21**: 363–95.

Grine, F., Pearson, O., Klein, R. *et al.* (1998). Additional human remains from Klasies River mouth, South Africa. *Journal of Human Evolution*, **35**: 95–107.

Grün, R. and Stringer, C. (1991). Electron spin resonance dating and the evolution of modern humans. *Archaeometry*, **33**: 153–99.

Grün, R., Brink, J., Spooner, N. *et al.* (1996). Direct dating of Florisbad hominid. *Nature*, **382**: 500–1.

Grün, R., Beaumont, P., Tobias, P. *et al.* (2003). On the age of Border Cave 5 human mandible. *Journal of Human Evolution*, **45**: 155–67.

Haile-Selassie, Y., Asfaw, B. and White, T. (2004). Hominid cranial remains from Upper Pleistocene deposits at Aduma, Middle Awash, Ethiopia. *American Journal of Physical Anthropology*, **123**: 1–10.

Hassan, F. (1981). *Demographic Archaeology*. New York: Academic Press.

Hublin, J.-J. (1985). Human fossils from the North African Middle Pleistocene and the origin of *Homo sapiens*. In Delson, E. (ed.), *Ancestors: the Hard Evidence*. New York: Liss, pp. 283–8.

(1993). Recent human evolution in Northwest Africa. In Aitken, M., Stringer, C. and Mellars, P. (eds.), *The Origins of Modern Humans and the Impact of Chronometric Dating*. Princeton: Princeton University Press, pp. 118–31.

(2000). Modern–nonmodern hominid interactions: a Mediterranean perspective. In Bar-Yosef, O. and Pilbeam, D. (eds.), *The Geography of Neandertals and Modern Humans in Europe and the Greater Mediterranean*. Cambridge: Harvard Peabody Museum Bulletin Number 8, pp. 157–82.

Hublin, J.-J. and A.-M. Tillier (1981). The Mousterian juvenile mandible from Irhoud (Morocco): a phylogenetic interpretation. In Stringer, C. (ed), *Aspects of Human Evolution*. London: Taylor and Francis, pp. 176–85.

Hutchinson, V. (2000). Circum-Mediterranean population dynamics in the Late Pleistocene: evidence from the Tangier (Morocco) maxilla. Unpublished MA thesis, Northern Illinois University.

Jabbour, R., Richards, G. and Anderson, J. (2002). Mandibular condyle traits in Neanderthals and other *Homo*: a comparative, correlative and ontogenetic study. *American Journal of Physical Anthropology*, **119**: 144–55.

Janković, I. and Smith, F. (2005). Comparative morphometrics of Neandertal zygomatic bones. *American Journal of Physical Anthropology Supplement*, **40**: 121–2.

Kennedy, G. (1984). The emergence of *Homo sapiens*: the postcranial evidence. *Man*, **19**: 94–110.

Klein, R. (1983). The stone age prehistory of southern Africa. *Annual Review of Anthropology*, **12**: 25–48.

(1989). Biological and behavioral perspectives on modern human origins in southern Africa. In Mellars, P. and Stringer, C. (eds.), *The Human Revolution: Behavioral and Biological Perspectives on the Origins of Modern Humans.* Edinburgh: University of Edinburgh Press, pp. 547–64.

(2000). Archaeology and the evolution of human behavior. *Evolutionary Anthropology*, **9**: 17–36.

(2003). Whither the Neanderthals? *Science*, **299**: 1525–7.

(2009). *The Human Career. Human Biological and Cultural Origins*, 3rd edn. Chicago: University of Chicago Press.

Lam, Y., Pearson, O. and Smith, C. (1996). Chin morphology and sexual dimorphism in the fossil hominid mandible sample from Klasies River Mouth. *American Journal of Physical Anthropology*, **100**: 545–57.

Levin, D. (2002). Hybridization and extinction. *American Scientist*, **90**: 254–61.

Manega, P. (1993). Geochronology, geochemistry and isotopic study of the Plio-Pleistocene hominid sites and the Ngorongoro volcanic highlands in Northern Tanzania. Unpublished PhD dissertation, University of Colorado.

McBrearty, S. and Brooks, A. (2000). The revolution that wasn't: a new interpretation of the origin of modern human behavior. *Journal of Human Evolution*, **39**: 453–563.

McBurney, C. (ed.) (1967). *The Haua Fteah (Cyrenaica) and the Stone Age of the South-East Mediterranean.* Cambridge: Cambridge University Press.

McDermott, F., Stringer, C., Grün, R. *et al.* (1996). New Late Pleistocene uranium–thorium and ESR dates for the Singa hominid (Sudan). *Journal of Human Evolution*, **31**: 507–16.

McDougall, I., Brown, F. and Fleagle, J. (2005). Stratigraphic placement and age of modern humans from Kibish, Ethiopia. *Nature*, **433**: 733–6.

(2008). Sapropels and the age of Omo I and II, Kibish, Ethiopia. *Journal of Human Evolution*, **55**: 409–20.

Miller, G., Beaumont, P., Jull, A. *et al.* (1993). Pleistocene geochronology and palaeothermometry from protein diagenesis in ostrich eggshells: implications for the evolution of modern humans. In Aitken, M., Stringer, C. and Mellars, P. (eds.), *The Origins of Modern Humans and the Impact of Chronometric Dating.* Princeton: Princeton University Press, pp. 49–68.

Minugh-Purvis, N. (1993). Re-examination of the immature hominid maxilla from Tangier, Morocco. *American Journal of Physical Anthropology*, **92**: 449–61.

Morris, A. (1992). Biological relationships between Upper Pleistocene and Holocene populations in southern Africa. In Bräuer, G. and Smith, F. (eds.), *Continuity or Replacement? Controversies in* Homo sapiens *Evolution.* Rotterdam: Balkema, pp. 131–43.

Myster, S. and Smith, F. (1990). The taxonomic dilemma of the Tangier maxilla: a metric and non-metric assessment. *American Journal of Physical Anthropology*, **81**: 273–4.

Passarino, G., Semino, O., Quintana-Murci, L. *et al.* (1998). Different genetic components in the Ethiopian population, identified by mtDNA and Y-chromosome polymorphisms. *American Journal of Human Genetics*, **61**: 1015–35.

Pearson, O. (2004). Has the combination of genetic and fossil evidence solved the riddle of modern human origins? *Evolutionary Anthropology*, **13**: 145–59.

Pearson, O., Royer, D., Grine, F. *et al.* (2008). A description of the Omo I postcranial skeleton, including newly discovered fossils. *Journal of Human Evolution*, **55**: 421–37.

Protsch, R. (1974). Florisbad: its paleoanthropology, chronology and archaeology. *Homo*, **25**: 68–78.

Quintana-Murci, L., Semino, O., Bandelt, H. *et al.* (1999). Genetic evidence of an early exit of *Homo sapiens sapiens* from Africa through eastern Africa. *Nature Genetics*, **23**(4): 437–41.

Rak, Y. (1998). Does any Mousterian cave present evidence of two hominid species? In Akazawa, T., Aoki, K. and Bar-Yosef, O. (eds.), *Neandertals and Modern Humans in Western Asia*. New York: Plenum, pp. 353–66.

Relethford, J. (1999). Models, predictions and the fossil record of modern human origins. *Evolutionary Anthropology*, **8**: 7–10.

(2001). *Genetics and the Search for Modern Human Origins*. New York: Wiley-Liss.

Rightmire, G. P. (1976). Relationships of Middle and Upper Pleistocene hominids from sub-Saharan Africa. *Nature*, **260**: 238–40.

(1978). Florisbad and human population succession in southern Africa. *American Journal of Physical Anthropology*, **48**: 475–86.

(1979). Implications of the Border Cave skeletal remains for later Pleistocene human evolution. *Current Anthropology*, **48**: 23–35.

(1983). The Lake Ndutu cranium and early *Homo sapiens* in Africa. *American Journal of Physical Anthropology*, **61**: 245–54.

(1984). *Homo sapiens* in sub-Saharan Africa. In Smith, F. and Spencer, F. (eds.), *The Origins of Modern Humans. A World Survey of the Fossil Evidence*. New York: Liss, pp. 295–325.

Rightmire, G. P. and Deacon, H. (1991). Comparative studies of late Pleistocene human remains from Klasies River Mouth, South Africa. *Journal of Human Evolution*, **20**: 131–56.

Rosas, A., Bastir, M., Martínez-Maza, C. *et al.* (2002). Sexual dimorphism in the Atapuerca-SH hominids: the evidence from the mandibles. *Journal of Human Evolution*, **42**: 451–74.

Royer, D., Lockwood, C., Scott, J. *et al.* (2009). Size variation in early human mandibles and molars from Klasies River, South Africa: comparison with other Middle and Late Pleistocene assemblages and with modern humans. *American Journal of Physical Anthropology*, **140**: 312–23.

Schwartz, J. and Tattersall, E. (2010). Fossil evidence for the origin of *Homo sapiens*. *Yearbook of Physical Anthropology*, **53**: 94–121.

Semino, O., Santachiara-Benerecetti, A., Falaschi, F. *et al.* (2002). Ethiopians and Khoisan share the deepest clades of the human Y- chromosome phylogeny. *American Journal of Human Genetics*, **70**: 265–8.

Şenyürek, M. (1940). Fossil man in Tangier. *Papers of the Peabody Museum of Archaeology and Ethnology*, **16**(3): 1–27.

Serre, D., Langaney, A., Chech, M. *et al.* (2004). No evidence of Neandertal mtDNA contribution to early modern humans. *PLOS Biology*, **2**: 313–17.

Singer, R. and Wymer, J. (1982). *The Middle Stone Age at Klasies River Mouth in South Africa*. Chicago: University of Chicago Press.

Smith, F. (1976). The Neandertal remains from Krapina: a descriptive and comparative study. Knoxville: University of Tennessee Department of Anthropology Reports of Investigation 15.

(1985). Continuity and change in the origin of modern *Homo sapiens*. *Zeitschrift für Morphologie und Anthropologie*, **75**: 197–222.

(1993). Models and realities in modern human origins: the African fossil evidence. In Aitken, M., Stringer, C. and Mellars, P. (eds.), *The Origins of Modern Humans and the Impact of Chronometric Dating*. Princeton: Princeton University Press, pp. 234–48.

(1994). Samples, species and speculations in the study of modern human origins. In Nitecki, M. and Nitecki, D. (eds.), *Origins of Anatomically Modern Humans*. New York: Plenum, pp. 227–49.

(1997a). Modern human origins. In Vogel, J. (ed.), *Encyclopedia of Precolonial Africa*. Walnut Creek: Altamira Press, pp. 257–66.

(1997b). Modern human origins. In Spencer, F. (ed.), *History of Physical Anthropology. An Encyclopedia*. New York and London: Garland, pp. 661–72.

(2002). Migrations, radiations, and continuity: patterns in the evolution of Middle and Late Pleistocene humans. In Hartwig, W. (ed.), *The Primate Fossil Record*. Cambridge: Cambridge University Press, pp.437–56.

(2010). Species, populations and assimilation in later human evolution. In Larsen, C. (ed.), *A Companion to Biological Anthropology*. Hoboken: Wiley-Blackwell, pp. 357–78

Smith, F., Falsetti, A. and Donnelly, S. (1989). Modern human origins. *Yearbook of Physical Anthropology*, **32**: 35–68.

Smith, F., Falsetti, A. and Simmons, T. (1995). Circum-Mediterranean biological connections and pattern of Late Pleistocene human evolution. In Ullrich, H. (ed.), *Man and Environment in the Paleolithic*. Liège: ERAUL, pp.197–207.

Smith, F., Janković, I. and Karavanić, I. (2005). The assimilation model, modern human origins in Europe, and the extinction of the Neandertals. *Quaternary International*, **137**: 7–19.

Spoor, F., Stringer, C. and Zonneveld, F. (1998). Rare temporal bone pathology of the Singa calvaria from Sudan. *American Journal of Physical Anthropology*, **107**: 41–50.

Stringer, C. (1979). A re-evaluation of the fossil human calvaria from Singa, Sudan. *Bulletin of the British Museum of Natural History (Geology)*, **32**: 77–83.

(2002). Modern human origins: progress and prospects. *Philosophical Transactions of the Royal Society of London, Series B*, **357**: 563–79.

(2003). Out of Ethiopia. *Nature*, **423**: 692–5.

Stringer, C. and Andrews, P. (1988). Genetic and fossil evidence for the origin of modern humans. *Science*, **239**: 1263–8.

Stringer, C., Cornish, L. and Stuart-Macadam, P. (1985). Preparation and further study of the Singa skull from the Sudan. *Bulletin of the British Museum of Natural History (Geology)*, **38**: 347–58.

Stynder, D., Moggi-Cecchi, J., Berger, L. *et al.* (2001). Human mandibular incisors from the Middle Pleistocene locality of Hoedjiespunt, South Africa. *Journal of Human Evolution*, **41**: 369–83.

Templeton, A. (2002). Out of Africa again and again. *Nature*, **416**: 45–51.

(2005). Haplotype trees and modern human origins. *Yearbook of Physical Anthropology*, **48**: 33–59.

Tobias, P. (1967). The hominid skeletal remains of Haua Fteah. In McBurney, C. (ed.), *The Haua Fteah (Cyrenaica) and the Stone Age of the South-East Mediterranean*. Cambridge: Cambridge University Press, pp. 337–52.

Trinkaus, E. (2005). Early modern humans. *Annual Review of Anthropology*, **34**: 207–30.

Trinkaus, E. and Zilhão, J. (2002). Phylogenetic implications. In Zilhão, J. and Trinkaus, E. (eds.), *Portrait of the Artist as a Young Child. The Gravettian Human Skeleton from the Abrigo do Lagar Velho and its Archaeological Context*. Lisbon: Trabalhos de Arqueologia Number 22, pp. 497–518.

Underhill, P., Shen, P., Lin, A. *et al.* (2000). Y chromosome sequence variation and the history of human populations. *Nature Genetics*, **26**: 358–61.

Vermeersch, P. (2002). Two Upper Paleolithic burials at Nazlet Khater. In Vermeersch, P. (ed.), *Paleolithic Quarrying Sites in Upper and Middle Egypt*. Leuven: Leuven University Press, pp. 273–82.

Vermeersch, P., Paulissen, E., Stokes, S. *et al.* (1998). A Middle Paleolithic burial of a modern human at Taramsa Hill, Egypt. *Antiquity*, **72**: 475–84.

Weaver, T. D. and Roseman, C. C. (2008). New developments in the genetic evidence for modern human origins. *Evolutionary Anthropology*, **17**: 69–80.

White, T., Asfaw, B., DeGusta, D. *et al.* (2003). Pleistocene *Homo sapiens* from Middle Awash, Ethiopia. *Nature*, **423**: 742–7.

Willoughby, P. (2007). *The Evolution of Modern Humans in Africa*. Lanham: Altamira Press.

Wolpoff, M. and Caspari, R. (1990). On Middle Paleolithic/Middle Stone Age hominid taxonomy. *Current Anthropology*, **31**: 394–5.

Wolpoff, M., Hawks, J. and Caspari, R. (2000). Multiregional, not multiple origins. *American Journal of Physical Anthropology*, **112**: 129–36.

Wolpoff, M., Hawks, J., Frayer, D. *et al.* (2001). Modern human ancestry at the peripheries: a test of the replacement theory. *Science*, **291**: 293–7.

Wolpoff, M., Mannheim, B., Mann, A. *et al.* (2004). Why not the Neandertals? *World Archaeology*, **36**: 527–46.

20 Patterns of Middle Pleistocene hominin evolution in Africa and the emergence of modern humans

EMMA MBUA AND GÜNTER BRÄUER

Abstract

Over the last two decades, different views have emerged on the mode of Middle Pleistocene evolution in Africa, and the origin of modern humans. These mainly range from an evolutionary change within one species *Homo sapiens* over much of the Middle Pleistocene, to the existence of two or three different species during this time. This chapter presents the results of a new comprehensive study of the Middle and early Late Pleistocene cranial remains based on a large number of both non-metric and metric features of potential phylogenetic relevance. The aim of the study is to examine whether modern human cranial morphology is a result of long-term diachronic changes favouring a single evolving species, *H. sapiens*, or whether multiple Middle Pleistocene species were involved in the evolution to modern *H. sapiens*. Results from this study suggest that the origin of modern human anatomy is a product of a continuous remodelling of major aspects of vault and face from conditions seen in early Middle Pleistocene groups. The increasing mosaic-like emergence and accumulation of more derived, near-modern or modern morphology over this long period of time does not provide convincing evidence for any anagenetic or cladogenetic speciation events. Rather, it appears that any patterns or subdivisions were below the species level.

Introduction

The evolutionary history and taxonomy of the Middle and early Late Pleistocene hominins is a contentious topic. During the 1990s and 2000s, evidence accumulated that points to Africa as the place for the origin of modern anatomy between 200 to 150 ka. The latest evidence particularly from Ethiopia

African Genesis: Perspectives on Hominin Evolution, eds. Sally C. Reynolds and Andrew Gallagher. Published by Cambridge University Press. © Cambridge University Press 2012.

clearly indicates that modern humans developed in Africa much earlier than they appeared in any other part of the world (Bräuer *et al.*, 1997; White *et al.*, 2003; McDougall *et al.*, 2005; Bräuer, 2007). Nevertheless, over the last decade considerable debate has emerged on the mode of evolution for origin of modern anatomy in Africa and on the number of species involved in this process. Several authors favour a speciation event for the origin of *Homo sapiens* in Africa at the beginning of Middle Pleistocene and subsequent evolution to anatomically modern humans in Africa over several hundreds of thousands of years (e.g. Bräuer *et al.*, 1997; Klein, 1999; Bräuer, 2001; Turbón, 2006). It has also been suggested that this continuous evolutionary lineage could be subdivided into three grades. The first is early archaic *H. sapiens*, which includes specimens such as Bodo, Broken Hill (Kabwe) and Hopefield (Saldanha) that are clearly derived relative to *Homo erectus*. Another is late archaic *H. sapiens* (e.g. KNM-ER 3884, LH 18, Florisbad), which are again derived compared to the morphological pattern of the early archaics, and last are anatomically modern humans (e.g. Bräuer *et al.*, 1997; Bräuer, 2001). Because of their mosaic morphological pattern the late archaics have also been designated the 'African transitional group' (ATG) (Smith, 1993, 2002). Other authors (e.g. Rightmire, 1998) also see evidence for a speciation event from *H. erectus* at around 800 or 700 ka in Africa but designate the new species *Homo heidelbergensis*. They further assume two other speciation events, one in Africa leading to *H. sapiens* (anatomically modern humans) and another in Europe giving rise to *Homo neanderthalensis*. Foley and Lahr (1997, 2003) even distinguish three Middle Pleistocene species in Africa, *Homo heidelbergensis* (roughly equivalent to only the early archaics *sensu* Bräuer), *Homo helmei* (late archaics), and *H. sapiens* (anatomically modern humans). According to these authors, *H. helmei* was also present in Europe, but McBrearty and Brooks (2000) refer to this species as the immediate African ancestor of modern humans only. Stringer (2002) designates the late archaics as archaic *H. sapiens* and early archaics as *H. heidelbergensis*. Lieberman *et al.* (2002, 2004), however, see a major anatomical shift and speciation event somewhere between archaic *H. sapiens* *sensu* Stringer and anatomically modern *H. sapiens*.

Besides the current discussions regarding taxonomic diversity, further questions relate to the place for origin of modern humans within Africa. Eastern, southern and northwestern Africa have all been favoured by different authors in this respect (see e.g. Hublin, 1992; Rightmire, 1996; Bräuer, 2001; White *et al.*, 2003). The prevailing question is thus – did one part of the continent play a major role in this process, or did modernisation occur in a complex mosaic-like fashion in several parts of Africa? The present study aims to provide further evidence regarding these questions. Based on a new study approach involving comprehensive analysis of morphological traits, the study sets out to investigate whether modern cranial morphology is likely to have resulted from long-term diachronic changes, or from multiple speciation events. Results of the new approach would have implications for the currently discussed taxonomic alternatives and will give new insights regarding the geographic pattern of *H. sapiens* evolution. In order to obtain additional information on ancestral conditions of morphological features, we examined a number of African *Homo erectus* specimens as well. *Homo erectus* is regarded here as one species found in Asia, Africa and probably in Europe, thus including the early Turkana specimens (Bräuer and Mbua, 1992; Walker and Leakey, 1993; Bräuer, 1994; Rightmire, 1998; Asfaw *et al.*, 2002).

Material and features

The Middle to early Late Pleistocene cranial material used in this study comprises 23 specimens from eastern, southern and northwestern Africa (Table 20.1). In addition, six African *H. erectus* specimens were included. One of us (E.M.) obtained almost all the data from original fossils or high-quality casts housed in different museums and institutions within Africa and Europe. The present approach was restricted to cranial morphology. Thus, mandibles, dental remains and postcranial remains were not included.

Based on a review of published descriptions and analyses of all relevant fossil specimens, 47 non-metrical (Table 20.2) and 57 metrical (Table 20.3) variables were chosen for the study. Selection of features is based on their potential phylogenetic relevance for this part of human evolution. For assessment of non-metrical variables new scoring methods were developed or published schemes used (information on the scoring categories are given only for those features that showed clear changes; see legends on Figures 20.1, 20.2 and text). Most of the categories were defined based on the occurrence and variation of the features as published for both Middle/early Late Pleistocene hominins from Africa and *H. erectus*. The character states distinguish between ancestral and derived modern conditions, as well as intermediate states. As indicated in Table 20.3, the measurements used are defined by Howells (1973) and Bräuer (1988).

Results

In order to test for morphological changes over time among the 104 non-metrical and metrical variables considered, we used bivariate graphs. In addition, we computed Spearman's correlation coefficient (r_s) for the measurements. The

Table 20.1. *African cranial remains used in the study (o = original; c = cast; l = literature/slides).*

Specimen	Element	Dating (Ma)	References
East Africa			
Bodo (o)	Partial cranium	0.6	Clark *et al.* (1994); Rightmire (1996)
Ndutu (o)	Partial cranium	0.4	Manega (1995)
Eyasi 1 (o)	Partial cranium	0.4–0.3	Bräuer and Mabulla (1996)
Eyasi 2 (o)	Occipital fragment	0.4–0.3	Bräuer and Mabulla (1996)
LH 18 (o)	Cranium	0.3–0.2	Magori and Day (1983); Manega (1995)
Eliye Springs (o)	Cranium	>0.2	Bräuer and Leakey (1986)
Ileret/ER 3884 (o)	Partial cranium	0.27	Bräuer *et al.* (1997)
Singa (c)	Cranium	0.15	McDermott *et al.* (1996)
Omo 1 (o)	Cranium	0.2	Day and Stringer (1982); McDougall *et al.* (2005)
Omo 2 (o)	Cranium	0.2	Day and Stringer (1982); McDougall *et al.* (2005)
Omo 3 (o)	Cranium	0.1	Day and Stringer (1982); McDougall *et al.* (2005)
South Africa			
Hopefield (o)	Cranium	0.4	Klein (1999)
Broken Hill 1 (c)	Cranium	0.4–0.3	Klein (1999)
Broken Hill 2 (c)	Maxilla	0.4–0.3	Klein (1999)
Florisbad (c)	Partial cranium	0.26	Clarke (1985); Grün *et al.* (1996)
KRM 16425 (o)	Frontal piece	0.085	Rightmire and Deacon (1991); Grün and Stringer (1991)
SAM-AP 6269 (o)	Right temporal	0.085	Grün and Stringer (1991)
Border Cave 1 (o)	Partial cranium	0.115–0.09	Grün and Beaumont (2001)
Northwest Africa			
Salé (c)	Partial cranium	0.4	Hublin (1989); Klein (1999)
Thomas Quarry (l)	Frontal fragment	0.4	Hublin (1989); Klein (1999)
Jebel Irhoud 1 (c)	Cranium	0.19	Hublin (1992); Grün and Stringer (1991)
Jebel Irhoud 2 (c)	Partial cranium	0.19	Hublin (1992)
Dar es Soltane 2 (c)	Partial skull	0.09–0.06	Hublin (1992); McBrearty and Brooks (2000)
Homo erectus			
ER 3733 (o)	Cranium	1.78	Wood (1991); Feibel *et al.* (1989)
ER 3883 (o)	Cranium	1.57	Wood (1991); Feibel *et al.* (1989)
OH 9 (o)	Cranium	1.48	Leakey and Hay (1982); Delson *et al.* (2000)
WT 15000 (o)	Cranium	1.5	Walker and Leakey (1993); Feibel *et al.* (1989)
OH 12 (o)	Cranial fragments	0.7	Leakey and Hay (1982)
Tighenif (c)	Parietal	0.8–0.7	Geraads *et al.* (1986)

Table 20.2. *Non-metrical features used in this study.*

	Feature	Selected references
F1	Anterior border of glabellar torus	Santa Luca (1980), Bräuer (1984b), Wu and Bräuer (1993)
F2	Superior surface of glabellar torus	Rightmire (1990), Wu and Bräuer (1993)
F3	Supraorbital torus in superior view	Hublin (1986)
F4	Supraorbital torus in anterior view	Bräuer (1984a) Hublin (1986)
F5	Position of maximum thickness of supraorbital torus	Bräuer (1984a), Rightmire (1996)
F6	Shape of supraorbital torus	Bräuer (1984b), Rightmire (1996)
F7	Course of supratoral sulcus	Weidenreich (1943), Rightmire (1984b)
F8	Depth of supratoral sulcus	Weidenreich (1943)
F9	Course of inferior supraorbital margin	Rightmire (1979), Groves (1989)
F10	Location of supraorbital tubercle	Weidenreich (1943)
F11	Degree of supraorbital tubercle development	Weidenreich (1943)
F12	Location of the supraorbital notch	Santa Luca (1980)
F13	Degree of supraorbital notch development	Weidenreich (1943), Santa Luca (1980)
F14	Glabella projection relative to nasion	Santa Luca (1980), Lahr (1996)
F15	Bregmatic eminence	Weidenreich (1943), Bräuer and Mbua (1992)
F16	Coronal extension of bregmatic eminence	Weidenreich (1943), Lahr (1996)
F17	Frontal keel	Andrews (1984), Bräuer and Mbua (1992)
F18	Location of frontal keel along the frontal arc	Bräuer and Mbua (1992)
F19	Parasagittal flattening/depression	Weidenreich (1943), Lahr (1996)
F20	Development of temporal crests/lines	Rightmire (1990), Wu and Bräuer (1993)
P1	Parietal sagittal keel	Santa Luca (1980), Bräuer and Mbua (1992)
P2	Parasagittal flattening/depression	Weidenreich (1943), Bräuer and Mbua (1992)
P3	Orientation of the lateral cranial walls	Rightmire (1983), Bräuer (1994)
P4	Parietal bossing	Aiello and Dean (1990), Rightmire (1990)
P5	Position of maximum cranial breadth	Andrews (1984), Wood (1984), Bräuer (1994)
P6	Angular torus	Andrews (1984), Wood (1984), Rightmire (1990)
P7	Location of angular torus	Santa Luca (1980), Aiello and Dean (1990)
T1	Course of the squamosal suture	De Villiers (1968), Stringer (1984), Hublin (1986)
T2	Thickness of anterior tympanic plate	Bräuer (1984a), Rightmire (1984b), Stringer (1984)
T3	Angulation between tympanic (fissure Glaser) and petrous bone	Weidenreich (1943), Kimbel *et al.* (1984), Stringer (1984), Wood (1984), Rightmire (1990)
T4	Depth of glenoid fossa/development of articular tubercle	Andrews (1984), Kimbel *et al.* (1984)

Table 20.2. (*cont.*)

	Feature	Selected references
T5	Occipitomastoid/juxtamastoid eminence	Kimbel *et al.* (1984), Rightmire (1990)
T6	Posterior aspect of the mastoid process	Rightmire (1990)
T7	Strength of the supramastoid crest	Santa Luca (1980), Rightmire (1984b), Hublin (1986)
T8	Depth of the supramastoid sulcus	Santa Luca (1980), Bräuer (1984b), Clarke (1990)
O1	Occipital curvature and orientation of the upper scale	Bräuer (1984b, 1994) Rightmire (1984a,b)
O2	Shape of the occipital torus	Weidenreich (1943), Wu and Bräuer (1993), Bräuer (1994)
O3	Projection of occipital torus	Rightmire (1990), Wu and Bräuer (1993)
O4	Course of the occipital torus	Bräuer (1984b), Wu and Bräuer (1993)
O5	Connection of occipital torus to occipitomastoid, mastoid, supramastoid crests or angular torus	Santa Luca (1980), Bräuer (1984b)
O6	Depth of supratoral sulcus centrally and laterally	Weidenreich (1943), Bräuer (1984b), Lahr (1994)
Fa1	Shape of nasal bones	De Villiers (1968), Aiello and Dean (1990)
Fa2	Nasal bridge	Habgood (1989), Groves (1989), Lahr (1996)
Fa3	Shape of lower nasal margin	Gower (1923), Stringer *et al.* (1984), Hublin (1986), Lahr (1996)
Fa4	Shape of orbits	Wolpoff (1989), Lahr (1996)
Fa5	Inframalar curvature	Wu and Bräuer (1993), Nara (1994)
Fa6	Canine fossa	De Villiers (1968), Bräuer (1984a,b), Stringer *et al.* (1984)

analyses showed that 16 non-metrical, and 17 metrical variables might be significant in the modernisation process, and only these are considered here. The non-metrical traits (Table 20.4) demonstrate that all major cranial regions examined played an important role in the anatomical changes. In addition, principal components analysis (PCA) was done to analyse the morphology of the cranial vault in a more complex way using both raw data as well as shape-transformed data.

Non-metrical features

Major elements of the supraorbital morphology underwent changes in shape and size. In eastern Africa, a mosaic-like pattern of change (Figure 20.1a) is seen

Table 20.3 *Metrical variables used in the present study.*

Feature		Reference	
		Bräuer (1988)	Howells (1973)
V1	Thickness of supraorbital torus at midorbit	Bräuer (1984a)	–
V2	Thickness of supraorbital torus lateral segment	Bräuer (1984a)	–
V3	Bistephanic breadth	10b	STB
V4	Outer biorbital breadth	43	–
V5	Postorbital breadth	9(1)	–
V6	Minimum frontal breadth	9	–
V7	Thickness of vault bones at bregma	–	–
V8	Frontal sagittal chord (nasion-bregma)	29	FRC
V9	Frontal subtense	29b	FRS
V10	Nasion-subtense fraction	29c	FRF
V11	Frontal angle (nasion-bregma)	32(5)	FRA
V12	Glabella-bregma chord	29d	–
V13	Glabella-bregma subtense	29e	–
V14	Glabella-subtense fraction	29f	–
V15	Frontal angle (glabella-bregma)	32e	–
V16	Parietal chord	30	PAC
V17	Parietal subtense	30a	PAS
V18	Bregma-subtense fraction	30b	PAF
V19	Parietal angle	33e	PAA
V20	Bregma-asterion chord	30c	–
V21	Bregma-asterion arc	27a	–
V22	Lambda-inion chord	32(1)	–
V23	Lambda-inion arc	28(1)	–
V24	Inion-opisthion chord	31(2)	–
V25	Inion-opisthion arc	28(2)	–
V26	Lambda-opisthion chord	31	–
V27	Lambda-opisthion arc	28	–
V28	Occipital angle	33d	OCA
V29	Occipital subtense	31a	OCS
V30	Lambda-subtense fraction	31b	OCF
V31	Biasterionic breadth	12	ASB
V32	Thickness of vault bones at lambda	–	–
V33	Maximum height of occipital torus	–	–
V34	Simotic chord	57	WNB
V35	Simotic subtense	57a	SIS
V36	Simotic angle	75b	SIA
V37	Upper breadth of nasal bones (at frontonasal suture)	analogous to (57)	–
V38	Nasion-subtense on upper nasal breadth	analogous to (57a)	–
V39	Lower breadth of nasal bones	–	–
V40	Nasal breadth	54	NLB
V41	Nasal height	55	NPH
V42	Nasion-prosthion height	48	NHP
V43	Basion-nasion length	5	BNL
V44	Basion-prosthion length	40	BPL
V45	Nasion angle	72b	NAA
V46	Prosthion angle	72(5)	PRA
V47	Bifrontal breadth	43a	FMB

Table 20.3. (*cont.*)

Feature		Reference	
		Bräuer (1988)	Howells (1973)
V48	Nasiofrontal subtense	43b	NAS
V49	Nasio-frontal angle	77a	NFA
V50	Bimaxillary breadth	46b	ZMB
V51	Bimaxillary subtense	46c	SSS
V52	Zygomaxillary angle	76a	SSA
V53	Bidacryal breadth	49a	DKB
V54	Anterior interorbital breadth	50	–
V55	Bregma-asterion chord/arc index	V20/ V21 × 100	–
V56	Postorbital index	V5/ V4 × 100	–
V57	Lower/upper scale chord index	V 24/ V22 × 100	–

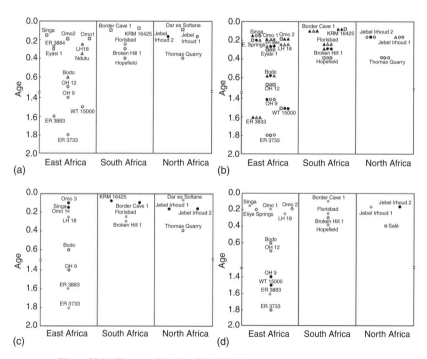

Figure 20.1. Changes of various frontal features.

(a) Shape of supraorbital torus (○: continuous torus, ●: continuous torus with groove/foramen, Δ: torus devided by groove/foramen, □: supraorbital region devided into medial and lateral segment).

(b) Depth of supratoral sulcus at glabella, midorbit and lateral segments (○: deep, ●: marked, Δ: weak, ▲: absent, □: broken off).

(c) Glabella projection relative to nasion (○: strong, ◉: moderate, ●: weak).

(d) Frontal keel (○: strong, ◉: weak, ●: absent).

Table 20.4 *Major non-metrical features showing temporal changes.*

Shape of supraorbital torus
Depth of supratoral sulcus
Glabella projection relative to nasion
Frontal keel
Orientation of lateral cranial walls
Parietal bossing
Position of maximum cranial breadth
Angular torus
Course of the squamosal suture
Posterior aspect of the mastoid process
Occipital curvature and orientation of the upper scale
Shape of occipital torus
Depth of supratoral sulcus centrally and laterally
Shape of lower nasal margin
Inframalar curvature
Canine fossa

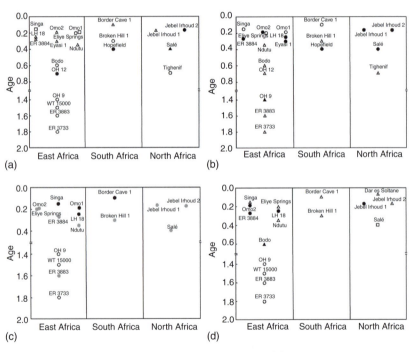

Figure 20.2. Changes of various parietal and temporal features.

(a) Orientation of lateral walls (○: converging, ●: vertical but slightly converging, △: vertical, ▲: vertical but slightly diverging, □: diverging).
(b) Parietal bossing (○: strong, ●: moderate, △: weak, ▲: absent).
(c) Position of maximum cranial breadth (○: mastoid, ◉: supramastoid crests, ●: parietal).
(d) Course of squamosal suture (○: superior limb horizontal/posterior limb oblique, ●: curved/oblique, △: curved/curved, ▲: curved/broken off, □: defective/curved).

from a continuous torus morphology in *H. erectus*, through tori that are divided into medial and lateral segments by a midorbital groove or depression (Bodo, Ndutu, LH 18), to those that are fully modern in morphology. Remarkably, the ancestral condition of the torus persists in early and late archaic specimens from southern and northern Africa, with some differentiation in the Jebel Irhoud 2 specimen. Temporal changes of the depth of supratoral sulcus are observed in eastern and southern Africa ranging from deep or marked sulci at glabella and mid-orbit, to shallow or absent (Figure 20.1b). Here, the three northern African archaic *H. sapiens* retain rather deep depressions. Interestingly, Bodo exhibits a derived condition by lacking a clear sulcus above the glabellar torus, which only becomes more common in later specimens. As regards the glabella prominence relative to nasion (Figure 20.1c), a clear decrease is evident from strong and moderate projections in the *H. erectus* and earliest archaics, to moderate and weak conditions in late archaics and early moderns.

A frontal keel is often regarded as mainly or exclusively an East Asian feature but has been shown to occur frequently in Africa as well (Bräuer and Mbua, 1992). This feature occurs in 15 of 18 specimens included ranging from weak to strong keeling (Figure 20.1d). The youngest *H. erectus* included in the study (OH 12) exhibits a strong keel that is similar in prominence to those found in early archaic specimens like Bodo, Broken Hill 1 and Salé. Although marked keeling occurs in younger specimens such as Omo 2, the late archaics as well as early moderns generally have weak ridges. We do not observe any clear differences between the major geographic regions.

The parietal morphology similarly suggests clear diachronic changes. Regarding the orientation of the lateral walls (Figure 20.2a), change is noticeable from generally upwards converging walls characteristic of *H. erectus,* and some early and late archaic *H. sapiens*, to vertical and diverging walls common in early moderns. Although the fragmentary condition of the Bodo cranium prevents a complete shape study, the parietals appear to converge upwards. Intermediate vertical walls with slight convergence are also present in late *H. erectus* and in various archaics (e.g. Hopefield, Jebel Irhoud 2). This change of vault shape occurs in individuals from all three geographic regions. There appears to be a link between the shape of the lateral walls and the development of the parietal eminences (Figure 20.2b). Parietal bosses are either lacking or weakly developed in *H. erectus*. The shift towards development of pronounced bossing obviously occurred in archaic *H. sapiens*. In this group, parietal bossing ranges from weak to strong, with intermediate moderate conditions also present. The early moderns from both eastern and southern Africa exhibit strong bosses. The position of the maximum cranial breadth is associated with parietal expansion. In early moderns the position for maximum cranial breadth is located more superiorly (Figure 20.2c), whereas in *H. erectus* it was found to occur either across the mastoids or the supramastoid crests. In all early archaics the greatest breadth is situated on the supramastoid crests, whereas in later archaics it is either on these crests or more superiorly on the parietals (LH 18), similar to the condition found in early moderns. A large number of eastern African specimens clearly document this change, but it is seen as well in the few specimens from the South.

The occurrence and development of an angular torus has been discussed in the context of suggested differences between the Asian and African specimens of *H. erectus*. This feature is not only found in East Asia but has also been identified in African *H. erectus* and archaic *H. sapiens* (Bräuer and Mbua, 1992). In the present study, weak to strong angular tori occur in most *H. erectus* specimens. Among the early archaics only Bodo exhibits a strongly developed angular ridge. Despite the great variability of this feature among archaic *H. sapiens* (including a moderate development in Broken Hill 1 and absence in LH 18), weak tori are common in this group. Further reductions finally led to a complete loss of the angular torus in the early modern humans.

A number of features of the temporal and occipital bones were similarly found to demonstrate changes during the modernisation process. A fairly straight course of the squamosal suture is characteristic of *H. erectus* (e.g. Rightmire, 1990). The course of superior and posterior limbs of the squamosal suture demonstrated an interesting pattern (Figure 20.2d). In the *H. erectus* crania examined, the morphology of the superior limb generally follows a straight course, while that of the posterior limb follows an oblique course downwards. In contrast, all early and late archaics in which this feature can be reliably observed, have curved superior limbs whereas the posterior course varies from oblique to curved. Among the early moderns from all three regions, the suture is curved in both superior and posterior parts. This feature thus demonstrates a polarity from a straight and oblique ancestral condition, to curved on both superior and posterior segments, as seen in modern humans. Variability in course of the posterior limb of the suture are evident within the archaic *H. sapiens* since both curved and oblique forms are present.

The posterior aspect of the mastoid process is flat and continuous with the nuchal plane in *H. erectus*. A change was observed from flattened conditions (see also Rightmire, 1990: 65) to a rounded condition that is discontinuous to the nuchal plane. The *H. erectus* specimens studied exhibit ancestral flat morphology, as do the early archaics from all three regions. The morphology is rather variable within late archaics with the flattened condition seen on Eliye Springs, while other specimens (e.g. KNM-ER 3884, LH 18, Omo 2, Jebel Irhoud 1 and 2) show rounded conditions. The late archaics also show variation regarding the aspect of continuation or discontinuation with the nuchal plane. In early moderns, the posterior aspect is rounded and discontinuous to the nuchal plane. The few southern and northern specimens examined suggest a similar pattern.

Strong angulation between the occipital and nuchal planes accompanied with forward inclination of the upper occipital scale is common in the African *H. erectus* analysed. A clear reduction in angulation is evident within the early archaics. Moreover, the occipital plane is oriented vertically and more rounded around the medial and upper parts (e.g. Ndutu, Eyasi). The late archaics exhibit a strong reduction of occipital angulation relative to early archaics except for Omo 2. The upper occipital scale in late archaics was rather vertical and curved. The early moderns (Singa, Omo 1) exhibit rounded mid-sagittal curvature. Although this feature could mainly be studied in eastern African specimens, the condition in the Hopefield specimen fits well within the range of variation for the early archaics from the eastern African sample.

In spite of considerable variation in the general shape of the occipital torus, we see an obvious change within Early and Middle Pleistocene hominins. In KNM-ER 3733 the torus is strongly developed, especially in its central part, and shows some basic similarities in shape to that of OH 9 although the latter is damaged around its central region. The early archaics similarly exhibit well developed tori (e.g. Ndutu) with their prominences restricted more centrally (e.g. Hopefield) or even much weaker developments as seen in the Eyasi specimen. In late archaics, torus formations range from weak to absent (e.g. KNM-ER 3884, LH 18, Eliye Springs, Jebel Irhoud) as seen in early moderns (Omo 1, Singa). Omo 2 fits within this range of variation. Associated with a torus development there can be a supratoral sulcus. This feature was examined along the central and lateral parts of the occipital bone and shows a general decrease in depth from moderate to weak sulci in *H. erectus* and early archaics, to weak or absent in late archaics and early moderns.

Although the sample size of diagnostic facial remains was small, relevant changes can be demonstrated. For example, the shape of the lower nasal margin shows a rather consistent pattern of change. The lower nasal border in *H. erectus* lacks well defined narial margins. In two early archaics that could be studied (Bodo, Broken Hill 1), the spinal and tubinal crests appear to merge while the lateral crests run more or less parallel downwards beyond the lower border of the aperture. In three late archaics (LH 18, Florisbad, Jebel Irhoud 1) the lateral, tubinal and spinal crests merge to a single crest. Although the condition in Jebel Irhoud 1 differs somewhat with lateral crests that slightly project inferiorly below the level of the anterior nasal spine, the condition is close to that seen in the LH 18 and Florisbad specimens.

Features of the mid-facial region that suggested diachronic changes include degree of inframalar curvature, and development of the canine fossa. Both show clear changes from ancestral to modern conditions. Among the specimens studied, the shape of the lower border of the zygomatic process was distinguished into two categories: slightly arched and strongly arched. Among the *H. erectus,* only KNM-WT 15000 could be examined for this feature and shows very weak inframalar curvature. The shape of this feature in Bodo and Broken Hill 1 is more derived with a slightly arched curvature. Although the facial region in Ndutu is fragmentary, a more strongly developed curvature is assumed, and may approach the conditions seen in late archaics and early modern crania (e.g. LH 18, Eliye Springs, Florisbad, Jebel Irhoud 1, Dar-es-Soltane 2).

It was possible to study the development of a canine fossa in nine specimens. Only in the *H. erectus* specimen, KNM-WT 15000, is the respective facial region preserved, and exhibits a slight canine concavity. Similar conditions are also present in the Bodo and Broken Hill 1 specimens (see also Wu and Bräuer, 1993), whereas Ndutu and Broken Hill 2 appear to have more clearly defined, but weak, canine fossae. All late archaic specimens exhibit either well defined, or weak to moderately expressed fossae (LH 18, Eliye Springs, Florisbad, Jebel Irhoud 1), characteristic of a modern anatomy (see Stringer *et al.*, 1984).

Although we found 16 non-metrical traits that show clear basic changes of cranial morphology, it is likely that other features could similarly demonstrate changes towards modern morphology. However, due to the fragmentary nature of the specimens and small sample sizes, it was not possible to document these changes.

Metrical variables

In addition to changes observed on non-metrical features, we found significant correlation coefficients for 17 measurements (Table 20.5), which describe major aspects of vault morphology. Three variables relating to the frontal breadth document evolutionary trends of coronal enlargement, and show considerable overlap between early and late archaics and early moderns (Figure 20.3a). Other measurements show an increased curvature of the frontal squama towards a more rounded shape seen in archaic and modern humans. Diachronic changes of five mid-sagittal frontal measurements demonstrate considerable overlap between the archaic and modern samples (Figure 20.3b).

Among the variables of the parietal bone, five show significant correlations. A clear increase in length of the parietal bone is observable from Hopefield to Omo 1 fossils (Figure 20.3c). There is also close similarity within all groups, supporting a pattern of continuous change. Similarities between the derived morphology are clear among the early and late archaics, as demonstrated by the coronal expansion of the parietals, as seen in the bregma-asterion dimensions and bregma-asterion chord/arc index (Figure 20.3d).

Table 20.5. *Spearman's correlation coefficients for features that show significant correlation with time.*

Variable	r_s	p	n
Bistephanic breadth STB (10b)	−0.680[a]	0.011	13
Postorbital breadth (9(1))	−0.681[a]	0.015	12
Minimum frontal breadth (9)	−0.747[b]	0.000	18
Frontal subtense FRS (29b)	−0.896[b]	0.000	10
Frontal angle FRA (32(5))	0.720[a]	0.019	10
Glabella-bregma subtense (29e)	−0.856[b]	0.001	11
Gabella-subtense fraction (29f)	0.693[a]	0.018	11
Parietal chord PAC (30)	−0.733[b]	0.010	11
Bregma-subtense fraction PAF (30b)	−0.831[b]	0.002	11
Bregma-asterion chord (30c)	−0.830[a]	0.011	8
Bregma-asterion arc (27a)	−0.928[b]	0.001	8
Bregma-asterion chord/arc index	0.810[a]	0.015	8
Lambda-inion chord (31(1))	−0.818[b]	0.004	10
Lambda-inion arc (28(1))	−0.729[a]	0.017	10
Lambda-opisthion chord OCC (31)	−0.879[b]	0.002	9
Lambda-opisthion arc (28)	−0.755[a]	0.031	8
Biasterionic breadth ASB (12)	−0.687[a]	0.020	11

[a] $p<0.05$; [b] $p<0.01$

In addition to changes observed on the parietal bone, five measurements of the occipital bone showed significant correlations. The length of the occipital upper scale as demonstrated by lambda-inion chord and arc show a remarkable increase from early archaics to modern humans (Figure 20.4a). The relative long upper scale on Omo 2 is closer to other derived modern conditions despite the angulated occipital region. A continuous increase in lengths of the occipital chord and arc is noticeable (Figure 20.4b) from early archaics to early moderns, with late archaics exhibiting intermediate conditions. An interesting distribution of the specimens is observable for the biasterionic breadth (Figure 20.4c). Whereas the three *H. erectus* specimens show a wide range of variation, a trend is apparent from the early archaic Ndutu to early moderns, e.g. Singa and Omo 1. Once again, the late archaics exhibit intermediate conditions. Again, Omo 2 appears similar to Omo 1, with a derived modern condition.

To study the affinities of the Middle Pleistocene specimens with regard to their frontal, parietal and occipital morphology in a more complex way, three PCAs were performed. The measurements used in the PCAs were those that showed significant correlation in a Spearman's correlation coefficients analysis (Table 20.5). The PCAs were calculated based on both raw data and shape-transformed data (log-shape data) following the methods described by Darroch and Mosimann (1985; see Kidder *et al.*, 1992; Bräuer and Mímisson, 2004).

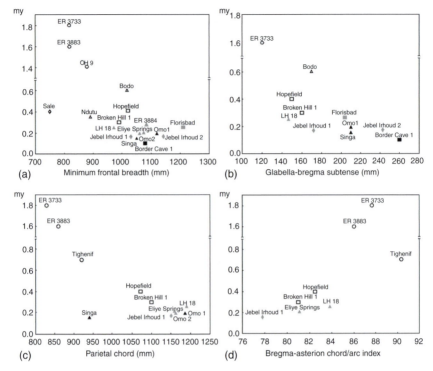

Figure 20.3. Temporal trends of various frontal and parietal metrical variables
(○: *Homo erectus*; Δ: eastern African early archaics, ▲: eastern African late archaics,
▲: eastern African early moderns; □: southern African early archaics, ■: southern
African late archaics, ■: southern African early moderns; ◊: northern African early
archaics, ◆: northern African late archaics, ◆: northern African early moderns).

Controlling for individual size is an important modification for studying samples of great variability (see also Bräuer *et al.*, 2006). Due to the fragmentary
condition of many of the specimens, only a small number of individuals ($n = 7$)
could be included in the different multivariate analyses.

The first analysis (PCA1) is based on five variables (Table 20.6) describing
coronal and sagittal dimensions of the frontal bone. Analysis of the raw data
yielded high loadings (>0.71) for all variables on the first component. The distribution of the specimens along this component (Figure 20.5a) shows remarkably close affinities between all early and late archaics. Differences are mainly
present on the second component, which, however, only represents 13.5% of
the total variance within the dataset. The shape-based analysis shows more
differentiated, but essentially similar, patterns of distribution (Figure 20.5b).
This analysis supports strong similarities between Bodo and Broken Hill 1

Table 20.6. *Principal component analysis 1 (PCA 1) based on* [a]*raw and* [b]*log-shape data of five frontal variables (for numbers see Table 20.3).*

Variable		[a]PC1	[a]PC2	[b]PC1	[b]PC2
V3	Bistephanic breadth	0.89	0.37	0.74	−0.40
V5	Postorbital breadth	0.89	0.22	0.20	0.97
V6	Minimum frontal breadth	0.98	0.07	0.69	0.70
V13	Glabella-bregma subtense	0.87	−0.12	0.83	−0.40
V14	Glabella-subtense fraction	−0.71	0.68	−0.99	0.06

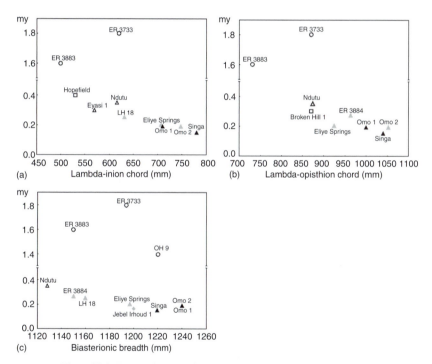

Figure 20.4. Temporal trends of various occipital measurements (for symbols see Figure 20.3).

specimens. Somewhat closer affinities are observable between Hopefield, LH 18 and Jebel Irhoud 1, in terms of coronal and sagittal shape. All the variables except for the postorbital breadth, have high loadings (>0.69) on PC1 (Table 20.6). Principal component 2 is mainly determined by postorbital breadth and minimum frontal breadth.

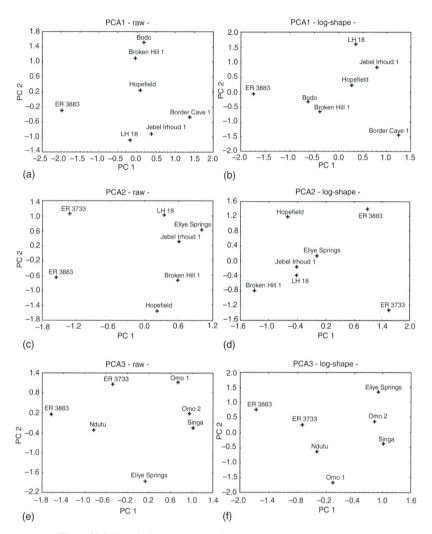

Figure 20.5. Principal components analyses based on raw data and log-shape data. (a) PC1 accounts for 76% and PC2 for 13.5% of the total variance; (b) PC1: 54.8%, PC2: 35.2%; (c) PC1: 88%, PC2: 5.4%; (d) PC1: 53%, PC2: 22.8%; (e) PC1: 71.8%, PC2: 17.6%; (f) PC1: 63.2%, PC2: 28.4%.

The second analysis (PCA2) is based on six dimensions of the parietal bones and postorbital region (Table 20.7). Results based on raw data show high loadings (>0.85) on the first component for all six variables. The distribution of the specimens (Figure 20.5c) points to close affinities between early and late archaics and shows great differences from early *H. erectus* specimens (represented

Table 20.7. *Principal components analysis 2 (PCA 2) based on ᵃraw and ᵇlog-shape data of six variables of the parietal bone and postorbital region.*

Variable		ᵃPC1	ᵃPC2	ᵇPC1	ᵇPC2
V3	Bistephanic breadth	0.85	−0.51	−0.68	0.48
V5	Postorbital breadth	0.99	0.07	0.98	−0.02
V16	Parietal chord	0.95	0.07	−0.61	0.13
V18	Bregma-subtense fraction	0.89	0.22	−0.01	−0.98
V20	Bregma-asterion chord	0.96	0.10	0.94	0.14
V21	Bregma-asterion arc	0.98	0.01	0.72	0.38

Table 20.8. *Principal components analysis 3 (PCA 3) based on ᵃraw and ᵇlog-shape data of six occipital variables.*

Variable		ᵃPC1	ᵃPC2	ᵇPC1	ᵇ PC2
V22	Lambda-inion chord	0.98	−0.18	0.98	0.01
V24	Inion-opisthion chord	−0.53	0.79	−0.95	0.11
V26	Lambda-opisthion chord	0.98	0.01	0.97	−0.15
V27	Lambda-opisthion arc	0.94	−0.02	0.76	0.58
V30	Lambda-subtense fraction	0.67	0.58	−0.19	−0.96
V31	Biasterionic breadth	0.89	0.23	−0.59	0.65

by KNM-ER 3733 and KNM-ER 3883). Based on shape analysis, all variables except for bregma-subtense fraction have high loadings (>0.61) on PC1 (Table 20.7). The distribution of the specimens (Figure 20.5d) is essentially similar to results based on the raw data. The early and late archaics are clearly separate from early *H. erectus,* with Broken Hill 1 deviating a little further from late archaics than in the previous raw data analysis.

In the third analysis (PCA3), six occipital variables (Table 20.8) were used (correlation coefficients for V24 (inion-opisthion chord) and V30 (lambda-subtense fraction) were not included in Table 20.5 since they are significant only at $p<0.1$). Based on raw data high loadings (>0.67) were yielded for all variables on the first component except for inion-opisthion chord. Interestingly, Ndutu exhibits closer affinities to KNM-ER 3733 than to late archaics and early moderns (Figure 20.5e). Omo 2, Singa and Omo 1 are close due to their derived near-modern morphology of the occipital bone. In the shape-transformed data all variables except for lambda-subtense fraction and biasterionic breadth have high loadings (>0.76) on the first component (Table 20.8). The biasterionic breadth loads similarly high (*c.* 0.6) on PC1 and PC2. Although Ndutu again shows close affinities to KNM-ER 3733, it occupies an intermediate position within the graph between *H. erectus* and Omo 1 (Figure 20.5f). Omo 2 and Singa show close affinities as demonstrated by the analysis of the raw data.

Discussion

A large number of general morphological aspects and detailed features have been used over the decades to describe individual morphology of African Pleistocene hominins or their evolutionary changes (e.g. Howell, 1978; Bräuer, 1984a; b; 1994; Rightmire, 1984a,b, 1990). In the present study, more than one hundred such features were examined in African Early to early Late Pleistocene hominins with the aim to test them for long-term changes during this period, particularly the Middle Pleistocene, which could possibly be linked to the origin of modern morphology. Results of this new comprehensive analysis indeed indicate basic remodelling of cranial vault and face. Thirty-three non-metrical and metrical features of major anatomical regions show clear diachronic changes. These changes demonstrate that the anatomical modern character states or conditions had developed from ancestral conditions in a post-*Homo erectus* evolutionary lineage during much of the Middle Pleistocene. In addition to the 33 variables showing significant changes, several others indicate diachronic trends as well. However, these changes are less clear, often due to the small number of specimens examined for respective traits. Consequently, it could certainly be that the 33 variables presented here represent a minimum number of traits showing diachronic changes, among the total number of features studied.

As previously outlined, it is possible to trace the evolution of the derived modern cranial form back to early Middle Pleistocene post-*Homo erectus* hominins. This is indicated by the results of non-metrical and metrical features and analyses within the present study. The frontal bone including the postorbital region expanded. This is observable among early archaics, e.g. Bodo, Hopefield and Broken Hill 1, which show considerably increased frontal breadths (Figure 20.3a). The squama also becomes more rounded over time as shown by midsagittal measurements. For instance, Bodo, Hopefield and Broken Hill 1 are similar to each other with regard to glabella-bregma subtense (Figure 20.3b) and are close to late archaics such as LH 18 or Jebel Irhoud 1. The supraorbital torus reveals incipient mid-orbital division that is noticeable on Bodo and other early and late archaics (Figure 20.1a). There is a clear reduction in the projection of the supraorbital torus and the depth of the supratoral sulcus (Figures 20.1b and c). A clear reduction of the frontal keel is also evident from strongly developed ridges among early archaics to weaker or absent conditions in late archaics and early moderns (Figure 20.1d).

Expansion of parietal bones both sagittally and coronally is noticeable from early archaics (e.g. Hopefield and Broken Hill 1) to late archaics and early moderns (Figures 20.3c and d). In spite of these temporal trends the conditions seen in the three chrono-groups or grades are closely related with considerable overlap. The metrical changes are reflected by more vertical orientation of the lateral cranial walls, the increased parietal bossing and the upwards movement of the maximum cranial breadth (Figures 20.2a–c). A mosaic-like pattern of reduction of the angular torus is apparent from the fossils examined. Among the early archaics only Bodo exhibits a strongly developed angular torus.

Regarding the temporal bone, *H. erectus* and early Middle Pleistocene specimens differ in the course of the squamosal suture. In all early and late archaics examined, the superior border is curved in contrast to the straight course observed in *H. erectus*. The posterior limb of the squamosal suture among these groups appears variable and shows change towards a modern curved suture. The mastoid processes also show interesting changes in the shape of their posterior aspect. While the mastoid is generally flattened and its posterior plane continuous with the nuchal plane in both *H. erectus* and early archaics, a shift is observed towards a rounded mastoid process whose posterior aspect is discontinuous with the nuchal plane in later populations.

Changes within the occipital bone are demonstrated by diachronic enlargement of its basic dimensions. A clear increase in length is visible regarding the upper scale and mid-sagittal curvature of the occipital bone (Figures 20.4a and b, Table 20.5), and in biasterionic breadth (Figure 20.4c). In addition, a general reduction in occipital angulation is clearly noticeable. Early archaics such as the Ndutu cranium have an occipital plane that is oriented more vertically and rounded in its middle and upper parts. Most of late archaics have a vertical and curved upper scale that approaches the shape of modern humans. Further changes are seen in the shape of the occipital torus, which is remodelled from a well developed torus formation around mid-region, especially common in early archaics (e.g. Ndutu), to weak or absent ridges in late archaics (e.g. LH 18, KNM-ER 3884). Associated with torus reduction is the decrease of the depth of the supratoral sulcus.

Changes are also visible in facial morphology. Some early archaics (Bodo, Broken Hill 1) have slight concavities in the region of the canine fossa and slightly arched inframalar curvatures, although Ndutu exhibits some derived conditions such as arched inframalar curvature. The late archaics generally exhibit well defined canine fossae associated with strongly developed inframalar curvatures identical to modern morphology. The lower border of the nasal aperture shows changes that involve fusion of the spinal, tubinal and lateral crests into a single crest.

The pattern of changes of major and minor morphological features presented here, and the close affinities between the groups of specimens studied, suggest that the origin of modern morphology was a continuous mosaic-like evolutionary process that can be traced back to early Middle Pleistocene. The presence of a large number of derived near-modern or modern character states among the specimens over a period of 400 ka does not suggest any anagenetic or cladogenetic speciation events. It thus appears plausible that any subdivisions should be below the species level.

It is widely accepted that it is possible to subdivide the fossil record of the African Middle Pleistocene into three groups. The composition of the groups does not differ much between the authors (e.g. Bräuer *et al.*, 1997; McBrearty and Brooks, 2000; Bräuer, 2001; Foley, 2001; Smith, 2002; Stringer, 2002). Based on this study the early group includes Bodo, Ndutu, Eyasi, Hopefield, Broken Hill, Salé and Thomas Quarry. The subsequent group includes LH 18, KNM-ER 3884, Omo 2, Eliye Springs, Florisbad, Jebel Irhoud and the early moderns Omo 1 and 3, Klasies River, Border Cave, Dar-es-Soltane 2 (see Bräuer, 2001).

If one accepts a continuous modernisation process without clear-cut distinctions as suggested by the present study, a sequence of three evolutionary grades or morphs within one biological species *H. sapiens* appears in agreement with the current evidence for Africa. The grade mode neither suggests anything about the underlying factors of the modernisation process nor whether there are any parts of the lineage that show more intensive changes toward the modern morphology than others. Thus, factor analysis and other studies by other workers (e.g. Lieberman *et al.*, 2002) are useful for identifying anatomical complexes in this process. Indeed, it is obvious that some of the features analysed in this study might show a complex pattern of inter-correlations. However, since many of the morphological changes obviously occurred in a gradual or mosaic-like pattern over hundreds of thousands of years, we suggest that the origin of modern cranial morphology did not result from a few major adjustments within a short period of time associated with a speciation event, as proposed by Lieberman *et al.* (2002). Regarding this debate Brooks (cited by Balter, 2002:1221) contends that in Africa 'we don't see any sudden leaps' in the emergence of modern humans. She rather sees a long gradual process of both physical and behavioural change.

The continuous evolutionary process in Africa as suggested by this study did not occur simultaneously in all parts of the continent. Rather, results of the present study suggest that the changes towards modern anatomy are most clearly demonstrable for eastern Africa. This is supported by diachronic changes observed for many of the features that show changes from ancestral to derived modern conditions. Similar trends although not as clear are observable for some traits in southern Africa despite the small sample size. The trends are less clear in northern Africa from where, however, only a few cranial speci-mens exist. Despite the small regional sample sizes, a progressive modernisa-tion process in East Africa is in agreement with proposals by other workers who see an early transition to modern humans in this region based on fossil discoveries from Herto, Ethiopia, and new dating evidence for the Omo Kibish specimens (e.g. White *et al.*, 2003; McDougall *et al.*, 2005).

Although three chronologically subsequent groups are widely recognised by several authors, their taxonomic classification has remained a contentious topic. The main questions regard whether the alternative phylogenies currently discussed are more plausible than the assumption of three grades of an evolv-ing species *H. sapiens*. Although Foley (2001: 9–11) favours a phylogeny of three species, *H. heidelbergensis*, *H. helmei* and *H. sapiens*, he concedes:

> Indeed, continuity between them, rather than discontinuity, is the reason for the per-sistent problem of delimiting the taxonomic units in the later stages of human evo-lution and gives rise to the question of whether the species concept, which lies at the heart of macroevolutionary theory, is sufficiently fine-tuned to cope with evolution at this scale. The lineages of later human evolution seem to show simultaneously *continuously evolving lineages* and very distinctive derived endpoints, which are exactly what would be expected within the modern synthesis. They certainly high-light the problems of reconciling terminology with process. (emphasis ours)

Stringer (2002: 568) also recognises a gradual mosaic-like evolution to modern humans in Africa, and therefore uses the term 'archaic *Homo sapiens*' for the transitional later specimens. In fact, there appears to be little justification to distinguish this transitional group as a distinct species, *H. helmei*. According to McBrearty and Brooks (2000: 480), *H. helmei* is a 'problematic taxon with no formal diagnosis'. They merely use the name '*Homo helmei* or *Homo sapiens*' for their morphologically intermediate 'Group 2' of African fossils, which is equivalent to late archaic *H. sapiens*. Foley and Lahr's use of *H. helmei* appears even more problematic because they included European fossils as well in their hypodigm. As Stringer (2002: 567) critically pointed out, 'Neanderthal charac-teristics were already evolving in Europe prior to the hypothesized appearance and dispersal of "*Homo helmei*"…(and) African specimens such as Florisbad and Jebel Irhoud make unparsimonious ancestors for the Neandertals, since not only do they post-date the appearance of Neanderthal clade characters in Europe, but they appear to lack Neanderthal morphological characteristics that might be expected in a common ancestor'. Thus, the use of *H. helmei* either for Africa alone or for Europe as well cannot be regarded as a conclusive taxo-nomic solution.

Problems also exist with regard to the species *H. heidelbergensis* as favoured by Rightmire (1998). He sees a speciation event from *H. heidelbergensis* to *H. sapiens* at *c.* 150 ka (or possibly 200 ka according to the new dates for Omo).

Thus, he includes all African specimens from Bodo to Omo 2 in one species, *H. heidelbergensis* (Rightmire, 2002) and the anatomically modern remains in the other. However, as shown by the present study there is clear evidence for considerable continuity between the late archaics and early moderns making a distinction on the species level between for example Omo 1 and Omo 2, artificial and unsubstantiated. These two crania exhibit many shared derived features. Trinkaus (2005) would regard the differences between these specimens as merely a reflection of considerable intrapopulational variation. As problematic as a speciation event in Africa at around 200 to 150 ka appears, so is the assumed speciation event from *H. heidelbergensis* to *H. neanderthalensis* in Europe. Hublin (1998: 302) emphasised that it is quite artificial to trace any clear divisions along the pre-Neandertal/Neandertal lineage, and Manzi (2004: 21–2) suggests an anagenetic evolution 'which could be more reasonably considered a sequence of chrono-subspecies'. Condemi (2003) divides the European lineage into three groups, early pre-Neandertals, late pre-Neandertals and proto-Neandertals implying that, over several hundreds of thousands of years a Neandertalisation process might have occurred, without speciation in parallel to, and largely isolated from, the anatomical modernisation process in Africa. Similar to Europe, the evidence from Africa shows a mosaic-like continuous process or even a kind of accretional mode (see Stringer, 2002: 568), providing no justification for any subdivisions on the species level (Bräuer, 2007, 2008, 2010).

Further problems regarding *H. heidelbergensis* are the different hypodigms used. Several authors (e.g. Bermúdez de Castro *et al.*, 2004) disagree with the assumption of a single widespread species, *H. heidelbergensis*, in Africa, Europe and parts of East Asia. They favour a separate morph, *Homo rhodesiensis*, for African *Homo heidelbergensis sensu* Rightmire. McBrearty and Brooks (2000), however, use the term *H. rhodesiensis* only for the African specimens equivalent to the early archaics *sensu* Bräuer. White *et al.* (2003) also use this name for early archaic specimens cautiously ('*Homo rhodesiensis*'). Thus, in view of the evidence from the present study and the considerable problems and disagreements regarding the suggested splitting of the Middle Pleistocene evolutionary lineage into several species (Bräuer, 2007, 2008, 2010), it remains most plausible to regard the African lineage from Bodo to modern humans as demonstrating one chronospecies, *Homo sapiens*.

Acknowledgements

We would like to thank Sally Reynolds and Andrew Gallagher for their invitation to contribute to the Proceedings as well as for their kind cooperation. One of us (G.B.) also thanks Francis Thackeray, Andrew, Sally and Colin Menter for the invitation to participate in the great African Genesis Symposium in honour of Phillip Tobias, to whom I am very grateful for his friendship and support over more than three decades.

During this new study of the African fossil material, many persons were of great help by granting permission to study the specimens under their care or by supporting this research in different ways as well as with the analysis of the data. We would like to thank all of them, particularly Dr Idle O. Farah, Director National Museums of Kenya; Drs Margaret and Graham Avery of Iziko Museum, Cape Town; Dr Berhane Asfaw of National Museum of Addis Ababa; Dr N. Kayombo, Director, National Museums of Tanzania; Professor Lee Berger and Professor Beverly Kramer of Medical School, University of Witwatersrand; Maximilian von Harling, Juliette Kober, Angelika Kroll, Hermann Müller, all of Hamburg University; colleagues in the Palaeontology Department, National Museums of Kenya; Dr Meave Leakey, Professor Fred Spoor, Mr Ari Grossman as well as Professor Tim White and Professor Clark Howell.

The study was supported through a Mosher Baldwin Fellowship of the Leakey Foundation as well as by Diana Holt, the Kenya Museum Society, and the Institute of Human Biology at Hamburg University. We thank Maximilian von Harling and Frederik Jessen for their valuable help with the final version of the chapter. Finally, we would like to thank the reviewers as well as the editors for their useful comments.

References

Aiello, L. and Dean, C. (1990). *An Introduction to Human Evolutionary Anatomy.* London: Academic Press.

Andrews, P. (1984). An alternative interpretation of the characters used to define *Homo erectus*. *Courier Forschungs-Institut Senckenberg*, **69**: 167–75.

Asfaw, B., Gilbert, W. H., Beyene, Y. *et al.* (2002). Remains of *Homo erectus* from Bouri, Middle Awash, Ethiopia. *Nature*, **416**: 317–20.

Balter, M. (2002). What made humans modern? *Science*, **295**: 1219–25.

Bermúdez de Castro, J. M., Martinon-Torres, M., Carbonell, E. *et al.* (2004). The Atapuerca sites and their contribution to the knowledge of human evolution in Europe. *Evolutionary Anthropology*, **13**: 25–41.

Bräuer, G. (1984a). A craniological approach to the origin of anatomically modern *Homo sapiens* in Africa and implications for the appearance of modern Europeans. In Smith, F. H. and Spencer, F. (eds.), *The Origins of Modern Humans: A World Survey of the Fossil Evidence*. New York: Alan R. Liss, pp. 327–410.

   (1984b). The 'Afro-European *sapiens*-hypothesis', and hominid evolution in East Asia during the late Middle and Upper Pleistocene. *Courier Forschungs-Institut Senckenberg*, **69**: 145–65.

(1988). Osteometrie. In Knußmann, R. (ed.), *Anthropologie. Handbuch der vergleichenden Biologie des Menschen*. Volume 1. Stuttgart: Gustav Fischer Verlag, pp. 160–231.

(1994). How different are Asian and African *Homo erectus*? *Courier Forschungs-Institut Senckenberg*, **171**: 301–18.

(2001). The KNM-ER 3884 hominid and the emergence of modern anatomy in Africa. In Tobias, P. V., Raath, M. A., Moggi-Cecchi, J. and Doyle, G. A. (eds.), *Humanity from African Naissance to Coming Millennia*. Firenze: Firenze University Press, pp. 191–7.

(2007). Origin of modern humans. In Henke, W. and Tattersall, I. (eds.), *Handbook of Paleoanthropology*. Volume 3. Heidelberg: Springer, pp. 1749–79.

(2008). The origin of modern anatomy: by speciation or intraspecific evolution? *Evolutionary Anthropology*, **17**: 22–37.

(2010). The Out of Africa model for modern human origins: basics and current perspectives. In Bajd, B. (ed.), *Where Did We Come From? Current Views on Human Evolution*. Ljubljana: University of Ljubljana, pp. 127–57.

Bräuer, G. and Leakey, R. E. (1986). The ES-11693 cranium from Eliye Springs, West Turkana, Kenya. *Journal of Human Evolution*, **15**: 289–312.

Bräuer, G. and Mabulla, A. (1996). New hominid fossil from Lake Eyasi, Tanzania. *Anthropologie (Brno)*, **34**: 47–53.

Bräuer, G. and Mbua, E. (1992). *Homo erectus* features used in cladistics and their variability in Asian and African hominids. *Journal of Human Evolution*, **22**: 79–108.

Bräuer, G. and Mímisson, K. (2004). Morphological affinities of early modern crania from China. In Baquedano, E. and Rubio Jara, S. (eds.), *Miscelánea en homenaje a Emiliano Aguirre*. Vol III: Paleoantropología, Henares: Museo Arqueologico Regional. pp. 59–70.

Bräuer, G., Yokoyama, Y., Falguères, C. *et al.* (1997). Modern human origins backdated. *Nature*, **386**: 337–8.

Bräuer, G., Broeg, H. and Stringer, C. B. (2006). Earliest Upper Paleolithic crania from Mladeč, Czech Republic, and the question of Neanderthal-modern continuity: metrical evidence from the fronto-facial region. In Harvati, K. and Harrison, T. (eds.), *Neanderthals Revisited: New Approaches and Perspectives*. Heidelberg: Springer, pp. 277–88.

Clark, J. D., de Heinzelin, J., Schick, K. D. *et al.* (1994). African *Homo erectus*: old radiometric ages and young Oldowan assemblages in the Middle Awash Valley, Ethiopia. *Science*, **264**: 1907–10.

Clarke, R. J. (1985). A new reconstruction of the Florisbad cranium, with notes on the site. In Delson, E. (ed.), *Ancestors: the Hard Evidence*. New York: Alan R. Liss, pp. 301–5.

(1990). The Ndutu cranium and the origin of *Homo sapiens*. *Journal of Human Evolution*, **19**: 699–736.

Condemi, S. (2003). Les Néandertaliens. In Susanne, C., Rebato, E. and Chiarelli, B. (eds.), *Anthropologie Biologique: Evolution et biologie humaine*. Bruxelles: De Boeck and Larcier, pp. 271–9.

Darroch, J. and Mosimann, J. (1985). Canonical and principal components of shape. *Biometrika*, **72**: 241–52.

Day, M. H. and Stringer, C. B. (1982). *A reconsideration of the Omo Kibish remains and the erectus–sapiens transition*. Nice: I. Congrès International de Paléontologie Humaine. pp. 814–46.

De Villiers, H. (1968). *The Skull of the South African Negro: a Biometrical and Morphological Study*. Johannesburg: Witwatersrand University Press.

Delson, E., Tattersall, I., Van Couvering, J. A. *et al.* (eds.) (2000). *Encyclopedia of Human Evolution and Prehistory*, 2nd edn. New York and London: Garland Publishing, Inc.

Feibel, C. S., Brown, F. H. and McDougall, I. (1989). Stratigraphic context of fossil hominids from the Omo Group deposits: Northern Turkana Basin, Kenya and Ethiopia. *American Journal of Physical Anthropology*, **78**: 595–622.

Foley, R. (2001). In the shadow of the modern synthesis? Alternative perspectives on the last fifty years of paleoanthropology. *Evolutionary Anthropology*, **10**: 5–14.

Foley, R. A. and Lahr, M. M. (1997). Mode 3 technologies and the evolution of modern humans. *Cambridge Archeological Journal*, **7**: 3–36.

Foley, R. and Lahr, M. M. (2003). On stony ground: lithic technology, human evolution, and the emergence of culture. *Evolutionary Anthropology*, **12**: 109–22.

Geraads, D., Hublin, J. J., Tong, H. *et al.* (1986). The Pleistocene hominid site of Ternifine, Algeria: new results on the environment, age and human industries. *Quaternary Research*, **25**: 380–91.

Gower, C. D. (1923). A contribution to the morphology of the apertura piriformis. *American Journal of Physical Anthropology*, **6**: 27–36.

Groves, C. P. (1989). A regional approach to the problem of the origin of modern humans in Australasia. In Mellars, P. and Stringer, C. B. (eds.), *The Human Revolution*. Edinburgh: Edinburgh University Press, pp. 274–85.

Grün, R. and Beaumont, P. (2001). Border Cave revisited: a revised ESR chronology. *Journal of Human Evolution*, **40**: 467–82.

Grün, R. and Stringer, C. B. (1991). Electron spin resonance dating and the evolution of modern humans. *Archaeometry*, **33**: 153–99.

Grün, R., Brink, J. S., Spooner, N. A. *et al.* (1996). Direct dating of Florisbad hominid. *Nature*, **382**: 500–1.

Habgood, P. J. (1989). The origin of anatomically-modern humans in Australasia. In Mellars, P. and Stringer, C. B. (eds.), *The Human Revolution*. Edinburgh: Edinburgh University Press, pp. 245–73.

Howell, F. C. (1978). Hominidae. In Maglio, V. J. and Cooke, H. B. S. (eds.), *Evolution of African Mammals*. Cambridge: Harvard University Press, pp. 154–248.

Howells, W. W. (1973). *Cranial Variation in Man. A Study by Multivariate Analysis of Patterns of Differences Among Recent Human Populations*. Cambridge, MA: Harvard University, Peabody Museum of Archaeology and Ethnology.

Hublin, J. J. (1986). Some comments on the diagnostic features of *Homo erectus*. *Anthropos (Brno)*, **23**: 175–87.

(1989). *Les origines de l'Homme moderne: Europe occidentale et Afrique du Nord*. In Giacobini, G. (ed.), Hominidae. Milano: Jaca Book, pp. 423–30.

(1992). Recent human evolution in northwestern Africa. In Aitken, M. J., Stringer, C. B. and Mellars, P. A. (eds.), *The Origin of Modern Humans and the Impact of Chronometric Dating*. Princeton, New Jersey: Princeton University Press, pp. 118–31.

(1998). Climatic changes, paleogeography, and the evolut.on of the Neandertals. In Akazawa, T., Aoki, K. and Bar-Yosef, O. (eds.), *Neandertals and Modern Humans in Western Asia*. New York: Plenum Press, pp. 295–310.

Kidder, J. H., Jantz, R. L. and Smith, F. H. (1992). Defining modern humans: a multivariate approach. In Bräuer, G. and Smith, F. H. (eds.), *Continuity or Replacement. Controversies in* Homo sapiens *evolution*. Rotterdam and Brookfield: A. A. Balkema, pp. 157–77.

Kimbel, W. H., White, T. D. and Johanson, D. C. (1984). Cranial morphology of *Australopithecus afarensis*: a comparative study based on a composite reconstruction of the adult skull. *American Journal of Physical Anthropology*, **64**: 337–88.

Klein, R. G. (1999). *The Human Career. Human Biological and Cultural Origins*, 2nd edn. Chicago and London: The University of Chicago Press.

Lahr, M. M. (1994). The multiregional model of modern human origins: a reassessment of its morphological basis. *Journal of Human Evolution*, **26**: 23–56.

(1996). *The Evolution of Modern Human Diversity: a Study of Cranial Variation*. Cambridge: Cambridge University Press.

Leakey, M. D. and Hay, R. L. (1982). The chronological position of the fossil hominids of Tanzania. In De Lumley, M. A. (ed.), *L' Homo erectus et la place de l'homme de Tautavel parmi les hominidés fossiles*. Nice: Premier Congrès International de Paléontologie Humaine, pp. 753–65.

Lieberman, D.E., McBratney, B. M. and Krovitz, G. (2002). The evolution and development of cranial form in *Homo sapiens*. *Proceedings of the National Academy of Sciences of the United States of America*, **99**: 1134–9.

Lieberman, D. E., Krovitz, G. E. and McBratney-Owen, B. (2004). Testing hypotheses about tinkering in the fossil record: the case of the human skull. *Journal of Experimental Zoology (Mol. Dev. Evol.)*, **302B**: 284–301.

Magori, C. C. and Day, M. H. (1983). Laetoli Hominid 18: an early *Homo sapiens* skull. *Journal of Human Evolution*, **12**: 747–53.

Manega, P. C. (1995). *New Geochronological Results from the Ndutu, Naisiusiu and Ngaloba Beds at Olduvai and Laetoli in Northern Tanzania: Their Significance for Evolution of Modern Humans*. Bellagio Conference, Italy.

Manzi, G. (2004). Human evolution at the Matuyama–Brunhes boundary. *Evolutionary Anthropology*, **13**: 11–24.

McBrearty, S. and Brooks, A. S. (2000). The revolution that wasn't: a new interpretation of the origin of modern human behavior. *Journal of Human Evolution*, **39**: 453–563.

McDermott, F., Stringer, C. B., Grün, R. *et al.* (1996). New late Pleistocene Uranium–Thorium and ESR dates for the Singa hominid (Sudan). *Journal of Human Evolution*, **31**: 507–16.

McDougall, I., Brown, F. and Fleagle, J. G. (2005). Stratigraphic placement and age of modern humans from Kibish, Ethiopia. *Nature*, **433**: 733–6.

Nara, M. T. (1994). Etude de la variabilité de certains caractères métriques et mor-
phologiques des Néandertaliens. PhD thesis, Bordeaux.

Rightmire, G. P. (1979). Cranial remains of *Homo erectus* from Beds II and IV, Olduvai
Gorge, Tanzania. *American Journal of Physical Anthropology*, **51**: 99–116.

(1983). The Lake Ndutu cranium and early *Homo sapiens* in Africa. *American
Journal of Physical Anthropology*, **61**: 245–54.

(1984a). *Homo sapiens* in sub-Saharan Africa. In Smith, F. H. and Spencer, F. (eds.),
The Origins of Modern Humans. A World Survey of the Fossil Evidence. New York:
Alan R. Liss, pp. 295–325.

(1984b). Comparisons of *Homo erectus* from Africa and Southeast Asia. In Andrews,
P. and Franzen J. L. (eds.), The early evolution of man with special emphasis on
Southeast Asia and Africa. *Courier Forschungs-Institut Senckenberg*, **69**: 83–98.

(1990). *The Evolution of* Homo erectus. *Comparative Anatomical Studies of an
Extinct Human Species*. Cambridge: Cambridge University Press.

(1996). The human cranium from Bodo, Ethiopia: evidence for speciation in the
Middle Pleistocene? *Journal of Human Evolution*, **31**: 21–39.

(1998). Human evolution in the Middle Pleistocene: the role of *Homo heidelbergensis*. *Evolutionary Anthropology*, **6**: 218–27.

(2002). Les plus anciens *Homo erectus* d'Afrique et leur rôle dans l'évolution
humaine. In Grimaud-Hervé, D., Marchal, F., Violet, A. and Détroit, F. (eds.),
Le deuxième homme en Afrique: Homo ergaster, Homo erectus. Paris: Editions
Artcom, pp. 123–6.

Rightmire, G. P. and Deacon, H. J. (1991). Comparative studies of Late Pleistocene
human remains from Klasies River Mouth, South Africa. *Journal of Human
Evolution*, **20**: 131–56.

Santa Luca, A. P. (1980). The Ngandong fossil hominids. *Yale University Publications
in Anthropology*, **78**: 1–175.

Smith, F. H. (1993). Models and realities in modern human origins: the African fossil
evidence. In Aitken, M., Stringer, C. and Mellars, P. (eds.), *The Origins of Modern
Humans and the Impact of Chronometric Dating*. Princeton: Princeton University
Press, pp. 234–48.

(2002). Migrations, radiations and continuity: patterns in the evolution of Middle
and Late Pleistocene humans. In Hartwig, W. C. (ed.), *The Primate Fossil Record*.
Cambridge: Cambridge University Press, pp. 437–56.

Stringer, C. B. (1984). The definition of *Homo erectus* and the existence of the species
in Africa and Europe. *Courier Forschungs-Institut Senckenberg*, **69**: 131–44.

(2002). Modern human origins: progress and prospects. *Philosophical Transactions
Royal Society London (B)*, **357**: 563–79.

Stringer, C. B., Hublin, J. J. and Vandermeersch, B. (1984). The origin of anatomically
modern humans in Western Europe. In Smith, F. H. and Spencer, F. (eds.), *The
Origins of Modern Humans. A World Survey of the Fossil Evidence*. New York:
Alan R. Liss, pp. 51–135.

Trinkaus, E. (2005). Early modern humans. *Annual Review Anthropology*, **34**: 207–30.

Turbón, D. (2006). *La evolución humana*. Barcelona: Editorial Ariel.

Walker, A. and Leakey, R. (eds.) (1993). *The Nariokotome* Homo erectus *skeleton.* Berlin: Springer Verlag.

Weidenreich, F. (1943). The skull of *Sinanthropus pekinenesis*: a comparative study on a primitive hominid skull. *Palaeontologia Sinica D*, **10**: 1–485.

White, T. D., Asfaw, B., DeGusta, D. *et al.* (2003). Pleistocene *Homo sapiens* from Middle Awash, Ethiopia. *Nature*, **423**: 742–7.

Wolpoff, M. H. (1989). Multiregional evolution: the fossil alternative to Eden. In Mellars, P. and Stringer, C. B. (eds.), *The Human Revolution*. Edinburgh: Edinburgh University Press, pp. 62–108.

Wood, B. A. (1984). The origins of *Homo erectus*. *Courier Forschungs-Institut Senckenberg*, **69**: 99–112.

Wood, B. (1991). *Koobi Fora Research Project. Volume 4. Hominid Cranial Remains.* Oxford: Clarendon Press.

Wu, X. and Bräuer, G. (1993). Morphological comparison of archaic *Homo sapiens* crania from China and Africa. *Zeitschrift für Morphologie und Anthropologie*, **79**: 241–59.

21 Integration of the genetic, anatomical and archaeological data for the African origin of modern humans: problems and prospects

OSBJORN M. PEARSON

Abstract

In the early to mid 1990s many anthropologists and geneticists concluded that a synthesis of the origin of modern humans was possible: modern humans evolved in Africa between 200 000 and 100 000 years ago, migrated to Israel by 100 000 years ago, and completed the colonisation of the Old World between 50 000 and 30 000 years ago. However, by the late 1990s to early 2000s, genetic and archaeological evidence had made many aspects of this synthesis debatable. Mitochondrial DNA (mtDNA) and Y-chromosome data provided different ages for their last common ancestors; that of the Y-chromosome was probably too young to support a 100 000-year-old exodus from Africa. There was also a delay of at least 50 000 years between the appearance of anatomically modern morphology in Africa and the successful colonisation of much of Eurasia and Australia. New finds of early anatomically modern humans from Herto and revised dates for the Omo Kibish specimens from Ethiopia increase the length of this delay to 100 000 to 150 000 years. Great controversy surrounds the issue of how to identify fully modern behavioural patterns in the African and Eurasian archaeological record, but whether they view the behaviour of earlier Middle Stone Age (MSA) humans as fully modern or not, most archaeologists agree that the behavioural record between 70 000 to 40 000 years ago in Africa demonstrates the capacity for a variety of sophisticated behaviours present in later humans. New data from mtDNA on the age of the modern human settlement of Eurasia indicates a rapid settlement starting at around 63 000 years ago. Other data from mtDNA hints that there may have been a contemporaneous expansion of people through Africa bringing with

African Genesis: Perspectives on Hominin Evolution, eds. Sally C. Reynolds and Andrew Gallagher. Published by Cambridge University Press. © Cambridge University Press 2012.

423

them new Y-chromosomes and perhaps a novel form of the *FOXP2* gene, which may have been a crucial component of fully modern language. Industries from Tanzania to South Africa dating to 55 000 to 70 000 years ago such as the Howiesons Poort in South Africa, the Lupembo-Tshitolian in northern Angola, and Tshangulan in Zimbabwe, and Mumba Industry in Tanzania all feature the prominent use of backed blades, segments and crescents in addition to generic sidescrapers. Unifacial or bifacial points may be the archaeological handiwork of this expanding population. However, the absolute ages of many of these assemblages need further clarification before this hypothesis can be accepted unreservedly. It is still possible that the capacity for 'modern' behaviour was in place long before this date, perhaps even before the appearance of anatomically modern humans.

Introduction

By the early to mid 1990s, genetic, fossil and archaeological evidence provided a unified and coherent picture of the origin of modern humans. Modern humans had arisen in Africa sometime between 200 ka and 100 ka years ago (Stringer and Andrews, 1988; Clark, 1992; Stringer, 1993; Klein, 1995). The fossil record known at that time suggested that 100 000 years ago was a better estimate for the date for the first appearance of anatomically modern morphology, with MSA specimens from Klasies River Mouth and Border Cave (South Africa), and Omo 1 from the Kibish Formation (Ethiopia) providing the earliest examples of anatomically modern humans in Africa (Day, 1969; Rightmire, 1984; Bräuer 1984; Day and Stringer, 1991; Day *et al.*, 1991). These dates were closely approximated by 100 ka-year-old modern humans from the sites of Skhul and Qafzeh in Israel (Valladas *et al.*, 1988; Stringer *et al.*, 1989; Bar-Yosef, 1998; Shea, 2003). The MSA provided evidence of precociously early 'modern' behaviours including stylistic variation in projectile points perhaps indicating the persistence of regional identities (Clark, 1988, 1989, 1992). Skhul and Qafzeh provide evidence of the use of red ochre (Hovers *et al.*, 2003), at least some shellfish collecting and deliberate burials, some of which contain grave goods such as deer antlers or a boar's mandible (Mellars, 1989, 2006). Many researchers considered these examples of 'symbolic' behaviour to be a likely indication that these early, anatomically modern people were also capable of fully modern thought and behaviour, traits that almost certainly required these people to have had a fully modern form of language. Modern patterns of behaviour seemed to have clear antecedents in the MSA (Deacon, 1989; Deacon and Geleijnse, 1988), supporting the conclusions drawn from modern humans' genes and the geographical location of the earliest fossils of the taxon (Bräuer, 1989).

In Africa, the MSA lasts from *c*. 250 ka until between 45 and 20 ka and is broadly equivalent to the Middle Palaeolithic of Eurasia (Clark, 1988; McBrearty and Brooks 2000). The MSA and Middle Palaeolithic feature reliance upon flake-tools, sometimes but not always made with a prepared-core technique, occasional use of hafting and a relatively slow pace of technological change. The Later Stone Age (LSA) begins around 45 ka in East Africa (Ambrose, 1998), although the MSA persists as late as 22 ka in the Drakensberg Mountains of South Africa (Opperman and Heyenrych, 1990). The LSA differs from the MSA by its much more frequent use of microlithic tools, ubiquitous hafting, frequent use of bone tools, a much more rapid pace of stylistic change, and substantially greater number of distinctive and geographically more restricted cultures. Klein (1995, 1999, 2000) has frequently emphasised that evidence of symbolic behaviours, including representational art and the use of items of personal adornment, also become prevalent only in the LSA and that the LSA represents a major increase in cognitive ability and cultural complexity relative to the MSA. Many aspects of that view have been challenged by McBrearty and Brooks's (2000) synthesis of the evidence, which demonstrates a gradual accretion of 'LSA' behavioural and technological traits within the MSA rather than their sudden appearance at the transition from the MSA to the LSA.

Disintegration and debate

The internally consistent synthesis of the genetic, morphological and archaeological evidence drew criticism from its inception (Wolpoff, 1989; Clark and Lindley, 1989; Templeton, 1993), but cracks in the foundation of the unified synthesis of the African origin of modern humans also appeared as the result of new research and long-standing disagreements among those who accepted the fundamental proposition that modern humans had arisen in Africa. In the field of genetics, a feeling of unease set in with the realisation that the inferred ages of the most recent common ancestor (MRCA) of mtDNA and Y-chromosomes did not really agree.

Debate continued among archaeologists on the issue of whether the conventional differences between the MSA and LSA (e.g. Klein, 1979, 1995), although certainly linked to differences in behaviour, were necessarily tied to absolute differences in the *capacity* for behaviour, or truly provided clear evidence of a substantial behavioural difference between MSA and LSA peoples. This debate stemmed from two opposing models for the timing of the appearance of modern behaviour, a 'late and sudden' model championed by Richard Klein (1995, 2000, 2003) and an 'early and gradual' model advocated by Sally McBrearty, Alison Brooks, Lawrence Barham and the late Hilary Deacon among others (Deacon and Geleijnse, 1988; Deacon, 1989; McBrearty and Brooks, 2000; McBrearty, 2001, 2003; Barham, 2001, 2002a). Given the observation that modern anatomy had evolved before 'modern' patterns of behaviour could be inferred from the archaeological record, Klein (1995) proposed that there may have been an invisible neural mutation around 50 ka that led to substantial behavioural change without perceptible morphological change.

The alternative to a late and sudden origin of modern behaviour is that the numerous archaeological traits that characterise human behaviour in the LSA and Upper Palaeolithic of Europe appeared very gradually in Africa between 500 and 20 ka (McBrearty and Brooks, 2000). These behavioural traits and items of material culture include the use of red ochre and backed pieces in Africa by 300 ka (Barham, 2002a,b), a precociously early appearance of pre-pared core technology and blade production in the Late Acheulean (between 500 and 400 ka) of the Kapthurin Formation, Kenya (McBrearty, 2001), the use of bone to make harpoon points at Katanda, Democratic Republic of the Congo at 90 ka (Brooks *et al.*, 1995; Yellen *et al.*, 1995) and at Blombos, South Africa by 75 ka. The same archaeological levels at Blombos also feature evidence of active fishing of ocean fish (Henshilwood and Sealy, 1997) and the production of items that may have symbolic meanings such as cross-hatching on ochre pieces and pierced shells for personal adornment (Henshilwood *et al.*, 2002, 2004; Jacobs *et al.*, 2003; d'Errico *et al.*, 2005; Tribolo *et al.*, 2006). Fragments of engraved ostrich eggshells date from 60 ka from Diepkloof (Texier *et al.*, 2010), pierced snail-shell beads are known from Blombos (Henshilwood *et al.*, 2004; d'Errico *et al.*, 2005), the Stillbay and Howiesons Poort levels of Sibudu (d'Errico *et al.*, 2008), as well as from the 82 ka levels at the Moroccan site of Grotte des Pigeons (Bouzouggar *et al.*, 2007). Pressure-flaked artefacts at Blombos date to 70 ka, and pieces of engraved ochre dating to as early as 100 ka have recently been reported from Blombos (Henshilwood *et al.*, 2009; Mourre *et al.*, 2010) and Pinnacle Point, which also preserves evidence of marine resource exploitation as early as 164 ± 12 ka (Marean *et al.*, 2007).

Important caveats to this view of an increase in behavioural complexity stem from the appearance and loss in the African archaeological record of many of these technological and behavioural innovations. Rather than their retention, they may have been re-invented at a later date (d'Errico, 2003). This pattern of innovation and loss may, in part, be a by-product of population size, density and the rate of extinction of local populations (Shennan, 2001; Powell *et al.*, 2009).

Nevertheless, Ambrose (2001a, 2002, 2006; Ambrose and Lorenz, 1990) has proposed the intriguing argument that the procurement of exotic raw materials likely corresponds to an elaboration of human social networks and a 'troop-to-tribe transition' (Ambrose, 2002: 22). Separating demographic effects from changes in hominin cognitive abilities currently presents a key challenge for archaeologists who study the MSA. An additional problem is that a case for the gradual appearance of 'modern' behavioural traits or technology can be made for Neandertals in Europe (d'Errico, 2003), raising the question of whether the African Middle Palaeolithic record truly presents the only possible source for the origin of modern behaviour.

Since the early 2000s, new developments and discoveries have added additional pieces to the puzzle of modern human origins. Some of the discoveries have added new complications. One is Shen *et al.*'s (2002) conclusion that the anatomically modern hominin from Liujiang, southern China probably dates between 150 to 110 ka; another is Liu *et al.*'s (2010) announcement of human remains including a mandible bearing a small but modern chin from Zhirendong in southern China dating to 100 ka. Both discoveries imply there may have been a much wider geographic dispersal of modern humans than admitted by the current consensus. However, other studies, particularly from genetic evidence and new dates for key archaeological assemblages in South Africa, have begun to paint a coherent picture that may mean that the genetic, fossil and archaeological data for the origin of modern humans can be successfully re-integrated (Mellars, 2006) after a decade of debate.

New hominins and dates

Recently one new fossil discovery and better dates for another set of finds have pushed back the timing of the first appearance of anatomically modern morphology, each by roughly 50 ka years from the previously accepted consensus, moving the date from 100 ka in the mid 1990s to 195 ka today. The first major advance came with the announcement of the discovery and dating of three fossil crania from the Herto formation of the Middle Awash succession in Ethiopia (White *et al.*, 2003; Clark *et al.*, 2003). Argon–Argon (Ar–Ar) isotopic dates bracket the Herto crania between 160 ± 2 ka and 154 ± 7 ka (Clark *et al.*, 2003). The finds are associated with a surprisingly late Acheulean industry, although one that includes prepared core technology and a substantial number of 'light-duty', flake-based tools.

The second major jump in age came with the announcement of revised dates for the Omo Kibish fossils, also from Ethiopia (McDougall *et al.*, 2005). For many years, the age of the Kibish fossils had been the subject of controversy

(Wolpoff, 1989; Smith *et al.*, 1989; Smith, 1993), primarily fueled by the multiregionalists' contention that anatomically modern humans did not appear in Africa substantially earlier than elsewhere. Butzer and his colleagues divided the Kibish Formation into four members; and the specimens Omo I and II, the most important hominins, both came from the lowest member, Member I (Butzer *et al.*, 1969). Butzer *et al.* (1969) reported an Uranium–Thorium (^{230}Th/^{234}U) isotopic date derived from fresh water mollusc shells of 130 ± 5 ka from essentially the same level as the Omo I hominin specimen. This date became the focal point of multiregionalists' criticisms, because as ground water conditions fluctuate, uranium can either be deposited or removed from the shells. Renewed work in the Kibish Formation identified a tuff dated by Ar–Ar methods to 195.8 ± 1.6 ka, which underlies the Omo I and II specimens, and a second tuff 46 metres higher in Member III that dates to 103.7 ± 0.9 ka (McDougall *et al.*, 2005, 2008; Brown and Fuller, 2008). These ages correlate well with specific sapropels, layers of sediments rich in organic material that were deposited on the sea floor of the eastern Mediterranean during intervals of increased flow in the Nile river, which, in turn, stemmed from greater precipitation in Ethiopia. Specifically, the tuffs underlying and overlying Omo I and II correlate with sapropels S7 (195 ka) and S4 (102 ka) (McDougall *et al.* 2005; 2008).

The dates of the Kibish and Herto finds create an even longer temporal period between the first appearance of anatomically modern humans and the full suite of archaeological traits that some archaeologists insist must be present to demonstrate modern behavioural patterns. There are at least two additional implications of these older dates. First, the evolution of a modern anatomy occurred earlier and perhaps more gradually than was generally believed in the early 1990s. Second, if the dates for the Omo I hominin are correct, then the cooling, drying and contraction of the suitable habitat for humans during Oxygen Isotope Stage 6 (OIS 6) could not be the trigger for a population bottleneck, or speciation event that produced anatomically modern morphology, since modern morphology was present in Ethiopia at the beginning of OIS 6. If the new date for Omo I is too old, it would still be possible that range contraction, a population bottleneck and/or selection during OIS 6 played a key role in the emergence of modern humans, but the age of the Herto remains implies that the process was essentially complete by the middle of the OIS 6 period. The best current genetically based evidence for the origin of modern humans is 141 ka (95% CI: 186–104 ka) (Fagundes *et al.*, 2007), which also points to the most likely time of origin lying within OIS 6.

Another interesting issue concerning these surprisingly early anatomically modern humans arises from an increasing awareness among anthropologists that perhaps not all African MSA humans are really 'anatomically modern', at least in the sense of being indistinguishable from recent humans. For example, the observation that the best preserved Herto cranium could be readily distinguished from recent humans in multivariate analyses led White *et al.* (2003) to propose that the specimens should be placed in a separate sub-species, *Homo sapiens idaltu*. Other examples of distinctive morphology in MSA hominins include individuals with small to very small teeth in comparison to extant African populations, whereas most other human teeth from the MSA tend to be fairly large (Grine *et al.*, 1991, 2000; Grine and Klein, 1993; Grine, 1998; Rightmire and Deacon, 2001; Grine and Henshilwood, 2002). Examples of the small-toothed hominins are known from Klasies River Mouth (Singer and Wymer, 1982; Rightmire and Deacon, 1991; Lam *et al.*, 1996), Mumba Rock Shelter in Tanzania (Bräuer and Mehlman, 1988), and Witkrans Cave (McCrossin, 1992). Many of the mandibles from Klasies River Mouth have very weakly developed chins (Smith, 1993; Schwartz and Tattersall, 2000) and a high degree of sexual dimorphism (Lam *et al.*, 1996). Human postcranial remains from the MSA also tend to possess some archaic features (Churchill *et al.*, 1996; Pearson and Grine, 1996, 1997; Pearson, 2000; Pearson *et al.*, 2008a,b) that argue in favour of Klein's (1999) proposal that these specimens should be described as 'near-modern' rather than clearly anatomically modern.

New genetic data

In recent years, genetic studies have provided some of the greatest insights into the origin of modern humans (Mellars, 2006). Several research foci have been particularly revealing: work on human mtDNA, Y-chromosomes, simulations of genetic patterns expected under competing models of modern human origins (Satta and Takahata, 2002, 2004; Eswaran, 2002; Eller *et al.*, 2004; Eswaran *et al.*, 2005; Fagundes *et al.*, 2007), and findings from *FOXP2*, a gene possibly associated with the origin of language as we know it today (Lai *et al.*, 2001; Enard *et al.*, 2002; Zhang *et al.*, 2002; MacDermot *et al.*, 2005). Mutations in *FOXP2* are associated with errors or deficits in speech in humans (Lai *et al.*, 2001; Zhang *et al.*, 2002; MacDermot *et al.*, 2005) and problems in vocalization in other mammals (Lai *et al.*, 2001; Shu *et al.*, 2005), and *FOXP2* expression correlates with acoustic learning in birds (Haesler *et al.*, 2004; Scharff and Haesler, 2005). Mutations in *FOXP2* or surrounding regions on chromosome 7 are also associated with autism in humans in some studies (e.g. Gong *et al.*, 2004; Li *et al.*, 2005), but not all (Marui *et al.*, 2005). *FOXP2* appears to exert its effects by influencing the expression of other genes in key parts of the developing brain including the basal ganglia and inferior frontal cortex (Spiteri *et al.*, 2007; Konopka, 2009; Enard, 2009).

Enard *et al.* (2002) found that *FOXP2* has been highly conserved in mammalian evolution, with only one amino acid difference between mice and catarrhines including chimpanzees, gorillas and macaques (humans and orang-utans are exceptions) but that the gene had undergone an acceleration in change in humans following our split with chimpanzees. Two additional amino acid changes accumulated in the human lineage. Enard *et al.* (2002) also studied variability in the gene in modern humans and found almost none. The few mutations that existed allowed Enard *et al.* (2002) to calculate a very recent date for the origin of the recent form of *FOXP2* at 0 ka (which is obviously impossible) with a 95% confidence interval of 120 to 0 ka. Strong selection on the allele makes more precision difficult because there has been very little time for mutations, even synonymous ones, to accumulate. Given its importance in producing language and its recent origin, the modern human allele for *FOXP2* has been widely touted as the smoking gun for the origin of language (Klein, 2003; Mellars, 2004, 2005). However, the recovery of two partial sequences of Neandertal *FOXP2* that appear to belong to the 'modern' allele of the gene (Krause *et al.*, 2007) challenge the notion that the new form of *FOXP2* alone can account for the success of modern humans in their colonisation of Africa.

Another key, recent development in genetics has been the use of the sequence variation present in mtDNA in Africa and many parts of Eurasia and Australia to obtain much more precise estimates for the date at which the bearers of modern mtDNA left Africa and colonised the rest of the world. Studies of the mtDNA of Andaman Islanders (Thangaraj *et al.*, 2003, 2005) and the Orang Asli, dark-skinned, curly haired aboriginal inhabitants of the Malaysian peninsula (Macauley *et al.*, 2005) have led to better estimates for the age at which mtDNA haplogroups M and N, which contain all mtDNAs of populations outside of Africa, began to differentiate from closely related African sequences belonging to haplogroup L3 (Watson *et al.*, 1997; Salas *et al.*, 2002; Macauley *et al.*, 2005). The results show that haplogroups M and N each have a most recent common ancestor (MRCA) at around 63 000 BP (62 900 ± 5200 BP for M; 62 800 ± 5000 for N) (Macauley *et al.*, 2005). These ages for the origin of Eurasian mtDNA clades suggest a very rapid coastal settlement; the journey from India to Australia may have only taken 13 000 to 3000 years (Macauley *et al.*, 2005; Forster and Matsumura, 2005). At the moment, this detail from the impressive set of inferences derived from mtDNA greatly exceeds our ability to test this scenario with archaeological evidence. Very few sites along the putative coastal route from eastern Africa to the easternmost islands of Indonesia have been uncovered and firmly dated within 10 000 years of the inferred dispersal event. New evidence from Jwalapuram in southern India shows that the hominins who inhabited the subcontinent at the time of the massive eruption of Mount Toba at 74 ka were able to persist there through the changes caused

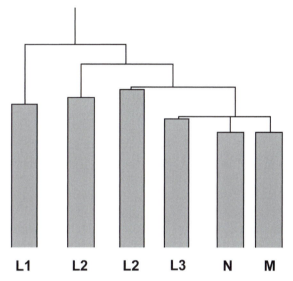

L1   L2   L2   L3   N   M

Figure 21.1. Phylogeny of mtDNA haplogroups. L1 here is equivalent to L0 of Behar *et al.* (2008).

by the ashfall and volcanic winter that followed the eruption (Petraglia *et al.*, 2007). However, if the mtDNA data are correct, these hominins may have been archaic rather than modern, or, if they *were* modern, they made very little genetic contribution to the later population of South Asia.

Turning to the search for the closest relatives of migrants from Africa, haplogroup L3 contains the closest African cousins of the non-African mtDNA lineages (Figure 21.1). The most sequence variation and most divergent haplotypes in L3 currently occur in eastern Africa, lending weight to the inference that the L3 lineage originated in East Africa (Watson *et al.*, 1997; Salas *et al.*, 2002). Macauley *et al.* (2005) calculated the MRCA of L3 haplotypes: 83.5 ± 8.4 ka. Haplogroups L1 (L0 of Behar *et al.*, 2008) and L2 are the other major mtDNA haplogroups present in sub-Saharan Africa. L2 has a MRCA of 56 ± 3 ka (Watson *et al.*, 1997). Haplogroup L1 (L0 of Behar *et al.*, 2008) contains the deepest lineages of human mtDNA, with an MRCA around 111 ka (Watson *et al.*, 1997), but an inferred coalescent age with other African lineages between 143 ka (Horai *et al.*, 1995) and 204.7 ± 22.1 ka (Macauley *et al.*, 2005). In Africa, haplogroups L2 and L3 are common in western, eastern, central and the northernmost part of southern Africa; haplogroup L1 (L0 of Behar *et al.*, 2008) is common only in southern Africa among Khoe-san populations, although it occurs in low frequencies across the continent (Salas *et al.*, 2002; Behar *et al.*, 2008).

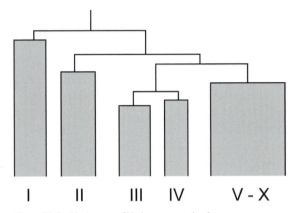

Figure 21.2. Phylogeny of Y-chromosome haplogroups.

The inferred common ancestor of human Y-chromosomes is much more recent, with a coalescent age at 59 ka (95% confidence interval: 140 to 40 ka) (Underhill *et al.*, 2001). As is the case for mtDNA, three main haplogroups of Y-chromosomes dominate sub-Saharan African populations. These are designated Groups I, II and III; Group I is the most ancient and divergent and is found only in African populations (Underhill *et al.*, 2001). Group II forms the sister group of a major cluster containing additional African and virtually all non-African Y-chromosomes (Groups III–X; see Figure 21.2). As is the case for mtDNA, in Africa Y-chromosomes of Group I are common only among Khoe-san people of southern Africa, although they also occur elsewhere and are moderately prevalent in Ethiopia (Semino *et al.*, 2002).

Taken together, these genetic results suggest that new Y-chromosomes, L2 and L3 mtDNA lineages, and perhaps the new form of *FOXP2* all may have spread through Africa at approximately 60 000 BP (see Mellars, 2006 for a similar argument regarding mtDNA). The new Y-chromosomes and *FOXP2* appear to have supplanted all previous alleles, but the effect on mtDNA of this hypothetical migration would have been much less pronounced because L1 (L0 of Behar *et al.*, 2008) mtDNAs remain in high frequency in most Khoe-san-speaking peoples of southern Africa. Outside of Africa, all three genetic systems swept away all previously existing alleles. Thus, as Fred Smith suggested at the conference in honour of Tobias (Smith, 2006; this volume), and others have argued based on genetic simulations (Eswaran, 2002; Satta and Takahata, 2004; Eswaran *et al.*, 2005; Plagnol and Wall, 2006), the evolution of modern humans in Africa may well have involved a subdivided population even in sub-Saharan Africa and proceeded along similar lines as the assimilation model proposed by Smith *et al.* (1989) for Eurasia, albeit with less substantial replacement of pre-existing African alleles.

Towards a new synthesis

Are there any archaeological correlates of a possible spread of people, genes and new behaviours through Africa at *c*. 60 000 BP when modern humans' Y-chromosomes and form of *FOXP2* were spreading throughout the continent? The genetic data strongly hint at substantial population mixture – or even upheaval – around 60 ka in Africa. The expansion of mtDNA and Y-chromosomes in eastern Africa coincides with the return of wet conditions in equatorial Africa after a series of prolonged mega-droughts between 135 and 75 ka that have been discovered through the study of cores from Lakes Malawi and Tanganyika in eastern Africa and Lake Bosumtwi in Ghana (Scholz *et al.*, 2007; Cohen *et al.*, 2007).

If the establishment of these genetic patterns corresponded to the physical movement of people, it is reasonable to hypothesise that it ought to have an archaeological signature. Nevertheless, one should bear in mind that, to the great frustration of archaeologists working to discover traces of modern humans' rapid dispersal along the Indian Ocean littoral from Africa to Australia, the same hypothesis can be made for the out of Africa movement, but has yet to be validated by archaeological finds.

Given the diversity and geographic distribution of mtDNA L3 haplotypes in Africa, it is likely that an eastern African population was the source of the modern humans who colonised the rest of the word and perhaps concurrently spread through much of the rest of Africa (Watson *et al.*, 1997; Salas *et al.*, 2002; Macauley *et al.*, 2005), with the exception of southern Africa (Behar *et al.*, 2008). In comparison to the southern African archaeological sequence, the MSA of eastern Africa presents an impressive diversity of industries (Clark, 1988; McBrearty and Brooks, 2000; Ambrose, 2002). The highlands of eastern Africa were continuously occupied during the MSA; the human population tracked environmental zones, moving up or down slope to stay in optimal ecological zones (Isaac, 1972; Ambrose, 2001a). In contrast, much of southern Africa was abandoned during the driest periods save the highlands around the Drakensberg Mountains in the eastern escarpment region of southern Africa (Deacon and Lancaster, 1988; Kaplan, 1990).

However, the South African archaeological record has also received considerable attention for an industry known as the Howiesons Poort, which occurred during the MSA (Figure 21.3). Many authors herald this industry as a precociously early appearance of archaeological traits more commonly associated with the LSA including the standardisation of formal tool types, the extensive use of exotic, high-quality raw material for lithic artefacts, and the extensive use of backed crescents, segments and blades (Singer and Wymer, 1982; Wurz, 1999; Ambrose, 2001b, 2002, 2006; Barham, 2002b). The backed pieces were almost certainly fitted into hafts to form compound tools, requiring a more

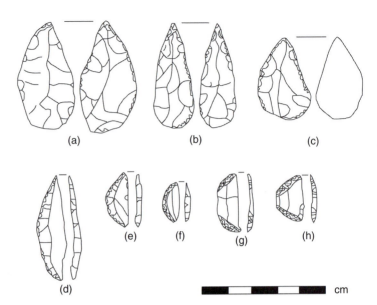

(a)   (b)   (c)

(e)   (f)   (g)   (h)

(d)   cm

Figure 21.3. Howiesons Poort artefacts from Layer 26 of Umhlatuzana rockshelter, Natal Province, Republic of South Africa: (a, b) bifacial points; (c) unifacial point; (d, e, f) backed crescents; (g, h) trapezoids (after Kaplan, 1990).

sophisticated sequence of actions and planning that Ambrose (2001b) has likened to the mental processes necessary to produce language. The procurement of raw materials from greater distances than was the norm in earlier MSA assemblages from the same sites in South Africa (but see Minichillo, 2006) may also indicate that Howiesons Poort people had wider social networks than earlier people and had perhaps undergone a key 'troop to tribe' transition that had fundamentally reorganised relationships among groups and may only have been possible with a fully modern capacity for language (Ambrose and Lorenz, 1990; Ambrose, 2000, 2001b, 2002, 2006).

New excavations at Rose Cottage Cave in the eastern Free State Province of South Africa have facilitated the establishment of a series of TL dates for the Howiesons Poort levels at the site to between 60.4 ± 4.6 ka and 56.3 ± 4.5 ka (Valladas *et al.*, 2005). In a review of other TL assays and amino acid racemisation dates derived from ostrich eggshells (Brooks and Robertshaw, 1990; Miller *et al.*, 1999), Valladas *et al.* (2005) concluded that the best dates for the Howiesons Poort in South Africa and the Apollo 11 rock shelter in Namibia bracket the industry between 71 to 56 ka, indicating it persisted for 15 000 years. More recent work by Jacobs *et al.* (2008) dated Howiesons Poort sites in southern Africa by means of single grain OSL, constraining the industry to a narrower age range of 65 to 60 ka and placing the earlier Still Bay variant of the MSA to a narrow (<5 ka) band of time around 70 ka. Given the possible techno-logical innovations and possible cognitive importance of the Howiesons Poort, and the new dates that place it around the same time that modern humans left Africa to colonise Eurasia, can any link be established between the Howiesons Poort and other earlier, or even contemporaneous, archaeological assemblages to the northern and eastern regions of Africa?

In his 1974 synthesis of the Stone Age of Southern Africa, Garth Sampson noted that numerous typological similarities existed between the Howiesons Poort of South Africa and assemblages from Botswana, Zambia, Zimbabwe, Angola and territory all the way north to the southern shore of Lake Tanganyika, commenting, 'an alarming variety of names is in current use to describe materials similar in typological composition' (Sampson, 1974: 232). These broadly similar industries include the Howiesons Poort, Umguzan, Tshangula, Bambatan/Tshangulan, Magosian, Rhodesian Magosian, Second Intermediate and a variety of other names (Clark, 1966, 1970; Sampson, 1974; Cooke, 1978; Ervedrosa, 1980; Barham, 2000). All of these assemblages feature bifacial or unifacial points, sidescrapers, curve-backed knives, and backed crescents and blades (Sampson, 1974). The geographic range of these industries could per-haps even be extended further to the north if the Mumba Industry from Mumba Höhle in Tanzania (Mehlman, 1989) is added to the list (Figure 21.4). The small assemblage from the Naisiusiu Beds at Olduvai Gorge (Leakey *et al.*, 1972) also contains microliths and crescent forms; it was thought to date to the early LSA but has been dated recently to 62 ± 5 ka by ESR on teeth, assuming linear uptake of uranium (Skinner *et al.*, 2003).

The Howiesons Poort features a high degree of standardisation in the types and shapes of formal tools (Wurz, 1999) as well as the extensive use of exotic raw materials, features that lend weight to the hypothesis that it represents an early example of truly modern behavioural capacity (Ambrose and Lorenz, 1990; Wurz, 1999; Ambrose, 2002, 2006). This degree of standardisation and use of exotic raw materials are not necessarily prominent features of the other assemblages that bear typological similarities to the Howiesons Poort.

A key problem that Sampson (1974) faced in his attempt to draw connec-tions between these industries – and which still plagues efforts to synthesise this period – is its absolute chronology. The fundamental problem in argu-ing for an association between these industries is that some or many of them may, in fact, belong to the LSA rather than the MSA, but in most cases the industries are either poorly dated via old, conventional radiocarbon techniques (which may have yielded falsely young ages) or have sharply conflicting age estimates from radiocarbon and newer techniques such as electron spin reson-ance (ESR), thermoluminescence (TL) and optically stimulated luminescence

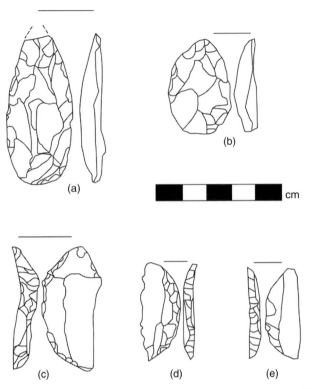

Figure 21.4. A selection of implements from the Mumba Industry, Bed V, Mumba Höhle,Tanzania: (a) bifacial, elongate foliate point; (b) unifacial point; (c, d, e) backed crescents (after Mehlman, 1989).

(OSL) (Sampson, 1974; Brooks and Robertshaw, 1990; Brooks *et al.*, 1990; Barham, 2000). As a case in point, Mehlman (1989) reported radiocarbon ages of 37 to 21 ka for the Mumba Industry at Mumba Höhle but newer dating methods frequently produce older ages. Uranium series dates for the same strata at Mumba placed them between 66 and 23 ka, and amino acid racemisation dates on ostrich eggshell from Level V at Mumba, which contains the Mumba Industry, bracket the age of the level between 65 and 45 ka (McBrearty and Brooks, 2000). Miller *et al.* (1999) used amino acid racemisation on ostrich eggshell to date a Bambatan assemblage from the open air at ≠Gi in Botswana to between 80 and 70 ka, which would place this assemblage slightly before the Howiesons Poort in South Africa. After surveying the available literature including recent arguments for industrial associations advanced by Larsson (1996), Barham (2000) tentatively proposed that the Lupembo-Tshitolian of Central Africa dated to late OIS 5 through OIS 4 (while assigning the Tshitolian proper to the LSA), and hypothesised that the Lupembo-Tshitolian might correlate with the Tshangulan in Zimbabwe, the Howiesons Poort in South Africa and the Mumba Industry in Tanzania. If these tentative correlations are correct, the archaeological record may well have preserved the cultural signature of people who spread from eastern into southern Africa at approximately 60 ka, bringing new tools, genes and behaviours with them (Mellars, 2006).

This hypothesis, however, should not be accepted uncritically. It needs to be tested much more rigorously, which will require the chronology of the MSA in the southern half of Africa to be refined. In addition, it faces a host of problems with respect to the fundamental issues of how one should identify 'modern' behaviour in the archaeological record and, given those criteria, whether the Howiesons Poort and related industries truly record a quantum advance in behavioural sophistication over earlier archaeological assemblages in the African MSA. Earlier assemblages from Blombos, Klasies River Mouth, Die Kelders, Mumbwa and Mumba all provide fairly clear evidence of other precociously 'modern' behaviours in an earlier MSA context than the Howiesons Poort or the putative age of the spread of modern humans out of (and possibly throughout) Africa around 60 ka.

The Howiesons Poort and related industries may simply be additional manifestations of a modern capacity for behavioural flexibility that had been present since at least 120 ka, if not earlier (McBrearty and Brooks, 2000; Ambrose, 2001a,b; Barham, 2002b). The Howiesons Poort is associated with OIS 4 and, although it is important to bear in mind that the terrestrial record of climate change may be substantially more complex than the marine isotope curves might lead one to believe (e.g. Butzer, 2004), climatic conditions may have required the development of wider social networks and planning that presumably underlie the technology and patterns of procurement of high-quality raw material (especially silcrete) that distinguish the Howiesons Poort from earlier or later MSA industries in southern Africa. When climatic conditions improved, these elaborate social networks may simply have no longer been needed: the effort needed to maintain them may have no longer been worth the benefit they provided. The recent history of the *hxaro* exchange system of the !Kung San provides an example of how this process could operate.

Traditionally in !Kung San society, each adult had several trading partners, some of whom resided over a hundred kilometres away, with whom he or she exchanged gifts (the *hxaro* system) and who also served as a social safety net for the individual if local conditions became unfavourable (Wiessner, 1982, 1986). With the recent settlement of !Kung San bands and supplementation of their diet by the government, the importance of the *hxaro* system for survival has been undermined. *Hxaro* exchanges now tend to be made with those living nearby rather than far away, and, if food supplementation were to suddenly end, the ability of the system to manage risk in the face of a local shortfall has been largely destroyed (Wiessner, 2003). From an ecological perspective, food supplementation by the government or climatic change leading to richer and more consistently available local resources might be expected to exert similar pressure on social institutions. If this model is correct, then the Howiesons Poort is simply one more manifestation of a capacity for modern behaviour rather than a watershed period marking the first appearance in southern Africa of people with those abilities.

Further work will be needed to decide between the two main hypotheses. New archaeological researches that seek to untangle the potentially confounding effects of population size and density are badly needed. Additional studies of human genetics and the fossil record (especially new fossil finds) could also be of great importance. If the modern form of *FOXP2* arose in Africa, it is possible that the most ancient diversity in synonymous mutations is still present in African populations and thus work on the phylogeny of *FOXP2* in Africa might be enlightening. With respect to the fossil record, if humans physically spread from eastern Africa around 60 ka, it may well be that this migration should correspond to morphological change in MSA southern Africans, perhaps in the form of indisputably anatomically modern humans associated with the Howiesons Poort and later industries. These fully modern populations may have replaced or absorbed the near-modern humans before this period (e.g. the hominin fossils from Klasies River Mouth). This hypothesis is currently untestable given the scarce fossil record from this period. The Fish Hoek cranium was once thought to be possibly associated with the Howiesons Poort (Sampson, 1974), but this attribution is erroneous: direct radiocarbon assays date the cranium to 7.3 to 7.1 ka (calibrated and adjusted for marine diet) (Stynder *et al.*, 2009). The cranium is large relative to extant Khoe-san peoples, but morphologically similar (Keith, 1931). Given the dearth of data on the morphology of MSA and early LSA populations in southern Africa, the analyses of the Hofmeyr cranium (Grine *et al.*, 2007, 2010); Tuinplaas (Hughes, 1990; Pike *et al.*, 2004) and the LSA crania from Malawi (Morris and Ribot, 2006) are all valuable and indicate that anthropologists still have a great deal left to learn about the emergence of extant African populations as well as the patterns of variation that existed before the Bantu expansion that dramatically remodelled the genetic landscape of southern Africa (Salas *et al.*, 2002; Beleza *et al.*, 2005; Tishkoff *et al.*, 2007, 2009).

Acknowledgements

My sincere thanks to the organisers of the conference for their invitation to participate and to Professor Phillip V. Tobias, who warmly welcomed me on my trips to collect data in the University of the Witwatersrand Dart Collection when I was a graduate student. Alison Brooks, Chris Henshilwood, Andrew Gallagher and Sally Reynolds provided useful comments on the manuscript. I also wish to thank the organisers of a 2005 conference on the MSA in East Africa hosted by the National Museums of Kenya, and the National Museum of Ethiopia. Many of the ideas presented here began to coalesce as a result of that conference and interactions with its many participants. I am very grateful to Alison Brooks for the invitation to participate in the MSA conference and to John C. Pearson for financial support to attend it.

References

Ambrose, S. H. (1998). Chronology of the Later Stone Age and food production in East Africa. *Journal of Archaeological Science*, **25**: 377–92.

(2000). Change in Middle Stone Age settlement patterns in the central Rift Valley, Kenya. *Journal of Human Evolution*, **38**: A4.

(2001a). Middle and Later Stone Age settlement patterns in the Central Rift Valley, Kenya: comparisons and contrasts. In Conard, N. J. (ed.), *Settlement Dynamics of the Middle Paleolithic and Middle Stone Age*. Tübingen: Kerns Verlag, pp. 21–43.

(2001b). Paleolithic technology and human evolution. *Science*, **291**: 1748–53.

(2002). Small things remembered: origins of early microlithic industries in sub-Saharan Africa. In Elston, R. G. and Kuhn, S. L. (eds.), *Thinking Small: Global Perspectives on Microlithization* (Archaeological Papers of the American Anthropological Association Number 12). Washington, DC: American Anthropological Association, pp. 9–29.

(2006). Howiesons Poort lithic raw material procurement patterns and the evolution of modern human behavior: a response to Minichillo (2006). *Journal of Human Evolution*, **50**: 365–9.

Ambrose, S. H. and Lorenz, K. G. (1990). Social and ecological models for the Middle Stone Age in Southern Africa. In Mellars, P. (ed.), *The Emergence of Modern Humans: an Archaeological Perspective*. Ithaca: Cornell University Press, pp. 3–33.

Bar-Yosef, O. (1998). The chronology of the Middle Paleolithic of the Levant. In Akazawa, T., Aoki, K. and Bar-Yosef, O. (eds.), *Neandertals and Modern Humans in Western Asia*. New York: Plenum Press, pp. 39–56.

Barham, L. (2000). A speculative summary. In Barham, L. (ed.), *The Middle Stone Age of Zambia, South Central Africa*. Bristol: Western Academic and Specialist Press Limited, pp. 237–50.

(2001). Central Africa and the emergence of regional identity in the Middle Pleistocene. In Barham, L. and Robson-Brown, K. (eds.), *Human Roots: Africa and Asia in the Middle Pleistocene*. Bristol, England: Western Academic & Specialist Press Limited, pp. 65–80.

(2002a). Systematic pigment use in the Middle Pleistocene of South-Central Africa. *Current Anthropology*, **43**: 181–90.

(2002b). Backed tools in Middle Pleistocene Central Africa and their evolutionary significance. *Journal of Human Evolution*, **43**: 585–603.

Behar, D. M., Villems, R., Soodyall, H. *et al.* (2008). The dawn of human matrilineal diversity. *American Journal of Human Genetics*, **82**: 1130–40.

Beleza, S., Gusmão, L., Amorim, A. *et al.* (2005). The genetic legacy of western Bantu migrations. *Human Genetics*, **117**: 366–75.

Bouzouggar, A., Barton, N., Vanhaerem, M. *et al.* (2007). 82,000-year-old shell beads from North Africa and implications for the origins of modern human behavior. *Proceedings of the National Academy of Sciences of the USA*, **104**: 9964–9.

Bräuer, G. (1984). A craniological approach to the origin of anatomically modern *Homo sapiens* in Africa and implications for the appearance of modern Europeans. In Smith, F. H. and Spencer, F. (eds.), *The Origins of Modern Humans: a World Survey of the Fossil Evidence*. New York: Alan R. Liss, pp. 327–410.

(1989). The evolution of modern humans: a comparison of the African and non-African evidence. In Mellars, P. and Stringer, C. (eds.), *The Human Revolution*. Princeton: Princeton University Press, pp. 123–54.

Bräuer, G. and Mehlman, M. J. (1988). Hominid molars from a Middle Stone Age level at Mumba Rock Shelter, Tanzania. *American Journal of Physical Anthropology*, **75**: 69–76.

Brooks, A. S. and Robertshaw, P. (1990). The glacial maximum in tropical Africa: 22,000–12,000 BP. In Gamble, C. and Soffer, O. (eds.), *The World at 18,000 BP. Volume 2. Low Latitudes*. London: Unwin Hyman, pp. 121–69.

Brooks, A. S., Hare, P. E., Kokis, J. E. *et al.* (1990). Dating Pleistocene archaeological sites by protein diagenesis in ostrich eggshell. *Science*, **248**: 60–4.

Brooks, A. S., Helgren, D. M., Cramer, J. S. *et al.* (1995). Dating and context of three Middle Stone Age sites with bone points in the Upper Simliki Valley, Zaire. *Science*, **268**: 548–53.

Brown, F. H., and Fuller, C. R. (2008). Stratigraphy and tephra of the Kibish Formation, southwestern Ethiopia. *Journal of Human Evolution*, **55**: 366–403.

Butzer, K. (2004). Coastal eolian sands, paleosols, and Pleistocene geoarchaeology of the Southwestern Cape, South Africa. *Journal of Archaeological Science*, **31**: 1743–81.

Butzer, K. W. (1969). Geological interpretation of two Pleistocene hominid sites in the lower Omo Basin. *Nature*, **222**: 1133–5.

Butzer, K. W., Brown, F. H. and Thurber, D. L. (1969). Horizontal sediments of the lower Omo valley: the Kibish Formation. *Quaternaria*, **9**: 15–29.

Churchill, S. E., Pearson, O. M., Grine, F. E. *et al.* (1996). Morphological affinities of the proximal ulna from Klasies River Mouth Main Site: archaic or modern? *Journal of Human Evolution*, **31**: 213–37.

Clark, G. A. and Lindley, J. M. (1989). The case of continuity: observations on the bio-cultural transition in Europe and Western Asia. In Mellars, P. and Stringer, C. (eds.), *The Human Revolution*. Princeton: Princeton University Press, pp. 626–76.

Clark, J. D. (1966). *The Distribution of Prehistoric Culture in Angola*. Lisboa: Museu do Dunda and Companhia de Diamantes de Angola.

(1970). *The Prehistory of Africa*. New York: Praeger.

(1988). The Middle Stone Age of East Africa and the beginnings of regional identity. *Journal of World Prehistory*, **2**: 235–305.

(1989). The origins and spread of modern humans: a broad perspective on the African evidence. In Mellars, P. and Stringer, C. B. (eds.), *The Human Revolution*. Princeton, NJ: Princeton University Press, pp. 565–88.

(1992). African and Asian perspectives on the origins of modern humans. *Philosophical Transactions of the Royal Society of London*, **337**: 201–16.

Clark, J. D., Beyene, Y., WoldeGabriel, G. *et al.* (2003). Stratigraphic, chronological and behavioral contexts of Pleistocene *Homo sapiens* from Middle Awash, Ethiopia. *Nature*, **423**: 747–52.

Cohen, A. S., Stone, J. R., Beuning, K. R. M. *et al.* (2007). Ecological consequences of early Late Pleistocene megadroughts in tropical Africa. *Proceedings of the National Academy of Sciences of the USA*, **104**: 16422–7.

Cooke, C. K. (1978). The Redcliff Stone Age Site, Rhodesia. *Occasional Papers of the National Museums and Monuments of Rhodesia, Series A, Human Sciences*, **4**: 43–80.

d'Errico, F. (2003). The invisible frontier. A multiple species model for the origin of behavioral modernity. *Evolutionary Anthropology*, **12**: 188–202.

d'Errico, F., Henshilwood, C., Vanhaerem, M. *et al.* (2005). *Nassarius kraussianus* shell beads from Blombos Cave: evidence for symbolic behaviour in the Middle Stone Age. *Journal of Human Evolution*, **48**: 3–24.

d'Errico, F., Vanhaeren, M. and Wadley, L. (2008). Possible shell beads from the Middle Stone Age layers of Sibudu Cave, South Africa. *Journal of Archaeological Science*, **35**: 2675–85.

Day, M. H. (1969). Omo human skeletal remains. *Nature*, **222**: 1135–8.

Day, M. H. and Stringer, C. B. (1991). Les restes crâniens d'Omo-Kibish et leur classification à l'intérieur du genre *Homo*. *L'Anthropologie*, **95**: 573–94.

Day, M. H., Twist, M. H. C. and Ward, S. (1991). Les vestiges post-crâniens d'Omo I (Kibish). *L'Anthropologie*, **95**: 595–610.

Deacon, H. J. (1989). Late Pleistocene palaeoecology and archaeology in the Southern Cape, South Africa. In Mellars, P. and Stringer, C. (eds.), *The Human Revolution: Behavioural and Biological Perspectives on the Origins of Modern Humans*. Princeton: Princeton University Press, pp. 547–64.

Deacon, H. J. and Geleijnse, V. B. (1988). The stratigraphy and sedimentology of the main site sequence, Klasies River Mouth, South Africa. *South African Archaeological Bulletin*, **43**: 5–14.

Deacon, J. and Lancaster, N. (1988). *Late Quaternary Palaeoenvironments of Southern Africa*. Oxford: Oxford University Press.

Eller, E., Hawks, J. and Relethford, J. H. (2004). Local extinction and recolonization, species effective populations size, and modern human origins. *Human Biology*, **76**: 689–709.

Enard, W., Przeworski, M., Fisher, S. E. *et al.* (2002). Molecular evolution of *FOXP2*, a gene involved in speech and language. *Nature*, **418**: 869–72.

Enard, W., Gehre, S., Hammerschmidt, K. *et al.* (2009). A humanized version of Foxp2 affects cortico-basal ganglia circuits in mice. *Cell*, **137**: 961–71.

Eswaran, V. (2002). A diffusion wave out of Africa: the mechanism of the modern human revolution? *Current Anthropology*, **43**: 749–74.

Eswaran, V., Harpending, H. and Rogers, A. R. (2005). Genomics refutes an exclusively African origin of humans. *Journal of Human Evolution*, **49**: 1–18.

Ervedosa, C. (1980). *Arqueologia Angolana*. Lisboa: Edições 70, Limitada.

Fagundes, N. J. R., Ray, N., Beaumont, M. *et al.* (2007). Statistical evaluation of alternative models of human evolution. *Proceedings of the National Academy of Sciences of the USA*, **104**: 17614–19.

Forster, P. and Matsumura, S. (2005). Did early humans go North or South? *Science*, **308**: 965–6.

Gong, X., Jia, M., Ruan, Y. *et al.* (2004). Association between the FOXP2 gene and autistic disorder in Chinese population. *American Journal of Medical Genetics. Part B, Neuropsychiatric Genetics*, **127**: 113–16.

Grine, F. E. (1998). Additional human fossils from the Middle Stone Age of Die Kelders Cave 1, South Africa: 1995 excavation. *South African Journal of Science*, **94**: 229–35.

Grine, F. E. and Henshilwood, C. S. (2002). Additional human remains from Blombos Cave, South Africa: (1999–2000 excavations). *Journal of Human Evolution*, **42**: 293–302.

Grine, F. E. and Klein, R. G. (1993). Late Pleistocene human remains from the Sea Harvest site, Saldanha Bay, South Africa. *South African Journal of Science*, **89**: 145–252.

Grine, F., Klein, R. G. and Volman, T. P. (1991). Dating, archaeology and human fossils from the Middle Stone Age levels of Die Kelders, South Africa. *Journal of Human Evolution*, **21**: 363–95.

Grine, F. E., Henshilwood, C. S. and Sealy, J. C. (2000). Human remains from Blombos Cave, South Africa: (1997–1998 excavations). *Journal of Human Evolution*, **38**: 755–65.

Grine, F. E., Bailey, R. M., Harvati, K. *et al.* (2007). Late Pleistocene human skull from Hofmeyr, South Africa, and modern human origins. *Science*, **315**: 226–9.

Grine, F. E., Gunz, P., Betti-Nash, L. *et al.* (2010). Reconstruction of the late Pleistocene human skull from Hofmeyr, South Africa. *Journal of Human Evolution*, **59**: 1–15.

Haesler, S., Wada, K., Nshdejan, A. *et al.* (2004). *FOXP2* expression in avian vocal learners and non-learners. *Journal of Neuroscience*, **24**: 3164–75.

Henshilwood, C. and Sealy, J. (1997). Bone artefacts from the Middle Stone Age at Blombos Cave, Southern Cape, South Africa. *Current Anthropology*, **38**: 890–5.

Henshilwood, C. S., d'Errico, F., Yates, R. *et al.* (2002). Emergence of modern human behavior: Middle Stone Age engravings from South Africa. *Science*, **295**: 1278–80.

Henshilwood, C. S., D'Errico, F., Vanhaeren, M. *et al.* (2004). Middle Stone Age shell beads from South Africa. *Science*, **304**: 404.

Henshilwood, C. S., d'Errico, F. and I. Watts, I. (2009). Engraved ochres from the Middle Stone Age levels at Blombos Cave, South Africa. *Journal of Human Evolution*, **57**: 27–47.

Horai, S., Hayasaka, K., Kondo, R. *et al.* (1995). Recent African origin of modern humans revealed by complete sequences of hominoid mitochondrial DNAs. *Proceedings of the National Academy of Sciences of the USA*, **92**: 532–6.

Hovers, E., Ilani, S., Bar-Yosef, O. *et al.* (2003). An early case of color symbolism: ochre use by modern humans in Qafzeh Cave. *Current Anthropology*, **44**: 491–522.

Hughes, A. R. (1990). The Tuinplaas human skeleton from the Springbok Flats, Transvaal. In Sperber, G. H. (ed.), *From Apes to Angels: Essays in Anthropology in Honor of Phillip V. Tobias*. New York: Wiley-Liss, pp. 197–214.

Isaac, G. L. (1972). Comparative studies of site locations in East Africa. In Ucko, P. J., Tringham, R. and Dimbleby, G. W. (eds.), *Man, Settlement and Urbanism*. London: Duckworth, pp. 165–76.

Jacobs, Z., Wintle, A. G. and Duller, G. A. T. (2003). Optical dating of dune sand from Blombos Cave, South Africa: I – multiple grain data. *Journal of Human Evolution*, **44**: 599–612.

Jacobs, Z., Roberts, R. G., Galbraith, R. F. *et al.* (2008). Ages for the Middle Stone Age of southern Africa: implications for human behavior and dispersal. *Science*, **322**: 733–5.

Kaplan, J. M. (1990). The Umhlatuzana rock shelter sequence: 100,000 years of Stone Age history. *Natal Museum Journal of Humanities*, **2**: 1–94.

Keith, A. (1931). *New Discoveries Relating to the Antiquity of Man*. London: Williams and Norgate.

Klein, R. G. (1979). Stone age exploitation of animals in Southern Africa. *American Scientist*, **67**: 151–60.

Klein, R. G. (1995). Anatomy, behavior, and modern human origins. *Journal of World Prehistory*, **9**: 167–98.

(1999). *The Human Career*, 2nd edn. Chicago: University of Chicago Press.

(2000). Archaeology and the evolution of human behavior. *Evolutionary Anthropology*, **9**: 17–36.

(2003). Whither the Neanderthals? *Science*, **299**: 1525–7.

Konopka, G., Bomar, J. M., Winden, K. *et al.* (2009). Human-specific transcriptional regulation of CNS development genes by FOXP2. *Nature*, **462**: 213–17.

Krause, J., Lalueza-Fox, C., Orlando, L. *et al.* (2007). The derived *FOXP2* variant of modern humans was shared with Neandertals. *Current Biology*, **17**: 1–5.

Lai, C. S., Fisher, S. E., Hurst, J. A. *et al.* (2001). A forkhead-domain gene is mutated in a severe speech and language disorder. *Nature*, **413**: 519–23.

Lam, Y. M., Pearson, O. M. and Smith, C. M. (1996). Chin morphology and sexual dimorphism in the fossil hominid mandible sample from Klasies River Mouth. *American Journal of Physical Anthropology*, **100**: 545–57.

Larsson, L. (1996). The Middle Stone Age of Zimbabwe: some aspects of former research. In Pwiti, G. and Soper, R. (eds.), *Aspects of African Archaeology*. Harare: University of Zimbabwe Publications, pp. 201–6.

Leakey, M. D., Hay, R. L., Thurber, R. *et al.* (1972). Stratigraphy, archaeology, and age of the Ndutu and Naisiusiu beds, Olduvai Gorge, Tanzania. *World Archaeology*, **3**: 328–41.

Li, H., Yamagata, T., Mori, M. *et al.* (2005). Absence of causative mutations and presence of autism-related allele in *FOXP2* in Japanese autistic patients. *Brain & Development*, **27**: 207–10.

Liu, W., Jin, C.-Z., Zhang, Y.-Q. *et al.* (2010). Human remains from Zhirendong, South China, and modern human emergence in East Asia. *Proceedings of the National Academy of Sciences of the USA*, **107**: 19201–6.

Macauley, V., Hill, C., Achilli, A. *et al.* (2005). Single, rapid coastal settlement of Asia revealed by analysis of complete mitochondrial genomes. *Science*, **308**: 1034–6.

MacDermot, K. D., Bonora, E., Sykes, N. *et al.* (2005). Identification of *FOXP2* truncation as a novel cause of developmental speech and language deficits. *American Journal of Human Genetics*, **76**: 1074–80.

Marean, C. W., Bar-Matthews, M., Bernatchez, J. *et al.* (2007). Early human use of marine resources and pigment in South Africa during the Middle Pleistocene. *Nature*, **449**: 905–8.

Marui, T., Koishi, S., Funatogawa, I. *et al.* (2005). No association of *FOXP2* and *PTPRZ1* on 7q31 with autism from the Japanese population. *Neuroscience Research*, **53**: 91–4.

McBrearty, S. (2001). The Middle Pleistocene of East Africa. In Barham, L. and Robson-Brown, K. (eds.), *Human Roots: Africa and Asia in the Middle Pleistocene*. Bristol, England: Western Academic & Specialist Press Limited, pp. 81–98.

(2003). Patterns of technological change at the origin of *Homo sapiens*. *Before Farming*, **9**: 1–5.

McBrearty, S. and Brooks, A. S. (2000). The revolution that wasn't: a new interpretation of the origin of modern human behavior. *Journal of Human Evolution*, **39**: 453–563.

McCrossin, M. L. (1992). Human molars from later Pleistocene deposits of Witkrans Cave, Gaap Escarpment, Kalahari margin. *Human Evolution*, **7**: 1–10.

McDougall, I., Brown, F. H. and Fleagle, J. G. (2005). Stratigraphic placement and age of modern humans from Kibish, Ethiopia. *Nature*, **433**: 733–6.

McDougall, I., Brown, F. H. and Fleagle. J. G. (2008). Sapropels and the age of hominins Omo I and Omo II, Kibish, Ethiopia. *Journal of Human Evolution*, **55**: 409–20.

Mehlman, M. J. (1989). Late Quaternary archaeological sequences in northern Tanzania. Unpublished PhD thesis, Department of Anthropology, University of Illinois, Urbana.

Mellars, P. (1989). Major issues in the emergence of modern humans. *Current Anthropology*, **30**: 349–85.

(2004). Neanderthals and the modern human colonization of Europe. *Nature*, **432**: 461–5.

(2005). The impossible coincidence. A single-species model for the origins of modern human behavior in Europe. *Evolutionary Anthropology*, **14**: 12–27.

(2006). Why did modern human populations disperse from Africa ca. 60,000 years ago? A new model. *Proceedings of the National Academy of Sciences of the USA*, **103**: 9381–6.

Miller, G. H., Beaumont, P. B., Brooks, A. S. *et al.* (1999). Earliest modern humans in South Africa dated by isoleucine epimerization in ostrich eggshell. *Quaternary Science Reviews*, **18**: 1537–48.

Minichillo, T. (2006). Raw material use and behavioral modernity: Howiesons Poort lithic foraging strategies. *Journal of Human Evolution*, **50**: 359–64.

Morris, A. G. and Ribot, I. (2006). Morphometric cranial identity of prehistoric Malawians in the light of sub-Saharan African diversity. *American Journal of Physical Anthropology*, **130**: 10–25.

Mourre, V., Villa, P. and Henshilwood, C. S. (2010). Early use of pressure flaking on lithic artifacts at Blombos Cave, South Africa. *Science*, **330**: 659–62.

Opperman, H. and Heyenrych, B. (1990). A 22,000 year-old Middle Stone Age camp site with plant food remains from the north-eastern Cape. *South African Archaeological Bulletin*, **45**: 93–9.

Pearson, O. M. (2000). Postcranial remains and the origin of modern humans. *Evolutionary Anthropology*, **9**: 229–47.

Pearson, O. M. and Grine, F. E. (1996). Morphology of the Border Cave hominid ulna and humerus. *South African Journal of Science*, **92**: 231–6.

(1997). Re-analysis of the hominid radii from Cave of Hearths and Klasies River Mouth, South Africa. *Journal of Human Evolution*, **32**: 577–92.

Pearson, O. M., Grine, F. E., Fleagle, J. G. *et al.* (2008a). A description of the Omo 1 postcranial skeleton, including newly discovered fossils. *Journal of Human Evolution*, **55**: 421–37.

(2008b). Further new hominin fossils from the Kibish Formation, southwestern Ethiopia. *Journal of Human Evolution*, **55**: 444–7.

Petraglia, M., Korisettar, R., Boivin, N. *et al.* (2007). Middle Paleolithic assemblages from the Indian subcontinent before and after the Toba super-eruption. *Science*, **317**: 114–16.

Pike, A. W. G., Eggins, S., Grün, R. *et al.* (2004). U-series dating of TP1, an almost complete human skeleton from Tuinplaas (Springbok Flats), South Africa. *South African Journal of Science*, **100**: 381–3.

Plagnol, V. and Wall, J. D. (2006). Possible ancestral structure in human populations. *PLoS Genetics*, **2**: e105.

Powell, A., S. Shennan, S. and Thomas, M. G. (2009). Late Pleistocene demography and the appearance of modern human behavior. *Science*, **324**: 1298–301.

Rightmire, G. P. (1984). *Homo sapiens* in sub-Saharan Africa. In Smith, F. H. and Spencer, F. (eds.), *The Origins of Modern Humans: a World Survey of the Fossil Evidence*. New York: Alan R. Liss, pp. 295–325.

Rightmire, G. P. and Deacon, H. J. (1991). Comparative studies of late Pleistocene human remains from Klasies River Mouth, South Africa. *Journal of Human Evolution*, **20**: 131–56.

(2001). New human teeth from Middle Stone Age deposits at Klasies River, South Africa. *Journal of Human Evolution*, **41**: 535–44.

Salas, A., Richards, M., De la Fe, T. *et al.* (2002). The making of the African mtDNA landscape. *American Journal of Human Genetics*, **71**: 1082–111.

Sampson, C. G. (1974). *The Stone Age Archaeology of Southern Africa*. New York: Academic Press.

Satta, Y. and Takahata, N. (2002). Out of Africa with regional interbreeding? Modern human origins. *BioEssays*, **24**: 871–5.

(2004). The distribution of the ancestral haplotype in finite stepping-stone models with population expansion. *Molecular Ecology*, **13**: 877–86.

Scharff, C. and Haesler, S. (2005). An evolutionary perspective on *FOXP2*: strictly for the birds? *Current Opinion in Neurobiology*, **15**: 694–703.

Scholz, C. A., Johnson, T. C., Cohen, A. S. *et al.* (2007). East African megadroughts between 135 and 75 thousand years ago and bearing on early-modern human origins. *Proceedings of the National Academy of Sciences of the USA*, **104**: 16416–21.

Schwartz, J. H. and Tattersall, I. (2000). The human chin revisited: what is it and who has it? *Journal of Human Evolution*, **38**: 367–409.

Semino, O., Santachiara-Benerecetti, A. S., Falaschi, F. *et al.* (2002). Ethiopians and Khoisan share the deepest clades of the human Y-chromosome phylogeny. *American Journal of Human Genetics*, **70**: 265–8.

Shea, J. J. (2003). Neandertals, competition, and the origin of modern human behavior in the Levant. *Evolutionary Anthropology*, **12**: 173–87.

Shen, G., Wang, W., Wang, Q. *et al.* (2002). U-series dating of Liujiang hominid site in Guangxi, southern China. *Journal of Human Evolution*, **43**: 817–29.

Shennan, S. (2001). Demography and cultural innovation: a model and its implications for the emergence of modern human culture. *Cambridge Archaeological Journal*, **11**: 5–16.

Shu, W., Cho, J. Y., Jiang, Y. *et al.* (2005). Altered ultrasonic vocalization in mice with a disruption in the *FOXP2* gene. *Proceedings of the National Academy of Sciences of the USA*, **102**: 9643–8.

Singer, R. and Wymer, J. (1982). *The Middle Stone Age at Klasies River Mouth*. Chicago: University of Chicago Press.

Skinner, A. R., Hay, R. L., Masao, F. *et al.* (2003). Dating the Naisiusiu Beds, Olduvai Gorge, by electron spin resonance. *Quaternary Science Reviews*, **2003**: 1361–6.

Smith, F. H. (1993). Models and realities in modern human origins: the African fossil evidence. In Aitken, M. J., Stringer, C. B. and Mellars, P. A. (eds.), *The Origin of Modern Humans and the Impact of Chronometric Dating*. Princeton: Princeton University Press, pp. 234–48.

(2006). Assimilation and modern human origins in the African peripheries. In Reynolds, S. C., Menter, C. G., Robinson, M. S. and Hemingway, J. (eds.), *African Genesis. A Symposium on Hominid Evolution in Africa. Abstracts & Information. 8th-14th January 2006, University of the Witwatersrand Medical School, Johannesburg, South Africa*. Johannesburg: University of the Witwatersrand, p. 40.

Smith, F. H., Falsetti, A. B. and Donnelly, S. M. (1989). Modern human origins. *Yearbook of Physical Anthropology*, **32**: 35–68.

Spiteri, E., Konopka, G., Coppola, G. *et al.* (2007). Identification of the transcriptional targets of *FOXP2*, a gene linked to speech and language, in developing human brain. *American Journal of Human Genetics*, **81**: 1144–57.

Stringer, C. B. (1993). Reconstructing recent human evolution. In Aitken, M. J., Stringer, C. B. and Mellars, P. A. (eds.), *The Origin of Modern Humans and the Impact of Chronometric Dating*. Princeton: Princeton University Press, pp. 179–95.

Stringer, C. B. and Andrews, P. (1988). Genetic and fossil evidence for the origin of modern humans. *Science*, **239**: 1263–8.

Stringer, C. B., Grün, R., Schwarcz, H. P. *et al.* (1989). ESR dates for the hominid burial site of Es Skhul in Israel. *Nature*, **338**: 756–8.

Stynder, D. D., Brock, F., Sealy, J. C. *et al.* (2009). A mid-Holocene AMS 14C date for the presumed Upper Pleistocene human skeleton from Peers Cave, South Africa. *Journal of Human Evolution*, **56**: 431–4.

Templeton, A. R. (1993). The 'Eve' hypothesis: a genetic critique and reanalysis. *American Anthropologist*, **95**: 51–72.

Texier, P.-J., Porraz, G., Parkington, J. *et al.* (2010). A Howiesons Poort tradition of engraving ostrich eggshell containers dated to 60,000 years ago at Diepkloof Rock Shelter, South Africa. *Proceedings of the National Academy of Sciences of the USA*, **107**: 6180–5.

Thangaraj, K., Singh, L., Reddy, A. G. *et al.* (2003). Genetic affinities of the Andaman Islanders, a vanishing human population. *Current Biology*, **13**: 86–93.

Thangaraj, K., Chaubey, G., Kivisild, T. *et al.* (2005). Reconstructing the origin of Andaman Islanders. *Science*, **308**: 996–7.

Tishkoff, S. A., Gonder, M. K., Henn, B. M. *et al.* (2007). History of click-speaking populations of Africa inferred from mtDNA and Y chromosome genetic variation. *Molecular Biology and Evolution*, **24**: 2180–95.

Tishkoff, S. A., Reed, F. A., Friedlaender, F. R. *et al.* (2009). The genetic structure and history of Africans and African Americans. *Science*, **324**: 1035–44.

Tribolo, C., Mercier, N., Selo, M. *et al.* (2006). TL dating of burnt lithics from Blombos Cave (South Africa): further evidence for the antiquity of modern human behaviour. *Archaeometry*, **48**: 341–57.

Underhill, P. A., Passarino, G., Lin, A. A. *et al.* (2001). The phylogeny of Y chromosome binary haplotypes and the origins of modern human populations. *Annals of Human Genetics*, **65**: 43–62.

Valladas, H., Reyss, J. L., Joron, J. L. *et al.* (1988). Thermoluminescence dating of Mousterian 'Proto-Cro-Magnon' remains from Israel and the origin of modern man. *Nature*, **331**: 614–15.

Valladas, H., Wadley, L., Mercier, N. *et al.* (2005). Thermoluminescence dating on burnt lithics from Middle Stone Age layers at Rose Cottage Cave. *South African Journal of Science*, **101**: 169–74.

Watson, E., Forster, P., Richards, M. *et al.* (1997). Mitochondrial footprints of human expansions in Africa. *American Journal of Human Genetics*, **61**: 691–704.

White, T. D., Asfaw, B., DeGusta, D. *et al.* (2003). Pleistocene *Homo sapiens* from Middle Awash, Ethiopia. *Nature*, **423**: 742–7.

Wiessner, P. (1982). Risk, reciprocity and social influences on !Kung San economics. In Leacock, E. and Lee, R. (eds.), *Politics and History in Band Societies*. Cambridge and Paris: Cambridge University Press and Éditions de la Maison des Sciences de l'Homme, pp. 61–84.

   (1986). !Kung San networks in a generational perspective. In Biesele, M., Gordon, R. and Lee, R. (eds.), *The Past and Future of !Kung San Ethnography* (Quellen zur Khoisan-Forschung, Band 4). Hamburg: Helmut Buske Verlag, pp. 103–36.

   (2003). Owners of the future? Calories, cash, casualties and self-sufficiency in the Nyae Nyae area between 1996 and 2003. *Visual Anthropology Review*, **19**: 149–59.

Wolpoff, M. H. (1989). Multiregional evolution: the fossil alternative to Eden. In P. Mellars and C. B. Stringer (eds.), *The Human Revolution*. Princeton, NJ: Princeton University Press, pp 62–108.

Wurz, S. (1999). The Howiesons Poort backed artefacts from Klasies River: an argument for symbolic behaviour. *South African Archaeological Bulletin*, **54**: 38–50.

Yellen, J. E., Brooks, A. S., Cornelissen, E. *et al.* (1995). A Middle Stone Age worked bone industry from Katanda, upper Semliki Valley, Zaire. *Science*, **268**: 553–6.

Zhang, J., Webb, D. M. and Podlaha, O. (2002). Accelerated protein evolution and origins of human-specific features: *FOXP2* as an example. *Genetics*, **162**: 1825–35.

Part IV

*In search of context: hominin environments,
behaviour and lithic cultures*

22 Animal palaeocommunity variability and habitat preference of the robust australopiths in South Africa

DARRYL J. DE RUITER, MATT
SPONHEIMER AND JULIA LEE-THORP

Abstract

The palaeoenvironments associated with *Australopithecus* (*Paranthropus*) *robustus* have generally been reconstructed as habitat mosaics; typically open, arid grasslands in the vicinity of woodlands or forests with a nearby source of permanent water. Disentangling which aspect(s) of these mosaics might have been preferred by the hominins presents a significant challenge. The aim of this study is to enhance our resolution of animal palaeocommunity structure in the Bloubank river valley of South Africa in order to test which ecological conditions might have been favoured or avoided by *A. robustus*. Faunal assemblage data were collected from a series of hominin-bearing deposits including Kromdraai, Swartkrans, Sterkfontein and Coopers (locality D). Taphonomic data revealed the presence of a potential bias resulting from depositional matrix, though our analysis demonstrated there was no association between taphonomic conditions and taxonomic composition. A selection of environmentally sensitive taxa was assigned to a series of ecological categories based on isotopic, ecomorphological and taxonomic evidence. Correspondence analysis was used to assess changes in faunal composition between assemblages. Results indicate that the more open, arid-adapted taxa there are in a given assemblage, the fewer hominins there tend to be. Rather than reflecting the habitat preference of *A. robustus*, these data indicate a pattern of habitat avoidance that is inconsistent with a reconstruction of this hominin as an open, arid specialist. We conclude that the hominins were capable of subsisting in sub-optimal habitats as a result of their capacity to significantly alter their dietary patterns in favour of less preferred food items when conditions dictated.

African Genesis: Perspectives on Hominin Evolution, eds. Sally C. Reynolds and Andrew Gallagher. Published by Cambridge University Press. © Cambridge University Press 2012.

Introduction

Australopithecus (Paranthropus) robustus is typically reconstructed as a species that occupied an open, arid grassland habitat (Cooke, 1952, 1963; Shipman and Harris, 1988; Vrba, 1975, 1980, 1985a,b), though several recent studies have documented a more diverse habitat mosaic associated with these early hominins (Avery, 1995, 2001; Reed, 1997; Watson, 2004). These habitat mosaics are reconstructed as predominantly open grasslands in the vicinity of woodlands or forests with a nearby source of permanent water. Disentangling which aspect(s) of these mosaics might have been preferred by the hominins presents a significant challenge, as some have questioned the validity of the association of *A. robustus* with open grasslands (Shipman and Harris, 1988). In this chapter we document fluctuations in the abundance of *A. robustus* relative to a series of taxa belonging to the Cercopithecidae, Equidae, Suidae and Bovidae in order to investigate patterns in diet, habitat preference or avoidance, and water dependence in the fossil palaeocommunities.

The study sample

For this study, we recorded faunal assemblage data from a selection of *A. robustus*-bearing deposits in the Cradle of Humankind World Heritage Site (Gauteng, South Africa), including Kromdraai, Swartkrans, Sterkfontein and Coopers. Faunal assemblage data are unavailable from Drimolen, and the association between the fauna and the hominins recovered from Gondolin is unclear, therefore these latter sites are excluded from this analysis. Some of these deposits are subdivided into lithostratigraphic members, thus our combined dataset represents eight discrete faunal assemblages (Table 22.1). The assemblages were arranged in what we consider to be the most probable chronological sequence: KB–ST5OL–COD–SKLB–SKHR–SKM2–SKM3–KA (see Table 22.1 for abbreviations and age estimates used in this text). Assemblage data were recorded by the first author for all but ST5OL; this deposit was analysed by Pickering (1999) using comparable data collection techniques. Data collection involved a manual overlap approach as recommended by Bunn (1982, 1986) to document both the minimum number of elements (MNE) and the comprehensive minimum number of individuals (cMNI) in each assemblage. Details of the procedure are presented in de Ruiter (2004). A combined total of 24 211 specimens were identified to skeletal part and taxonomic family, representing 1266 individual animals from the Cercopithecidae, Equidae, Suidae and Bovidae (Table 22.2).

Table 22.1. *Faunal assemblages examined in this study with probable age estimates.*

Site	Member/deposit	Abbreviation	Age estimate (Ma)
Sterkfontein	Member 5, Oldowan Infill	ST5OL	2.0–1.7
Kromdraai	Kromdraai A	KA	1.5
	Kromdraai B	KB	1.9
Swartkrans	Member 1, Lower Bank	SKLB	1.7
	Member 1, Hanging Remnant	SKHR	1.6
	Member 2	SKM2	1.5
	Member 3	SKM3	1.5
Coopers	Coopers D	COD	1.9–1.6

Faunal assemblage data for ST5OL from Pickering, 1999. Age estimates are from White and Harris, 1977; Vrba, 1981, 1985a, 1995; Delson, 1984; Kuman and Clarke, 2000; Curnoe *et al.*, 2001; Thackeray *et al.*, 2002; de Ruiter, 2003; Berger *et al.*, 2003; Brain, 2004.

These families represent some of the most common taxa known from the cave infills of the Cradle of Humankind World Heritage Site, representing 68% of the combined fauna. They are generally regarded as being ecologically sensitive (e.g. Bobe *et al.*, 2002), by which we mean that alterations in the availability of the vegetation that these animals feed upon will significantly impact on population density and distribution. This is in contrast to less sensitive mammalian groups, such as carnivores, which are more adept at altering their behavioural patterns to suit changing environmental conditions. By way of example, if the preferred vegetation of a given bovid disappears from an area, individuals of that particular bovid species must seek sustenance elsewhere. In contrast, carnivores feeding on this transient bovid species can respond by shifting their diet to a different food resource (i.e. other animal species), and thus are not as directly affected by prevailing ecological conditions, an advantage derived from their position at a higher trophic level. And, while isotopic evidence indicates that members of the Cercopithecidae are dietarily insensitive (Codron *et al.*, 2006), they do have particular habitat requirements that make them useful for this analysis. We therefore use these ecologically sensitive animals as proxies for investigating prevailing environmental conditions. Where ecological requirements were identical, species were grouped into genera for primates, equids and suids, and into tribes for the bovids. Taxa that varied in their ecological requirements were computed separately. For instance, members of the Tragelaphini were considered as individual species rather than as a tribe owing to their varying dietary adaptations and water requirements. The tribe Hippotragini includes only the genus *Hippotragus*, as the other members of this tribe (*Oryx*, *Addax*) that have

Table 22.2. *Comprehensive minimum numbers of individuals (cMNI) of select mammalian taxa with associated ecological categories.*

	Fossil deposit									Ecological category		
	KB	ST5OL	COD	SKLB	SKHR	SKM2	SKM3	KA	Total	Diet	Preferred habitat	Water requirements
Australopithecus robustus	6	2	2	9	58	8	6	0	91	–	–	–
Papio	32	0	12	13	47	21	23	16	164	MF	W	PWD
Gorgopithecus	2	0	0	0	0	0	0	10	12	MF	W	PWD
Theropithecus	0	1	8	4	16	2	7	0	38	MF	W	PWD
Small Papionin	0	7	0	0	7	0	0	2	16	B	W	PWD
Cercopithecoides	5	0	0	1	0	4	0	0	10	MF	W	PWD
Equus	1	3	2	3	6	16	8	30	69	G	G	WD
Eurygnathohippus	0	0	0	1	2	1	1	1	6	G	G	WD
Phacochoerus	1	0	0	1	0	7	1	1	11	G	W	PWD
Metridiochoerus	0	2	10	1	7	1	1	2	24	G	W	PWD
Alcelaphini	5	25	43	44	112	76	73	101	479	G	G	WD
Antilopini	6	3	30	21	52	27	47	27	213	MF	G	WI
Neotragini	0	3	2	2	2	13	5	1	28	B	W	WI
Bovini	1	0	1	2	2	3	3	3	15	G	W	WD
Taurotragus oryx	1	2	1	0	0	1	2	3	10	MF	W	PWD
Tragelaphus strepsiceros	0	0	3	0	7	6	2	6	24	B	W	PWD
Tragelaphus scriptus	0	0	2	0	0	4	0	1	7	B	CW	WD
Hippotragini	0	0	2	0	3	9	4	2	20	G	CW	WD
Reduncini	1	0	2	0	1	1	1	1	7	G	CW	WD
Peleini	0	0	2	1	3	10	2	4	22	MF	G	WI
Total	61	48	122	103	325	210	186	211	1266			
Chord distance		1.284	0.609	0.290	0.272	0.434	0.303	0.393				

Abbreviations: B = browser, MF = mixed feeder, G = grazer, CW = closed/wet, W = woodland, WD = water dependent, PWD = partially water dependent, WI = water independent. The last row in each of the columns gives the chord distances computed from taxonomic abundance. Chord distance values are calculated between the site at the head of the column and the site in the column to the left.

contrasting ecological requirements have not been recovered in any of the fossil caves of the Cradle of Humankind sites.

Taphonomic factors

Before we can begin to examine taxonomic abundance in the faunal assemblages, we must address the potential impact of taphonomic factors such as bone accumulating agent and depositional matrix on assemblage composition. A variety of bone collecting agents have been implicated in the accumulation of the South African cave infills (Brain, 1981; Pickering, 1999; de Ruiter and Berger, 2000; de Ruiter, 2004; Newman, 2004; Pickering *et al.*, 2004). As a result, it is difficult to determine a predominant or consistent bone accumulating agent in individual assemblages. Indeed, as Brain (1980) has noted, most of the caves were likely open to the surface for millennia, and thus were likely to have been utilised by numerous carnivorous agents over time. In addition, abiotic factors such as slope wash were also likely to have been important. We hypothesise that the combined impact of numerous agents over long spans of time will minimise the idiosyncratic influence of any individual accumulating agent, and that any taphonomic bias introduced as a result of bone accumulating agents will have an approximately equivalent impact across assemblages. We test below for the existence of such isotaphonomic conditions. The depositional matrix from which the fossils were extracted can also influence the composition of assemblages. Hard breccia requires laborious manual or chemical extraction of fossils. Fossils recovered from hard breccia are often relatively intact, though the difficulty inherent in fossil preparation often precludes recovery of more fragmented materials. Decalcified sediments allow for complete fossil recovery, though the decalcification process often leads to severe fragmentation of fossil remains.

Skeletal part representation is a particularly useful indicator of taphonomic bias, as significant differences in the proportions of elements recovered from discrete deposits might signal the existence of differing taphonomic conditions (Voorhies, 1969; Behrensmeyer, 1991; Bobe and Eck, 2001; Bobe *et al.*, 2002). For this study we examine the relative abundance of a series of skeletal parts spanning a range of transportability, destructibility and carnivore attraction. These include maxillae, mandibulae, isolated teeth, longbones of fore and hind limbs, and astragali (Table 22.3). These elements were chosen as they tend to be well represented, and cover a variety of physical shapes (e.g. cylinders, cubes, irregular shapes). We use 95% confidence intervals to document the statistical significance of differences in skeletal part representation across assemblages using the following formula:

$$p \pm 1.96 \times \mathrm{SQRT}[(p \times q)/(n-1)],$$

Table 22.3. *Abundance of skeletal elements (MNE) in each of the faunal assemblages.*

	KB	ST5OL	COD	SKLB	SKHR	SKM2	SKM3	KA	Total
Maxilla	18	10	23	24	164	30	46	14	329
Mandible	39	30	49	55	222	73	105	39	612
Isolated teeth	310	380	557	679	1020	598	1123	426	5093
Humerus	6	32	30	64	30	71	49	26	308
Radius	10	27	24	37	14	41	93	15	261
Metacarpal	21	26	46	29	14	37	94	16	283
Femur	9	15	35	39	32	31	81	24	266
Tibia	4	20	28	33	16	24	52	11	188
Metatarsal	25	27	44	49	16	22	110	20	313
Astragalus	12	27	46	31	32	16	47	16	227
Total	454	594	882	1040	1560	943	1800	607	7880
Chord distance (taphonomy)		0.106	0.053	0.069	0.208	0.184	0.106	0.088	

The last row in each column gives the chord distances computed from skeletal part data. Chord distance values are calculated between the site at the head of the column and the site in the column to the left.

where p is the proportion of a given skeletal element, q is equal to $1 - p$, and n represents the total sample size (Buzas, 1990).

The relative abundance of skeletal elements with associated 95% confidence intervals (Figure 22.1) displays no temporal trends, although a significant difference is evident in terms of depositional matrix. In broad terms, it appears that hard breccia deposits show a relative over-abundance of craniodental remains and a paucity of post-cranial remains, while decalcified deposits show the opposite pattern. This difference relates, at least in part, to the difficulty encountered while extracting fragmented post-cranial remains from hard breccia. There is a tendency to focus on more diagnostic cranio-dental remains, thus post-cranial elements tend to be under-represented. Decalcified deposits, on the other hand, allow for complete fossil recovery, including fragmented post-cranial remains. Since taxonomic identification relies in large part on cranio-dental remains, this represents a potentially significant biasing factor. It is therefore necessary to test whether there is any relationship between taphonomic conditions and taxonomic abundance. Chord distance is a measure of faunal dissimilarity that allows us to quantify differences in skeletal part or taxonomic representation across a series of faunal assemblages (Ludwig and Reynolds, 1988; Bobe *et al.*, 2002). Chord distance values are computed between assemblage j and assemblage k by the formula:

$$CRDjk = SQRT[2(1 - ccos_{jk})]$$
$$\text{with } ccos_{jk} = \Sigma^S(Xij \times Xik)/SQRT[\Sigma^S X^2 ij \Sigma^S X^2 ik]$$

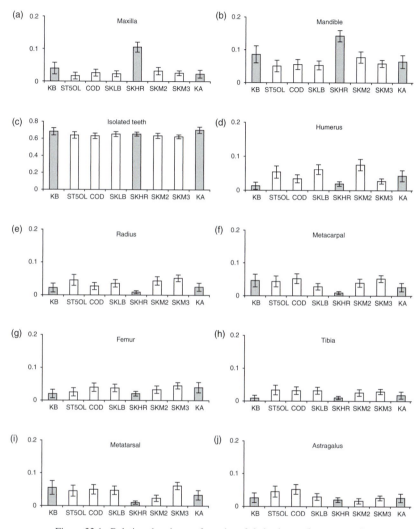

Figure 22.1. Relative abundance of a series of skeletal parts from across the assemblages examined in this study as a measure of isotaphonomic conditions. Skeletal part data based on entire assemblages, not just select taxonomic families. Numbers are calculated from data in Table 22.3. Binomial error bars indicate 95% confidence intervals. Shaded boxes denote hard breccia assemblages, unshaded boxes denote uncalcified/decalcified assemblages.

where Xij represents the abundance of the ith taxon or skeletal element in the jth assemblage, Xik represents the abundance of the ith taxon or skeletal element in the kth assemblage, and S is the total number of taxa or skeletal elements common to the two assemblages. Chord distance values range from zero for assemblages with identical composition, i.e. 100% shared characteristics, to the square root of 2 ($\approx$1.414) for assemblages with zero commonalities, or shared characters, between assemblages. Each chord distance value represents the difference between a pair of faunal assemblages.

Figure 22.2 is a plot of chord distance values computed for taxonomic abundance data from Table 22.2 and skeletal part data from Table 22.3. The low skeletal part chord distance values indicate that taphonomic conditions are not dramatically different between the various assemblages. The higher chord distances for taxonomic data indicate that there are moderate differences in taxonomic representation across the assemblages. However, the most important feature of Figure 22.2 is the lack of correspondence between taxonomic and taphonomic conditions. Kromdraai B-Sterkfontein Member 5 Oldowan Infill represents the largest taxonomic chord distance, though the taphonomic chord distance is one of the lowest. At the same time, Swartkrans Member 1 Lower Bank and Swartkrans Member 1 Hanging Remnant exhibit the highest taphonomic, but the lowest taxonomic, chord distances. This is an unsurprising result given that these are sub-assemblages of the same lithostratigraphic member that are composed of uncalcified versus hard breccia sediments respectively. The different depositional matrices have produced a high taphonomic chord distance, while the similar assemblages recovered from Member 1 result in a low taxonomic chord distance. Testing for a correlation between taphonomic and taxonomic chord distances reveals no significant association (Spearman's $r_s = -0.214$, $p = 0.645$). What is evident from this data is that there is no link between taphonomic conditions and taxonomic composition. In other words, although a taphonomic bias likely exists as a result of the individual characteristics of the depositional matrix between the sites, and perhaps the actions of differing bone accumulating agents, this bias has not significantly altered the taxonomic composition of any particular assemblage. As a result, we conclude that fluctuations in taxonomic abundance across these assemblages reflect real biological responses to changing environmental conditions, rather than any form of taphonomic bias.

Ecological composition of the assemblages

We investigate indicators of environmental change across the assemblages by assigning the selected taxonomic families to a series of broadly defined ecological classes reflecting diet, habitat preference and water requirements (Table 22.2). Assignment of taxa to dietary categories is based on isotopic evidence (Sponheimer, 1999; Sponheimer *et al.*, 1999, 2003; Luyt, 2001; Harris and Cerling, 2002). Assignment to habitat categories is based on taxonomic

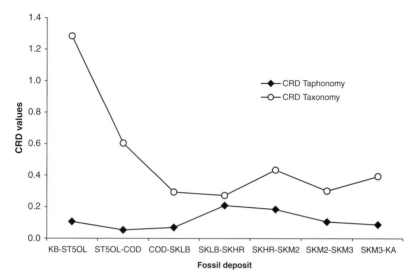

Figure 22.2. Plots of chord distances for taxonomic and taphonomic data. Taphonomic chord distance values are computed for skeletal part data from Table 22.3; taxonomic chord distance values are computed for abundance data from Table 22.2. The lack of correlation ($r_s = -0.214$, $p = 0.645$) between taphonomic and taxonomic chord distances indicate that fluctuations in taxonomic abundance are not linked to taphonomic conditions.

uniformitarian evidence (Greenacre and Vrba, 1984; Cooke, 1976; Shipman and Harris, 1988; Skinner and Smithers, 1990; Estes, 1991; Bobe *et al.*, 2002). By this we mean that fossil representatives of living taxa are assumed to have exhibited similar habitat preferences as their modern descendants, while extinct taxa are assumed to have preferred an environment similar to their closest living relatives. Testing for habitat preferences in modern African mammals confirms the assignments provided in Table 22.2 (Alemseged, 2003; de Ruiter *et al.*, 2008). Water requirements are likewise based on a taxonomic uniformitarian approach (data from Skinner and Smithers, 1990), though isotopic evidence is used to confirm assignments where data are available (Sponheimer, 1999). We made no assumptions about any ecological characteristics of *A. robustus*. Ecological classes are modified from Pratt *et al.* (1966), Foley (1983), Reed (1997) and Bobe *et al.* (2002). Definitions of groupings within the ecological classes as used in this study are as follows. Diet: browsers (B) selectively feed on trees and shrubs; grazers (G) consume mostly grasses; mixed feeders (MF) include components of both browse and graze, often on a seasonally rotating basis. Habitat preference: woodlands (W) are characterised by relatively dense tree coverage (~20 to 40% of land surface); grasslands (G) exhibit sparse

vegetational coverage ranging from bushy grasslands to relatively open savan-
nahs; closed/wet (CW) habitats are typified by either very dense tree coverage
(>40% of land surface) or an abundance of permanent water. Water requirements: water dependent (WD) mammals must drink regularly, usually daily,
or else rely on vegetation growing near a permanent water source for their
food source; partially water dependent (PWD) mammals might normally drink
water when available, but can subsist for long periods (several days to weeks)
without drinking water; water independent (WI) are capable of surviving without drinking water, instead obtaining moisture mainly from their food.

We recognise that taxonomic abundance estimates cannot reproduce the
actual composition of an animal palaeocommunity. However, fluctuations in
proportions of mammalian taxa can be used as proxy evidence for changing
palaeoenvironmental conditions over time (Klein, 1980). For this study, we
use correspondence analysis (CA) to investigate the relationship between fossil
deposits and taxonomic/ecological classes. Correspondence analysis is a visual
ordination technique that graphically displays groupings of points representing
closely related variables (Greenacre, 2007). When plotted, groups with similar abundance profiles will cluster more closely together, while groups with
dissimilar abundance profiles will be positioned further apart. It is important
to note that when examining a correspondence analysis plot, row and column
coordinates must be considered separately. As a result, one should interpret
either the distances between row points or the distances between column
points, but not the distances between row points and column points together. In
this study, abundance data from Table 22.2 are arranged in a contingency table,
relating combined frequency counts of taxa representing particular ecological
categories to fossil assemblages. Each ecological grouping is examined as a
unit (e.g. dietary preferences), and values for *A. robustus* are inserted as supplementary points so that they will not influence the outcome of the analysis.
This allows us to view the position of *A. robustus* in a plot without including
the hominin values in the actual ecological category separation. In the course
of computation, correspondence analysis calculates deviations in observed
values relative to expected values, as in a Chi-squared test (χ^2). As a result, we
can use χ^2 residual (observed minus expected) values as a proxies for original
abundance estimates.

This is particularly important as proportional data represent a zero sum relationship; fluctuations in one category result in changes in all other categories, reducing the available degrees of freedom. Such a computational bias has
been recognised as a significant limiting factor in the use of proportional data
(Grayson, 1984). Fortunately, the use of χ^2 residual values negates this limitation, allowing us to normalise the dataset relative to an independent standard, and thereby avoiding exclusive reliance on proportional data. During the

course of computing a correspondence analysis, a set of observed and expected values are created, thus allowing the researcher to examine observed minus expected residual values (this is automatically done in Statistica™). By using such χ^2 residual values, we are able to examine fluctuations in numbers without having to first convert those numbers into percentage values, and thereby avoiding an additional transformation of the data. It allows us to test the correlation values that we obtain from percentage values with the same set of data prior to conversion of that data.

Figure 22.3 displays the results of the correspondence analyses for the three ecological classes, with *A. robustus* values added as supplementary points in all three plots. Beginning with diet, it is clear that *A. robustus* groups most closely with the mixed feeders along axis 1 (which explains 81.57% of the inertia, an approximation of the variance described by the axis). This indicates that across the assemblages, *A. robustus* has an abundance profile that is most similar to that of mixed feeder species. In other words, the relative representation of hominins is most consistent with the relative representation of mixed feeders across assemblages. This does not indicate dietary affinities, but rather that *A. robustus* is commonly found in assemblages where mixed feeding species are more abundant. The low inertia value represented by axis 2 indicates that this axis explains only a small proportion of the data. Considering habitat, *A. robustus* plots closest to the woodland category along axis 1 (explaining 77.35% of inertia). The next closest category along axis 1 is closed/wet, while grasslands are the most distant. Along axis 2, *A. robustus* is approximately equidistant to both woodland and grassland, though this axis explains far less of the available data than axis 1. Turning to water requirements, *A. robustus* clearly groups with partially water dependent taxa along both axis 1 and axis 2. In summary, the relative representation of *A. robustus* is most similar to the relative representation of mixed feeders, woodland adapted taxa and partially water dependent taxa across the assemblages. These data therefore demonstrate that sites with an abundance of mixed feeders, woodland taxa and partially water dependent taxa also tend to have an abundance of hominins, particularly of *A. robustus*, but perhaps also of early *Homo*.

When we compute χ^2 residual values from the correspondence analysis data, a trend becomes evident (Table 22.4). Regarding diet, *A. robustus* shows a statistically significant negative relationship with grazers, while the relationships with browsers (−) and mixed feeders (+) are insignificant. Examining habitat preference, there is a statistically significant negative relationship between *A. robustus* and grassland adapted taxa, and insignificant correlations with closed/wet (−) and woodland (+) adapted taxa. For water requirements there is a statistically significant negative relationship with water dependent taxa, a significant positive relationship with partially water dependent taxa and an insignificant

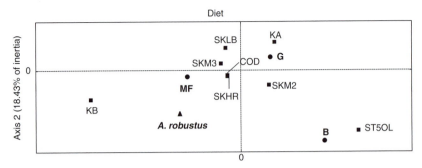

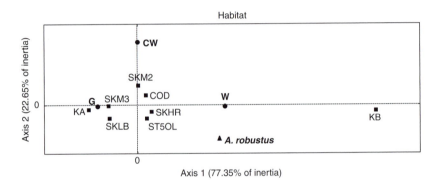

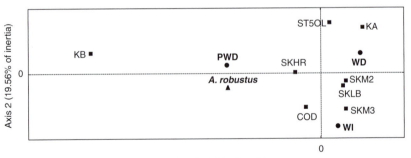

Figure 22.3. Correspondence analyses of diet, habitat and water requirements for the faunal assemblages examined in this study in relation to *A. robustus*. Data computed from Table 22.2. Squares represent faunal assemblages, circles represent group centroids for ecological categories and triangles represent the relative position of *A. robustus* when the hominin values are inserted as supplementary points. Inertia values are an approximation of the variance described by each individual axis. In all three plots, axis 1 accounts for the majority of the inertia, thus the relative position of *A. robustus* to ecological categories along axis 1 is the most informative.

Table 22.4. *Correspondence analysis χ^2 residual values and Spearman's r_s values correlating A. robustus and each individual ecological category.*

	Fossil deposit									
	KB	ST5OL	COD	SKLB	SKHR	SKM2	SKM3	KA	Spearman's r_s	*p*-level
A. *robustus*	1.615	−1.450	−6.769	1.596	34.639	−7.095	−7.370	−15.167	–	–
B	−3.469	7.270	0.062	−3.858	−2.483	8.057	−3.578	−2.000	−0.26	0.53
MF	23.258	−11.896	7.515	1.599	−3.169	−10.294	11.654	−18.667	0.33	0.42
G	−21.404	6.076	−0.807	0.663	−28.987	9.332	−0.706	35.833	−0.74	0.04[a]
A. *robustus*	1.615	−1.450	−6.769	1.596	34.639	−7.095	−7.370	−15.167	–	–
CW	−0.638	−1.289	2.724	−2.766	−4.728	8.360	0.005	−1.667	−0.48	0.23
W	25.039	1.654	3.079	−4.638	−2.363	−0.389	−7.716	−14.667	0.52	0.18
G	−26.017	1.085	0.967	5.808	−27.547	−0.877	15.081	31.500	−0.76	0.03[a]
A. *robustus*	1.615	−1.450	−6.769	1.596	34.639	−7.095	−7.370	−15.167	–	–
WD	−21.055	5.137	−6.109	0.941	−28.799	9.976	1.408	38.500	−0.83	0.01[a]
PWD	26.111	0.284	4.223	−5.140	4.675	−9.256	−9.398	−11.500	0.88	0.003[a]
WI	−6.672	−3.972	8.656	2.603	−10.516	6.374	15.360	−11.833	−0.29	0.49

Note: [a] denotes statistically significant values. Abbreviations as in Table 22.2.

relationship (–) with water independent taxa. These data indicate that the more grazers and grassland preferring animals there are in a given assemblage, the fewer hominins there tend to be. In addition, assemblages with greater numbers of water dependent animals tend to have fewer hominins, while those with greater numbers of partially water dependent animals have an abundance of hominins. The overall trend that becomes apparent is that ecological features common to water dependent, grassland-inhabiting grazers are those that were *not* preferred by the hominins. These data are inconsistent with a hypothesis that *A. robustus* were grassland habitat specialists. Rather than reflecting their habitat preference, the negative relationship between the hominins and grassland adapted taxa in particular indicates a pattern of avoidance of more open habitats.

Isotopic evidence for *A. robustus* diet

The prevailing environment reflected in the taxonomic abundance of macromammals associated with *A. robustus* appears to have been a relatively open grassland, a conclusion consistent with most palaeoenvironmental reconstructions (Cooke, 1952, 1963; Vrba, 1975, 1980, 1985a,b; Shipman and Harris, 1988). However, our data suggest that *A. robustus* likely found this to be a relatively unfavourable habitat. At the same time, there are indications of a more wooded component in the habitat mosaic (Avery, 1995, 2001; Reed, 1997; Watson, 2004), thus it is possible that the hominins preferred a more closed habitat. Recent investigation into the isotopic composition of dental enamel carbonates in the hominins from Swartkrans has revealed significantly greater dietary variability in the robust australopiths than was previously assumed (Lee-Thorp *et al.*, 1994; Sponheimer and Lee-Thorp, 1999; Sponheimer *et al.*, 2007). In particular, we have been able to document significant variability in the *A. robustus* diet over the lifetimes of individual animals, at both seasonal and annual scales (Sponheimer *et al.*, 2006a). These hominins consumed a predominantly C_3 browse based diet, though they incorporated as much as 35% C_4 grasses, C_4 sedges or animals that ate these foods, in their diets. Recent evidence demonstrates that while C_4 sedges and termites might have been significant components of early hominin diets, neither can account for the C_4 signal on their own (Sponheimer *et al.*, 2005). C_4 vegetation is virtually absent in the diet of chimpanzees, thus representing a significant dietary difference between hominins and our chimpanzee cousins (Sponheimer *et al.*, 2006b). These data lead us to conclude that the hominins were capable of surviving in the face of deteriorating environmental conditions by placing increased reliance on fallback foods (i.e. C_4 foods) when necessary. In other words, they could survive environmental change by shifting the focus of their foraging strategies to less preferred food items. We therefore suggest that the capacity to consume significant quantities of C_4 foods during times of resource stress is a fundamental hominin characteristic, a hypothesis that might be tested using high-resolution sampling of additional hominin taxa elsewhere in Africa.

Summary and conclusion

Based on the evidence presented above, we formulate a tentative scenario of the palaeoecology of *A. robustus* in relation to its surrounding environment. Although *A. robustus* existed in a predominantly grassland environment, this did not constitute their specific habitat preference. The negative correlation between the numbers of hominins and the numbers of grassland adapted taxa indicates that the more grassland animals there are in an assemblage, the fewer hominins there tend to be. Therefore we suggest that as conditions became more suitable for grassland adapted taxa, they became less favourable for the hominins, the latter responding by reducing their population densities. The close grouping of the hominins with woodland adapted taxa in Figure 22.3 suggests that they preferred a more closed portion of the habitat mosaic, though the positive correlation between hominins and woodland taxa is statistically insignificant. When conditions were favourable, the robust australopiths would have subsisted on C_3 foods, switching to C_4 foods when their preferred resources became depleted. The high degree of dietary variability evident in the diets of *A. robustus* from Swartkrans demonstrates their capacity to alter their subsistence patterns in ways not seen in modern chimpanzees. The association of the hominins with partially water dependent taxa raises the possibility that they were not as closely tied to permanent water as the strictly water dependent taxa. This is corroborated by a significant correlation between $\delta^{13}C$ and $\delta^{18}O$ values (Sponheimer *et al.*, 2006a), suggesting that the hominins were capable of varying their daily water intake to match environmental conditions. The hominins were therefore capable of surviving fluctuating environmental conditions by altering their behavioural patterns. When conditions deteriorated, resulting from either seasonal or longer term climatic changes, *A. robustus* would have been forced into less favoured environments to satisfy their nutritional requirements. At these times, they ranged into more open habitats to acquire such fallback resources as tubers, sedges, insects and perhaps some form of meat, and perhaps drinking water. Despite dwindling supplies of preferred food items, the variable diet of *A. robustus* would have remained highly resilient in the face of environmental fluctuations.

Acknowledgements

Special thanks go to Sally Reynolds and Andy Gallagher for organising this conference, and for editing this volume. The tremendous effort that they went to is truly appreciated. Special thanks also go to Professor Phillip Tobias not only for inspiring this conference, but for inspiring generations of palaeoanthropologists. We are grateful to Bob Brain, Francis Thackeray, Stephany Potze and Teresa Kearney of the Transvaal Museum for access to fossil and modern comparative materials in their care. Mike Raath, Bruce Rubidge, Lee Berger and Rodrigo Lacruz gave us access to the fossil materials housed at the University of the Witwatersrand. We thank Kathy Kuman for sharing the details of the excavations in the Oldowan Infill of Sterkfontein, and the nature of its depositional matrix. Sheela Athreya and David Carlson provided invaluable statistical advice, though any errors remain our responsibility. The correspondence analyses were performed using Statistica 6.0™. Travis Pickering, Kaye Reed, Kevin Kuykendall, Sally Reynolds and Andy Gallagher all provided useful data, insight and critical commentary on earlier drafts of this chapter. This research was funded by the Wenner-Gren Foundation (USA), the National Research Foundation (RSA), the Paleoanthropology Scientific Trust (RSA) as well as the Faculty Research Enhancement Program and the International Research Travel Assistance Grant programs of Texas A&M University.

References

Alemseged, Z. (2003). An integrated approach to taphonomy and faunal change in the Shungura Formation (Ethiopia) and its implications for hominid evolution. *Journal of Human Evolution*, **44**: 451–78.

Avery, D. M. (1995). Southern savannas and Pleistocene hominid adaptations: the micromammalian perspective. In Vrba, E. S., Denton, G. H., Partridge, T. C. and Burckle, L. H. (eds.), *Paleoclimate and Evolution, with Emphasis on Human Origins*. Yale University Press, New Haven, pp. 459–78.

Avery, D. M., (2001). The Plio-Pleistocene vegetation and climate of Sterkfontein and Swartkrans, South Africa, based on micromammals. *Journal of Human Evolution*, **41**: 113–32.

Behrensmeyer, A. K., (1991). Terrestrial vertebrate accumulations. In Allison, P. A. and Briggs, D. E. G. (eds.), *Taphonomy: Releasing the Data Locked in the Fossil Record*. New York: Plenum Press, pp. 291–335.

Berger, L. R., de Ruiter, D. J., Steininger, C. *et al.* (2003). Preliminary results of excavations at the newly investigated locality Coopers D, Gauteng, South Africa. *South African Journal of Science*, **99**: 276–8.

Bobe, R. and Eck, G. G. (2001). Responses of African bovids to Pliocene climatic change. *Paleobiology* **27** (Suppl. to No. 2). *Paleobiology Memoirs*, **2**: 1–47.

Bobe, R., Behrensmeyer, A. K. and Chapman, R. E. (2002). Faunal change, environmental variability and late Pliocene hominin evolution. *Journal of Human Evolution*, **42**: 475–97.

Brain, C. K. (1980). Some criteria for the recognition of bone-collecting agencies in African caves. In Behrensmeyer, A. K. and Hill, A. P. (eds.), *Fossils in the Making*. Chicago: University of Chicago Press, pp. 107–30.

(1981). *The Hunters or the Hunted?* Chicago: University of Chicago Press.

(2004). Structure and stratigraphy of the Swartkrans Cave in light of the new excavations. In Brain, C. K. (ed.), *Swartkrans: a Cave's Chronicle of Early Man*, 2nd edn. Transvaal Museum Monograph No. 8, Pretoria, pp. 7–22.

Bunn, H. T. (1982). Meat-eating and human evolution: studies on the diet and subsistence patterns of Plio-Pleistocene hominids in East Africa. PhD dissertation, University of California, Berkeley.

(1986). Patterns of skeletal representation and hominid subsistence activities at Olduvai Gorge, Tanzania and Koobi Fora, Kenya. *Journal of Human Evolution*, **15**: 673–90.

Buzas, M. A. (1990). Another look at confidence limits for species proportions. *Journal of Paleontology*, **64**, 842–3.

Codron, D., Lee-Thorp, J. A., Sponheimer, M. *et al.* (2006). Inter- and intrahabitat dietary variability of chacma baboons (*Papio ursinus*) in South African savannas based on fecal d13C, d15N and %N. *American Journal of Physical Anthropology*, **129**: 204–14.

Cooke, H. B. S. (1952). Mammals, ape-men and stone age men in southern Africa. *South African Archaeological Bulletin*, **26**: 59–69.

(1963). Pleistocene mammal faunas of Africa, with particular reference to southern Africa. In Howell, F. C. and Bourliére, F. (eds.), *African Ecology and Human Evolution*. New York: Wenner-Gren Foundation, pp. 65–116.

(1976). Suidae from Plio-Pleistocene strata of the Rudolf Basin. In Coppens, Y., Howell, F. C., Isaac, G. L. and Leakey, R. E. F. (eds.), *Earliest Man and Environments in the Lake Rudolf Basin*. Chicago: University of Chicago Press, pp. 251–63.

Curnoe, D., Grun, G., Taylor, L. *et al.* (2001). Direct ESR dating of a Pliocene hominin from Swartkrans. *Journal of Human Evolution*, **40**: 379–91.

Delson, E. (1984). Cercopithecid biochronology of the African Plio-Pleistocene: correlation among eastern and southern hominid-bearing localities. *Courier Forschungs Institut Senckenberg*, **69**: 199–218.

de Ruiter, D. J. (2003). Revised faunal lists for Members 1–3 of Swartkrans, South Africa. *Annals of the Transvaal Museum*, **40**, 29–41.

(2004). Relative abundance and skeletal part representation of macromammals from Swartkrans. In Brain, CK. (ed.), *Swartkrans: a Cave's Chronicle of Early Man*, 2nd edn. Pretoria: Transvaal Museum Monograph No. 8, pp. 265–78.

de Ruiter, D. J. and Berger, L. R. (2000). Leopards as taphonomic agents in dolomitic caves: implications for bone accumulations in the hominid-bearing deposits of South Africa. *Journal of Archaeological Science*, **27**: 665–84.

de Ruiter, D. J., Sponheimer, M. and Lee-Thorp, J. A. (2008). Indications of habitat preference or avoidance by *Australopithecus robustus* in the Bloubank Valley, South Africa. *Journal of Human Evolution*, **55**(6): 1015–30.

Estes, R. D. (1991). *The Behavior Guide to African Mammals*. Berkeley: University of California Press.

Foley, R. (1983). Modeling hunting strategies and inferring predator behaviour from prey attributes. In Clutton-Brock, J. and Grigson, C. (eds.), *Animals and Archaeology: Hunters and Their Prey*. Oxford: Oxford University Press, pp. 63–76.

Grayson, D. K. (1984). *Quantitative Zooarchaeology: Topics in the Analysis of Archaeological Faunas*. Orlando: Academic Press.

Greenacre, M. J. (2007). *Correspondence Analysis in Practice*. London: Chapman and Hall.

Greenacre, M. J. and Vrba, E. S. (1984). Graphical display and interpretation of antelope census data in African wildlife areas, using correspondence analysis. *Ecology*, **65**, 984–97.

Harris, J. M. and Cerling, T. E. (2002). Dietary adaptations of extant and Neogene African suids. *Journal of Zoology (London)*, **256**, 45–54.

Klein, R. G. (1980). Environmental and ecological implications of large mammals from Upper Pleistocene and Holocene sites in southern Africa. *Annals of the South African Museum*, **81**: 223–83.

Kuman, K. and Clarke, R. J. (2000). Stratigraphy, artefact industries and hominid associations for Sterkfontein, Member 5. *Journal of Human Evolution*, **38**: 827–47.

Lee-Thorp, J. A., van der Merwe, N. J. and Brain, C. K. (1994). Diet of *Australopithecus robustus* at Swartkrans from stable carbon isotopic analysis. *Journal of Human Evolution*, **27**, 361–72.

Ludwig, A. J. and Reynolds, J. F. (1988). *Statistical Ecology: a Primer on Methods and Computing*. New York: Wiley.

Luyt, J. (2001). Revisiting the palaeoenvironments of the South African hominid-bearing Plio-Pleistocene sites: new isotopic evidence from Sterkfontein. MSc thesis, University of Cape Town, Cape Town.

Newman, R. (2004). The incidence of damage marks on Swartkrans fossil bones from the 1979–1986 excavations. In Brain, C. K. (ed.), *Swartkrans: a Cave's Chronicle of Early Man*, 2nd edn. Pretoria: Transvaal Museum Monograph No. 8, pp. 217–28.

Pickering, T. R. (1999). Taphonomic interpretations of the Sterkfontein early hominid site. PhD dissertation, University of Wisconsin, Madison.

Pickering, T. R., Dominguez-Rodrigo, M., Egeland, C. P. *et al.* (2004). Beyond leopards: tooth marks and the contribution of multiple carnivore taxa to the accumulation of the Swartkrans Member 3 fossil assemblage. *Journal of Human Evolution*, **46**: 595–604.

Pratt, D. J., Greenway, P. J. and Gwynne, M. D. (1966). A classification of East African rangeland with an appendix on terminology. *Journal of Applied Ecology*, **3**: 369–82.

Reed, K. E. (1997). Early hominid evolution and ecological change through the African Plio-Pleistocene. *Journal of Human Evolution*, **32**: 289–322.

Shipman, P. and Harris, J. M. (1988). Habitat preference and paleoecology of *Australopithecus boisei* in Eastern Africa. In Grine, FE. (ed.), *Evolutionary History of the 'Robust' Australopithecines*. New York: Aldine de Gruyter, pp. 343–81.

Skinner, J. D. and Smithers, R. H. N. (1990). *The Mammals of the Southern African Subregion*. Pretoria: University of Pretoria Press.

Sponheimer, M. (1999). Isotopic paleoecology of the Makapansgat Limeworks fauna. PhD dissertation, Rutgers University, New Brunswick.

Sponheimer, M. and Lee-Thorp, J. A. (1999). Isotopic evidence for the diet of an early hominid, *Australopithecus africanus*. *Science*, **283**: 368–70.

Sponheimer, M., Reed, K. E. and Lee-Thorp, J. A. (1999). Combining isotopic and ecomorphological data to refine bovid paleodietary reconstruction: a case study from the Makapansgat Limeworks hominin locality. *Journal of Human Evolution*, **36**: 705–18.

Sponheimer, M., Lee-Thorp, J. A., de Ruiter, D. J. *et al.* (2003). Dietary preferences of Southern African Bovidae: the stable isotope evidence. *Journal of Mammalogy*, **84**: 471–9.

(2005). Hominins, sedges, and termites: new carbon isotopic data from the Sterkfontein valley and Kruger National Park. *Journal of Human Evolution*, **48**: 301–12.

Sponheimer, M., Passey, B. H., de Ruiter, D. J. *et al.* (2006a). Isotopic evidence for dietary variability in the early hominin *Paranthropus robustus*. *Science*, **314** : 980–2.

Sponheimer, M., Loudon, J. E., Codron, D. *et al.* (2006b). Do 'savanna' chimpanzees consume C4 resources? *Journal of Human Evolution*, **51**: 128–33.

Sponheimer, M., Lee-Thorp, J. A. and de Ruiter, D. J. (2007). Icarus, isotopes and australopithecine diets. In Ungar, P. (ed.), *Evolution of Hominin Diet: the Known, the Unknown and the Unknowable*, Oxford University Press, pp. 132–49.

Thackeray, J. F., Kirschvink, J. L. and Raub, T. D. (2002). Palaeomagnetic analyses of calcified deposits from the Plio-Pleistocene hominid site of Kromdraai, South Africa. *South African Journal of Science*, **98**: 537–40.

Voorhies, M. R. (1969). Taphonomy and population dynamics of an early Pliocene vertebrate fauna. Knox County, Nebraska. University of Wyoming Contributions to Geology Special Paper 1, 1–69.

Vrba, E. S. (1975). Some evidence of chronology and palaeoecology of Sterkfontein, Swartkrans and Kromdraai from the fossil Bovidae. *Nature*, **254**: 301–4.

(1980). The significance of bovid remains as indicators of environment and predation patterns. In Behrensmeyer, A. K. and Hill, A. P. (eds.), *Fossils in the Making*. Chicago: University of Chicago Press, pp. 247–71.

(1981). The Kromdraai australopithecine site revisited in 1980: recent investigations and results. *Annals of the Transvaal Museum*, **33**: 17–60.

(1985a). Early hominids in southern Africa: updated observations on chronological and ecological background. In Tobias, P.V. (ed.), *Hominid Evolution: Past, Present and Future*. New York: Alan R. Liss, pp. 195–200.

(1985b). Ecological and adaptive changes associated with early hominid evolution. In Delson, E. (ed.), *Ancestors: the Hard Evidence*. New York: Alan R. Liss, pp. 63–71.

(1995). The fossil record of African antelopes (Mammalia, Bovidae) in relation to human evolution and paleoclimate. In Vrba, E. S., Denton, G. H., Partridge, T. C. and Burckle, L. H. (eds.), *Paleoclimate and Evolution, with Emphasis on Human Origins*. New Haven: Yale University Press, pp. 385–424.

Watson, V. (2004). Composition of the Swartkrans bone accumulations, in terms of skeletal parts and animals represented. In Brain, C. K. (ed.), *Swartkrans: a Cave's Chronicle of Early Man*, 2nd edn. Pretoria: Transvaal Museum, pp. 35–73.

White, T. D. and Harris, J. M. (1977). Suid evolution and correlation of African hominid localities. *Science*, **198**: 13–21.

23 Impacts of environmental change and community ecology on the composition and diversity of the southern African monkey fauna from the Plio-Pleistocene to the present

SARAH ELTON

Abstract

The southern African cercopithecid (monkey) fauna has undergone a profound change in composition and diversity since the Plio-Pleistocene, with modern species representing only a small part of the diversity that existed in the past. During the Plio-Pleistocene, eleven cercopithecid species were found in southern Africa, as many as six of which might have been contemporaneous. The move to more open environments, plus dispersal from and to southern Africa, have probably contributed significantly to changes in monkey diversity over the past three million years. Some of the Plio-Pleistocene cercopithecids are likely to have lived in the same ecological communities as hominins. In modern primate communities, niche partitioning is sometimes used as a way to minimise competition for resources. This would have been a plausible way to maintain relatively high species diversity in the Plio-Pleistocene primate fauna of southern Africa. Nonetheless, the presence of hominins in the generalist feeder niche could have affected the behaviour of other primates in their communities, specifically the monkeys that today have an eclectic diet. It is also possible that Plio-Pleistocene hominins influenced community structure and behaviour through predation. In conclusion, environmental changes as well as interaction with hominins each contributed to shaping the community structure that is seen in South African monkeys today, but further work is required to reconstruct in more depth the interactions of the ecological communities to which hominins belonged.

African Genesis: Perspectives on Hominin Evolution, eds. Sally C. Reynolds and Andrew Gallagher. Published by Cambridge University Press. © Cambridge University Press 2012.

471

Introduction

The southern African monkey fauna has undergone a profound change in composition and diversity since the Plio-Pleistocene. Only three species of Cercopithecidae, *Chlorocebus aethiops* (the vervet monkey), *Papio hamadryas* – as the subspecies *P. h. ursinus* (the chacma baboon) – and *Cercopithecus mitis* (the blue monkey), are currently found in South Africa (International Union for Conservation of Nature and Natural Resources, 2006), none of which are endemic. Lower species richness is often seen at higher latitudes (Eeley and Foley, 1999), so the relatively small number of living monkey species in South Africa compared to Uganda, for example, where eleven species are found (International Union for Conservation of Nature and Natural Resources, 2006), might be expected. However, much greater diversity was evident in the Plio-Pleistocene, with at least eleven species identified from the southern African fossil record, possibly as many as six of these existing contemporaneously (Elton, 2007).

Hominins were the other large-bodied primates found in southern Africa during the Plio-Pleistocene, with *Australopithecus africanus* recovered from certain Pliocene sites, including Makapansgat and Sterkfontein Member 4, and *Paranthropus robustus* and *Homo* identified at localities that date from the early Pleistocene, such as Swartkrans. The recent discovery of *Australopithecus sediba* (a gracile hominin that shares features with both *A. africanus* and *Homo*), found at Malapa (about 15 km from the major fossil sites in the Cradle of Humankind World Heritage Site) and dated to around 1.95 million years ago, further increases early Pleistocene hominin diversity in southern Africa (Berger *et al.*, 2010). In southern as well as eastern Africa, cercopithecid and hominin fossils are often found associated in time and space, and as a result it has been argued that cercopithecid evolutionary histories and adaptive strategies can be used to contextualise those of hominins (Foley, 1993; Elton, 2000, 2006). In addition, the ecology of cercopithecids past and present might make them the most suitable primate referents for early hominins (Aiello *et al.*, 2000; Lee-Thorp *et al.*, 2003; Codron, *et al.*, 2005; Elton, 2006). Bearing such issues in mind, this brief review has two main aims. The first is to assess how South African cercopithecid diversity has changed since the Pliocene, considering palaeobiology and dispersals from and to southern Africa, as well as speciation and extinction events. The second aim is to suggest how the presence of hominins might have influenced southern African cercopithecid communities and niches in the Plio-Pleistocene.

Southern African cercopithecid diversity from the Pliocene to the present

The South African cercopithecid fossil record in the past 3 million years (Ma) is characterised by high species diversity at the beginning of the period followed by a reduction in diversity in the Pleistocene (Table 23.1), although this reduction was not necessarily gradual (Elton, 2007). The patterns observed are also complicated by the estimation of species numbers (Elton, 2007; also see Figure 23.1). Correct taxonomic identification of fossil material lies at the heart of discussions of past diversity, and there is ongoing debate about the recognition and validity of some Plio-Pleistocene cercopithecid species from southern Africa. *Papio h. robinsoni* has been identified from various southern African sites, including Sterkfontein Member 4 (Delson, 1984), but its presence at Sterkfontein Member 4 has been questioned (McKee, 1993). In addition to this, there is an ongoing debate about how many *Parapapio* species there were, which would also affect the estimation of diversity at Sterkfontein Member 4, as well as at other sites such as the Makapan Valley Limeworks. Although many workers accept four species of *Parapapio* in southern Africa (*Pp. jonesi, Pp. broomi, Pp. whitei* and *Pp. antiquus*), it has been argued that the range of size variation found in a combined sample of *Pp. jonesi* and *Pp. broomi* specimens from Sterkfontein could be contained in a single, sexually-dimorphic species (Thackeray and Myer, 2004). However, recent work on guenon skull morphology in species with very similar mean body masses has indicated that it is often subtle morphological differences that reflect species boundaries in closely related monkeys (Cardini and Elton, 2008). Thus, although size was used as a basis for initially assigning cercopithecid specimens to different species of *Parapapio*, more sophisticated shape analysis, now used routinely in palaeontology, might benefit our understanding of the taxonomy of the genus.

One of the main drivers of the *Parapapio* multiple species debate is the question over whether three congeners could live in close proximity. Brain (1981:152), for example, commented that it appeared 'remarkable' to find three synchronous species of *Parapapio* at Sterkfontein and other sites in southern Africa. However, arboreal guenons in Africa often aggregate in multispecies groups that offer access to resources (Cords, 1987) and protection from predation (Gautier-Hion, 1988). These two factors, as discussed below, would have exerted significant pressures on southern African cercopithecids. To mitigate the effects of multiple sympatric species, modern cercopithecids often adjust their behaviours, for example by having larger home ranges (Waser, 1987). This would have been a mechanism available to Plio-

Table 23.1. *Primate species occurrences at some major southern African Plio-Pleistocene palaeoanthropological sites. Sites are listed in chronological order from left to right. Data are taken from the Paleobiology Database, (http://paleodb.org) based on Vrba (1975), Butler and Greenwood (1976), Brain (1976, 1981, 1994), Partridge (1978, 1982), Jones, Brock and McFadden (1986). Supplemented by Delson (1984), Turner et al. (1999), Elton (2001), Jablonski (2002) and de Ruiter (2003).*

	Makapansgat	Taung	Sterkfontein Member 4	Swartkrans Member 1	Kromdraai B	Kromdraai A	Swartkrans Member 2	Swartkrans Member 3
T. darti	+							
Pp. whitei	+	+	+					
Pp. broomi	+		+					
Pp. jonesi	+	+	+	+				
C. williamsi	+		+	+	+	+	+	
Pp. antiquus		+						
P. izodi		+	+	+	+	+		
P. h. robinsoni			+	+	+	+	+	+
T. oswaldi			+	+			+	+
D. ingens				+	+		+	
G. major						+		
A. africanus	+	+	+					
P. robustus				+	+		+	+
Homo sp.				+			+	

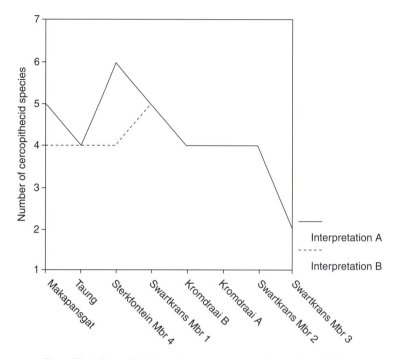

Figure 23.1. Cercopithecid species counts at some major southern African Plio-Pleistocene palaeoanthropological sites. Primary data are taken from the Paleobiology Database (http://paleodb.org), supplemented as listed in Table 23.1. Sites are shown in chronological order from earliest to most recent. Interpretation A uses a traditional estimate of species numbers at these sites, Interpretation B a more conservative estimate in which specimens assigned to *Pp. broomi* and *Pp. jonesi* are treated as conspecific (after Thackeray and Myer, 2004) and *P. h. robinsoni* is not recognised at Sterkfontein Member 4 (McKee, 1993). The significant reduction in species count over time is evident. In the mid or late Pleistocene, *P. hamadryas* (as the subspecies *P. h. ursinus*) was joined by two guenon species that dispersed into southern Africa, *C. aethiops* and *C. mitis* (not shown).

Pleistocene cercopithecids. Some *Parapapio* species seem to have had distinct adaptive strategies, with dietary and locomotor differences observed between specimens likely to belong to the contemporaneous species *Pp. jonesi* and *Pp. broomi* (Elton, 2001; Codron *et al.*, 2005; El-Zaatari *et al.*, 2005). If this were the case, sympatry, if it occurred, would also have been possible, with alternative modern cercopithecid models being sympatric Asian macaques: *Macaca fascicularis* and *M. nemestrina* are just one example of sympatric congeners that show significant differences in locomotion and habitat use. Thus, given the need for further morphological study of *Parapapio* to investigate its taxonomy, plus observations on modern cercopithecids that demonstrate that sympatry between several species of the same genus is possible, it will be assumed in this review that the four recognised species of *Parapapio* were present in Plio-Pleistocene southern Africa, some of which may have coexisted in the same ecosystem.

During the Plio-Pleistocene there was considerable species turnover in southern African monkeys. *Parapapio*, speciose in Pliocene deposits in southern Africa, had largely disappeared by the early Pleistocene. The genus *Theropithecus*, found at Makapansgat, Swartkrans and Sterkfontein Member 5, but not in the intermediate Sterkfontein Member 4 fauna, was represented by two species, *T. darti* at Makapansgat and *T. oswaldi* at the other sites. At or shortly after 1.75 Ma, there was a radiation of large terrestrial papionins (baboon-like monkeys), with *Dinopithecus ingens* and *Gorgopithecus major*, which were likely to have originated in southern Africa, joining the two *Papio* species (also probably a southern African native) and the terrestrial colobine *Cercopithecoides williamsi* in the cercopithecid fauna. However, by around or just after 1.0 Ma, the number of cercopithecid species in southern Africa had declined markedly. *Theropithecus oswaldi* and *P. h. robinsoni* are the only monkeys recovered from the Swartkrans Member 3 faunal assemblage. *Theropithecus oswaldi* is also found at the later site of Hopefield, dated to around 0.7 to 0.4 Ma (Klein and Cruz-Uribe, 1991); this occurrence might represent either a 'residual' population from the original *T. oswaldi* colonisation of southern Africa or a 'third wave' of *Theropithecus* movement into southern Africa (Pickford, 1993).

The turnover observed prior to 1.0 Ma was due in part to regional environmental change (Elton, 2007). Palaeoecological reconstructions indicate wooded, relatively closed environments at Makapansgat (Sponheimer *et al.*, 1999; Sponheimer and Lee-Thorp, 2003) and Sterkfontein Member 4 (Bamford, 1999), with southern African environments becoming more open after 2 Ma (Watson, 1993; Avery, 1995; Reed, 1997; Luyt and Lee-Thorp, 2003). Palaeobiological studies of Plio-Pleistocene monkeys from southern Africa indicate the presence of a range of adaptive strategies, at least in the Pliocene. Ecomorphic analysis of postcranial elements sampled from Makapansgat, Sterkfontein Member 4 and Bolt's Farm suggests that cercopithecids from these sites exploited grassland, bushland/open woodland and forest environments, with some species using arboreal locomotion and others using predominantly terrestrial locomotion (Elton, 2000, 2001). In contrast, the cercopithecid assemblages from the more recent sites of Kromdraai and Swartkrans are dominated by species that apparently preferred terrestrial locomotion in more open habitats (Elton, 2000, 2001). Direct dietary evidence, from tooth microwear (El-Zaatari *et al.*, 2005) and stable carbon isotopes (Codron *et al.*, 2005), also indicates that there was significant inter- and intraspecific variation in the dietary strategies of southern

African cercopithecids during the Plio-Pleistocene. One of the most striking results is the ability of these monkeys to use C_4 resources (tropical grasses) in their diets (Codron *et al.*, 2005). This, plus the shift in locomotor strategies and habitat preferences through time, suggests that the evolution of the cercopithecid community in this region was closely tied to the expansion of more open habitats (Elton, 2001, 2007; Codron *et al.*, 2005).

In addition to species turnover, dispersals from other parts of Africa contributed to southern African cercopithecid diversity in the Plio-Pleistocene. Such dispersals were not confined to monkeys: faunal exchange between southern and eastern Africa occurred in a number of mammalian groups, including hominins, during this period (Turner and Wood, 1993; Strait and Wood, 1999; Foley, 1999). The major cercopithecid interchanges were the expansion of *T. darti* and *T. oswaldi* from eastern to southern Africa, probably in two waves (Pickford, 1993; Hughes *et al.*, 2008), movement of *Cercopithecoides williamsi*, possibly out of eastern Africa (Benefit, 1999), and the dispersals of *Parapapio* and *Papio* from southern Africa (Benefit, 1999). Nonetheless, two essentially different cercopithecid communities existed in these continental regions during the Plio-Pleistocene: eastern and southern Africa remained the strongholds for *Theropithecus* and *Parapapio/Papio* respectively, and the large colobines were consistently more abundant and speciose in East Africa (Benefit, 1999).

Notwithstanding dispersals into southern Africa during the Plio-Pleistocene, by the Middle Pleistocene cercopithecid diversity appeared to reduce dramatically, with *P. hamadryas* being the only Plio-Pleistocene species to survive to the present day in South Africa. The modern southern African subspecies *P. h. ursinus* co-occurs with another modern monkey species, *C. aethiops*, in the fossil record from the Late Pleistocene. Both are found at Border Cave (Klein, 1977), and *Cercopithecus* (probably more accurately designated as *Chlorocebus*) and *Papio* have been identified from Black Earth Cave (Peabody, 1954). At least seven more Pleistocene/Middle Stone Age sites including Swartkrans Member 5 have yielded *P. h. ursinus*, some in association with *H. sapiens* (Peabody, 1954; Humphreys, 1974; Klein, 1979; Singer and Wymer, 1982; Grine and Klein, 1991, 1993; Klein *et al.*, 1991; Brain, 1993). *Papio hamadryas ursinus* probably evolved in southern Africa (Newman *et al.*, 2004) whereas *C. aethiops*, found in the Middle Pleistocene record of Ethiopia (Alemseged and Geraads, 2000) and able to disperse widely in the increasingly open environments of Pleistocene Africa, was very probably a Middle to Late Pleistocene immigrant (Elton, 2007). There is no obvious fossil record for the third species, *Cercopithecus mitis*, which probably radiated in the late Quaternary, with the current distribution in South Africa dating to after the last glacial maximum (Lawes, 1990, 2002).

Today, the three monkey species found in South Africa are all relatively ecologically flexible, and are widespread in sub-Saharan Africa. *Cercopithecus mitis* (the blue monkey), although being dependent on forest habitats and found mainly in the far east of South Africa (Lawes, 1990, 2002), is often regarded as one of the most ecologically flexible arboreal guenons. The most abundant South African monkeys, *P. h. ursinus* (the baboon) and *C. aethiops* (the vervet), are eurytopic. Primarily adapted to open environments, they nonetheless exploit a range of habitats and are distributed widely across South Africa, with *P. h. ursinus* having the greater geographic range. Both species feed eclectically and can exist in environments that are heavily modified by human activity. The ecological and behavioural flexibility that is evident to a greater or lesser extent in all the modern South African cercopithecids could have been key to their survival outside Central African forest refugia in the climatic fluctuations of the Pleistocene. Another key to their success, at least in *P. h. ursinus* and *C. aethiops*, was probably the ability to live alongside humans. Some of the most successful modern non-human primates are those that can adapt to environments modified by humans. Baboons and vervets are so good at exploiting human environments that they are regarded by many communities as 'pest' species (Fedigan and Fedigan, 1988; Hill, 2002). Given their association with *H. sapiens* in the fossil record, it is likely that they have been coexisting closely with humans since at least the Late Pleistocene.

Large-bodied primate communities and niches in the Plio-Pleistocene of southern Africa

Close association between monkeys and hominins probably began much earlier than the Late Pleistocene. Cercopithecids are found at most of the major southern African Plio-Pleistocene hominin sites, so it is likely that in some areas monkeys and hominins belonged to the same ecological community, although association in the fossil record is no guarantee of coexistence in either time or space. It is difficult to judge sympatry from the evidence available in the fossil record (Elton, 2006), but coexistence of, and interaction between, contemporaneous hominins and cercopithecids was possible, if not probable. For example, at the East African archaeological site of Olorgesailie, butchery marks on *Theropithecus oswaldi* bones (Shipman *et al.*, 1981) indicate sympatry between at least one hominin and one monkey species during the Pleistocene. In areas of high species diversity, modern African primate communities often contain representatives of several primate radiations, including apes, monkeys and strepsirhines (Reed and Bidner, 2004). There is no reason to suppose that similar sympatry could not have occurred in southern Africa during the Plio-Pleistocene.

Organisms that form part of the same ecological community can have a profound impact on one another, influencing feeding behaviour, group structure and habitat use. Having access to resources is fundamental to survival and reproduction, so consideration of diet and feeding behaviour is essential when exploring the possible relationships within past communities. Plio-Pleistocene hominins were probably generalist feeders, exploiting C_3 and C_4 foods (Wood and Strait, 2004; Peters and Vogel, 2005). Dietary components might have included vertebrates, invertebrates, fruits and tubers (Sponheimer and Lee-Thorp, 1999; Backwell and d'Errico, 2001; Lee-Thorp *et al.*, 2003; Wood and Strait, 2004; Plummer, 2004; Peters and Vogel, 2005). Several modern cercopithecid species also forage eclectically, and dental microwear indicates that at least one Plio-Pleistocene papionin from southern Africa, *Dinopithecus ingens*, had a very varied diet (El-Zaatari *et al.*, 2005). In addition, stable carbon isotope evidence indicates that, like hominins, many Plio-Pleistocene cercopithecids from southern Africa exploited C_4 foods to a greater or lesser extent (Codron *et al.*, 2005). Competition for resources within large-bodied primate communities, and within the faunal community as a whole, could therefore have been a very real possibility. In an extreme form, this might have led to competitive exclusion of one or more species. Niche partitioning, whereby coexistence is facilitated through altering the way or frequency in which resources are used, might have been an alternative solution, and a way in which southern African primates might have avoided competition for identical resources. This approach is certainly used in modern African primate communities (for example, guenons: Buzzard, 2006), and probably helps to maintain species diversity.

There is some evidence for niche partitioning in Plio-Pleistocene southern African monkeys. At Makapansgat, for example, the diets of *Pp. jonesi* and *Pp. broomi* were probably quite different, with *Pp. jonesi* being a grass or leaf eater and *Pp. broomi* preferring fruit (El-Zaatari *et al.*, 2005). Assuming sympatry, the four large terrestrial cercopithecids at Swartkrans, *P. h. robinsoni*, *Cercopithecoides williamsi*, *D. ingens* and *Theropithecus oswaldi*, may have reduced competition through altering the frequencies in which certain resources were used. *Papio. h. robinsoni* and *D. ingens*, primarily C_3 consumers (Codron *et al.*, 2005), could have partitioned resources through differential consumption of fruit and leaves, with *P. h. robinsoni* being more folivorous and *D. ingens* more frugivorous (El-Zaatari *et al.*, 2005). *Cercopithecoides williamsi* and *T. oswaldi* both appear to have included substantial proportions of C_4 foods in their diets, although the *C. williamsi* data suggest highly variable consumption of tropical grass-based resources (Codron *et al.*, 2005). Dental microwear indicates that whereas *C. williamsi* was primarily a leaf or grass eater, *T. oswaldi* had a reasonably varied diet, possibly consuming some fruit in addition to grass and/or leaves (El-Zaatari *et al.*, 2005). These interpretations largely fit with observations based on gross molar morphology (Benefit, 1999), and are also consistent with stable carbon isotope analyses that indicate that some C_3 foods were incorporated into the diets of both *C. williamsi* and *T. oswaldi* (Codron *et al.*, 2005). The *T. oswaldi* findings from southern Africa also fit with microwear data from eastern Africa, that point to a greater degree of variability in the diet of *T. oswaldi* compared to that of the one modern species, *T. gelada* (Teaford, 1993), supporting assertions that the ecology of *T. gelada* is not analogous to those of the extinct *Theropithecus* species (Elton, 2000, 2002; Codron *et al.*, 2005). Thus, by varying the proportions of different plant types in the diet and using different plant parts, it is not implausible that the four large terrestrial cercopithecids at Swartkrans could have been sympatric whilst avoiding direct competition.

What, then, were the likely roles of hominins in southern African primate communities? In eastern Africa, although the palaeobiologies of Plio-Pleistocene primates are not as well studied as those in southern Africa, it is possible that hominins filled the generalist dietary niche to the exclusion of monkey generalists (Elton, 2006). However, there are differences between the hominin fauna of eastern and southern Africa. As many as four contemporaneous hominin species have been recorded in parts of East Africa, such as the Upper Burgi and KBS Members at Koobi Fora (Turner *et al.*, 1999). In southern Africa, the maximum apparent number of synchronous species was two, for example at Swartkrans (de Ruiter, 2003), although the recent discovery of *A. sediba* may increase this number. Due to this, cercopithecids might have faced less competition from hominins in southern Africa than in eastern Africa, allowing certain species, such as *D. ingens*, to radiate into terrestrial niches and exploit a wide range of dietary resources. Nonetheless, on current evidence, few monkey species at southern African Plio-Pleistocene sites appear to have been highly generalist, although they might have been very flexible in their feeding behaviours. One very interesting finding to emerge from recent dietary work is that *P. h. robinsoni* at Swartkrans was more folivorous than suggested by previous studies (El-Zaatari *et al.*, 2005). Observations on modern *P. hamadryas* subspecies demonstrate an impressive amount of dietary diversity, including consumption of numerous plant species, insects, eggs and birds (Altman, 1998).However, in times of food scarcity, many baboon populations exploit increased quantities of 'fallback' items such as grass corms (Alberts *et al.*, 2005). This is observed today in seasonal environments (Alberts *et al.*, 2005), but could also have been a strategy used by extinct baboons in the face of competition from other animals, including hominins.

Modern humans undoubtedly influence the primate communities around them in a variety of ways, including providing access to cultivated foods such as crops, through hunting, and by encroaching on habitats because of settlement or logging. Thus, competition for resources apart, the presence of Plio-Pleistocene hominins might have affected primate communities. The most obvious way by which this could have occurred was through hunting. There is good evidence for hominin predation on large monkeys in eastern Africa (Shipman *et al.*, 1981), and evidence for hominin modification of ungulate bone has been found in southern Africa, such as at Swartkrans Member 3 (Pickering *et al.*, 2004). Analogy with modern chimpanzees suggests that hominins may have hunted other primates, and this could well have affected cercopithecid populations; at Gombe National Park (Tanzania), for example, chimpanzee predation pressure has a significant limiting effect on group size in red colobus monkeys (Stanford, 1995). Thus, although much work remains to be done on hominin predation of monkeys in Plio-Pleistocene southern Africa, the possibility that hominins were not only cercopithecid competitors but also predators, helping to shape group structures and behaviour patterns, cannot be dismissed.

Summary and conclusions

The modern cercopithecid fauna of South Africa represents only a small part of the diversity that existed in the past. Environmental changes, including the move to more open habitats in southern Africa (Elton, 2007) as well as interaction with hominins, the other large-bodied primates to be found in southern Africa, both contributed to shaping the community structure that is seen in monkeys today. Attention must now be paid to examining in more detail the evolutionary histories, taxonomies and palaeobiologies of Plio-Pleistocene monkeys in southern Africa and elsewhere, in order to build more robust models of community ecology and help reconstruct the interactions of the ecological communities to which hominins belonged.

Acknowledgements

The work on which this chapter was based was funded by the Leverhulme Trust and by the NERC EFCHED programme. I thank Ruliang Pan, Jeff McKee and Sally Reynolds for useful comments on this manuscript. I also thank Andy Gallagher, Sally Reynolds and Colin Menter for their kind invitations to participate in the African Genesis meeting and the resulting volume, and also for their generous hospitality in South Africa. This is Paleobiology Database official Publication number 147.

References

Aiello, L. C., Collard, M., Thackeray, J. F. *et al.* (2000). Assessing exact randomization-based methods for determining the taxonomic significance of variability in the human fossil record. *South African Journal of Science*, **96**: 179–83.

Alberts, S. C., Hollister-Smith, J., Mututua, R. S. *et al.* (2005). Seasonality and long term change in a savannah environment. In Brockman, D. K. and van Schaik, C. P. (eds.), *Seasonality in Primates: Studies of Living and Extinct Human and Non-Human Primates*. Cambridge: Cambridge University Press, pp. 157–96.

Alemseged, Z. and Geraads, D. (2000). A new Middle Pleistocene fauna from the Busidima-Telalak region of the Afar, Ethiopia. *Comptes rendus de l'Academie des sciences Paris, Sciences de la Terre et des planetes*, **331**: 549–56.

Altman, S. A. (1998). *Foraging for Survival: Yearling Baboons in Africa*. Chicago: University of Chicago Press.

Avery, D. M. (1995). Southern savannas and Pleistocene hominid adaptations: the micromammalian perspective. In Vrba, E. S., Denton, G. H., Partridge, T.C. and Burckle, L. H. (eds.), *Paleoclimate and Evolution, with Emphasis on Human Origins* New Haven: Yale University Press, pp. 459–78.

Backwell, L. R. and d'Errico, F. (2001). Evidence of termite foraging by Swartkrans early hominids. *Proceedings of the National Academy of Sciences*, **98**: 1358–63.

Bamford, M. (1999). Pliocene fossil woods from an early hominid cave deposit, Sterkfontein, South Africa. *South African Journal of Science*, **95**: 231–7.

Benefit, B. R. (1999). Biogeography, dietary specialization, and the diversification of African Plio-Pleistocene monkeys. In Bromage, T. G. and Schrenk, F. (eds.), *African Biogeography, Climate Change and Evolution*. Oxford: Oxford University Press, pp. 172–88.

Berger, L. R., de Ruiter, D. J., Churchill, S. E. *et al.* (2010). *Australopithecus sediba*: a new species of *Homo*-like australopith from South Africa. *Science*, **328**: 195–204.

Brain, C. K. (1976). Re-interpretation of the Swartkrans site and its remains. *South African Journal of Science*, **72**: 141–6.

(1981). *The Hunters of the Hunted? An Introduction to African Cave Taphonomy*. Chicago: University of Chicago Press.

(1993). *Swartkrans: a Cave's Chronicle of Early Man*. Pretoria: Transvaal Museum Monograph, No. 8.

(1994). The Swartkrans Palaeontological Research Project in perspective: results and conclusions. *South African Journal of Science*, **90**: 220–3.

Butler, P. M. and Greenwood, M. (1976). Elephant shrews (Macroscelididae) from Olduvai and Makapansgat. In Savage R. J. G. and Coryndon S. C. (eds.), *Fossil Vertebrates of Africa*, Volume 4. London: Academic Press, pp. 1–56.

Buzzard, P. (2006). Ecological partitioning of *Cercopithecus campbelli*, *C. petaurista*, and *C. diana* in the Tai Forest. *International Journal of Primatology*, **27**: 529–58.

Cardini, A. and Elton, S. (2008). Variation in guenon skulls I: species divergence, ecological and genetic differences. *Journal of Human Evolution*, **54**: 615–37.

Codron, D., Luyt, J., Lee-Thorp, J. A. *et al.* (2005). Utilizations of savanna-based resources by Plio-Pleistocene baboons. *South Africa Journal of Science*, **101**: 245–8.

Cords, M. (1987). Mixed-species association of *Cercopithecus* monkeys in the Kakamega Forest, Kenya. *University of California Publications in Zoology*, **117**: 1–109.

Delson, E. (1984). Cercopithecid biochronology of the African Plio-Pleistocene: correlation among eastern and southern hominid-bearing localities. *Courier Forschung Institute Senckenberg*, **69**: 199–218.

de Ruiter, D. J. (2003). Revised faunal lists for Members 1–3 of Swartkrans, South Africa. *Annals of the Transvaal Museum*, **40**: 29–41.

Eeley, H. A. C. and Foley, R. A. (1999). Species richness, species range size and ecological specialisations among African primates: geographical patterns and conservation implications. *Biodiversity and Conservation*, **8**: 1033–56.

El-Zaatari, S., Grine, F. E., Teaford, M. F. *et al.* (2005). Molar microwear and dietary reconstructions of fossil Cercopithecoidea from the Plio-Pleistocene deposits of South Africa. *Journal of Human Evolution*, **49**: 180–205.

Elton, S. (2000). Ecomorphology and Evolutionary Biology of African cercopithecoids: providing an ecological context for hominin evolution. Unpublished PhD thesis, University of Cambridge, UK.

  (2001). Locomotor and habitat classification of cercopithecoid postcranial material from Sterkfontein Member 4, Bolt's Farm and Swartkrans Members 1 and 2, South Africa. *Palaeontologia Africana*, **37**: 115–26.

  (2002). A reappraisal of the locomotion and habitat preference of *Theropithecus oswaldi*. *Folia Primatologica*, **73**: 252–80.

  (2006). Forty years on and still going strong: the use of the hominin-cercopithecid comparison in palaeoanthropology. *Journal of the Royal Anthropological Institute*, **12**: 19–38.

  (2007). Environmental correlates of the cercopithecoid radiations. *Folia Primatologica*, **78**: 344–64.

Fedigan, L. and Fedigan, L. M. (1988). *Cercopithecus aethiops*: a review of field studies. In Gaultier-Hion, A., Bourliere, F., Gautier, J-P. and Kingdon, J. (eds.), *A Primate Radiation: Evolutionary Biology of the African Guenons*. Cambridge: Cambridge University Press, pp. 394–411.

Foley, R. A. (1993). Comparative evolutionary biology of *Theropithecus* and the Hominidae. In Jablonski, N. G. (ed.), *Theropithecus: the Rise and Fall of a Primate Genus*. Cambridge: Cambridge University Press, pp. 254–70.

  (1999). Evolutionary geography of Pliocene African hominids. In Bromage, T. G. and Schrenk, F. (eds.), *African Biogeography, Climate Change and Evolution*. Oxford: Oxford University Press, pp. 328–48.

Gautier-Hion, A. (1988). Polyspecific associations among forest guenons. In Gaultier-Hion, A., Bourliere, F., Gautier, J-P. and Kingdon, J. (eds.), *A Primate Radiation: Evolutionary Biology of the African Guenons*. Cambridge: Cambridge University Press, pp. 452–76.

Grine, F. E. and Klein, R. G. (1991). Dating, archaeology and human fossils from the Middle Stone Age levels of Die Kelders, South Africa. *Journal of Human Evolution*, **21**: 363–95.

(1993). Late Pleistocene humans remains from the Sea Harvest Site, Saldanha Bay, South Africa. *Suid-Afrikaanse Tydskrif vir Wetenskap*, **89**: 145–52.

Hill, C. M. (2002). Primate conservation and local communities: ethical issues and debates. *American Anthropologist*, **104**: 1184–94.

Hughes, J. K., Elton, S. and O'Regan, H. R. (2008). *Theropithecus* and 'Out of Africa' dispersal in the Plio-Pleistocene. *Journal of Human Evolution*, **54**: 43–77.

Humphreys, J. B. (1974). A preliminary report on test excavations at Dikbosch Shelter 1, Herbert District, Northern Cape. *South African Archaeological Bulletin*, **29**: 115–19.

International Union for Conservation of Nature and Natural Resources (2006). 2006 IUCN Red List of Threatened Species. www.iucnredlist.org. [Downloaded 29 September 2006].

Jablonski, N. G. (2002). Fossil Old World monkeys: the late Neogene radiation. In Hartwig, W. C. (ed.), *The Primate Fossil Record*. Cambridge: Cambridge University Press, pp. 255–99.

Jones, D. L., Brock, A. and McFadden, P. L. (1986). Palaeomagnetic results from the Kromdraai and Sterkfontein hominid sites. *South African Journal of Science*, **82**: 160–3.

Klein, R. G. (1977). The mammalian fauna from the Middle and Later Stone Age (Later Pleistocene) levels of Border Cave, Natal Province, South Africa. *South African Archaeological Bulletin*, **32**: 14–27.

(1979). Paleoenvironmental and cultural implications of Late Holocene archaeological faunas from the Orange Free State and North Central Cape Province, South Africa. *South African Archaeological Bulletin*, **34**: 34–49.

Klein, R. G. and Cruz-Uribe, K. (1991). The bovids from Elandsfontein, South Africa, and their implications for the age, palaeoenvironment, and origins of the site. *African Archaeological Review*, **9**: 21–79.

Klein, R. G., Cruz-Uribe, K. and Beaumont, P. B. (1991). Environmental, ecological and paleoanthropological implications of the Late Pleistocene mammalian fauna from Equus Cave, Northern Cape Province, South Africa. *Quaternary Research*, **36**: 94–119.

Lawes, M. J. (1990). The distribution of the Samango monkey (*Cercopithecus mitis erythrarchus* Peters, 1852 and *Cercopithecus mitis labiatus* I. Geoffroy, 1843) and forest history in southern Africa. *Journal of Biogeography*, **17**: 669–80.

(2002). Conservation of fragmented populations of *Cercopithecus mitis* in South Africa: the role of reintroduction, corridors and metapopulation ecology. In Glenn, M. E. and Cords, M. (eds.), *The Guenons: Diversity and Adaptation in African Monkeys*. New York: Kluwer Academic/Plenum Publishers, pp. 375–92.

Lee-Thorp, J. A., Sponheimer, M. and van der Merwe, N. J. (2003). What do stable isotopes tell us about hominid dietary and ecological niches in the Pliocene? *International Journal of Osteoarchaeology*, **13**: 104–13.

Luyt, J. and Lee-Thorp, J. A. (2003). Carbon isotope ratios of Sterkfontein fossils indicate a marked shift to open environments ca. 1.7 Ma. *South African Journal of Science*, **99**: 271–3.

McKee, J. M. (1993). Taxonomic and evolutionary affinities of *Papio izodi* fossils from Taung and Sterkfontein. *Palaeontologica Africana*, **30**: 43–9.

Newman, T. K., Jolly, C. J. and Rogers, J. (2004). Mitochondrial phylogeny and systematics of baboons (*Papio*). *American Journal of Physical Anthropology*, **124**: 17–27.

Partridge, T. C. (1978). Re-appraisal of lithostratigraphy of Sterkfontein hominid site. *Nature*, **275**: 282–7.

(1982). Brief comments on 'sedimentological characteristics of the "Red Muds" at the Makapansgat Limeworks', by B. R. Turner. *Palaeoecology of Africa*, **15**: 45–7.

Peabody, F. E. (1954). Travertines and cave deposits of the Kaap Escarpment of South Africa, and the type locality of *Australopithecus africanus* (Dart). *Bulletin of the Geological Society of America*, **65**: 671–706.

Peters, C. R. and Vogel, J. C. (2005). Africa's wild C4 plant foods and possible early hominid diets. *Journal of Human Evolution*, **48**: 219–36.

Pickering, T. R., Dominguez-Rodrigo, M., Egeland, C. P. *et al.* (2004). Beyond leopards: toothmarks and the contribution of multiple carnivore taxa to the accumulation of the Swartkrans Member 3 fossil assemblage. *Journal of Human Evolution*, **46**: 595–604.

Pickford, M. (1993). Climatic change, biogeography and *Theropithecus*. In Jablonski, N. G. (ed.), *Theropithecus: the Rise and Fall of a Primate Genus*. Cambridge: Cambridge University Press, pp. 227–43.

Plummer, T. (2004). Flaked stones and old bones: biological and cultural evolution at the dawn of technology. *Yearbook of Physical Anthropology*, **47**: 118–64.

Reed, K. E. (1997). Early hominid evolution and ecological change through the African Plio-Pleistocene. *Journal of Human Evolution*, **32**: 289–322.

Reed, K. E. and Bidner, L. R. (2004). Primate communities: past, present and possible future. *Yearbook of Physical Anthropology*, **47**: 2–39.

Shipman, P., Bosler, W. and Davis, K. L. (1981). Butchering of giant geladas at an Acheulean site. *Current Anthropology*, **22**: 257–68.

Singer, R. and Wymer, J. (1982). *The Middle Stone Age at Klasies River Mouth in South Africa*. Chicago: University of Chicago Press.

Sponheimer, M. and Lee-Thorp, J. A. (1999). Isotopic evidence for the diet of an early hominid, *Australopithecus africanus*. *Science*, **283**: 368–9.

Sponheimer, M. and Lee-Thorp, J. (2003). Using carbon isotope data of fossil bovid communities for palaeoenvironmental reconstruction. *South African Journal of Science*, **99**: 273–5.

Sponheimer, M., Reed, K. E. and Lee-Thorp, J. A. (1999). Combining isotopic and ecomorphological data to refine bovid palaeodietary reconstruction: a case study from the Makapansgat Limeworks hominin locality. *Journal of Human Evolution*, **36**: 705–18.

Strait, D. S. and Wood, B. A. (1999). Early hominid biogeography. *Proceedings of the National Academy of Sciences*, **96**: 9196–9200.

Stanford, C. B. (1995). The influence of chimpanzee predation on group size and anti-predator behaviour in red colobus monkeys. *Animal Behaviour*, **49**: 577–87.

Teaford, M. F. (1993). Dental microwear and diet in extant and extinct *Theropithecus*: preliminary analyses. In Jablonski, N.G. (ed.), *Theropithecus: the Rise and Fall of a Primate Genus*. Cambridge: Cambridge University Press, pp. 331–49.

Thackeray, J. F. and Myer, S. (2004). *Parapapio broomi* and *Parapapio jonesi* from Sterkfontein: males and females of one species? *Annals of the Transvaal Museum*, **41**: 79–82.

Turner, A. and Wood, B. A. (1993). Taxonomic and geographic diversity in robust australopithecines and other African Plio-Pleistocene mammals. *Journal of Human Evolution*, **24**: 147–68.

Turner, A., Bishop, L. C., Denys, C. *et al.* (1999). A locality-based listing of African Plio-Pleistocene mammals. In Bromage, T. G. and Schrenk, F. (eds.), *African Biogeography, Climate Change and Evolution*. Oxford: Oxford University Press, pp. 369–99.

Vrba, E. S. (1975). Some evidence of chronology and paleoecology of Sterkfontein, Swartkrans and Kromdraai from the fossil Bovidae. *Nature*, **254**: 301–4.

Waser, P. M. (1987). Interactions among primate species. In Smuts, B. B., Cheney, D. L., Seyfarth, R. M., Wrangham, R.W. and Struhasker, T. T. (eds.), *Primate Societies*. Chicago: University of Chicago Press, pp. 219–26.

Watson, V. (1993). Composition of the Swartkrans bone accumulations, in terms of skeletal parts and animals represented. In Brain, C. K. (ed.), *Swartkrans: a Cave's Chronicle of Early Man*. Transvaal Museum Monograph, No. 8. Pretoria: Transvaal Museum. pp. 35–73.

Wood, B. and Strait, D. (2004). Patterns of resource use in early *Homo* and *Paranthropus*. *Journal of Human Evolution*, **46**: 119–62.

24 African Genesis revisited: reflections on Raymond Dart and the 'predatory transition from ape(-man) to man'

TRAVIS R. PICKERING

Abstract

It is impossible to overstate Raymond Dart's contributions to the field of palaeoanthropology. Not only did his 1924 discovery of the Taung child (*Australopithecus africanus*) verify Darwin's prediction that Africa was the birthplace of humanity, but by the mid twentieth century he had also developed an influential hypothesis of early hominid behaviour. The 'killer ape' hypothesis, popularised in Robert Ardrey's book *African Genesis*, contended that an inherent violence in early hominids propelled the evolution of our lineage. *Australopithecus africanus* was conceptualised as a murderous species, members of which regularly cannibalised other hominids and curated their heads as trophies. A more prosaic, but fundamental, component of the hypothesis argued that *A. africanus* was also a proficient hunter. In support of this contention, Dart argued that large faunal assemblages associated with *A. africanus*, such as those from Makapansgat, were its feeding residues. These ideas so provoked Bob Brain, at the time a young South African naturalist, that he tested them at the *Paranthropus robustus* and *Homo erectus* site of Swartkrans (South Africa). Brain's work ushered into palaeoanthropology the developing discipline of taphonomy, resulting ultimately in a new standard of scientific rigour for the field. Further, the data Brain generated at Swartkrans, including numerous *Paranthropus* fossils damaged by the teeth of large carnivores, falsified Dart's imaginative hypothesis of australopithecines as mighty hunters, and suggested they were instead common prey of large carnivores. Since Brain's seminal work, other taphonomic studies elsewhere in Africa have concluded that even members of the genus *Homo* were acquiescent in competition with carnivores for carcass resources. These results were largely embraced by non-specialists (including, prominently, textbook authors) throughout the 1980s and 1990s, to the disregard of contradictory studies that concluded early and

African Genesis: Perspectives on Hominin Evolution, eds. Sally C. Reynolds and Andrew Gallagher. Published by Cambridge University Press. © Cambridge University Press 2012.

profitable access to animal carcasses by East African *Homo*. Until our recent re-analyses of the Swartkrans faunas, the South African record has been comparatively less informative on the issue of hunting in post-*Australopithecus africanus* hominids. This chapter summarises some of our results, which conclude that Swartkrans hominids regularly gained early access to fleshed carcasses and exploited them effectively for food. These zooarchaeological results make sense in light of what is known of the palaeobiology of *H. erectus*, a species with high energy needs, which, in turn, necessitated a high-quality diet. Our current knowledge suggests strongly that that necessity was satisfied by the consumption of meat and marrow. Brain's important work, falsifying the 'killer ape' hypothesis, has allowed palaeoanthropologists to consider early hominid hunting and aggressive scavenging on its own merits, unburdened by the more imaginative aspects of Dart's idea regarding australopithecine inter-personal violence. In doing so, recent data have revealed that Dart was likely correct in the broadest sense when he postulated a 'predatory transition' from the ape-like adaptations of the first hominids to a human-like pattern for the first 'men', *H. erectus*.

From dominance to obeisance: changing perceptions of the 'African genesis' *c.* 1950–1990s

This volume celebrates two benchmarks in the history of palaeoanthropology, the 80th birthday of Phillip V. Tobias and the coinciding 80th anniversary of the Taung child's discovery by Raymond Dart. The lives and careers of Tobias and Dart are intertwined in other, deeper ways as well. While their detailed anatomical and systematic works on South African early hominids come readily to mind, this chapter is dedicated in appreciation of their efforts to reconstruct the behavioural patterns of our distant ancestors. In particular, Dart (e.g. 1949a,b; 1953a,b; 1956a,b; 1957a–c; 1958a,b; 1959a–f; 1960a,b; 1961a,b; 1962a–c;1964a–c; 1965a,b) was unyielding in promoting his view that the humanity of modern people emanated from a violent and predatory disposition inherent to our early African forebears. Dart argued that the palaeoanthropological record of Makapansgat (South Africa) supported this contention, with the thousands of animal bones recovered there representing the feeding residues of carcasses acquired through hunting by *Australopithecus africanus*. The incredible series of publications produced by Dart between 1949 and the mid 1960s espousing his views are engrossing to read in their luridness. As if more provocation was needed, Dart found in Robert Ardrey, the American playwright, a popular voice for the further dissemination of the 'killer ape' hypothesis. Ardrey's best known work is his 1961 book, *African Genesis*, which drips with the same garish verbosity as is in Dart's scientific writings.

But, also as with Dart, the central message from Ardrey (1961: 316), when stripped to its essence, is crystalline in its simplicity: 'Man is a predator whose natural instinct is to kill with a weapon.'

Bob Brain, a third towering figure in the history of South African palaeo-anthropology, was so stimulated by the writings of Dart and Ardrey that he set out to test the idea that australopithecines were proficient predators at a series of cave sites in South Africa's Sterkfontein Valley. Brain's (e.g. 1981, 1993a) taphonomic interpretations of faunal assemblages from Sterkfontein, Swartkrans and Kromdraai suggested that far from being regular hunters, *A. africanus* and the later species *Paranthropus robustus*, like the other animals whose fossils have been recovered from these sites, were more often the prey of large carnivores. Coincident with 1981 publication of *The Hunters or the Hunted?*, Brain's classic treatise summarising his results, was Lewis Binford's (1981) book *Bones*. Binford went beyond Brain in arguing for a lack of hunting prowess in even more recent hominids of the genus *Homo*.

However, actual archaeological investigation of the behavioural capacities of early *Homo* preceded Binford's claims. As early as the mid to late 1970s, Glynn Isaac sponsored taphonomic and site-formation research in East Africa to test his home base model of hominid sociality (e.g. Isaac and Isaac, 1997). One trend that emerged from the taphonomic research environment initiated by the combined influences of Brain, Isaac and Binford was a body of work that focused on understanding the ecological parameters of passive scavenging by early hominids and assessing its taphonomic signatures in East African, open-air contexts, such as the *c.* 1.75 million year old (Ma) site of FLK 22 *Zinjanthropus*, at Olduvai Gorge (Tanzania). Rob Blumenschine and his collaborators (e.g. Blumenschine, 1988, 1991, 1995; Blumenschine and Marean, 1993; Selvaggio, 1994; Capaldo, 1997, 1998) led this work during the 1980s and 1990s, which focused mainly on carnivore tooth mark and hominid hammerstone percussion mark frequencies (but largely disregarded cutmark data) in experimental and naturalistic bone assemblages.

Blumenschine and his colleagues arrived at a model of Earlier Stone Age (ESA) archaeofaunal formation in which hominids scavenged abandoned carcass residues from primary carcass consumers, especially lions (*Panthera leo*), sometimes with a third stage of carcass use in which spotted hyenas (*Crocuta crocuta*) then scavenged grease-laden bone sections after hominids had abandoned them. In the wake of this multistage passive scavenging model, support for the alternative scenario, often characterised as a hunting/aggressive scavenging (also referred to as confrontational or power scavenging; Bunn, 2001) hypothesis, had largely fallen away by the late 1980s.

In my opinion, the near wholesale acceptance of the multistage passive scavenging model by palaeoanthropologists, informed lay people and especially textbook writers and other producers of secondary literature was due not just to Blumenschine's compelling argumentation, but also because his work was inventive, dynamic and rooted in foraging theory. However, a host of less obvious, perhaps even subconscious, factors probably also ensured the wide-scale abandonment of the hunting/aggressive scavenging hypothesis. There has always been a strong intuitive sense that small-bodied, blunt-toothed and slow-running early hominids lacked the physical, cognitive and cultural capabilities to hunt fleet-footed prey and/or drive large, dangerous predators from carcasses of animals that they killed. In addition, no lithic projectile technology is known for the ESA (although some researchers contend that unmodified manuports qualify). Until such time as possible evidence of lithic projectiles emerges, the only plausible hunting and confrontational scavenging weapons for ESA hominids might have been pointed sticks (rudimentary spears) and clubs. Spears, clubs and stones could have been thrown at prey animals and competitors for carcasses. Spears could also have been implemented as pikes in pit traps. Regardless, claims that early hominids were physically capable of effective weapon throwing (e.g. Isaac, 1987; Calvin, 1992; Bingham, 2000; Cannell, 2002) and inferences of possible spear production in the Early Pleistocene (Domínguez-Rodrigo *et al.*, 2001) have thus far had little effect on the perception of ineffective hunting and confrontational scavenging potentials for ESA hominids. In addition, rejection by some of the hunting/aggressive scavenging hypothesis is probably also a long lingering effect of the feminist backlash (e.g. Tanner, 1979, 1981; Dahlberg, 1981) against the 'man the hunter' paradigm (Lee and DeVore, 1968), in which hunting by males overshadowed the role played by females in our evolutionary history.

A most elusive record: inferences of hominid carcass foraging in South Africa, *c.* 1975–2006

In contrast to the eventual ascendancy of the multistage passive scavenging hypothesis among East Africanists, Elisabeth Vrba's (e.g. 1975, 1976) important studies of bovid fossils indicated a variety of modes by which South African early *Homo* acquired carcasses – including hunting at Kromdraai and Swartkrans to passive scavenging at Sterkfontein. These early conclusions were based on the analyses of mortality profiles and animal body size representation. However, due to factors such as differential body part transport and preservation biases, it is highly unlikely that mortality and body size profiles represent a perfect record of age and body size groups acquired by taphonomic agent(s) (Marean, 1995). Even if this were not the case, assigning hominids credit for faunal assemblage formation simply because of the co-occurrence of their remains and stone tools with the bones of other animals is inappropriate and insufficient (e.g. Binford 1981, 1985). Thus, in retrospect, Vrba's results lack inferential power compared to studies focused on skeletal part representation and bone surface modifications. The latter type of study usually includes data on various types of damage that are taxonomically diagnostic – allowing particular taphonomic agents to be linked securely to various stages of assemblage formation. Of particular relevance in this category of damage are stone tool cut and percussion marks, inflicted by hominids while butchering carcasses. The advantage of using butchery mark data to build inferences of early hominid foraging capabilities is that those marks are *directly attributable* to hominid behaviour, and hominid behaviour alone. Thus, they are more immediately informative to questions of hominid carcass foraging than are inferences extrapolated from the indirect evidence of carnivore tooth mark frequencies, such as was done in some multistage passive scavenging models (see expanded discussions in Domínguez-Rodrigo, 1999a,b, 2002; Domínguez-Rodrigo and Pickering, 2003; Egeland *et al.*, 2004; Pickering *et al.*, 2004a, 2005a; Pickering and Domínguez-Rodrigo, 2006).

The extensive South African cave faunas are extreme examples of archaeological palimpsests, the frequency of their hominid-derived components 'swamped' by osseous contributions from many other types of taphonomic agents and processes (e.g. Brain, 1981; Pickering, 1999). In addition, except possibly in the case of Swartkrans Member 3 (e.g. Brain, 1993a; Pickering *et al.*, 2004a), it is very unlikely that hominids ever actually dwelled in the caves of the Sterkfontein Valley. Taphonomic evidence suggests that the caves were dangerous places, the haunts of large predators (e.g. Brain, 1981, 1993a). In addition, the form of many Pleistocene caves, with steeply vertical entrances, was unlikely to have been conducive to hominid occupation (e.g. Pickering, 2002), and analyses of recovered lithic assemblages indicate that they are secondarily derived (e.g. Kuman, 2003, 2007). As a result, archaeological indications of hominid activity preserved in the caves, even at their best, are ephemeral. That said, diligent search for traces of hominid butchery has still proven very profitable.

While a few butchered bones are known from the Oldowan and Acheulean levels of Sterkfontein Member 5 (*c.* 2.0–1.7 Ma) (Brain, 1981; Pickering, 1999), Swartkrans has yielded the largest collections to date (Brain, 1993a; Pickering *et al.*, 2004a,b, 2005a,b, 2007, 2008). The initial sample described from Swartkrans includes 16 cut- and chop-marked specimens identified by Bob Brain and Pat Shipman from Member 3, the cave's most recently deposited Early Pleistocene unit (*c.* 1.8–1.0 Ma) (Brain, 1993a). Working within an actualistic framework constructed by Shipman (1986), Brain and Shipman concluded that:

the position of cut marks on [limb bones] can be instructive in deciding between [passively] scavenged or hunted meat: a concentration of cut marks near joints indicates systematic butchering following hunting, while the presence of cut marks on mid-shaft portions suggests opportunistic utilization of scavenged carcasses. The great majority of the Member 3 cut marks are on mid-shaft bone [fragments], suggesting that [passive] scavenging was probably the means of meat acquisition during Member 3 times at Swartkrans, although the sample size of cut-marked bones is very small.

(Brain, 1993a: 263)

I agree that the position of cut marks on bones is highly informative about the timing of hominid access to carcasses (i.e. early = hunting and/or aggressive scavenging, versus, late = passive scavenging) (e.g. Bunn, 1982, 1991; Bunn and Kroll, 1986; Domínguez-Rodrigo, 1997, 1999a,b, 2002; Domínguez-Rodrigo and Pickering, 2003; Pickering and Domínguez-Rodrigo, 2006; Pickering *et al.*, 2004a, 2007). However, some important ethnoarchaeological and experimental work not considered in Brain and Shipman's initial study concludes with contradictory predictions of how a hunted/aggressively scavenged archaeofauna should appear taphonomically (e.g. Bunn, 1982, 1986, 1991; Bunn and Kroll, 1986; Domínguez-Rodrigo, 1997, 1999a,b; Nilssen, 2000). As illustrated in Figure 24.1, meat and marrow are differentially distributed across the limbs of ungulates. Upper (i.e. humerus and femur) and intermediate (i.e. radius and tibia) limb bones are encased in thick muscle masses and possess large medullary cavities, in contrast to the metapodials, which are meatless and have relatively small marrow chambers. Thus, it is unsurprising that when large African carnivores feed on complete carcasses the abundant flesh of upper and intermediate limbs is consumed early and usually in its entirety (e.g. Blumenschine, 1986; Domínguez-Rodrigo, 1997, 1999a,b). Once sated, primary consumers then usually abandon the metapodials untouched, and often the marrow of all limb bones. Further, Manuel Domínguez-Rodrigo's (1999b) study of nearly 30 medium-sized ungulate carcasses showed that when small meat scraps did occasionally persist on limb bones after carcass abandonment by primary consumers, those scraps adhered to the proximal and distal epiphyseal/metaphyseal sections of those bones. More importantly for the following discussion, *no* midshaft sections of any upper limb bone retained meat scraps upon abandonment by primary consumers.

The relevance of this actualistic work is that if Pleistocene hominids were acting as passive scavengers, little to no flesh would have been available to them from the upper and intermediate limb bones of abandoned carcasses. The test implication is that a passively scavenged fauna should not preserve cut-marked upper and intermediate limb bone specimens, especially midshaft ones; why, after all, would a hominid put a stone flake to a bone already defleshed? This

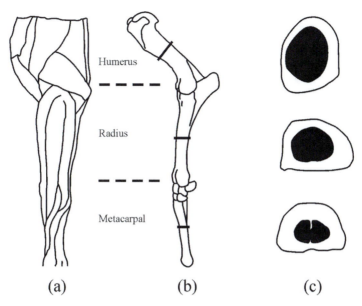

Figure 24.1. Differential distribution of edible tissues across the length of an ungulate forelimb. Proximodistally, note the heavy meat cover on the humerus and radius, while the metacarpal has no overlying muscle (a, b). Cross-sectional views of the midshaft of each bone reveal the large medullary cavities of the humerus and radius versus the more restricted volume of the metacarpal's marrow chamber (c). These differences are mirrored in the ungulate hindlimb, with the femur and tibia possessing thick overlying musculature and large medullary cavities and the metatarsal lacking these features.

would only result in dulling the tool's edge, with no significant nutritional or energetic benefit to the hominid in return. Henry Bunn, a pioneer of the ethno-archaeological and experimental approach in zooarchaeology, best expresses the irresistible logic, in summing up this idea:

> It is, of course, possible to start with a largely defleshed bone and then experimen-tally slice away at the visible muscle attachment areas, as Selvaggio (1994) has shown…I would suggest, however, that butchers with any interest in preserving the sharpness of their knife blades are not going to repeatedly hack into the visible bone surfaces when the adhering meat can be shaved free without hitting the bone directly enough to produce cut-marks…Cut-marks are mistakes; they are acciden-tal miscalculations of the precise location of the bone surface when muscle masses obscured it. As soon as a butcher can see the bone surface, few if any cut-marks will be inflicted thereafter in that area.

(Bunn, 2001: 206–7)

Grounded on this actualistic base, I, with Bob Brain, Manuel Domínguez-Rodrigo, Charles Egeland and Amy Schnell conducted a zooarchaeological

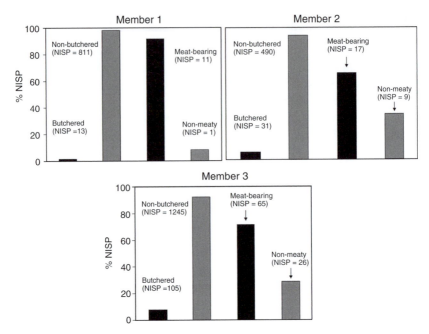

Figure 24.2. Graphic representations of the proportion of butchered versus non-butchered limb bone shaft fragments (left side of each graph) and proportion of meat-bearing versus non-meaty specimens (right side of each graph) for Members of 1, 2 and 3, Swartkrans Cave. NISP = number of identified specimens: raw NISP values appear in parentheses, while bar heights indicate percentages of total NISPs. Butchered specimens = fossils bearing stone cut marks and/or hammerstone percussion damage. Meat-bearing elements = humerus, radius, femur and tibia; non-meaty elements = metapodials (see Figure 24.1). Limb bone fragments that were not assignable to a more specific level of identification were excluded from analyses of meat-bearing versus non-meaty element representation. Two important patterns are apparent in these data. First, the overall number of butchered bones is very low in each member. The Swartkrans faunas are palimpsests created by multiple taphonomic agents and processes, with only minimal contribution from hominids in each. However, those fossils that were modified by prehistoric hominids are informative behaviourally. The second significant pattern is that the total butchered samples in each member are composed of high proportions of meat-bearing elements – indicating early access to carcasses by hominid foragers at Swartkrans *c*.1.8–1.0 Ma. Data from Pickering *et al.* (2004a, 2007, 2008).

re-analysis of the limb bone midshaft samples from Swartkrans Members 1 to 3. Our results are well published (Pickering *et al.*, 2004a,b, 2005a,b, 2007, 2008), but I summarise a few pertinent conclusions here. Figure 24.2 presents the frequency of butchered fossil specimens broken down by limb bone type – meat-bearing (i.e. upper and intermediate limb bones combined) versus non-meaty (i.e. metapodials). A couple of interesting points emerge from our analyses of butchery patterns (tooth mark patterns and inferred carnivore behaviour are being dealt with in a forthcoming paper). First, we identified for the first time ever, butchered fossils from Swartkrans Members 1 and 2. Although Members 1, 2 and 3 cannot be differentiated chronometrically (based on biostratigraphy, each is *c.* 1.8–1.0 Ma), a combination of studies on sedimentology, stratigraphy, faunal seriation and archaeology suggests that the units are discrete and time successive, with the Member 1 sediments representing the first of the three infills, followed by Member 2 and most recently by Member 3 (Brain, 1993a,b; McKee *et al.*, 1995). Second, meat-bearing bone specimens comprise 91.7%, 65.4% and 71.4% of the total butchered samples (minus skeletally unidentifiable specimens) in Members 1, 2 and 3 respectively. The differences in percentages are not statistically significant (chi-squared test, $\chi^2 = 2.8$; 2 d.f.; $p < 0.5$), suggesting a similar degree of high competence in carcass acquisition abilities for Swartkrans hominids (i.e. early access to preferred, heavily muscled carcass parts) through the time span covered by Members 1 to 3.

Our results have important implications for the behavioural capabilities of *H. erectus*, assuming the commonly held understanding that it was predominantly this species, and not *P. robustus*, which generated the lithic and zooarchaeological record at Swartkrans (e.g. Klein, 1999; Kuman, 2003; Plummer, 2004). This view is, however, open to debate. Susman (1988a,b, 1994), in particular, has voiced a strong opinion that *P. robustus* was capable of producing the simple stone tools found at Swartkrans. The question, though, is whether that capability equates with their actual production and use by *P. robustus*? Earlier Stone Age lithic assemblages consist of sharp-edged cutting flakes and cobbles, which, respectively, are well suited for defleshing and demarrowing the carcasses of large animals (e.g. Schick and Toth, 1993; Isaac and Isaac, 1997). In addition, these stone tools are associated from their very first appearance *c.* 2.6 Ma with the butchered remains of animal bones at Gona, Ethiopia (Domínguez-Rodrigo *et al.*, 2005; see also de Heinzelin *et al.*, 1999). It does seem likely that *P. robustus* was more omnivorous than previously supposed (reviewed in Pickering, 2006). However, the fact that ESA technology and butchered bone assemblages persist *after* its extinction (e.g. Bunn 1982, 1997; Brain, 1993a; Asfaw *et al.*, 2002; Domínguez-Rodrigo *et al.*, 2002; Fiore *et al.*, 2004; Pickering *et al.*, 2004a, 2005a; Lordkipanidze *et al.*, 2005) indicates absolutely that meat eating was an important part of the dietary adaptations of its collateral relative, *H. erectus*, which went extinct much more recently, disappearing from the fossil record *c.* 0.5 Ma. Based on the preponderance of currently available data, it thus seems reasonable to hypothesise that although *P. robustus* may have contributed to the zooarchaeological record of Swartkrans, *H. erectus* surely did.

As a species, *H. erectus* was the first hominid to closely approach or meet modern *H. sapiens* standards in body size and proportions, neonate brain size (with its associated maternal costs) and geographic spread (reviewed in Antón, 2003). In that sense, it is appropriate to conceive of *H. erectus* as a 'human species' (contra, Walker and Shipman, 1996). It is in this context that the Swartkrans zooarchaeological results meet current expectations of the dietary adaptations of *H. erectus*. Routine consumption of animal product by the species has been predicted on theoretical grounds because it was an animal that 'was large [-bodied] and wide-ranging, had a high total energy expenditure, and required a high-quality diet' (Plummer, 2004: 118; see also, Antón, 2003; Walker and Leakey, 1993; Rogers *et al.*, 1994). In addition, the species' eventual occupation of temperate latitudes with markedly seasonal environs and plant food availability, such as those along the southern slopes of the Caucasus Mountains at prehistoric Dmanisi (e.g. Gabunia *et al.*, 2001), attests to the need for a reliable and regular strategy of carcass acquisition (e.g. Shipman and Walker, 1989). On balance, it is likely that *H. erectus* could only achieve its 'human status' through the consistent attainment and consumption of high-quality animal product. In other words, Raymond Dart seems to have, in fact, been correct when he postulated that the transition from animality to humanity involved a vital predatory component.

Raymond Dart's last laugh: evidence of expanded dietary breadth at Sterkfontein Cave?

An integral part of Dart's 'killer ape' hypothesis was the concept of the Osteodontokeratic Culture, a fanciful bone, tooth and horn tool industry that *A. africanus* supposedly employed in its murderous activities. Bob Brain likes to tell the story of showing Dart *genuine* bone tools Brain discovered at Swartkrans (e.g. Brain *et al.*, 1988; Brain and Shipman, 1993):

> At that stage, Raymond Dart's eyesight was starting to fail, but as he felt the smooth points of many of the tools with his fingers, his face lit up with excitement. Then he said: 'Brain, I always told you that *Australopithecus* made bone tools, but you did not believe me. What were they used for?' I replied that I thought that they had been used for digging in the ground. Dart slumped back in his chair with a look of disbelief on his face. 'That is the most unromantic explanation I have heard of in my life!' he said, and, picking up the longest of the bone points, he rammed it between my ribs, saying, 'Brain, I could run you through with this!'

(Brain, 2007: 4–5)

This anecdote illustrates two of the most extraordinary characteristics of Dart noted by his contemporaries: first was the unshakable optimism he had in himself and his ideas; second, was his remarkable magnanimity, expressed in his ultimate acceptance of Brain's interpretation of the Swartkrans bone tools. A third trait revealed is Dart's uncanny ability to be right in the end, even if that accuracy was sometimes not recognised for years by the rest of palaeoanthropology (e.g. the long-delayed acceptance of the Taung child as a legitimate hominid). Another characteristic of Dart's eventual rightness on various issues is that it is not always for entirely accurate reasons. The data and discussion presented in the previous section illustrate both these points with regard to the prosaic aspect of the 'killer ape' hypothesis. Dart's conviction that predation and meat eating were integral parts of what made us human was largely ignored or rejected for several long decades. Dart was also almost certainly wrong in believing that the 'predatory transition' took place between non-hominid hominoids and *Australopithecus*; current data suggests the transition was between *Australopithecus* and *H. erectus*. But, in the broadest (and most important) sense Dart was right about the crucial role that the regular acquisition and consumption of meat and marrow played in the transformation from 'ape(-man) to man'.

In closing, I would suggest that Dart may have even had it right (in a sense, at least) about one of the more dramatic aspects of the 'killer ape' hypothesis: hominid cannibalism. In another example of great magnanimity, Tim White and Nick Toth became my partners on a project for which they actually had priority. Ten years before I began my research on the large vertebrate faunas of Sterkfontein Member 5 (Pickering, 1999), White and Toth identified a series of linear striations on a zygomaticomaxillary specimen from the partial hominid skull StW 53, *c.*2.4–2.0 Ma. They did not publish their observations until I corresponded with them about my independent, corroborating assessment that the striations are stone tool cut marks. Our report on the damage included the carefully worded conclusion: 'It is not possible to infer the reason(s) for the cutmarks observed on the StW 53 hominid specimen. Reasonable hypotheses include cannibalism, curation, mutilation and/or funerary practices' (Pickering, *et al.*, 2000: 583).

The most convincing cases in which prehistoric cannibalism has been inferred are based on demonstrations of hominid remains having been treated in the same manner as co-occurring non-hominid animal bones (e.g. White, 1992; Turner and Turner, 1998; Defleur *et al.*, 1999; Fernández-Jalvo *et al.*, 1999). Many critical thinkers have little problem with the inference that animal bones scarred by defleshing cut marks and percussion marks and then dumped unceremoniously in the site represent refuse from hominid meals. Proponents of cannibalism hypotheses argue that rejecting cannibalism in these cases, in which there is identical treatment of hominid and animal bones, is to deny that we can make any inferences at all about early hominid diet from humanly modified bones.

I agree. Unfortunately, though, the faunal assemblage from the StW 53 deposit is very small (Pickering, 1999), so building the contextual case for cannibalism is not possible. In fact, the *only* cut-marked specimen from the StW 53 breccia is the hominid. That said, if I had to choose between the 'reasonable hypotheses' offered above for the StW 53 cut marks, cannibalism seems the *most* reasonable. My rationale for that choice is based on the deep antiquity from which StW 53 derives and because the frequency and intensity of cut-marking on it is moderate, indicating it was probably inflicted unintentionally. There is no other convincing indication of symbolic behaviour in the palaeo-anthropological record at this time period. It is not until *c.* 0.6 Ma, with the hominid cranium from Bodo (Ethiopia), that cut-marking beyond what I would expect from simple subsistence-driven butchery is evident (White, 1986). And it is only much more recently (*c.* 0.15–0.16 Ma) that taphonomic indications of curation, in the form of defleshing cut marks and handling polish (on the cranial remains of *H. sapiens idaltu* from the Middle Awash, Ethiopia) appear (Clark *et al.*, 2003). It seems likely that Dart would have approved of this interpretation of the StW 53 data, confirming his view that hominid cannibalism, consistently evident in more recent phases of human evolution (e.g. White, 1992; Turner and Turner, 1998; Defleur *et al.*, 1999; Fernández-Jalvo *et al.*, 1999), had its origin deep in the Pleistocene.

On the other hand, disagreement with the idea is likely, given that cannibalism is such a controversial issue. I contend, however, that it will be a considerable challenge to falsify a hypothesis of cannibalism for StW 53. Emerging evidence from South Africa continues to validate Raymond Dart's prescience in his vision of an 'African Genesis' not just for humanity, but also for humanity's humanness, in all its majestic and lowly expressions.

Acknowledgements

I thank the organisers of the African Genesis Conference and editors of this volume for the invitation to contribute to both and for financial support to attend the conference. Special thanks to Phillip Tobias, the honoree of both projects; in 1997, Professor Tobias granted me permission to conduct my dissertation work at Sterkfontein Cave, which launched my career in South African palaeoanthropology. The new butchery data from Swartkrans summarised in this chapter is the product of the labours of a team of collaborators and friends, which I am honoured to direct; the Swartkrans Palaeoanthropological Research Project includes or has included (in alphabetical order), Bob Brain (project coordinator), Ron Clarke, Manuel Domínguez-Rodrigo, Charles Egeland, Jason Heaton, Kathy Kuman, Amy Schnell and Morris Sutton. Thank you to our all-important field assistants Andrew Phaswana, Isaac Makhele, Hendrick Dingiswayo, Nkwane Molefe and Stephen Motsumi, and to the students of the 2005 Swartkrans-Limpopo River Valley Field School for additional help in the field. I am most grateful to John Cruise and Dusty van Rooyen of John Cruise Mining (Johannesburg) for their invaluable help, advisement and camaraderie, and to African Explosives. Thanks to the Department of Archaeology and the Institute for Human Evolution, University of the Witwatersrand for continued support of my work. Thanks to the Transvaal Museum and especially Francis Thackeray and Stephany Potze for permission to study the curated Swartkrans fauna and for logistical support of that work. Wendy Voorvelt is thanked for her assistance with Figure 24.1. Funding for the Swartkrans Palaeoanthropological Research Project has been provided through grants from the National Science Foundation, the LSB Leakey Foundation and the Palaeontology Scientific Trust (PAST). Three good friends, Henry Bunn, Manuel Domínguez-Rodrigo and Charles Egeland, deserve special recognition for influencing my thoughts on and approach to studying early hominid carcass foraging. Thanks to Tim White and Nick Toth, my collaborators on the StW 53 cutmark project. Nick Toth and Kathy Schick provided encouragement from the Stone Age Institute. Last, but certainly not least, I offer continued thanks to my family in the USA, and to my dearest friends in South Africa, the Brains, Clarkes, Suttons and Shuna Huffman, for their patience, support and good humour.

References

Antón, S. C. (2003). Natural history of *Homo erectus*. *Yearbook of Physical Anthropology*, **46**: 126–69.

Ardrey, R. (1961). *African Genesis: a Personal Investigation into the Animal Origins and Nature of Man*. New York: Atheneum.

Asfaw, B., Gilbert, W. H., Beyne, Y. *et al.* (2002). Remains of *Homo erectus* from Bouri, Middle Awash, Ethiopia. *Nature*, **416**: 317–20.

Binford, L. R. (1981). *Bones: Ancient Men and Modern Myths*. New York: Academic Press.

(1985). Human ancestors: changing views of their behavior. *Journal of Anthropological Archaeology*, **4**: 292–327.

Bingham, P. M. (2000). Human evolution and human history: a complete theory. *Evolutionary Anthropology*, **9**: 248–57.

Blumenschine, R. J. (1986). Carcass consumption sequences and the archaeological distinction of scavenging and hunting. *Journal of Human Evolution*, **15**: 639–59.

(1988). An experimental model of the timing of hominid and carnivore influence on archaeological bone assemblages. *Journal of Archaeological Science*, **15**: 483–502.

(1991). Hominid carnivory and foraging strategies, and the socio-economic function of early archaeological sites. *Philosophical Transactions of the Royal Society (London)*, **334**: 211–21.

(1995). Percussion marks, tooth marks and experimental determinations of the timing of hominid and carnivore access to long bones at FLK *Zinjanthropus*, Olduvai Gorge, Tanzania. *Journal of Human Evolution*, **29**: 21–51.

Blumenschine, R. J. and Marean, C. W. (1993). A carnivore's view of archaeological bone assemblages. In Hudson, J. (ed.), *From Bones to Behavior: Ethnoarchaeological and Experimental Contributions to the Interpretation of Faunal Remains.* Carbondale, IL: Center for Archaeological Investigations, Southern Illinois University, pp. 271–300.

Brain, C. K. (1981). *The Hunters or the Hunted? An Introduction to African Cave Taphonomy.* Chicago: University of Chicago Press.

(1993a). A taphonomic overview of the Swartkrans fossil assemblages. In Brain, C. K. (ed.), *Swartkrans: a Cave's Chronicle of Early Man.* Pretoria: Transvaal Museum, pp. 257–64.

(1993b). Structure and stratigraphy of the Swartkrans Cave in the light of the new excavations. In Brain, C. K. (ed.), *Swartkrans: a Cave's Chronicle of Early Man.* Pretoria: Transvaal Museum, pp. 23–33.

(2007). Fifty years of fun with fossils: some cave taphonomy-related ideas and concepts that emerged between 1953 and 2003. In Pickering, T. R., Schick, K. and Toth, N. (eds.), *Breathing Life into Fossils: Taphonomic Studies in Honor of C. K. (Bob) Brain.* Bloomington, IN: Stone Age Institute Press, pp. 1–24.

Brain, C. K. and Shipman, P. (1993). The Swartkrans bone tools. In Brain, C. K. (ed.), *Swartkrans: a Cave's Chronicle of Early Man.* Pretoria: Transvaal Museum, pp. 195–215.

Brain, C. K., Churcher, C. S., Clark, J. D. *et al.* (1988). New evidence of early hominids, their culture and environment from the Swartkrans Cave, South Africa. *South African Journal of Science*, **84**: 828–35.

Bunn, H. T. (1982). Meat-eating and human evolution: studies on the diet and subsistence patterns of Plio-Pleistocene hominids in East Africa. PhD thesis, University of California, Berkeley.

(1986). Patterns of skeletal representation and hominid subsistence activities at 5 Olduvai Gorge, Tanzania and Koobi Fora, Kenya. *Journal of Human Evolution*, **15**(6): 673–90.

(1991). A taphonomic perspective on the archaeology of human origins. *Annual Review of Anthropology*, **20**: 433–67.

(1997). The bone assemblages from the excavated sites. In Isaac, G. Ll. and Isaac, B. (eds.), *Koobi Fora Research Project, Volume 5: Plio-Pleistocene Archaeology.* Oxford: Claredon Press, pp. 402–44.

(2001). Hunting, power scavenging, and butchering by Hadza foragers and by Plio-Pleistocene *Homo*. In Stanford, C. B and Bunn, H. T. (eds.), *Meat-eating and Human Evolution.* New York: Oxford University Press, pp. 199–218.

Bunn, H. T. and Kroll, E. M. (1986). Systematic butchery by Plio-Pleistocene hominids at Olduvai Gorge, Tanzania. *Current Anthropology*, **27**: 431–52.

Calvin, W. H. (1992). *A Brain for All Seasons: Human Evolution and Abrupt Climate Change.* Chicago: University of Chicago Press.

Cannell, A. (2002). Throwing behaviour and the mass distribution of geological hand samples, hand grenades and Olduvian manuports. *Journal of Archaeological Science*, **29**: 335–9.

Capaldo, S. D. (1997). Experimental determinations of carcass processing by Plio-Pleistocene hominids and carnivores at FLK 22 (*Zinjanthropus*), Olduvai Gorge, Tanzania. *Journal of Human Evolution*, **33**: 555–97.

(1998). Methods, marks and models for inferring hominid and carnivore behavior. *Journal of Human Evolution*, **35**: 323–6.

Clark, J. D., Beyene, Y., WoldeGabriel, G. *et al.* (2003). Stratigraphic, chronological and behavioural contexts of Pleistocene *Homo sapiens* from Middle Awash, Ethiopia. *Nature*, **423**: 747–52.

Dahlberg, F. (ed.) (1981). *Woman the Gatherer*. New Haven: Yale University Press.

Dart, R. A. (1949a). The predatory implemental technique of *Australopithecus*. *American Journal of Physical Anthropology*, **7**: 1–38.

(1949b). The bone-bludgeon hunting technique of *Australopithecus*. *South African Journal of Science*, **2**: 150–2.

(1953a). The predatory transition from ape to man. *International Anthropological and Lingusitic Review*, **1**: 201–18.

(1953b). The proto-human inhabitants of southern Africa. In *Africa's Place in the Human Story*. Johannesburg: South African Broadcasting Corporation, pp. 19–22.

(1956a). The myth of the bone-accumulating hyena. *American Anthropologist*, **58**: 40–62.

(1956b). Cultural status of the South African man-apes. *Smithsonian Report*, **4240**: 317–38.

(1957a). The Makapansgat australopithecine osteodontokeratic culture. In *Proceedings of the Third Pan-African Congress on Prehistory (Livingstone, 1955)*. London: Chatto and Windus.

(1957b). *The Osteodontokeratic Culture of* Australopithecus prometheus. Pretoria: Transvaal Museum.

(1957c). An australopithecine object from Makapansgat. *Nature*, **179**: 693–5.

(1958a). The minimal bone-breccia content of Makapansgat an the australopithecine predatory habit. *American Anthropologist*, **60**: 923–31.

(1958b). Bone tools and porcupine gnawing. *American Anthropologist*, **60**: 715–24.

(1959a). *Africa's Place in the Emergence of Civilization*. Johannesburg: South African Broadcasting Corporation.

(1959b). The ape-man tool-makers of a million years ago: South African *Australopithecus* – his life, habits and skills. *Illustrated London News*, **234**: 798–801.

(1959c). An australopithecine scoop from Herefordshire. *Nature*, **183**: 844.

(1959d). Cannon-bone scoops and daggers. *South African Journal of Science*, **55**: 79–82.

(1959e). Osteodontokeratic ripping tools and pulp scoops for edentulous australopithecines. *Journal of the Dental Association of South Africa*, **14**: 164–78.

(1959f). Further light on australopithecine humeral and femoral weapons. *American Journal of Physical Anthropology*, **17**: 87–94.

(1960a). The bone tool-manufacturing ability of *Australopithecus prometheus*. *American Anthropologist*, **62**: 134–43.

(1960b). The persistence of some tools and utensils found first in the Makapansgat grey breccia. *South African Journal of Science*, **56**: 71–4.

(1961a). An australopithecine scoop made from a right australopithecine upper arm bone. *Nature*, **191**: 372–3.

(1961b). Further information about how *Australopithecus* made bone tools and utensils. *South African Journal of Science*, **57**: 127–34.

(1962a). Substitution of stone tools for bone tools at Makapansgat. *Nature*, **196**: 314–16.

(1962b). Stalactites as tool material for australopithecines: a missing cultural link between skeletal and stone tool-making from the Makapansgat stalactite cavern. *Illustrated London News*, **242**: 1052–5.

(1962c). From cannon-bone scoops to skull bowls at Makapansgat. *American Journal of Physical Anthropology*, **20**: 287–96.

(1964a). A brief review of the Makapansgat investigations, 1925–1963. *Academia das Ciências de Lisboa, Memorias*, **9**: 1–17.

(1964b). The Abbé Breuil and the Osteodontokeratic Culture. *Instituto de Prehsitoria y Arqueologia, Monografias*, **11**, 347–70.

(1964c). The ecology of the South African man-apes. In Davis, D. H. S. (ed.), *Ecological Studies in Southern Africa*. Den Haag: Junk Publishers, pp. 49–66.

(1965a). Pounding as a process and producer of other artefacts. *South African Archaeological Bulletin*, **20**: 141–7.

(1965b). Tree chopping with an elephant rib. *South African Journal of Science*, **61**: 395.

Defleur, A., White, T., Valensi, P. *et al.* (1999). Neanderthal cannibalism at Moula-Guercy, Ardèche, France. *Science*, **286**: 128–31.

Domínguez-Rodrigo, M. (1997). Meat-eating by early hominids at the FLK 22 Zinjanthropus site, Olduvai Gorge, Tanzania: an experimental approach using cut mark data. *Journal of Human Evolution*, **33**: 669–90.

(1999a). Flesh availability and bone modification in carcasses consumed by lions. *Palaeogeography, Palaeoclimatology, Palaeoecology*, **149**: 373–88.

(1999b). Meat-eating and carcass procurement by hominids at the FLK Zinj 22 site, Olduvai Gorge (Tanzania): a new experimental approach to the old hunting-versus-scavenging debate. In Ullrich, H. (ed.), *Lifestyles and Survival Strategies in Pliocene and Pleistocene Hominids*. Schwelm: Edition Archaea, pp. 89–111.

(2002). Hunting and scavenging in early hominids: the state of the debate. *Journal of World Prehistory*, **16**: 1–56.

Domínguez-Rodrigo, M. and Pickering, T. R. (2003). Early hominid hunting and scavenging: a zooarchaeological review. *Evolutionary Anthropology*, **12**: 275–82.

Domínguez-Rodrigo, M., Serrallonga, J., Juan-Tresserras, J. *et al.* (2001). Woodworking activities by early humans: a plant residue analysis on Acheulian stone tools from Peninj (Tanzania). *Journal of Human Evolution*, **40**: 289–99.

Domínguez-Rodrigo, M., de Luque, L., Alcalá, L. *et al.* (2002). The ST site complex at Peninj, West Lake Natron, Tanzania: implications for early hominid behavioral models. *Journal of Archaeological Science*, **29**: 639–65.

Domínguez-Rodrigo, M., Pickering, T. R., Semaw, S. *et al.* (2005). Cutmarked bones from Pliocene archaeological sites at Gona, Afar, Ethiopia: implications for the function of the world's oldest stone tools. *Journal of Human Evolution*, **48**: 109–21.

Egeland, C. P., Pickering, T. R., Domínguez-Rodrigo, M. *et al.* (2004). Disentangling Early Stone Age palimpsests: determining the functional independence of hominid- and carnivore-derived portions of archaeofaunas. *Journal of Human Evolution*, **47**: 343–57.

Fernández-Jalvo, Y., Díez, J. C., Cáceres, I. *et al.* (1999). Human cannibalism in the Early Pleistocene of Europe (Gran Dolina, Sierra de Atapuerca, Burgos, Spain). *Journal of Human Evolution*, **37**: 591–622.

Fiore, I., Bondioli, L., Coppa, A. *et al.* (2004). Taphonomic analysis of the Late Early Pleistocene bone remains from Buia (Dandiero Basin, Danakil Depression, Eriteria): evidence for large mammal and reptile butchering. *Rivista Italiana di Paleontologia e Stratigrafia*, **110**: 89–97.

Gabunia, L., Anton, S. C., Lordkipanidze, D. *et al.* (2001). Dmanisi and dispersal. *Evolutionary Anthropology*, **10**: 158–70.

de Heinzelin, J., Clark, J. D., White, T., *et al.* (1999). Environment and behavior of 2.5-million-year-old Bouri hominids. *Science*, **284**: 625–9.

Isaac, A. B. (1987). Throwing and human evolution. *African Archaeological Review*, **5**: 3–17.

Isaac, G. L. and Isaac, B. (eds.) (1997). *Koobi Fora Research Project, Volume 5: Plio-Pleistocene Archaeology*. Oxford: Claredon Press.

Klein, R. G. (1999). *The Human Career: Human Biological and Cultural Origins*. Chicago: University of Chicago Press.

Kuman, K. (2003). Site formation in the early South African Stone Age sites and its influence on the archaeological record. *South African Journal of Science*, **99**: 251–4.

(2007). The Earlier Stone Age in South Africa: site context and the influence of cave studies. In Pickering, T. R., Schick, K. and Toth, N. (eds.), *Breathing Life into Fossils: Taphonomic Studies in Honor of C.K. (Bob) Brain*. Bloomington, IN: Stone Age Institute Press, pp. 181–98.

Lee, R. B. and DeVore, I. (eds.) (1968). *Man the Hunter*. New York: Aldine de Gruyter.

Lordkipanidze, D., Vekua, A., Ferring, R. *et al.* (2005). The earliest toothless hominin skull. *Nature*, **434**: 717–18.

McKee, J. K., Thackeray, J. F. and Berger, L. R. (1995). Faunal assemblage seriation of southern African Pliocene and Pleistocene fossil deposits. *American Journal of Physical Anthropology*, **96**: 235–50.

Marean, C. W. (1995). Of taphonomy and zooarchaeology. *Evolutionary Anthropology*, **4**: 64–72.

Nilssen, P. J. (2000). An actualistic butchery study in South Africa and its implications for reconstructing hominid strategies of carcass acquisition and butchery in the Upper Pleistocene and Plio-Pleistocene. PhD thesis, University of Cape Town.

Pickering, T. R. (1999). Taphonomic interpretations of the Sterkfontein early hominid site (Gauteng, South Africa) reconsidered in light of recent evidence. PhD thesis, University of Wisconsin, Madison.

(2002). Reconsideration of criteria for differentiating faunal assemblages accumulated by hyenas and hominids. *International Journal of Osteoarchaeology*, **12**: 127–41.

(2006). Subsistence behaviour of South African Pleistocene hominids. *South African Journal of Science*, **102**: 205–10.

Pickering, T. R. and Domínguez-Rodrigo, M. (2006). The acquisition and use of large mammal carcasses by Oldowan hominids in eastern and southern Africa: a selected review and assessment. In Toth, N. and Schick, K. D. (eds.), *The Oldowan: Studies into the Origins of Human Technology*. Bloomington, IN: Stone Age Institute Press, pp. 113–28.

Pickering, T. R., White, T. D. and Toth, N. (2000). Cutmarks on a Plio-Pleistocene hominid from Sterkfontein, South Africa. *American Journal of Physical Anthropology*, **111**: 579–84.

Pickering, T. R., Domínguez-Rodrigo, M., Egeland, C. P. *et al.* (2004a). New data and ideas on the foraging behaviour of Early Stone Age hominids at Swartkrans Cave, South Africa. *South African Journal of Science*, **100**: 215–19.

(2004b). Beyond leopards: tooth marks and the relative contribution of multiple carnivore taxa to the accumulation of the Swartkrans Member 3 fossil assemblage. *Journal of Human Evolution*, **46**: 595–604.

(2005a). The contribution of limb bone fracture patterns to reconstructing early hominid behavior at Swartkrans Cave (South Africa): archaeological application of a new analytical method. *International Journal of Osteoarchaeology*, **15**: 247–60.

(2005b). The earliest evidence of hominid butchery in southern Africa: new zooarchaeological and taphonomic data on the use of large animal carcasses at Swartkrans Members 1–3. Paper presented at the Annual Meeting of the Paleoanthropology Society, held in Milwaukee, Wisconsin, April 4–6, 2005.

Pickering, T. R., Domínguez-Rodrigo, M., Egeland, C. P. *et al.* (2007). Carcass foraging by early hominids at Swartkrans Cave (South Africa): a new investigation of the zooarchaeology and taphonomy of Member 3. In Pickering, T. R., Schick, K. and Toth, N. (eds.), *Breathing Life into Fossils: Taphonomic Studies in Honor of C. K. (Bob) Brain*. Bloomington, IN: Stone Age Institute Press, pp. 233–53.

Pickering, T. R., Egeland, C. P., Domínguez-Rodrigo, M. *et al.* (2008). Testing the 'shift in the balance of power' hypothesis at Swartkrans, South Africa: hominid cave use and subsistence behavior in the Early Pleistocene. *Journal of Anthropological Archaeology*, **27**: 30–45.

Plummer, T. (2004). Flaked stones and old bones: biological and cultural evolution at the dawn of technology. *Yearbook of Physical Anthropology*, **47**: 118–64.

Rogers, M. J., Harris, J. W. K. and Feibel, C. S. (1994). Changing patterns of land use by Plio-Pleistocene hominids in the Lake Turkana basin. *Journal of Human Evolution*, **27**: 139–58.

Schick, K. D. and Toth, N. (1993). *Making Silent Stones Speak: Human Evolution and the Dawn of Technology*. New York: Touchstone.

Selvaggio, M. M. (1994). Identifying the timing and sequence of hominid and carnivore involvement with Plio-Pleistocene bone assemblages from carnivore tooth marks and stone-tool butchery marks on bone surfaces. PhD thesis, Rutgers University, New Brunswick.

Shipman, P. (1986). Scavenging or hunting in early hominids: theoretical frameworks and tests. *American Anthropologist*, **88**: 27–43.

Shipman, P. and Walker, A. (1989). The costs of becoming a predator. *Journal of Human Evolution*, **18**: 373–92.

Susman, R. L. (1988a). Hand of *Paranthropus robustus* from Member 1, Swartkrans: fossil evidence for tool behavior. *Science*, **240**: 781–4.

(1988b). New postcranial remains from Swartkrans and their bearing on the functional morphology and behavior of *Paranthropus robustus*. In Grine, F. E. (ed.), *Evolutionary History of the 'Robust' Australopithecines*. New York: Aldine de Gruyter, pp. 149–72.

(1994). Fossil evidence for hominid tool use. *Science*, **265**: 1570–3.

Tanner, N. M. (1979). Gathering by females: the chimpanzee model revisited and the gathering hypothesis. In Kinzey, W. G. (ed.), *The Evolution of Human Behavior: Primate Models*. New York: SUNY Press, pp. 3–27.

(1981). *On Becoming Human*. Cambridge: Cambridge University Press.

Turner, C. G. II and Turner, J. A. (1998). *Man Corn: Cannibalism and Violence in the Prehistoric American Southwest*. Salt Lake City: University of Utah Press.

Vrba, E. S. (1975). Some evidence of the chronology and palaeoecology of Sterkfontein, Swartkrans and Kromdraai from the fossil Bovidae. *Nature*, **254**: 301–4.

(1976). *The Fossil Bovidae of Sterkfontein, Swartkrans and Kromdraai*. Pretoria: Transvaal Museum.

Walker, A. and Leakey, R. E. F. (eds.) (1993). *The Nariokotome* Homo erectus *Skeleton*. Cambridge: Harvard University Press.

Walker, A. C. and Shipman, P. (1996). *The Wisdom of the Bones: in Search of Human Origins*. New York: Alfred A. Knopf.

White, T. D. (1986). Cutmarks on the Bodo cranium: a case of prehistoric defleshing. *American Journal of Physical Anthropology*, **69**: 503–9.

(1992). *Prehistoric Cannibalism at Mancos 5MTUMR-2346*. Princeton: Princeton University Press.

25 Shared intention in early artefacts: an exploration of deep structure and implications for communication and language

JOHN A. J. GOWLETT

Abstract

Recent researches in neurosciences and comparative primatology have reinforced appreciation of the importance of object manipulation and artefact use in the shaping of human intelligence, especially in the social contexts of shared knowledge. Archaeology has datasets of primary significance, which allow us to chart developments through time, and particularly the emergence or enhancement of shared concepts. When early Pleistocene artefacts are studied in sets, they exhibit some deep regularities that appear to show the operation of particular principles or concepts. The chapter uses African Acheulean datasets applying Principal Components Analysis (PCA) to explore the extent to which deeply seated elements of design form recur, whether under cultural control or reinforced by functional constraints. It highlights particular evidence that points towards shared activities and shared perceptions of rules, and the nature of the communications involved. The data are taken from sites ranging across Africa – Casablanca in the north, Kariandusi, Kilombe and Baringo in Kenya, and from two sites at Kalambo Falls in Zambia. The biface sets were measured by up to 11 variables. In general, three principal components emerge, with very similar characteristics. They indicate that the toolmakers tended to handle thickness separately from planform, to keep the butt region of the biface less variable than other areas, and to pay particular attention to the tip thickness. As this pattern is maintained almost regardless of the specific tool-form (hand-axe, cleaver, pick) and of site age, technology and refinement, it appears that the underlying concepts were strongly reinforced by external experience, as well as cultural tradition.

African Genesis: Perspectives on Hominin Evolution, eds. Sally C. Reynolds and Andrew Gallagher. Published by Cambridge University Press. © Cambridge University Press 2012.

Introduction

Artefacts – material culture – are projections of behaviour into the world. An essential point about their three-dimensional reality is that they are multi-variate, possessing at least several characteristics that the maker/user must manage. This fact makes artefacts valuable for evaluating the complexity of behaviour shared through cultural means (Wynn, 2002; Johnson-Frey, 2004; Gowlett, 2006, 2009). Even modern humans are not too good at the multivari-ate – handling more than three or four variables at once creates a processing bottleneck, to which we tend to respond by simplification. Indeed that is often the rationale for applying multivariate analytical techniques – they will take a large set of variables, and then for analysis and presentation aim to present the essentials as something like a two-dimensional plot. Early humans, however, were forced to deal with the pressures created by the multivariate nature of artefacts, probably sequencing their operations so that the shaping of essen-tial features did not create excessive cognitive load. Such elements can be explored in artefacts of early humans and for comparative purposes in apes (Joulian, 1996; Gowlett, 2002). This chapter uses PCA techniques to examine Acheulean datasets in the time range *c.* 1.1 to 0.2 Ma. They represent a good proportion of past human time, and also – it will be argued – clearly shared sets of needs and responses.

The approach is emphasised particularly because there is also a conceptual correlation between handling numbers of variables, and operating levels of intentionality, as studied in psychology. Levels of intentionality reflect the degree of insight and overview, as well as being closely linked with language in modern humans. Again, handling several levels of intentionality (I think he believes that you think…etc.) presents a heavy cognitive load (Kinderman *et al.*, 1998; Dunbar, 2004). For most people understanding collapses at around five levels of intentionality (Kinderman *et al.*, 1998). Similarly, it is difficult to consider interactions of more than four variables in artefacts (Gowlett, 2006).

Background: the social, the technical and the role of artefacts

Artefacts, the material record, should be ideal for these studies, but at times artefacts have been almost everything for archaeologists, so much so that their description (typology and technology) has been a barrier and irritation to other scientists. In the 1970s and 1980s, they came to have diminished importance, particularly with a strong focus on animal behaviour, and the dominance of a social archaeology (Hinde, 1979; Thorpe, 1979; Gamble, 1979). Early stone tools seemed to be technology that got in the way of a common framework of understanding. There are much stronger grounds for consensus now, in which to a surprising extent artefacts resume centre stage – well established now because of the agreed importance of tool-use in the great apes, and the extent of manipulations among other primates (Parker and Poti, 1990; McGrew, 1992; Boesch, 1993, 1996; Visalberghi and Limongelli, 1996; Whiten *et al.*, 1999, 2005; Mercader *et al.*, 2002; Sanz *et al.*, 2004).

Recent developments in neurosciences offer a much fuller evolutionary context. The discovery and studies of mirror neurons in monkeys emphasise the importance of understanding the activities of others, and the crucial importance of being able to share understanding of object manipulation (Gallese *et al.*, 1996, 2004; Rizzolatti and Arbib, 1998; Tettamanti *et al.*, 2005; Tomasello *et al.*, 2005). Furthermore, an important link is that the brain areas concerned appear to be those that lead to language in humans: it has been surmised that the precursor of Broca's area was endowed before speech evolved with a mechanism for recognising actions made by others (Rizzolatti and Arbib, 1998). More recently Tomasello and others have argued that this ability is central to the context of linguistic development (Tomasello and Rakocsy, 2003; Tomasello *et al.*, 2005).

For all the changes of emphasis just noted, some workers have argued the importance of artefacts in cognitive terms throughout. Holloway (1969) emphasised a role for the larger brain in concentration. Tobias (1981, 1991) placed an emphasis on hand–eye coordination – and feedback loops involving tool use. Wynn has explored many issues of concept handling (Wynn, 1979, 1985, 1995, 2002; cf. Wynn and McGrew, 1989), and the author and colleagues the importance of size transformations in showing the ability to project a single design at different scales (Gowlett, 1982, 1984, 1996; Crompton and Gowlett, 1993). There remain different views about the relationship between toolmaking processes and the processes of language production and use (Leroi-Gourhan, 1993), with Tobias and Holloway stressing similarities, and Wynn (e.g. 1985) emphasising differences.

Finally, the thrust of studies in evolutionary psychology has clearly had a huge social emphasis – first in terms of social competition models (Alexander, 1979, 1989), and then in terms of the management of social interactions (Byrne and Whiten, 1992; Dunbar, 1993, 1998, 2004). Despite efforts in gene-culture studies (e.g. Wilson, 1983, 1998) there is a great challenge remaining to integrate a social view of evolution with one that is technologically driven. This chapter addresses the need to work towards combined and interlinking models, stressing the theme of artefacts and shared intention, and aiming through studies of these concepts to explore the link with sociality and language. It argues that early artefacts allow us to monitor at least the emergence of shared concepts through the Pleistocene.

The archaeological record and shared intention

Artefacts of the Oldowan and Acheulean in the time range 2.5 to 0.2 Ma provide extensive records that allow archaeology to keep up with the developments described above (Figure 25.1). Although the point is not often drawn out, they show evidence of shared intention in a number of important respects. It is shown, for example, in the systematic group work necessary for early hominins in finding and moving large quantities of raw materials over long distances. When hundreds of kilograms of artefacts are transported over many kilometres, it has to be seen as a joint exercise in which there are mutual understandings. The systematic activities have to be seen as strategic, and could not realistically be explained as 'multiple individual intention'. There is similar shared purpose in activities of use – shown when large numbers of artefacts are found together, as on the major Acheulean sites, or even when tools cluster around a single animal carcass in numbers too large to be made by one individual.

This chapter is more concerned with aspects of shared knowledge in the concepts of manufacture. The question of design form in the artefacts is closely bound to the nature of shared cultural information necessary for sustaining the activities, as well as to functional issues. Specific design form may be limited to a few elements in early Oldowan artefacts (Toth, 1985), but Acheulean industries (*c.* 1.7–0.15 Ma) are generally accepted to show far stronger patterning in manufacture, use and discard activities.

Artefacts are multivariate, and their manufacture is likely to involve multiple concepts (variables). One task is to find out how many variables or concepts were seen as important – an exercise in unravelling multidimensional thinking. Another is to establish how closely these pivotal ideas or concepts were shared. Among many possible approaches, it seems essential to examine dimensions or axes of variation, as these elements give some indication of complexity in design, and of the way in which variation was handled. In the course of hominin evolution, as language emerges, it might be expected that such variables would be firmed up or fine tuned via verbally labelled concepts. Experiments in neuroscience indicate that human subjects are able to recognise an object from a picture or from a written label equally quickly (cf. Lambon-Ralph *et al.*,

2001). Such results suggest that language is very closely mapped into object recognition and classification, and that a long evolutionary history for this linkage may be implied.

The form in tools is nearly always recognisable – to the extent that one individual can recognise the purpose of a tool made by another. (For L. A. White, this fell within the scope of 'symboling', see papers in White, 1987.) It implies a cognitive analysis of the properties of a tool, not necessarily at a conscious level. For example, it has been demonstrated that modern humans approach different tools (such as pliers or a hammer) differently with the hand according to an anticipation of the function (Johnson-Frey, 2004).

This principle of shared recognition appears to extend to chimpanzee technology. Certainly, when two chimpanzees are working together in termite fishing or ant dipping, Chimp A appears to know what Chimp B is using. In the case of ant dipping or termite fishing, the tools are likely to be based on the same selected plant species, trimmed to a similar length and similarly cleaned of side shoots (McGrew, 1992:170–5; Bermejo and Illera, 1999; Sanz *et al.*, 2004). The actions would imply culturally shared 'concepts' about key dimensions and properties, e.g. length, stoutness and smoothness (some might dispute this). Such culturally derived information might of course be refined or modified by individual experience, both in chimpanzees and humans. Among archaeologists problems of further analysis may be partly verbal, relating for example to differing ideas of what 'design' entails. A chimp seems well able to appreciate the significance of the butt end and tip end of a human artefact, and in tool use in the wild, may well have similar appreciations about its own artefacts. These can be seen as the simplest elements of design (emphasising once more the multivariate nature of even the most rudimentary artefact). The distinction between theoretically-held and practical design points is not therefore obvious: it seems likely that even simple forms of shared knowledge may be sufficient to convey and reinforce points that amount to design rules, and equally that such shared knowledge may be a necessity. The challenge is to isolate such rules, and provide evidence for them.

Biface measurements

The focus of this study is the Acheulean biface, but that focus does not diminish the importance of other artefacts and variability in the period (Dominguez-Rodrigo *et al.*, 2002; de la Torre *et al.*, 2003) or of ethnographic studies on somewhat comparable tools (Stout, 2002). In popular literature, the bifaces are often regarded as all the same, but all Palaeolithic archaeologists are aware of their variation. Acheulean artefacts, although made in the distant past, allow us much fuller opportunities to explore some problems of managing 'multivariate load'. They give an essential continuity through the period from about 1.7 million to *c.* 150 000 years ago. They also embody various design features, which indicate that the multivariate challenge for early humans was much more demanding than for ape artefacts, although these present similar issues (Gowlett, 2009).

Acheulean bifaces have been studied through measurement schemes since the 1950s. There is no need to recapitulate beyond expressing that the schemes ideally throw a mesh around the bifaces in a consistent way, which gives enough detail to the study. This study is based on a standard scheme following the measurements used by Isaac (1968, 1977) at Olorgesailie, and largely coinciding with those used by Roe (1964, 1968). The approach relies on initial identification of a long axis by the measurer; breadth and thickness measurements are taken at intervals in relation to this long axis. Not surprisingly the approach can now be bettered in many ways, as fully digitised images become available, but it is still useful for comparative consistency across numerous collections.

There is, of course, a danger of taking more measurements than have any real-world significance. Ideally one would hope to identify and measure the variations that were important to the makers. There are, however, few landmarks in the sense that often applies in biology. Length, breadth and thickness have obvious real importance, as does weight. Most other characteristics that are chosen for study may or may not correspond to features seen as important by the makers – the study is aimed to elucidate those that were.

The role of variation

Why should the artefacts vary, and why indeed should they vary in similar ways, as is the case with many different biface sets? The chief causes normally given are:

Function – e.g. the nature of the edge required for particular tasks
Raw material – affecting size, edge and finish
Style – aspects chosen to be done one way, which could also be done in other ways

To these can be added 'individual need/preference' (Gowlett, 1996). It could be argued that this last is a consequence of the first three. As every artefact is made by an individual, the individual will always need to balance the potential challenges and opportunities of the situation. Somewhat similarly, Sackett argues that style is the perfect complement of function (Sackett, 1977, 1982). In one sense anything that is determined by function cannot be determined by style, but in another, style represents the choice of ways of approaching function. Taking this view, raw material variation would appear to be subsidiary, rather than an equal factor.

Size variation is consistently a major aspect of biface variation – nearly all assemblages vary through a factor of three in linear dimensions. At Kilombe, for example, the range is approximately 8 to 24 cm in length. Here the makers encountered a challenge – how to reconcile weight with linear dimensions. Essentially, doubling linear dimension entails weight rising by a factor of eight, unless design compensations are made, such as making long specimens thinner (Crompton and Gowlett, 1993).

However it is that these factors relate to one another, it is unquestionable that some degree of variation matters to all archaeologists. For example: some authors see 'weak' and 'strong' cultural traditions, perhaps in different environments (e.g. Mithen, 1996; McNabb *et al.*, 2004). Archaeologists often wonder whether/how the late Sangoan fits in the Acheulean (McBrearty, 1988; Clark, 2001: 643) and how far 'true' Acheulean extends as a single tradition in time and space (Lycett and Gowlett, 2008). Questions arise especially at the geographic margins of the biface distribution, for example in the Far East (Hou *et al.*, 2000; Norton *et al.*, 2006; Lycett and Bae, 2010), or in NW Europe (Monnier, 1996; Wenban-Smith, 1998; White, 2000). We have seen that the bifaces can be measured by a set of chosen attributes. But are these real variables? How can the issue be tested, when there is nobody to tell us about their importance? The key points are that the bifaces may show different degrees of control in different parts of the specimen. By recognising this, we might be able to partition variation, so as to recognise concepts and goals underlying the manufacturing process.

Principal Components Analysis (PCA) has been selected as a tool for this analysis, because of the insights that it provides into axes of variation within multivariate datasets. It has limitations as well as strengths, but its principal benefit is that it reduces complex datasets to a series of new components that better explain the variation within the dataset. The technique has been described many times since its early applications (Marriott, 1974; Kendall, 1975). From the starting set of variables, it makes a new series of variables which 'mop up' variance in descending order, and are uncorrelated with one another. The hope here is that the technique may allow us to depart from our own arbitrarily selected variables, and to identify larger patterns of variation, as axes or components, within the dataset that might indicate which sets of characteristics were important to the makers. There are of course some caveats – PCA is merely a tool, with distinct limitations.

It is important to say what PCA does and does not do. The technique is not an index of design complexity per se. As an illustration, one can take a complex object, such as a statue, and a simple brick, and vary them in scale (only). However complex the object, and however many attributes are measured, a PCA will account for all the variance, which is simply related to size, and not shape. If a set of hand-axes is generated that vary isometrically (in scale only), then a single principal component would explain 100% of all variation. On the other hand, even in a simple object, if there are aspects of both size and shape variation present, then these will emerge as separate components (as happens if the simple bricks have different proportions).

The analyses are presented visually as a percentage of original variance accounted for by the first three components, and also as selected scatter plots of components two and three (see Figures 25.2 to 25.4). Plots of all individual specimens against components have not been given, because of the large numbers and the large overlaps. A combined analysis of all the samples could have been set up, but it seemed preferable to run a separate analysis for each biface set. In this way, if similar features recur from assemblage to assemblage, it is evident that they do so because they occur independently, not because they are all in some way products of the common analysis. *A priori*, the separate assemblages could vary in all kinds of different ways.

In biological analyses, it is often assumed that the first principal component (PC1) will represent size variation alone, and can be discarded for the purpose of standardisation. Then, the main interest comes from a plot of PC2 and PC3, which are taken to reflect primarily shape variation. In a biological organism, there may be definite landmarks, and restrictions on the nature of three-dimensional variation. The same need not be the case for artefacts – landmarks may not be fixed (but need investigation), and the maker may have wide latitude to make major variations in some particular variable. Hence – as found here – PC1 may contain important information. The approach of plotting of the PC2 against the PC3 was also tested, however, with useful results.

The dataset

The dataset provides a quite broad sampling of the African Acheulean, both geographically, in time range and by raw materials (Figure 25.1). The two Kalambo Falls assemblages are the most southerly samples, the Casablanca assemblages the most northern. The oldest assemblages, from Kariandusi, are aged probably a little over one million years (Gowlett and Crompton, 1994; Evernden and Curtis, 1965; Trauth *et al.*, 2005). The youngest is likely to be

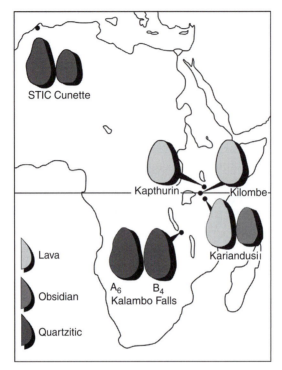

Figure 25.1. The biface datasets seen against a map of Africa. The symbols indicate relative size, planshape and raw material of each assemblage.

that from Kapthurin, at around 280 000 years (Deino and McBrearty, 2002). In all, then, the series ranges through approximately 60% of the total Acheulean time range. The Kilombe series are towards the older end of the spectrum, and have the value of measuring contemporary variation on one extensive site (Gowlett, 2005). The dataset includes three local pairings of very different assemblages (Figure 25.1).

The Kariandusi assemblages are most likely the oldest (Evernden and Curtis, 1965; Gowlett and Crompton, 1994). They are based on local trachyte lava in the case of the lower site, and on obsidian, probably from Mount Eburu about 15 km away, in the case of the Upper site. Kariandusi was originally investigated by Louis Leakey. It lies to the east of the present-day Lake Elmenteita, and would have been close to the shore of a much larger and deeper Pleistocene lake occupying most of the Nakuru-Elmenteita basin (perhaps similar to the early Holocene lake). The lower site was found in the 1970s; it is slightly lower in the sequence of pumice gravels that overlies diatomite and tuffs, but is likely to be of broadly similar age (Gowlett and Crompton, 1994).

Table 25.1. *Key data for all biface localities. Figures for length, and the thickness/breadth ratio are means and standard deviations. Thickness and breadth were treated separately in the analyses, but are presented as a ratio here for easy interpretation.*

Locality	Number	Length (mm)	Thickness/ breadth ratio	PC1 (%)	PC2 (%)	PC3 (%)
Kilombe EH	106	152 ± 31	0.47 ± 0.11	60	25	6
Kilombe AH	36	151 ± 41	0.44 ± 0.16	65	17	6
Kilombe AC/AD	121	150 ± 30	0.47 ± 0.09	61	16	13
Kilombe Z	18	161 ± 26	0.55 ± 0.12	54	16	14
Kilombe MM	33	142 ± 28	0.56 ± 0.11	55	18	9
Kilombe DJ	12	144 ± 24	0.42 ± 0.08	68	17	7
Kalambo Falls A6	47	169 ± 26	0.46 ± 0.11	42	21	16
Kalambo Falls B	25	170 ± 52	0.54 ± 0.15	65	22	6
Kariandusi obsidian	60	125 ± 24	0.47 ± 0.07	60	16	8
Kariandusi lava	126	164 ± 22	0.52 ± 0.11	39	23	14
Kapthurin	35	147 ± 39	0.40 ± 0.17	66	22	7
Sidi Abderrahman STIC	299	161 ± 29	0.60 ± 0.15	47	16	15
Sidi Abderrahman Cunette D2	126	114 ± 39	0.47 ± 0.09	78	10	6

The next pairing comes from Morocco. The Casablanca sites were explored and described by P. Biberson (1961). Later investigations have been conducted by Raynal and colleagues (Raynal and Texier, 1989; Raynal *et al.*, 1995; Geraads *et al.*, 2004). The STIC site is stratified below the 'Grand Dune H' of Sidi Abderrahman. Later, sea caves were eroded in this great consolidated dune. The Cunette D2 assemblage comes from the filling within one of the caves. Both of these Casablanca series are based on quartzitic rocks, but they show completely different approaches to refinement. The early STIC series is simply made, mainly from large flakes from which just a few further flakes were removed, but also with a good proportion of cobble blanks, often retaining cortex on the butt. The Cunette D2 bifaces in contrast are very well made and relatively small (in most analyses they appear very similar to the Kariandusi obsidian series (Tables 25.1 and 25.2).

The third pairing comes from Kalambo Falls in Zambia, where again the rocks are chiefly quartzitic (Clark, 2001: 63). The Kalambo Falls sites lie in a small basin just above the point that the river plunges down to Lake Tanganyika. They have been described definitively by Clark (2001) following many studies. A series of Acheulean sites is overlain by a further series described as belonging to the Sangoan tradition.

One of the Kalambo sets studied is designated as Acheulean (A6), the other as Sangoan (B4). Even after repeated recent studies it is far from certain that

Table 25.2. *Eigenvalues correspond with the percentage variance accounted for, as shown in Table 25.1. In PCA a component is often taken as significant if it accounts for more variance than one of the original variables on average (i.e. for 10 variables 100%/10 = 10% or eigenvalue of 1.0). PC1 and PC2 show a far stronger pattern than this. PC3 is here taken as significant as it recurs in similar form in numbers of separate samples.*

Locality	Number of specimens	Number of variables	Eigenvalue PC1	Eigenvalue PC2	Eigenvalue PC3
Kilombe EH	106	11	6.64	2.77	0.66
Kilombe AH	36	11	7.12	1.92	0.67
Kilombe AC/AD	121	9	5.50	1.44	1.13
Kilombe Z	18	11	5.89	1.80	1.50
Kilombe MM	33	11	6.08	1.99	1.01
Kilombe DJ	12	11	7.45	1.85	0.72
Kalambo Falls A6	47	11	4.62	2.32	1.80
Kalambo Falls B	25	11	7.12	2.41	0.71
Kariandusi obsidian	60	11	6.55	1.80	0.89
Kariandusi lava	126	11	4.25	2.54	1.53
Kapthurin	35	10	6.58	2.21	0.66
Sidi Abderrahman STIC	299	10	4.73	1.60	1.52
Sidi Abderrahman Cunette D2	126	9	7.02	0.90	0.53

the Sangoan is a unified or homogeneous phenomenon. It is known originally from Uganda, but best defined through the work at Kalambo Falls (Clark, 2001), and in western Kenya (cf. McBrearty, 1988). The Kalambo occurrences may, however, be older than usually suspected, and it has not been clearly demonstrated that the heavy-duty Sangoan features, including core axes, come only at the end of the Acheulean. A cluster analysis of the Sangoan assemblages from Kalambo distinguished clearly between large heavy pick-like specimens, and ordinary bifaces indistinguishable from the Acheulean *sensu lato* (Gowlett *et al.*, 2001). In this instance, then, the Sangoan is a 'classic' Acheulean plus heavy core-axes. There are signs of a similar heavy component at Kilombe, and at other sites, so it must yet be retained as a hypothesis that the Sangoan is simply an Acheulean facies.

The other sites come from the central Rift Valley in Kenya. Kilombe lies about 50 km north of Kariandusi, and Kapthurin in the Baringo basin about 80 km north again. The assemblages are made from fine-grained lavas. At Kilombe the main rock is a local trachyphonolite, and a trachyte was also used from the base of Kilombe mountain several kilometres away (Bishop, 1978; Gowlett, 2005).

Kilombe was discovered in the 1970s and it is estimated to date between 1.0 to 0.8 Ma. Unlike most sites, the finds are distributed across a clayey surface, sealed in by a volcanic tuff. The outstanding value of the site lies in the insights that it provides into contemporaneous variation across a local palaeolandscape preserved over distances of some hundreds of metres (Gowlett, 2005). So far this circumstance is almost unique and scarcely represented in other Acheulean sites. The sites are probably distributed in a broad drainageway at the edge of standing water. In total seven different biface assemblages have been sampled and studied (augmented in new studies in 2009–10).

The Kapthurin sites have been known since the 1960s and the assemblages are well known from recent investigation, representing a late Acheulean industry with Levallois technique used for the production of both bifaces and flakes, and dating to about 280 000 years ago (McBrearty *et al.*, 1996; McBrearty, 1999; Deino and McBrearty, 2002). The dataset of bifaces used in the study is as in Leakey *et al.* (1969).

Interpretation

Analyses of the results shows both impressive consistencies of pattern, and some significant differences. The various Kilombe assemblages show a very similar pattern (Figure 25.2).

The first principal component (PC1) – shows how far isometric variation is approached, and which variables depart from it most. In the great majority of samples the variables defining biface planform (length, breadth, breadth at 0.2, 0.5 and 0.8 of length from butt) are very strongly represented in PC1, with usually 70 to 80% of variance accounted for (Figures 25.2 and 25.3). In contrast, the thickness variables – four in number – are far less accounted for (usually less than half of total variance). These findings indicate that basic planform varies largely isometrically in most characters, but that thickness variation is affected by at least one other major influence. In the second principal component (PC2) this thickness element is normally strongly expressed. PC2 also generally appears to map elements of allometry (including probably a change in breadth–length relation with size: cf. Crompton and Gowlett, 1993). It appears to be consistently 'the same' component in most of the sets, with variable loadings seriated in a similar order. The third principal component (PC3) appears to separate the different areas of a biface from butt to tip, often with width at the butt (BB) at one extreme, and thickness at the tip (TA) at the other.

Plots of both PC2 and PC3 are informative for showing the relationships of variables, especially as the underlying pattern shows through minor rotations

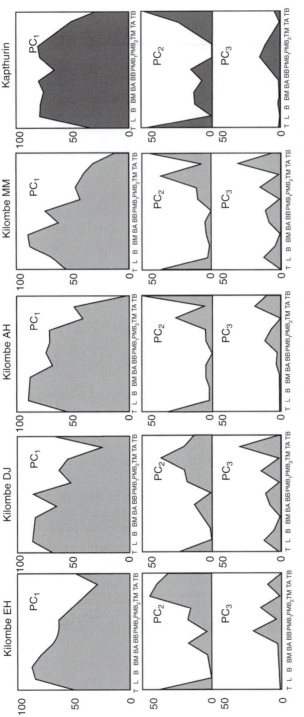

Figure 25.2. Graphical plot of PC1, PC2 and PC3 for four Kilombe assemblages and for the much later Baringo Kapthurin. For each principal component the loading or contribution of each original variable is shown as a percentage of variance accounted for.

Variables: T Thickness; L Length; B Breadth; BM Breadth at 0.5 L; BA Breadth at 0.8 L (from butt); BB Breadth at 0.2 L; PMB1 Point of maximum breadth (first side); PMB2 Point of maximum breadth (second side); TM Thickness at 0.5 L; TA Thickness at 0.8 L; TB Thickness at 0.2 L.

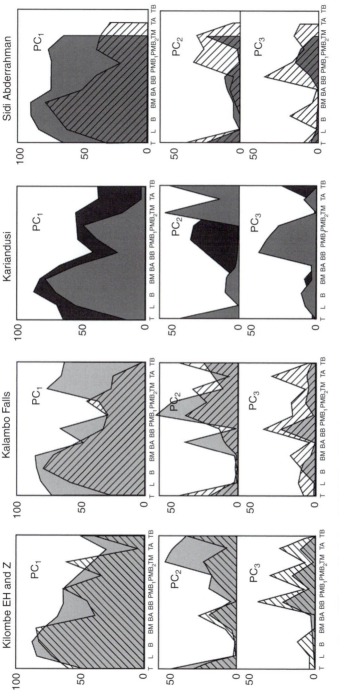

Figure 25.3. Graphical plot of PC1, PC2 and PC3 for several sites, which allow examination of pairs of assemblages: Kilombe, Kariandusi, Kalambo Falls and Sidi Abderrahman.

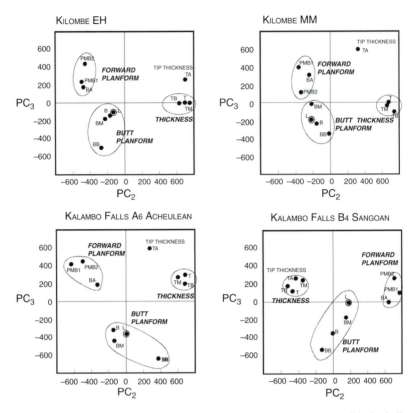

Figure 25.4. Plot of PC2 versus PC3 for four assemblages. Note the strikingly similar patterns of variables (in the fourth diagram PC2 mirrors the arrangement in the other sets). TA, thickness near the tip, is conspicuously separated, except in the Sangoan assemblage.

and inversions. In the examples given (Figure 25.4), the pattern is remarkably consistent from assemblage to assemblage.

A major outcome of the analysis is that, time and again, thickness at the tip is seen to be a very different element from thickness of the piece as a whole (Figure 25.5). That becomes especially apparent when the second and third components are plotted against each other. The two exceptions are: first, occasionally TA is so strongly differentiated that it draws its own separate component; and, second, in the assemblages with heavy-duty picks, there is much less evidence of thinning near the tip.

In PCA, a component is usually regarded as insignificant, or uninformative, if it accounts for less variance than one of the original variables. Among the bifaces, there is rarely a fourth component (PC4) making any substantial

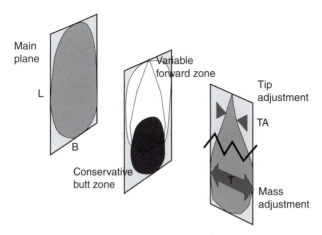

Figure 25.5. An interpretation of the meaning of data in the principal components extracted: the paper argues for a fairly 'locked' basic planform, conjunction of conservative butt area and variable 'front end', for a main thickness consideration that provides appropriate mass, and a second thickness consideration that adjusts tip thickness.

contribution to variance. Does this mean that just three 'axes' of variation account for most of the variation that we see in bifaces? The answer would be no. They are three dimensions of variation now firmly and repeatedly established, but they are only part of the whole picture. They have to be added to other obvious individual variables such as length, breadth and thickness, each of which might be separately appreciated by the makers. The components, that are so consistent from assemblage to assemblage, can be interpreted as additional but fundamental rule packages transmitted as learned information.

Conclusions

Shared intention – even collective intention – is very clearly demonstrated in Acheulean artefacts, in the overall strategy of manufacture, and in the systematic process of both manufacture and use. The whole process of manufacture–use–discard was extended in space and time, having an immediate scale of days and many kilometres for individual groups on their landscapes, and must therefore have embraced various sets of shared concepts. The analysis focused more specifically on sets of Acheulean bifaces, separating those from each locality. A set of concepts is needed for the manufacture of a biface, or it could not be a biface, but an issue was to explore how closely these are shared. The analyses showed that even within single sets of bifaces there are deep patterns.

It demonstrated that most of these specific concepts recur, sometimes in strikingly similar fashion, on far-distant sites. There are two points to highlight: first, the consistency of the patterns can be accounted for by postulating that the makers needed to deal with bundles of characteristics that were each quite necessary in the artefacts, and which therefore tend to recur as similar constellations of variables or attributes. Second, the considerable cognitive load of achieving control, so as to 'engineer' these bundles as artefacts, was one that had to pay off in selective terms. As modern humans find it difficult to oversee several variables at the same time, it seems reasonable to infer that the task was at least as difficult for earlier hominins (Gowlett, 2006). Ancient humans were, however, able to manage around four or five variables at the same time, by setting up their position very carefully (Figure 25.6). At best, well struck

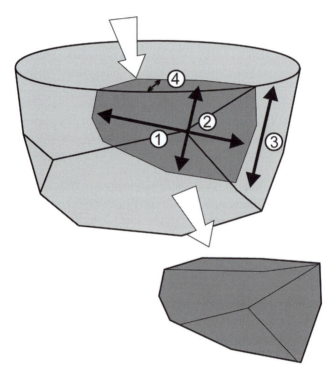

Figure 25.6. The multivariate problem illustrated by an idealised view of the striking of a large biface blank from a core. The result is a flake 15 to 20 cm long, with the essential form of a biface. Although modern humans find difficulty in dealing with several variables at the same time, adjustment of the core and of the striking position allowed the setting up of a single strike, such that the resulting artefact would be highly controlled in form, in at least five variables. This control was often achieved so successfully that the resulting piece has very little secondary trimming.

Acheulean biface blanks achieve control of length, breadth, thickness, tip-thickness and edge, all from one blow.

The Acheulean extends over a huge domain. There is thus an issue of 'how' the concepts were shared. Were they entirely transmitted culturally, or were they reinforced deterministically by use needs? Perhaps these are not altogether alternatives: in a system of strong cultural transmission there can nevertheless be strong constraints to cultural drift in the form of inescapable realities. Thus in a modern context, someone may tell me 'don't make it too thin'. I may also discover through rare errors that if I make it too thin, it breaks/does not work, etc. The cultural message would thus be reinforced ('I ought to have listened…'), or discarded if inappropriate. The word 'concept' in neuroscience is taken to be an idea or notion that is held within the brain, built up and reinforced by external experience. In modern human language, words that are rarely used are found to be vulnerable to dropping out of the concept system (Lambon-Ralph *et al.*, 2001). If, as the analyses show, the same concepts are repeated through a million years, it can only be because they are reinforced through repeated experience. That is, Acheulean bifaces are so similar in deep structure across vast areas of space and time, probably because makers were forced to take into account similar sets of requirements, time and again. We start from the point of a stone tool needing a good deal of mass, and with a longitudinal extension that allows both application of force and leverage. The analyses strongly suggest that even when bifaces are not superficially similar, they share elements of pattern that are deeply embedded. To a large extent these transcend factors such as refinement of finish, or proportions of hand-axes to cleavers. Yet, as the deep pattern unites sets of bifaces that look very different, it follows that the 'socio-technological packaging' of a locally prevalent industry depends on a further set of social conventions, more potentially alterable than the deep-seated ones. These might include more superficial aspects of style.

Further detailed study might do more to isolate these, but the overall 'shape' of the Acheulean in time and space has not been much explored, with rare exceptions (e.g. Wynn and Tierson, 1990; Noll and Petraglia, 2003; Lycett and Gowlett, 2008). Those papers suggest that there may be true regional variations, both in shape and technical habits. Along the timescale, it seems that through the middle part of Acheulean time (to which most of the assemblages studied here belong), there was little change, at least from about 1.0 to 0.4 Ma (Leakey, 1971; Isaac, 1977). The earliest bifaces may have been systematically thicker, as shown by Olduvai EF-HR and by the Ubeidiya samples from Israel (Leakey, 1971; Bar-Yosef and Goren-Inbar, 1993). Caution is necessary, however – Kilombe, for example, shows variation in thickness/breadth ratios between 0.56 and 0.35 in different areas that are contemporary (Gowlett, 2005), demolishing the idea that thickness/breath is an index of either refinement or chronology. It would be useful to make further comparisons with non-African material to determine how widely similar characters are shared (see e.g. Ashton and McNabb, 1994; Goren-Inbar and Saragusti, 1996; Gamble and Marshall, 2001; Noll and Petraglia, 2003; McPherron, 2006; Petraglia and Shipton, 2008).

In the later Acheulean, it has been demonstrated that bifaces became generally smaller, also with a shape shift that may reflect the allometry of smaller specimens (Gilead, 1970; Crompton and Gowlett, 1994; McPherron, 2000, 2006). The Sangoan phenomenon recognised in Africa seems to run counter to this trend, since it is characterised by heavy core-axes and picks. J. D. Clark explained these as wood-working tools, signs of a more recent human expansion into the forests (Clark, 1959, 2001). The analyses presented here bolster the idea that this 'Sangoan' pattern can occur alongside Acheulean and within it.

It would be surprising if questions did not remain about the nature and extent of shared intention in early artefacts. Shared intention is strongly documented in chimpanzees in the wild, shown especially well in boundary patrols. The chimps are aware of their role, and maintain silence and vigilance accordingly (Goodall *et al.*, 1979). Similar shared intention is shown by early humans in the transport of masses of raw material, as already noted. Does the artefact evidence show us something further? One could contend that it shows us merely repeated pattern. After all, individuals make stone tools for individual purpose. I would argue, however, that the constellations of concepts demonstrated in bifaces could only be handled in a functioning society by groups of interacting individuals, conscious of group norms and group needs. Members of a task group manufacturing a set of bifaces for butchery (for example), might be aware of their distinct individual roles, and tailor their products appropriately. Research on small sets of bifaces from good contexts might elucidate whether or not they are simply random samples of larger populations such as those analysed here.

After the Acheulean, the principles of concept-sets and transformations (variable manipulations) underlie many later developments in technology. For the most part these are similarly socially mediated. Do the results take us closer to understanding whether the sets of concepts correlate with spoken language? In the case of bifaces the principles extend too widely to relate to any one language. Their number and their definiteness are, however, redolent of language, and crucially they are externally projected or imposed 'outside the head'. Theory of mind is largely about mind reading, but language is largely about externalisation, in the cause of linking insulated minds. Artefacts that demonstrate externalisation of similar concepts at least fit into a similar scenario. Arguably it is more important to have this evidence of systematic or collective social communication than to be able to demonstrate the specific channels of communication, especially considering that the roles of visual and language-based learning are not easily partitioned even in modern humans.

Acknowledgements

I would like to express thanks to the Royal Society for conference support. The late P. Biberson and the late J. D. Clark gave permission for studies based on their data, and much encouragement. I am also grateful to Derek Roe, especially for making measurements available from Kalambo Falls material; to Andy Gallagher, Francis Thackeray, Stephen Lycett, Terry Hopkinson and Chris Henshilwood for discussion and/or suggestions; and particularly to Sally Reynolds. At various stages research has been supported by the British Academy and AHRC. In relation to work at Kilombe and Kariandusi I also thank National Museums and Government of Kenya, Maura Butler, and Ray and Barbara Terry.

References

Alexander, R. D. (1979). *Darwinism and Human Affairs*. London: Pitman.
  (1989). Evolution of the human psyche. In Mellars, P. and Stringer C., (eds). *The Human Revolution: Behavioural and Biological Perspectives on the Origins of Modern Humans*. pp. 455–513. Edinburgh: Edinburgh University Press.
Ashton, N. M. and McNabb, J. (1994). Bifaces in perspective. In: Ashton, N. and David, A., (eds). *Stories in Stone*. pp. 182–191. London: Lithic Studies Society.
Bar-Yosef, O. and Goren-Inbar, N. (1993). The Lithic Assemblages of 'Ubeidiya: a Lower Palaeolithic Site in the Jordan Valley. Qedem, Monographs of the Institute of Archaeology, Hebrew University of Jerusalem, No. 34.
Bermejo, M. and Illera, G. (1999). Tool-set for termite-fishing and honey extraction by wild chimpanzees in the Lossi Forest, Congo. *Primates*, **40**: 619–27.
Biberson, P. (1961). Le Paléolithique inférieur du Maroc atlantique. Rabat: Publications du Service des Antiquités du Maroc, Fascicule 17.
Bishop, W. W. (1978). Geological framework of the Kilombe Acheulian Site, Kenya. In Bishop, W. W. (ed.), *Geological Background to Fossil Man*. Edinburgh: Edinburgh University Press, pp. 329–36.
Boesch, C. (1993). Aspects of transmission of tool use in wild chimpanzees. In Gibson, K. and Imgold, T. (eds.), *Tools, Language and Cognition in Human Evolution*. Cambridge: Cambridge University Press, pp. 171–83.
  (1996). Three approaches for assessing chimpanzee culture. In Russon, A. E., Bard, K. and Parker, S. T. (eds.), *Reaching into Thought: the Minds of the Great Apes*. Cambridge: Cambridge University Press, pp. 404–29.
Byrne, R. W. and Whiten, A. (1992). Cognitive evolution in primates: evidence from tactical deception. *Man*, **27**: 609–27.

Clark, J. D. (1959). *The Prehistory of Southern Africa*. Harmondsworth: Penguin.

(ed.) (2001). *Kalambo Falls*, Volume 3. Cambridge: Cambridge University Press.

Crompton, R. H. and Gowlett, J. A. J. (1993). Allometry and multidimensional form in Acheulean bifaces from Kilombe, Kenya. *Journal of Human Evolution*, **25**: 175–99.

de la Torre, I., Mora, R., Domínguez-Rodrigo, M. *et al.* (2003). The Oldowan industry of Peninj and its bearing on the reconstruction of the technological skills of Lower Pleistocene hominids. *Journal of Human Evolution*, **44**: 203–24.

Deino, A. L. and McBrearty, S (2002). 40Ar/39Ar dating of the Kapthurin Formation, Baringo, Kenya. *Journal of Human Evolution*, **42**: 185–210.

Domínguez-Rodrigo, M., de la Torre, I., Luque, L. *et al.* (2002). The ST site complex at Peninj, West Lake Natron, Tanzania: implications for early hominid behavioural models. *Journal of Archaeological Science*, **29**: 639–65.

Dunbar, R. (1993). Coevolution of neocortex size, group size and language in humans. *Behavioral and Brain Sciences*, **16**: 681–735.

(1998). The social brain hypothesis. *Evolutionary Anthropology*, **6**: 178–90.

Dunbar, R. I. M. (2004). *The Human Story*. London: Faber and Faber.

Evernden, J. F. and Curtis, G. H. (1965). Potassium-argon dating of late Cenozoic rocks in East Africa and Italy. *Current Anthropology*, **6**: 343–85.

Gallese, V., Fadiga, L., Fogassi, L. *et al.* (1996). Action recognition in the premotor cortex. *Brain*, **119**: 593–609.

Gallese, V., Keysers, C. and Rizzolatti, G. (2004). A unifying view of the basis of social cognition. *Trends in Cognitive Sciences*, **8**: 396–403.

Gamble, C. S. (1979). Hunting strategies in the central European Palaeolithic. *Proceedings of the Prehistoric Society*, **45**: 35–52.

Gamble, C. S. and Marshall, G. D. (2001). The shape of handaxes, the structure of the Acheulian World. In Milliken, S. and Cook, J. (eds.), *A Very Remote Period Indeed: Papers on the Palaeolithic Presented to Derek Roe*. Oxford, Oxbow Books, pp. 19–27.

Geraads, D., Raynal, J. P. and Eisenmann, V. (2004). The earliest human occupation of North Africa: a reply to Sahnouni *et al.* (2002). *Journal of Human Evolution*, **46**: 751–61.

Gilead, D. (1970). Handaxe industries in Israel and the Near East. *World Archaeology*, **2**: 1–11.

Goodall, J., Bandora, A., Bergmann, E. *et al.* (1979). Intercommunity interactions in the chimpanzee population of the Gombe National Park. In Hamburg D. A. and McCown, E. R. (eds.), *The Great Apes*. Menlo Park, CA: Benjamin, pp 13–53.

Goren-Inbar, N. and Saragusti, I. (1996). An Acheulian biface assemblage from the site of Gesher Benot Ya'aqov, Israel: indications of African affinities. *Journal of Field Archaeology*, **23**, 15–30.

Gowlett, J. A. J. (1982). Procedure and form in a Lower Palaeolithic industry: stone-working at Kilombe, Kenya. *Studia Praehistorica Belgica*, **2**: 101–9.

(1984). Mental abilities of early man: a look at some hard evidence. In Foley, R. A. (ed.), *Hominid Evolution and Community Ecology*. London: Academic Press, pp. 167–92.

(1996). Rule systems in the artefacts of *Homo erectus* and early *Homo sapiens*: constrained or chosen. In Mellars, P. and Gibson, K. (eds.), *Modelling the Early Human Mind*. Cambridge: McDonald Institute for Archaeological Research, pp. 191–215.

(2002). Apes, hominids and technology. In Harcourt, C. S. and Sherwood, B. R. (eds.), *New Perspectives in Primate Evolution and Behaviour*. Otley, West Yorkshire: Westbury Academic, pp. 147–71.

(2005). Seeking the Palaeolithic individual in East Africa and Europe during the Lower-Middle Pleistocene. In Gamble, C. S. and Porr, M. (eds.), *The Hominid Individual in Context: Archaeological Investigations of Lower and Middle Palaeolithic Landscapes, Locales and Artefacts*. London: Routledge, pp. 50–67.

(2006). The elements of design form in Acheulian bifaces: modes, modalities, rules and language. In Goren-Inbar, N. and Sharon, G. (eds.), *Axe Age: Acheulian Toolmaking from Quarry to Discard*. London: Equinox, pp. 50–67.

(2009). Artefacts of apes, humans and others: towards comparative assessment. *Journal of Human Evolution*, **57**: 401–10.

Gowlett, J. A. J. and Crompton, R. H. (1994). Kariandusi: Acheulean morphology and the question of allometry. *African Archaeological Review*, **12**: 1–40.

Gowlett, J. A. J., Crompton, R. H. and Li Yu (2001). Allometric comparisons between Acheulean and Sangoan large cutting tools at Kalambo Falls. In Clark, J. D. (ed.), *Kalambo Falls Prehistoric Site, Volume 3: the Earlier Cultures: Middle and Earlier Stone Age*. Cambridge: Cambridge University Press, pp. 612–19.

Hinde, R. A. (1979). The nature of social structure. In Hamburg D. A. and McCown, E. R. (eds.), *The Great Apes*. Menlo Park, CA: Benjamin, pp. 295–315.

Holloway R. L. (1969). Culture: a human domain. *Current Anthropology*, **10**: 395–412.

Hou, Y., Potts, R., Yaun, B. *et al.* (2000). Mid-Pleistocene Acheulean-like stone technology of the Bose Basin, South China. *Science*, **287**: 1622–6.

Isaac, G. L. l. (1968). The Acheulian site complex at Olorgesailie: a contribution to the interpretation of Middle Pleistocene culture in East Africa. Unpublished PhD dissertation, University of Cambridge.

(1977). *Olorgesailie: Archaeological Studies of a Middle Pleistocene Lake Basin*. Chicago: University of Chicago Press.

Johnson-Frey, S. H. (2004). The neural bases of complex tool use in humans. *Trends in Cognitive Science*, **8**: 71–8.

Joulian, F. (1996). Comparing chimpanzee and early hominid techniques: some contributions to cultural and cognitive questions. In Mellars, P. and Gibson, K. (eds.), *Modelling the Early Human Mind*. Cambridge: McDonald Institute for Archaeological Research, pp. 173–89.

Kendall, M. G. (1975). *Multivariate Analysis*. London: Griffin.

Kinderman, P., Dunbar, R. I. M. and Bentall, R. P. (1998). Theory-of-mind deficits and causal attributions. *British Journal of Psychology*, **89**: 191–204.

Lambon-Ralph, M. A., McClelland, J. L., Patterson, K. *et al.* (2001). No right to speak? The relationship between object naming and semantic impairment:

neuropsychological evidence and a computational model. *Journal of Cognitive Neuroscience*, **13**: 341–56.

Leakey, M., Tobias, P. V., Martyn, J. E. *et al.* (1969). An Acheulian industry with prepared core technique and the discovery of a contemporary hominid at Lake Baringo, Kenya. *Proceedings of the Prehistoric Society*, **35**: 48–76.

Leakey, M. D. (1971). *Olduvai Gorge. Volume III. Excavations in Beds I and II, 1960–1963*. Cambridge: Cambridge University Press.

Leroi-Gourhan, A. (1993). *Gesture and Speech*. (Translation from the French by A. B. Berger). Cambridge, MA: October Books.

Lycett, S. J. and Bae, C. J. (2010). The Movius Line controversy: the state of the debate. *World Archaeology*, **42**: 521–44.

Lycett, S. J. and Gowlett, J. A. J. (2008). On questions surrounding the Acheulean 'tradition'. *World Archaeology*, **40**: 295–315.

McBrearty, S. (1988). The Sangoan-Lupemban and Middle Stone Age sequence at the Muguruk site, western Kenya. *World Archaeology*, **19**: 379–420.

(1999). The archaeology of the Kapthurin formation. In Andrews, P. and Banham, P. (eds.), *Late Cenozoic Environments and Hominid Evolution: a Tribute to Bill Bishop*. London: Geological Society of London, pp. 143–56.

McBrearty, S., Bishop, L. and Kingston, J. (1996). Variability in traces of Middle Pleistocene hominid behavior in the Kapthurin Formation, Baringo, Kenya. *Journal of Human Evolution*, **30**: 563–80.

McGrew, W. C. (1992). *Chimpanzee Material Culture: Implications for Human Evolution*. Cambridge: Cambridge University Press.

McNabb, J., Binyon, F. and Hazelwood, L. (2004). The large cutting tools from the South African Acheulean and the question of social traditions. *Current Anthropology*, **45**: 653–78.

McPherron, S. P. (2000). Handaxes as a measure of the mental capabilities of early hominids. *Journal of Archaeological Science*, **27**: 655–63.

(2006). What typology can tell us about Acheulian handaxe production. In Goren-Inbar, N. and Sharon, G. (eds.), *Axe Age: Acheulian Tool-making from Quarry to Discard*. London: Equinox, pp. 267–85.

Marriott, F. H. C. (1974). *The Interpretation of Multiple Observations*. London: Academic Press.

Mercader, J., Panger, M. and Boesch, C. (2002). Excavation of a chimpanzee stone tool site in the African rainforest. *Science*, **296**: 1452–5.

Mithen, S. (1996). Social learning and cultural tradition: interpreting early Palaeolithic technology. In Steele, J. and Shennan, S. (eds.), *The Archaeology of Human Ancestry: Power, Sex and Tradition*. London: Routledge, pp. 207–29.

Monnier, J. L. (1996). Acheuléen et industries archaïques dans le Nord-Ouest de la France. In Tuffreau, A. (ed.), *L'Acheuléen dans l'Ouest de l'Europe*Lille: Publications du CERP, Université des Sciences et Technologies de Lille, 4, pp. 145–53.

Noll, M. and Petraglia, M. P. (2003). Acheulean bifaces and early human behavioural patterns in East Africa and South India. In Soressi, M. and Dibble, H. (eds.), *Multiple Approaches to the Study of Bifacial Technologies*. Philadelphia: Museum of Archaeology and Anthropology, pp. 31–53.

Norton, C. J., Bae, K., Harris, J. W. K. *et al.* (2006). Middle Pleistocene handaxes from the Korean Peninsula. *Journal of Human Evolution*, **51**: 527–36.

Parker, S. T. and Poti, P. (1990). The role of innate motor patterns in ontogenetic and experiential development of intelligent use of sticks in cebus monkeys. In Parker, S.T. and Gibson, K. R. (eds.), *'Language' and Intelligence in Monkeys and Apes*. Cambridge: Cambridge University Press, pp. 219–43.

Petraglia, M. D. and Shipton, C. (2008). Large cutting tool variation west and east of the Movius Line. *Journal of Human Evolution*, **55**: 962–6.

Raynal, J.-P. and Texier, J.-P. (1989). Découverte d'Acheuléen ancien dans la Carrière Thomas 1 à Casablanca et problème de l'ancienneté de la présence humaine au Maroc. *Comptes Rendus Académie des Sciences Paris (Série II)*, **308**: 1743–9.

Raynal, J.-P., Magoga, L., Sbihi-Alaoui, F.-Z. *et al.* (1995). The earliest occupation of Atlantic Morocco: the Casablanca evidence. In Roebroeks, W. and van Kolfschoten, T. (eds.), The earliest occupation of Europe: Proceedings of the European Science Foundation Workshop at Tautavel (France), 1993. *Analecta Praehistorica Leidensia* 27. Leiden: University of Leiden, pp. 255–62.

Rizzolatti, G. and Arbib, M. A. (1998). Language within our grasp. *Trends in Neurosciences*, **21**: 188–94.

Roe, D. A. (1964). The British Lower and Middle Palaeolithic: some problems, methods of study and preliminary results. *Proceedings of the Prehistoric Society*, **30**: 245–67.

(1968). British Lower and Middle Palaeolithic handaxe groups. *Proceedings of the Prehistoric Society*, **34**: 1–82.

Sackett, J. R. (1977). The meaning of style in archaeology: a general model. *American Antiquity*, **42**: 369–80.

(1982). Approaches to style in lithic archaeology. *Journal of Anthropological Archaeology*, **1**: 59–122.

Sanz, C., Morgan, D. and Gulick, S. (2004). New insights into chimpanzees, tools, and termites from the Congo Basin. *American Naturalist*, **164**: 567–81.

Stout, D. (2002). Skill and cognition in stone tool production: an ethnographic case study from Irian Jaya. *Current Anthropology*, **43**(5): 693–722.

Tettamanti, M., Buccino, G., Saccuman, M. C. *et al.* (2005). Listening to action related sentences activates fronto-parietal motor circuits. *Journal of Cognitive Neuroscience*, **17**: 273–81.

Thorpe, W. H. (1979). *The Origins and Rise of Ethology*. London: Heinemann.

Tobias, P. V. (1981). The emergence of man in Africa and beyond. *Philosophical Transactions of the Royal Society of London, Series B*, **292**: 43–56.

(1991). The emergence of spoken language in hominid evolution. In Clark, J. D. (ed.), *Approaches to Understanding Early Hominid Life-ways in the African Savanna*. UISSP, 11 Kongress, Mainz 1987, Monographien Band 19. Bonn: Dr Rudolf Habelt, pp. 67–78.

Tomasello, M. and Rakocsy, H. (2003). What makes human cognition unique? From individual to shared to collective intentionality. *Mind and Language*, **18**: 121–47.

Tomasello, M., Carpenter, M., Call, J. *et al.* (2005). Understanding and sharing intentions: the origins of cultural cognition. *Behavioral and Brain Sciences*, **28**: 675–735.

Toth, N. (1985). The Oldowan reassessed: a close look at early stone artefacts. *Journal of Archaeological Science*, **12**: 101–21.

Trauth, M. H., Maslin, M. A., Deino, A. *et al.* (2005). Late Cenozoic moisture history of East Africa. *Science*, **309**: 2051–3.

Visalberghi, E. and Limongelli, L. (1996). Acting and understanding: tool-use revisited through the minds of capuchin monkeys. In Russon, A. E., Bard, K. and Parker, S.T. (eds.), *Reaching into Thought: the Minds of the Great Apes.* Cambridge: Cambridge University Press, pp. 404–29.

Wenban-Smith, F. (1998). Clactonian and Acheulian industries in Britain: their chronology and significance reconsidered. In Ashton, N. M., Healy, F., and Pettitt, P. (eds.), *Stone Age Archaeology. Essays in Honour of John Wymer.* Oxford: Oxbow Monograph 102, pp. 90–7.

White, L. A. (1987). Dillingham, B. and Carneiro, R. L. (eds.), *Leslie A. White's Ethnological Essays.* Albuquerque: University of New Mexico Press.

White, M. J. (2000). The Clactonian question: on the interpretation of core and flake assemblages in the British Isles. *Journal of World Prehistory*, **14**: 1–63.

Whiten, A., Goodall, J., McGrew, W. *et al.* (1999). Cultures in chimpanzees. *Nature*, **399**: 682–5.

Whiten, A., Horner, V. and de Waal, F. B. M. (2005). Conformity to cultural norms of tool use in chimpanzees. *Nature*, **437**: 737–40.

Wilson, E. O. (1983). Sociobiology and the Darwinian approach to mind and culture. In Bendall, D. S. (ed.), *Evolution from Molecules to Men.* Cambridge: Cambridge University Press, pp. 545–53.

(1998). *Consilience:the Unity of Knowledge.* London: Little, Brown.

Wynn, T. (1979). The intelligence of later Acheulian hominids. *Man*, **14**: 371–91.

(1985). Piaget, stone tools and the evolution of human intelligence. *World Archaeology*, **17**: 32–43.

(1995). Handaxe enigmas. *World Archaeology*, **27**: 10–24.

(2002). Archaeology and cognitive evolution. *Behavioural and Brain Sciences*, **25**: 389–438.

Wynn, T. and McGrew, W. C. (1989). An ape's view of the Oldowan. *Man*, **24**: 383–98.

Wynn, T. and Tierson, F. (1990). Regional comparison of the shapes of later Acheulean handaxes. *American Anthropologist*, **92**: 73–84.

26 Sibudu Cave: recent archaeological work on the Middle Stone Age

LYN WADLEY

Abstract

The Middle Stone Age (MSA) sequence at Sibudu Cave, KwaZulu-Natal, South Africa, includes pre-Still Bay, Still Bay and Howiesons Poort assemblages that pre-date 60 ka. More recent MSA lithic assemblages have ages of ~58 ka, ~48 ka and ~38 ka derived from luminescence dating of quartz grains. Discrete hearths and ash-patches are present throughout, while palimpsests of hearths characterise the ~48 ka occupations. The people who lived at Sibudu were skilled encounter-hunters who killed a wide range of animals of all sizes. Their prey included zebra and dangerous animals such as buffalo and bushpig. Unifacially or bifacially retouched lithic points were parts of weapons for hunting, but, sometimes, points seem to have been used as butchery implements. Use-trace analysis supports both interpretations. Points were absent during the Howiesons Poort Industry when small animals, from moist, evergreen forests, were the focus of hunters whose toolkits contained backed stone implements and worked bone. Bedding made from sedges seems present throughout the sequence. The environmental setting for cultural activities changed through time. Combined evidence from magnetic susceptibility, phytoliths, charcoal, pollen, seeds, mineralogy, macromammals and micromammals suggests that cold Marine Isotope Stage 4 (MIS 4) and warmer MIS 3 conditions are represented at the site. The changing temperatures, moisture availability and distance from the coast during MIS 4 and MIS 3 influenced vegetation, sediments and animal populations. Much of the sequence from ~58 ka onwards was associated with open grassland and with more large grazers than is the case in the area today. Proportions of evergreen and deciduous taxa fluctuated, with an increase of deciduous taxa possibly coinciding with warmer temperatures and increased evapotranspiration at ~48 ka.

African Genesis: Perspectives on Hominin Evolution, eds. Sally C. Reynolds and Andrew Gallagher. Published by Cambridge University Press. © Cambridge University Press 2012.

Introduction

Sibudu is a large rock shelter situated on the Tongati River, north of Durban
in KwaZulu-Natal, South Africa (Figures 26.1 and 26.2). The uppermost
occupation is from the Iron Age and directly below this is the MSA with a
long and detailed cultural sequence. Recent multidisciplinary archaeological
research has enabled reconstruction of the site's environmental conditions, its
cultural succession and its chronology (Allott, 2006; Cain, 2006; Cochrane,
2006; Delagnes *et al.*, 2006; Glenny, 2006; Herries, 2006; Lombard 2006a;b;
Pickering, 2006; Plug, 2006; Renaut and Bamford, 2006; Reynolds, 2006;
Schiegl and Conard, 2006; Sievers, 2006; Villa and Lenoir, 2006; Wadley,
2005, 2006; 2007; Wadley and Jacobs, 2006; Wells, 2006).

Sibudu is important not only because of its rich artefactual content and its
good organic preservation, which has encouraged multidisciplinary research,
but also because it is far from the Cape where most other MSA research is
being conducted. It therefore provides a cultural and environmental archive in
a setting quite different from that of the Cape sites. Furthermore, its sequence
includes extensive occupations from periods (~58 ka, ~48 ka and ~38 ka) that
are not well represented at other South African MSA sites. The scale of the
excavations (21 m²), which have been ongoing since 1998, means that large
samples are available for analysis and that spatial studies can be conducted in

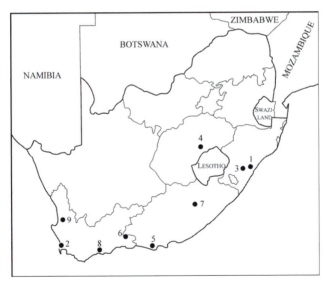

Figure 26.1. South African Middle Stone Age sites mentioned in the text. 1. Sibudu;
2. Peers Cave; 3. Umhlatuzana; 4. Rose Cottage; 5. Klasies River; 6. Boomplaas; 7.
Strathalan Cave B; 8. Blombos; 9. Diepkloof.

Figure 26.2. Sibudu Cave excavations. (See plate section for colour version.)

future. Two square metres (the trial trench) have been excavated to the base of the shelter's deposit so that predictions can be made about the sequence of layers elsewhere in the larger excavation grid.

The southern African MSA record has, until very recently, been sparse and poorly dated, with a few tantalising indications from the Cape that modern behaviour may pre-date ~70.5 ka (Mitchell, 2002). More evidence for the Still Bay and Howiesons Poort succession is particularly needed and the presence of both these industries at Sibudu helps to underline the importance of this site.

Dating of the MSA at Sibudu

The deepest MSA occupation (Figure 26.3), containing a pre-Still Bay industry (layer BS) has ages of 77.2 ± 2.1, 73.2 ± 2.3 and 72.5 ± 2.0 ka (Table 26.1; Jacobs *et al.*, 2008a) . The Still Bay Industry (Wadley, 2007) above this (layers RGS2 and RGS) has an age of 70.5 ± 2.0 ka age calculated from optically stimulated luminescence (OSL) dating of quartz grains. This age is within the range of ages published for Blombos Cave, i.e. >70 ka (Jacobs, pers. comm.; Jacobs *et al.*, 2003a,b; Tribolo *et al.*, 2005; Jacobs *et al.*, 2006; Tribolo *et al.*, 2006; Wadley and Jacobs, 2006). Howiesons Poort ages are 64.7 ± 1.9, 63.8 ± 2.5 and 61.7 ± 1.5 ka (Jacobs *et al.*, 2008a,b) the ages of a suite of layers with post-Howiesons Poort lithic assemblages has a weighted mean average of 58.5 ± 1.4 ka (Wadley and Jacobs, 2006; Jacobs *et al.*, 2008a). Jacobs has used OSL to provide 20 ages for the long Sibudu sequence above the

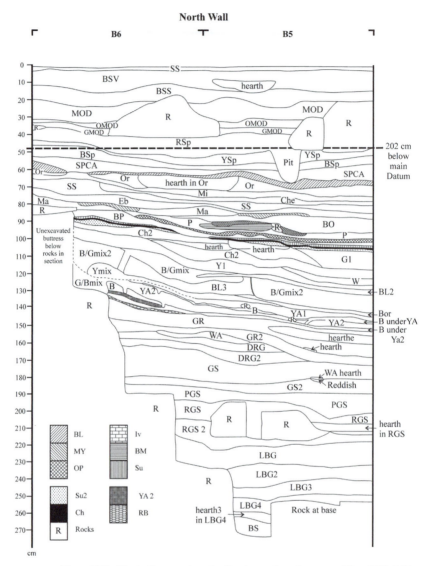

Figure 26.3. Sibudu Cave stratigraphy. Howiesons Poort layers are GR to PGS; Still Bay layers are RGS and RGS 2. See Table 26.1 for the ages associated with the more recent MSA layers.

Howiesons Poort Industry (Wadley and Jacobs, 2006; Jacobs *et al.*, 2008a,b). There are three age clusters of ~58 ka (weighted mean average of 58.5 ± 1.4 ka), ~48 ka (weighted mean average 47.7 ± 1.4 ka) and ~38 ka (weighted mean average 38.6 ± 1.9 ka) (Table 26.1), each separated by a long hiatus (10.8 ± 1.3 ka and 9.1 ± 3.6 ka) (Jacobs *et al.*, 2008a,b).

Table 26.1. *Sibudu Cave: layers, grid position, age and informal lithic designation; simplified mineralogy, charcoal, fauna and magnetic susceptibility. Only four taxa have been selected from the charcoal analysis:* Acacia spp., Erica spp., Podocarpus spp. *and* Leucosidea sericea. Podo. = Podocarpus sp.; Leuco. = Leucosidea sericea.

Layer	Grid position	Age in ka	Informal lithic designation	Mineralogy	Charcoal	Fauna	Magnetic susceptibility
Co	EAST	38.0 ± 2.6	**final MSA**	calcite	Acacia, Erica		
Bu		39.1 ± 2.6		high calcite, low gypsum			
LBMOD		49.9 ± 2.5		high calcite			
Es							
Mou, DMou							
PB	EAST		**late MSA**	high calcite, high gypsum			
Ore, Ore2				high calcite, high gypsum			
RD		49.4 ± 2.3		calcite, high gypsum			
Cad, Pu				gypsum			
MOD	NORTH	49.1 ± 2.5		high calcite, gypsum	Acacia, Erica	large and med. bovid	warmer
OMOD		46.6 ± 2.3		high calcite, high gypsum	Acacia, Erica	large and med. bovid	warmer
OMODBL		47.6 ± 1.9				large and med. bovid	
OMOD2						large and med. bovid	
OMOD2BL							
GMOD, BMOD							
RSp		46.6 ± 1.9		calcite, high gypsum	Acacia, Podo., Erica	large and med. bovid	warmer
YSp				gypsum		bovid	
BSp	NORTH	57.6 ± 2.1	**post-Howiesons Poort**	high calcite, gypsum	Erica, Acacia	large and med. bovid	
BSp2				calcite, gypsum		bovid	
SPCA				high calcite, high gypsum	Erica, Podo., Leuco.	large and med. bovid	
BL, Or					.	bovid	
Mi				high gypsum		large bovid	
SS				high gypsum		large bovid	
Che, Eb		59.6 ± 2.3		gypsum	Erica, Acacia, Leuco.	large bovid	cool
Ma, MY				gypsum		large bovid	
BO				gypsum		large bovid	

Table 26.1. (*cont.*)

Layer	Grid position	Age in ka	Informal lithic designation	Mineralogy	Charcoal	Fauna	Magetic susceptibility
P		59.0 ± 2.2		gypsum		large bovid	warm
OP				high gypsum		large bovid	warm
BP				gypsum		large bovid	
Iv				gypsum		large bovid	
BM				gypsum		large bovid	
Ch				high gypsum		large bovid	
Su, Su2				high gypsum		large bovid	warming
G1				high gypsum		large bovid	cold
Ch2		58.3 ± 2.0		high gypsum		large bovid	cold
Y1		58.6 ± 2.1		high gypsum		large bovid	cold
B/Gmix		58.2 ± 2.4		high gypsum		large bovid	cold
BL2, BL3				high gypsum		large bovid	cold
Bor, Yrmix				gypsum		large bovid	cold
YA1				calcite, gypsum		large bovid	cold
YA2				calcite, gypsum		large bovid	cold
Br under YA2							
GR	NORTH		**Howiesons Poort**	calcite, gypsum	*Podo.*	small bovid	
GR2		61.7 ± 1.5		calcite, gypsum		small bovid	
GS				calcite		small bovid	
GS2		63.8 ± 2.5		calcite		small bovid	
PGS		64.7 ± 1.9		high calcite		small bovid	
RGS	NORTH	70.4 ± 2.0	**Still Bay**				
RGS2				high calcite			
LBG	NORTH	72.5 ± 2.0	**pre-Still Bay**	calcite			
LBG2, LGB3		73.2 ± 2.3		calcite			
LGB4				calcite			
BS		77.2 ± 2.1					
BEDROCK?							

If the calcite deposits in sediments can be interpreted as secondary precipitation at the top of occupation surfaces exposed for a long time (Goldberg and Macphail, 2006), this has implications for the site's age clusters. The calcite deposits support the presence of hiatuses between ~58 ka and ~48 ka, between ~48 ka and ~38 ka and between ~38 ka and AD 1000.

The cultural sequence

At the base of the excavation in the trial trench (2 m²), on a rock floor that could be bedrock, there is an industry with unifacial points that at present can only be called pre-Still Bay. Above this is a Still Bay assemblage that is overlain by a Howiesons Poort Industry. In the Western Cape, Peers Cave (Figure 26.1; Minichillo, 2005) and Diepkloof (Figure 26.1; Rigaud *et al.*, 2006) have also yielded stratified Still Bay and Howiesons Poort sequences. The collection of Still Bay tools is small at Sibudu because thus far it has been excavated from the trial trench only (Wadley, 2007). The majority of tools are broken bifacial points (including proximal ends of double-pointed points), but there are also two whole double-pointed bifacial points and some bifacial tools (Figure 26.4). Some of the bifacial Still Bay points from Sibudu have use-wear traces that

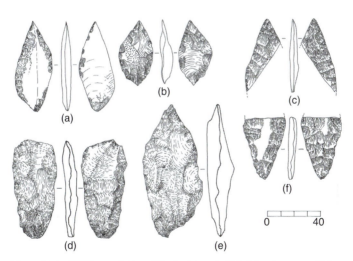

Figure 26.4. Still Bay tools from Sibudu. (a) partly bifacial point, square B5a RGS2, dolerite; (b) bifacial point (with rejuvenated tip), square B6a, RGS, hornfels; (c) distal tip, square B6a, RGS2, quartzite; (d) bifacial tool, square B6a, RGS, dolerite; (e) bifacial tool, square B5d, RGS2, dolerite; (f) proximal end, square B5c, RGS, dolerite. Scale in mm.

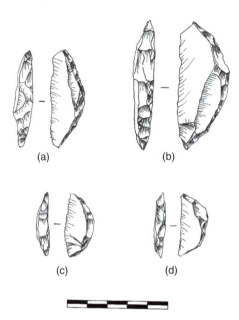

Figure 26.5. Howiesons Poort backed tools from Sibudu.

suggest that they were hafted and used as stone-tipped weapons, but others appear to have been used as butchery knives (Lombard, 2006a).

The Howiesons Poort layers are thicker than those of the Still Bay Industry and they contain many segments and other backed tools (Figure 26.5). Use-traces on 53 segments show that 80% and 87% of ochre and resin residues, respectively, occur on the backed portions of the tools (Lombard, 2006b). Thus segments seem to have been hafted along their backed edges, as was also the case at Rose Cottage in the Free State (Figure 26.1; Gibson *et al.*, 2004) and Enkapune ya Muto in Kenya (Ambrose, 1998).

The younger deposits contain post-Howiesons Poort (~58 ka), late MSA (~48 ka) and final MSA (~38 ka) assemblages. These assemblage names are informal and are intended for use only at Sibudu where the three age clusters (Jacobs *et al.*, 2008; Wadley and Jacobs, 2006) suggest that some lithic differences might be expected. The ~48 ka and ~38 ka assemblages are indeed typologically distinct, but the relationship between the ~58 ka and ~48 ka assemblages is uncertain and will remain so until larger ~58 ka samples are excavated and analysed. Quartz and quartzite tools are most common in the basal ~58 ka layers of the trial trench (Cochrane, 2006) and this might signify that a technological difference will be found between these and the uppermost ~58 ka layers where dolerite and hornfels tools are more common.

The quartz- and quartzite-rich assemblage examined by Cochrane (2006) contains unifacial points ($n = 30$), partly bifacial points ($n = 3$), distal ends of broken points ($n = 22$), scrapers (mostly convex sidescrapers) and grindstones. Only one segment and one backed blade occur in the ~58 ka post-Howiesons Poort layers studied by Cochrane (2006); thus, the Howiesons Poort backed tool technology disappeared completely at Sibudu by ~58 ka.

The lithics from layer RSp in the ~48 ka cluster of layers are published else-where (Villa *et al.*, 2005). The 344 formal tools in RSp include 32.8% pointed forms (unifacial points, one bifacial point and some triangular Levallois flakes), 7.3% broken tips of points, some burins, *pièces esquillées* (scaled pieces), scrapers and one segment (Villa *et al.,* 2005).

The ~38 ka assemblage is informally termed the final MSA, but this name implies only that it is the youngest MSA occurrence at Sibudu. Younger MSA assemblages occur, for example, at Boomplaas (Figure 26.1; Deacon, 1995), Strathalan Cave B (Figure 26.1; Opperman and Heydenrych, 1990; Opperman, 1996) and Rose Cottage (Figure 26.1; Wadley, 1997). At Sibudu the final MSA contains many bifacial as well as unifacial points, sidescrapers, deep seg-ments and *pièces esquillées*, together with rare bifacial 'hollow-based' points and small bifacial tools (Wadley, 2005; Figure 26.6). This distinctive MSA assemblage, which occurs only in the eastern part of the excavation grid, may represent a local industry that is also present at Umhlatuzana (Kaplan, 1990), approximately 90 km from Sibudu, between Durban and Pietermaritzburg.

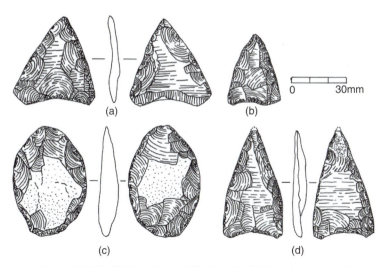

Figure 26.6. Final MSA tools from Sibudu: (a, b, d) hollow-based points from square C2a, layers Co, Mou and Bu; (c) bifacial tool, square C2c, Es. All are made of hornfels.

Faunal analysis

Faunal analyses of Still Bay and Howiesons Poort layers are incomplete, but the animals represented here include a wide range of species, with the little blue duiker (*Philantomba monticola*) predominating (Clark and Plug, 2008). Bone in these older layers is less fragmented than bone in younger layers, possibly because gypsum, which cracks bones in the other layers (Cain, 2006; Schiegl and Conard, 2006), is absent. Instead of gypsum, these older layers are enriched with calcite (Schiegl and Conard, 2006), which shows that the Sibudu lower deposits are dry and unusually well preserved.

Sibudu's occupants were skilled encounter-hunters between ~58 ka and ~38 ka. Their prey included dangerous species such as extinct and modern buffalo (*Pelorovis antiquus* and *Syncerus caffer*, respectively) and bushpig (*Potamochoerus larvatus*), and, on occasion, they also obtained meat from giraffe (*Giraffa camelopardalis*) and hippopotamus (*Hippopotamus amphibius*) (Plug, 2004; Cain, 2006; Wells, 2006). *Syncerus/Pelorovis* account for 10% of the identifiable species, and size class IV (body mass 300–1000 kg, for example Cape buffalo and eland) and size class V (body mass more than 1000 kg, for example hippopotamus and rhinoceros) (Brain, 1981) animals account for a further 10% of the Sibudu faunal sample. Studies of cut marks, percussion marks, carnivore gnawing, bone smashing and burning suggest that humans were the primary agents of accumulation of the bone in the cave (Plug, 2004; Cain, 2006; Wells, 2006).

There is no evidence to suggest that MSA methods of hunting changed between ~58 ka and ~38 ka at Sibudu and hunters probably used stone-tipped spears throughout this period. Tip cross-sectional area (TCSA) calculations for the ~58 ka points (137.8 mm^2) are larger than those of the more recent points (109.4 and 101.1 mm^2) (Villa and Lenoir, 2006), yet all these TCSA values for Sibudu fall within the range of thrusting/throwing spears according to Shea's (2006) calculations. This interpretation is supported by use-trace studies of MSA points from Sibudu (Lombard, 2004, 2005, 2006a,b). However, not all MSA points from all sites were necessarily used as thrusting/throwing spears. Some small points at sites such as Aduma, Ethiopia, may have been for darts or even arrows (Brooks *et al.*, 2006). The small size of some points at Rose Cottage Cave may also support the use of darts (Villa and Lenoir, 2006) or even arrows at this site (Mohapi, 2007).

Worked bone, shell and sedge

Worked bone is uncommon in Sibudu's MSA sequence. No worked bone has yet been found in the Still Bay Industry, although ground bone points and other

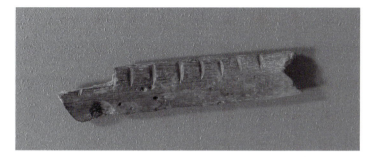

Figure 26.7. Notched bone (length 22 mm) from ~58 ka layer at Sibudu.

worked bone was found in this industry at Blombos (Henshilwood and Sealy, 1997; d'Errico *et al.*, 2001; d'Errico and Henshilwood, 2007). Several broken bone points were recovered from the Sibudu Howiesons Poort Industry and they are being refitted and analysed in detail by Lucinda Backwell (for the initial study see Backwell *et al.*, 2008).

Some worked marine shell is present in the Sibudu MSA and it seems likely that shell was deliberately transported from the coast as a raw material (Plug, 2006). *Nassarius kraussianus* (tick shells) shell beads have been recovered from Still Bay layers at Blombos Cave (Henshilwood *et al.,* 2004; d'Errico *et al.*, 2005). A few similar perforated shells have been found at Sibudu, but they are *Afrolittorina africana* marine shells and not *Nassarius* (d'Errico *et al.*, 2008). Engraved eggshell was found in the Howiesons Poort Industry at Diepkloof (Parkington *et al.*, 2005; Rigaud *et al.*, 2006), but ostrich eggshell is entirely absent from Sibudu MSA layers, perhaps because ostriches did not thrive in this area in the past (they do not thrive there now either).

Layer BSp2, with an age of ~58 ka, yielded a fragment of caudal rib with ten parallel notches that were made with a retouched stone tool (Cain, 2004; Figure 26.7). The notches lack residues (B. Williamson, pers. comm.) and there does not seem to be an obvious function for the piece. Notched rib bone was also found in the MSA at Klasies River (Singer and Wymer, 1982). A thin bone pin that may have been ground and polished was found in layer Co (Cain, 2004) that has an age of ~38 ka (Jacobs *et al.*, 2008b).

The presence of hundreds of sedge seeds (mostly *Schoenoplectus* sp.) in almost all MSA layers (Sievers, 2006) is intriguing. The sedge seeds, which are whole and do not appear to have been consumed by birds or animals, may have come into the shelter on bundles of sedges that were laid down for bedding. Pollen from sedges is present in some MSA layers, too (Renaut and Bamford, 2006). Today these sedges are particularly popular for weaving traditional Zulu sleeping mats (Van Wyk and Gericke, 2000), but there is no evidence, as yet, for woven mats at Sibudu.

Hearths and burning events

Circular to subcircular fireplaces are present in all the MSA occupations (Figure 26.8). Their bases are always flat and they never have stone foundations or surrounds. These 10 to 15 cm thick hearths are often stratified into a basal reddish-brown, burnt earth layer, a central brown-black layer with charcoal and an upper white ash layer. Ephemeral ash-smears and lenticular ashy lenses also occur. The Howiesons Poort and older industries have hearths and ash-smears that are well preserved and easily recognisable as separate and dispersed features. However, these old industries have been recovered only in the 2 m^2 trial trench, which may not be representative of the industries as a whole. As indicated earlier, there is a complete absence of gypsum in the older layers (Schiegl and Conard, 2006) and this may have helped to preserve hearth shape. Gypsum growth can crack bone (Cain, 2006; Schiegl and Conard, 2006) and distort deposits and hearths.

The ~58 ka layers have more hearths per square metre than the earlier layers and complex ash and hearth units often overlap. Burning intensity becomes greater through time and the younger ~48 ka occupations have palimpsests of burnt deposits that occur roughly in the centre of the excavation grid. They are at most about 60 cm thick and they contain stratified, but interfingering, whitish, orange-brown and brown-black layers. Repeated burning episodes appear to be represented. As in other sites (Speth, 2006), these Sibudu hearth palimpsests are set on the floor of the cave well away from the walls.

Figure 26.8. Hearth from Howiesons Poort layer GS (Howiesons Poort), Sibudu.

Cain suggests that bone was deliberately burnt in the hearths to clear away refuse and his proposal is supported by experimental work to explain the contents of Mesolithic hearths (Sergant *et al.*, 2006). Cain (2005) also studied ash-patches; these seldom contain bone fragments larger than 2 cm, suggesting that they are the result of sweeping out old hearths and redepositing debris away from areas that were being used. This suggested pattern of use supports the phytolith evidence for the spreading of ash away from recognisable hearths (Schiegl and Conard, 2006).

A wide range of fuel woods was used through time and it is not presently possible to distinguish between wood selection based on choice and wood selection based on environmental availability (Allott, 2006). People do select preferred firewood types (Archer, 1990), but wood availability is often the determining issue (Van Wyk and Gericke, 2000). Thus, charcoal from the MSA hearths is likely to reflect a component of woody vegetation at any given time even though firewood is collected by people.

Environmental evidence

Environmental interpretations made from archaeologically recovered data can be fraught with problems, particularly bias, which can include differential selection by a variety of natural agents and by people in prehistory, as well as by excavators and/or sorters during the excavation. Sibudu researchers (e.g. Allott, 2006; Cain, 2006; Glenny, 2006; Renaut and Bamford, 2006; Schiegl and Conard, 2006; Sievers, 2006; Wells, 2006) discuss specific issues of bias and sample preservation individually and they are not dealt with here.

A mosaic of habitats was almost certainly present at all times represented by the sequence of occupations at Sibudu Cave. The mosaic was, and still is, affected in part by the location of the site. The south-west facing cliff and shelter are shaded until afternoon and this aspect creates cool conditions with little evapotranspiration. Cool, moist locales encourage forest growth, particularly evergreen forest; even today there is evergreen forest around the shelter. In contrast, the northern slopes of the hill opposite the shelter are sunny, warm and dry and, under suitable rainfall and temperature regimes, they promote deciduous woodland and grassland.

Riverine habitat is likely to have been relatively constant: sedge seeds from *Schoenoplectus* sp. that only grows in standing water (Sievers, 2006) are present in most layers, with the exception of some in the ~58 ka suite. This is a strong indicator that water was close to the shelter for most of the time that it was occupied. Riverine forest taxa are present (sometimes together with *Erica* spp. [heather]) amongst the charcoal identifications throughout the MSA sequence from before 60 ka to ~38 ka (Allott, 2006) and sedges are present in the pollen profiles as well as amongst the seeds (Renaut and Bamford, 2006; Sievers, 2006). As might be expected, vlei rats (*Otomys irroratus*) occur throughout the sequence as the most common micromammals (Glenny, 2006).

The pre-60 ka layers

The presence of freshwater molluscs (Plug, 2006) and the Gambian giant rat (*Cricetomys gambianus*; Glenny, 2006) implies that humid or moist conditions occurred in pre-Howiesons Poort layers with an age of >70 ka. The giant rat seems to be a useful environmental indicator because today it only lives in evergreen forest and woodland in areas where rainfall is greater than 800 mm annually (Skinner and Chimimba, 2005: 193). It cannot tolerate temperatures above 34°C, suggesting that maximum summer temperatures prior to 60 ka must have been cooler than those of the present. Geoffroy's horseshoe bat (*Rhinolophus clivosus*), occurs in the Howiesons Poort layers (Glenny, 2006) and this bat prefers sandstone caves (Skinner and Chimimba, 2005: 339), preferably those with high humidity (Rautenbach, 1982: 36). The absence of gypsum, but presence of calcite, in these deeper layers (Schiegl and Conard, 2006: 157 their Table 2) also supports the idea of greater than usual humidity in the shelter because calcite is less soluble than gypsum (Goldberg and Macphail, 2006: 113). The presence of *Podocarpus* spp. (Yellowwood) and the absence of *Acacia* charcoal (Allott, 2006) corroborates the interpretation of evergreen forest around Sibudu during the Howiesons Poort Industry. The occurrence of many blue duiker and other forest-dwelling animals in Howiesons Poort layers (I. Plug and J. Clark, pers. comm.) also implies that forest was near the shelter.

The ~58 ka layers

Magnetic susceptibility data for the earliest of the ~58 ka layers (YA2 to G1) imply that this period was the coldest represented in the shelter (Herries, 2006), although susceptibility readings have not yet been analysed below YA2. The youngest of the layers laid down during the cold episode, G1, may mark the boundary between cold Marine Isotope Stage (MIS) 4 and warmer MIS 3. Type 5 (possibly *Olea* sp. [wild olive]) seeds (Sievers, 2006) and equids and large to very large bovids, including buffalo (Plug, 2004; Cain, 2006), are especially well represented here.

Magnetic susceptibility data for younger layers Su and P, directly above YA2 to G1, suggest warmer conditions than previously (Herries, 2006), though temperatures within OIS 3 did not reach those of today. All of the P layers (P, OP and BP) contain highly visible gypsum nodules (Pickering, 2006; Schiegl and Conard, 2006) and they demonstrate change between these and the earlier layers. Gypsum accumulations are a useful indicator of past arid conditions (Goldberg and MacPhail, 2006: 43, 70).

Higher in the ~58 ka sequence, charcoal evidence from layer Eb (Allott, 2006) suggests a vegetation community unknown in the area today. *Podocarpus* spp. are absent from the charcoal, implying that conditions were too dry for this genus. *Leucosidea sericea* (Oldwood) was present; this potential pioneer species does not occur near the coast today and is more often found above 400 m above mean sea-level. The Natal multimammate mouse (*Mastomys natalensis*), also found in an upper 58 ka layer (Glenny, 2006), is a pioneer species, too. *Mastomys natalensis* establishes itself in areas recovering from habitat destruction, thus, it occurs in the early stage of secondary succession (De Graaff, 1981: 211).

In the penultimate 58 ka layer, SPCA, large- to medium-sized bovids occur in place of large and very large bovids (Plug, 2004). Amongst the taxa in the charcoal record are *Podocarpus* spp. and *Leucosidea sericea* (Allott, 2006), but *Acacia* is absent. The re-appearance of *Leucosidea sericea* may imply another succession change, but on this occasion conditions may have been moist enough to allow the growth of *Podocarpus* spp.

In the final ~58 ka layers, BSp2 to BSp, dry, open grassland is implied by the high frequencies of grazers (Plug, 2004; Cain, 2006) and the absence of *Podocarpus* spp. (Allott, 2006). *Acacia* spp. occur here (Allott, 2006) and the absence of sedge seeds (*Schoenoplectus* sp.; Sievers, 2006) implies that there may not have been standing-water year round. BSp seems to have been the open surface of the shelter floor for 9.1 ± 3.6 ka (Wadley and Jacobs, 2006; Jacobs *et al.*, 2008) before occupation of the shelter resumed at ~48 ka and the high percentages of secondary minerals in BSp (Schiegl and Conard, 2006) seem to confirm this suggestion.

The ~48 ka layers

The magnetic susceptibility readings show a substantial warming trend in RSp (Herries, 2006). *Acacia* spp., *Erica* spp. and a *Podocarpus* sp. (a single charcoal fragment) co-occur in the charcoal sample (Allott, 2006); this is the only time that this happens in the sequence (based on the charcoal analysis of relatively few layers). In all other layers where charcoal has been analysed, *Podocarpus* and *Acacia* charcoals are mutually exclusive. No *Podocarpus* occurs anywhere in the site more recently than layer RSp. There is an increase in deciduous taxa amongst both the charcoal and seed identifications in RSp, but the variety of both evergreen and deciduous taxa increases (Allott, 2006; Sievers, 2006). *Pavetta* sp. (Bride's bush) seeds are especially common (Sievers, 2006). Deciduous woodland may have increased near the site, but the interpretation must be made cautiously. The presence in RSp of *Mastomys natalensis,* the pioneering micromammal, suggests that this may have been another period of change to secondary succession.

Suids become more frequent here than before, giraffe are present and there is an increase in equids, reptiles and frogs (Plug, 2004; Cain, 2006; Wells, 2006). Bushpig, blue duiker, red duiker (*Cephalophus natalensis*), bushbuck (*Tragelaphus scriptus*) and giant rat suggest forest or woodland habitats (Wells, 2006) and the giant rat implies rainfall above 800 mm per annum, while zebra (*Equus quagga*), warthog (*Phacochoerus africanus*), blue wildebeest (*Connochaetes taurinus*) and buffalo suggest grassland and woodland or savannah communities (Wells, 2006). Such variety is to be expected under conditions not dissimilar from those of today because currently there are complex habitats within the Sibudu area, which encompasses riverine, cliff and plateau localities.

The ~38 ka layers, eastern grid

Charcoal from layer Bu, which has an age of 39.1 ± 2.5 ka (Wadley and Jacobs, 2006; Jacobs *et al.*, 2008a,b) contains taxa that indicate drier than present conditions in the Sibudu region: *Brachylaena* spp. (Silver oak), *Acacia* spp, *Clerodendrum glabrum* (Tinderwood) and *Kirkia* sp. (Seringa) (Allott, 2006). High frequencies of *Otomys irroratus* (vlei rat) were present (Glenny, 2006) suggesting that moist conditions continued around the local river system.

Discussion and conclusions

Diverse agents of accumulation for the plants, animals, rocks and minerals in Sibudu have contributed to the strength of the combined environmental evidence presented here. The agents have, between them, exploited several potential habitats that may have been close to the shelter in the past. Sibudu is unusual in the KwaZulu-Natal context, and indeed in the wider southern African context, because high-resolution proxy environmental data are not readily available. The best non-archaeological environmental information in KwaZulu-Natal comes from stratigraphic sequences exposed in erosional gullies (dongas), where palaeosols alternate with colluvial deposits. Colluvial deposits indicate aridity or periods of transitional climate and reduced vegetation, but palaeosols suggest hill-slope stability when it was humid and vegetation was thicker (Botha *et al.*, 1992; Wintle *et al.*, 1995; Botha, 1996; Botha and Partridge, 2000; Clarke *et al.*, 2003). Distinct phases of colluviation appear to have occurred at ~110 to 96 ka, 56 to 52 ka, 47 to 41 ka and ~11 ka (Botha and Partridge, 2000). Fourteen Sibudu Cave age estimates divide naturally into three clusters, ~58 ka, ~48 ka and ~38 ka with lengthy hiatuses between the age clusters (Wadley and Jacobs, 2006; Jacobs *et al.* 2008a,b). Two of KwaZulu-Natal's colluviation phases correspond to the Sibudu hiatuses between 58 and 48 ka and between 48 and 38 ka. The stratigraphy of the geological site Voordrag (Clarke *et al.*, 2003) contains an undated colluvial deposit between two ^{14}C dated palaeosols; the evidence implies that the period between ~42 ka and 35 ka was also arid. The MSA occupations at Sibudu seem to correspond to periods of pedogenesis. Thus, climate and environmental forces may have contributed to determining periods of occupation in Sibudu (Wadley and Jacobs, 2006).

The varied data available at Sibudu suggest that there were sometimes material culture changes alongside environmental changes, although this does not imply that behaviour is driven by the environment. Few detailed environmental results are yet available for the earliest part of the sequence that contains pre-Still Bay, Still Bay and Howiesons Poort industries, but there have been intensive environmental studies of the occupations from ~58 ka to ~38 ka. Thus far we suspect that the Howiesons Poort at Sibudu was created in an environment that included moist, evergreen forest (Allott, 2006) with giant rat, blue duiker and other forest animals (Glenny, 2006; I. Plug and J. Clark, pers. comm.). The Howiesons Poort industry, with its small backed tools, directly preceded the ~58 ka occupations, which coincide (in layers YA2 to G1) with a weak magnetic susceptibility signal, implying a cold climate. At ~58 ka the hunting emphasis switched from small browsers to large- and medium-sized animals and, from this time on, though perhaps earlier, the people who lived at Sibudu were competent encounter-hunters who were able to kill a wide range of animals, including zebra, buffalo and bushpig (Plug, 2004; Cain, 2006; Wells, 2006). Concurrently, backed tools disappeared, points were re-introduced and quartz and quartzite predominated amongst the rock types used for stone tools in the earliest of the ~58 ka layers, YA2 to Y1 (Cochrane, 2006). Quartz and quartzite are not an important part of the lithic industries anywhere else in the sequence, where dolerite is usually the principal rock that was knapped, followed by hornfels. Thus the most dramatic environmental change in the Sibudu sequence coincides with transformations in both material culture and subsistence strategies.

Correspondence analysis shows development from an open environment in the first part of the ~58 ka age set to a more wooded environment from ~48 ka onwards (Reynolds, 2006). As suggested before, the increased woodland at ~48 ka seems to have contained more deciduous taxa than previously. This trend correlates with the magnetic susceptibility data, which show a gradual warming in the ~48 ka age set that coincides with part of OIS 3 (Herries, 2006). Warmer temperatures and increased evapotranspiration at ~48 ka may have resulted in an expansion of deciduous woodland and an increase in associated animals, but hunting with points continued and dolerite and hornfels remained the principal rock types. Indeed, from ~58 ka to ~38 ka, unifacially or bifacially retouched lithic points seem to have been consistently used as parts of weapons for hunting (Villa *et al.*, 2005; Wadley, 2005; Villa and Lenoir, 2006). Use-trace analysis supports this interpretation (Lombard, 2004, 2005, 2006a).

The combination of good organic preservation, deep deposits and many clearly defined stratigraphic layers at ~58 ka and ~48 ka implies fine resolution of data. Some data link environmental and cultural information: the sedge seeds (Sievers, 2006) provide proof of standing-water near the shelter through most of the sequence but, more importantly, they may provide the first such evidence in the MSA for the use of mats or bedding. Research on the cultural material from the site is not yet complete and larger samples need to be excavated from the deepest industries before behavioural patterns can be confirmed. However, the worked bone points from the Howiesons Poort Industry, the notched caudal bone from a ~58 ka layer (Cain, 2004) and worked marine shell from other layers in the trial trench (Plug, 2006) hold promise for future interpretations of behaviour in the deep past.

Acknowledgements

The Natal Museum and AMAFA have supported the Sibudu research in many ways and I thank both organisations. The National Research Foundation (NRF) has funded the Sibudu research since its inception, but views expressed here are not necessarily shared by the NRF. The School of Geography, Archaeology and Environmental Studies has provided logistical support. I thank Peter Mitchell, Nick Conard and Sally Reynolds for suggestions that have improved this chapter.

References

Allott, L. F. (2006). Archaeological charcoal as a window on palaeovegetation and wood use during the Middle Stone Age at Sibudu Cave. *Southern African Humanities*, **18**(1): 173–201.

Ambrose, S. H. (1998). Chronology of the Later Stone Age and food production in East Africa. *Journal of Archaeological Science*, **25**: 377–92.

Archer, F. (1990). Planning with people: ethnobotany and African uses of plants in Namaqualand (South Africa). *Mitteilungen aus dem Institute für Allgemeine Botanik Hamburg*, **23**(b): 959–72.

Backwell, L., d'Errico, F. and Wadley, L. (2008). Middle Stone Age bone tools from the Howiesons Poort layers, Sibudu Cave, South Africa. *Journal of Archaeological Science*, **35**: 1566–80.

Botha, G. A. (1996). The geology and palaepedology of Late Quaternary colluvial sediments in northern KwaZulu-Natal/Natal. *Council for Geoscience Memoires*, **83**: 1–165.

Botha, G. A. and Partridge, T. C. (2000). Colluvial deposits. In Partridge, T. C. and Maud, R. R. (eds.), *The Cenozoic of Southern Africa*. New York: Oxford University Press, pp. 88–99.

Botha, G. A., Scott, L., Vogel, J. C. *et al.* (1992). Palaeosols and palaeoenvironments during the Late Pleistocene Hypothermal in northern Natal. *South African Journal of Science*, **88**: 508–12.

Brain, C. K. (1981). *The Hunters or the Hunted? An Introduction to African Cave Taphonomy*. Chicago: University of Chicago Press.

Brooks, A. S., Yellen, J. E., Nevell, G. *et al.* (2006). Projectile technologies of the African MSA: implications for modern human origins. In Hovers, E. and Kuhn, S. L. (eds.), *Transitions before the Transition*. New York: Springer, pp. 233–56.

Cain, C. R. (2004). Notched, flaked and ground bone artefacts from Middle Stone Age and Iron Age layers of Sibudu Cave, KwaZulu-Natal, South Africa. *South African Journal of Science*, **100**: 195–7.

  (2005). Using burned bone to look at Middle Stone Age occupation and behavior. *Journal of Archaeological Science*, **32**: 873–84.

  (2006). Human activity suggested by the taphonomy of 60 ka and 50 ka faunal remains from Sibudu Cave. *Southern African Humanities*, **18** (1): 241–60.

Clark, J. L. and Plug, I. (2008). Animal exploitation strategies during the South African Middle Stone Age: Howiesons Poort and post-Howiesons Poort fauna from Sibudu Cave *Journal of Human Evolution*, **54**: 886–98.

Clarke, M. L., Vogel, J. C., Botha, G. A. *et al.* (2003). Late Quaternary hillslope evolution recorded in eastern South African colluvial badlands. *Palaeogeography, Palaeoclimatology, Palaecology*, **197**: 199–212.

Cochrane, G. W. G. (2006). An analysis of lithic artefacts from the ~58 ka layers of Sibudu Cave. *Southern African Humanities*, **18**(1): 69–88.

De Graaff, G. (1981). *The Rodents of Southern Africa*. Durban: Butterworths.

Deacon, H. J. (1995). Two late Pleistocene-Holocene archaeological depositories from the Southern Cape, South Africa. *South African Archaeological Bulletin*, **50**: 121–31.

Delagnes, A., Wadley, L., Villa, P. *et al.* (2006). Crystal quartz backed tools from the Howiesons Poort at Sibudu Cave. *Southern African Humanities*, **18**: 43–56.

D'Errico, F. and Henshilwood, C. (2007). Additional evidence for bone technology in the southern African Middle Stone Age. *Journal of Human Evolution*, **52**: 142–63.

D'Errico, F., Henshilwood, C. and Nilssen, P. (2001). An engraved bone fragment from ca. 75 kyr Middle Stone Age levels at Blombos Cave, South Africa: implications for the origin of symbolism and language. *Antiquity*, **75**: 309–18.

D'Errico, F., Henshilwood, C., Vanhaeren, M. *et al.* (2005). *Nassarius kraussianus* shell beads from Blombos Cave: evidence for symbolic behaviour in the Middle Stone Age. *Journal of Human Evolution*, **48**: 2–14.

D'Errico, F., Vanhaeren, M., Wadley, L. (2008). Possible shell beads from the Middle Stone Age layers of Sibudu Cave, South Africa. *Journal of Archaeological Science*, **35**(10): 2675–85.

Gibson, N. E., Wadley, L. and Williamson, B. S. (2004). Residue analysis of backed tools from the 60 000 to 68 000 year-old Howiesons Poort layers of Rose Cottage Cave, South Africa. *Southern African Humanities*, **16**: 1–11.

Glenny, W. (2006). Report on the micromammal assemblage analysis from Sibudu Cave. *Southern African Humanities*, **18**(1): 270–88.

Goldberg, P. and Macphail, R. I. (2006). *Practical and Theoretical Geoarchaeology*. Oxford: Blackwell.

Henshilwood, C. and Sealy, J. (1997). Bone artefacts from the Middle Stone Age at Blombos Cave, Southern Cape, South Africa. *Current Anthropology*, **38**: 890–5.

Henshilwood, C., d'Errico, F., Vanhaeren, M. *et al.* (2004). Middle Stone Age shell beads from South Africa. *Science*, **304**: 404.

Herries, A. I. R. (2006). Archaeomagnetic evidence for climate change at Sibudu Cave. *Southern African Humanities*, **18**(1): 131–47.

Jacobs, Z., Duller, G. A. T. and Wintle, A. G. (2003a). Optical dating of dune sand from Blombos Cave, South Africa: II – single grain data. *Journal of Human Evolution*, **44**: 613–25.

Jacobs, Z., Wintle, A. G. and Duller, G. A. T. (2003b). Optical dating of dune sand from Blombos Cave, South Africa: I – multiple grain data. *Journal of Human Evolution*, **44**: 599–612.

Jacobs, Z., Duller, G. A. T., Wintle, A. G. *et al.* (2006). Extending the chronology of deposits at Blombos Cave, South Africa, back to 140 ka using optical dating of single and multiple grains of quartz. *Journal of Human Evolution*, **51**: 255–73.

Jacobs, Z., Roberts, R. G., Galbraith, R. F. *et al.* (2008a). Ages for the middle stone. Age of Southern Africa: Implications for human behavior and dispersal. *Science*, **322**: 733–5.

Jacobs, Z., Wintle, A.G., Duller, G.A.T. *et al.* (2008b). New ages for the post-Howiesons Poort, late and final Middle Stone Age at Sibudu Cave, South Africa. *Journal of Archaeological Science*, **35**: 1790–807.

Kaplan, J. (1990). The Umhlatuzana Rock Shelter sequence: 100 000 years of Stone Age history. *Natal Museum Journal of Humanities*, **2**: 1–94.

Lombard, M. (2004). Distribution patterns of organic residues on Middle Stone Age points from Sibudu Cave, KwaZulu-Natal, South Africa. *South African Archaeological Bulletin*, **59**: 37–44.

(2005). Evidence of hunting and hafting during the Middle Stone Age at Sibudu Cave, KwaZulu-Natal, South Africa: a multinanalytical approach. *Journal of Human Evolution*, **48**: 279–300.

(2006a). First impressions on the functions and hafting technology of Still Bay pointed artefacts from Sibudu Cave. *Southern African Humanities*, **18**(1): 27–41.

(2006b). Direct evidence for the use of ochre in the hafting technology of Middle Stone Age tools from Sibudu Cave, KwaZulu-Natal. *Southern African Humanities*, **18**(1): 57–67.

Minichillo, T. J. (2005). Middle Stone Age lithic study, South Africa: an examination of modern human origins. Unpublished PhD thesis, University of Washington.

Mitchell, P. J. (2002). *The Archaeology of Southern Africa*. Cambridge: Cambridge University Press.

Mohapi, M. (2007). Rose Cottage Cave MSA lithic points: does technological change imply change in hunting techniques? *South African Archaeological Bulletin*, **62**: 9–18.

Opperman, H. (1996). Strathalan Cave B, north-eastern Cape Province, South Africa: evidence for human behaviour 29,000–26,000 years ago. *Quaternary International*, **33**: 45–54.

Opperman, H. and Heydenrych, B. (1990). A 22,000 year old Middle Stone Age camp site with plant food remains from the north-eastern Cape. *South African Archaeological Bulletin*, **45**: 93–9.

Parkington, J., Poggenpoel, C., Rigaud, J-P. *et al.* (2005). From tool to symbol: the behavioural context of intentionally marked ostrich eggshell from Diepkloof, Western Cape. In d'Errico, F. and Backwell, L. (eds.), *From Tools to Symbols: from Early Hominids to Modern Humans*. Johannesburg: Witwatersrand University Press, pp. 475–92.

Pickering, R. (2006). Regional geology, setting and sedimentology of Sibudu Cave. *Southern African Humanities*, **18**(1): 123–9.

Plug, I. (2004). Resource exploitation: animal use during the Middle Stone Age at Sibudu Cave, KwaZulu-Natal. *South African Journal of Science*, **100**: 151–8.

(2006). Aquatic animals and their associates from the Middle Stone Age levels at Sibudu Cave. *Southern African Humanities*, **18**(1): 289–99.

Rautenbach, I. L. (1982). *Mammals of the Transvaal*, Ecoplan Monograph 1. Pretoria: Ecoplan.

Renaut, R. and Bamford, M. (2006). Results of preliminary palynological analysis of samples from Sibudu Cave. *Southern African Humanities*, **18**(1): 235–40.

Reynolds, S. C. (2006). Temporal changes in vegetation and mammalian communities during Oxygen Isotope Stage 3 at Sibudu Cave, KwaZulu-Natal. *Southern African Humanities*, **18**(1): 301–14.

Rigaud, J-P., Texier, P.-J., Parkington, J. *et al.* (2006). Le mobilier Stillbay et Howiesons Poort de l'abri Diepkloof. La chronologie du Middle Stone Age sud-africain et ses implications. *Palevol,* **5**: 839–49.

Schiegl, S. and Conard, N. J. (2006). The Middle Stone Age sediments at Sibudu: results from FTIR spectroscopy and microscopic analyses. *Southern African Humanities,* **18**(1): 149–72.

Sergant, J., Crombé, P. and Perdaen, Y. (2006). The 'invisible' hearths: a contribution to the discernment of Mesolithic non-structured surface hearths. *Journal of Archaeological Science,* **33**: 999–1007.

Shea, J. J. (2006). The origins of lithic projectile point technology: evidence from Africa, the Levant and Europe. *Journal of Archaeological Science,* **33**: 823–46.

Sievers, C. (2006). Seeds from the Middle Stone Age layers at Sibudu Cave. *Southern African Humanities,* **18**(1): 203–22.

Singer, R. and Wymer, J. (1982). *The Middle Stone Age at Klasies River Mouth in South Africa.* Chicago: Chicago Press.

Skinner, J. D. and Chimimba, C. T. (2005). *The Mammals of the Southern African Subregion,* 3rd edn. Cape Town: Cambridge University Press.

Speth, J. D. (2006). Housekeeping, Neandertal style: hearth placement and midden formation in Kebara cave (Israel). In Hovers, E. and Kuhn, S. L. (eds.), *Transitions before the Transition.* New York: Springer, pp. 171–88.

Tribolo, C., Mercier, N. and Valladas, H. (2005). Chronology of the Howiesons Poort and Still Bay techno-complexes: assessment and new data from luminescence. In d'Errico, F. and Backwell, L. (eds.), *From Tools to Symbols: From Early Hominids to Modern Humans.* Johannesburg: Witwatersrand University Press, pp. 493–511.

Tribolo, C., Mercier, N., Selo, M. *et al.* (2006). TL dating of burnt lithics from Blombos Cave (South Africa): further evidence for the antiquity of modern human behaviour. *Archaeometry,* **48**: 341–57.

Van Wyk, B.-E. and Gericke, N. (2000). *People's Plants: a Guide to Useful Plants of Southern Africa.* Pretoria: Briza.

Villa, P. and Lenoir, M. (2006). Hunting weapons of the Middle Stone Age and the Middle Palaeolithic: spear points from Sibudu, Rose Cottage and Bouheben. *Southern African Humanities,* **18**(1): 89–122.

Villa, P., Delagnes, A. and Wadley, L. (2005). A late Middle Stone Age artefact assemblage from Sibudu (KwaZulu-Natal): comparisons with the European Middle Palaeolithic. *Journal of Archaeological Science,* **32**: 399–422.

Wadley, L. (1997). Rose Cottage Cave: archaeological work 1987 to 1997. *South African Journal of Science,* **93**: 439–44.

(2004). Vegetation changes between 61 500 and 26 000 years ago: the evidence from seeds in Sibudu Cave, KwaZulu-Natal. *South African Journal of Science,* **100**: 167–73.

(2005). A typological study of the final Middle Stone Age stone tools from Sibudu Cave, KwaZulu-Natal. *South African Archaeological Bulletin,* **60**: 51–63.

(2006). Partners in grime: results of multi-disciplinary archaeology at Sibudu Cave. *Southern African Humanities,* **18**(1): 315–41.

(2007). Announcing a Still Bay Industry at Sibudu Cave, *Journal of Human Evolution*, **52**: 681–9.

Wadley, L. and Jacobs, Z. (2006). Sibudu Cave: background to the excavations, stratigraphy and dating. *Southern African Humanities*, **18**(1): 1–26.

Wells, C. R. (2006). A sample integrity analysis of faunal remains from the RSp layer at Sibudu Cave. *Southern African Humanities*, **18**(1): 261–77.

Wintle, A. G., Botha, G. A., Li, S.-H. *et al.* (1995). A chronological framework for colluviation during the last 110 kyr in KwaZulu-Natal. *South African Journal of Science*, **91**: 134–9.

27 The oldest burials and their significance

AVRAHAM RONEN

Abstract

The oldest burials are found in the Middle Palaeolithic of Mt. Carmel and the Galilee, in Israel, 130 to 100 ka ago. Two populations, modern humans and Neandertals are involved, with a total of some 40 individuals. The burial practices of the two populations are similar and consist of placing the corpse in a prepared pit, sometimes inserting grave goods, then filling the pit. Protecting the corpse from scavenging animals, the burial reflects the oldest concern for human dignity. The gifts offered to the dead might be alluding to some kind of religious belief in rebirth and afterlife. Accordingly, the use of an advanced syntactic language is suggested for both modern humans and Neandertals in the Levant.

Background

Burial is here understood as a place where a corpse was intentionally buried. The oldest burials currently known are found in the Middle Palaeolithic period in a restricted geographical area of Israel, Mount Carmel and the Galilee (Figure 27.1) (henceforth the core area). The oldest burials in the core area, dated 130 to 100 ka ago (Grün *et al.*, 2005) contain some 30 modern human individuals and about 6 Neandertals. The inhumations were found in three largely contemporaneous burial sites, Tabun (Garrod and Bate, 1937), Skhul (McCown, 1937) and Qafzeh (Vandermeersch, 1981). At the seashore cave of Tabun a single Neandertal burial was discovered (Garrod and Bate, 1937: 64). In the nearby cave of Skhul, some ten modern-type individuals were buried (McCown and Keith, 1939), making it 'the most ancient prehistoric necropolis' (McCown, 1937: 94). At Qafzeh Cave in the Galilee, *c.* 35 km inland, an even larger necropolis containing some 15 modern human individuals was unearthed (Vandermeersch, 1981: 33; Hovers, 2006).

African Genesis: Perspectives on Hominin Evolution, eds. Sally C. Reynolds and Andrew Gallagher. Published by Cambridge University Press. © Cambridge University Press 2012.

Figure 27.1. The earliest burial sites (*c.* 100 ka ago) and later (*c.* 60 ka) in the Levant.

The buried Neandertal at Tabun was dated by ESR of tooth enamel to 122 ± 16 ka ago (Grün and Stringer, 2000). Isolated Neandertal teeth from Tabun were subsequently dated 90^{+30}_{-16} ka by uranium-series disequilibrium (Coppa *et al.* 2005; 2007). Hence the Tabun Neandertals are placed between 130 and 100 ka (Grün and Stringer, 2000). Direct dating of the modern human remains at Skhul by uranium series–ESR suggests 102 ± 26 ka ago as the best estimate (Grün *et al.*, 2005). Hence the Skhul and Tabun populations seem roughly contemporaneous. The modern humans at Qafzeh were directly dated by ESR of teeth to 100 ± 10 and 120 ± 8 ka (Grün and Stringer, 1991). The above estimates combine to suggest that the oldest burials at Tabun, Skhul and Qafzeh were roughly contemporaneous within the range of 130 to 100 ka (Grün *et al.*,

2005). These dates are in agreement with the suggestion that modern humans could have reached the Levant during the Last Interglacial, *c*. 125 ka ago (Vaks *et al.* 2007).

In the course of the Middle Palaeolithic, Neandertal burials spread over a larger area in the Levant and into Europe. In the core area, later Neandertal burials were found in Kebara Cave in Mount Carmel (Bar-Yosef *et al.*, 1992) and in Amud Cave in the Galilee (Suzuki and Takai, 1970; Rak *et al.*, 1994), both dated around 60 ka ago (Valladas *et al.*, 1998). Neandertal burials also occur outside the core area (Figure 27.2), in Shanidar Cave in Iraq (Solecki, 1953, not securely dated) and in Dederiyeh Cave in Syria (Akazawa *et al.*, 1993, 2002, dated 60 to 50 ka ago). Modern human burials were not found in the Levant apart from those at Skhul and Qafzeh. Hence in the Levant, Neandertals have apparently outlived modern humans (Shea, 2010). This chapter will focus on the oldest burials in the core area, with occasional reference to some later Middle Palaeolithic burials in the Levant.

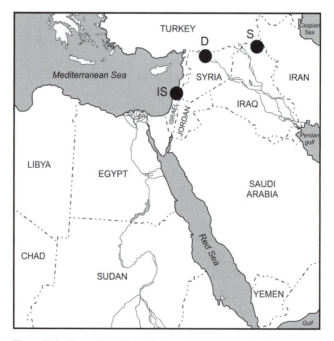

Figure 27.2. The earliest Middle Palaeolithic burial sites in the core area (*c*. 100–60 ka ago). (IS – sites in the core area shown in Figure 27.2; D – Dederiyeh; S – Shanidar).

The burial

The oldest burials consist of two facets: disposal of the corpse, and the occasional provision of grave goods. The corpse was disposed of by placing it in a pit (Figure 27.3), which was subsequently refilled with dirt. The pit is either visible or else may be deduced by the position of the bones. Among the oldest burials, pits are present in Tabun (Garrod and Bate, 1937: 64), Skhul 1, 4 and 5 (McCown, 1937: 99–100), Qafzeh 9 and 10 (a female and a child, the only double inhumation in the Middle Palaeolithic) and the adolescent Qafzeh 11 (Vandermeersch, 1970). Among the later burials, Kebara 2 (Bar-Yosef *et al.*, 1992) and the Dederiyeh 2 infant (Akazawa *et al.*, 2002: 80) were clearly buried in pits (Figure 27.3). Occasionally stones were placed on the skeleton or on top of the pit's fill. Skhul 3 may have been associated with a heap of stones (McCown, 1937: 98). Stones were placed on the skeletons of Qafzeh 8 and Qafzeh 11 (Vandermeersch, 1970). Pits and stones are construction elements of the first facet of the burial as mentioned above.

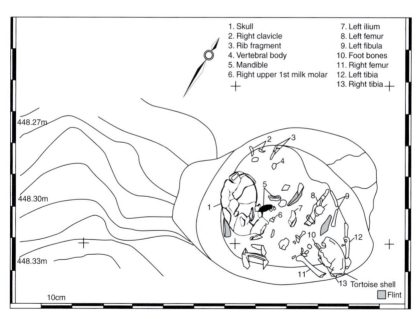

Figure 27.3. The pit containing the Dederiyeh child burial.

Grave goods

In the second facet, grave goods were sometimes placed in the grave. To accept objects as grave goods, these objects must be exceptional either by their context, size or their arrangement in the grave (Vandermeersch, 1976: 727). Two major types of objects were used as grave goods in the oldest burials: animal parts and objects of a symbolic significance like ochre, adornments or engraved notations. While the animal parts may represent provision of food, the symbolic objects were probably not intended for the physical wellbeing of the deceased.

Well documented faunal grave goods placed with the earliest burials in the core area include a boar's mandible held in the arm of Skhul 5 (Figure 27.4; Figure 27.5; McCown, 1937: 101). A large bovid skull was placed near the feet of Skhul 9 (McCown, 1937: 103; though a doubtful association) and a pair of deer antlers was placed across the chest of the adolescent Qafzeh 11 (Figure 27.6). The antlers were held in the hand of the deceased, augmenting the credibility of a deliberate association between the antlers and the deceased (Vandermeersch, 1970, 2006). Somewhat later, a deer mandible was placed on the pelvis of the Amud 7 Neandertal infant (Rak *et al.*, 1994).

It is important to note that the boar's mandible at Skhul and the antlers in Qafzeh were both qualified by the excavators, 40 years apart, as belonging to 'very large' animals (McCown, 1937: 100; Vandermeersch, 1970). These offerings were far larger than the equivalent food refuse in those sites. The exceptional size led Vandermeersch to suggest that a special hunting mission

Figure 27.4. Skhul, preservation 100 000 years after burial.

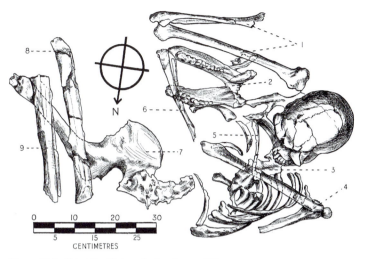

Figure 27.5. Skhul 5, offering of a boar's mandible.

Figure 27.6. Qafzeh 11, offering of deer antlers.

was apparently launched as part of the burial ceremony (Vandermeersch, 1970). Whether through hunting or a tedious search for appropriate faunal grave goods, the earliest burials in the core area already involved a complex ceremony demanding a considerable investment of time and effort by the

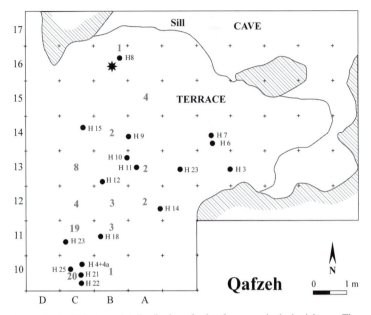

Figure 27.7. Qafzeh, spatial distribution of ochre fragments in the burial zone. The star indicates location of the engraved artefact.

community. All the faunal grave goods associated with the oldest burials are head parts – skull, mandibles and antlers. This fact and the exceptional size mentioned above incite us to consider these objects as status symbols rather than a simple provision of food.

Pigments were identified in the modern humans' burial zone at Qafzeh, with as many as 85 pieces of red ochre concentrated around the burials (Hovers *et al.*, 2003; Figure 27.7). The largest ochre at the site was near the individual Qafzeh 8, with striations due to the extraction of powder (Vandermeersch, 1969). Additional ochre fragments in Qafzeh had grooves and striations (Hovers *et al.*, 2003). Pigments were recently identified also in the other early modern human necropolis at Skhul (d'Errico *et al.*, 2010). Beads made of seashells were also found with modern human burials in the core area: in the Qafzeh burial zone, some 35 km from the seashore, *Glycimeris* shells were uncovered (Hovers *et al.*, 2003; Bar-Yosef Mayers *et al.*, 2009). At the coastal site of Skhul, the modern humans' necropolis contained pierced *Nassarius gibbosulus* shells (Vanhaeren *et al.*, 2006). *Glycimeris* shells (pierced ?) were also found in the 120 ka old seashore site of Atlit (Figure 27.8), though with no burial (Ronen *et al.*, 2008). An attempt was recently made to attribute the shells found in the coastal cave of Skhul to a natural cause, the Last Interglacial

Figure 27.8. Marine shells modified by Middle Palaeolithic humans (Ronen *et al.*, 2007). (See plate section for colour version.)

marine transgression *c.* 120 ka ago (Vita-Finzi and Stringer, 2007). Vita-Finzi and Stringer's idea would imply a tectonic uplift of Mount Carmel of some 35 m at 120 ka, which is contradicted by strong evidence for tectonic stability of Mount Carmel since the Last Interglacial (Galili *et al.*, 2007; Ronen *et al.*, 2007, 2008). As the seashells found in Qafzeh were certainly manuports, so were in all likelihood those of Skhul too.

Flint artefacts rarely served as grave goods in the Levant: a racloir was placed in the hands of Skhul 4 (McCown, 1937: 99; Garrod, 1957: 165) and a flake was placed on the chest of the Dederiyeh 1 infant (Akazawa *et al.*, 2002: 78; Figure 27.9). Other grave goods include an engraved stone, the oldest yet found, with 27 grooves found near Qafzeh 8 (Hovers *et al.*, 1997) and a roughly rectangular flat limestone placed near the head of the Dederiyeh 1 infant (Akazawa *et al.*, 2002: 75). Finally, medicinal plants were apparently placed in the grave of Shanidar 4 (Solecki, 1975; Lietava, 1992).

Personal ornaments are an important unspoken system of visual communication via symbols (Wright, 2011). Thus, the Middle Palaeolithic hominids in the Levant shared a symbolic system that must have been maintained through a developed, syntactical language. The symbolic message conveyed by the 100 ka old Qafzeh notations, as well as by the 70 ka old notations unearthed in Blombos Cave in South Africa (Henshilwood *et al.*, 2002; Figure 27.10) is lost, but it was certainly shared by members of those communities, again attesting to the use of fully advanced language in the Middle Palaeolithic (Noble and Davidson, 1996; Aiello, 1998; Enard *et al.*, 2002).

The distinction between 'practical' and 'symbolic' grave goods may be false, as shown by the faunal offerings discussed above. The stone slab near

Figure 27.9. The engraved artifact from Qafzeh 8 burial.

Figure 27.10. Engraved ochre 70 ka old from Blombos Cave, South Africa. (See plate section for colour version.)

the Dederiyeh child may seem of 'practical' intent ('pillow'?, Akazawa *et al.*, 2002: 75) but, having been transported over a distance of 30 km (Muhesen, pers. comm.) perhaps endows that stone with some special significance (Figure 27.11). The symbolic nature of the entire act of burial renders all its attributes symbolic as well. Grave goods were oddly placed with persons who could not have used them there and then. They make sense only if meant for some later time, for an afterlife (Tattersall, 1998). Hence, 100 ka ago death may have been

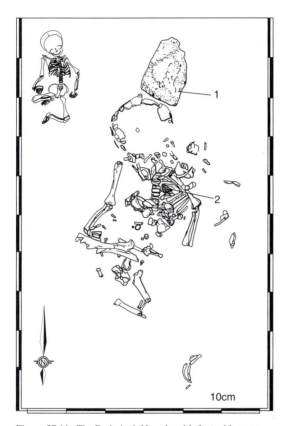

Figure 27.11. The Dederiyeh Neandertal infant with stone.

perceived as a temporary, transitional state between two forms of existence. A gift for the dead may be considered a particular case of social exchange, with delayed reciprocity. To give something is to give a part of oneself, which retains a magical and religious hold over the recipient (Mauss, 1967: 10). Finally, grave offerings may indicate the possible existence in the Middle Palaeolithic some 100 ka ago of a formal exchange system perhaps involving women in some form of 'marriage'.

The meaning of burial

The most obvious outcome of the burial is the disposal of a dead body. Accordingly, the burial was sometimes explained simply as a practical means to dispose of a corpse (e.g. Boyer, 2001: 211). But a corpse could have been disposed of as effectively, and at a far lower cost, by simply placing it outside the residence. A mere disposal of a corpse furthermore fails to account for the complex act of burial and the grave goods. Another practical explanation of the burial maintains that 'burial and cremation were invented…[to stop] scavenging predators from acquiring a dangerous taste for human flesh' (Goudsblom, 1992: 101), to avoid predator attacks on living humans. This explanation, too, fails to account for the grave goods. Finally, a practical explanation is contrasted by the visibly non-practical aspect of the whole act of burial. The burial was in fact the earliest case in human history of efforts invested with no clear benefit in the material world of quest for food, shelter or defence.

In the impossibility to use the language, concepts and metaphors of 100 ka ago, our own notions must be called upon. The pit protected the corpse from scavenging animals and other destructive elements. Hence, the burial is the oldest manifestation of a concern for human dignity. The protection proved highly effective as after 100 ka, Middle Palaeolithic buried individuals have reached modern archaeologists complete and articulated (Figure 27.4). Had the protection of the dead been the sole aim of the burial, the act could have ended there and then. The grave goods indicate, however, that a burial was not meant merely for protection.

On the cognitive side, the burial reflects a distinction between the states of 'life' and 'death'. That distinction necessarily leads to the human awareness of death and its inevitability, which constitute the principal anxiety rooted in the human condition (Becker, 1973). Awareness of one's own death furthermore implies having attained the concept of the future. The future, like the past, is only accessible through language. Here again we are led to conclude that Middle Palaeolithic humans used an advanced language. All cultures seek to appease the paralysing fear of death by admitting some form of an afterlife. Likewise, the oldest burials deny the finality of death. There is thus no escape from concluding that the oldest burials were for religious, not for practical, purpose.

Fire and death

The control of fire and the awareness of death are universal human monopolies and both constitute the formidable divide between humans and the non-human world. The control of fire and the awareness of death are the contradicting poles of human cognition: while the control of fire made humans the mightiest creatures on earth, the awareness of death revealed their inherent weakness.

Simultaneously almighty and weak, there lies the human paradox and therein may lie the threshold of religious thought. Humans have controlled fire for about 1 million years (Alperson-Afil, 2007). The eternally warm, ever-consuming and never-resting fire is the ultimate contrast to the cold and motionless death. Fire may be perceived as life itself. Fire is, furthermore, the only 'life' that humans can kill and revive at will (Ronen, 1998). Thus, manipulating fire may have initiated reflections on the 'presence/absence' dichotomy, as well as on that of 'life/death'. Fire is a social phenomenon and a symbolic entity. The stepwise technology involved in its maintenance required social interaction and, hence, an adequate language (Ronen, 1998).

Early burials were frequently located close to hearths. For example, the burial layer at Skhul contained abundant burnt and pitted flints, charred animal bones and charcoal fragments (McCown, 1937: 95). A hearth was close to the burial of Dederiyeh infant 1 (Akazawa and Muhesen, 2002: 20) and there were ashes in the burial pit at Tabun (Garrod and Bate, 1937: 67). Found in habitation sites, these and similar occurrences were generally dismissed by archaeologists as accidental. A deliberate association of fire and burial in the Middle Palaeolithic is hard to demonstrate. Two cases seem, however, to strongly suggest non-accidental association, the caves of Qafzeh and Kebara. In Qafzeh, all the burials are located in the lower part of the terrace, layers XXIV–XVII, with none in the upper layers XV–II (Hovers *et al.*, 2003: 500). The intensity of habitation, estimated by the quantity of lithics and faunal remains per sediment volume, does not change across the entire depth of the terrace (Hovers *et al.*, 2003). And yet, numerous hearths were unearthed in the lower layers surrounding the burials while none had been found in the upper, burial-free layers (Hovers, 2006). At Qafzeh, then, hearths are not correlated with the intensity of habitation but are significantly associated with burials.

In Kebara, a hearth was lit 4 cm above the Kebara 2 burial, apparently with no sediments in between. Consequently, some bones of the skeleton were burnt, suggesting a direct contact between the fire and the dead (Defleur, 1993: 266). Kebara apparently offers another example of a deliberate association between a hearth and a burial. That early burial ceremony may have involved fire (Frazer, 1957: 921) should come as no surprise, given the frequent association of fire with death in our present day rituals. Eternal flames near significant burial grounds (Figure 27.12) and the *Yarzeit* in our cemeteries are widespread examples of the association.

Fire and death are again brought together in our time in a peculiar setting: on the Sabbath, lighting fire and using it are strictly forbidden (Exodus 35, 3). At the same time, the thought of death and indeed any sadness is also forbidden on the Sabbath. The obligatory seven-day mourning period is interrupted by the Sabbath (Shulhan Aruch, Yoreh De'ah 400:1). Stripped of the central poles

Figure 27.12. The eternal flame at the Kennedy memorial.

of humanness, the control of fire and the awareness of death, on the seventh day of each week humans become even with the animal world. With no might or fear, humans are placed in a peculiar time slot, a remote past before fire and death became known. Put differently, on the seventh day of the week humans are placed in Eden.

Conclusions

The existence of Middle Palaeolithic burials was admitted by the scientific community following the 1908 discovery of the Neandertal inhumation at La Chapelle-aux-Saints (Bouyssonie and Bardon, 1909). A century later, the mental capacity of Neandertals to use symbols is still questioned by some researchers (e.g. Chase and Dibble, 1987: 280). Gargette (1989) went as far as rejecting the very act of Neandertal burial, claiming that natural and accidental events were mistaken for deliberate burials. In a similar vein, Conard has doubted (2005: 309) the Neandertal ability for ritual practices involving grave goods. These reservations ignore the remarkable similarity of Neandertal and modern human behaviour patterns in the Levant *c.* 100 ka ago (Kaufman, 1999; Henry, 2003: 25). As shown above, Neandertals and modern humans alike have, some 100 ka ago, symbolically treated their dead as if they were alive, indicating the symbolic and linguistic abilities of both hominin species. Obviously, only

Table 27.1. *Features of the oldest burials in the Levant. SKHUL and QAFZEH denote the entire burial zone with no clear relation to a specific grave. (after Defleur, 1993, Tables 23 and 24, with additions).*

Burial	Flint	Shells	Ochre	Bone	Stones	Pit deduced	Pit	Other
Tabun 1						*		
SKHUL		*	*					
Skhul 1						*		
Skhul 3					*			
Skhul 4	*					*		
Skhul 5				Boar mandible		*		
Skhul 9				Bovid skull				
QAFZEH		*	*					
Qafzeh 8			*		*		*	Engraved stone
Qafzeh 9-Oct						*		
Qafzeh 11				Deer antlers	*		*	
Qafzeh 15						*		
Amud 7				Deer maxilla				
Kebara 2							*	
Shanidar 4								Flowers
Dederiyeh 2	*						*	Flat stone

a small fraction of the Middle Palaeolithic population was buried, including individuals of both sexes and of all ages from infants to old age. Only a few of those were endowed with grave goods (summarised in Table 27.1). Yet who was buried and who was given goods remains enigmatic. It is perhaps no accident that the oldest burials and the oldest personal adornments appeared in the Levant, where a unique co-existence of two hominin species could have triggered territorial competition.

Acknowledgements

My sincere thanks to Daniel Kaufman and two anonymous reviewers for useful comments on an earlier version of this article. Thanks are due to M. Pachter and M. Kellner for their help with the laws of mourning and Sabbat.

References

Aiello, L. C. (1998). The foundation of human language. In Jablonski, N. G. and Aiello, L. (eds.), *The Origin and Diversification of Language*. San Francisco: California Academy of Science, pp. 21–34.

Akazawa, T. and Muhesen, S. (eds.) (2002). *Neanderthal Burials*. Kyoto: International Research Center for Japanese Studies.

Akazawa, T., Dodo, Y., Muhesen, S. *et al.* (1993). The Neanderthal remains from Dederiyeh Cave, Syria: interim report. *Anthropological Science*, **101**: 361–87.

Akazawa, T., Muhesen, S., Kondo, O. *et al.* (2002). Neanderthal burials of the Dederiyeh Cave. In Akazawa, T. and Muhesen, S. (eds.), *Neanderthal Burials*. Kyoto: International Research Center for Japanese Studies, pp. 75–83.

Alperson-Afil, N., Richter, D. and Goren-Inbar, N. (2007). Phantom hearths and the use of fire at Gesher Benot Ya'acov, Israel. *PaleoAnthropology*, **2007**: 1–15.

Bar-Yosef, O., Vandermeersch, B., Arensburg, B. *et al.* (1992). The excavations in Kebara Cave, Mt. Carmel. *Current Anthropology*, **33**: 497–550.

Bar-Yosef Mayer, D. E., Vandermeersch, B. and Bar-Yosef, O. (2009). Shells and ochre in Middle Paleolithic Qafzeh Cave, Israel: indications for modern behavior. *Journal of Human Evolution*, **56**: 307–14.

Becker, E. (1973). *The Denial of Death*. New York: The Free Press.

Bouyssonie, A., Bouyssonie, J. and Bardon, L. (1909). Decouverte d'un squelete humain mousterien a la Bouffia de la Chapelle-aux-Saints (Correze). *L'Anthropologie*, **19**: 513–18.

Boyer, P. (2001). *Religion Explained*. New York: Basic Books.

Chase, P. C. and Dibble, H. L. (1987). Middle Paleolithic symbolism: a review of current evidence and interpretation. *Journal of Anthropology and Archaeology*, **6**: 363–96.

Conard, N. J. (2005). An overview of the patterns of behavioural change in Africa and Eurasia during the Middle and Late Pleistocene. In d'Errico, F. and Backwell, L. (eds.), *From Tools to Symbols*. Johannesburg: Witwatersrand University Press, pp. 294–332.

Coppa, A., Grün, R., Stringer, C. *et al.* (2005). Newly recognized Pleistocene human teeth from Tabun Cave, Israel. *Journal of Human Evolution*, **49**: 301–15.

Coppa, A., Manni, F., Stringer, C. *et al.* (2007). Evidence for new Neanderthal teeth in Tabun Cave (Israel) by the application of self-organizing maps (SOMs). *Journal of Human Evolution*, **52**: 601–13.

Defleur, A. (1993). *Les sépultures moustériennes*. Paris: Editions CNRS.

d'Errico, F., Salomon, H., Vignaud, C. *et al.* (2010). Pigments from the Middle Palaeolithic levels of Es-Skhul (Mount Carmel, Israel). *Journal of Archaeological Science*, **37**: 3099–110.

Enard, W., Przeworski, M., Fisher, S. E. *et al.* (2002). Molecular evolution of *FOXP2*, a gene involved in speech and language. *Nature*, **418**: 869–72.

Frazer, J. G. (1957). *The Golden Bough*. London: Macmillan Press.

Galili, E., Zvieli, D., Ronen, A. *et al.* (2007). Beach deposits of MIS 5e high sea stand as indicators for tectonic stability of the Carmel coastal plain, Israel. *Quaternary Science Reviews*, **26**(19/21): 2544–57.

Gargette, R. H. (1989). Grave shortcomings. The evidence for Neandertal burials. *Current Anthropology*, **30**: 157–90.

Garrod, D. A. E. (1957). *Les rites funéraires des hommes fossils du Mont-Carmel*. Mélanges Pittard, Imprimerie Chastrusse, Brive, pp. 183–68.

Garrod, D. A. E. and Bate, D. M. A. (1937). *The Stone Age of Mount Carmel*, Volume I. Oxford: Clarendon Press.

Goudsblom, J. (1992). *Fire and Civilization*. London: Allen Lane.

Grün, R. and Stringer, C. B. (1991). ESR dating and the evolution of modern humans. *Archaeometry*, **33**: 153–99.

  2000). Tabun revisited: revised ESR chronology and new ESR and U-series analyses of dental material from Tabun C1. *Journal of Human Evolution*, **39**: 601–12.

Grün, R., Stringer, C., McDermott, F. *et al.* (2005). U-series and ESR analyses of bones and teeth relating to the human burials from Skhul. *Journal of Human Evolution*, **49**: 316–34.

Henry, D. O. (2003). *Neanderthals in the Levant*. London: Continuum.

Henshilwood, C. S., d'Errico, F., Yates, R. *et al.* (2002). Emergence of modern human behaviour: Middle Stone Age engravings from South Africa. *Science*, **295**: 1278–80.

Hovers, E. (2006). Neandertals and modern humans in the Middle Paleolithic of the Levant: what kind of interaction? In Conard, N. (ed.), *When Neandertals and Moderns Met*. Tübingen: Kerns Verlag, pp. 65–86.

Hovers, E., Vandermersch, B. and Bar-Yosef, O. (1997). A Middle Palaeolithic engraved artefact from Qafzeh Cave, Israel. *Rock Art Research*, **14**: 79–87.

Hovers, E., Ilani, S., Bar-Yosef, O. *et al.* (2003). An early case of color symbolism. Ochre use by modern humans in Qafzeh Cave. *Current Anthropology*, **44**: 491–522.

Kaufman, D. (1999). *Archaeological Perspectives on the Origins of Modern Humans*. Westport: Bergin and Garvey.

Lietava, J. (1992). Medicinal plants in a Middle Paleolithic grave Shanidar IV. *Journal of Ethnopharmacology*, **35**: 263–6.

Mauss, M. (1967). *The Gift*. New York: The Norton Library.

McCown, T. D. (1937). Mugharet es Skhul. Description and excavations. In Garrod, D. A. E. and Bate, D. M. A. (eds.), *The Stone Age of Mount Carmel*, Volume I. Oxford: Clarendon Press, pp. 91–17.

McCown, A. and Keith, T. (1939). *The Stone Age of Mount Carmel*, Volume II. Oxford: Clarendon Press.

Noble, W. and Davidson, I. (1996). The evolutionary emergence of modern human behaviour: language and its archaeology. *Man*, **26**: 223–53.

Rak, Y., Kimbel, W. H. and Hovers, E. (1994). A Neandertal infant from Amud Cave, Israel. *Journal of Human Evolution*, **26**: 313–24.

Ronen, A. (1998). Domestic fire as evidence for language. In Akazawa, T., Aoki, K. and Bar-Yosef, O. (eds.), *Neandertals and Modern Humans in Western Asia*. New York: Plenum Press, pp. 439–47.

Ronen, A., Zviely, D. and Galili, E. (2007). Did the Last Interglacial sea penetrate Mount Carmel Caves? *Quaternary Science Reviews*, **26**: 2684–5.

Ronen, A., Neber, A., Mienis, H. K. *et al.* (2008). Mousterian occupation on an OIS 5e shore near the Mount Carmel Caves, Israel. In Sulgostowska, Z. and Tomaszewski, A. J. (eds.), *Man – Millennia – Environment*. Warsaw: Polish Academy of Sciences, pp. 199–206.

Shea, J. J. (2010). Neanderthals and Early *Homo sapiens* in the Levant. In Garcea, E. A. A. (ed.), *South-Eastern Mediterranean Peoples Between 130,000 and 10,000 Years Ago*. Oxford: Oxbow Books, pp. 126–43.

Solecki, R. (1953). The Shanidar Cave sounding, 1953 season, with notes concerning the discovery of the first Paleolithic skeleton in Iraq. *Sumer*, **9**: 229–32.

Solecki, R. S. (1975). Shanidar IV, a Neanderthal flower burial in northern Iraq. *Science*, **190**: 880–1.

Suzuki, H. and Takai, F. (eds.) (1970). *The Amud Man and His Cave Site*. Tokyo: University of Tokyo Press.

Tattersall, I. (1998). *Becoming Human: Evolution and Human Uniqueness*. New York: Harcourt Inc.

Valladas, H., Mercier, N., Joron, J.-L. *et al.* (1998). GIF Laboratory dates for Middle Palaeolithic Levant. In Akazawa, T., Aoki, K. and Bar-Yosef, O. (eds.), *Neandertals and Modern Humans in Western Asia*. New York: Plenum Press, pp. 69–75.

Vandermeersch, B. (1969). Decouverte d'un objet en ocre avec traces d'utilisation dans le mousteerien de Qafzeh (Israel). *Bulletin Societe Prehistorique Francaise*, **66**: 57–8.

(1970). Une sepulture mousterien avec offtrandes decouverte dans la grotte de Qafzef. *Comptes rendus de l'Académie des Sciences*, **268**: 298–301.

(1976). Les sépultures néandertaliennes. *La Préhistoire Francaise* I. Paris: Editions CNRS, pp. 725–7.

(1981). *Les hommes fossils de Qafzeh (Israel)*. Paris : CNRS Editions.

(2006). Ce que nous apprennent les premières sépultures. *Comptes rendus Palevol*, **5**: 161–7.

Vanhaeren, M., d'Errico, F., Stringer, C. *et al.* (2006). Middle Paleolithic shell beads in Israel and Algeria. *Science*, **312**: 1785–8.

Vaks, A., Bar-Matthews, M., Ayalon, A. *et al.* (2007). Desert speleothems reveal climatic window for African exodus of early modern humans. *Geology*, **35**: 831–4.

Vita-Finzi, C. and Stringer, C. (2007). The setting of the Mt. Carmel caves reassessed. *Quaternary Science Reviews*, **26**: 436–40.

Wright, K. I. (in press, 2011). Beads and the body: ornamental technologies of the BACH Area buildings at Çatalhöyük. In Tringham, R. and Stevanovic, M. (eds.), *House Lives: Building, Inhabiting, Excavating a House at Çatalhöyük, Turkey. Reports from the Bach Area, Çatalhöyük, 1997–2003 (Çatalhöyük Vol. 7)*. Monumenta Archaeologica. UCLA, Los Angeles, CA: Cotsen Institute of Archaeology Publications.

Index

571